Essential Introductory Linguistics

ESSENTIAL
INTRODUCTORY
LINGUISTICS

Grover Hudson

Michigan State University

© 2000 by Grover Hudson

BLACKWELL PUBLISHING
350 Main Street, Malden, MA 02148-5020, USA
9600 Garsington Road, Oxford OX4 2DQ, UK
550 Swanston Street, Carlton, Victoria 3053, Australia

First published 2000

10   2006

Library of Congress Cataloging-in-Publication Data

Hudson, Grover.
    Essential introductory linguistics / Grover Hudson.
        p. cm.
    Includes bibliographical references and index.
    ISBN 0-631-20303-6 (hbk: alk. paper) — ISBN 0-631-20304-4 (pbk: alk. paper)
    1. Linguistics. I. Title.
    P121.H746   1999
    410—dc21   98–51949
                                                                          CIP

ISBN-13: 978-0-631-20303-2 (hbk: alk. paper) — ISBN-13: 978-0-631-20304-9 (pbk: alk. paper)

A catalogue record for this title is available from the British Library.

Set in 10 on 13 pt Sabon
by Graphicraft Ltd, Hong Kong
Printed and bound in Singapore
by Fabulous Printers Pte Ltd

The publisher's policy is to use permanent paper from mills that operate a sustainable forestry policy, and which has been manufactured from pulp processed using acid-free and elementary chlorine-free practices. Furthermore, the publisher ensures that the text paper and cover board used have met acceptable environmental accreditation standards.

For further information on
Blackwell Publishing, visit our website:
www.blackwellpublishing.com

CONTENTS

LIST OF FIGURES

LIST OF TABLES

PREFACE

Knowledge in linguistics has grown greatly since, in the early 1970s, introductory linguistics courses began to be commonly taught to college undergraduates, and introductory linguistics textbooks have tried to present more and more of this knowledge, much of it in increasingly abbreviated form.

In this time, also, the place of linguistics in the college curriculum, and students of linguistics, have changed. Linguistics has become perceived as less arcane and esoteric, and student life is more competitive. More students enroll in introductory linguistics classes because they need these, whether as the foundation of their major field of study, as a requirement of a major in another field, or because linguistics is perceived as relevant for a career – in language teaching or other areas of education, in audiology and speech science, communication fields, computer science, and cognitive psychology, for example. As a result, students are more demanding; they want teachers and textbooks to be very clear about both the content and the goals of lessons. Reasonably, they want to know what the point is, and they want to get to the point.

The structure and method of this book, therefore, is somewhat different from that of other introductory linguistics textbooks. First, it is more selective in its inclusion of topics and subtopics, limiting these, with reasonable consideration to the tradition and expectations of the field, strictly to what the author considers to be essentials. Second, with this selectivity, it has been possible to present each topic with sufficient clarity and thoroughness, and, importantly, to organize, relate, and integrate topics with one another.

Please notice that:

- Chapters are numerous compared to other such books, 28, but relatively short, as seems appropriate for units of study.
- Each chapter is strictly organized, and this organization is made very clear: each chapter begins with a statement of its major content and goals, and

the structure of each chapter is overt with use of numbered and labeled sections, each of which rarely exceeds a few paragraphs in length.

- Wherever possible, information is presented as a list of points and subpoints.
- Points are amply exemplified and illustrated, often in numbered lists.
- When first raised, new concepts and terms are in bold type, and defined. A number of topics reappear from chapter to chapter, and are cross-referenced.
- New concepts and terms are also listed at the end of each chapter.
- The outline of each chapter is presented at the end of each, as a basis for review. Topics of the outlines can be readily rephrased as study questions.
- Finally, at the end of each chapter there are recommended readings, and a number of fairly short, often objective, exercises. Sometimes secondary points which expand on those of the main text are raised in conjunction with these exercises.

It is hoped, therefore, that the book will serve as a study guide as well as the textbook for a course.

Chapters on 'core linguistics' areas of phonology, morphology, and syntax are distributed as follows: After chapters 2–7, two each on phonetics–phonology, morphology, and syntax, there are chapters on language acquisition, brain and language, and animal communication. Then follow six more chapters on core linguistics, two each on phonology, morphology, and syntax–semantics. The 12 chapters on core linguistics have been broken up in this way in order to illustrate applications and to motivate the study of descriptive and theoretical linguistics topics, as well as to more evenly distribute these more technically oriented chapters.

Of course, teachers rarely agree completely on the proper content of the introductory linguistics course, and many will disagree with the present selection. But with the strict and overt structure of this textbook, and with its short chapters, it should be relatively easy for teachers to omit chapters and/or their subunits, and to introduce and integrate additional topics in a coherent way. No doubt many teachers will choose to omit one or both of the chapters on writing (21, 22), that on the history of linguistics (28), perhaps that on animal communication (12), on language families (25), or on universals of language (20).

In a few ways, the content of introductory linguistics as well as its selection and presentation is differently conceived in this book.

- Chapter 1 provides a thorough introduction to the background concepts of the sign and sign systems, using the original terminology of C. S. Peirce: icon, index, and symbol. Other textbooks have avoided these terms, because of their different meanings in ordinary language. Here, this difference between technical, linguistic, and ordinary language usage has been made an emphasis, and the nature of the sign is a topic which is returned to in several chapters, as one which connects areas of linguistics from structure, to learning, to change.

- Chapter 1 also introduces the general nature of language through the six characteristics of arbitrariness, creativity, openness, duality, grammaticality, and cultural transmission, and these topics also come up again and again in subsequent chapters – particularly that of the probable innateness of language in contrast to the more obvious characteristic of cultural transmission.
- Chapter 2, concerning phonetics, presents the palatal glide in its IPA [j] symbolization versus more typical Anglocentric [y], in order to acknowledge international versus American usage, and to emphasize the difference between phonetic and alphabetic writing.
- Chapter 14 provides a thorough introduction to phonological (distinctive) features, despite the difficulty of this topic and its perceived technical nature by students, in the belief that this important aspect of the unique structure of language is essential and must be made clear.
- Chapters 15 and 16 introduce topics in morphology by a thorough survey of processes of new word formation in English.
- Chapters 21 and 22 provide a more complete treatment of writing systems than is usual. It is well known that students usually find this topic of interest, if most linguists do not. It seems important both to satisfy the student interest, and to take advantage of it to emphasize the difference between language and writing, and to emphasize for native English readers the efficacy of non-alphabetic and non-European writing systems.

Finally, I hope that teachers will forgive, as a necessity, some simplification in the treatment here of a few important but potentially over-complex topics, including:

- the set of universal phonological features, for example, concerning their binarity or not, phonological markedness, and the feature (here [peripheral]), which distinguishes English 'tense/lax' vowel pairs;
- the nature of lexical entries, presented here as traditional pairings of form and meaning;
- the nature and representation of morphophonemic alternations, with suppression of the possibility of rule ordering;
- the proper relation between syntactic representation and sentence meaning; and
- the treatment of several syntactic rules as raisings to 'specifier' nodes, and the suppression of X-bar theory.

ACKNOWLEDGMENTS

The contributions of many persons must be very gratefully acknowledged, none of whom has any responsibility for flaws of the book: Barbara Abbott, Malik Balla, Raimund Belgardt, Mayrene Bentley, Alan Beretta, Mutsuko Endo Hudson, Norman Gary, David Lockwood, David Magier (fig. 22.3), Alan Munn, Ok-suk Park (fig. 22.4), Li-Jiuan Wang, and hundreds of students of my LIN 200 and LIN 401 Michigan State University classes since 1995, who have used the book in its earlier stages.

The author and publishers gratefully acknowledge the following for permission to reproduce copyright material: International Phonetic Association (for fig. 2.1); Allyn and Bacon (fig. 9.1); *American Scientist* (fig. 10.4); John Bradshaw, Lesley J. Rogers, and Academic Press, Inc. (fig. 10.5); Elissa L. Newport and Academic Press, Inc. (figs 11.1–3); Blackwell Publishers and *Language Learning* (figs 11.4); Miriam Rothman for the estate of Sol Mednick (fig. 12.2); Lawrence Erlbaum Associates, Inc. (fig. 12.3); Harvard University Press and the President and Fellows of Harvard College (figs 12.7 and 12.11); Eric Mose, Jr. for the estate of Eric Mose (fig. 12.8); John Wiley and Sons, Inc., and the Language Research Center, Georgia State University (fig. 12.9); Alfred A. Knopf, Inc. (fig. 12.10); Dept of Hebrew and Semitic Studies, University of Wisconsin (fig. 21.2); Denise Schmandt-Besserat, courtesy of German Archaeology Institute, Division Baghdad (fig. 21.3); University of Nebraska Press (figs 21.4–5); Harvard University Press and the President and Fellows of Harvard College (fig. 21.6); Blackwell Publishers (fig. 21.7); Stanford University Press; Peters, Fraser and Dunlap; and Geoffrey Sampson (figs 21.8 and 21.12); the British Museum, British Museum Press (fig. 21.10); Harcourt Brace and Company (fig. 23.5); Stanford University Press, Hodder Headline Group, and Merritt Ruhlen (fig. 25.2).

The publishers apologize for any errors or omissions in the above list and would be grateful to be notified of any corrections that should be incorporated in the next edition or reprint of this book.

The author welcomes all suggestions from users of the book.

SIGNS AND SIGN SYSTEMS

This chapter introduces basic concepts of language, especially the *sign*, and presents the basic structure and general nature of language.

1. THREE BASIC CONCEPTS: SIGN, COMMUNICATION, AND LANGUAGE

1.1. Sign

In ordinary language a sign is a notice placed for the public to see. Here, however, following technical and linguistic usage, let **sign** mean 'an intersection or relationship of **form** and **meaning**', where form is something concrete, including writing, sound, and gestures, and meaning is something mental or cognitive.

Examples of signs in this sense include:

'∞', which means 'infinity',
'©', which means 'copyrighted',
'♥', which means 'love', as in 'I ♥ New York',
'*sign*', which means 'an intersection or relationship of form and meaning'.

As in the last example, a sign may be a word. A sign does not have to be seen; it could be heard, as is the usual case with words, which are more often spoken than read.

A sign is neither form nor meaning, but simultaneously both: the intersection or relationship of form and meaning. A form without a meaning is not a sign, nor is a meaning without a form. It may be argued that form and meaning cannot exist apart from one another, and it is not easy to argue otherwise. But this rather difficult and profound matter cannot be considered here.

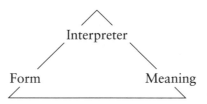

Figure 1.1   The three parts of a sign

1.2.   Communication

The notion 'sign' is fundamental to understanding human communication, and upon the basis of the above understanding, we can define **communication** as 'the use of signs'. In communication, one presents the form of signs to others, and so invokes their meanings.

But communication is seldom perfect, and this can be understood as resulting from the third dimension of a sign, the interpreter; see figure 1.1. The relationship between the form of a sign and its meaning must be part of the knowledge of its interpreter. The interpreter adds an aspect or dimension of variability to our understanding of *sign*, because different interpreters may recognize different aspects of meaning in association with particular forms, and different forms in association with particular meanings. This variability is probably apparent with some of the four signs '∞', '©', '♥', and '*sign*'. Some interpreters of these may not recognize the meaning 'infinity' of the ∞ form, and some may be unfamiliar with the still somewhat novel extension of '♥' to mean 'love'. As for the fourth sign, '*sign*', the meaning of this as a technical term has only just been introduced to most readers, whose interpretations undoubtedly vary considerably at this time.

1.3.   Language

Language, then, can be simply defined as a sign system. Usually, however, *language* means specifically the customary sign system of humankind, and here we shall follow this usage. Sometimes language, in this sense, is termed **speech**, a term which properly refers just to the vocal medium typically employed to form the natural signs of human languages.

2.   SIGNS

2.1.   Three types of signs

There are three types of signs (as recognized by the philosopher Charles Sanders Peirce (1839–1914)), which differ according to the three types of relationship that exist between form and meaning: icon, index, and symbol.

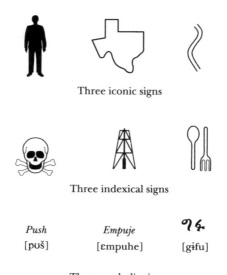

Three iconic signs

Three indexical signs

Push   *Empuje*   ？ᎇ

[pʊš]   [ɛmpuhe]   [gɨfu]

Three symbolic signs:
'Push!' in English, Spanish and Amharic

Figure 1.2   The three types of signs

2.1.1. *Icon*

An **icon** is a sign whose form has actual characteristics of its meaning. See three examples of iconic signs in figure 1.2. The first means 'man', the second 'Texas', and the third 'winding road'. These three signs can have the meanings 'man', 'Texas', and 'winding road', respectively, since, obviously enough, the forms have actual characteristics of these meanings. The third may not be so obvious, in fact, but when seen posted at the side of a highway, in a mountainous area, its iconic characteristic may be apparent enough.

2.1.2. *Index*

An **index** is a sign whose form has characteristics which are only associated in nature with its meaning. Recognizing indexical signs can be a little tricky. See three examples of indexical signs in figure 1.2. The first example is a skull and crossed bones, traditionally a sign meaning 'poison'. Notice the indexical, natural, relation between this form and its meaning: 'if you drink the contents of this bottle, in a few months you will look like this'. Similarly, an oil well could mean 'Texas', since oil wells are something naturally associated with Texas. The third sign, when seen posted at the side of a highway, will suggest 'restaurant' or 'food (service)', by the natural association of spoons and forks with these meanings.

The difference between icon and index is not always perfectly clear. A spoon and fork may be considered an actual characteristic (icon) of restaurants, if only an association (index) with food. The interpreter/interpretation is crucial to the determination of a sign as icon, index, or symbol. The difference between icon and index is especially problematic when meanings are abstract. Take the meaning 'liberty', for example, and its occasional form of 'breaking chains'. Such a picture/form may be associated with 'liberty' because such an event is an actual characteristic of this otherwise somewhat abstract idea, or, if 'liberty' is essentially something quite abstract (personal, and emotional), because the breaking of chains is just an occasional association with 'liberty' as a precondition in history.

2.1.3. Symbol

A **symbol** is a sign whose form is arbitrarily or conventionally associated with its meaning. See three examples of symbolic signs in figure 1.2. These are necessarily presented here in their secondary, written, forms, as ordinarily spelled, and in phonetic writing. The first example, the written English word *push* [puš], only means 'push' by a completely arbitrary or conventional association of this form, whether spoken or written, with this meaning. Nothing in nature associates this word with this meaning. In fact, to those who have grown up in the English-speaking world it may seem completely normal that this form should have this meaning. On reflection, however, it must be clear that there is nothing intrinsic to the natural world about this normality, which results entirely from the customary usage or convention of English-speaking communities. The other examples, the Spanish and Amharic (a language of Ethiopia) written words for 'push' – like the English words, those which would be written on a door, as an instruction – are also such symbolic signs.

2.2. Linguistic signs

2.2.1. Morphemes

The simplest sort of sign in (human) languages is a **simple word**. An example of a simple word is *sea*, which contrasts with a **complex word** like *seashell*. *Sea* has one meaning and *seashell* has two. But linguistic signs don't have to be words: the *un-* and the *-ly* of *unhappily*, for example, are meaningful too, and these are not words. A linguistic sign, whether of the word type, like *sea* and *shell*, or the sub-word type, like *un-* and *-ly*, is a **morpheme** (*morph* is from Greek, 'form'). There are two morphemes in the word *seashell* (*sea, shell*) and three in *unhappily* (*un-, happy, -ly*).

Although here on the pages of this book it is necessary to present words and morphemes in their written or **orthographic form**, these are ordinarily more common in their spoken or **phonetic form**, a pattern of sound produced by a set of articulations of the physiological apparatus of speech including the lungs, larynx, tongue, velum, lips, etc.

2.2.2. Symbolic nature of morphemes

With rare exception, the typical signs of human language, morphemes, are symbolic signs, like *push, sea, un-*, or other examples of English or of any other language you know. That is, there is no characteristic of their meaning in their form (whether spoken or written), nor any natural association between their form and meaning.

There are two good reasons why linguistic signs should typically be symbolic. First, we have to process these signs at a rapid average rate of two to three per second, so there is just no time to make use of their iconic and/or indexical aspects. Second, most linguistic meanings don't have iconic or indexical formal properties which could be expressed as vocalizable sounds.

2.2.3.   Evidence for the symbolic nature of linguistic signs

There are four sorts of clear evidence that morphemes (and words) are typically symbolic: translation equivalents, synonyms, and iconically expressible meanings, and the rarity of plainly iconic and indexical morphemes.

2.2.3.1.   Translation equivalents.   Translation equivalents are words with

approximately the same meanings in different languages. If words were typically iconic or indexical, then translation equivalents from language to language would be similar in form as well as meaning. The word meaning 'dog', for example, should sound (or look) the same in different languages. But in English, a dog is called a *dog*, in French *chien*, in Spanish *perro*, and in Arabic *kalb*. This is typical for translation equivalents: the words don't sound (or look) similar at all.

2.2.3.2.   Synonyms.   Synonyms are words with same or similar meanings within

a language, for example *sick* and *ill*, and *twelve* and *dozen*. If morphemes were typically iconic or indexical, words with the similar meaning within a language should have similar form. But again there is little or no similarity of form; *sick* doesn't sound like (and isn't spelled like) *ill*, etc.

2.2.3.3.   Iconically expressible meanings.   Consider meanings that, theoretically,

could be readily expressed as pronunciations. An example would be numbers, such as 'one', 'two', etc. If morphemes were iconic or indexical, the form of 'two' would be twice as big as the form of 'one', and the form of 'four' would be twice as big as the form of 'two'. But this isn't so. True, *twenty* is bigger than *ten*, but not twice as big, and *thirty* is not bigger than *twenty* at all. Another example is physical quality opposites like *narrow/wide* and *big/small*. If morphemes were iconic or indexical, the word for 'narrow' should be narrower than the word for 'wide', and the word for 'big' bigger than the word for 'small'. Instead, *narrow* is wider than *wide*; *wide* is narrower than *narrow*, etc.

2.2.3.4.   Exceptionality of iconic and indexical morphemes.   There are some

words which are iconic signs, termed mimetic words (also called onomatopoeic words). Mimetic words sound like what they mean, for example, *bow-wow*, *tick-tock*, and *bam*. The phonetic forms of such words have actual characteristics of their meanings, which are sounds; mimetic words sound something like the sounds they mean. *Bow-wow*, at least, sounds more like the sound of a dog than does *meow* and *meow* sounds more like the sound of a cat than does *bow-wow*. Indeed, in many languages around the world, the word for the sound of a dog is mimetic, and thus somewhat similar to *bow-wow*:

French: wah-wah
Arabic: ʔaw-ʔaw
Japanese: wan-wan
Chinese: wãw-wãw

Another case of iconicity in morphemes is drawing out the pronunciation of the word *long* so that the form of the word, like the meaning, is long: *loooong* ('I mean, like, reeeally looong, man'). To call a dog a *bow-wow* or a cow a *moo* is also to use iconic signs, since the sound of these words is at least an attempt to give form to an actual quality of the meaning.

But mimetic words are exceptional words! It should be clear that most word-meanings are not – and cannot be – modeled in the forms of the words.

There is rarely some indexicality in words, too. For example, if you want to get someone's attention you might say 'Hey!' If you really want to get their attention you might say it a bit louder, 'HEY!' And if you really, desperately, want to get their attention you might say it even louder, '**HEY!**'. This is indexicality; the volume or intensity of the voice naturally rises in association with the intensity of meaning. Notice that this is not iconicity, since the meaning associated with increased loudness is increased interest in getting someone's attention, and loudness is not an actual characteristic of that interest – it's just naturally associated with it. Saying *Oh!* with rising or falling pitch, when excited or disappointed, respectively, gives the word indexical form, in which the pitch is associated with the rise or fall of emotion which may be noted by a hearer as part of the meaning of the word. As with iconic signs, obviously such indexical signs are exceptional cases.

3. LANGUAGE

3.1. Two-part structure of sign systems

Language was defined above as a sign system. Every sign system has two parts:

a. a **lexicon**, or dictionary, the inventory of its signs, and
b. a **grammar**, the **rules** for the construction of its signs and for their combination into messages.

Consider an example of a very simple sign system, the traffic light. Its lexicon has three signs and, in one version, its grammar has three rules, as follows:

Lexicon: *Meanings*   *Forms*
            'stop'   red light
            'go'   green light
            'caution'   yellow light

Rules: 1. From top to bottom, the signs are ordered red-yellow-green.
        2. One color is lighted at a time.
        3. The sequence of lights is green-yellow-red, repeatedly.

Adding possibilities to the lexicon such as a flashing mode, or an arrow-shaped light, and possibilities to the rules such as simultaneous signs (green and yellow at the same time), increases the expressiveness and the complexity of the system. Finally, remember that a sign, or sign system, has a third component, the interpreter. Signs and sign systems are useless unless users have shared knowledge of them.

3.2. Three substructures of language

Within and cutting across this two-part structure of inventory and rules, language has three sorts of substructure: phonology, morphology, and syntax.

3.2.1. *Phonology*

Phonology concerns the sounds of the forms of language. The few languages that lack phonology are the manually signed languages of the deaf, which instead have, parallel to phonological rules, rules which concern the sub-parts of the discrete gestures of the hands (discussed in chapter 12, §4.1).

Phonological form consists of **phones**, for example the phones [m], [æ] and [p] of *map*, and phones consist of even smaller units, **phonological features**, for example:

[labial], the feature present at the start of the words *map, bad* and *wag*;
[voiced], the feature present at the start of the words *bad* and *dad* and absent at the start of *pad* and *tad*;
[nasal], the feature of the first phone of *map* and the first and last phones of *name*.

These three features are simultaneously present in the phone [m], the first sound of *map*, the voiced labial nasal [m]. (Phonetic writing is typically shown within square brackets, [ ].) Languages differ in the phonological features they employ, and in the possibilities for simultaneous or sequential cooccurrence of features.

The possibilities of combination or cooccurrence of phonological features in morphemes are expressed by **phonological rules**. In English, for example, the feature [nasal] is present in vowels which precede nasal consonants, as in the vowel of *pan* and *bin*. You can confirm this for yourself by comparing the vowel sounds of these two words to those of *pad* and *bid*, which lack the final nasal consonant.

Four chapters of this book present phonology: 2, 3, 13, and 14.

3.2.2. Morphology

Morphology concerns the classes of morphemes, and their cooccurrence in sentences and combination as words. Among the English morphemes, for example, are the following four, where elements of form are in square brackets, [ ], and elements of meaning in braces, { }:

[dɔg], {noun, 'dog', animate, non-human, . . . }
[go], {verb, 'go', intransitive, . . . }
[z], {plural suffix of nouns}
[z], {present tense suffix of verbs with third-person singular subject}

Morphological rules express the possible combinations of morphemes as words. For example, the first and third morphemes above, [dɔg] and [z], combine according to rules of English to produce the word [dɔgz] *dogs*, and the second and fourth morphemes [go] and [z] combine to produce the present tense verb [goz] *goes*. Don't let English spelling mislead you; the last consonant is pronounced [z], not [s].

Other languages have different forms for similar meanings, for example French *chien* 'dog' (pronunciation: [šjẽ]), and simple words for meanings which English expresses by combining words, for example Amharic *ayat* 'grandparent'. But all languages have the capability to express the meanings expressed in other languages. The meaning of Amharic *ayat* English expresses with the combination of words *grand + parent*.

Four chapters of this book present morphology: 4, 5, 15, and 16.

3.2.3. Syntax

Syntax concerns the combinations of words as phrases and of phrases as sentences. Every language has words, which combine as phrases and sentences. The possibilities of combination are strictly limited, so every language has syntax, or sentence structure.

Words come in different types based upon their possibilities of combination with other words in sentences. These types are the **parts of speech**: noun, verb, adjective, etc. Nouns, for example (such as English *circus*, *pajamas*, and *story*), combine with determiners (such as English *the*, *these*, *my*) and adjectives (such as English *big*, *red*, *extraordinary*) to make noun phrases, such as *the big circus*, *these red pajamas*, and *my extraordinary story*, and verbs combine with auxiliary verbs (such as English *can*, *might*, *will*, and *have*) and adverbs (such as

English *always*, *then*, and *surely*) to make verb phrases, such as *has already eaten*, *will leave then*, and *surely can't go*.

Syntactic rules specify the possible combinations of words as phrases and as sentences of general types, such as affirmative and negative, statements, commands, questions, etc. In English, for example, questions answerable by *yes* or *no* are typically sentences in which a so-called 'auxiliary' verb appears before the noun phrase subject of the sentence, as in these examples:

Statement	*Yes/No question*
The big circus is opening today.	Is the big circus opening today?
These red pajamas wouldn't fit.	Wouldn't these red pajamas fit?

Four chapters of this book present syntax: 6, 7, 17, and 18.

3.3. Other types of linguistic structure

In addition to phonology, morphology, and syntax, other types of linguistic structure may be recognized: semantic structure, concerning word and sentence meaning and their interpretation (chapter 17); orthographic structure, concerning writing (chapters 21, 22); pragmatics, concerning how we use language to get meanings beyond those given form by language (chapter 19); and discourse structure, concerning how sentences are fitted to longer stretches of language, as in conversation and arguments.

A basic understanding of the structure of language is necessary for understanding most other aspects of language taken up in this book.

3.4. Six aspects of the general nature of language

Partly as a result of their unique three-part substructure (phonology, morphology, syntax), languages have unique characteristics of a more general nature, and these characteristics tend strongly to distinguish (human) language from other sign systems and from communication in other animal species (the latter the topic of chapter 12). Of many characteristics that have been proposed as unique to language, six are **arbitrariness**, **displacement**, **creativity**, **duality**, **grammaticality**, and **cultural transmission**.

3.4.1. Arbitrariness

Arbitrariness is the above-noted characteristic that the signs of languages (morphemes) are typically **symbolic**: typically, that is, the forms of morphemes are only arbitrarily related to their meanings. Because the form of morphemes is phonetic (vocal sound), only mimetic morphemes can be iconic, and relatively few meanings, otherwise, can be expressed indexically, like the different degrees of intensity/insistence in 'Hey!'.

3.4.2. Displacement

language divorced from immediate stimulus [handwritten annotation]

Displacement is the characteristic that in languages meanings are expressed which are 'displaced' or removed from the concrete or physical presence of the object or stimulus, outside the individual, of those meanings. Having symbolic signs means that we can give form to abstract meanings like 'past' and 'future', and associate other signs with these. Indeed, all languages have morphemes and constructions which make it possible to talk about the past and future as well as the present, and so to talk about persons and places not present, and even about hypothetical things, like 'golden mountains' and 'the present king of France'.

3.4.3. Creativity

Creativity is the characteristic of languages that they readily and regularly permit the expression of new meanings. In fact, the finite forms of language are able to express a non-finite (unbounded) number of meanings. The creativity of language is owed particularly to the two properties of **openness** and **recursion**.

3.4.3.1. Openness.

Openness is the characteristic of languages that they are always able to come up with new morphemes to express new ideas and new things in the world, and new ways, also, of expressing old ones. A couple of somewhat recent examples in English are *'toon*, a clipped and casual way of saying 'cartoon', and *schmooz*, which seems to mean something like 'entertaining and getting entertained by lobbyists'. The many ways that languages have of fulfilling the property of openness are the topic of chapters 15 and 16.

3.4.3.2. Recursion.

Recursion allows phrases to expand by the expansion of phrases within themselves. For example, the phrase *a friend* may expand as *a friend of mine*, and this may be an expansion in another phrase *friend of a friend of mine*. The property of recursion makes it impossible to set a limit on the length of sentences, or, therefore, on the number of sentences. Although the signs of languages exist in a limited number of categories, such as noun, verb, and adjective, and although these categories combine with one another in fixed ways, as where a sentence may consist of a noun and a verb (*Dogs bark; Ideas abound*) and a noun phrase may consist of an adjective and a noun (*lucky dog, crazy ideas*), because of recursion nothing limits the length of sentences except the limits of our patience and memory. Recursion is discussed further in chapters 6 and 7.

3.4.4. Duality

Duality is the characteristic of linguistic signs that these have a two-part or dual structure, in which the meaningful whole is made up of meaningless parts. Morphemes, that is, are meaningful, but the phones and features which make up the phones are meaningless. Meaningless units [labial], [stop], [voiceless] make up [p], which is still meaningless, but meaningless [p], [t] and [a] combine as

[pat] 'pot', [apt] 'opt', and [tap] 'top'. (By the rules of English phonology, the three other possibilities [pta], [tpa], and [atp] are impossible.)

3.4.5. Grammaticality

Grammaticality is the characteristic of languages that they have rather strict rules about how things may be said. Only certain sounds may be combined in words, and meanings have to be combined in certain ways, in words and sentences. As just noted, [pat] is a possible English word, but [pta] is not. To form a question in English, one can say *Are they here?*, inverting the subject and verb, but not *Came they here?*. As a consequence of choosing to express certain meanings, languages require that certain other aspects of meaning, so-called 'grammatical' meaning, be expressed. In English, for example, if a noun with plural meaning is mentioned its plurality must be expressed as a suffix on the noun. One can't say *I ate two pear*, even though the plurality of *pear* is obvious given mention of '*two*', but must say *I ate two pears*. Other languages may not have this requirement, but they have others. The difference between grammatical and lexical meaning is a topic of chapter 4.

All languages – and all stages of language including the earliest child language – have their particular such 'rules' of grammar. Utterances in the language which follow the rules are said to be **grammatical**, and those which don't follow the rules are **ungrammatical**.

3.4.6. Cultural transmission

Languages differ from place to place in the world, and we have to learn the form appropriate for the place. This learning is called **cultural transmission**. If languages were completely instinctive or innate (genetically encoded in us), like knowing how to swallow, digest, or to recognize faces, languages wouldn't differ this way, and we wouldn't need to learn them.

This cultural transmission of language in humankind contrasts with the **innateness** of the typical signs of nonhuman species, for example the basic songs of most birds or the signs of chimpanzees including facial expressions and a few vocalizations. Animal communication is the topic of chapter 12.

Because language learning by children is almost completely spontaneous, very regular, and seemingly effortless, especially when considered in relation to the complexity of human language, it is certain that we come into the world with a considerable amount of innate knowledge that makes language learning possible: in some sense, expectations about what is a possible language. Perhaps even a significant if highly abstract part of our adult linguistic knowledge is innate to the human species – a controversial issue which comes up elsewhere in this book (chapters 9 and 20). But it is also certain that a significant part of language, also, is not genetically encoded but culturally transmitted, intensively if effortlessly, especially before age four, but throughout life.

Because languages vary, and are learned, they always differ from generation to generation (the topic of chapters 23 and 24). The changed forms of language persist as variants which distinguish the different varieties of language of social groups, including dialects (the topic of chapter 26), and as the different forms of language by which we express our understanding of different social circumstances (the topic of chapter of 27).

Suggestions for
ADDITIONAL READING

Charles Sanders Peirce's writings on his philosophy are notoriously obscure. His basic ideas on his theory of signs may be found in the chapter 'Logic as semiotic: the theory of signs' (1897), in *Philosophical Writings of Peirce*, ed. by Justus Buchler (1955, pp. 98–120). A presentation of Peirce's theory in relation to language is found in chapter 1 of Raimo Anttila's *Historical and Comparative Linguistics* (1989). There is also James Jakob Liszka's *A General Introduction to the Semeiotic of Charles Sanders Peirce* (1996).

There are other compact introductions to linguistics, for example Jean Aitchison's *Teach Yourself Linguistics* (1992), Richard Hudson's *Invitation to Linguistics* (1984), and R. L. Trask's *Language: the Basics* (1995). There are many textbooks of introductory linguistics which, like this one, are written for students and include exercises, for example, Edward Finegan's *Language: its Structure and Use* (1994).

On the characteristics of the nature of language, see the first chapter of Anttila (1972). Convenient reference works in which to find more information on this and other specific topics of this book are the *International Encyclopedia of Linguistics* (1992) edited by William Bright, *The Linguistics Encyclopedia* (1992) edited by Kirsten Malmkjaer, and *The Cambridge Encyclopedia of Language*, edited by David Crystal (1987).

IMPORTANT CONCEPTS AND TERMS IN THIS CHAPTER

- sign
- form
- meaning
- communication
- language
- speech
- icon
- index
- symbol
- simple word
- complex word
- morpheme

- phonology
- phone
- phonological feature
- phonological rule
- morphology
- morphological rule
- syntax
- parts of speech
- syntactic rule
- arbitrariness
- displacement
- creativity

- orthographic form
- phonetic form
- translation equivalent
- synonym
- mimetic word
- lexicon
- grammar
- rule

- openness
- recursion
- duality
- grammaticality
- grammatical
- ungrammatical
- cultural transmission
- innateness

OUTLINE OF
CHAPTER 1

1. **Three basic concepts: sign, communication, and language**
   1. Sign
   2. Communication
   3. Language
2. **Signs**
   1. Three types of signs
      1. Icon
      2. Index
      3. Symbol
   2. Linguistic signs
      1. Morphemes
      2. Symbolic nature of morphemes
      3. Evidence for the symbolic nature of linguistic signs
         1. Translation equivalents
         2. Synonyms
         3. Iconically expressible meanings
         4. Exceptionality of iconic and indexical morphemes
3. **Language**
   1. Two-part structure of sign systems
   2. Three substructures of language
      1. Phonology
      2. Morphology
      3. Syntax
   3. Other types of linguistic structure
   4. Six aspects of the general nature of language
      1. Arbitrariness
      2. Displacement
      3. Creativity
         1. Openness
         2. Recursion
      4. Duality
      5. Grammaticality
      6. Cultural transmission

EXAMPLES AND PRACTICE

EXAMPLE

1. Logos for international development communication. The journal *Development Communication Report* introduced in its June 1981 issue the set of 'logos' presented in figure 1.3. The *Report* defined *logo* as a 'visual symbol representing an idea or concept'. According to the *Report*, the logos were 'created for the Clearinghouse on Development Communication by Washington designer Timothy Bradford Ward'. It says that logos are 'a kind of visual shorthand', which 'guide readers quickly to subjects of special interest to them', and 'make it easier for readers to scan the newsletter to get an idea of the content of the articles'.

Notice some of the iconic, indexical, and symbolic aspects of these 'logos for international development communication'.

   a.   The 'audiocassette' logo is basically iconic. It has the actual appearance of an audiocassette.
   b.   The 'nutrition' logo is basically indexical. It has pictures of a fish, a fruit or vegetable (a pineapple?), and a bowl of rice.
   c.   The 'information' logo is basically symbolic. It consists of the letter *i*, which is only arbitrarily – in the English language – associated with this meaning.

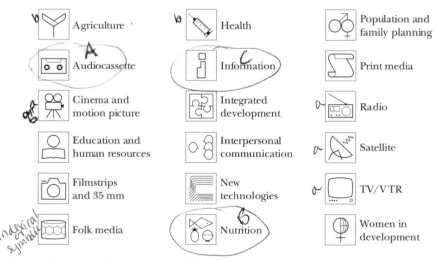

Figure 1.3   Logos for international development communication
Source: Development Communication Report, June 1981

PRACTICE

Identify six more of the logos for international development communication, two which are basically iconic, two which are basically indexical, and two of which are at least partly symbolic, and for each one say, as in the three examples above, what makes it iconic, indexical, or symbolic.

EXAMPLE

2. Corporation logos. Corporation logos are visual signs whose meaning is the corporation. A pair of examples is shown in figure 1.4, for Travelers Insurance and AT&T.

Often these logos mix iconic, indexical, and symbolic aspects with the intention to present a quick and clear impression of the product(s), service(s), name, and/or intended image of the corporation. Thus:

a. The Travelers Insurance logo is an umbrella (red in color, actually). An umbrella gives protection and so does insurance, so this may be understood as an indexical sign. The umbrella also looks sort of like a letter 'T', possibly a symbolic sign, the initial letter of the word 'Travelers'.

b. The AT&T logo has the English letters 'A', 'T', and 'T', a symbolic sign, and also a circle with lines crossing it. Perhaps the circle represents the world, and the lines represent electronic communication lines. These may be indexical signs, associations with the international electronic business of this corporation.

Figure 1.4   Two corporation logos: Travelers and AT&T

PRACTICE

Find in a magazine or an old (!) telephone book two more corporation logos which mix symbolic, indexical, and/or iconic aspects. Draw them or cut them out and attach them to a piece of paper, and briefly describe, as in the examples (a) and (b) above, the types of signs which they illustrate.

EXAMPLE

3. The ten most frequent words of English. (This exercise anticipates discussion in chapter 4.) The ten most frequent words of English in written texts – and they are very, very frequent – are the following, in order of first to tenth most frequent: *the, of, and, to, a/an, in, that, is, was, he* (Francis and Kučera 1967). Not only are the words frequent, but, because they are essential to expression in the language, they show this frequency very regularly, in any English text of sufficient size and whatever type.

PRACTICE

Take a 250-word text from a newspaper and underline all occurrences of these ten words. Attach the text to a page on which you list the number of occurrences of each, add them up, and calculate the total as a percentage of 250. See the 150-word example below (from *Newsweek*, May 15, 1995). Unless you choose an unusual text, this percentage will almost certainly be between 17% and 21%.

Parking is one of suburbia's highest achievements. In the United States the humblest copy-shop or pizzeria boasts as much space for cars as the average city hall. But it is also a curse that the vast acreage given over to asphalt is useless for any other purpose, and goes unused more than half the time anyway.

Most planners regard parking as a prerequisite for economic growth, like water. But downtown Portland, Ore., which strictly regulates parking, has been thriving with essentially the same space for cars as it had 20 years ago. Developers often build more parking than they actually need; a half-empty lot is presumed to reassure prospective tenants that they'll never run out of space for their cars. Yet a bank, a movie theater and a church are all full at different times. One simple improvement towns can make is to look for ways to share . . . (150 words)

the	6	in	1
of	2	that	2
and	2	is	4
to	4	was	0
a/an	5	he	0
			26

26 / 150 = 17.3%

EXAMPLE

4. Grammar of a fragment of English. Consider these eight sentences, a tiny fragment of the utterances of the English language.

1. Pat taps Sam.
2. Sam taps Pat.
3. Pat tapped Sam.
4. Sam tapped Pat.
5. Pat naps.
6. Sam naps.
7. Pat napped.
8. Sam napped.

Following is a grammar of these few sentences, including rules of spelling, phonology, morphology, and syntax.

Grammar of the eight sentences

1. Lexicon
   a. *Pat*, a noun
   b. *Sam*, a noun
   c. *tap*, a verb followed by a noun
   d. *nap*, a verb not followed by a noun
   e. *s*, verb present tense suffix
   f. *ed*, verb past tense suffix

2. Rules (a partial list)
   A. Phonology and spelling
      a. Words consist of the consonant phones written *p*, *m*, *t*, *n*, *s*, and *d*, and the vowel phones written *a* and *e*.
      b. Every word begins with a consonant.
      c. Every word has *a* after the initial consonant.
      d. Every word ends with a consonant.
   B. Morphology:
      f. Verbs are followed by *s* or *ed*.
   C. Syntax:
      g. Every sentence begins with a noun (the subject).
      h. Every subject is followed by a verb.
      i. Some sentences have a second noun (the direct object) after the verb.

This grammar is simple but still longer and more complicated than the eight-sentence language that it describes! However, as the language is a fragment of English, so the grammar is a fragment of English grammar, and just like all grammars it expresses the characteristic of language known as **creativity**: its generalizations about the eight sentences effectively predict, or generate, new sentences. Four sentences not in the list above but which the grammar generates are:

Pat taps Pat.   Pat tapped Pat.
Sam taps Sam.   Sam tapped Sam.

There is also the creative characteristic of **openness**, such that if we just add to the dictionary the verb *pat*, a verb which, like *tap*, takes an object, the grammar would generate four additional sentences:

Sam pats Pat.   Sam patted Pat.
Pat pats Sam.   Pat patted Sam.

PRACTICE

Answer questions 1–4.

1. How does the grammar of the language – that is, statements of the grammar – have to be changed if:

    a. We add a new noun, *Tad*?
    b. We add a new verb *fan*, a verb with an object?
    c. We add a new noun *Jan*?
    d. We add a new verb *gab*, a verb with no object?
    e. We add a new verb *pay*, a verb with an object?

2. List ten additional sentences which the grammar now generates and describes.

3. Suppose we want to incorporate sentences like:

    Sam and Pat pat Tad and Jan.   Jan and Pat fan Sam.
    Tad and Sam nap.   Sam and Jan gabbed.
    Jan and Sam paid Pat and Tad.

State the new rules of grammar that will be necessary, if we want the sentences of the language to continue to be a subset of those of English.

4. Assume that in the world of this grammar there is only one Pat, one Sam, one Jan, and one Tad, and therefore, as in English generally, instead of saying *Pat fanned Pat*, speakers of the language say *Pat fanned himself*, or *herself*. Add *himself* and *herself* to the lexicon, and add to the meanings of names their appropriate genders, masculine or feminine. Let 'Pat' be either masculine or feminine. Write out a statement or 'rule' of the grammar that will appropriately substitute *herself* or *himself* for a name. State the rule clearly and carefully, so that it will yield English-like sentences.

EXAMPLE

5. Comparative grammar. The **arbitrariness** characteristic of language is usually evident in a comparison of languages, which typically express similar meanings very differently. Compare the following sentences of Amharic, an Ethiopian language, with their English translations. The Amharic sentence is written phonetically; *ə* is a vowel as in English *but*, *i* is a vowel not ordinarily heard in English, and *č* is the consonant usually spelled *ch* in English. Within words morphemes are separated by a hyphen, and a morpheme by morpheme translation of the Amharic sentences is provided to show how its organization differs from that of the English sentences.

Even though the languages are very different from one another, the sentences have almost the same number of morphemes with approximately the same meanings.

English	Amharic
They are Mary-'s sister-s.	jə-marjam ɨhɨt-oč n-aččəw.
	of-Maryam sister-s be(pres. tense)-they
She is Mary-'s sister.	jə-marjam ɨhɨt n-at.
	of-Maryam sister be(pres. tense)-she

The statement of the rules of grammar which describe such short English sentences is not simple.

a. A pronoun *they* or *she* is first in the sentence.
b. This is followed by the present tense verb, *is* after *she*, and *are* after *they*.
c. The verb is followed by the possessing noun.
d. The possessing noun has the suffix -*'s*.
e. This is followed by the possessed noun, a singular noun if the first word (subject of the sentence) is *she* and a plural noun if this is *they*.
f. If the possessed noun is plural it has the suffix -*s*.

PRACTICE

Using similar statements, carefully describe the two Amharic sentences.

PHONETICS

This chapter provides an understanding of the physiological basis of language in the units of vocal sound, phones, and their articulation. For many readers these topics seem packed with detail and new terminology. This is necessary here, however, because an understanding of phonetics is required to fully grasp examples and discussion in later chapters. At first the phones of English are presented, and then a sample of phones of other languages.

Unless stated otherwise, phonetically written English words here (and elsewhere in this book) are as in typical American English.

1. PHONES

Speech is commonly thought of as a sequence of **phones,** more or less unitary segments of the stream of speech. Phones are typically represented as symbols of the **International Phonetic Alphabet** (IPA), for which see figure 2.1, IPA charts of places and manners of articulation of common consonants and vowels of languages of the world.

In fact, the unitary qualities of phones are quite transitory, because the physiology of speech is constantly in motion during speech, so that at any moment of time each phone is being influenced by and influencing neighboring phones. Furthermore, it was noted in chapter 1, §3.2.1 that phones are made up of more elementary units, phonological features. This chapter is concerned with phones; phonological features will be presented in chapter 14.

2. SPEECH PHYSIOLOGY

See the diagram of speech physiology, figure 2.2.

The International Phonetic Alphabet (revised to 1993)

Consonants (pulmonic) _→ lungs (air)_ *(handwritten)*

	Bilabial	Labiodental	Dental	Alveolar	Postalveolar	Retroflex	Palatal	Velar	Uvular	Pharyngeal	Glottal
Plosive	p b			t d		ʈ ɖ	c ɟ	k ɡ	q ɢ		ʔ
Nasal	m	ɱ		n		ɳ	ɲ	ŋ	N		
Trill	ʙ			r					ʀ		
Tap or Flap				ɾ		ɽ					
Fricative	ɸ β	f v	θ ð	s z	ʃ ʒ	ʂ ʐ	ç ʝ	x ɣ	χ ʁ	ħ ʕ	h ɦ
Lateral fricative				ɬ ɮ							
Approximant		ʋ		ɹ		ɻ	j	ɰ			
Lateral approximant				l		ɭ	ʎ	L			

Where symbols appear in pairs, the one to the right represents a voiced consonant. Shaded areas denote articulations judged impossible.

Consonants (non-pulmonic) _→ not w/ lungs (air)_ *(handwritten)*

Clicks	Voiced implosives	Ejectives
ʘ Bilabial	ɓ Bilabial	ʼ as in:
ǀ Dental	ɗ Dental/alveolar	pʼ Bilabial
ǃ (Post)alveolar	ʄ Palatal	tʼ Dental/alveolar
ǂ Palatoalveolar	ɠ Velar	kʼ Velar
ǁ Alveolar lateral	ʛ Uvular	sʼ Alveolar fricative

Vowels

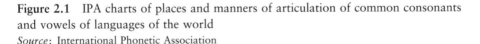

Where symbols appear in pairs, the one to the
right represents a rounded vowel.

Figure 2.1 IPA charts of places and manners of articulation of common consonants and vowels of languages of the world

Source: International Phonetic Association

2.1. Pulmonic egressive airstream

Essential for communication by sound is an airstream. Compression of the lungs creates a **pulmonic egressive airstream**. All languages base the majority of their phones on a pulmonic egressive airstream, and most, like English, employ it exclusively. There are two other ways by which languages create an airstream, and these are described in §6, below, along with presentation of other aspects of phonetics which happen to be absent in English.

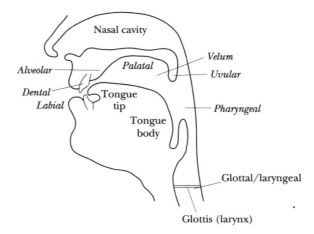

Figure 2.2 Diagram of speech physiology

2.2. Voiced and voiceless phones

When the airstream passes through the **larynx**, or, more specifically, the **glottis**, the opening of the larynx, it passes between the **vocal folds**, two hinged planes of tissue which open and close the glottis.

If the vocal folds are relatively closed and not too tense, the airstream produces vibration of the vocal folds known as **voicing**, the usual frequency of which in human speech is from 80 to 400 cycles per second (cps). Phones produced with this vibration are termed **voiced** and those without it, when the vocal folds are relatively open, **voiceless**. For example, [p, t, k, f, s] are voiceless, and [b, d, g, v, z] are identical, respectively, except for being voiced.

Notice that silence must result when a consonant fully interrupts the airstream, as in [p, t, k] and [b, d, g]: if there is no airstream there can be no sound. Thus the sound of such a consonant is that which it gives to the airstream (a) as the closure is being made, (b) upon release of the closure as the airstream is reinitiated, or, (c) in the case of [b, d, g], in the split second of time after the closure but before the voiced airstream fills the airspace behind the closure.

2.3. Oral and nasal phones

The **velum** or soft palate is the soft flap of tissue that separates the **nasal cavity** from the **oral cavity**. When the velum is down, or open, the airstream is directed, at least in part, into the nasal cavity. If the velum is up, or closed, the airstream is directed fully orally. When you say *Bob* [bɑb] the velum is closed. By contrast, when you say *mom* everything remains the same except that the velum is open, the airstream is directed into the nasal cavity and exits by the nose, and the consonants and the vowel are nasal: [mãm].

2.4. Four articulators

There are four articulators, which modify the airstream: the larynx, the tongue body, the tongue tip, and/or the lips. Phones articulated with the larynx, back of the tongue, tongue tip, and lips are termed, respectively, **laryngeal, dorsal, coronal,** and **labial.**

—Stop= bringing lips together to create break in air

2.5. Eight places of articulation

The airstream may be modified at eight places of articulation: the glottis, pharynx, uvula, velum, palate, alveolum, teeth, and lips. Consonant phones produced at these places are termed, respectively: **glottal, pharyngeal, uvular, velar, palatal, alveolar, dental,** and **labial.** Consonants may be produced at places intermediate to these, including alveopalatal, between the alveolum and palate, and labiodental, with the lower lip touching the upper teeth.

3. TYPES OF PHONES

Recall that **phones** are more or less unitary segments of the stream of speech. In this section, different types of phones are illustrated from English. Some of the important phones of other languages are illustrated in §6, below.

3.1. Consonants

Five types of **consonants** are usually recognized, which differ by their **manner of articulation**: stops, fricatives, affricates, nasals, and approximants.

3.1.1. *Stops*

Full closure or interruption results in a **stop**. If the stop is released with or without voicing, the result is a voiced or voiceless stop, respectively.

With a pulmonic airstream and with the velum closed, so that the airstream is directed orally, complete interruption by closure of the two lips produces the oral bilabial stops [p] (voiceless) and [b] (voiced). Complete interruption at the alveolum, by the tongue tip, produces the oral alveolar stops [t] (voiceless) and [d] (voiced). Complete interruption at the velum by the dorsum, or tongue body, produces the velar oral stops [k] (voiceless) and [g] (voiced). Finally, full interruption of the airstream at the glottis, by the vocal folds, produces the necessarily voiceless glottal stop [ʔ]. With the velum open, so that the airstream is directed nasally, the same bilabial, alveolar, and velar closures produce the bilabial **nasal stop** [m], the alveolar nasal stop [n], and the velar nasal stop [ŋ]. Because these are usually termed simply 'nasals', the oral stops are often termed simply 'stops'.

For examples of words with these stops, and for example words with other phones mentioned below, refer to tables 2.1 and 2.2 of consonant and vowel phones of English.

Table 2.1 Consonant phones of English

Consonant	Description	Example words
[p]	voiceless labial stop	*pie, pop, puppy*
[b]	voiced labial stop	*be, Bob, Bobby*
[t]	voiceless alveolar stop	*toe, tight, tapestry*
[d]	voiced alveolar stop	*do, did, dry-dock*
[k]	voiceless velar stop	*key, kick, crooked*
[g]	voiced velar stop	*go, gag, groggy*
[ʔ]	glottal stop (necessarily voiceless)	*unh-unh, uh-oh*
[f]	voiceless labiodental fricative	*free, fife, fifty-five*
[v]	voiced labiodental fricative	*view, valve, vivacious*
[θ]	voiceless dental fricative	*thin, thick, thirty-three*
[ð]	voiced dental fricative	*though, this, leather*
[s]	voiceless alveolar fricative	*sew, slice, sister*
[z]	voiced alveolar fricative	*zoo, zones, zigzag*
[š] (= [ʃ])	voiceless alveopalatal fricative	*show, shore, ship-shape*
[ž] (= [ʒ])	voiced alveopalatal fricative	*azure, measure, prestige*
[h]	voiceless glottal fricative	*hi, hop, hedgehog*
[č] (= [ʧ])	voiceless alveopalatal affricate	*chew, church, choo-choo*
[ǰ] (= [ʤ])	voiced alveopalatal affricate	*jaw, judge, Georgia*
[m]	labial nasal	*my, most, mammal*
[n]	alveolar nasal	*no, noon, nanny*
[ŋ]	velar nasal	*wing, song, singing*
[l]	alveolar lateral approximant	*low, lot, lately*
[r]	alveopalatal approximant (glide)	*row, roar, rotary*
[w]	labiovelar approximant (glide)	*we, wow, westward*
[j]	palatal approximant (glide)	*you, yard, yesteryear*

3.1.2. Fricatives

The airstream may be forced through a narrow closure, with less than complete interruption, resulting in a **fricative**, with or without voicing. Labiodental fricatives, formed with the lower lip on the upper teeth, are voiceless [f] and voiced [v]. Dental (or interdental) fricatives, formed by the tongue on or between the teeth, are voiceless [θ] and voiced [ð]. Alveolar fricatives are voiceless [s] and voiced [z]. Alveopalatal fricatives are voiceless [š] and voiced [ž]. The voiceless glottal fricative [h] is produced by friction at the vocal folds of the open glottis.

3.1.3. Affricates

A combination stop + fricative is termed an **affricate**. The most common affricates are articulated at the juncture of the alveolum and palate. Without voicing this **alveopalatal** affricate is [č], and with voicing it is [ǰ].

3.1.4. Nasals

Often the nasal stops, English [m, n, ŋ], are termed simply **nasals**.

Table 2.2 Vowel phones of English

Vowel	Description	Example words
American and British		
[i]	high front tense vowel	*see, beat, teen*
[ɪ]	high front lax vowel	*sip, bit, tin*
[e]	mid front tense vowel	*say, bait, taint*
[ɛ]	mid front lax vowel	*said, bet, ten*
[æ]	low front vowel	*sad, bat, tan*
[ə]	mid central vowel	*sup, but, ton*
[ɔ]	mid back lax vowel	*saw, bought, taught*
[o]	mid back tense vowel	*so, boat, tone*
[ʊ]	high back lax vowel	*foot, book, took*
[u]	high back tense vowel	*soon, boot, too*
[ɑ]	low back unrounded vowel	*sod, pot*
British only		
[ɒ]	low back rounded vowel	*sort, part*

3.1.5. Approximants

Lateral (l-like), rhotic or retroflex (r-like) phones, and so-called 'glides' or 'semivowels' are termed **approximants**, because they lack full oral closures as in oral and nasal stops and fricatives.

3.1.5.1. Lateral approximants.   The **lateral** phones are so termed because they are formed with the sides of the tongue lowered, so that the airstream passes laterally around a central closure, usually at the alveolum. The typical lateral phone is alveolar [l], as in English *lip* and *roll*. If the lateral lowerings of these words are absent, the result is [d] instead of [l]: *dip* and *rode*.

3.1.5.2. Retroflex/rhotic approximants.   Typical pronunciations of [r], as in Spanish *pero* 'but' and *caro* 'car', consist of a light tap of the tongue blade on the alveolar ridge. There is often some retroflexion, or turning back of the tongue blade, and bunching of the tongue body. English [r] at the beginning and end of *roar* [ror] consists of such a gesture, without contact, in which the blade of the tongue curls back from the alveolum, toward the palate, and/or the back of the tongue body is bunched (the IPA symbol for this English phone is properly [ɹ]). Phones with this articulation and resulting acoustic quality are termed **retroflex** (turning back of the tongue blade) or **rhotic** (bunching of the tongue body).

3.1.5.3. Glide approximants.   **Glides**, or 'semivowels', have no steady state, but consist entirely of a dynamic motion of an articulator. If the tongue blade gestures toward the palate, behind the alveopalatal area of [r], the result is the palatal glide [j] (the phone ordinarily spelled *y* in English). If the tongue-body gesture is high and back, toward the velum, and the lips are rounded, the result is the labiovelar glide approximant [w]. English [r] involves such a dynamic gesture of the tongue blade toward the alveolum, and may be considered a glide like [j] and [w].

3.2. Vowels

A momentary shaping of the airstream, without interruption, results in **vowels**. Vowels may be **high** or **low** and **front** or **back**, depending, respectively, on whether during their articulation the body of the tongue is raised or lowered and fronted or backed. Vowels with neither fronting nor backing are **central**, and vowels with neither raising nor lowering are **mid**. These six dimensions define vowels in nine places of the oral vowel-space, as follows:

	Front	Central	Back
High	i	ɨ	u
Mid	e	ə	o
Low	æ	a	ɑ

Back non-low vowels are typically accompanied by lip-rounding, as in [u, o], above; these are called **round** or rounded vowels. If the velum is down during a vowel, so that the airstream is directed though the nose, the result is a **nasal vowel,** written with [˜], for example [ĩ, ɔ̃, ũ,]. The high central vowel [ɨ] is not ordinarily heard in English.

3.3. Obstruents and sonorants

Stops, affricates, and fricatives are formed by articulations which completely obscure the airstream frequencies, and are appropriately termed **obstruents**. Oral (but not nasal) stops interrupt the airstream altogether, creating airstream turbulence upon release, and fricatives compress it so greatly that friction or turbulence is also introduced. Affricates, recall, are stop + fricative combinations. Obstruents may be voiced or voiceless.

All other types of phones – nasal 'stops', approximants, and vowels – have sonorous airstreams and are appropriately termed **sonorants**. Sonorants don't interrupt the airstream, so they have a sonorous aural quality. Sonorants are ordinarily voiced, but may exceptionally be voiceless.

4.   SUPRASEGMENTALS

In addition to phones, there are **suprasegmental** qualities, which are spread over more than one phone. These are also known as **prosodies**. The most common of these are length, stress, and pitch.

4.1. Length

Some phones are about twice as long as others of the same quality. The IPA phonetic symbol for this extra length is [ː]. Long consonant phones are heard in English when consecutive words end and begin with the same consonant, as in:

[bʊkːes]	'bookcase'	[parkːɑrz]	'park cars'
[pɛnːɑjf]	'penknife'	[fʊlːitər]	'full liter'

Long phones are sometimes written by doubling the phonetic symbol: [bʊkkes] 'bookcase', [pɛnnɑjf] 'penknife'.

4.2. Stress

Syllables, especially the vowels of these syllables, may differ by degree of **stress**. Stress is the intensity, or loudness (volume/time ratio), of the airstream. Compare these three three-syllable English words, which have greatest stress on their first, second, and third vowels, respectively (underlined letters):

a. canopy   [kǽnəpi]
b. atomic   [ətámɪk]
c. disappoint   [dɪsəpɔ́jnt]

The third, *disappoint*, may be pronounced with a third degree of stress: secondary stress, in the first syllable, [dìsəpɔ́jnt]. The three degrees of stress are clearer in *elevate* [ɛ́ləvèt]. The three levels of stress are written with the acute accent mark [´] for primary, the grave accent mark [`] for secondary, and no mark for no stress.

4.3. Pitch

Pitch is the frequency of vibration of the vocal folds. The regular patterns of these frequencies over a phrase or sentence are termed **intonation**. A short phrase like English 'You know' can be said with various intonations, and these provide somewhat different meanings, including

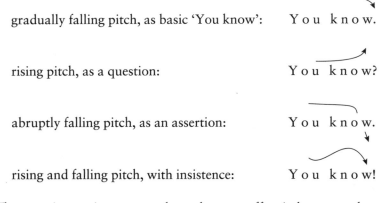

gradually falling pitch, as basic 'You know':   Y o u   k n o w.

rising pitch, as a question: Y o u   k n o w?

abruptly falling pitch, as an assertion: Y o u   k n o w.

rising and falling pitch, with insistence: Y o u   k n o w!

The same intonation patterns have the same effect in longer or shorter utterances:

It's already four o'clock. Yes.

It's already four o'clock? Yes?

Such a pattern of pitch when applied to differentiate meanings of words rather than phrases and sentences is termed **tone**. Tone is not employed in English, and examples from other languages are given below (§6.3.1).

5. PHONES OF ENGLISH

Exemplification above was mainly with English examples. In fact, the phones of English include most of those which are common in languages of the world, and some which are not.

5.1. English consonants

The consonants of a language are concisely presented in a place and manner of articulation chart. The typical set of 25 English consonants is seen in the place and manner of articulation chart of figure 2.3. For description of these, and three words exemplifying each one, see table 2.1 of the consonant phones of English. Many phones other than these are heard in English, but these are basic, and, for this introduction, sufficient.

The chart of consonants of figure 2.3 may differ in the following ways from similar charts in other books:

a. [f, v] are termed labial but to be precise are **labiodental**, articulated with the lower lip on the upper teeth. Compare them to the **bilabial stops** [p, b], articulated with closure of the two lips.

b. [ʔ] is not very important in English, and some accounts omit it.

c. [š, ž] may also be written with the IPA symbols [ʃ, ʒ]. Writing these [š, ž] makes clear their shared alveopalatal aspect, and their similarity to [s, z], respectively.

d. [č, ǰ] may also be written with the IPA symbols [ʧ, ʤ], which makes clear their stop + fricative composition. Writing these as [č, ǰ] makes clear their similarity to [š, ž], respectively, and their similarity in English to single phones.

e. [w] is labial and velar, and in the labial place here; it has lip rounding plus a velar gesture of the back of the tongue blade.

f. [ʍ], a voiceless version of [w], appears in some English dialects in pronunciations of words like *when* and *where*, spelled with *wh*. Here this phone is considered to be to be [h] followed by [w]. (In fact, it was spelled *hw* in English from the 10th to 13th centuries.)

		Labial	Dental	Alveolar	Alveo-palatal	Palatal	Velar	Glottal
Obstruents								
Stops	vl	p		t			k	ʔ
	vd	b		d			g	
Affricates	vl				č			
	vd				ǰ			
Fricatives	vl	f	θ	s	š			h
	vd	v	ð	z	ž			
Sonorants								
Nasals		m		n			ŋ	
Lateral				l				
Glides		w			r	j		

vl = voiceless, vd = voiced

Place and manner of articulation chart of 25 consonants of English

	Front	Central	Back
High	i ɪ		ʊ u
Mid	e ɛ	ə	ɔ o
Low	æ		ɑ

	Front	Central	Back
High	i ɪ		ʊ u
Mid	e ɛ	ə	ɔ o
Low	æ		ɑ ɒ

Diphthongs: ɑj, ɑw, ɔj

Diphthongs: ɑj, ɑw, ɔj, ɪə, ɛə, ɑə

Eleven vowels of typical
American English

Twelve vowels of typical British English

Figure 2.3   Consonants and vowels of English

5.2. English vowels

See the two vowel charts, also in figure 2.3: one for the 11 vowels of typical American English and another for the 12 vowels of typical British English. These vowels are described and exemplified in table 2.2 of the vowel phones of English. Many vowel phones other than these are heard in English, but these are basic, and, for this introduction, sufficient.

Notice that there are two high front vowels [i, ɪ], two high back vowels [ʊ, u], two mid front vowels [e, ɛ], and two mid back vowels [ɔ, o]. The second, more central, of each of the pairs [i, ɪ], [e, ɛ], and [u, ʊ], is often termed a **lax** vowel, and the first, more peripheral, member, [i, u, e], plus [o, ɔ], is often termed a **tense** vowel. The so-called lax vowels are generally speaking somewhat centralized in place of articulation, and their characterization as 'lax' is mainly impressionistic; they cannot be final in English words. The 'tense' or peripheral vowels may be final in English words, as in *see* [si], *say* [se], *sue* [su], *so* [so], and *saw* [sɔ].

5.2.1. American English vowels

The vowels of American English of figure 2.3 may differ from other such accounts you see in other books, as follows:

a. Sometimes one sees two mid central vowels, [ə] and [ʌ]. Basically [ʌ] is [ə] with stress, as in *but* and *son*, and the first vowel of *funny*. If stress is shown as a stress mark ([bə́t], [sə́n]), as in this book, [ʌ] is unnecessary.

b. Sometimes there are phonetic symbols for retroflex mid central vowels: stressed as in *bird* [bɝd] and unstressed as in *father* [fáðɚ]. In this book, these are treated as sequences [ə́r] and [ər], respectively: [bə́rd], [fáðər].

c. [ɔ] is absent in the speech of some Americans, especially in the West, who have [ɑ] in words like *saw* and *caught*, so that *caught* sounds just like *cot*.

d. Sometimes the so-called tense and lax pairs are symbolized differently; for example, instead of [i, ɪ], one may see [iʸ, i]. This is appropriate, because often the tense vowel has a dynamic rising quality. Writing [i, ɪ] is perhaps simpler.

e. American [ɑ] is often less back than typical British [ɑ], and is sometimes written [a] (IPA [a] is a front vowel, but not as front as [æ]).

There are vowel + glide sequences known as **diphthongs**, of which the second part is [w] or [j]. Sometimes the diphthongs are written with two vowel symbols, [ɑi, ɑu, ɔi], which contradicts a useful generalization preserved by writing [ɑj, ɑw, ɔj], that each vowel represents one syllable. American English has three frequent diphthongs, as in the following words:

[ɑj]:	night	[nɑjt]	kite	[kɑjt]
[ɑw]:	now	[nɑw]	south	[sɑwθ]
[ɔj]:	toy	[tɔj]	soil	[sɔjl]

5.2.2.   British English vowels

A common variety of British English has a vowel additional to those of American, making 12: [ɒ], a low back vowel with rounding, which typically appears in words for which American has [ɑ] + [r], such as *tart* and *park*. In words for which American has [ə] + [r] (= [ɝ]) in words such as *bird* and *work*, varieties of British which lack [r] in such words are usually considered to have a 13th vowel, often longer and perhaps higher than [ə], written [ɜ]. Standard British parallel to American [o] is ordinarily diphthongal [əo], or [əʊ], and there are other, smaller and variable, quality differences.

British has **diphthongs** with [ə] in words in which American has final [r]:

[ɪə]:	tear (n.)	[tɪə]	fear	[fɪə]
[ɛə]:	bear	[bɛə]	tear (v.)	[tɛə]
[ɑə]:	tire	[tɑə]	fire	[fɑə]

6. OTHER LANGUAGES

6.1. Airstream

All languages employ, for the majority of their phones, the pulmonic airstream employed by English, and some languages make use of two other airstream types: **glottalic** and **velaric**.

A **glottalic airstream** is produced in a number of languages, by closing the vocal folds and raising or lowering the larynx during an oral closure. (Consonants with a glottalic airstream are shown in a separate chart in figure 2.1.) Raising the glottis compresses air behind the closure, and when the closure is released while the glottis remains closed there is a sudden audible outrushing or explosion of air. Consonants so produced are termed glottalic ejectives, or **ejectives**. Here are examples of ejective stops and an ejective fricative in words of Amharic, a Semitic language of Ethiopia:

[t']:	[t'im]	'hair'	[mətː'a]	'he came'
[k']:	[k'ən]	'day'	[ruk']	'far'
[s']:	[s'əhay]	'sun'	[məs'ɨhaf]	'book'

When the closed glottis is lowered during an oral closure, which is then released, the result is a sudden audible inrushing or implosion of air. Consonants so produced are termed glottalic **implosives**. Here are examples of implosive labial and alveolar stops [ɓ, ɗ], and implosive glide ['j] in words of Hausa, a Chadic language of Nigeria and neighboring west African countries:

[ɓ]:	[ɓawnaː]	'buffalo'	[haɓàː]	'chin',
[ɗ]:	[ɗawkàː]	'take'	[ɗajɗaj]	'one by one'
['j]:	['jantʃi]	'freedom'	['ja'ja]	'daughters'

A **velaric ingressive airstream** is employed in the small group of Khoisan languages of southeast Africa and some of their neighboring Bantu languages, notably Zulu. When the tongue blade is pressed against the velum or palate and then withdrawn, the resulting airspace is a momentary relative vacuum into which air rushes. Velaric ingressive stops so produced are termed **clicks**. Examples of dental, alveolar, and palatal clicks, with typical velar [k] onsets, in words of Nama, a Khoisan language of Namibia and South Africa, are [kǀoa] 'put into', [kǃoas] 'hollow', and [kǂais] 'calling' (Ladefoged and Maddieson 1996, p. 263).

6.2. Phones

6.2.1. Consonants

A number of consonants absent in English are relatively common in the world's languages, including consonants at places of articulation not employed in English. Following is a sample of these.

a. Bilabial fricatives. Recall that English labial fricatives are labiodental, not bilabial: [f, v]. English speakers readily produce a voiceless bilabial fricative [ɸ] when blowing out candles, but the phone has no role in the language. A language with bilabial voiceless and voiced fricatives [ɸ, β] as well as labiodental fricatives [f, v] is Ewe, of Ghana and Togo. Example Ewe words (from Ladefoged 1993, p. 282) are [éɸá] 'he polished' and [èβè] 'Ewe (language)'. Ewe words which differ from these just by labiodental rather than labial fricatives are [éfá] 'he was cold' and [èvè] 'two'.

b. Velar fricatives. Recall that English has velar stops [k, g] but no velar fricatives. A language with voiceless and voiced velar fricatives [x, ɣ], respectively, is Arabic. Example Arabic words are [xubz] 'bread' and [ɣaːli] 'expensive'. German has a voiceless velar fricative, written *ch*, when this follows back vowels as in [buːx] *Buch* 'book', and Spanish has a voiced velar fricative, written *g*, when this is between vowels as in [laɣo] *lago* 'lake'.

c. Voiceless uvular stop and fricative. A language with a voiceless uvular stop [q] and voiceless and voiced uvular fricatives [χ, ʁ] is Yupik Eskimo. Here is a short Yupik sentence with all three of these: [qaja čuaχ tuŋunʁituq] 'The little kayak is not black'. The standard French phone spelled *r* is the voiced uvular fricative [ʁ], as in [paʁi] 'Paris'.

d. Pharyngeal fricatives. A language with voiceless and voiced pharyngeal fricatives [ħ, ʕ], respectively, is Arabic. Example Arabic words are [baħr] 'sea' and [ʕajn] 'eye'.

e. Retroflex tap and trill. The *r* of perhaps most languages, such as that written *r* in Spanish (as in *pero* 'but', *caro* 'expensive'), is a **tap** [r], articulated with a single tap of the tongue tip at or slightly behind the alveolar ridge; its IPA symbol is [ɾ]. Multiple or 'trilled' taps are a **trill** [r]. The phone written *rr* in Spanish is a trill, as in *perro* 'dog', *carro* 'car'.

6.2.2. *Vowels*

There are vowels absent in English but relatively common in the world's languages. Following is a sample of these.

a. Round front vowels. A language with high and mid round front vowels [y, ø], respectively, is French. Pronounce these by articulating [i] and [e], respectively, with lip rounding. Example French words with these are [sy] *su* 'known' and [sø] *ceux* 'those'. Lacking the rounding but otherwise identical to [sy] is [si] *si* 'if'; being back instead of front but otherwise identical to [sy] is [su] *sou* 'sou' (five centime coin).

b. High central vowel. Recall that English has a mid central vowel and high front and back vowels but no high central vowel [ɨ]. A language with this vowel is Amharic. Example Amharic words are [wɨdː] 'expensive', and [ɨwnət] 'true'.

6.3. Suprasegmentals

Two suprasegmental features important in other languages but not in English are **tone** and **length**.

6.3.1. Tone

The rate of vibration of the vocal folds provides pitch, heard especially on vowels. When used to distinguish words this is termed **tone** (versus the distinctive pitch pattern of a phrase or clause, termed **intonation**). Languages which use pitch in this way are termed 'tone languages'. Chinese is an example. The following somewhat famous quartet of Chinese words differ just by their tone:

[mā] 'mother'   [mǎ] 'horse'
[má] 'hemp'   [mà] 'scold'

[ˉ] in 'mother' shows a high tone, [ˊ] in 'hemp' rising tone, [ˇ] in 'horse' falling-rising tone, and [ˋ] in 'scold' falling tone.

Another tone language is Hausa, of northern Nigeria, in which one finds the three tones high, low, and falling (and in which tones are marked differently from Chinese):

[wàː] 'who?'   [sakaː] 'put on'
[wâː] 'elder brother'   [sàkaː] 'release'

'Who?' has (long) [aː] with low tone [ˋ] and 'release' has (short) [a] with low tone [ˋ]. 'Elder brother' has [aː] with falling tone [ˆ]. The first and last vowels of 'put on' and the last vowel of 'release' have high tone, which is unmarked.

6.3.2. Length

We saw that English **long consonants** only occur when two like consonants meet at a word-boundary, as in *bookcase* [bʊkːes]. In other languages, however, long consonants may be heard within single words, as in Amharic, with pairs of words like the following:

[səfi]   'tailor'   [səfːi]   'wide'
[wɑnɑ]   'swimming'   [wɑnːɑ]   'most important'
[ɑlə]   'he/it said'   [ɑlːə]   'he/it is present'

In English, very **long vowels** can sometimes be heard when two words respectively end and begin in a vowel of the same quality, such as *see East* [siːst], which contrasts with *ceased* [sist]. Also, English vowels differ in length depending on following consonants: that of *bid*, for example, is audibly longer than that of *bit*.

In many languages, however, vowel length may be the meaningful difference between words, as in Japanese, with pairs of words like the following:

[i]	'stomach'	[iː]	'good'
[obɑsɑn]	'aunt'	[obɑːsɑn]	'grandmother'
[kuki]	'stem'	[kuːki]	'air'

Long vowels are sometimes written with a line (macron) over them: Japanese [ī] 'good', [obāsɑn] 'grandmother'.

Suggestions for
ADDITIONAL READING

A good introductory phonetics textbook is Peter Ladefoged's *A Course in Phonetics* (1993). A very readable introduction to English phonetics is Charles Kreidler's *Describing Spoken English: an Introduction* (1997). For the terminology of phonetics see *A Dictionary of Linguistics and Phonetics* by David Crystal (1991), and for an advanced, thorough, treatment of phonetics, see John Laver's *Principles of Phonetics* (1994). The phonetics of the world's languages is surveyed in Ladefoged and Ian Maddieson's *The Sounds of the World's Languages* (1996). Regarding stress in English words, see *English Word-stress*, by Eric Fudge (1984).

IMPORTANT CONCEPTS AND TERMS IN THIS CHAPTER

- phone
- International Phonetic Alphabet
- pulmonic airstream
- larynx
- glottis
- vocal fold
- voicing
- voiced
- voiceless
- velum
- nasal cavity
- oral cavity
- articulators
- laryngeal
- glide
- retroflex
- rhotic
- vowel
- high
- low
- front
- back
- central
- mid
- round
- nasal vowel
- obstruent
- sonorant
- dorsal
- coronal
- labial
- glottal
- pharyngeal
- uvular

- velar
- palatal
- alveolar
- dental
- consonant
- manner of articulation
- stop
- nasal stop
- fricative
- affricate
- alveopalatal
- nasal
- approximant
- lateral
- suprasegmental
- prosody
- length

- stress
- intonation
- tone
- labiodental
- bilabial
- lax
- tense
- diphthong
- glottalic airstream
- ejective
- implosive
- velaric ingressive airstream
- click
- tap
- trill
- long consonant
- long vowel

OUTLINE OF
CHAPTER 2

1. **Phones**
2. **Speech physiology**
   1. Pulmonic egressive airstream
   2. Voiced and voiceless phones
   3. Oral and nasal phones
   4. Four articulators
   5. Eight places of articulation
3. **Types of phones**
   1. Consonants
      1. Stops
      2. Fricatives
      3. Affricates
      4. Nasals
      5. Approximants
         1. Lateral approximants
         2. Retroflex/rhotic approximants
         3. Glide approximants
   2. Vowels
   3. Obstruents and sonorants
4. **Suprasegmentals**
   1. Length
   2. Stress
   3. Pitch

5. **Phones of English**
    1. English consonants
    2. English vowels
        1. American English vowels
        2. British English vowels
6. **Other languages**
    1. Airstream
    2. Phones
        1. Consonants
        2. Vowels
    3. Suprasegmentals
        1. Tone
        2. Length

EXAMPLES AND PRACTICE

EXAMPLE

As above, typical American English is assumed in these examples and exercises.

1. Read phonetic English I. Following are some English two-word phrases, written phonetically using the 36 phonetic symbols of the place and manner of articulation chart of consonants and American English vowel chart of figure 2.3. No spaces are written between the words, since no spaces are pronounced, and phonetic writing properly represents pronunciations, not spellings. The words are written according to the pronunciation of the author. You may have different pronunciations. The first phrase is also written in ordinary orthography, as an example.

1. maskawrəšə   Moscow, Russia
2. ləndənɪŋlənd   London, England.
3. hɛlsɪŋkifɪnlənd   Helsinki, Finland
4. viɛnəɔstriə   Viena, Austria
5. romɪtali   Rome, Italy
6. kopənhagəndɛnmark   Kopenhajan,
7. azlonorwe   Oslo, norwe Denmark
8. dəblɪnajrlənd   dublin, Irland.
9. brəsəlzbɛljəm   brussels, belgium
10. barsəlonəspen   Barcalona, spain

11. æθənzgris   *ʲʰ* anthes, Green
12. krakawpolənd   Crac
13. bərlɪnjərməni   Berlin, Germany
14. stakhomswidən   stockolm
15. budəpesthəŋgəri   Budapest
16. pragčɛkripəblɪk   Prag.
17. jənivəswɪtsərlənd Geneva
18. æmstərdæmhalənd Ams
19. lɪzbənporčugəl
20. rigalætvia   Riga, Lat'ia

PRACTICE

Write 2–20 in ordinary orthography.

EXAMPLE

2. Read phonetic English II. Following are ten English phrases, written phonetically. The words are written according to the pronunciation of the author, still using the basic 36 consonant and vowel symbols. The first is written in ordinary orthography, as an example.

1. dontstapnaw Don't stop now.
2. ɪzðɪsrajt *Is this right.*
3. husɛdðæt ~~How is that~~ *who said that.*
4. ajθɪŋkso *I think so*
5. ðætstuməč *that's too much*
6. lɛtsgɛtgoɪŋ *let's get going*
7. fɪlɪtʔəp *Fill it up.* (=stop)
8. ɪtsnəmbəret *it's number 8*
9. jʊrkɪdɪŋmi *You're kidding me*
10. ðizlʊkgʊd *These look good.*

PRACTICE

Write 2–10 in ordinary orthography.

EXAMPLE

3. Read phonetic English III. Following is a short English text (IPA 1949, p. 1), written phonetically using the basic 36 phonetic symbols as above. Pronunciation is according to the author's careful speech. To make it easier to read, there are spaces between words and extra space between sentences.

ðə nanromən lɛdərz əv ði ɪntərnæšənəl fənɛdɪk ælfəbɛt hæv bɛn dɪzajnd
The non roman letters of the international phonetig alphabet have been disigned.
æz far æz pasɪbəl tə harmənajz wɛl wɪθ romən lɛdərz ði əsosiešən dəz nat
as fassi possible to harmonize well with roman letters the associal does not
rɛkəgnajz mekšɪft lɛdərz ɪt rɛkəgnajzɪz onli lɛdərz hwɪč hæv bɛn
recognize make shift letters. It reconizes only letters which have been.
kærfəli kət so æz tə bi ɪn harməni wɪθ ði əðər lɛdərz
carefully cut so as to be in harmony with the others letters.

PRACTICE

Write the text in ordinary orthography.

EXAMPLE

4. Read phonetic English IV. Following is another, longer, English text written phonetically. Here pronunciation is according to the author's somewhat casual speech. Casual speech has many modifications and even omissions of the phones heard in careful speech. Here spaces are provided only at possible pauses between sentences and phrases.

ðənɔrθwɪnd ənðəsən wərargjuɪŋwənde əbawthwɪčəvðəmwəzstrɔŋgər
and the Sun were arguing one day about which one of them was stronger
hwɛnətrævlərkeməlɔŋ ræptəpɪnɪzovərkot ðeəgrɪdðæt ðəwənhukʊdmekðə
when a traveler came along rapidly they agreed that they the one who could make
trævlərtekɪzkotəf wʊdbikənsɪdərdstrɔŋgər ðænðiəðərwən ðɛnðənɔrθ
traveler to take his coat off Re
wɪndblu æzhardæzhikʊd bətðəhardərhiblu ðətajtərðətrævlərræptɪzkot
wind blue as hard as he could but the harder Re blew the

ərɑwndhɪm ænætlæst ðɛnðənɔrθwɪndgevəptrɑjɪŋ ðɛnðəsənbəgæntəšɑjnhat

ə ᴀᴏund hɪm

ən rɑjtəwe ðətrævlərtukhɪzkotɔf ənsoðənɔrθwɪnd hædtuædmɪt ðætðəsən

wəzstrɔŋgər ðænhiwəz

Write the text in ordinary orthography.

---

5. English word stress. *Happy* has the same pattern of stress as *writer*, with stress on the first syllable. *Desire* has the same pattern of stress as *resolve*, with stress on the second syllable. The words *salivate*, *entirely*, and *resurrect* have first, second, and third-syllable stress, respectively.

The following three-syllable words also have first, second, or third-syllable stress.

a. Mark the stressed syllable of each.

educate, engineer, contagious, cortisone, linguistic, serenade, simplify, decision, picturesque, cigarette, mesmerize, collection, debonair, catalog, examine, absentee, government, computer

b. List three more words with first-syllable stress, three more with second-syllable stress, and three more with third-syllable stress.

---

6. Main stress in English words. The acute accent ´ over a vowel shows the primary or main stress of a word, and the grave accent ` over a vowel shows secondary stress. *Arkansas* has three vowels, one with primary, one with secondary, and one with no stress. In *Arizona* also three levels of stress are audible. The unmarked vowels are unstressed.

árkənsɔ̀ Arkansas   æ̀rɪzónə Arizona

Mark the primary and secondary stress of the vowels in these names of states. Some have no secondary stress.

1.	nəbræskə	Nebraska	6.	mæsəčusəts	Massachusetts
2.	flɔrədə	Florida	7.	mɪšəgən	Michigan
3.	kælɪfɔrnjə	California	8.	numɛksiko	New Mexico
4.	sɑwθdəkotə	South Dakota	9.	dɛləwær	Delaware
5.	pɛnsəlvenjə	Pennsylvania	10.	luwiziænə	Louisiana

EXAMPLE

7. Sounds and English spellings. Because the relation between phones and English spelling is inconsistent, there may be more than one spelling for one pronunciation, or two pronunciations for one spelling. Thus [sin] is the pronunciation of *seen* or *scene*, and *lead* is the spelling of both [lid] and [lɛd].

PRACTICE

a. Give two spellings for each pronunciation 1–20.

1.	[flɑwər]	11.	[rod]
2.	[fɪl]	12.	[hol]
3.	[tiz]	13.	[sɛnt]
4.	[rɛd]	14.	[pen]
5.	[rɑjt]	15.	[brek]
6.	[sin]	16.	[prɪns]
7.	[jǐɪm]	17.	[sid]
8.	[for]	18.	[trækt]
9.	[bɑw]	19.	[tɔt]
10.	[no]	20.	[gret]

b. Give two pronunciations for each spelling 1–5.

1. wind
2. read
3. bass
4. entrance
5. does

EXAMPLE

8. Articulatory descriptions I. Our mental dictionaries must associate the meanings of simple words with their pronunciations. It is difficult to imagine what meanings might look like, but forms may be thought of as descriptions of phonetic articulations.

PRACTICE

Match 1–26, English spelled words, with articulatory descriptions (a)–(z). The first answer is given as an example.

_m_	1.	top	___	11.	see	___	21.	big
___	2.	tree	___	12.	need	___	22.	now
___	3.	road	___	13.	run	___	23.	soon
___	4.	car	___	14.	move	___	24.	wool
___	5.	key	___	15.	play	___	25.	then
___	6.	note	___	16.	take	___	26.	thin
___	7.	gate	___	17.	red			
___	8.	lake	___	18.	hat			
___	9.	feed	___	19.	old			
___	10.	know	___	20.	new			

very important — on Mid-term [handwritten annotation]

    voiceless alveolar fricative, high front tense vowel

    voiced velar stop, mid front tense vowel, voiceless alveolar stop

    voiceless alveolar stop, mid front tense vowel, voiceless velar stop

    voiceless velar stop, low back vowel, retroflex approximant

    voiced dental fricative, mid front lax vowel, alveolar nasal

    alveolar nasal, low back vowel, labial glide

    voiceless alveolar stop, retroflex approximant, high front tense vowel

    labial nasal, high back tense vowel, voiced labial fricative

    voiceless labial fricative, high front tense vowel, voiced alveolar stop

    lateral approximant, mid front tense vowel, voiceless velar stop

    labial glide, high back lax vowel, lateral approximant

    alveolar nasal, high front tense vowel, voiced alveolar stop

    voiceless alveolar stop, low back vowel, voiceless labial stop

    voiceless dental fricative, high front lax vowel, alveolar nasal

    glottal fricative, low front vowel, voiceless alveolar stop

    alveolar nasal, mid back tense vowel, voiceless alveolar stop

    retroflex approximant, mid central vowel, alveolar nasal

    voiceless labial stop, lateral approximant, mid front tense vowel

    alveolar nasal, high back tense vowel

    mid back tense vowel, lateral approximant, voiced alveolar stop

    retroflex approximant, mid front lax vowel, voiced alveolar stop

    voiceless velar stop, high front tense vowel

    voiced labial stop, high front lax vowel, voiced velar stop

    voiceless alveolar fricative, high back tense vowel, alveolar nasal

    alveolar nasal, mid back tense vowel

    retroflex approximant, mid back tense vowel, voiced alveolar stop

EXAMPLE

9. Articulatory descriptions II.

PRACTICE

Give articulatory descriptions, like those above, for *go, to, pay, fee, odd, us, in,* and *am*.

EXAMPLE

10. Example words for English consonants and vowels. Notice the example words which illustrate the English consonants and vowels in tables 2.1 and 2.2.

PRACTICE

(a) Write these example words as they are spelled. (b) Add two words to each list of three, writing them both as spelled and phonetically, using just the 36 phonetic symbols of these examples.

Examples of words illustrating English consonants

1 [p] paj, pap, pəpi   3 [t] to, tajt, tæpəstri
2 [b] bi, bab, babi   4 [d] du, dɪd, drajdak

ଓ[k] ki, kɪk, krʊkəd	\ᕼ[h] haj, hap, hɛjhɔg
ᕚ[g] go, gæg, grɑgi	\ᕆ[č] ču, čərč, čuču
𝈎[f] fri, fajf, fɪftifajv	\𝈎[ǰ] ǰɔj, ǰəǰ, ǰorǰə
ᕝ[v] viw, vælv, vɪvešəs	\ᕝ[m] maj, most, mæməl
ᕕ[θ] θɪn, θɪk, θərtiθri	\ᕘ[n] no, nun, næni
\ᕔ[ð] ðo, ðɪs, lɛðər	2ᕔ[ŋ] wɪŋ, sɔŋ, rɪŋɪŋ
\\[s] so, slajs, sɪstər	2⅃[l] lo, lɑt, lɛtli
\²[z] zon, zɪgzæg, dɔgz	2²[r] ro, ror, rotəri
\ᕄ[š] šo, šor, šɪpšep	2ᕄ[w] wi, wɑw, wɛstwərd
\ᕀ[ž] æžər, mɛžər, prɛstiž	2ᕀ[j] ju, jɑrd, jɛstərjɪr

Examples of words illustrating English vowels

[i]	si, bit, tin	[ɔ]	sɔ, bɔt, tɔt
[ɪ]	sɪp, bɪt, tɪn	[o]	so, bot, ton
[e]	se, bet, tent	[ʊ]	fʊt, bʊk, tʊk
[ɛ]	sɛd, bɛt, tɛn	[u]	sud, but, tun
[æ]	sæd, bæt, tæn	[aj]	tajd, bajt, krajm
[ə]	səp, bət, tən	[aw]	lawd, ǰawst, sawnd
[ɑ]	sad, pat, tap	[ɔj]	kɔjl, bɔjld, pɔjzd

> EXAMPLE

11. Write phonetic English I.

> PRACTICE

Write the following text phonetically, as read in your normal speech, using just the 36 basic phonetic symbols for English. Provide spaces between words. Don't neglect [ə], the most frequent English vowel. You needn't mark stress. Be guided by the examples above, especially practice 3 and practice 4.

> I am a part of all that I have met, yet all experience is an arch wherethrough gleams that untravelled world whose margin fades forever and forever when I move.
>
> (from 'Ulysses', Alfred, Lord Tennyson)

> EXAMPLE

12. Write phonetic English II.

> PRACTICE

Take a 25-word text from a newspaper, attach it to a page, and write it phonetically, as read in your own normal speech, again using just the 36 basic phonetic symbols for English. This time, provide spaces only where you pause in reading. Notice that if your text includes a number, such as '112', you have to write this phonetically, like any other word: [ə həndrəd ən twɛlv]. Again, don't mark stress and don't neglect [ə].

PHONES AND PHONEMES

This chapter presents phonetics in more detail, and shows how we classify phones and organize them into a much smaller number of units, phonemes, by important universal principles of learning.

1. BROAD AND NARROW PHONETIC WRITING

Discussion above has concerned rather rough phonetic writing. Many phonetic characteristics of the stream of speech were ignored, and only a small number of the phones made possible by the physiology of speech were illustrated, including an idealized set of phones of English. Numerous phones heard in English speech were ignored. In fact, the phones of even one language are so many as to be almost innumerable.

1.1. Coronal nasal consonants

Consider the consonant employed as the first and last phone of the English words *none* and *nine*, [n]. This phone is coronal (articulated with the tongue blade) and nasal (the velum is lowered, so that the airstream is directed through the nose). The tongue blade makes a stop closure at the alveolum, the ridge just back of the upper teeth, while the velum is lowered. There are a number of coronal nasal phones very similar to this one, but different. A coronal nasal may be:

    a. somewhat forward, so that the blade contacts the teeth. This phone is written [n̪], and is heard in English when a coronal nasal precedes a dental consonant [θ, ð], as in *tenth*, [tɛn̪θ].

    b. somewhat back on the alveolar ridge, termed retroflex and written [ɳ]. This phone is heard in English when a coronal nasal follows [r], as in *earn*, [ərɳ].

c. articulated with the tongue body raised, so that it contacts the palate. This phone is written [ɲ], and is heard in English when a coronal nasal precedes [j], as in *onion*: [ɲ], [əɲjən].

d. articulated with the length of a vowel, as a syllable, for which the phonetic symbol is [n̩], and heard in English when word-final after other alveolar consonants as in *button* [bətn̩] and *hidden* [hɪdn̩].

In broad, rough, phonetic writing, the simple phonetic symbol [n] might be written for any one of the dental [n̪], retroflex [ɳ], palatal [ɲ], syllabic [n̩], or voiced alveolar nonsyllabic [n] phones. But in careful, detailed, phonetic writing in which all these different coronal nasal phones are distinguished, [n] must be specifically understood as voiced, alveolar, and nonsyllabic.

1.2. High front lax vowels

Consider the vowel phone in the middle of the English words *bid* or *sit*. This phone is articulated by raising and fronting the tongue blade, though not so high or forward as in [i] of *bead* and *seat*. This vowel, described as high, front, and lax, whose phonetic symbol is [ɪ], may be modified in various ways; it may be articulated:

a. nasalized, with the velum somewhat open, when a nasal consonant precedes or follows, as in *knit* or *kin*, respectively; this phone is written [ɪ̃]: [nɪ̃t], [kɪ̃n].

b. lengthened, when stressed and a single voiced consonant follows in the syllable, as in *bid*; this phone is written [ɪ́ː], [bɪ́ːd].

c. voiceless, when it is unstressed between two voiceless consonants as in *anticipate*, written [ɪ̥], [æntɪ̥spèt].

d. somewhat raised and fronted but not to the extent of [i], when final in a word such as *funny*: [ɪ˔], [fʌnɪ˔]. (This phone may sound to you like [i], in fact, but many phoneticians and English dictionaries consider it to be [ɪ], if a fronted and raised variety of this, as the little IPA symbol [˔] suggests.)

1.3. Narrow phonetic writing

If we listen carefully and take note of all such qualities in even a few words of English speech, the resulting **narrow phonetic writing** would be quite detailed, as for the following phrase:

Anticipate the tenth bid: [æ̀ntʰísɪ̥pʰèt̪ðətḛ́n̪θbɪ̀ːd]

Notice in the above narrow phonetic writing a few phones which were not mentioned above:

a. nasalized vowels [æ̃, ɛ̃] which occur in English before nasal consonants instead of plain [æ, ɛ] (the high front vowels tend to be nasalized even after a nasal consonant, as in *knit* [nĭt], as mentioned above);

b. aspirated stops [pʰ, tʰ] which occur in English before stressed vowels instead of the plain stops [p, t]. Aspirated stops will be discussed below.

1.4. Broad phonetic writing

Without extensive training and experience it is impossible to hear and to write such narrow, detailed, phonetic writing, accurately differentiating the different phones. Instead, rough or **broad phonetic writing** is common, as used in exercises of the previous chapter, which employed broad phonetic writing of English, using just 37 phonetic symbols (36 for American English). In broad phonetic writing, for example, all the *n*-like phones appear as simply [n], all the *ɪ*-like phones appear as simply [ɪ], etc.: [æ̀ntísɪp̀ètðəténθbɪ̀d].

2. PHONEMIC WRITING

2.1. Contrast

Detailed or narrow phonetic writing is not just difficult. It is quite impractical, because the range of phonetic variation is vast and the differences between many of the variants are impossible to hear consistently or reliably even with training and experience. More important, however, there is a significant systematic difference between narrow phonetic writing and a certain kind of broad phonetic writing. This difference concerns the fact that many of the phonetic details in the stream of speech are present for one of two reasons:

a. the obligatory pronunciation rules of the language, or

b. idiosyncratic or momentary characteristics of the speaker.

Here are examples of each of these two sorts of cases, concerning the *n*-like phones of English.

a. When a coronal nasal stop precedes the dental fricative [θ], in words such as *tenth* and *enthusiasm*, the dentally articulated [n̪] is pronounced.

b. When the speaker has a cold, which tends to block the nasal cavity, coronal [n] may lose some of its nasal quality and an only somewhat nasalized [d], which might be written [d̃], occurs; 'My nose is runny' will sound like 'By dose is ruddy' (with [b̃] also replacing [m]).

Such phonetic characteristics of speech are **noncontrastive**. Their presence is determined by neighboring phones or by the individuality of the speaker, so they are not associated with the meanings of morphemes as part of their particular form, and being present by necessity of their neighboring phones, or as a characteristic of the speaker's voice, they cannot make a difference of linguistic meaning between one utterance or another. In this sense they are **noncontrastive**.

Other characteristics of phones are **contrastive**. They are contrastive because they are not required by neighboring phones in an utterance nor are they determined by the individuality of a speaker. They are associated with morphemes as form to meaning. They distinguish or contrast meanings. The contrastive characteristics are said to be **phonemic**, and the noncontrastive characteristics are said to be **nonphonemic**. In English, for example, the difference between [m] and [n] is contrastive/phonemic, but the difference between [n] and [n̪] is noncontrastive/nonphonemic; the difference between [ɪ] and [i] is contrastive/phonemic, but the difference between [ĩ] and [ɪ] is noncontrastive/nonphonemic.

2.2.   Phonemes and their allophones

The sets of phonetically similar noncontrastive phones are termed **phonemes**, and the separate phones of the set, which make up a phoneme, are termed its **allophones**. Thus [n̪], [n], [ɲ], [n̥], [d̃], and [n] are all allophones of the English phoneme /n/, and the phones [ĩ], [ɪː], [ɪ̥], and [ɪ˔] are all allophones of the English phoneme /ɪ/.

2.2.1.   Noncontrastive distribution of allophones
Allophones are in **noncontrastive distribution**. Noncontrastive distribution is either **complementary distribution**, or **free variation**.

Complementary distribution is the typical case for allophones – when their places of occurrence in words are such that where one is pronounced the other is not. For example, dental [n̪] of English is pronounced before the dental fricatives [θ, ð], where the other allophones of the phoneme /n/ are not. Similarly the nasalized vowel phones of English occur before nasal consonants where the oral vowel phones do not.

Free variation exists between pairs of allophones when one or the other can occur without affecting the meaning of morphemes. For example, for all speakers of English, but especially those in parts of the American southwest, both **oral vowels** and somewhat **nasal vowels** may occur before oral consonants. Another example of free variation concerns the retroflex liquid phones [ɾ] and [r] of Spanish, a **tap** and **trilled** *r*, respectively, either of which may appear at the beginning of words, where one hears, for example, both [ɾopɑ] or [ropɑ] 'clothes'. (Between vowels, though, [ɾ] and [r] are contrastive – if you pronounce [peɾo] you say 'but' (spelled *pero*) but if you pronounce [pero] you say 'dog' (*perro*).)

2.2.2.   Phonemic writing
Writing which systematically lacks the noncontrastive or nonphonemic details is termed **phonemic writing**, and is ordinarily written within 'slash' brackets, //.

The broad phonetic writing above of the utterance *anticipate the tenth bid*, is equivalent to phonemic writing: /æntɪsɪpetðətɛnθbɪd/.

2.3.   Another example: aspirated stops

A voiceless stop is said to be 'aspirated' when it is followed by voiceless-ness heard as a momentary puff of air [ʰ], as in the English word *pan* [pʰæn]. A **voiceless aspirated** phone with this sort of release is written with [ʰ], as in [pʰ, tʰ, kʰ].

2.3.1.   Aspirated stops in English

The three phones [pʰ, tʰ, kʰ] are heard in English at the beginning of words including *pan*, *tan*, and *can*: [pʰæn, tʰæn, kʰæn], respectively. If [s] precedes the stops at the beginning of such words, there is no aspiration, as in *span*, *Stan*, and *scan*: [spæn, stæn, skæn]. English speakers can confirm this for themselves by holding a piece of paper loosely in front of their lips while pronouncing the words with and without initial [s].

Consider the following English words, all with voiceless stops, [p], [t], or [k]. Stops of the first row are **aspirated** and those of the second row are **unaspirated**.

a. [tʰǽb] tab,   [pʰín] pin,   [kʰón] cone,   [pʰúl] pool
b. [stǽb] stab, [spín] spin,   [skón] scone, [spúl] spool

The aspiration must occur in English when voiceless stops occur before stressed vowels, as in *tab*, unless [s] precedes in the same syllable, as in *stab*. An English speaker has to aspirate or not, depending on the phonetic context.

So aspiration in English is noncontrastive, or nonphonemic, and we say that English voiceless stop phonemes /p/, /t/, and /k/ have aspirated and unaspirated allophones:

/p/ is a phoneme with the allophones [pʰ] and [p];
/t/ is a phoneme with the allophones [tʰ] and [t];
/k/ is a phoneme with the allophones [kʰ] and [k].

2.3.2.   Aspirated stops in Thai

In Thai (of Thailand), aspirated stops function differently. In speaking you either pronounce an aspirated or unaspirated stop depending on what words you choose, or what meanings you intend. For example:

Words with unaspirated stops	*Words with aspirated stops*
[pàa] 'forest'	[pʰàa] 'to split'
[tam] 'to do'	[tʰam] 'to pound'
[kàt] 'to bite'	[kʰàt] 'to interrupt'

In other words, aspiration is phonemic in Thai, and /pʰ, tʰ, kʰ/ and /p, t, k/ are all phonemes. The word *Thai* is written with an *h*, because the *t* of this word is aspirated in Thai.

2.4.   Another example: dental fricatives in Spanish and English

Spanish has a voiced dental fricative [ð] in words such as *lado* [laðo] 'side', *caldo* [kalðo] 'hot' and *perdon* [pɛrðon] 'pardon'. This phone is more or less the same as that heard in English words such as *lather* [læðər], *those* [ðoz], and *breathe* [brið].

The important difference is that in Spanish [ð] is an allophone of /d/, and in English /ð/ is a phoneme. In Spanish, when you pronounce a coronal (tongue-tip articulated) voiced obstruent, this is [ð] or [d] depending on neighboring phones. At the beginning of a word or after [n], Spanish /d/ is [d]: *dar* [dar] 'to give', *dando* [dando] 'giving'. After a vowel, [r], and often /l/, /d/ is typically [ð]: *lado* [laðo] 'side', *perdon* [pɛrðon] 'pardon', *caldo* [kalðo] 'hot'.

English employs [ð] or [d] depending on what words we choose, or what meanings we intend. *Laid* is [led] but *lathe* is [leð]; *ladder* is [lædər] but *lather* is [læðər]; and *doze* is [doz] but *those* is [ðoz].

2.5.   Minimal pairs

Pairs of words like the following differ minimally, by one phone, and the difference of phones corresponds to a difference of meaning.

English:	[led]	'laid'	[lædər]	'ladder'
	[leð]	'lathe'	[læðər]	'lather'
Thai:	[pàa]	'forest'	[tam]	'to do'
	[pʰàa]	'to split'	[tʰam]	'to pound'
Spanish:	[peɾo]	'but'	[kaɾo]	'expensive'
	[pero]	'dog'	[karo]	'cart'

Such a word-pair is evidence that the difference of the two phones is contrastive of meaning, or phonemic, since the two phones which distinguish the members of such a pair are clearly not in noncontrastive distribution. Reasonably enough, such word-pairs are called **minimal pairs**.

3.   ALLOPHONIC RULES

We have seen that in English a voiceless stop is aspirated when it is first in its syllable and precedes a stressed vowel. This is a **rule** of English pronunciation.

Since it concerns a noncontrastive feature of English, it is an **allophonic rule**. We have seen that in Spanish a voiced coronal obstruent is a fricative when it follows a vowel, [r], or [l], according to a rule of Spanish pronunciation, again an allophonic rule, since it also concerns a noncontrastive feature. Every language has allophonic rules.

3.1.   Some English allophonic rules

See the lists of Some Allophonic Rules for American English Consonants and American English Vowels.

SOME ALLOPHONIC RULES FOR AMERICAN ENGLISH CONSONANTS

1. A coronal nasal /n/ is dental before a dental fricative [θ, ð]: *te*[n̪]*th*, *a*[n̪]*them*.
2. A voiceless stop /p, t, k/ may be glottalized (have a glottal onset) when unreleased at the end of a syllable: *sto*[ˀp], *wai*[ˀt], *kic*[ˀk].
3. An approximant /l, r, w, j/ is voiceless (or mostly voiceless) after a voiceless aspirated stop in its syllable: *p*[l̥]*ay*, *c*[r̥]*y*, *q*[w̥]*ick*, *c*[j]*ute*.
4. A syllable-initial voiceless stop /p, t, k/ (not preceded by [s] in its syllable) is aspirated before a stressed vowel: *p*[ʰ]*ot*, *t*[ʰ]*op* (compare *s*[p]*ot*, *s*[t]*op*, without aspiration), *p*[ʰ]*lan*, *t*[ʰ]*rick*, [kʰ]*rib*.
5. Adjacent-like consonants form one long such consonant: *pe*[nː]*ife*, *boo*[kː]*ase*.
6. A coronal consonant (/t, d, s/) is retroflex before [r]: [t]*ruck*, [d]*rink*.
7. A coronal sonorant consonant /n, l/ is syllabic in an unstressed syllable after a coronal obstruent [t, d, s (etc.)]: *hidd*[n̩], *miss*[l̩]*e*.
8. A velar stop /k/ is fronted (pronounced somewhat forward on the velum) before a high front vowel: [kˑ]*eep*, [kˑ]*ey*.
9. A velar stop /k/ is rounded before [u]: [kʷ]*oo*, [kʷ]*oop* (compare [k]*lue*).
10. A consonant is rounded before [w]: [tʷ]*win*, [kʷ]*uote*, [hʷw]*ich* (*which*).
11. A retroflex liquid /r/ is rounded when word initial: [rʷ]*ed*, [rʷ]*un*.
12. A lateral liquid /l/ is velarized at the end of a word or before a consonant: *fee*[ɫ], *to*[ɫ]*d* (compare [l]*eaf*, [l]*ine*, with unvelarized [l]).
13. A glottal fricative /h/ may be voiced between vowels after an unstressed vowel: *be*[ɦ]*ind*, *a*[ɦ]*ead*.
14. A labial nasal /m/ may be labiodental [ɱ] before labiodental /f, v/: *sy*[ɱ]*phony*, *e*[ɱ]*phatic*.
15. A coronal stop /t, d, n/ is very lax and short – said to be 'flapped' – before an unstressed vowel: *wai*[ɾ]*er*, *wa*[ɾ]*er*, *di*[ɾ]*er*. A flapped /t/ is also voiced, so that flapped /t/ and /d/ are often the same in casual speech.
16. A coronal consonant is retroflex after /r/: *earn* [ərn̩], *third* [θərd].

SOME ALLOPHONIC RULES FOR AMERICAN ENGLISH VOWELS

17. A vowel is nasalized before a nasal consonant: c[æ̃]n, b[õ]ne.
18. A high front vowel is nasalized after a nasal consonant: n[ĩ]t (neat), n[ĩ]ce (niece), kn[ĩ]t.
19. A stressed vowel is lengthened before a voiced single consonant in its syllable: b[ɪː]d, p[eː]ys (compare b[ɪ]t, p[e]ce).
20. A unstressed vowel may be voiceless between voiceless consonants: p[ə̥]tato, symp[ə̥]thy.
21. A stressed tense vowel has a central off-glide before [r]: b[iə]r (beer), t[oə]r (tore).
22. A stressed front tense vowel has a central off-glide before [l]: f[iə]l (feel), p[eə]l (pail).
23. A stressed mid front tense vowel /e/ has a high off-glide: l[eʲ]ke (lake), b[eʲ]t (bait).
24. A high front lax vowel /ɪ/ is raised when word-final: happ[ɪ̟], funn[ɪ̟].
25. A mid central vowel plus following /r/ is a retroflex such vowel: b[ɝ]d (bird), lab[ɚ] (labor).

3.2. Functions of allophonic rules

Allophonic rules often reflect the effect of phones on neighboring phones. Notice rules of the list of English allophonic rules for which this is so. Such rules integrate the stream of speech, merging and overlapping phones with other phones. This presumably makes speech more efficient, and faster, and adds redundancy which is good for understanding. For example, we may not hear a nasal consonant, yet still notice its presence by its effect as nasalization on a neighboring vowel. Many other allophonic rules apply at the beginnings and ends of words, and reasonably serve to mark the beginning and end of words, which is also helpful for comprehension.

3.3. English phonemes

When all the noncontrastive phones of English including those mentioned by these and other English allophonic rules are collected into phonetically similar sets, the result is 37 sets, or 37 phonemes (36 of British and American English, plus one in British), as follows (in which '. . .' represents allophones not mentioned above):

PHONEMES OF TYPICAL ENGLISH

/p/: [ˀp, pʰ, p, . . .]	/z/: [z, . . .]	/i/: [iː, ĩ, iə, . . .]
/b/: [b, . . .]	/š/: [š, . . .]	/ɪ/: [ɪ̟, ɪː, ɪ̩, ɪ̥, ĩ, . . .]

/t/: [ˀt, tʰ, t̪, ✗, . . .] /ž/: [ž, . . .] /e/: [eː, ẽ, eʲ, eˀ, e, . . .]
/d/: [d, d̪, ᴅ, . . .] /h/: [ɦ, h, . . .] /ɛ/: [ɛː, ɛ̃, ɛ, . . .]
/k/: [ˀk, kʰ, k<, kʷ, k, . . .] /č/: [č, . . .] /æ/: [æː, æ̃, æ, . . .]
/g/: [g, . . .] /ǰ/: [ǰ, . . .] /ə/: [əː, ə̧, ə̃, ə, . . .]
/ʔ/: [ʔ, . . .] /m/: [m̥, m, . . .] /ɔ/: [ɔː, ɔ̃, ɔ, . . .]
/f/: [f, . . .] /n/: [n̥, n̪, n̩, ɳ, ɴ, n, . . .] /o/: [oː, õ, oˀ, o, . . .]
/v/: [v, . . .] /ŋ/: [ŋ, . . .] /ʊ/: [ʊː, ʊ̃, ʊ, . . .]
/θ/: [θ, . . .] /l/: [l̥, ɫ, l, l̩, l, . . .] /u/: [uː, ũ, uˀ, u, . . .]
/ð/: [ð, . . .] /r/: [r̥, rʷ, r, . . .] /a/: [ɑː, ã, ɑ, . . .]
/s/: [s, . . .] /w/: [w̥, w̃, w, . . .] /ɒ/: [ɒː, ɒ̃, ɒ, . . .]
  /j/: [j, j̃, j, . . .] (British)

These 37 English phonemes are written with the 37 phonetic symbols of broad phonetic writing introduced in chapter 2, §5.

4.   LETTERS AND PHONEMES

Notice an important difference between English spelling and phonemic writing. Phonemic writing gives a consistent or regular presentation of the sounds, but English spelling is quite irregular. Our spelling does not provide a regular or consistent presentation of speech sounds. For example,

a.   /f/ is sometimes spelled *ph* and sometimes *f*.
b.   /s/ is sometimes spelled *s* and sometimes *c*.
c.   /e/ is sometimes spelled *ai* as in *bait*, sometimes *a* as in *late*, sometimes *ay* as in *say*, and sometimes otherwise (*ei*, *ey*, etc.).
d.   /ə/ is spelled in numerous ways: *u* in *sun*, *o* in *son*, *a* in *about*, *oe* in *does*, *ou* in *rough*, etc.

There are four reasons why the sound and symbol relationships of English spelling are so irregular or inconsistent:

a.   Our spelling has arisen by mixing spelling practices which arose at different times and places.
b.   English continues to borrow words from other languages, and sometimes keeps the spellings of the words in those languages.
c.   Pronunciation is regularly changing, and spelling rarely or only slowly reflects the changes of pronunciation.
d.   Most importantly, spelling has valid but different purposes from those of phonetic or phonemic writing:

1.   Phonemic writing attempts accurately to represent the distinctive or contrastive phones of speech, whereas:
2.   Spelling attempts to enable people of different generations and regions, who may speak differently, to communicate over time and space, despite their differences of speech.

Phonemes are units in a phonology (the grammar of sound) of a language, and represent a systematic or scientific phonological analysis. **Letters** are the units of our writing system, and are the much less systematic product of the long and varied history of that system. Since there are few regular correspondences between phonemes and letters, phonemes ought not be called 'letters'. (Some reasons for the poor English letter–sound correspondences are presented in chapter 21, §7.3.)

5. DERIVATIONS

One understanding of how we perform speech is that we take the phonemic forms of linguistic signs from our mental dictionary and apply the allophonic rules to these to derive pronunciations. The result of applying the rules to an abstract or mental phonemic representation is phonetic speech. For example, saying the English word *pin*, *cling*, and *stick* requires application of several allophonic rules, as shown in figure 3.1, which shows the **derivations** of these words: the application of allophonic rules to derive the three pronunciations from the three phonemic representations.

Phonemic representation	/pɪn/	/klɪŋ/	/stɪk/
Stress	í	í	í
Aspiration (4)	pʰ	kʰ	
Vowel nasalization (17)	ĩ	ĩ	
Vowel lengthening (19)	ĩː	ĩː	
Devoicing (3)		l̥	
Glottalization (2)			ˀk
Phonetic representation	[pʰĩːn]	[kʰl̥ĩːŋ]	[stíˀk]

Figure 3.1 Derivations of *pin*, *cling*, and *stick*

The first rule in each derivation, which assigns stress, wasn't mentioned above: since these nouns and verbs have only one vowel, this must be stressed. The other rules are as listed in §3.1, above.

Suggestions for
ADDITIONAL READING

Discussion of the difference between phones and phonemes is found in most of the textbook introductions to language and linguistics, such as *Language: its Structure and Use* (1994) by Edward

Finegan, *Contemporary Linguistics: an Introduction* (1993) by William O'Grady et al., and *An Introduction to Language* (1993) by Victoria Fromkin and Robert Rodman. The method of basic phonological analysis is presented in *Phonological Analysis: a Functional Approach* (1993) by Donald A. Burquest and David L. Payne. Somewhat more advanced is *An Introduction to Phonetics and Phonology* (1990) by John Clark and Colin Yallop. Concerning specifically English, see *English Phonology* (1993) by John T. Jensen and *The Pronunciation of English: a Coursebook in*

Phonology (1989) by Charles W. Kreidler. For introductory books more concerned with theories of phonology, see the suggestions for additional reading at the end of chapter 13.

For exercises on phonemic data analysis see section 2 of the *Source Book for Linguistics* (1987) by William Cowan and Jaromira Rakušan.

IMPORTANT CONCEPTS AND TERMS IN THIS CHAPTER

- narrow phonetic writing
- broad phonetic writing
- noncontrastive
- contrastive
- phonemic
- nonphonemic
- phoneme
- allophone
- noncontrastive distribution
- complementary distribution
- free variation
- oral vowel

- nasal vowel
- tap
- trill
- phonemic writing
- voiceless aspirated
- aspirated
- unaspirated
- minimal pair
- rule
- allophonic rule
- letter
- derivation

OUTLINE OF CHAPTER 3

1. **Broad and narrow phonetic writing**
    1. Coronal nasal consonants
    2. High front lax vowels
    3. Narrow phonetic writing
    4. Broad phonetic writing
2. **Phonemic writing**
    1. Contrast
    2. Phonemes and their allophones
        1. Noncontrastive distribution of allophones
        2. Phonemic writing
    3. Another example: aspirated stops
        1. Aspirated stops in English
        2. Aspirated stops in Thai

4. Another example: dental fricatives in Spanish and English
5. Minimal pairs
3. **Allophonic rules**
    1. Some English allophonic rules
    2. Functions of allophonic rules
    3. English phonemes
4. **Letters and phonemes**
5. **Derivations**

Let's go storm!!!

EXAMPLES AND PRACTICE

EXAMPLE

1. Minimal pairs for English phonemes.   *Come On!!*

PRACTICE

For each of the following pairs of English phonemes provide two minimal pairs. The first two are done as examples.

1. /t/, /d/: to, do; seat, seed
2. /i/, /ɪ/: seat, sit; greed, grid
3. /s/, /z/:
4. /k/, /g/:
5. /m/, /n/:
6. /n/, /ŋ/:
7. /l/, /r/:
8. /n/, /l/:
9. /a/, /æ/:
10. /a/, /ə/:
11. /g/, /ŋ/:
12. /w/, /j/:
13. /p/, /b/: *pig / big*
14. /b/, /m/: *lab / lam, be / me, crab / cram*
15. /č/, /ĵ/: *chang / jang.*
16. /æ/, /ɛ/: *men / man*
17. /ɛ/, /e/: *bad / bed, met / mate,*
18. /a/, /o/: *Rat / Roat.*
19. /o/, /u/: *Spoke / spook.*
20. /u/, /ʊ/: *Lut / look,*

EXAMPLE

2. Derivations. Consider in figure 3.2 the derivation of the English sentence *Send in the clowns, please.* Stress is provided. The rules are numbered according to the list of allophonic rules in §3.1, above.

/sèndɪnðək láwnzplìz/

Dentalization (1)	ṇ	
Aspiration (4)	kʰ	pʰ
Devoicing (3)	l̥	l̥
Nasalization (17)	ɛ̃ ĩ	ã w̃
Lengthening (19)		iː

[sɛ̀ndĩṇðəkʰ l̥ãw̃nzpʰ l̥ìːz]

Figure 3.2   Derivation of *Send in the clowns, please*

PRACTICE

As in figure 3.2, provide the complete derivation for the English sentence *The rain in Spain stays mainly in the plain.*

/ ð ə r è n ɪ n s p é n s t è z m é n l ɪ ì n ð ə p l é n /

EXAMPLE

3. Phonemic analysis I. Consider the following phonetically written words of a hypothetical language.

[tʰi ɬ	it	tʰĩn	nĩn	liḷ
ni ‚	ĩn	tʰit	nit	lĩn
li	iḷ̥	tʰiḷ̥	niḷ̥	lit]

The words include seven phones: [tʰ, t, i, ĩ, n, l, ḷ]. Some of these phones are phonetically similar: obviously [tʰ] and [t] are similar, as are [ḷ] and [l], and [ĩ]. and [i]. The [n], too, is somewhat phonetically similar to other phones: it is a sonorant consonant like the laterals [l] and [ḷ], a coronal stop like [tʰ] and [t], and, indeed, a nasal phone like [ĩ].

When we study the places of occurrence of the phonetically similar pairs, we see that [tʰ] and [t], [ḷ] and [l], and [i] and [ĩ] are noncontrastive: in environments where one occurs the other doesn't, and vice versa.

But [n] contrasts with [l] and [tʰ]; in fact there are minimal pairs [niḷ] and [tʰiḷ] and [niḷ] and [liḷ]. Thus we can group the phonetically similar noncontrastive phones into the four phonemes 1–4, three of which have two allophones. Then, using just these four phonemic symbols, we can rewrite the first row of words of the hypothetical language as 5.

1. /t/: [tʰ] at the beginning of words, and [t] elsewhere
2. /l/: [ḷ] at the end of words, and [l] elsewhere
3. /i/: [ĩ] before [n], and [i] elsewhere
4. /n/: [n]
5. /ti it tin nin lil/

It is customary to write the phoneme with the symbol of the most typical or simplest allophone, thus the four phonemes are written as /t, n, l, i/.

PRACTICE

The following phonetically written words of a hypothetical language include eight phones. But there are only four phonemes: one has four allophones, one has two, and two have only one allophone.

List the phonemes and their allophones as 1–4 (4 is already done) and rewrite the first row of words in phonemic writing as 5.

How to do this? As in the example above, find pairs of phonetically similar phones which are noncontrastive – where one occurs the other doesn't, and vice versa. These are allophones of a phoneme. In phonemic writing, write them both with the phonetic symbol of one, preferably the simplest.

Y

[pʰaː ap   pʰap   mãw   pʰãmãː
mãː   ãm   pʰãm   mãm   pʰapʰaː
waː   aw   pʰaw   mãp   pʰawaː]

2 allophones.

1. /pʰ/: *pʰ*
2. /nt/: /only one allophone.*
3. /m/:   *a has 4 allophones.*
4. /a/: [ãː] after [m] at the end of words, [aː] after consonants other than [m] at the end of words, [ã] before and after [m] but not at the end of words, and [a] elsewhere.
5. /

phonemes

---

4. Phonemic analysis II. The following phonetically written words of a hypothetical language include seven phones. There are only four phonemes, three of which have two allophones. The phonemes with their allophones are listed as 1–4, and the first row of words is rewritten in phonemic writing as 5 (that is, writing which uses only the four phonemic symbols).

ignore

[it   mɪr   dɪr   dɪrt   rɪli   idi   ilɪt
di   rɪt   rɪr   irt   dɪli   imi   ilɪr
ri   dɪt   rɪrt   rɪdi   dɪdɪm   idɪt   idɪr]

1. /t/: [d] at the beginning of words and between vowels, and [t] elsewhere
2. /m/: [m]
3. /r/: [l] between vowels, and [r] elsewhere
4. /i/: [ɪ] between consonants, and [i] elsewhere
5. /it mir tir tirt riri iti irit/

Notice that the allophones are phonetically similar: [i, ɪ] are both high front vowels; [t, d] are both alveolar stops; [l, r] are both liquids. Don't be misled by the existence of distinct phonetic symbols for phonetically very similar phones; [t], for example, could be written as [d̥], with the little subscript symbol for voicelessness ([d̥] = [t]).

The following phonetically written words of a hypothetical language also include seven phones. The seven phones may be grouped into four phonemes, three of which have two allophones each.

List the phonemes and their allophones as 1–4 and rewrite just the first row of seven words in phonemic writing, as 5. Hint: remember that allophones are phonetically similar phones, so look for pairs of phonetically similar phones which are noncontrastive – that is, their occurrence in the data seems to be according to some rule.

[sizi pubi nizi izup nin subi si
pup ubi nubi nup pini pis sizi
up nis pizi ubin izi ubup izup]

EXAMPLE

5. Phonemic analysis III. The following phonetically written words of a hypothetical language also include seven phones. Again the seven phones may be grouped into four phonemes, three of which have two allophones each.

PRACTICE

List the phonemes and their allophones as 1–4 and rewrite just the first row of seven words in phonemic writing as 5.

*W= bf ter [a], θ
end of word;
w/ consonant*

✗ minimal pairs

[daw va vaθ tawð aθa taθ ta
dað aða awða da aθaw vaθa awθaʔ
vaw vava tað vaða aðaw tawða tava]

EXAMPLE

6. Phonemic analysis IV. Consider the following data of a hypothetical language. There are 13 phones but only 8 phonemes.

PRACTICE

List the phonemes and their allophones as 1–8, and rewrite just the first row of five words in phonemic writing as 9.

[nan kin soda piŋgo timbi
tan naŋga nada soga tibi
nambi saŋgo nanda nan po
taŋgo san ani kaŋga kona
tambo namba pana soba nimba
tidi koda nani kida pogi]

EXAMPLE

7. Phonemic analysis V. Consider the following data of a hypothetical language. There are 23 phones, [p pʰ t tʰ č čʰ k kʰ s š h m n i í e é a á o ó u ú], but only 12 phonemes.

[kʰóhi óči híši nína pʰáši
mín méni tʰému séšinu sótu
tʰóku hátu kʰína kʰéme tʰóte
čʰíku tʰú pʰú mépo tʰúna
pʰéme nóka sósa héte čʰí]

PRACTICE

List the phonemes and their allophones as 1–12, and rewrite just the first two rows of ten words in phonemic writing as 13.

MORPHEMES

This chapter classifies the signs of language, morphemes, into their important types, in terms of form and meaning, and illustrates these mainly from English. It shows how languages differ concerning their morphology, and how morphemes, like phonemes, may have different forms.

1. MORPHEMES

A **sign** of language – an association of linguistic meaning and its forms – is termed a **morpheme**. The forms of a morpheme of vocal language may be thought of as sequences of phonemes, perhaps with associated stress and/or tone. Linguistic meaning also includes characteristics of relation to other morphemes, expressed as membership in a part of speech such as noun, verb, etc.

The English sentence *The pigs cannot fly* has six morphemes, the forms and meanings of which are listed below. The form is shown in phonemic writing within '/ /' brackets, and the meaning, roughly expressed as words, is within quotation marks.

/ðə/, 'definite article'
/pɪg/, 'pig, noun'
/z/, 'noun plural'
/kæn/, 'can, auxiliary verb'
/nɑt/, 'negative of verb'
/flɑj/, 'fly, verb'

The words 'pig', 'can', and 'fly' included within the quotation marks represent aspects of meaning which might be further analyzed, but this is omitted here. The form of a morpheme, in addition to its representation in phonemes, includes its spelling. Morphemes are typically represented in short, as often below in this book, just by their underlined or italicized spellings: *the*, *pig*, *-s*, *can*, *not*, and *fly*.

2.   MORPH, MORPHEME, AND ALLOMORPH

As phonemes may have more than one allophone, morphemes may have more than one phonemic form, each of which is an **allomorph** of the morpheme. Here are three examples of allomorphs of English morphemes:

a.   the 'indefinite article', *a/an*, which has the two forms *a* /ə/ and *an* /æn/, the former for use before words beginning with consonants (*a car*, *a dog*), and the latter for use before words beginning with vowels (*an apple*, *an eagle*).

b.   the noun plural suffix spelled *-s* and pronounced /ɪz/ (or /əz/) in words like *kisses* and *catches*, which end in alveolar and alveopalatal fricatives (known as 'sibilants'), /s/ in words like *cats* and *walks*, which end in voiceless consonants, and /z/ in words like *dogs* and *runs*, which end in voiced consonants.

c.   the free morpheme *exit*, which some speakers pronounce sometimes /ɛksɪt/ and sometimes /ɛgzɪt/.

This characteristic of morphemes presents a parallel in morphological structure to the phones, phonemes, and allophones of phonological structure. A meaningful form is a **morph**. The set of morphs of similar form, like meaning, and complementary (noncontrastive) distribution make up a **morpheme**, and the different forms of a morpheme are its **allomorphs**. Thus as there are phones, phonemes, and allophones, there are morphs, morphemes, and allomorphs. As phones are grouped into phonemes as allophones of a phoneme, morphs are grouped into morphemes as allomorphs of a morpheme. Here are some examples of the latter relationship:

a.   Morphs: /ə/ 'indefinite article', /æn/ 'indefinite article', /s/ 'noun plural suffix', /z/, 'noun plural suffix' /ɪz/, 'noun plural suffix', /ɛksɪt/ 'exit', /ɛgzɪt/ 'exit', /dɔg/ 'dog', . . .

b.   Morphemes:
/ə/, /æn/ 'indefinite article' (/ə/ and /æn/ are allomorphs)
/ɪz/, /s/, /z/ 'noun plural suffix' (/ɪz/, /s/, /z/ are allomorphs)
/ɛksɪt/, /ɛgzɪt/ 'exit (verb)' (/ɛksɪt/, /ɛgzɪt/ are allomorphs)
/dɔg/ 'dog' (/dɔg/ is the only allomorph of this morpheme)

The English **contractions** provide additional examples. These are allomorphs of morphemes the other allomorphs of which are full words, for example:

	Contracted form	Word form
a.	/nt/, spelled *n't*	/nɑt/, *not*
b.	/z/, spelled *'s*	/ɪz/, *is*
c.	/l/, spelled *'ll*	/wɪl/, *will*
d.	/d/, spelled *'d*	/wʊd/, *would*
e.	/v/, spelled *'ve*	/hæv/, *have*

Given some data of a language, whether spoken or written, a learner at first recognizes the occasions of meaningful form, the morphs. Eventually the learner groups the morphs with similar form, like meaning, and complementary distribution as morphemes, recognizing the different forms as its allomorphs.

Morphemes are not always distinct from one another. While /dɔgz/ *dogs* is readily analyzed into /dɔg/ *dog* 'dog' and /z/ -s 'noun plural', in /mɛn/ the forms of the meanings 'man' and 'noun plural' are indistinct, or fused.

3. TYPES OF MORPHS ACCORDING TO FORM: FREE AND BOUND

The form of a morph may be **free** or **bound**. A **free morph** is a **simple word**, a word consisting of a single morpheme (and necessarily one morph). A **bound morph** must always be combined with another morph within a word. The bound morphs are of three types: **prefixes**, **suffixes**, and **stems**. Here are some English examples:

ENGLISH FREE AND BOUND MORPHS

Free morphs

/dɔg/ *dog*, /it/ *eat*, /ðə/ *the*, /ləv/ *love*, /grin/ *green*, etc.

Bound morphs

1. **Prefixes**, such as /ri/ *re-* of *rearrange*, /ən/ *un-* of *unhappy*, and /ænti/ *anti-* of *antivirus*;
2. **Suffixes**, such as /ɪŋ/ *-ing* of *running*, /s/ *-s* of *tapes*, and /mənt/ *-ment* of *government*;
3. **Stems**, such as /dɪsɪz/ *decis-* of *decision*, a bound-form of *decide*; /rəsɛp/ *recep-* of *reception*, a bound form of *receive*, and /kɛp/ *kep-* of *kept*, a bound form of *keep* (assuming *-t* of *kept* is the past tense suffix).

Some morphemes have both free and bound allomorphs, such as:

a. 'decide': /dɪsɑjd/ *decide* and /dɪsɪz/ *decis-* (of *decision*)
b. comparative of adjectives: /mor/ *more* and /ər/ *-er*
c. negative of verbs: /nɑt/ *not* and /nt/ *-n't*

Since morphemes often have either free or bound allomorphs, and only occasionally both free and bound allomorphs, it is common to speak of morphemes, as well as morphs, as free and bound.

3.1. Free forms

A **free morph** is termed 'free' because it occurs relatively freely with other words or morphemes. There is little restriction on what can occur before and after such a form. It has a degree of independence from other forms which provides it the status of a **word**. For example, a word like *dog* can be preceded by words of various sorts, including pronouns (*my*, *her*, etc.), determiners (*the*, *this*), and adjectives (*old*, *friendly*), and followed by an even greater variety. In writing (in English and many other languages), the status of a morph or combination of morphs as a word is shown by providing spaces at the beginning and end of the word.

3.2. Bound forms

A **bound morph** is a form which must always be combined with another morpheme within a word. It has very restricted cooccurrence with other morphemes – so little such freedom that it is considered to be attached to the morphs with which it regularly cooccurs. For example, in English:

a. The prefix *re-* is almost always attached to a verb, as in *rearrange* and *redesign*, and the prefix *un-* ordinarily to an adjective, as in *unhappy* and *unusual*.
b. The suffix *-ing* is always attached to a verb, as in *eating*, and the suffix *-s* which means 'plural' to a singular noun, as in *dogs*.
c. The stem /dɪsɪz/ *decis-* of *decision* must be followed by a suffix: /jən/ *-ion*, and the stem /dɪsays/ *decis-* of *decisive* by /ɪv/ *-ive* (the stem has one spelling but different phonemic forms in the two cases); and the stem *kep-* /kɛp/ of *kept* must be followed by the past tense suffix, *-t*.

4. SIMPLE AND COMPLEX WORDS

A **word** is one or more morphemes with the freedom of occurrence of a single free morpheme. A **simple word** consists of a single free morpheme, for example *dog*, and *eat*, and a **complex word** (also a 'free form') consists of two or more morphemes, like *dogs*, with two (*dog-s*), *unhappily*, with three (*un-happi-ly*), or *disagreements*, with four (*dis-agree-ment-s*).

Consider the example of *seashell*. This word consists of two morphemes: *sea* /si/ with the meaning 'sea', and *shell* /šɛl/, with the meaning 'shell'. Compare *season*. *Season* is only one morpheme. The syllable /si/ of this word doesn't mean 'sea' and the syllable /zən/ doesn't mean 'son', despite its spelling; there is only one meaning, 'season', associated with the form /sizən/.

Sometimes breaking down a word into its morphemes leaves a form which seems to be meaningless and, being so, is not a morpheme in the usual sense. *Blueberries*, for example, breaks down into *blue*, *berrie* (= *berry*), and *s*. Similarly *boysenberries* seems to break down into *boysen*, *berrie*, and *s*. But what does *boysen-* mean? Since this form doesn't exist apart from its combination with *berries*, it is difficult to say. Such left-over forms may be considered the **residue** of analysis: *berries* is removed, and *boysen* is left.

5. TYPES OF MORPHEMES ACCORDING TO MEANING: LEXICAL AND GRAMMATICAL

There are two types of morphemes according to meaning: lexical and grammatical. Here are some English examples:

ENGLISH LEXICAL AND GRAMMATICAL MORPHEMES

Lexical morphemes

1. Free: *dog, eat, love, green, tomorrow*, etc.
2. Bound: *re-* (*reattach, retest*), *dis-* (*disagree, disqualify*), *-ment* (*government, easement*), *-er* (*hunter, filler*), etc.

Grammatical morphemes:

1. Free: *I, she, the, to, of, and, so*, etc.
2. Bound: *-s* (*dogs, cats*), *-s* (*walks, rides*), *-ing* (*singing, knowing*), *-er* (*older, bigger*), etc.

5.1. Lexical morphemes

5.1.1. *Five characteristics of lexical morphemes*
Lexical morphemes are those showing, at least as tendencies, five characteristics.

a.   The essential characteristic of **lexical morphemes** is that their presence is directly determined by what we are talking about. Because of this, lexical morphemes have three other characteristics.

b.   Concreteness. They tend to express somewhat concrete meanings, like *Evelyn*, *food*, *eat*, *decide*, *green*, *sudden*, *quickly*, and *today*.

c.   Infrequency. Individually, they are very infrequent, certainly compared to grammatical morphemes.

d.   Open-set membership. They are members of large sets which regularly get new members, basically nouns, verbs, adjectives, adverbs, and so-called derivational affixes.

e.   In languages which, like English, distinguish stressed and unstressed syllables, lexical morphemes almost always have a stressed syllable.

The ten most frequent lexical morphemes of written English (according to Kučera and Francis 1967) are *man*, *time*, *go*, *year*, *new*, *take*, *come*, *see*, *get*, and *have*.

5.1.2.   *Derivational (lexical) affixes*

The affixal forms of lexical morphemes are termed **derivational affixes**. Derivational affixes have three characteristics:

a.   Function change. Derivational affixes typically change the part of speech of the word or morpheme to which they are added, thus 'deriving' new words. For example, *energy* is a noun, but *energy + ize* yields a verb; *govern* is a verb, but *govern + ment* yields a noun. The English derivational *prefixes* don't conform to this generalization: *assign* is a verb and *re + assign* is still a verb; *happy* is an adjective and *un + happy* yields another adjective. There are other exceptions to this generalization, including -*let* (*piglet*, like *pig* a noun), and -*ish* (*smallish*, like *small* an adjective).

b.   **Nonproductivity**. One can't readily or confidently 'produce' or predict novel uses of the derivational affixes. For example, imagine a new noun *glick*; a verb derived from this might be *glickify*, *glickize*, or *glickate*.

c.   Suffixability. The derivational suffixes may be followed by other suffixes. The adjective *formal* may be followed by the derivational suffix -*ize*: *formalize*, which may be followed by -*able*: *formalizable*, and this may be followed by a third derivational suffix -*ity*: *formalizability*.

5.2. Grammatical morphemes

5.2.1. *Five characteristics of grammatical morphemes*

Like lexical morphemes, grammatical morphemes have five characteristic tendencies.

a. The essential characteristic of **grammatical morphemes** is that their presence is obligated by the grammar of the language. Because of this basic characteristic, grammatical morphemes have three other characteristics.

b. Abstractness. They express rather abstract meanings, having to do with relationships of the grammar, such as tense of verbs (*-ed* in *walked*), hearer-knowledge of nouns (*a* or *the* in *a/the guy*), and clause conjunction (*if*, *so*, *because*).

c. Frequency. Grammatical morphemes are *very* frequent, as a group and individually, certainly compared to lexical morphemes.

d. Closed-set membership. The grammatical morphemes are members of sets which get new members relatively infrequently, including pronouns, determiners, prepositions, and affixes expressing categories like verb tense and noun plurality.

e. In languages which, like English, distinguish stressed and unstressed syllables, grammatical morphemes typically lack stressed syllables.

Some free grammatical morphemes of English are *the*, *to*, and *and*. In the sentence *The cat and the dog like to fight*, *cat*, *dog*, *like* and *fight* concern a speaker's choice of topic, but *the*, *to* and *and* concern how English grammar associates these ideas. The most frequent words of written English are all simple grammatical morphemes (in the study of Kučera and Francis 1967): *the*, *of*, *and*, *to*, *a/an*, *in*, *that*, *is*, *was*, and *he* (as noted in practice 3 of chapter 2; these results are based on American English texts; for similar results based on British English texts, see Johansson and Hofland 1989).

5.2.2. *Inflectional (grammatical) affixes*

The bound forms of grammatical morphemes are known as **inflectional affixes**. Like derivational affixes, inflectional affixes have three general characteristics:

a. No function change. Inflectional affixes don't change the function (part of speech) of the word or morpheme to which they are added. Thus *guy* is a noun, and *guys* is a plural noun; *jump* is a verb and so is *jumped*.

b. **Productivity.** One predicts new uses of the inflectional affixes in new words. Thus given a new (imaginary) verb *glock*, its past tense will be *glocked*. If *glock* is a new noun, its plural will be *glocks*.

c. Nonsuffixability. The English inflectional suffixes may not ordinarily be followed by other suffixes. *Formalizability* has three derivational suffixes (*formal-iz-abil-ity*), but adding the plural suffix closes the word: *formalizabilities*.

Some affixes may have both inflectional and derivational characteristics. The suffix *-ly*, for example, fulfills the inflectional characteristic of productivity and the derivational characteristic of function change: new adjectives will form adverbs by suffixing *-ly*.

6. ENGLISH INFLECTIONAL AFFIXES

All the **English inflectional affixes**, of which there are typically said to be eight, are suffixes. Here is the whole list as often recognized; the usual pronunciation is given first, in phonemic form, followed by the usual spelling:

THE EIGHT ENGLISH INFLECTIONAL SUFFIXES

a. /z/ *-s*, the plural suffix of nouns, as in *pigs* and *cows*
b. /z/ *-'s*, the possessive suffix, ordinarily of nouns, as in *Jackson's* and *New York's*, but in fact suffixable to whatever word ends the possessor phrase, as in *the person we visited's house* and *the person I thought of's picture*
c. /z/ *-s*, the present tense 3rd-person singular suffix of verbs, as in *walks* and *runs*
d. /d/ *-ed*, the past tense suffix of verbs, as in *arrived* and *waited*
e. /ɪŋ/ *-ing*, the present participle suffix of verbs, as in *walking* and *running*
f. /ər/ *-er*, the comparative suffix of adjectives, as in *quicker* and *earlier* (This *-er* should not be equated with the *-er* which forms 'agents' of verbs, such as *finder* and *doer*; the latter is a derivational suffix.)
g. /əst/ *-est*, the superlative suffix of adjectives, as in *quickest* and *earliest*
h. /n/ *-n*, the past participle suffix of some verbs, as in *broken* and *eaten*

Notice how all but the last of these suffixes strongly fulfill the three characteristics of inflectional affixes: they don't change the part of speech, are very productive, and are last in their words. The past participle suffix /n/ *-n* is not productive: it is not being employed with new verbs which come into English, which instead form their past participle, like their past tense form, with /d/ *-ed*.

7. MORPHOLOGICAL DIFFERENCES AMONG LANGUAGES

7.1. General differences

It was necessary above to introduce concepts of morphology by use of English examples, but it must be emphasized that English morphology, like other aspects of English grammar, is not often typical of languages of the world. Languages differ morphologically in a number of ways, for example:

a. the types of grammatical meaning that must be expressed,
b. how much grammatical and inflectional morphology they have,
c. how much bound morphology they have,
d. whether there tend to be prefixes or suffixes, and/or stems, and
e. how much **morphological fusion** there is (as in a word like *men*, in which forms of the two meanings 'man' and 'noun plural' are not neatly separable, but are fused.

We will see many examples of such differences in chapters below.

7.2. Amharic verbs

Following is an example of a language with aspects of morphology different from English. Carefully study the following phonemically written verbs of Amharic, a Semitic language of Ethiopia already exemplified in previous chapters. Notice the regularities. In the first column are past tense verbs and in the second column present tense verbs. (The data are slightly regularized to avoid a couple of complexities.)

AMHARIC PRESENT AND PAST TENSE VERBS

a.	/səbbərš/	'you-f. broke'	/tɨsəbɨri/	'you-f. break'
b.	/səbbərk/	'you-m. broke'	/tɨsəbɨr/	'you-m. break'
c.	/səbbərku/	'I broke'	/ɨsəbɨr/	'I break'
d.	/dəkkəmš/	'you-f. tired'	/tɨdəkɨmi/	'you-f. tire'
e.	/dəkkəmk/	'you-m. tired'	/tɨdəkɨm/	'you-m. tire'
f.	/dəkkəmku/	'I tired'	/ɨdəkɨm/	'I tire'
g.	/samš/	'you-f. kissed'	/tɨsɨmi/	'you-f. kiss'
h.	/samk/	'you-m. kissed'	/tɨsɨm/	'you-m. kiss'
i.	/samku/	'I kissed'	/ɨsɨm/	'I kiss'

j.	/sabš/	'you-f. pulled'	/tɨsɨbi/	'you-f. pull'
k.	/sabk/	'you-m. pulled'	/tɨsɨb/	'you-m. pull'
l.	/sabku/	'I pulled'	/ɨsɨb/	'I pull'
m.	/nəkkaš/	'you-f. touched'	/tɨnəki/	'you-f. touch'
n.	/nəkkah/	'you-m. touched'	/tɨnəka/	'you-m. touch'
o.	/nəkkahu/	'I touched'	/ɨnəka/	'I touch'
p.	/səmmaš/	'you-f. heard'	/tɨsəmi/	'you-f. hear'
q.	/səmmah/	'you-m. heard'	/tɨsəma/	'you-m. hear'
r.	/səmmahu/	'I heard'	/ɨsəma/	'I hear'

English present tense verbs (*walk*, *open*, etc.) must have a suffix if the subject is 'he, she, it' (*walks*, *opens*, etc.), and, similarly but more extensively, Amharic verbs must ordinarily have suffixes and/or prefixes, depending on the subject of the verb. Notice that the first, second, and third rows of each set of verbs above show, respectively, verbs with the subjects 'you-feminine', 'you-masculine', and 'I'. The different verb forms of these rows reflect these different verb subjects.

English past tense verbs differ (almost always) from present tense verbs, usually by having a suffix (*walked*, *opened*, etc.; a few, including *set* and *hit*, however, are unchanged in past and present). Amharic past tense verbs differ from present tense verbs also, but by differences within the stem as well as by different affixes.

The Amharic verbs above consist of combinations of allomorphs of twelve morphemes: six lexical and six grammatical, as follows.

Lexical morphemes (verb stems)

a. 'break': /səbbər/ if past tense, /səbɨr/ if present tense
b. 'tire': /dəkkəm/ if past tense, /dəkɨm/ if present tense
c. 'kiss': /sam/ if past tense, /sɨm/ if present tense
d. 'pull': /sab/ if past tense, /sɨb/ if present tense
e. 'touch': /nəkka/ if past tense, /nək/ if present tense and subject is 'you-f.', /nəka/ if present tense and subject is 'you-m.' or 'I'
f. 'hear': /səmma/ if past tense, /səm/ if present tense and subject is 'you-f.', /səma/ if present tense and subject is 'you-m.' or 'I'

Grammatical morphemes (suffixes and prefixes)

g. 'you-feminine' of past tense verbs: /-š/
h. 'you-feminine' of present tense verbs: /-i/
i. 'you-feminine and masculine' of present tense verbs: /tɨ-/
j. 'you-masculine' of past tense verbs: /-k/ after consonants and /-h/ after /a/

k.   'I' of past tense verbs: /-ku/ after consonants and /-hu/ after /ɑ/
l.   'I' of present tense verbs: /ɨ-/

There are generalizations which can simplify this analysis. For example, stem allomorphs of some of the verbs are in a regular relationship: compare /səbbər/ 'broke' with /dəkkəm/ 'tired', and /səbɨr/ 'break' with /dəkɨm/ 'tire'. If we looked at many more verbs with these lexical meanings, we would see that the form common to all of them consists of consonants only, so that the form of 'break' is just /sbr/ 'break', and of 'tire' just /dkm/.

There is another generalization concerning the fact that both /-k/ and /-ku/ appear after consonants and both /-h/ and /-hu/ appear after /ɑ/ (or any vowel). This aspect of language, phonological rules, is the topic of chapter 13. The comparision of these English and Amharic verbs is perhaps sufficient to suggest the extent to which morphology can differ from language to language.

Suggestions for
ADDITIONAL READING

Introductions to the study of morphology are *Morphology* (1990) by John T. Jensen and *Introducing Linguistic Morphology* (1988) by Laurie Bauer. Also see chapter 2 of *Fundamentals of Linguistic Analysis* (1972) by Ronald W. Langacker. The latter also includes data analysis problems concerning morphemes and their allomorphs, for which also see section 3 of *Source Book for Linguistics* (1987) by William Cowan and Jaromira Rakušan.

For the frequency analysis of English words, see *Frequency Analysis of English Usage: Lexicon and Grammar* (1982) by W. Nelson Francis and Henry Kučera. These authors' earlier *Computational Analysis of Present-day American English* (1967) was mentioned above. A similar study of British English is *Frequency Analysis of English Vocabulary and Grammar* (1989) by Stig Johansson and Knut Hofland.

Also see suggestions for additional reading at the end of chapter 5.

IMPORTANT CONCEPTS AND
TERMS IN THIS CHAPTER

- sign
- morpheme
- allomorph
- morph
- contraction
- free

- word
- complex word
- residue
- lexical morpheme
- derivational affix
- nonproductivity

- bound
- simple word
- prefix
- suffix
- stem

- grammatical morpheme
- inflectional affix
- productivity
- English inflectional affix
- morphological fusion

OUTLINE OF CHAPTER 4

1. **Morphemes**
2. **Morph, morpheme, and allomorph**
3. **Types of morphs according to form: free and bound**
   1. Free forms
   2. Bound forms
4. **Simple and complex words**
5. **Types of morphemes according to meaning: lexical and grammatical**
   1. Lexical morphemes
      1. Five characteristics of lexical morphemes
      2. Derivational (lexical) affixes
   2. Grammatical morphemes
      1. Five characteristics of grammatical morphemes
      2. Inflectional (grammatical) affixes
6. **English inflectional affixes**
7. **Morphological differences among languages**
   1. General differences
   2. Amharic verbs

EXAMPLES AND PRACTICE

EXAMPLE

1. Dividing English words into morphs. Consider the following 25-word sentence:

> Our program offers prompt, all-day service and free repairs on covered parts of your gas furnace or hot water heater, range, and clothes dryer.

The morphs of this sentence are listed and their forms classified as follows, where F = free form, B = bound form, L = lexical, G = grammatical, and R = residue.

Our	F, G	repair	F, L	or	F, G
program	F, L	-s	B, G	hot	F, L
offer	F, L	on	F, G	water	F, L
-s	B, G	cover	F, L	heat	F, L
prompt,	F, L	-ed	B, G	-er	B, L
all	F, L	part	F, L	range	F, L
day	F, L	-s	B, G	and	F, G
serv	F, L	of	F, G	cloth-	B, L
-ice	B, R	your	F, G	-es	B, G
and	F, G	gas	F, L	dry	F, L
free	F, L	furnace	F, L	-er	B, L

The 25 words of the sentence are made up of 33 morphs. Notice that:

a. *-ice* of *service* is listed as residue since it doesn't seem to be a recognizable suffix, but the first part of this word seems to be the word *serve*.

b. *cloth-* /klo(ð)/ of *clothes* is listed here as a bound form, as if /z/ at the end of this word is the plural suffix.

c. *repair* is listed as a free morph; the hypothetical parts *re* and *pair* don't have the meanings of the prefix *re-* and the word *pair*.

PRACTICE

Cut a sentence of 20 words or more from a newspaper, attach it to a page, and list and label the morphs and their forms as above. If your sentence includes contractions, such as *don't* or *she's*, treat the latter part as suffixes.

EXAMPLE

2. Allomorphs of English plural and past tense suffixes. The English plural suffix morpheme has three allomorphs:

a. /ɪz/ (or /əz/) after /s, z, š, ž, č, ǰ/, as in *kisses* /kɪsɪz/, *rashes* /ræšɪz/, and *patches* /pæčɪz/;

b. /s/, after other voiceless consonants, as in *lips* /lɪps/, *cats* /kæts/ and *books* /bʊks/; and

c. /z/, after other consonants and vowels, as in *dogs* /dɔgz/, *bears* /bɛrz/, and *fleas* /fliz/.

The possessive suffix of nouns and the present tense 3rd-person-singular suffix of verbs have the same allomorphs:

Possessive suffix of nouns	*3rd-person-sing. of verbs*
fish's /fɪšɪz/, Tess's /tɛsɪz/	catches /kæčɪz/, races /resɪz/
cat's /kæts/, Nick's /nɪks/	takes /teks/, drops /drɑps/
dog's /dɔgz/, people's /pipəlz/	falls /fɑlz/, knows /noz/

The past tense suffix of verbs has three somewhat similar allomorphs, similarly distributed:

a. /ɪd/ or /əd/, after /t, d/, the two alveolar stops, as in *waited* /wetɪd/ and *added* /ædɪd/;
b. /t/, after other voiceless consonants, as in *laughed* /læft/, *locked* /lakt/, and *pushed* /pušt/; and
c. /d/, otherwise, as in *rubbed* /rəbd/, *phoned* /fond/, and *tried* /trɑjd/.

PRACTICE

(a) Identify the plural suffix allomorph /z/, /s/, or /ɪz/ appropriate for each of the nouns 1–15, and (b) identify the past tense suffix allomorph /d/, /t/, or /ɪd/ appropriate for each of the verbs 16–30:

1.	book	6.	train	11.	bow
2.	lane	7.	tray	12.	bell
3.	knee	8.	fork	13.	car
4.	loss	9.	garage	14.	axe
5.	fiddle	10.	tenth	15.	latch

16.	walk	21.	fix	26.	lapse
17.	row	22.	clasp	27.	try
18.	load	23.	allocate	28.	rattle
19.	roast	24.	possess	29.	roar
20.	rob	25.	sympathize	30.	match

EXAMPLE

3. Frequency of allomorphs. Of the allomorphs of the plural and possessive suffixes of nouns and present tense suffix of verbs, the /z/ allomorph is most frequent. Of the allomorphs of the past tense suffix, /d/ is most frequent. For /z/ this is apparent in the following text (from *Newsweek* for May 15, 1995, p. 44), which is followed by a list of words in the text which include the four morphemes.

Left behind in this rush to embrace nature are thousands of 1960s-era ranch houses that are too old, small and unfashionable to attract middle-class buyers, and as a result are turning into that new American phenomenon, the suburban slum. This may be the fate of an area called Maryvale, which like all west-side suburbs suffers from the competitive disadvantage that commuters must drive into the sun both ways. Interspersed among the houses are large tracts . . .

1.	thousands	/θɑwzənz/	4.	buyers	/bajərz/
2.	1960s	/najntinsɪkstiz/	5.	suburbs	/səbərbz/
3.	houses	/hɑwzɪz/	6.	suffers	/səfərz/

7.	commuters	/kəmjudərz/	9.	houses	/hɑwzɪz/
8.	ways	/wez/	10.	tracts	/træks/

PRACTICE

Find a stretch of newspaper text in which are found at least 20 occurrences of the four suffix morphemes present tense, plural, possessive, and past tense. (a) Underline the 20 words in which the suffixes appear and attach the text to a page. As above, (b) make a list of these words and (c) write them phonemically, with special attention to the pronunciation of the suffix.

EXAMPLE

4. Morphological analysis. Morphemes in the stream of speech often follow one another without pause. Nor are there spaces as in writing to separate spoken words. Children learning their language come to recognize the morphemes by noticing and recording the recurrences of form–meaning pairs.

PRACTICE

Following is a three-sentence text of Amharic with an English translation. Because it has a number of proper nouns, or names, in it, by noticing these names, which are almost the same in Amharic and English, and using these as benchmarks in the transcription, it should be possible to identify (if with some guessing) most of the other morphemes, including the allomorphs of some of these proper nouns. Notice that 'Yohannis', 'mother' and 'and' occur three times each, and 'Dawit', 'Addis Ababa', 'Father', 'sent', 'house', and 'Mr' occur twice each. Expect all of these to be distributed in the three sentences as in the English translation. (In fact, one cannot ordinarily expect a translation to be such an accurate reflection of the original, but in this case it is.)

1. jəjohanːisabːaʈinːainːat atodawitinːawəjzərohanːa
johanːisinwədəadːisababalakut.
2. johanːisadːisababasidərs wədəatodawitinːatbethedə.
3. kəbetaččəwlabːatunːainːatudəbdabːelakə.

1. 'Yohannis's father and mother, Mr Dawit and Ms Hanna, sent Yohannis to Addis Ababa.
2. When Yohannis arrived in Addis Ababa, he went to Mr Dawit's mother's house.
3. From her house, he sent a letter to his father and mother.'

List as many of the Amharic morphemes as you can, including the four names, with their English translations. You can't expect the order of Amharic morphemes to be like that of English, but you can, generally, expect morphemes associated in meaning to be associated in time and space (in time in speech, and in space in writing).

EXAMPLE

5. Amharic past tense verbs. Some of the morphology of Amharic past tense verbs was presented in §7.2, above. Following are eight more Amharic past tense verbs with suffixes of four subjects whose English translation equivalents are 'he', 'she', 'we', and 'they'.

	'he'	'she'	'we'	'they'	
a.	/kəffələ/	/kəffələč/	/kəffəlin/	/kəffəlu/	'pay'
b.	/fəlləgə/	/fəlləgəč/	/fəlləgin/	/fəlləgu/	'want'
c.	/bəlla/	/bəllač/	/bəllan/	/bəllu/	'eat'
d.	/ləkka/	/ləkkač/	/ləkkan/	/ləkku/	'measure'
e.	/k'omə/	/k'oməč/	/k'omin/	/k'omu/	'stand'
f.	/hedə/	/hedəč/	/hedin/	/hedu/	'go'
g.	/samə/	/saməč/	/samin/	/samu/	'kiss'
h.	/fənədda/	/fənəddač/	/fənəddan/	/fənəddu/	'burst'

PRACTICE

Review §7.2, then study the verbs above and identify the morphemes and their allomorphs. There are eight verb stems and four verb–subject suffixes. Three of the stems have two allomorphs, and three of the suffixes have two allomorphs. The 'he' suffix, for example, has allomorphs as follows:

'he': /-ə/ after consonants, Ø after vowels.

List the other three suffix morphemes with their allomorphs, and the eight verb stem morphemes with their allomorphs.

8 stems

Ayabu verbs

Kaffal (pay)
Fallag (want)

ball / balla (eat).
lakk / lakka (measure)
fanadd / fanadda

4 suffixes

he /ə/ø
she əč/č I'm bored in this class It's horrible!!!
we in/n
They u

Chapter 5

THE LEXICON AND MORPHOLOGICAL RULES

This chapter presents two aspects of the structure of the morphology of languages: the inventory of morphemes and the rules which combine morphemes as words. It presents some examples of how languages differ in their grammatical morphology, and shows how, given phonemic representations of words, these may be analyzed into morphemes.

1. LEXICON

The **lexicon** of a language is its morphemes, organized in a richly cross-classified **mental dictionary**, which enables us to find morphemes in many ways. A dictionary of the familiar sort, a book, presents a listing of morphemes, mostly words, which may be found only by their spellings, if one knows the alphabetical order according to which the spellings are arranged. A different sort of lexicon-book is a thesaurus, in which words are classified according to their synonyms and near synonyms. Most of the entries in an English dictionary are words, but in a good, lengthy, English dictionary-book, many of the bound morphemes may also be listed.

1.1. Organization of the lexicon

The **lexical entries** of our mental dictionary must be a lot more complex or richly structured than the entries of print dictionaries and thesauruses.

A dictionary-book makes us find meanings and pronunciations from spellings. If we don't know the spelling of the word we want to find, we have to use a trial-and-error method still based on spelling. Our mental dictionary has a lot more flexibility. Entries of the mental dictionary are represented in a system which enables us to access morphemes (basically words, really) in a number of ways, including:

    a.   by rhyme – one can think of words that rhyme with *dog*, *funny*, etc.

    b.   by initial sound – one can think of words that begin with /d/, /i/, etc.

    c.   by synonym – one can think of words that mean about the same as *sad*, *smart*, etc.

    d.   by rough opposites – one can think of words that mean the rough opposite of *sad*, *smart*, etc.

    e.   by other semantic features – one can think of words for names of animals, colors, bodies of water, capital cities, ice cream flavors, etc.

    f.   by context of occurrence – one can think of words for things found in a kitchen, at a wedding, etc.

    g.   by part of speech, noun, verb, etc. – one can think of nouns, like *dog*, *cat*, etc.; verbs, like *go*, *find*, etc.; prepositions; etc.

    h.   by spelling, left-to-right – one can think of words that begin with *d-*, *m-*, *e-*, etc.

1.2.   Lexical morphology: parts of speech

The major classes of lexical morphemes, which are the basis of words, are traditionally known as the **parts of speech**, the three most common of which are noun, verb, adjective. All languages have nouns and verbs and most, perhaps all, have adjectives. The parts of speech cannot be simply defined, but are characterized by a number of aspects of both form and meaning. Typically the formal characteristics are more reliable than those based on meaning.

1.2.1. *Nouns*

As for meaning, **nouns** are traditionally known to be names of persons, places, things, and ideas. But this meaning aspect of nouns remains rather vague – verbs, for example, may also be considered names of ideas – and the formal characteristics are often more reliable. Among the formal characteristics of English nouns are that they typically:

    a.   may be made definite in meaning by use of preceding *the* (the definite article), as in *the book*, *the guy*, *the answer*;

    b.   may be made possessive by suffixing *-'s*, as in *people's*, *Jane's*, *a politician's*;

    c.   may be made negative by prefixing *non-*, as in *nonbeliever*, *nonsense*, *nonunion*.

1.2.2. *Verbs*

Verbs are traditionally said to express action, being, and states of being, but some nouns, especially nouns derived from verbs, express the same ideas: *action*, *existence*, *happiness*. Fortunately, verbs also have formal characteristics, which are often more reliable. Among the formal characteristics of English verbs are that they typically:

a. may be made past in meaning by suffixing -(e)d as in *walked, opened, said*;

b. may be made into agents by suffixing -er as in *doer, walker, knower*;

c. may be made negative by prefixing *dis-* as in *disagree, disappear, dislike*.

1.2.3. Adjectives

In terms of meaning, **adjectives** are said to modify nouns, but this is problematic, since nouns also seem to modify nouns, in phrases like *fish dinner*, and *business deal*. Among their formal characteristics, English adjectives typically:

a. may be used in comparisons by suffixing -er or by use of *more*, as in *quicker, older, more extravagant*, etc.

b. may be modified by intensifiers like *very* and *too*, as in *very quick, very old, too extravagant*;

c. may often be made negative by prefixing *un-*, as in *unhappy, unusual, uncritical*, etc.

1.3. Nouns, verbs, and adjectives in Amharic

Amharic nouns are made definite by suffixing /-u/: /bet/ 'house', /betu/ 'the house', and possessive by prefixing /jə-/: /paulos/ 'Paul', /jəpaulos/ 'Paul's', /jəbetu/ 'of the house'. But there is no negative prefix for Amharic nouns. 'Nonbeliever', for example, would be expressed with a negative verb /jəmmajamɨn/ '(one) who does not believe'.

Amharic verbs distinguish present and past tense as described in chapter 4, §7.2, by changes in the form of the verb stem. Like English verbs, they can be made into agents, by suffixing /-i/ to a special stem, for example: /fəlləgə/ 'he sought, /fəllagi/ 'opener'; /səbbərə/ 'he broke', /səbbari/ 'breaker'. Amharic has nothing like the English prefix *dis-*, but Amharic 'reduplicative' verbs may be formed with a special stem as follows: /səbabbərə/ 'he broke here and there/ smashed', /fəlalləgə/ 'he looked here and there'.

Amharic has relatively few adjectives. Many ideas which English expresses with adjectives Amharic expresses with verbs. English 'he is sick', for example, may be expressed in Amharic as /amməməw/, 'it sickened him' (thus, 'he is sick'). English 'he is sad' would probably be expressed by the verb /azzənə/ 'he grieved' (thus 'he is sad').

1.4. Grammatical morphology in English and other languages

Languages typically have translation equivalents for the lexical morphemes of other languages, but they typically differ, often quite extensively, in the categories of their grammatical morphology. In other words, 'Languages differ essentially in what they must convey and not in what they *can* convey' (Jakobson 1959 [1971, p. 264]).

1.4.1. Subject–verb agreement

A prominent way that languages differ in their grammatical morphology is **subject–verb agreement,** the necessity to mark verbs differently, often with prefixes or suffixes, according to their subject. Compare the patterns of subject–verb agreement in regular present tense verbs of three languages: English, Spanish, and Amharic. Notice that Spanish has special forms for second-person ('you') familiar, whereas Amharic has special forms for second-person polite.

SUBJECT–VERB AGREEMENT IN PRESENT TENSE VERBS OF THREE LANGUAGES

Language	Subject of verb	Verb ('eat')
English	3rd person singular ('he, she, it')	eats
	Other subjects	eat
Spanish	1st person singular ('I')	como
	2nd person singular ('you') familiar	comes
	Other singular subjects*	come
	1st person plural ('we')	comemos
	2nd person plural ('you') familiar	coméis
	Other plural subjects**	comen

*2nd singular nonfamiliar and 3rd singular
**3rd plural and 2nd plural nonfamiliar

Amharic	1st person singular	/bəllahu/
	2nd person singular feminine	/bəllaš/
	2nd person singular masculine	/bəllah/
	3rd person singular feminine	/bəllač/
	3rd person singular masculine	/bəlla/
	1st person plural	/bəllan/
	2nd person plural	/bəllaččihu/
	Other subjects***	/bəllu/

***2nd and 3rd singular polite and 3rd plural

Languages have many categories of grammatical morphology unknown in English. Following are four examples, from Swahili (East Africa), Spanish, Japanese, and Amharic (Ethiopia).

1.4.2. Swahili noun classes

In Swahili, all nouns are members of 15 (or so, depending on how they are counted) **noun classes,** whose class-membership is shown by a prefix, which usually differs whether the noun is singular or plural. The classes are only very roughly based on meaning. For example:

Class	Singular noun		Plural noun
'Animate things'	msichana	'girl'	wasichana
(m-/wa-)	mvulana	'boy'	wavulana
	mtoto	'child'	watoto
	mtu	'man'	watu
'Plants, etc.'	mti	'tree'	miti
(m-/mi-)	mgomba	'banana tree'	migomba
	mguu	'foot'	miguu
'Useful things'	kitu	'thing'	vitu
(ki-/vi-)	kiti	'chair'	viti
	kitanda	'bed'	vitanda

The class prefix of a noun also appears on its modifiers, including adjectives, as in *m-tu m-zuri* 'a good man', *wa-tu wa-zuri* 'good men', and on verbs for which the noun is subject: *wa-mekwenda* 'they (the men) have gone'.

1.4.3. *Spanish verb classes*

There are three types of verbs in Spanish, which differ by the first vowel of their suffixes. Here are two examples of each of these three types of verb, as infinitives ('to-forms'), first person singulars ('I-forms') of the present tense, and past participles ('-*en*-forms' – in many English verbs, same as the past tense).

Infinitive		1st person sg. present		Past participle	
andar	'to walk'	ando	'I walk'	andado	'walked'
hablar	'to speak'	hablo	'I speak'	hablado	'spoken'
comer	'to eat'	como	'I eat'	comido	'eaten'
aprender	'to learn'	aprendo	'I learn'	aprendido	'learned'
sentir	'to feel'	siento	'I feel'	sentido	'written'
recibir	'to receive'	recibo	'I receive'	recibido	'received'

The three types are apparent in the infinitives, which end in -*ar*, -*er*, or -*ir*. The three types are not distinct in their 1st sg. present tense forms, all of which end in -*o*, and in the present participles the -*er* and -*ir* types are not distinct, both having the suffix -*ido*, though these two are distinct from -*ar* types, with -*ado*.

Membership in the three types has nothing to do with meaning. Thus the dictionary listing of a verb, its **citation form**, must reveal its type. The citation form of a Spanish verb is an infinitive, which reveals its type by one of the suffixes -*ar*, -*er*, or -*ir*.

1.4.4. *Japanese topics, subjects, and objects*

In Japanese, noun phrases are followed by morphemes which show whether they are the **topic** of the sentence, or the **subject** or **object** of the verb. Topics, those noun phrases which, roughly speaking, a speaker perceives to be the topic of discussion, are followed by /wa/. Subjects in Japanese are followed by /ga/, and objects by /o/. Here are two example sentences:

1. kinoo wa jooko ga piano o hiita
    Yesterday Top Yoko Subj piano DO played
    'As for Yesterday, Yoko played the piano.'

2. jooko-wa kinoo ǰon ni hana o ageta
    Yoko Top yesterday John to flowers DO gave
    'As for Yoko, yesterday she gave flowers to John.'

The first sentence is about yesterday, and the second is about Yoko. As the topic of the second sentence – and therefore marked by /wa/ – Yoko doesn't have the subject morpheme /ga/. Subject and topic are different things. Also notice how the Japanese topic suffix is translated in English: as 'as for', or 'regarding'. Japanese sentences typically have topics, but English sentences rarely have a noun phrase introduced by words like 'as for' or 'regarding'. That is, topic is expressed by a grammatical morpheme in Japanese (thus obligatorily expressed and very frequent), but by a syntactic phrase in English.

1.4.5. *Amharic causative verbs*

In Amharic, verbs may be made **causative** by prefixing /a-/ or /as-/. **Intransitive** verbs (verbs without objects, like 'come' and 'get well') are made causative by prefixing /a-/, and **transitive** verbs (verbs with objects, like 'send' and 'buy') are made causative by prefixing /as-/. Here are a few examples of past tense verbs with and without the causative prefix:

Simple past tense verb		*Causative past tense verb*	
/mətt'a-n/	'we came'	/a-mətt'a-n/	'we brought'
/dan-ə/	'he got well'	/a-dan-ə/	'he cured'
/dəkkəm-ə/	'he became tired'	/a-dəkkəm-ə/	'he caused to tire'
/lak-əč/	'she sent'	/as-lak-əč/	'she caused to send'
/gəzz-u/	'they bought'	/as-gəzz-u/	'they caused to buy'
/fərra-hu/	'I feared'	/as-fərra-hu/	'I frightened'

2. MORPHOLOGICAL RULES

Morphological rules are generalizations which express:

a. the necessary and possible combinations and temporal (or linear) order of morphemes which make up words, and

b. when a morpheme has allomorphs, the choice among these.

Rules of the latter type are also called **morphophonemic rules,** because they have both morphological and phonological aspects and effects (these are discussed further in chapter 13, §1.2). Following are two examples which illustrate these two rule-types in the formation of possessive nouns in two languages: English and Amharic.

2.1.   Morphology of possessive nouns in English

a.   A possessive noun consists of a noun plus the possessive suffix, basically /z/ (written *'s,* as in *Travis's, Smith's,* and *Miller's*).
b.   This possessive suffix has three pronunciations, or allomorphs:

1.   After sibilants /z/ is preceded by /ɪ/: /trævɪsɪz/ *Travis's,* /rozɪz/ *Rose's,* /nɔrɪšɪz/ *Norrish's,* /fɪtɪčɪz/ *Fittich's* (English sibilants are /s, z, š, ž, č, ǰ/; recall that /č/ = /tš/ and /ǰ/ = /dž/)
2.   After other voiceless consonants (/p, t, k, f/) the /z/ is made voiceless, /s/: /fɪlɪps/ *Philip's,* /kets/ *Kate's,* /nɪks/ *Nick's,* /rælfs/ *Ralph's*
3.   After voiced phones (which are all the rest) the simple /z/ remains: /frɛdz/ *Fred's,* /ǰenz/ *Jane's,* /halz/ *Hall's,* /mæriz/ *Mary's*

2.2.   Morphology of possessive nouns in Amharic

a.   A possessive noun consists of a noun plus the possessive prefix, basically /jə/.
b.   The possessive prefix of Amharic also has three allomorphs:

1.   If another prefix precedes, the possessive suffix is absent: /ləmarta abbat/ 'for Marta's father', /bəp'aulos bet/ 'at Paulos's house'
2.   Before vowels the /ə/ of /jə/ is absent: /jantə/ 'yours, sing. masc.' (/antə/ 'you, sing. masc.'), /janči/ 'yours, sing. fem.' (/anči/ 'you, sing. fem.'), /jitjopp'ja/ 'Ethiopia's' (/itjopp'ja/ 'Ethiopia')
3.   Before consonants the simple /jə/ remains: /jəmarta/ 'Marta's', /jəp'aulos/ 'Paulos's', /jəkeɲa/ 'Kenya's'

2.3.   Hierarchical structure of words

The result of the word-formation rules is sometimes more than just a string of morphemes. If there are three or more morphemes, it is often useful to consider the word to have a **hierarchical structure** in which some of the morphemes combine to make subparts to which others are attached. Consider the examples of *unenjoyable* and *resettlement.*

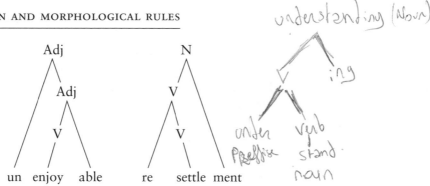

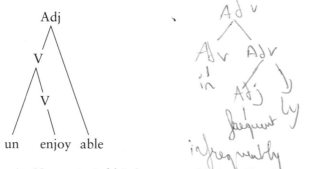

Unenjoyable may be understood to have the structure [*un*[*enjoy-able*]], which is clearer in the 'tree diagram', above. We know the structure is *not*,

that is, [[*un-enjoy*]*able*], because *-able* is suffixed to verbs, like *enjoy*, to make adjectives, and *un-* is prefixed to adjectives, like *enjoyable*, to make negative adjectives. Thus *unenjoy* is not a possible English word. The structure of *resettlement* is as shown because *re-* is prefixed to verbs, such as *settle*, but not to nouns, such as *settlement*.

3. MORPHOLOGICAL ANALYSIS OF LANGUAGES

An important part of learning a language consists of analyzing the stream of speech to discover and inventory its morphemes. Learning a first language as a child includes this sort of **morphological analysis**.

3.1. Morphological analysis in language learning

As young children, we do this analysis on pronunciations – on the stream of speech. Long before we go to school and learn to read and write, we have thoroughly mastered the basic spoken language, having analyzed and inventoried several thousand of the most important morphemes.

Ignorant of writing, the child analyzes the stream of speech and isolates the most important morphemes as form and meaning pairs, where form is a pronunciation, constructs the lexical entries of the mental dictionary, and constructs the grammar including rules for the combination of morphemes as words, their

Affaire Kraniel

Tidane

linear order, and for choosing among allomorphs. There is often good evidence for this when children say things like *rided*, *foots*, and *gooder*, instead of *rode*, *feet*, and *better*. When children have not heard the former, they must have formed these words as the products of the grammar they have created.

As adults we continue to do this sort of analysis, on speech and on written language. Hearing the pronunciation [ənáyshàws], for example, given its context of occurrence, we decide whether this represents 'a nice house' or 'an ice house'. Seeing words like *cyberspace*, *cybertalk*, and *cybersex*, we abstract knowledge of a new morpheme *cyber*, a noun-prefix meaning something like 'having to do with computer-assisted communication'.

3.2. Morphological analysis of language data: Sidamo verbs

3.2.1. Data

Consider the following quite typical morphological data concerning verbs of the Ethiopian language Sidamo, written phonemically. The linguistic analysis of these data involves the same learning process as the child's: isolating and listing the morphemes and finding the rules, or generalizations, necessary for combining these morphemes into words.

SIDAMO VERBS

1.	aganno	'he drinks'	11.	agí	'he drank'
2.	murí	'he cut'	12.	itanno	'he eats'
3.	giiranno	'he burns'	13.	murtú	'she cut'
4.	laʔí	'he saw'	14.	umí	'he dug'
5.	umanno	'he digs'	15.	ittú	'she ate'
6.	fantú	'she opened'	16.	runtú	'she cursed'
7.	rumí	'he cursed'	17.	runtanno	'she curses'
8.	murtanno	'she cuts'	18.	laʔanno	'he sees'
9.	untú	'she dug'	19.	untanno	'she digs'
10.	faní	'he opened'	20.	rumanno	'he curses'

3.2.2. Analysis

Notice in the data that the meaning 'drink' is always associated with the phoneme sequence /ag/. This morpheme, /ag/ 'drink', is a verb stem, always followed by something else within a word. Also notice in the data that the meaning 'he, past tense' is always associated with the form /í/. This morpheme, /í/ 'he, past tense', is a suffix, always attached to a verb stem.

3.2.2.1. Lexicon. Continuation of such analysis, matching meanings with forms, will result in the following list of associations: a partial lexicon of Sidamo consisting of 12 morphemes, eight verb stems and four verb–subject suffixes, again written phonemically.

LEXICON OF SIDAMO VERBS

ag-	'verb, drink'	ru{m, n}-	'verb, curse'
mur-	'verb, cut'	it-	'verb, eat'
giir-	'verb, burn'	-anno	'he, present'
laʔ-	'verb, see'	-í	'he, past'
u{m, n}-	'verb, dig'	-tanno	'she, present'
fan-	'verb, open'	-tú	'she, past'

Two of the verb morphemes each have two allomorphs, /um, un-/ 'dig' and /rum, run-/ 'curse'. Analysis will show that the forms that end in /n/ (/un-, run-/) appear before the two suffixes which begin with /t/, /-tú/ and /-tanno/, and the forms that end in /m/ (/um-, rum-/) appear before the suffixes which begin with vowels.

3.2.2.2. *Rules.*   Thus we can give the following morphological rules for Sidamo verbs employing the above twelve morphemes.

RULES FOR SIDAMO VERBS

a. A verb consists of a verb stem and another morpheme expressing person, gender and tense.
b. The person/gender/tense morpheme is a suffix on the verb stem.
c. Of morphemes ending in both /m/ and /n/, the allomorph with /n/ appears with suffixes beginning with /t/ and the allomorph with /m/ appears otherwise.

Analysis might be carried farther, and the rules might be stated differently. For example, we could separate the /t/ of -/tanno/ and /-tú/ as a separate morpheme meaning 'feminine', so that /-anno/ and /-ú/ are just '3rd person', understood as masculine ('he') when feminine /t-/ is absent. We could say that the verb-stem allomorph with final /m/ appears with suffixes beginning with vowels, and the allomorph with /n/ appears otherwise. We could even say that the /n/ of morphemes which end in /m/ is the result of changing the /m/ to /n/ when a following suffix begins with /t/. Such data typically present a number of possibilities of analysis. As more and more data are examined, some of these possibilities have to be rejected.

Suggestions for
ADDITIONAL READING

Words, and how we organize them in our mental dictionary, are the topic of *Words in the Mind* (1994) by Jean Aitchison. Two textbooks for the advanced study of morphology are *Morphological Theory* (1991) by Andrew Spencer, and *Current Morphology* (1992) by Andrew Carstairs-McCarthy. Lexical and grammatical categories in a variety of languages are surveyed in volume 3 of *Language Typology and Syntactic Description:*

Grammatical Categories and the Lexicon (1992) edited by Timothy Shopen.

At this point, some readers may want to refresh their study and understanding of English grammar. Good books for this purpose are *English Grammar: an Outline* (1995) by Rodney Huddleston, and *English Grammar: Principles and Facts* (1995) by Jeffrey P. Kaplan.

IMPORTANT CONCEPTS AND
TERMS IN THIS CHAPTER

- lexicon
- mental dictionary
- lexical entries
- parts of speech
- nouns
- verbs
- adjectives
- subject–verb agreement
- noun classes
- citation forms

- topic
- subject
- object
- causative
- intransitive verb
- transitive verb
- morphological rule
- morphophonemic rule
- hierarchical structure
- morphological analysis

OUTLINE OF
CHAPTER 5

EXAMPLES AND PRACTICE

EXAMPLE

1. Morphemes in the mental dictionary. Unlike in book-dictionaries, words can be accessed in our mental dictionaries in various ways: by first phoneme, first letter, synonymy, rhyme, semantic feature, association in a context, etc.

PRACTICE

Fill in the blanks with words which you access in your English mental dictionary according to the characteristic at the top of each column. A few of the blanks are filled in as examples.

		First phone	First letter	Synonym	Rhyme	Opposite	Associated word
a.	love	_____	_____	adore	dove	hate	_____
b.	send	sit	_____	_____	_____	_____	letter
c.	happy	_____	help	_____	_____	_____	_____
d.	cat	_____	_____	_____	_____	_____	_____
e.	apple	_____	_____	_____	_____	_____	_____
f.	quick	_____	_____	_____	_____	_____	_____
g.	over	_____	_____	_____	_____	_____	_____
h.	new	_____	_____	_____	_____	_____	_____
i.	harm	_____	_____	_____	_____	_____	_____
j.	road	_____	_____	_____	_____	_____	_____

2. Word structure. It was noted in §2.3, above, that *unenjoyable* may be said to have the structure [un [enjoy + able]] and *resettlement* the structure [[re + settle] ment]. This is so because *enjoy + able* is a likely combination but *un + enjoy* is not, and *re + settle* is a likely combination but *re + Noun* is not.

Match the six words (a)–(f) with the six word structures of figure 5.1, by writing the parts of the words in the blanks: (a) *engagements*, (b) *remagnetize*, (c) *winterizes*, (d) *nonconformist*, (e) *darkened*, (f) *predemocratic*. The first step should be to match the part of speech of each word (noun, verb, or adjective) with that shown at the top of each structure.

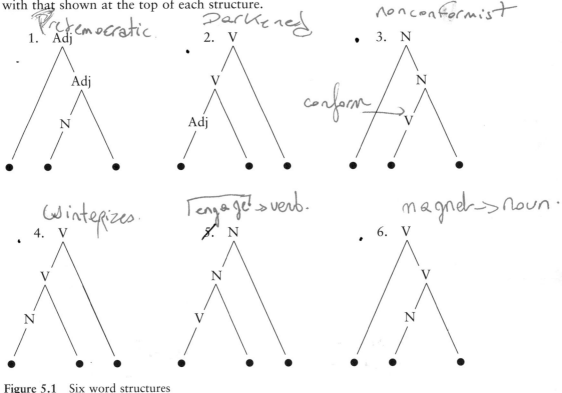

Figure 5.1   Six word structures

3. Data analysis I: Amharic nouns. The following list of Amharic nouns, written phonemically, includes twelve morphemes: five nouns and seven suffixes. 'M.sg.' and 'f.sg.' mean 'masculine singular' and 'feminine singular', respectively; /ɨ/ is a high central unrounded vowel, not ordinarily heard in English.

1. bet   'house'
2. bete   'my house'
3. betɨš   'your (f.sg.) house'
4. betɨh   'your (m.sg.) house'
5. fərəsɨč 'horses'
6. fərəse   'my horse'

7.	fərəsiš	'your (f.sg.) horse'	18. betu	'his house'
8.	fərəsih	'your (m.sg.) horse'	19. betoču	'his houses'
9.	kisoč	'pockets'	20. kiswa	'her pocket'
10.	kise	'my pocket'	21. kisočwa	'her pockets'
11.	kisiš	'your (f.sg.) pocket'	22. fərəswa	'her horse'
12.	kisih	'your (m.sg.) pocket'	23. fərəsočwa	'her horses'
13.	betoče	'my houses'	24. səʔataččin	'our clock'
14.	betočiš	your (f.sg.) houses'	25. fərəsoču	'his horses'
15.	betaččin	'our house'	26. zəməde	'my relative'
16.	fərəsaččin	'our horse'	27. zəmədoče	'my relatives'
17.	səʔatoč	'clocks'	28. zəmədočaččin	'our relatives'

PRACTICE

(a) Analyze the words into their morphemes and make a list of the morphemes (phonemic forms and meanings). Your list should include, for example:

/bet/ 'house'
/-e/ 'my'

(b) Suppose we add to the list the following vowel-final nouns and their plurals. How does the analysis have to be changed? (/k'/ is a glottalized ejective velar stop).

29.	bək'lo	'mule'	32.	eliwoč	'tortoises'
30.	bək'lowoč	'mules'	33.	wiša	'dog'
31.	eli	'tortoise'	34.	wišawoč	'dogs'

EXAMPLE

4. Data analysis II: Sidamo sentences expressing possession. In these phonemically written Sidamo sentences there are 18 morphemes: one verb stem, nine verb affixes including seven verb–subject suffixes, seven nouns, and one quantifier.

1.	basu nooʔe	'I have a cat.'
2.	mini noohe	'You (sg.) have a house.'
3.	saa noosi	'He has a cow.'
4.	waṭi noose	'She has money.'
5.	ǰiro noonke	'We have wealth.'
6.	mini nooʔne	'You (pl.) have a house.'
7.	ǰiro noonsa	'They have wealth.'
8.	basu dinooʔe	'I don't have a cat.'
9.	mini nooseni	'Does she have a house?'
10.	saa nooʔne	'You (pl.) have a cow.'
11.	saa dinoosini	'Doesn't he have a cow?'
12.	waši dinoose	'She doesn't have a dog.'
13.	ulla nooheni	'Do you (sg.) have land?'

14. lowo ullɑ dinooʔe   'I don't have much land.'
15. lowo sɑɑ noohe   'You (sg.) have many cattle.'

Analyze the Sidamo sentences and list the 18 morphemes (form and meaning). Your list should include, for example, /bɑsu/ 'cat'.

5. Data analysis III: Samoan sentences (data from Langacker 1972). Samoan is the language of Samoa. Study these Samoan sentences, written phonemically. There are 16 morphemes.

1.	e faʔapaʔū e faifeʔau le niu	'A missionary fells the coconut palm.'
2.	sa puʔe e le fafine le pusi	'The woman caught the cat.'
3.	e faʔapaʔū e le fafine niu	'The woman fells a coconut palm.'
4.	e puʔe upega siaosi	'A net catches George.'
5.	sa paʔū le pusi	'The cat fell.'
6.	sa puʔe le upega le faifeʔau	'The net caught the missionary.'
7.	e paʔū le upega	'The net falls.'
8.	sa faʔapaʔū e malia le laʔau	'Mary felled the tree.'
9.	sa puʔe e siaosi le pusi i le upega	'George caught the cat with the net.'
10.	e puʔe e le faifeʔau le pusi i upega	'The missionary catches the cat with a net.'

List the 16 Samoan morphemes (form and meaning). There are two morphemes with the form /e/. One of these has grammatical function unlike anything in English; describe its meaning as precisely and concisely as you can.

Chapter 6

SENTENCES AND SYNTAX

This chapter is about the nature of syntax, sentence structure, especially the unbounded length of sentences, how this unboundedness is possible, and how we deal with it through abstract knowledge.

1. UNBOUNDEDNESS OF SYNTAX

Every language has a certain number of phonemes, and an inventory of morphemes (a mental dictionary), but there can be no inventory of sentences. This is apparent in the fact that every day, repeatedly, we freely speak and understand sentences which we have never spoken or heard before. Probably, indeed, the reader has never before encountered any of the sentences in this book. Despite their complete novelty as whole sentences, hopefully you will have little difficulty understanding them. Take the following quite ordinary sentence, presumably new to you:

The corner grocery sells motor oil but it closes at ten.

The words are few and ordinary, and the topic mundane, just like most of the sentences we utter and encounter. It is likely, indeed, that most sentences which we encounter are new to us, because the number of sentences of a language is **unbounded**.

Even the length of sentences is unbounded. Given any sentence in any language, no speaker of the language will have difficulty adding one more word to it:

What? What happened? What happened next? Guess what happened next. I guessed what happened next. You know I guessed what happened next. Do you know I guessed what happened next? Don't you know I guessed what happened next? Don't you know I guessed what happened at the door next? Don't you know I guessed what happened there at the door next. Etc.

This unboundedness of syntax, of the number and length of sentences, is a result of the general characteristic of language known as **creativity** (chapter 1, §3.4.3): people are always saying things in new ways – especially always constructing new sentences. Even though we speak, write, hear, and read such new sentences continually, new sentences rarely catch our attention, unless they include new sounds or new words. Presumably this is because the most basic elements of sentence structure are relatively few and very, very familiar.

2. THREE ASPECTS OF SYNTAX

Syntax concerns sentence structure, and sentence structure may be said to have three aspects: grouping, function, and word order. These three aspects of syntactic structure are all represented in a **tree diagram** of a sentence. Figure 6.1 is an example: the tree diagram for the sentence *Those pesky beavers inhabit a narrow stream above the lake*.

2.1. Grouping

Grouping is the grouping of words into meaningful and functional **phrases**, which are members, or **constituents**, of larger phrases. Groupings recognized in

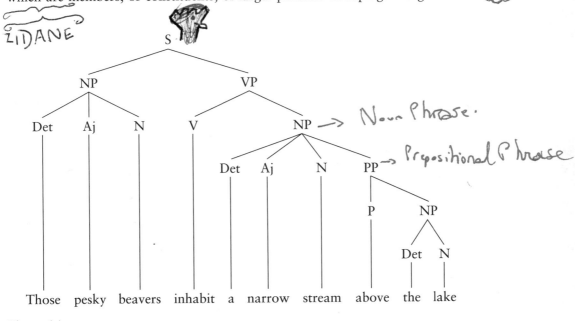

Figure 6.1

the above sentence are the sentence itself (S), noun phrase (NP), verb phrase (VP), and prepositional phrase (PP). Each of these is represented as a 'node', or branching point, in the tree diagram. Notice that in this sentence the prepositional phrase is included in or is a constituent of the lower noun phrase.

2.2. Function

(Function) concerns the relationship of the noun phrases to the verb and to other words and word groups in the sentences. There are three different kinds of functions in the sentence above: grammatical relations, parts of speech, and relations of head and modifier.

2.2.1. *Grammatical relations* Grammatical relations

(Grammatical relations) concern certain major types of phrases recognized by the grammar, apparent in their location in a tree diagram, and include the following traditionally recognized aspects of grammar:

a. (subject,) the noun phrase (NP) immediately under S,
b. (predicate) the verb phrase (VP) immediately under S,
c. (direct object) the noun phrase (NP) immediately under VP, and
d. (object of preposition,) the noun phrase (NP) immediately under PP.

2.2.2. *Parts of speech* lexical categories

Also recognized in the tree diagram are word types, including the traditionally recognized parts of speech:

a. **determiner** (Det): *those*, *a*, and *the*,
b. **adjective** (Aj): *pesky* and *narrow*,
c. **noun** (N): *beavers*, *stream*, and *lake*,
d. **verb** (V): *inhabit*,
e. **preposition** (P): *above*.

Noun and verb are word categories you could reasonably expect to find in all languages. Determiner and adjective are not always clearly recognized in languages, and instead of prepositions some languages have postpositions.

2.2.3. *Heads and modifiers*

head:
N of NP
V of VP
P of PP

A third sort of function presented by the tree diagram is **head** and **modifier**. Except for S, each word-group of the sentence is made up of a head and its modifiers. The (head) of a phrase is the word necessary for the phrase, which gives the phrase its name: the noun of an NP, the verb of a VP, and the preposition of a PP. The other words are the **modifiers** (or specifiers and modifiers) of the head.

Even when you combine two words of the same category, as in an English noun compound like *car phone* or *light switch*, one is the head and the other a modifier. Thus a *car phone* is a phone and not a car, and a *light switch* is a switch and not a light.

2.3. Word order

Word order is the temporal or linear sequence of words of the sentence. Word order is expressed in the tree diagram by the linear, left-to-right, arrangement of words on the page, which parallels the temporal order of these elements in speech.

In languages other than English, word order may often be different even when groupings and functions are the same. This is so, for example, in the following noun phrases of Spanish and Amharic, which, like their English translation, consist of a determiner (possessive pronoun), an adjective, and a noun:

a. Spanish: nuestro barrio hermoso 'our pretty neighborhood'
    our neighborhood pretty

b. Amharic: qonǰo səfər-aččɨn 'our pretty neighborhood'
    pretty neighborhood-our

In some languages there may be a lot of freedom of word order for the main constituents subject, verb, and direct object or other complement of the verb. Arabic is such a language, as seen in the following sentences, all three of which mean 'The girl saw a house' (recall that [ʔ] is a glottal stop).

a. raʔa-ti l-bint-u bajt-an
    saw-she the-girl-Subj house-Obj
b. il-bint-u bajt-an raʔa-ti
    the-girl-subj house-obj saw-she
c. bajt-an raʔa-ti l-bint-u
    house-Obj saw-she the-girl-Subj

Word-order freedom is made possible here by the noun suffixes /-u/ and /-an/, which mark the nouns as subject and object, so their function is apparent without fixed word order, as in English subject–verb–object. The different versions of the sentence would be especially appropriate in different contexts of discourse in which background information would be early in the sentence and foreground and/or contrastive information would be late. Thus the first example is appropriate where the context has established that 'somebody saw something', and the second that 'the girl did something'. (This topic comes up again in chapter 18, §5.)

3. RECURSION IN SYNTAX

It was emphasized above that the length of a sentence, like the number of sentences, is unbounded: no matter how long a sentence gets, it is always possible to add more words to it. The main reason for this unboundedness of sentence length is that aspect of the creativity of language known as **recursion** (chapter 1, §3.4.3). The recursiveness of syntax concerns the expansion of phrases by the expansion of phrases, including of their own types, within themselves. For example, there can be:

a. Sentences within sentences, such as:

[I said [I know]ₛ]ₛ
[I know [I said [I know]ₛ]ₛ]ₛ
[[I said it]ₛ and [I believe it]ₛ]ₛ

b. Noun phrases within noun phrases, such as:

[three coins in [the fountain]ₙₚ]ₙₚ
[[dear hearts]ₙₚ and [gentle people]ₙₚ]ₙₚ

c. Verb phrases within verb phrases, such as:

[likes to [play games]ᵥₚ]ᵥₚ
[[stop completely]ᵥₚ and [look both ways]ᵥₚ]ᵥₚ

d. Prepositional phrases within noun phrases within prepositional phrases, such as:

[for [a vacation [in [the month [of May]ₚₚ]ₙₚ]ₚₚ]ₙₚ]ₚₚ
[to [my family [in Texas]ₚₚ]ₙₚ]ₚₚ

Recursion of prepositional phrases – and people's amusement with this – is illustrated by the concluding words of a long, well-known song about things at the bottom of the sea: *a frog on a log in a hole in the bottom of the sea*, etc., the structure of which is shown in the tree diagram of figure 6.2.

In another example of such recursion, a well-known traditional poem, a sentence is included in a noun phrase and within the sentence is another noun phrase which includes another sentence, etc., so the sentences goes on and on; see figure 6.3, the tree diagram for the sentence which begins *This is the cat*.

Coordination is a <u>sort of recursion</u> according to which groups like sentence, noun phrase, verb phrase, and prepositional phrase may be expanded as a pair of such phrases joined by a **coordinating conjunction** such as *and* or *or*. In English, for example, there are:

Should I stay or should I go

a. Coordinated sentences: *Birds fly and fish swim. Stop or I'll shoot*
b. Coordinated noun phrases: *birds and bees, a fly and a flea*

love and money

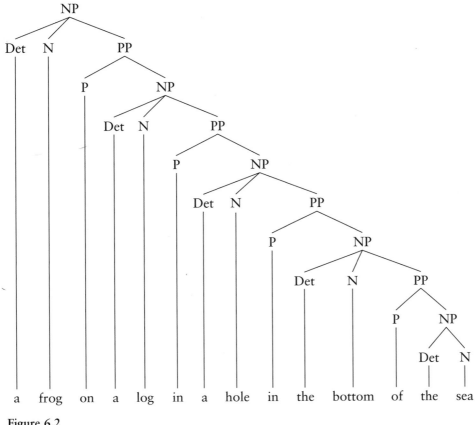

a   frog   on   a   log   in   a   hole   in   the   bottom   of   the   sea

Figure 6.2

c. Coordinated verb phrases: *sink or swim, praise the Lord and pass the ammunition*

d. Coordinated prepositional phrases: *by hook or by crook, on the beaches and in the towns*

e. Coordinated adjective phrases: *used but wearable, completely false and probably libelous*

*think of examples

4. ABSTRACTNESS OF SYNTAX

Not only are the sentences of languages an unbounded number, but the constituents and functions of sentences are not ordinarily concretely marked – not in speaking by pauses or other signals of pronunciation, nor in writing by punctuation. In this sense, syntax is characterized by **abstractness**.

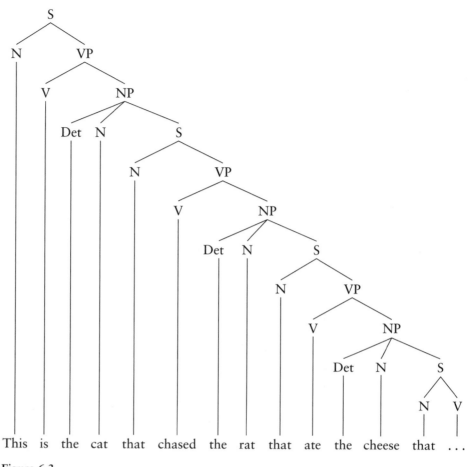

Figure 6.3

Nevertheless, syntactic groupings and functions must be real, since users of language give concrete evidence that their knowledge of syntax concerns constituents and functions, and not just knowledge of words and how to order words in sentences.

4.1. Knowledge of constituents

There are three kinds of evidence for groups and their constituents: ①replace-②ment, movement, and ③grouping ambiguity.

4.1.1. Replacement

(**Replacement**)concerns the fact that a group may ordinarily be replaced by a single word. In English, for example:

a. A sentence may be replaced by a noun or pronoun:

I said *I liked it*. I said *nothing*.
I said *I liked it*. I said *so*.
Koalas eat eucalyptus leaves. – *This* is true, but . . .

b. A noun phrase may be replaced by a pronoun:

Your cat hissed at me. *It* hissed at me.
I'll take *this one*. I'll take *yours*.

c. A verb phrase may be replaced by a form of the verb *do*.

Who *hissed at you*? – Your cat *did*.
Koalas *live in trees*. – They *do*?

d. A prepositional phrase may be replaced by an adverb:

I waited *at the corner of Grand River and Cedar*. I waited *there*.
You finally arrived *after midnight*. You arrived *then*.
Put them *by the door*. Put them *here*.

Such replacements are evidence for groupings, and for functions as well. That is, a clause is replaced by a noun, which is evidence that the clause functions as a noun. Verb phrases, of course, are replaced by verbs (in English, by forms of *do*).

Perhaps not all phrases can be replaced, but certainly no non-phrases can be replaced. For example, in *I waited at the corner of Grand River and Cedar* you can't replace *waited at the*, or *corner of Grand*, or *River and*, and these are certainly not phrases.

4.1.2. *Movement*

There may be movement of phrases, in the sense that these may appear in different places in different versions of a sentence. That is, if we think of one of the sentences as basic and the others as derived from this, then we will think of the phrase as having moved from the basic to the derived position. For example:

a. Local farmers sell vegetables at the city market on Saturday.
b. It is *local farmers* that sell vegetables at the city market on Saturday.
c. It is *vegetables* that local farmers sell at the city market on Saturday.
d. It is *at the city market* that local farmers sell vegetables on Saturday.
e. It is *on Saturday* that local farmers sell vegetables at the city market.

– proves what are phrases/ groups

Sentence (b) shows that *local farmers*, an NP, is a phrase in sentence (a); sentence (c) shows the same for *vegetables* (a phrase of one word); (d) shows that *at the city market*, a PP, is a group; and (e) shows the same for *on Saturday*.

Again the test may not work for every phrase, but it will never work for a non-phrase, as the following sentences show. The asterisk which precedes these sentences is to show that they seem impossible, or ungrammatical.

f.   *It is *stop at* that city buses most major intersections until midnight.
g.   *It is *intersections until midnight* that city buses stop at most major.

4.1.3. Grouping ambiguity

Ambiguity is when a word, phrase, or sentence has two distinct meanings. There are ambiguous words, like *wind* and [rod], for example: *wind* can be pronounced [wɪnd] or [waynd], and [rod] can be spelled *road* or *rode*. **Grouping ambiguity** is when the same string of words may have two meanings based upon different possible groupings of the words. Grouping ambiguity is a third sort evidence for groupings in syntactic structure. Two examples are *nutritious food and drink* and *We feed the pigs in clean clothes*. See the two tree diagrams for each of these, in figure 6.4.

According to 1a, *food* and *drink* are grouped and *nutritious* modifies both, but according to 1b *nutritious* modifies (is grouped with) only *food*. According to 2a the pigs are in clean clothes: *in clean clothes* modifies or is grouped with *pigs*. But according to 2b, *in clean clothes* is grouped with *feed*, so the phrase *in clean clothes* is about those doing the feeding. Our ability to recognize such ambiguities in a string of words may be understood as our awareness of the different possibilities for grouping in syntactic structure.

4.2. Knowledge of functions

We acquire our knowledge of abstract functions as a necessary part of learning our language, long before we go to school. This knowledge is revealed in various ways. For example, speakers of English show knowledge of:

a.   subjects, by making present tense verbs, and the *be*-verb in the past, agree with the subject, saying, for example, *robins are* . . . but *a robin is* . . . , and *city buses were...* but *a city bus was...*
b.   head and modifier, when we say *the weather in the mountains is...* (*is* is singular, like *weather*, the head of this phrase) and not *the weather in the mountains are...* (*are* is plural, like *mountains*, not *weather*).
c.   parts of speech, by using determiners with nouns and not with verbs, and auxiliary verbs with verbs and not with nouns, saying *the robin*, and not *the go*, and *might go* but not *might robin*.

Our knowledge of functions is sometimes apparent in our recognition of **function ambiguity**. These are cases in which an ambiguity is based not on an ambiguous word (**lexical ambiguity**) or an ambiguous grouping of words (**grouping ambiguity**), but strictly on an ambiguity of function. In such a case there are two

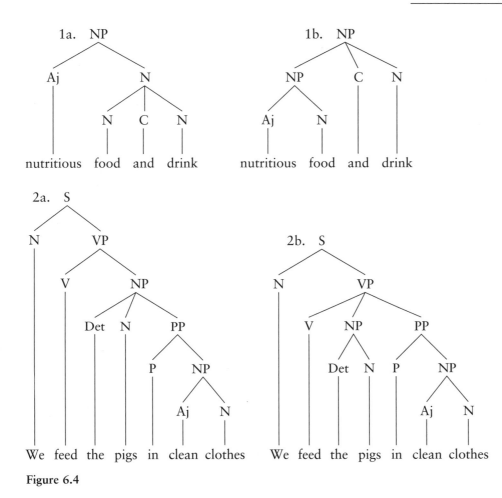

Figure 6.4

meanings but word groups and, in a sense, word meanings are the same in both – the two meanings are distinct only by the function, or grammatical function, of some word. For example, the following sentences are functionally ambiguous.

a. I need a criminal lawyer.
b. Visiting professors can be boring.
c. I like ice cream more than you.

In (a) the needed lawyer may be a specialist in criminal law, or a lawyer who is criminal. In (b) the mentioned professors can be understood as either the subject or object of *visiting*: the professors visit or get visited (and in either case this is boring). In (c) the ambiguity results from thinking of *you* as either the subject or object of *like*: I like ice cream more than you (subject of *like*) like ice cream, or I like it more than I like you (object of *like*).

Suggestions for
ADDITIONAL READING

Good introductions to the study of syntax are found in other introductory linguistics textbooks, such as those mentioned at the end of chapter 3, plus *Linguistics: an Introduction* by Donna Jo Napoli (1996). Textbooks of introductory syntax are *Beginning Syntax* (1993) by Linda Thomas, *Understanding Syntax* (1998) by Maggie Tallerman, *Generative Grammar* (1987) by Geoffrey Horrocks, and the *Practical Guide to Syntactic Analysis* by Georgia Green and Jerry Morgan (1996).

For English syntax, there is *Analysing Sentences: an Introduction to English Syntax* by Noel Burton-Roberts (1997), *Understanding English Grammar* (1995) by Ronald Wardhaugh, and *English Grammar: Principles and Facts* (1995) by Jeffrey Kaplan.

Chapters 17 and 18, below, continue the topic of syntax; see the suggestions for additional reading there.

IMPORTANT CONCEPTS AND TERMS IN THIS CHAPTER

- unbounded
- creativity
- tree diagram
- grouping
- phrase
- constituent
- function
- grammatical relation
- subject
- predicate
- direct object
- object of preposition
- part of speech
- determiner
- adjective
- noun
- verb
- preposition
- head
- modifier
- word order
- recursion
- coordination
- coordinating conjunction
- abstractness
- replacement
- movement
- ambiguity
- grouping ambiguity
- function ambiguity
- lexical ambiguity

OUTLINE OF
CHAPTER 6

EXAMPLES AND PRACTICE

EXAMPLE

1. Unboundedness of syntax. Sentence length is unbounded because words can always be added to a sentence. Take the sentence:

The quick brown fox jumped over the lazy dog.

Words can be added almost anywhere in the sentence.

a. *Then* the quick brown fox . . .
b. The *very* quick brown fox . . .
c. The quick *dark* brown fox . . .
d. The quick brown *bat-eared* fox jumped . . .
e. The quick brown fox *easily* jumped over . . .

PRACTICE

(a) List a word or words which can be added to the following sentence at the numbered places, and (b) do the same with another sentence of at least seven words, which you compose.

January $_1$ was $_2$ the $_3$ coldest $_4$ month $_5$ since $_6$ 1916.

EXAMPLE

2. Three types of ambiguity. There are three types of linguistic ambiguity:

a.   Lexical ambiguity occurs when a word has different meanings. In *We met at the bank*, *bank* might be the land at the side of a river or a financial institution. In [gìvmiðəfláwər], [fláwər] might be *flower* or *flour*.

b.   Grouping ambiguity occurs when words may have different groupings. In *They served expensive wine and cheese*, *expensive* could be grouped just with *wine*, [[expensive wine] and cheese], or *wine* and *cheese* could be grouped, so that *expensive* modifies both, [expensive [wine and cheese]].

c.   Function ambiguity is a bit trickier. It occurs when a word or phrase has different functions but not different meanings or different groupings. In *Visiting professors can be boring*, *professors* could be doing the *visiting* (in grammatical terms, *professors* is the subject of the verb *visit*), or professors could be getting visited (in grammatical terms, *professors* is the object of the verb *visit*). Note that *professor* has the same meaning in both cases, and the groupings are the same.

Lexical ambiguity depends entirely on the quite different meanings of a word. Grouping ambiguity depends on how the words are grouped. Function ambiguity depends, like lexical ambiguity, on a particular word, but on the word's different grammatical functions, not its lexical meaning. All three cases show that we have abstract knowledge – of meanings not reflected in audible or visible form.

PRACTICE

Each of the following 12 sentences is ambiguous. Figure out the ambiguity of each sentence and explain this, if more briefly than in the examples above, as lexical, grouping, or functional ambiguity. There are at least two ambiguities of each type; some might be explained in two ways.

1.   This pen is empty.
2.   Are the chickens ready to eat?
3.   Do you want to try on that dress in the window?
4.   This old car needs new brakes and antifreeze.
5.   Riddle: what gets wetter the more it dries? (Answer: a towel.)
6.   Don't sit on those glasses!
7.   I understand money matters.
8.   They read books.
9.   I know clever people like you.
10.   The dog looked at the snake longer than the cat.
11.   Mom's home cooking.
12.   That's [ənɑjshɑws].

EXAMPLE

3. Meaningfulness of groupings. The meaningfulness of different word groupings can be shown by parentheses. Compare the following pairs of phrases, with

basically the same sort of word composition but different groupings, as shown by the parentheses:

   a. see (whales) (from cruise ships)
   b. see (whales (from Alaska))
   c. adult (language learning)
   d. (foreign language) learning

In (a) *from cruise ships* is a group, a prepositional phrase. It is not about the whales but about the seeing, so this prepositional phrase is grouped apart from *whales*. In (b), however, *with newborn calves* IS about *whales*, so this prepositional phrase IS grouped together with *whales*. The phrase (c) is about 'language learning' by adults, and *language learning* is a group apart from *adult*. The phrase (d), however, is about the learning of 'foreign languages', so *foreign language* is a group apart from *learning*.

PRACTICE

Insert at least one pair of parentheses in each of the following phrases to show the likely contrast of meaning and of grouping between the pairs 1–2, 3–4, 5–6, 7–8, and 9–10.

  1. write a paper on the revolution
  2. write a paper on the weekend
  3. old or new movies
  4. books or new movies
  5. Chicago Welfare Department
  6. Child Welfare Department
  7. single parent family
  8. single migrant family
  9. garage door opener
10. electric can opener

EXAMPLE

4. Recursion. Recall the eight types of recursion exemplified in §3, above:

   a. Sentences within sentences
   b. Noun phrases within noun phrases
   c. Verb phrases within verb phrases
   d. Prepositional phrases within prepositional phrases
   e. Coordinated sentences
   f. Coordinated noun phrases
   g. Coordinated verb phrases
   h. Coordinated prepositional phrases

PRACTICE

In the following sentences identify cases of each of these sorts of recursion (a)–(h). Notice that one type may be within another. Each sentence exemplifies at least two types, and each type is exemplified in two sentences.

1. Fiona goes to church and eats out every Sunday, and Ray does too.
2. We met them on the ferry to the island.
3. They say they always try to see a movie Friday evening.
4. It seems we never see them on the train or at the station.
5. We see them on the boardwalk and in cafés near the harbor.
6. I believe they never eat anything but beer and pretzels.
7. They like going to bed early and they hate getting up late.
8. We left early and arrived before dark, and so did they.

EXAMPLE

5. Replacement and movement of phrases. It was mentioned above (§§4.1.1–2) that two tests which provide evidence that a group of words is a phrase, or unit of syntactic structure, are replacement and movement. In the sentence *These children love anything chocolate*, we can make three replacements:

a. *They* love anything chocolate.
b. They love *it*.
c. They *do*.

They replaces the subject noun phrase *these children*; *it* replaces the direct object noun phrase *anything chocolate*, and *do* replaces the verb phrase *love anything chocolate*.

Movement is a somewhat less reliable test than replacement, but take the sentence *These children play with matches*, which can be paraphrased:

d. It is *these children* who play with matches.
e. It is *matches* that these children play with.
f. *Play with matches* is what these children do.

PRACTICE

Identify as many phrases as you can in the following sentences, by performing the replacement or movement tests on them, as in (a)–(f), above.

1. Children who play with matches need lessons in fire safety.
2. Fire safety lessons may not work for all such children.
3. These children may need lessons of a different sort.

EXAMPLE

6. Grouping ambiguity. Another test of phrasehood is grouping ambiguity (§4.1.3). Sentences 1 and 2 below are ambiguous. They each have two interpretations depending on how words are grouped into meaningful phrases.

1. I know a café in the theater district near the metro station.

   a. *Near the metro station* is about *the theater district*. (It is grouped with *the theater district*.)
   b. *Near the metro station* is about *a café*. (It is grouped with *a café*.)

(How can *near the metro station* be grouped with *a café*, when *in the theater district* separates *a café* and *near the metro station*? – Because all of *a café in the theater district near the metro station* is a group, as evidenced by its replacement in *I know it*.)

2. Oh, that's just a crazy economist's idea.

   a. Crazy is about <u>economist</u>.
   b. Crazy is about <u>idea</u>.

PRACTICE

Similarly explain the grouping ambiguity in sentences 3–10.

3. They admitted that we had attended only with reluctance.
4. We watched a video of European automobile races.
5. I will teach your dog to potty in a box if requested.
6. Let's have chocolate cake and ice cream.
7. The Dean wants to eliminate sex and race bias in student organizations.
8. They ought to compete against more competitive teams.
9. We discovered that they lost the election by chance.
10. She fed her dog meat.

PHRASE STRUCTURE RULES

This chapter presents rules which describe the basic sentence types of languages, exemplified by those of English. These phrase structure rules provide language with the important property of recursion, and, within the structures which these rules generate, basic syntactic functions such as subject of the sentence and object of the verb are identifiable, and verbs are matched with their possible sentence types.

1. PHRASE STRUCTURE RULES

The basic possibilities of the structure of basic sentences of languages may be represented by **phrase structure rules**, for example:

    a.   A sentence consists of a subject and a predicate.
    b.   A noun may be modified by an adjective.
    c.   Every predicate has a verb.

There is a lot of controversy about phrase structure rules and particularly about their universality – the extent to which such rules, and the categories mentioned by such rules, are shared by all the languages of the world.

1.1. Sentences

Certainly all languages have sentences, and a more or less traditional idea about sentences is that:

A **sentence** is a relationship between a subject and a predicate.

A subject, in the traditional understanding, is a noun phrase, and a predicate is a verb phrase. Thus a minimal sentence is a two-part, hierarchical, structure like this:

This understanding about sentences is formalized as the following **phrase structure rule** 1 about the minimal composition of sentences.

1.   S → NP VP

In less than 20% of languages of the world, verbs typically precede subjects in sentences, so the rule is superficially false for these. This chapter exemplifies rules specific for English. Other languages have rules which differ in detail but probably not in their basic elements, and not in their specification of the basic possibilities of sentence structure and function.

1.2.   Two senses of grammar

There are two ways of thinking about such rules. The arrow can mean either 'consists of', or 'is rewritten as'. In the latter sense, rule 1 may be understood to 'generate', or build, a 'tree diagram' like that above, in which S branches as an NP and a VP. In this sense, the grammar is a device, or program, for producing sentences, and if a sentence is generated by the rules, it is **grammatical**; if not, it is **ungrammatical**. In the other way of thinking about such rules, they don't generate structures but just 'license' them: if a sentence is interpretable to have a structure consistent with the rule, it is so understood, and is grammatical. In this sense, the grammar is a device, or program, for interpreting sentences. It is usually possible, however, to think of the grammar as being both and doing both.

1.3.   Phrases in universal grammar

Noun and verb, and other major lexical categories or parts of speech including adjective, adverb, and, for English, preposition, are always expandable as phrases in which the noun, verb, etc., is the **head**, and other parts are specifiers or modifiers.

This understanding is formalized as the following rules 2 and 3 of the phrase structure of languages, which are interpreted as saying that members of the major lexical categories, abbreviated as 'X', may be expanded as a phrase, XP; and such a phrase consists of necessarily a word of category X, the **head** of the phrase, maybe a **specifier** (Spec) and maybe one or more **modifiers** (M^n). The parentheses mean that the parenthesized item may or may not be present, and the superscript n means 'some number including zero'.

2. $X \to XP$

3. $XP \to$ (Spec) X M^n

XP
Spec   X M^n

Modifiers of nouns are words like adjectives, and of verbs, adverbs, which are generally identifiable in all languages. Specifiers are a category of a less general or more abstract nature, concerning both the existence and membership of which there is controversy. The category is mentioned here just to give a more or less complete picture of phrase structure.

Rules like 2–3 are very general, and not obviously true of all languages. Our knowledge of the languages of the world is very incomplete, but such rules may provide interesting and helpful generalizations nevertheless. There is controversy, even, about whether there exists a **universal grammar**, valid for all the languages of the world, and, if there is, its nature is quite abstract and so little understood that many of our hypotheses about it are unsuitable for introductory purpose. Here we consider just the basic phrase structure of one language that we share, English.

1.4.   Phrase structure rules for English

Here for example are four very basic phrase structure rules for English noun phrases, verb phrases, prepositional phrases, and adjective phrases:

4. NP → (Det) (AjP) N (PP)

5. VP → V ({NP, S, AjP}) (PP) → a restaurant Ran

6. PP → P NP → a restaurant

7. AjP → (Deg) Aj → in Chicago

The parentheses mean 'maybe occurs', and the curly braces mean 'one of these'. So, respectively, rules 1 and 4–7 say:

1. A **sentence** consists of a noun phrase and a verb phrase.
4. A **noun phrase** consists of a noun, which may be preceded by a determiner and an adjective phrase, and followed by a prepositional phrase.
5. A **verb phrase** consists of a verb, which may be followed by a noun phrase, sentence, or adjective phrase, and, after one of these, maybe a prepositional phrase.

6.   A **prepositional phrase** consists of a preposition followed by a noun phrase. *in the cold*
7.   An **adjective phrase** consists of an adjective, which may be preceded by a 'degree' word, like *very, somewhat*, etc. → *very tall* → *absolutely right*

1.5.   Unboundedness of phrase structures: recursion

If we limit consideration to just the immediate output of rules 4 and 5 for the noun phrase and verb phrase, without considering the further possibilities of expansion of N, V, Aj, P, and S, the structural possibilities for sentences generated by the two rules of English are summarized as follows:

$$[\,[\,(\text{Det})\,(\text{AjP})\,\text{N}\,(\text{PP})\,]_{\text{NP}}\,[\,\text{V}(\{\text{NP, S, AjP}\})\,(\text{PP})\,]_{\text{VP}}\,]_{\text{S}}$$

Items within {} are alternatives, so {N, S, Aj} is three possibilities, and items within () may or may not be present (= two possibilities), so '({NP, S, AjP})' is four possibilities (NP, S, AjP, and none of these). Thus the number of sentence structures represented by the above formula is 64, without counting the many possibilities which arise with the further expansion of recursive phrases.

$$2 \times 2 \times 1 \times 2 \times 1 \times 4 \times 2 = 64$$

Five of these 64 possible sentence structures, or tree diagrams, with appropriate words provided at the bottom of each, are shown in figure 7.1.

Recursion is when a phrase appears within a phrase (chapter 1, §3.4.3, and chapter 6, §3). The phrase structure rules above establish a number of possible recursions, and because of any one of these, in fact, sentences are open-ended, and the number of sentence structures of the language is potentially unbounded. Notice the recursions in the rules above:

a.   S occurs in rule 1 and recurs as a possibility in rule 5.
b.   PP occurs in rules 4 and 5, and recurs as a possibility within all NP's and S's.
c.   NP occurs in rules 1 and 5, and 6, and recurs as a possibility within all S's and PP's.

There is no limit to these recursions, so there is no limit to the number of structures (tree diagrams) generated by the four rules. The phrase structures of all languages similarly provide for such recursion and therefore for such unboundedness of structure.

1.6.   Coordination

Coordination is another sort of recursion, also found in all languages, according to which phrase types including S, N, V, Aj may be split up as a pair of such

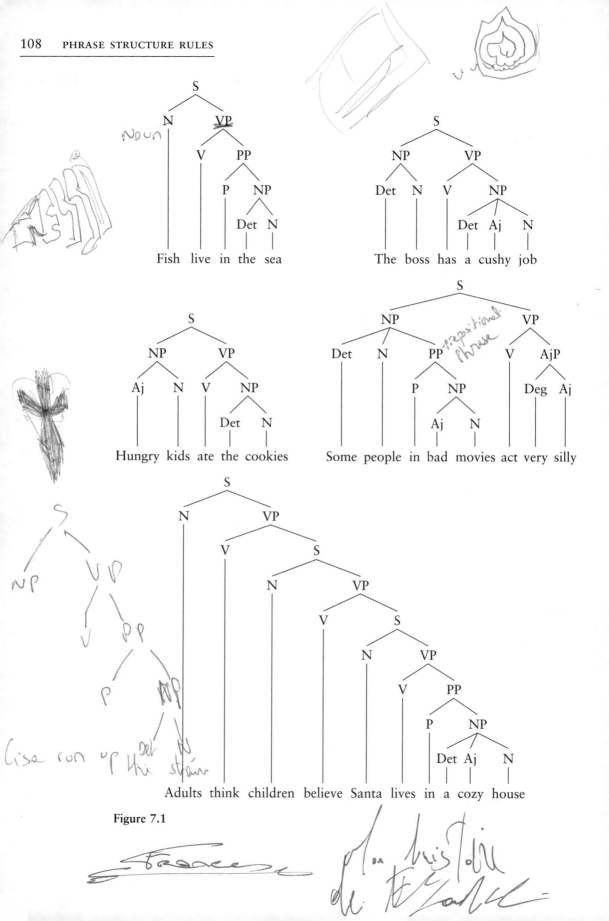

Figure 7.1

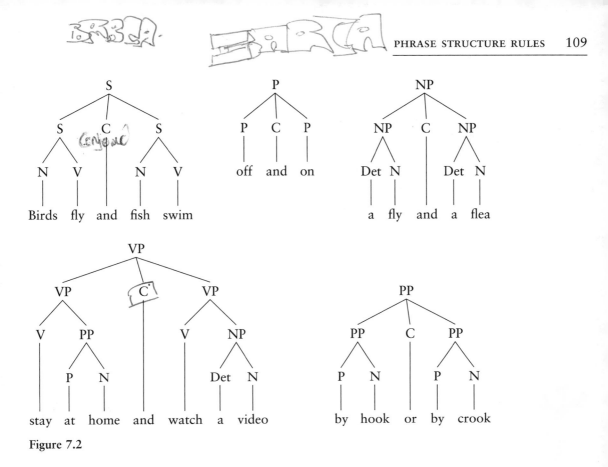

Figure 7.2

phrases (maybe of one word), joined by a **coordinating conjunction**, such as *and* or *or* in English. This is rule 8, where C is a coordinating conjunction:

8. X → X C X

Rule 8 generates coordinate structures like those of figure 7.2, for English.

2. FORMAL GRAMMAR AND SYNTACTIC FUNCTIONS

Rules such as 1–8 are a representation of linguistic knowledge, part of a **formal grammar**, which provides structures within which the types of **syntactic function** including grammatical relations, parts of speech, and head–modifier relations are well defined, and on the basis of which we can understand how language works, as a system of rules which provide possibilities which are limited in type but unlimited in number.

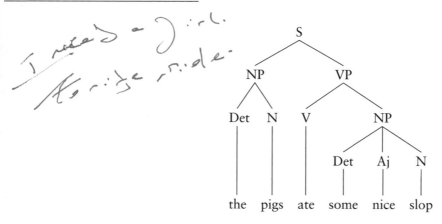

Figure 7.3

2.1. Grammatical relations

The grammatical relations include 'subject' and 'direct object'. People know what the subject and direct object of sentences are when they speak, even if they don't understand or don't even know these words. English speakers, for example, choose a present tense verb with an appropriate suffix: we say, for example, *he goes*, but *they go*. We specifically recognize objects – direct objects as well as objects of prepositions – as well as subjects when we choose different pronouns for these, saying *I see him* and not *Him sees me* (where the asterisk, '*', means 'ungrammatical'). In *I see him*, and *He sees me*, *I* and *he* are subject pronouns and *him* and *me* are object pronouns. In other languages, subjects and direct objects may be recognized in other ways. In Japanese, for example, the subject is followed by *ga* and the direct object by *o*: *Kazuko-san ga hon o agemashita* 'Ms Kazuko gave a book' (chapter 5, §1.4.4).

How we can make these numerous spontaneous and instantaneous determinations when we speak and when someone speaks to us is often very clear in formal grammar, through the phrase structure rules and the structures which they specify. For example:

a.   the subject of a sentence is the NP immediately under S, and
b.   the direct object is the NP immediately under VP.

Thus the subject of the sentence *The pigs ate some nice slop* must be *the pigs* and the direct object must be *some nice slop*, as the tree diagram of the sentence, figure 7.3, makes clear. No matter how lengthy and complex a sentence becomes, its subject and its direct object, if it has one, are unambiguously determined by their place in the structure of the sentence as determined by the phrase structure rules.

2.2.   Parts of speech

In our formal grammar with phrase structure rules, the parts of speech such as determiner, noun, and verb appear as the 'terminal nodes' at the bottom of the tree. We can partially understand our knowledge of the parts of speech, then, as knowledge of where words of particular types may be 'plugged in' at the bottom of tree diagrams. In the tree diagram of figure 7.3, *the* and *some* are determiners, *pigs* and *slop* are nouns, *ate* is a verb, and *nice* is an adjective. Provided we plug in the words appropriately, basic requirements of the grammar are fulfilled: *the nice slop ate some pigs* is somewhat sensible or grammatical, if a bit unusual, meaning-wise, whereas plugging in words in complete violation of their parts of speech yields a fully ungrammatical sentence, just a string of words, really, as in *some the nice ate slop pigs.

2.3.   Heads and modifiers

The head of a phrase is always the included word of the category of the phrase, and the other words are specifiers or modifiers, by rule 3 (a distinction not developed here). Thus the head of an NP is its N, of VP its V, etc. There is an ambiguity when we talk about subject, object, etc.: the subject of a sentence is the highest NP of that sentence, and the head of that NP.

3.   SYNTACTIC CATEGORIES OF VERBS

3.1.   Four types of verb complement

In addition to specifying syntactic functions, the phrase structure rules formalize our knowledge about verbs and their possible (verb complements) within the predicate (VP). This is so, because the phrase structure rules establish or define a relatively small number of structures, or frames, within which verbs may appear. Rule 5 for English, for example, defines the verb phrase as having, after the verb, maybe a noun, maybe an adjective, maybe a sentence, and maybe none of these. The rule thus defines four **syntactic categories** of verb: (a) verbs which take nouns as their complements, (b) those which take adjectives, (c) those which take sentences, and (d) those which have no complement. Following are five examples of each type:

EXAMPLES OF TYPES OF ENGLISH VERB ACCORDING TO THEIR COMPLEMENTS

Noun Complement	Adjective Complement	Sentence Complement	No Complement
see	be	say	fall
eat	look	imagine	smile

Noun Complement	Adjective Complement	Sentence Complement	No Complement
find	seem	think	sleep
take	feel	believe	laugh
send	become	promise	walk

Many verbs exist in more than one type. *Eat*, for example, may have a noun complement (*eat a candy bar?*), or no complement (*Did you eat?*). Not all nouns that have noun complements are like *eat* in this way. *Find* and *take*, for example, must have noun complements; a sentence without these is ungrammatical: **Did you find?*; **Did you take?*. Verbs which have sentence complements may also have simple noun complements (if of certain types), for example: *I said it; she imagined the event; we think such things often.*

3.2. Subcategorization features of verbs   *based on verb complement*

The phrase structure rule for VP defines the main syntactic categories of verbs, and enables us to classify verbs according to their complement types. Verbs may therefore be understood to be listed in the lexicon with notation of their complement type (along with other information, including their part of speech, V, pronunciation, and spelling). This notation is a subcategorization feature of the form '[__ X]', where '__' is the position of the verb, and 'X' is the type of complement which completes the verb phrase: N (or NP), Aj (or AjP), or S (sentence). For the example verbs above, these partial lexical entries of the four types of verb are as follows:

SUBCATEGORIZATION FEATURES OF 20 ENGLISH VERBS

see, V, [__ N]	be, V, [__ Aj]	say, V, [__ S]	fall, V
eat, V, [__ N]	look, V, [__ Aj]	imagine, V, [__ S]	smile, V
find, V, [__ N]	seem, V, [__ Aj]	think, V, [__ S]	sleep, V
take, V, [__ N]	feel, V, [__ Aj]	believe, V, [__ S]	laugh, V
send, V, [__ N]	become, V, [__ Aj]	promise, V, [__ S]	walk, V

Verbs of the general type of *see* and *say* are traditionally known as **transitive verbs**, those of the type of *be* as **linking verbs**, those of the type of *say* and *promise* as **verbs of communication**, those of the type of *imagine*, *think*, and *believe* as **psychological verbs**, and those of the type of *fall* as **intransitive verbs**.

Like the phrase structure rules, such formalization of verb categories further reflects our knowledge of **grammaticality** of our language (chapter 1, §3.4.5). We know not only the possible sentence structures, but which of these a particular verb can fulfill. In English, for example, *Astronauts see the moon* is grammatical and **Astronauts see happy* is ungrammatical; *The children become sad* is grammatical, and *The children think sad* is not; *The teacher thinks I believe her* is grammatical, and *The teacher breaks I believe her* is ungrammatical.

Suggestions for
ADDITIONAL READING

Introductions to the study of syntax were mentioned at the end of chapter 6, including *Practical Guide to Syntactic Analysis* (1996) by Georgia Green and Jerry L. Morgan, and *Beginning Syntax* (1993) by Linda Thomas. Somewhat more advanced and based on English is *English Grammar* (1998) by Liliane Haegeman and Jacqueline

Gueron. In more depth on English is *The Syntactic Phenomena of English* (2 vols, 1988) by James D. McCawley. With data from numerous languages and emphasizing functional explanation is *Syntax: a Functional-typological Introduction* (2 vols, 1984) by Talmy Givón.

IMPORTANT CONCEPTS AND TERMS IN THIS CHAPTER

- phrase structure rules
- sentence
- subject
- predicate
- grammatical
- ungrammatical
- head
- specifier
- modifier
- universal grammar
- noun phrase
- verb phrase
- prepositional phrase
- adjective phrase

- recursion
- coordination
- coordinating conjunction
- formal grammar
- syntactic function
- verb complement
- syntactic category
- subcategorization feature
- transitive verb
- linking verb
- verb of communication
- psychological verb
- intransitive verb
- grammaticality

OUTLINE OF CHAPTER 7

1. **Phrase structure rules**
   1. Sentences
   2. Two senses of grammar

EXAMPLES AND PRACTICE

EXAMPLE

1. Phrase structure rules and tree diagrams. Recall the four phrase structure rules:

S   → NP VP
NP → (Det) (AjP) N (PP)
VP → V ({NP, AjP, S}) (PP)
PP → P NP
AjP → (Deg) Aj

The rules may be said to generate tree diagrams, including figure 7.4, generated by these rules. Tree diagram (a) of figure 7.4 is the structure of sentence 1, and (b) is the structure of sentence 2:

1. Young beavers with appetites eat the fish with pleasure.
2. Beavers in this pond build dams with big rooms.

PRACTICE

Match tree diagrams (c)–(e) of figure 7.4 with three of sentences 3–6, and then draw the tree diagram for the unmatched sentence of 3–6.

3. The farmers believe the hungry beavers frighten the fish.
4. Those beavers in the tranquil pond built a dam.
5. The ambitious beavers in ponds near trees build dams.
6. These farmers say ambitious beavers build dams with enthusiasm.

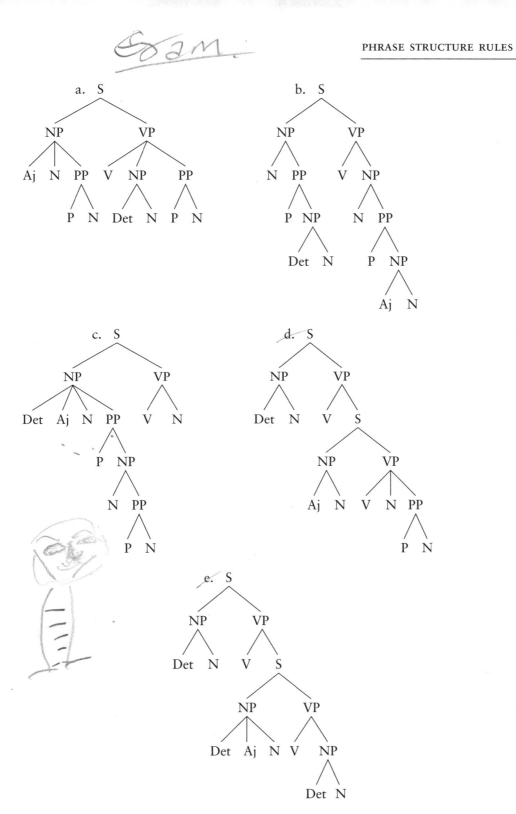

Figure 7.4

EXAMPLE

2. Groupings represented as bracketings. The groupings of sentence structure can be represented as a bracketed string of words, but this way of presenting grouping or phrase structure is less readable than a tree diagram, especially when parts of speech and labels of the groups are not shown. The sentence 'People say beavers live in this pond' can be represented as the bracketing

[People [say [beavers [live [in [this pond]]]]]]

in which 'this pond' is an NP within the PP 'in this pond', and 'in this pond' is a PP within the VP 'live in this pond', and 'live in this pond' is a VP within the S 'beavers live in this pond', and 'beavers live in this pond' is an S within the VP 'say beavers live in this pond', all of which is the VP of the highest S 'people say beavers live in this pond'.

PRACTICE

Match bracketed strings (a)–(d) with four of sentences 1–5. Then provide the bracketed string for the unmatched sentence.

a.   [X [X [X [X [X [X X]]]]]]

b.   [[X X X] [X [X [X X]]]]

c.   [[X X] [X X [X [X X]]]]

d.   [[X [X X]] [X X [X X]]]

1.   The ambitious beavers flee farmers with guns.
2.   Beavers with teeth chase fish with pleasure.
3.   Hungry beavers barricade streams with their dams.
4.   Fish in ponds with beavers eat bugs.
5.   People say beavers build dams with tunnels.

EXAMPLE

3. Unlabeled tree diagrams. See again the four phrase structure rules of §1.4, above. As interpreted by these four rules, sentences 1–2 could be matched with unlabeled tree diagrams (a)–(b), respectively.

1.   Beavers with appetites eat the fish with pleasure.
2.   Beavers in this pond build dams with rooms.

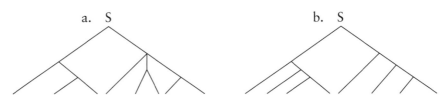

Notice that the first sentence has constituents 'Beavers with appetites', 'with appetites', 'eat the fish with pleasure', 'the fish', and 'with pleasure' which, unlike constituents of the second sentence, conform to the branchings of only the left-hand tree diagram.

Following the same logic, match tree diagrams (c)–(j) of figure 7.5 with sentences 3–10.

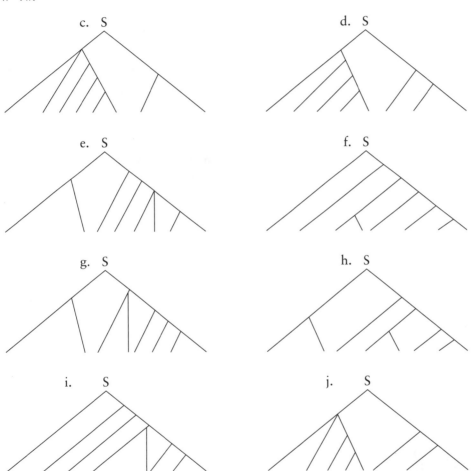

Figure 7.5

3. The farmers believe the beavers frighten the fish.
4. The beavers in the pond built a dam.
5. The people on farms near ponds frighten fish.
6. The farmers think beavers build dams with pleasure.
7. Farmers know the beavers swim under the ice.
8. Fish in ponds with beavers swim with caution.
9. The beavers build dams in ponds near rivers.
10. Beavers fish in the waterways near the dams.

EXAMPLE

4. More tree diagrams: complex sentences. Because of recursion, sentences may appear within sentences. The term 'compound sentence' traditionally means two sentences combined by coordination (§1.6), whereas a 'complex' sentence is one with two sentences combined otherwise.

PRACTICE

Provide tree diagrams for the following sentences.

    a.   Dolphins are mammals and unicorns are imaginary.
    b.   People believe dolphins are fish and tomatoes are vegetables.

EXAMPLE

5. Subcategorization of verbs. Verbs are fitted to their possible phrase structures by reference to their subcategorization features, as in the following examples of verbs of four types.

    a.   /drɑjv/, V, [__ N], as in *drive a car*, and /rəpǽr/, V, [__ N], as in *repair a window*;
    b.   /bɪlív/, V, [__ S], as in *believe you are right*, and /no/, V, [__ S], as in *know what happened*;
    c.   /gɛt/, V, [__ Aj], as in *get ready*, and /lʊk/, V, [__ Aj], as in *look sad*;
    d.   /rɛst/, V, as in *Let's rest* (that is, a verb with no complement), and /smɑjl/, V, as in *Everybody smile!*

Remember that a verb may be a member of more than one type: /bɪlív/, V, [__ N], as in *believe Bill*; /gɛt/, V [__ N], as in *get a life*.

PRACTICE

Write English verbs 1–12 as they are spelled, and match them with their subcategorization feature(s) (a)–(d).

    1. /rid/   7. /čenǰ/
    2. /fɪks/   8. /dəlívər/
    3. /slɪp/   9. /sim/
    4. /práməs/ 10. /ərájv/
    5. /fɪl/   11. /dəklǽr/
    6. /tərn/   12. /kwɪt/

    a.   V, [__ N]
    b.   V, [__ Aj]
    c.   V, [__ S]
    d.   V, (no complement, no subcategorization feature)

EXAMPLE

6. Phrase structure rules for a hypothetical language. Imagine a language in which the following is a sentence: *nu ke a li pe mo a.*

Assume that the the phrase structure rules and lexicon of the hypothetical language are as follows:

Phrase structure rules:
S   → AP BP
AP → A (BP) (CP)
BP → B (D)
CP → BP C

According to these rules, sentences consist of an A-phrase and a B-phrase. A-phrases consist of an A, maybe a B-phrase, and maybe a C-phrase. B-phrases consist of a B and maybe a D, and C-phrases consist of a B-phrase and a C.

Lexicon:
a,	D	*nu,*	A
ke,	B	*oa,*	A
li,	B	*pe,*	C
mo,	B	*qi,*	C

According to this lexicon, *a* is a D (member of the category D), *ke* is a B (member of the category C), *li* and *mo* are also B's, *nu* is an A, etc. (A–D are 'parts of speech'.) According to this two-part grammar, the sentence *nu ke a li pe mo a* must have the structure of figure 7.6.

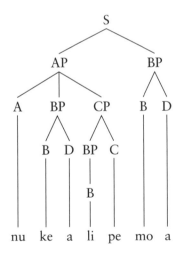

Figure 7.6

PRACTICE

Decide which of 1–6 are possible sentences in the language (two are not), and, using the phrase structure rules and lexicon for the imaginary language, provide tree diagrams for two of these.

1. oa li a qi mo   4. ke a li a pe
2. nu ke a ke a   5. nu mo pe li a
3. oa ke   6. nu ke a li mo

CHILD LANGUAGE LEARNING

This chapter presents some of the general characteristics of child language learning, and some specific regularities seen in the learning of English. Children appear to follow the same basic learning program, and progress regularly through some of the same stages of learning.

1. FOUR GENERAL CHARACTERISTICS OF CHILD LANGUAGE LEARNING

All over the world, normal children acquire fluent command of the language of the community into which they are born. Everywhere four important characteristics of this learning are evident, and distinguish this from other sorts of complex learning: child language learning is:

1. typical,
2. similar from child to child,
3. spontaneous, and
4. creative.

1.1. Typicality of language learning

We say that children learn their language *typically* because there are, indeed, exceptions, which always involve very exceptional circumstances: either great physical handicaps of the child, or family settings in which adequate input for learning is absent.

1.2.   Similarity of language learning

We say children learn languages *similarly*, because a somewhat regular schedule for language learning has been generally observed wherever in the world child language learning has been studied. This schedule can be recognized in five regularly seen stages.

a.   Babbling: about 6 months *6–12*
b.   First words: about 1 year *holographic: 12–18*
c.   First grammatical morphemes: about 2 years *36 months*
d.   Basic mastery: by about 4 years
e.   Continued learning, especially of vocabulary, indeed throughout life

telegraphic: 22 years 18–24

24+: wording exploded

For particular languages, sub-stages and details of the stages have been identified, as for English. Children differ, certainly (as must be emphasized), so that, for example, the first words of many children may appear some time before or after age one. But as a generalization, the appearance of first words at about age one is quite reliable, and this generalization is valid despite personality differences between children, and in learning environments. Some children are expressive and vocal, others reflective and quiet; the number of siblings, level of education in the family, amount of verbal play, etc., may differ, but it appears that this regularly observed schedule of language learning is fulfilled with remarkable regularity.

1.3.   Spontaneity of language learning

We say children learn languages *spontaneously* because there is obviously a drive, a strong natural or innate motivation, by children to learn language, so that instruction in the usual sense is unnecessary. This is evident when we compare the learning of speech and writing by children.

Except for the two sorts of exceptional circumstance mentioned above, all children learn to speak. Indeed, they start speaking, often before the end of their first year, when it is apparent that no instruction in the usual sense is possible. Parents may excitedly await the first words, and find each new linguistic achievement of the child a remarkable event. (In fact, while the specific events of language acquisition are unexpected, parents fully expect their children to acquire the language much the same as do other children.)

Writing, on the other hand, is something that most of us have to go to school to learn, and this may be at age five or six, or later, even in adulthood. A child may see people writing and spontaneously grasp a pencil or pen to try to write. But the result will never be writing, and indeed often the result, as on a wall or floor, or in an expensive book, is completely undesirable.

As language is not speech, learning language is not learning to speak. Deaf children are unable to speak because they are unable to receive the necessary aural input. But just as naturally as speaking children, and also without instruction in the usual sense, deaf children who receive suitable visual input learn language perfectly – manually signed language. This is an important point, which shows that language exists fully apart from speech. Speech is just a medium for language, a medium typically but not necessarily employed. Language then is not speech, but something abstract and mental, underlying speech (a system of signs, as it was defined in chapter 1, §1.3), and the forms, or medium, of language can as well be speech, writing, gestures, or, conceivably, some other.

1.4. Creativity of language learning

We say that child language learning shows **creativity** because it always results in utterances by children which they cannot have heard. They cannot be imitating these utterances, and so must be guessing, or creating, what would be said in their language. English-speaking children, for example, say things like *goed*, *mans*, and *mommy sock*, which they have not heard from others. That is, they *create* these words and phrases.

2.   STAGES IN THE LEARNING OF ENGLISH

Some of the general regularities noted below for child learning of English are found for other languages.

2.1. Language readiness

Before the first words of the English-learning child, a number of typical events show a readiness or preparation for language, and provide early evidence of the spontaneity, similarity, and creativity of child language learning:

2.1.1. Cooing
When they are six to eight weeks old, babies typically start '**cooing**'. In their cooing stage, they regularly produce combinations of velar consonants and back vowels, in utterances like [kuː], *coo*, [gaga] *ga-ga*, and [guː] *goo*.

2.1.2. Babbling
Babbling is a period of regular production by the child of unrecognizable but word-like vocalization, some of which may persist for years, but especially that which typically begins at about six months of age. During early babbling, English-learning children may even produce non-English phones, such as bilabial fricatives, front rounded vowels, and retroflex stops.

Early babbling has been extensively studied to find out whether this outpouring of sound represents an unstructured practice of speech physiology, during which a random collection of phones of languages of the world are produced, some basic set of presumably universal phones, or whether phones of the language(s) which children hear predominate. The conclusion appears to be that during babbling children particularly practice the phones of the language(s) they hear and will grow to speak.

Deaf children babble too, if they are exposed to signing, but their babbling is with their hands. As hearing children babble in phones of languages, not necessarily those of the languages they are learning, deaf children babble in manual gestures, which include some other than those of the sign language they are learning.

2.1.3. Word recognition

Before the end of the first year, most parents see signs that babies recognize words. Most of us have observed this in children. Saying the name of a family pet dog or cat, for example, seems regularly to produce an interest by the child, who looks around, or becomes excited, as if the dog or cat would appear. Saying *daddy* or *mommy* may produce the same result.

2.2. First words

2.2.1. First meanings

It was mentioned that the first words of the child, in English as in all languages studied, appear at about one year of age – though exceptions are many and occasionally extreme. According to common knowledge, among the first words are words such as *mommy* or *daddy*, if in fact rarely the very first. This is consistent with the strong generalization that the meanings of first words are overwhelmingly concrete, not abstract. In the child's early vocabulary, typically:

a. names (so-called proper nouns) are among the first words;
b. nouns are more common than verbs;
c. first verbs are action verbs such as *go* and *eat*; and
d. first adjectives concern vivid meanings such as *dirty* and *funny*.

It is notable that the most frequent words of adult language, grammatical morphemes such as *the* and *of*, are at first absent, though this is very reasonable, since these words are (a) abstract in meaning, (b) low in information value compared to lexical morphemes, and (c) short and unstressed.

2.2.2. Intonation

The first words may be heard as little sentences, having the intonation pattern of either statements or yes–no questions – statements with a rise and fall, and yes–no questions with a rise; for example:

[b æː f] 'Bath.'   [b æː f] 'Bath?'

2.2.3. *Phoneme learning order*

In child language learning around the world, there are regularities concerning phoneme acquisition, where phoneme means phones regularly found in particular words:

    a.   nasal and oral stops are relatively early, /m, n, p, b, k/.
    b.   early voiceless stops tend to be unaspirated.
    c.   early vowels are typically /ɑ/ and/or /i/, then often /u/.
    d.   labial consonants /p, b, f, m, w/ will often be mastered earlier than those at other places of articulation.
    e.   certain phones, including /l, r, θ, ð/ of English, are relatively late.

2.2.4. *Phoneme substitutions*

When words are pronounced in non-adult ways, certain **phoneme substitutions** are often observed. In the phenomenon known as **fronting**, consonants with more forward articulation replace those with less forward articulation; in **stopping**, stops replace other manners of articulation; in **perseverance**, a preceding phone replaces a following phone; and in **anticipation**, a following phone replaces a preceding one. Some examples are the following child pronunciations:

    a. (fronting:)   [ti] 'kick': alveolar [t] for back-articulated velar [k]
                           [fəm] 'thumb': labial [f] for dental [θ]
    b. (stopping:)   [dɛ] 'there': stop [d] for fricative [ð]
                           [ču] 'shoe': [č] (= [tš]) for [š]
    c. (perseverance:)   [gɑgi] 'glasses': [g] for [s] when [g] precedes
                           [dɑt] 'dog': alveolar [t] for velar [g] when alveolar [d] precedes
    d. (anticipation:)   [gɑjgə] 'tiger': [g] for [t] when [g] follows
                           [nəm] 'thumb': [n] for [θ] when nasal [m] follows

2.2.5. *Word structure*

There are generalizations concerning the phonological structure of words. The first words of first language learners, where C is for some consonant and V for some vowel:

    a.   especially take the form CV, of simple 'open' syllables or CVCV: [dɑ] 'father', [nɑ] 'not'
    b.   if CVCV, the consonants are often the same (because of the perseverance and anticipation phenomena): [kækæ] 'cracker', [gɑgi] 'glasses'
    c.   have few 'closed' syllables (syllables which end in consonants)

When closed syllables appear, in words of form CVC, such as [ʔuf] 'woof/dog' and [bɛt] 'bed', fricatives may first appear as final consonants.

2.2.6. Overextension and underextension of meaning

Phenomena known as overextension and underextension show that first language learners often have word meanings which are broader or narrower than those which adults have and which the children will, eventually, acquire.

In overextension a word has a broader range of meaning than the apparently equivalent adult word. The child's word for 'dog', for example, may be used for cats and various stuffed animals. Its meaning seems to be something like 'furry animal-like thing'. The child's word for 'daddy', unhappily for daddy, may be used for all large human males. Underextensions are also seen, in which a word has a narrower range of meaning than the apparently equivalent adult word. A child's word for 'dog', for example, may be used for a single dog, as if it were, in fact, the dog's name.

[handwritten margin note: ex: dog (all animals?) (one spec. dog?)]

2.2.7. MLU

'MLU' abbreviates 'mean length of utterance'. It expresses the average number of morphemes in one of the child's utterances – not always recognizable as sentences. MLU is difficult to calculate, but, counted according to strict understandings about what qualifies as a morpheme and as an occasion of use of a morpheme, it appears that by about eighteen months, a year and a half, an English-learning child's MLU may often average one and a half. The child has virtually no bound morphemes at this time, so each morpheme is a word, basically, and MLU expresses the average number of words per utterance. A good average for MLU at age three appears to be about three, or twice that of MLU at one and a half.

2.3. Two-word sentences

2.3.1. Telegraphic speech

The second stage of two-word sentences, from about 18 months, is characterized by **telegraphic speech,** so termed because the child learner's utterances at this time are like those of a telegram, lacking grammatical morphemes. Telegrams were paid for according to the number of words, so senders of telegrams would omit the unnecessary words and these were mostly grammatical morphemes: for example, 'Having wonderful time; wish you here', rather than 'we are having a wonderful time, and wish that you were here'. The absent words *are, a, and, that,* and *were* are all grammatical morphemes (and among the most frequent words of the language). A child at this stage says things like 'There rabbit', not 'There's a rabbit,' and 'Snowy gone', not 'Snowy is gone'.

2.3.2. Syntax of two-word sentences

When children first begin to assemble sentences with two or more words, there is already evidence of lexical and grammatical structure. Words appear to be classified by the child into two groups, which might be called **object words,** of a growing and relatively open-class (we might call these 'pre-nouns'), such as *pudding* and *baby*, and **relation words**, sometimes called 'pivot words', of a more closed class (which might be called 'pre-verbs'), such as *up* and *there*. Action words typically take first position and object words second position in little sentences like *Up baby*, and *There pudding*. The child's little sentences seem often to consist of an action word followed by an object word, and the reverse order is less often observed.

Action words	Object words
up	pudding
there	baby
bye-bye	shoes
allgone	Johnny
hi	juice
big	plane
night-night	Mommy

2.3.3. 200-word vocabulary

The child's vocabulary grows steadily and surprisingly for such an otherwise still very dependent little creature. By age two, the vocabulary of most children surpasses 200 words, a great majority of which are nouns, especially proper and concrete nouns, somewhat fewer verbs and a few adjectives, 'social words' like *yes*, *no*, *hey* and *good-bye*, and, until late in the second year, no grammatical morphemes.

Notice that even though from the point of view of adult language it is possible to classify much of the child's vocabulary into part-of-speech classes like noun and verb, many of the words do not function in adult ways, but do function, as in the little two-word-class grammar above, within a rudimentary syntactic system. *Up* and *down*, for example, are adverbs or prepositions in adult grammar, but perhaps are verb-like for the child, meaning something like 'pick up' and 'put down', respectively. From the beginning, children do not appear to be just stringing miscellaneous words together.

2.4. Basic mastery

2.4.1. Vocabulary growth

Between two and four the child's mastery of language seems typically to increase by leaps, as most parents will assert. Within these two years children become amazingly verbal. They seem driven to talk; increasingly rarely are they at a loss for words. The lexicon grows astoundingly at this stage: from 18 to 36 months vocabulary size approximately doubles every six months, and doubles again from 36 to 48 months.

TYPICAL VOCABULARY GROWTH, 18 TO 48 MONTHS

18 months	100 words
24	200
30	400
36	800
48	1,600

The spontaneous drive to learn language is often evident to parents in this period when, shortly after having been put to bed, children can be heard repetitively talking to themselves in events of private practice sometimes called 'sleepy-time monologues'.

2.4.2. First grammatical morphemes

For most English-speaking children, the first grammatical morpheme to appear is the *-ing* suffix of verbs. Other grammatical morphemes appear in a very regular order, by now observed in a number of children, girls and boys, from different family environments. The ten first-learned grammatical morphemes, in typical 1–10 learning order with two examples of each, are as follows, where the parentheses show the item's order of frequency of occurrence in ordinary speech, and the square brackets a typical age of acquisition [years; months] (from Brown 1973, p. 271).

TYPICAL LEARNING ORDER OF TEN ENGLISH GRAMMATICAL MORPHEMES

Morpheme	Example words
1. Verb suffix *-ing* (2) [2; 0]	*walking, playing*
2. Prepositions *in* and *on* (4)	*in the box, on the bed*
3. Noun plural suffix *-s* (3) [2; 0]	*car*[z], *truck*[s]
4. Irregular past tense of frequent verbs [2; 6]	*went, saw*
5. Noun possessive suffix *-'s* (5)	*Mom'*[z], *Kitty'*[z]
6. Uncontracted copula in questions	*Is Kitty here? Was it?*
7. Indefinite and definite articles *a/an, the* (1) [3; 0]	*a book, the books*
8. Regular verb past tense suffix *-ed* (6) [3; 6]	*walk*[t], *play*[d]
9. Regular verb present tense suffix *-s* (7)	*walk*[s], *play*[z]
10. Irregular present tense of frequent verbs	*does, has*

1	2	3	4	5	6
/bɔj/	/bɔj/	/bɔjz/	/bɔjzəz/	/bɔjz/	/bɔjz/
/kæt/	/kæt/	/kæts/	/kætsəz/, /kætəz/	/kæts/	/kæts/
/mæn/	/mɛn/	/mænz/	/mænzəz/, /mɛnəz/	/mænz/	/mɛn/
/haws/	/haws/	/haws/	/hawsəz/	/hawsəz/	/hawsəz/
/fʊt/, /fit/	/fʊt/, /fit/	/fʊts/, /fits/	/fʊtsəz/, /fitsəz/	/fits/	/fit/

Figure 8.1   Six stages in the learning of English plural nouns

Notice that the regular order of learning of English grammatical morphemes is not explained by the frequency order of the morphemes in the language. We saw that *the* is the most frequent word in English, but this word goes unlearned until about age three. This acquisition order must be explained by other factors, perhaps having to do with the structure and functions of language and/or the innate structure of the child's knowledge, or learning program. (The topic of the next chapter is explanations of child language learning.)

2.4.3.   *Overgeneralization of morphological rules*

Another regular phenomenon in children's learning of English concerns the rules for making plural nouns. The basic rule is to suffix /z/ or one of its allomorphs /s/ or /əz/: for example *dog*[z], *cat*[s], *hors*[əz]. Six stages leading to mastery of the rule have been often (not invariably!) observed, as shown in figure 8.1 (from Moskowitz 1978).

(1) At first the typical child has one plural noun – the irregular plural *feet*. This makes sense in that the plural of this word is as frequent as the singular. (2) Then another frequent irregular plural appears, *men*. Probably *men* is less frequent than *feet*, in the child's environment. (3) At the third stage the plural suffix appears, in typical nouns like *boy* and *cat*, but not in the less typical *house*, perhaps because the word ends already in a phone very like /z/ (/s/). The child has not yet learned the conditions for the [əz] allomorph of the suffix. Furthermore, now the plural of *man* is changed to *mans*! (4) At the next stage, *houses* is correct (that is, adult-like) but the rule for the use of [əz] is overgeneral. (5) Then, at the fifth stage, everything is right – even *foot* and *feet* have been sorted out and mastered – except *mans*, which is still overgeneralized. (6) Finally at the last stage *men*, which was mastered at stage 2, reappears. In overextension of meaning (§2.2.6, above), meanings are overextended; in these **overgeneralizations**, morphological rules are overgeneral.

2.4.4.   *Stages in the learning of questions and negatives*

Negative sentences appear at about 18 months, in which *no* or *not* is placed at the beginning or end of sentences: *No I can go*. Before age three, the negative word may appear after the subject, where it belongs, and the common negative auxiliary verbs *can't* and *don't* begin to be used: *He no bite you. I can't go. I don't want it.*

Children have questions, marked by intonation, with their early one-word sentences. Before age three, an English-learning child may acquire yes–no questions with inversion of the subject and auxiliary verb: *Can I go?*, *Is Daddy going?* Inversion in questions with wh-words typically takes a little longer: *Where I can go?* (without inversion) precedes *Where can I go?* Furthermore, the child will invert auxiliary verbs in so-called 'embedded questions', an inversion which must later be unlearned: *I know what can I do* precedes *I know what I can do.*

THREE STAGES IN THE ACQUISITION OF NEGATIVES AND QUESTIONS

	Negatives	*Questions*
1.	No I can go. Wear mitten no.	I can go? This is it? (Intonation only)
2.	I no can go. I don't want it.	Can I go? Where I can go?
3.	I can't go. I don't want it.	Can I go? Where can I go?

2.4.5. *MLU*

An easy-to-remember generalization about MLU is that this reaches a rough average of 3 at about age three. Since one-word utterances persist at this age, and later, an MLU of 3 means that many utterances of the three-year-old child are more than three words in length. The three-year-old child has proceeded through the stages above, has acquired the ten grammatical morphemes of §2.4.2, has many multi-word sentences including questions and negatives, and often a vocabulary of 800 words or more.

Since the 800 most frequent words of English are over 90% of all the words we use, the three-year-old often seems to talk like an adult. By age four, many children are so accomplished linguistically that they often seem to have fully learned the language.

2.5. Continued learning

The learning of our first language continues throughout life. A mid-teenager may begin to use complex tense sequences like 'If we had known, we would have told them', perhaps learned in English class at school. Importantly, we learn to vary our choice of words and phrasing in subtle ways, according to social circumstances (the subject of chapter 27). Reading and writing, of course, many of us begin to learn at school, and don't acquire fluency with until our college studies or careers require it.

As adults, we continue to learn: the names of new products and new ideas, and other new morphemes that enter the language – like the prefix *cyber-*, recently common in all sorts of vocabulary of the 'information age': *cyberspace*, *cyberpunk*, *cybertalk*, etc. (ways to get new words is the main topic of chapters 15 and 16).

The vocabulary of a college student grows with each new subject, and is probably easily a hundred thousand words, as shown by the fact that you recognize words that occur at a frequency rank of about one hundred thousand, such as *acquiesce* and *simmer*. The language is always changing (the topic of chapters 23 and 24), and, to some extent, older speakers acquire, if reluctantly, the changes initiated by younger speakers.

3.   EXPLANATIONS OF CHILD LANGUAGE LEARNING

Among the many languages the child's acquisition of which has been well studied are some quite different from English, including Finnish, Korean, and Hebrew. Many of the important generalizations which apply to the child's acquisition of English appear to be valid for these languages also, which suggests that the process is controlled by the nature of children, generally, rather than by particular circumstances of a child's environment. The following chapter will offer some explanations of child language learning, with evidence in particular that, in some sense, the child is born with significant predispositions for skillful language learning, expectations regarding language, or perhaps even some of its actual abstract forms of grammar.

Suggestions for
ADDITIONAL READING

A number of books present thorough surveys of child language learning, including *Language Development* (1986) by Peter A. Reich, *Language Acquisition: a Linguistic Introduction* (1991) by Helen Goodluck, and *First Language Acquisition: Method, Description, and Explanation* (1989) by David Ingram. A classic and still important book which emphasizes the growth of MLU and English morpheme acquisition order is *A First Language: the Early Stages* (1973) by Roger Brown.

Child phonological development is thoroughly presented in *Phonological Development: the Origins of Language in the Child* (1996) by Maryilyn May Vihman. One year of the growth of English is the focus of *Language Development from Two to Three* (1991) by Lois Bloom. Current surveys of twenty-five topics in child language acquisition are found in *The Handbook of Child Language* (1996) edited by Paul Fletcher and Brian MacWhinney.

IMPORTANT CONCEPTS AND TERMS IN THIS CHAPTER

- creativity
- babbling

- cooing
- overextension

- underextension
- MLU
- phoneme substitutions
- fronting
- stopping
- perseverance

- anticipation
- telegraphic speech
- object words
- action words
- sleepy-time monologues
- overgeneralization

OUTLINE OF
CHAPTER 8

1. **Four general characteristics of child language learning**
    1. Typicality of language learning
    2. Similarity of language learning
    3. Spontaneity of language learning
    4. Creativity of language learning
2. **Stages in the learning of English**
    1. Language readiness
        1. Cooing
        2. Babbling
        3. Word recognition
    2. First words
        1. First meanings
        2. Intonation
        3. Phoneme learning order
        4. Phoneme substitutions
        5. Word structure
        6. Overextension and underextension of meaning
        7. MLU
    3. Two-word sentences
        1. Telegraphic speech
        2. Syntax of two-word sentences
        3. 200-word vocabulary
    4. Basic mastery
        1. Vocabulary growth
        2. First grammatical morphemes
        3. Overgeneralization of morphological rules
        4. Stages in the learning of questions and negatives
        5. MLU
    5. Continued learning
3. **Explanations of child language learning**

EXAMPLES AND PRACTICE

EXAMPLE

1. Pronunciations of Kylie, a two-year-old. Consider the following words as pronounced by Kylie (from Bleile 1991, p. 61).

a.	[pʌpi]	'puppy'	l.	[bʌk]	'truck'
b.	[pʌzu]	'puzzle'	m.	[bwɛ]	'bread'
c.	[tɪtæ]	'kitty cat'	n.	[dejps]	'grapes'
d.	[tɔwi]	'Corrie'	o.	[dæsɪz]	'glasses'
e.	[tæni]	'candy'	p.	[muzɪk]	'music'
f.	[dadi]	'dolly'	q.	[bajbəbæs]	'bible class'
g.	[bʌfəfaj]	'butterfly'	r.	[mʌnki]	'monkey'
h.	[bɛd]	'bed'	s.	[fɛs]	'fish'
i.	[towzd]	'closed'	t.	[bəlu]	'blue'
j.	[mɔ]	'more'	u.	[tow]	'coat'
k.	[bwi]	'queen'	v.	[bæwum]	'bathroom'

PRACTICE

Find examples in Kylie's words (a)–(l) of each of the following characteristics of child speech, and write one example and its letter in the spaces provided. Some items may illustrate more than one characteristic. The first is answered already, as an example.

	Characteristic	Example	Letter
1.	Syllable-final [r] omitted	[mɔ] for 'more'	j
2.	[l] omitted after a consonant	_____ for _____	_____
3.	Single consonant for two consonants	_____ for _____	_____
4.	Alveolar stop for velar stop (fronting)	_____ for _____	_____
5.	Labial stop for alveolar stop (fronting)	_____ for _____	_____
6.	Labial stop for velar stop (fronting)	_____ for _____	_____
7.	Stop for non-stop (stopping)	_____ for _____	_____
8.	Following consonant substituted for preceding consonant (anticipation)	_____ for _____	_____
9.	Preceding consonant substituted for following consonant (perseverance)	_____ for _____	_____
10.	Word-final consonant omitted	_____ for _____	_____
11.	[w] for [r]	_____ for _____	_____
12.	Vowel inserted between consonants	_____ for _____	_____

2. Pronunciations of Paul, a two-year-old. Consider the following words as pronounced by Paul (Ohio State University Dept of Linguistics 1994, pp. 273–274) which illustrate typical simplifications of child speech.

a.	[sən]	'sun'	k.	[kay]	'sky'	u.	[dor]	'door'
b.	[si]	'see'	l.	[bəs]	'bus'	v.	[bokən]	'broken'
c.	[ɛk]	'egg'	m.	[bəs]	'buzz'	w.	[bawni]	'brownie'
d.	[təp]	'tub'	n.	[wɛt]	'wet'	x.	[butəpəl]	'beautiful'
e.	[bet]	'bed'	o.	[pen]	'plane'	y.	[ɔp]	'off'
f.	[kut]	'cute'	p.	[tɪk]	'twig'			
g.	[kæk]	'crack'	q.	[tək]	'truck'			
h.	[ke]	'clay'	r.	[kɔpi]	'copy'			
i.	[læp]	'laugh'	s.	[nek]	'snake'			
j.	[pun]	'spoon'	t.	[tap]	'stop'			

Answer these questions.

1. What are two examples of stops substituted for adult fricatives (stopping)?
2. What are two examples of consonants which are pronounced accurately at the beginning of words but inaccurately at the end of words?
3. What is substituted, respectively, for word-final [b], [d], [g], and [z]?
4. What generalization covers all four of the above substitutions?
5. What does Paul substitute for clusters of [s] + consonant at the beginning of words?
6. How does he deal with other clusters of two consonants at the beginning of words?
7. How does item f show this?
8. What about Paul's pronunciation of vowels?

3. A child phonemic system. A child vocabulary may consist of a few words only, and typically the phones employed for those words may be few and show considerable restrictedness of occurrence in the words. This suggests the existence of a phonemic system, as in the following example (from Winitz 1969, p. 66). Suppose the child's few words are as follows:

1. [da] or [pa] 'dog'
2. [sa] 'there'
3. [æt] 'up'
4. [fa] 'father'
5. [æs] or [æz] 'open'
6. [ta] 'cat'

Winitz notes that there are eight phones [d, a, p, s, æ, t, f, z], and he analyzes these as making up only five phonemes /d, s, f, t, a/.

Explain the suggested phonemic analysis. Study the distribution of the phones, and group them as allophones into the five phonemes suggested, according to their phonetic similarity and complementarity of distribution. Notice, for example, that there are two phonetically similar vowels in complementary distribution (chapter 3, §2.2), suggesting one vowel phoneme with two allophones.

EXAMPLE

4. Stages in the learning of past tense verbs (data from Moskowitz 1978). Compare the six stages in the learning of English past tense verbs, shown in figure 8.2, with the six stages in the learning of the plural nouns shown in figure 8.1 (discussed in §2.4.3, above).

1	2	3	4	5	6
/wɔk/	/wɔk/	/wɔkt/	/wɔktəd/	/wɔkt/	/wɔkt/
/ple/	/ple/	/pled/	/pledəd/	/pled/	/pled/
/nid/	/nid/	/nid/	/nidəd/	/nidəd/	/nidəd/
/kəm/	/kem/	/kəmd/	/kemdəd/, /kəmdəd/	/kəmd/	/kem/
/go/	/went/	/god/	/god/, /wɛntəd/	/god/	/wɛnt/

Figure 8.2   Six stages in the learning of English past tense verbs

PRACTICE

Answer these questions.

1.   Which past tense verbs are adult-like at stage 2?
2.   How are these verbs similar to one another?
3.   Which past tense verbs are adult-like at stage 3?
4.   How are these two verbs similar in their past tense forms?
5.   Only one verb at stage 3 lacks its past tense suffix. What characterizes this verb?
6.   How is this verb like *house* in stage 3 in the learning of plural nouns (see §2.4.3, above)?
7.   What can be said to be overgeneralized at stage 4?
8.   Which past tense verbs are not adult-like at stage 5?
9.   How is this like stage 5 in the learning of plural nouns?
10. Why might irregular past tense verbs like *went* and *came* be adult-like before regular verbs?

Chapter 9

EXPLANATIONS OF CHILD LANGUAGE LEARNING

This chapter discusses four general ideas about how children learn languages: conditioned-response learning, imitation, hypothesis testing, and innateness. There are arguments for and against each of these, but several arguments support the basic innateness of human language ability.

1. CONDITIONED-RESPONSE LEARNING

Learning is complex, and language is a particularly complex sort of knowledge, so equally complex theories of language learning have to be considerably simplified here. In **conditioned-response learning**, some naturally occurring **stimulus** ('unconditioned stimulus', US) produces a natural, 'unconditioned,' **response** (UR), aspects of which may receive **positive reinforcement** by some 'conditioned' aspects of the stimulus (CS), with which these then become associated as a 'conditioned' response (CR). In a popular example, college students attended (US) a professor's lecture (UR). But students responded to the lecture differently (CS). Those on one side of the classroom gave positive reinforcement by being attentive to the lesson, while those on the other side looked bored. After some days of this, according to the story, the teacher stopped lecturing to the frowning side altogether (CR).

It is doubtful that language is very much like orienting oneself toward students in a class. Adults talk to the child (US), who vocalizes in response (UR); adults positively reinforce progressively more language-like and grammatical talk by the child (CS), to which the child responds by speaking progressively more grammatically (CR). Following are some arguments both for and against the conditioned-response theory of language learning.

1.1. For conditioned-response learning

First, we do, obviously, learn some things in at least roughly this way, such as to answer the phone when it rings, and to look out when someone yells 'Look out!' Second, mothers and fathers surely do encourage speech, and when, at first, the child says almost anything they are likely to reinforce this behavior positively, by picking up, praising, and otherwise rewarding the child. Some words, of course, get more positive response than others.

1.2. Against conditioned-response learning

Against the general reasonability of conditioned-response learning of language, however, are a number of facts. First, it is difficult to recognize any relation between even the simplest early language and some possible stimulus for this in the child's environment. Parents do, indeed, encourage the conditions in which babies will speak. In English-speaking homes, for example, mothers may try to get the child to say *Mommy* and fathers try to get baby to say *Daddy*, modeling the word encouragingly, and using it over and over in reference to themselves. But it is notorious that when the child's first word is heard, this may be something unexpected and seemingly unstimulated, such as *pudding*, *dirty*, or *Mickey*.

Second, children regularly say completely unstimulated things, like *goed* and *mans*, as we have seen. Many English-learning children who cannot have heard **double negatives** may be heard, nevertheless, to say things like:

I'm not afraid of nothin.
I don't want no applesauce.
That's not no big one.

Third, a basic thing about language learning is the fact that, with exceptions, comprehension must precede naturalistic production. Children often give evidence of attention to language, and appear to comprehend before they start talking. A one-year-old doesn't just accidentally come out with the utterance /mami/, which her mother then, somehow, teaches to be a word referring to herself, but seems to say *Mommy* from the first as a comprehended and meaningful word. But first comprehensions can't be reinforced. Parents can't often know when comprehension occurs, in order to reinforce it.

Fourth and finally, is the fact that even though children don't learn just to speak, but to speak grammatically, according to the requirements of their particular language, parents at first reinforce all the language-like utterances of the child, not just the grammatical ones, which, in fact, are few at first. Child learners (in evidence reviewed by Foss and Hakes 1978, p. 269) says things like 'Her curl my hair' to which mother happily agrees; bare phrases like 'baby room' parents may readily interpret and reinforce with a reply like 'That's right, baby is in her room.' But saying something plainly untrue may get a negative response, for example 'There's the animal farmhouse' to which an adult replies 'No, that's a lighthouse'; or 'Walt Disney comes on Tuesday' (the Disney TV show), which gets the reply 'No, it doesn't.' It is something of a contradiction of conditioned-response learning, then, that we grow up to speak grammatically but not always truthfully.

2. IMITATION

Perhaps children learn language by imitating adults. Again there are arguments for and against this.

2.1. For learning by imitation

In support of the role of **imitation** is, first of all, the fact that imitation, like conditioned-response learning, is a common sort of learning. We learn many things by imitating, like how to light the oven and to flush the toilet. Besides, many children do seem actively to imitate, and perhaps all children do, obviously, imitate some of the things they hear, sometimes to the embarrassment of parents. Furthermore, we do acquire very specific characteristics of the language of our home and childhood environment, including local vocabulary and 'accent'. Finally, many parents do encourage their children to imitate, often instructing the child to say this and that, and giving models in a simple and salient manner of speech that has been called '**caregiver talk**'.

Caregiver talk, which research shows we typically use in modifying the things we say around or to small children, has certain regular characteristics, including these seven:

SEVEN CHARACTERISTICS OF CAREGIVER TALK

1. Exaggerated intonation
2. Slow rate and carefully pronounced words
3. Simple sentences
4. Proper nouns for pronouns
5. High percentage of questions and imperatives
6. Repetitions
7. Expansions

Expansions are as where the child says 'Baby sleep', and the parent replies, expanding this utterance, 'That's right; the baby is sleeping'.

Caregiver talk characteristics 1–5 are seen in a typical adult question to a child, not 'Are you hungry?' but 'Is baby hungry?', said with slow speed, high pitch, and sharply rising question intonation. Caregiver talk is of interest in a number of ways, but among these is the evidence it is for the theory that we naturally expect children to learn by imitation, and so provide simple, clear, models to imitate. But it could also be a response to our reasonable understanding that children can't know the language very well, so we had better speak simply and clearly.

Caregiver talk should be distinguished from **babytalk,** talking like a baby. Babytalk may be as useful for teaching babies to talk as driving like a 16-year-old would be for teaching a 16-year-old to drive.

2.2.   Against learning by imitation

Several facts argue that imitation can't go very far as an explanation of how children learn language. First, the fact must be again considered that, ordinarily, comprehension precedes production: for how could children imitate comprehension? Or how could they even recognize it, in order to imitate it? In this regard, dialogs like the following are interesting (Clark and Clark 1977, p. 385):

> David: [asks to ride the] mewy-go-wound.
> 2nd child: David wants to go on the mewy-go-wound.
> David: You didn't say it wight.

Notice that while David's pronunciation provides [w] for adult [r], he comprehends that [w] is not [r].

Second is the fact that the apparent imitativeness of children, who seemingly learn at roughly the same rate, varies greatly. Some children appear to imitate a lot, others hardly at all; but all learn.

Third and importantly, the imitations of children seem rarely to represent new or advanced learning. In fact, children typically imitate well only what they already know, and may seem not even to hear what they don't, as in this famous dialog concerning double negatives and the English present tense suffix (from McNeil 1966, p. 69):

> Child: Nobody don't like me.
> Mother: No, say 'Nobody likes me.'
> Child: Nobody don't like me.
> [Eight repetitions of this dialogue, then:]
> Mother: No, now listen carefully. Say 'Nobody likes me.'
> Child: Oh! Nobody don't *likes* me.

Children seem to ignore those aspects of a would-be imitated sentence which are beyond their level of competence, such as many grammatical morphemes in these imitations of Donnie, two and a half years old (Ervin 1964, p. 168):

Adult model	Donnie's imitation
This is a round ring.	This ring.
Where does it go.	Where's it go?
Is Donnie all-gone?	Donnie all-gone?
Is it a bus?	It a bus?
Is it broken?	It broken?

Fourth, children who cannot vocalize (for physiological reasons such as having an impaired or removed larynx) are found to learn the language, if at a slowed rate, and, when they get speech, are found to have learned a great deal of language.

A fifth fact arguing against the importance of imitation is that, if children learn by imitating, they might be expected to learn some grammatical morphemes, which are very frequent, very early. But as we have seen, the grammatical morphemes are largely ignored by children for almost two years.

A sixth argument concerns again the characteristically creative aspect of child language learning: children who don't hear such utterances cannot be imitating when they create utterances like *goed*, *mans*, double negatives, and questions like *What I can do?*

3. HYPOTHESIS TESTING

Hypothesis testing may also be called 'trial and error learning'. The child seems to be guessing about how the language works, and testing the guesses (hypotheses) in speech.

3.1. For learning by hypothesis testing

The clearest evidence for this is the creative utterances we have emphasized above; another example: a child was heard to say, 'I have not feeded a horse, but I have rided one.' The child may have heard an adult saying 'I have rode a horse', but is unlikely to have heard 'I have rided one'! Clearly the child, on the model of many regular past tense verbs, has figured out, consciously or not, that past tense verbs are formed by adding /əd/ to basic verbs ending in /d/.

Creative utterances of children like *mommy sock* and *boot paper* show a willingness to use new word combinations to express meanings also new to the child. Notice that children who say such things cannot be considered, even, to be employing the crude hypothesis that language is just stringing words together, because, already at the two-word stage of *allgone juice* and *bye-bye juice*, they appear to be classifying words into action words like *allgone* and *bye-bye* and object words like *juice*, and hypothesizing a rule of word order that action words precede object words (chapter 8, §2.3.2).

3.2.   Against learning by hypothesis testing

The first difficulty with the hypothesis-testing explanation of how children learn language is that it begs the question – the important question – of where the hypotheses come from. Obviously children are not trained and experienced linguists figuring out an unwritten language in some little-traveled corner of the world. It seems impossible to attribute to small children mature and rational inductive powers, so the unconsciously reached linguistic hypotheses of child learners must be considered instinctive.

A second difficulty is that, for some of the hypotheses, the evidence must seem very inadequate to take a chance on. For the formation of past tense verbs, for example, the evidence maybe is adequate: the past tense of many verbs is formed by adding /d/ or its allomorphs (*walk/t/*, *open/d/*, *need/əd/*), and though several other ways of forming the past tense are seen in relatively few verbs, among these are very frequent ones such as *drink/drank*, *eat/ate*, *see/saw*, and *go/went*.

The English articles *a/an* and *the*, for example, begin to be used by children by about age two, and with very few errors. However, the rules for using the articles are complex and abstract, and there are many exceptions, such as *rice* (**a rice* is ungrammatical, but *a bean*, and *a pea* are not), *the Hague* (not **the Paris*), and *the sun* and *the Earth* (but not **the Saturn*, or **the Mars*).

Concerning syntax, many examples like the following may be mentioned. We say *the child is ready* and *the child is sleeping*, and *the child looks ready*, but not **the child looks sleeping*. Child learners appear not to say the latter either, as a seemingly reasonable hypothesis suggests they should – just as *walked*, *opened* etc. suggest *rided*, which they do say. In short, children seem, often, to be guided to just the right hypotheses, and away from the bad ones, despite the seemingly poor data they have to work from.

Finally, when adults are testing a hypothesis, they are alert for evidence against the hypothesis. But children who say things like *goed* and *mans* will persist in using these forms in spite of being corrected, as in the example above (§2.2), concerning double negatives. With regard to phonology, sometimes children seem unable to correct themselves, even upon receiving negative evidence (Clark and Clark 1977, p. 385):

Father:	Say 'jump'.
Child:	Dup.
Father:	No, say 'jump'.
Child:	Dup.
Father:	No. JUMMP.
Child:	Only Daddy can say 'Dup'.

4. INNATENESS OF LANGUAGE

A fourth explanation of child language learning is **innateness**. According to this idea, much knowledge of language is genetically encoded in the child, as a member of the human species. The idea is that the child, relatively speaking, has little to learn, since much of the necessary knowledge – or at least a crucial amount – is present from birth, 'wired in', so to speak.

There is innate knowledge: some bird species know their songs without having heard them, and humans have innate knowledge of various sorts, for example to suckle, distinguish human faces, digest food, walk, and fear snakes. Clearly we don't have innate knowledge of particular languages, since we learn perfectly well whichever language we happen to grow up hearing. Thus if we have innate knowledge of language, this must be abstract and universal, underlying all languages.

4.1. For innateness of language

There is a variety of evidence for the innateness of language. Some of this is quite complex, and much of it is controversial. Let's consider evidence organized in relation to four criteria for the innateness of some behavior in a species (from Lenneberg 1964).

1.   Absence of history of development in the species
2.   Inherited predisposition in the species
3.   Absence of variation in the species
4.   Physiological correlates

For each criterion, below we will contrast the two behaviors walking, certainly an unlearned but innate behavior of humankind, and writing, a certainly learned and non-innate behavior, and then consider how language compares with these.

4.1.1. *Absence of history of development*
For an innate behavior, there will be no history of development in a species. There is no history of development of walking, and indeed, upright posture with walking is a defining characteristic of our species. The history of writing, however, we know from its beginnings about 5,000 years ago (chapter 21).

Language is more like walking than writing. As far back in the record of human history as we can go (the 5,000 years of writing), humans appear to have been using language as we know it today.   *humans always have used language*

4.1.2. *Inherited predisposition*
For an innate behavior, there will be an evident inherited predisposition in a species. There is certainly an inherited predisposition for walking: normal human

babies start trying to walk by about 10 months, and typically succeed by about 12 months. For writing, there is no such inherited predisposition: children will seize a pen or pencil and ruin a surface, but they have to be carefully and extensively taught before they begin to write. Again language is more like walking than writing.

Indeed, an inherited predisposition for language in humankind is apparent in three of the four general characteristics of child language learning mentioned at the outset of the previous chapter.

4.1.2.1. _Typicality._

The typicality of child language learning may be understood to result not from innateness, but from the more or less uniform circumstances, world-wide, of first language acquisition, including need for language, encouragement to learn, and sympathetic exposure to restricted, usually simplified, data. In fact, many believe that child language learning world-wide is considerably more uniform than the circumstances can explain. The spontaneity, similarity, and creativity of child learning more clearly seem to be evidence of a predisposition to learn.

4.1.2.2. _Similarity._

The similarity of child language learning is apparent in the regular stages of learning noted in the previous chapter, for example, the onset of babbling at about six months, and first words at about one year.

4.1.2.3. _Spontaneity._

The spontaneity of child language learning is evident in those aspects of language learning which go beyond what seems possible. For example, children appear to master the English definite article, _the_, with few errors, quite unlike adult learners of English, despite its considerable irregularities of usage. _The_, which roughly means 'noun phrase known to the hearer', is often used otherwise; thus we say _the moon_ (certainly known to the hearer, being unique) but not _the Venus_; we say _the Gulf of Mexico_ but not _the Lake Michigan_, and _the Netherlands_ but not _the Holland_. Furthermore, _the_ often appears in many common idioms (fixed phrases with specialized meaning) when there is no knowledge by the hearer of its noun phrase, as in _the hospital_ ('He went to the hospital' (American English)) and _the piano_ ('She plays the piano'). That children should eventually master _the_ is not surprising, but that they do so without evident overgeneralizations.

Such spontaneous mastery is more impressive in some aspects of the learning of syntax. For example, in English we typically contract a subject and following auxiliary verb, such as _will_, _have_, _are_, and _is_:

   a. OK, we'll go.
   b. I've eaten already.
   c. Yes, they're ready.
   d. Jimmy's up now.

But when the word which logically completes the verb phrase is absent, contraction becomes impossible:

   e.   Are you sure you won't go? – OK, we will. (*OK, we'll.)
   f.   Why don't you eat something? – I have already. (*I've already.)
   g.   Are they ready? – Yes, they are. (*Yes, they're.)
   h.   Who's up? – Jimmy is now. (*Jimmy's now.)

Notice that what is needed to make contraction possible, or grammatical, is presence of the logically required complement to the auxiliary verb (main verb *go* in the first example, main verb *eaten* in the second, adjective *ready* in the third, and prepositional adverb *up* in the fourth). The second and fourth examples show that not just any following word is sufficient. This is not a simple rule of English, but requires abstract analysis of the logic of sentences, yet it seems to be learned by English-learning children without any tendency to overgeneralize use of the typical, contracted, case, as in their overgeneralizing of regular past tense forms of verbs (*rided*) and regular plurals of nouns (*sheeps*). The rule cannot be taught, since English speakers are ordinarily unaware of it. Instead, the rule is learned spontaneously, and so appears to be predisposed in the child – made possible, somehow, by innate knowledge.

4.1.2.4.   *Creativity.*   The creativity of child language learning, in utterances like *rided* and *mommy sock*, is also good evidence for an inherited predisposition, since it is good evidence against the role of instruction and imitation. Also, as was noted above, if creative utterances are evidence of learning by the method of hypothesis testing, they raise the question of where the hypotheses come from. They appear to be part of a predisposition for language – for creative human language that is, not just for using signs.

4.1.3.   *Absence of variation*
   For an innate behavior, there will be little or no variation in the species. This is so for walking – all normal humans around the world walk – and not so for writing, since, while some humans write, many, perhaps a majority, do not.
   Superficially, variation seems to be the usual case for language, since there are perhaps 6,000 different languages in the world. But this variety concerns specifics of what is acquired, not whether there is acquisition. Every normal child learns the language of its home; concerning the learning process, there is remarkable regularity.

4.1.4.   *Physiological correlates*
   For an innate behavior, there may be expected to be found physiological correlates. There are certainly physiological correlates for walking, in the bone structures of our spine, legs and feet, and in the musculature of our legs and feet. But

there seem to be no physiological correlates of writing. The physiology of our hands is completely adequate for writing, but is as well suited for the general purpose of grasping and holding tools of all kinds.

Superficially this criterion seems to fail for language, there being for language no obvious parallels to the physiology of walking. In fact, the matter is complex. Let's consider the physiology of speech and, briefly, the areas of the human brain particularly involved in language, which will be taken up more fully in the next chapter.

4.1.4.1. *Speech physiology.*

The speech physiology of language (lungs, larynx, pharynx, tongue, velum, lips, etc.) appears to be entirely justified for the purposes of breathing and eating, and only secondarily adapted for the uses of vocal language. However, a couple of facts about speech physiology provide evidence that speech physiology has evolved, to some extent, specifically for language.

First, speech is produced and processed at a normal rate of about 15 phonemes per second. (Thus you should find yourself able to read aloud, at a normal rate, the preceding 70-phoneme sentence in about five seconds.) This rate of response to discrete processing units has been considered to be quite fast in comparison with other fine-grained motor behavior of humans, such as reading music, or typing. Since such rapidity appears to be necessary only for speech, the physical capability for this may, reasonably, be specific to the purposes of speech.

Second, in humans in comparison with our nearest mammalian relatives among the apes, the larynx is somewhat lowered in the throat, as seen in figure 9.1, which compares cross-sections of adult human and chimpanzee oral–laryngeal areas (Lieberman 1975, pp. 60, 106). A human child cross-section, before three months of age, would look a lot like that of the adult chimpanzee, in which the larynx is closer to the back of the tongue, which therefore effectively can prevent food and liquids in the mouth from dropping directly into the larynx! In his *Origin of Species* (1859 [1979, p. 113]), Charles Darwin had noted the problem which, by contrast, the adult human configuration presents: 'Every particle of food and drink which we swallow has to pass over the orifice of the trachea, with some risk of falling into the lungs' (with the result that many communities require restaurants to acquaint employees with the 'Heimlich maneuver' for correcting potentially fatal choking).

However – and this is the important point of evidence for human speech-specific physiology – the lowered adult human larynx, which can kill us, is apparently important for speech, since the relatively complex right-angle sounding chamber with which it coincides enables us to produce a variety of speech sounds impossible for the ape (and child before three months). Perhaps, thus, the lowered larynx is a physiological correlate of speech and so of language.

4.1.4.2. *Language centers of the brain.*

Specific areas of the human brain appear to be centers for language processing. These also are possible physiological correlates of language.

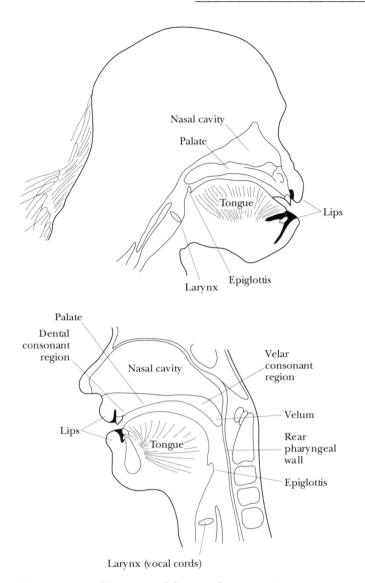

Figure 9.1 Chimpanzee and human oral–laryngeal cross-sections
Source: Reprinted by permission of Allyn & Bacon from *On the Origins of Language: An Introduction to the Evolution of Human Speech* by Philip Lieberman, copyright © 1975 by Allyn & Bacon

The brain is roughly a sphere, and has approximately symmetrical left and right hemispheres. In the great majority of humans, the left hemisphere is significantly more involved in language than the right. Furthermore, within the left hemisphere, two areas are particularly involved in language production and comprehension: an area approximately under the left ear known as **Wernicke's area**, and an area at the left front known as **Broca's area**. A left-hemisphere view of the human brain is provided as figure 10.1 of the next chapter. (We consider the evidence for the presence of these language centers in the brain, and the topic of language and the brain, generally, in the next chapter.)

4.2. Against innateness of language

Against innateness are the above-mentioned problems that (1) the variety of languages of the world means that language, if innate, is abstract universal language of a form which is yet to be revealed, and that (2) the existence of physiological correlates of language is controversial.

It has been argued that what is certainly abstract and universal about language are its functions, and that languages may therefore take the general form they do by necessity of expressing or fulfilling these functions. This explanation of language universals does not entail that aspects of language be innate in humankind. However, not all the universal aspects of language are obviously functional. This topic arises again in chapter 20.

But the seeming physiological correlates of language may have non-language origins. Perhaps the rapid rate of speech does not require but simply fully engages neural and articulatory capabilities which have evolved for evolutionarily more critical purposes including eating, and tool use. The brain centers which seem dedicated to language may be among those generally dedicated to symbolic communicative and analytic cognitive tasks of which language is a case. This topic is continued in the next chapter.

Suggestions for
ADDITIONAL READING

For a survey of the phenomena of child language learning plus explanations, see *Introduction to Language Development* (1998) by Scott McLaughlin. Also see the last chapter of *Language Development* (1986) by Peter A. Reich.

Three books which explain child language acquisition as involving a great deal of innateness of language are *Patterns in the Mind: Language and Human Nature* (1994) by Ray Jackendoff, *The Language Instinct* (1994) by Steven Pinker, and *Language and Mind* (1998) by Stephen Crain and Diane Lillo-Martin. The opposing viewpoint is expressed in *Educating Eve: the 'Language Instinct' Debate* (1997) by Geoffrey Sampson, and *Rethinking Innateness: a Connectionist Perspective on Development* (1997) edited by Jeffrey Elman and others. Evidence and arguments on both sides are also found in articles of the anthology *Language Acquisition: Core Readings* (1996), edited by Paul Bloom. A conversation between two leading scholars, Noam Chomsky and Jean Piaget, on opposite sides of the issue of the innateness of language, is found in *Language and Learning: the Debate between Jean Piaget and Noam Chomsky* (1980), edited by Massimo Piattelli-Palmarini.

IMPORTANT CONCEPTS AND TERMS IN THIS CHAPTER

- conditioned-response learning
- stimulus
- response
- positive reinforcement
- double negatives
- imitation
- caregiver talk

- expansions
- babytalk
- hypothesis testing
- innateness
- Broca's area
- Wernicke's area

OUTLINE OF CHAPTER 9

EXAMPLES AND PRACTICE

EXAMPLE

1. The rate of speech. It was suggested above that the surprisingly rapid human speech rate of about 15 phonemes per second is evidence of physiology for speech specific to the unusual demands of language, and therefore evidence of the innateness of, at least, this aspect of language.

PRACTICE

Choose a 50-word text from a newspaper, one dealing with an ordinary rather than a technical or obscure topic.

    a.   Write the text phonemically to see how long it is in phonemes (perhaps, on average, 300–350 phonemes).

    b.   Read it at normal rate, and time your reading, to see whether you read it at the approximate rate of 15 phonemes per second. (If the 50-word text consists of 300 phonemes, at this rate you would read it in about 12–14 seconds.)

    c.   Then, read it faster and faster, to determine at what rate accurate pronunciation begins seriously to break down.

    d.   Write down what you find and what happens, for discussion in class.

EXAMPLE

2. First-grader talk. First graders, about six years old, can talk very much like adults. Following is a phonemically written sample of first-grader talk (from Carterette and Jones 1974, slightly regularized).

    a.   wɛn wi wɔk hom frəm skuə ɑ wɔk om wɪθ tu frɛnz ən səmtajmz wi kænʔ

    b.   rən hom frəm skuə ðo, bikəz ʔəm wən gər wɛr ɛvi tajm ši wənʔ ə, rənz,

    c.   ši gɛts ðə wizəz ən stəf. ən ðɛn ši kænʔ əm, brið vɛri wɛl ən ši gɛts sɪk.

    d.   ðæs wɑj wi kænʔ rən. . . . aj lajk tə go tə mɑj grænməðərz hɑws. wɛə

    e.   bikəz ši gɪvz əs kændi. wɛəl ʔəm, wi ʔit ðɛr səmtajmz. səmtajmz wi slip

    f.   ovərnajt ðɛr. səmtajmz wɛn aj go tə, go tə mɑj kəzənz aj gɛt tə ple

    g.   sɔfbɔ ər plebædminən ən ɔl ðæt. . . . θɪŋ ɑ het tə ple ɪz daktər o. aj het

    h.   tə ple daktər ər hɑws ər, donʔ lajk ət ər stəf. . . . wi bɛn lərnən ə ladə

i.   spænɪš wərdz. ɑr tičǝr spiks spænɪš sǝmtɑjmz. so dǝz mɑj fɑðǝr. wɛǝl

j.   mɑj fɑðǝr dǝzǝnʔ no vɛrɪ mǝč spænɪš. bǝt hi dǝzǝnʔ no wǝt gre ɪz . . .

PRACTICE

Read the above text and answer these questions.

1. Several words lack final [l], which perhaps would appear in adult speech. Which?
2. A common young-people's word meaning 'suchlike' or 'like that' appears several times. What is the word? Do adults use this?
3. Words ending in /nt/ may often be pronounced [nʔ] in child or adult speech. What are some examples in this text?
4. Notice several hesitation words, typically spelled *uh*. Are these typical in adult as well as child speech?
5. In line h one might expect to see [wiv bɛn lǝrnɪŋ] but different pronunciations appear. Would adults say this?
6. How is *and* pronounced? Is this a child characteristic?
7. Notice the words *grandmother's* and *that's*. Are these pronunciations child characteristics?
8. What about the nature of the topics, or content: child-like or adult-like?

EXAMPLE

3. Phonological system in child pronunciations. Consider the following words of Joan, a child of 22 months (Velten 1943).

a.	[wuf]	'woof'	f.	[bɑt]	'bat'
b.	[wut]	'wet'	g.	[hut]	'head'
c.	[fus]	'face'	h.	[un]	'in'
d.	[hɑt]	'hot'	i.	[mun]	'moon'
e.	[nut]	'neat'	j.	[nu]	'no'

Only two vowels are used by Joan, but they are in a systematic relation to adult vowels: [ɑ] appears for the two adult low vowels [ɑ] and [æ], and [u] appears everywhere else. The child has a phonological system, not just a set of pronunciations in imperfect relation to adult language.

PRACTICE

Now consider the consonants of Christopher, a child of 36 months, and answer the questions. Christopher's consonants, like Joan's vowels, are in a regular relation to adult pronunciations.

a.	[dɪp]	'dip'	d.	[fwi]	'three'
b.	[dwɪp]	'drip'	e.	[bwiv]	'breathe'
c.	[twi]	'tree'	f.	[wǝf]	'rough'

g.	[wɪf]	'with'	j.	[dɑjv]	'five'
h.	[fɪn]	'thin'	k.	[do]	'four'
i.	[dæt]	'that'			

1. What does Christopher have for adult [r]?
2. There are three substitutions for adult [θ] and [ð]. Which of these occur at the beginning of words and which at the end of words?
3. What does he substitute for adult [f] in 'five' and 'four'?
4. We wouldn't want to say that Christopher 'can't pronounce [f]'. Why not?
5. What are Christopher's rules for pronouncing [f] of adult words?

EXAMPLE

4. Second and foreign language learning. As many of us have experienced in school language classes, when we get older our approach to learning languages is quite different from that which we adopted as first-language learning children – and so is the result, usually. There are differences in the manner of learning, in the sort of things learned, and in the way society encourages the learning.

PRACTICE

(a) Mention at least four ways that such learning of second and/or foreign languages by older people, especially adults, generally differs from child first-language learning as described in this chapter. (b) Also, suggest at least four explanations for the differences.

LANGUAGE AND THE BRAIN

This chapter concerns the special language centers of the brain which all humans have. It provides a survey of evidence for these language centers, including the main types of aphasia, the loss of language ability resulting from brain injuries. It is noted that the left hemisphere is specialized for analytic skills of which language is perhaps the best example.

1. STRUCTURE OF THE BRAIN

1.1. General structure

The human brain has only very approximately the shape of a sphere, but its two sides are referred to as the left and right hemispheres. With its two halves, it looks sort of like a pair of boxing gloves side by side, with the big thumbs outside and pointing forward. Figure 10.1 is a picture of the left hemisphere of the brain.

The two halves or hemispheres of the brain exercise **contralateral control** of the body. That is, the left and right hemispheres control their opposite sides of the body.

The outer layer of the brain, about $\frac{1}{4}$-inch thick, is the **cortex**. The cortex is multiply fissured or enfolded, and, compared with the rest of the brain, packed with nerves – about ten billion, it is estimated. The major visible parts of the brain, each with left and right hemisphere equivalents, are the following:

a. **temporal lobes,** the thumb-like shapes,
b. **frontal lobes,** above and in front of the temporal lobes,
c. **occipital lobes,** behind the temporal lobes,
d. **parietal lobes,** above and behind the temporal lobes.

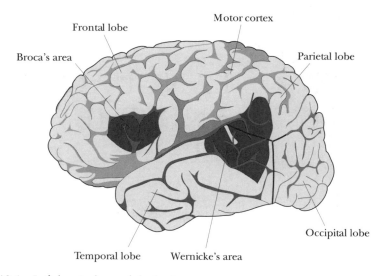

Figure 10.1 Left hemisphere of the brain

Separating the two hemispheres is the **corpus callosum**, a dense layer of tissue with relatively little nerve structure. Prominent fissures or enfoldings separate the temporal lobes from the frontal lobes, and others divide the main body of the brain into quarters. The **Sylvian fissure** separates the temporal lobe; the prominent **longitudinal fissure** runs from front to back on the surface of the brain along the line of the corpus callosum, and the less prominent **central fissure** separates the frontal and parietal lobes. The area just forward of and along the left-to-right central fissure is the **motor strip** (motor cortex), so called because it is particularly the location of motor or muscle control.

1.2. Language centers

In most persons, the left hemisphere is greatly more involved in language processing than the right. This rule is generally less valid for left-handers: while about 90% of right-handers have left-hemisphere language centers, only about 65% of left-handers do. Left-handers, especially those with left-handedness in their family, may have some right-hemisphere dominance for language, or language dominance somewhat evenly distributed between the left and right. A common generalization, which ignores the actuality of different kinds and degrees of left-handedness, is that about 10% of us are more or less left-handed. Thus about 88% of the population as a whole tends to be left-hemisphere dominant for language.

The reason for the strong correlations between hemisphere dominance for language and handedness is unknown and controversial, but it has been speculated that it may result from one of two factors in evolution, or both:

a. Perhaps detailed or fine-grained motor activity early in human evolution favored specialization of one hand or the other, since one hand will get more practice than two, and become more skilled, quicker. For whatever reason, perhaps by chance, this turned out to be the right hand in most of the population. The left hemisphere, which directs the right hand, then naturally came also to direct speech, another detailed motor activity, and thus language.

b. Perhaps language was originally gestural, or manual. Gestural language might have arisen more readily in prehistoric hunting societies, but the vocal medium would have developed secondarily, and eventually would have proven more adaptable, particularly with the engagement of the hand in other activities such as tool-making and carrying. The language centers remained those of the usually dominant, right, hand, after vocal language replaced the earlier manual language.

Two areas of the language-dominant hemisphere of the brain are known to be particularly involved in language processing.

a. **Broca's area** is on the language-dominant frontal lobe above the forward part of the temporal lobe. Broca's area is named for the French physician Paul Broca, who identified it as a language center in 1861.

b. **Wernicke's area** is on the language-dominant hemisphere in the area where the upper temporal lobe joins the parietal lobe. It is named for the German physician Carl Wernicke, who identified it as a language center in 1872.

2. TYPES OF EVIDENCE FOR LANGUAGE CENTERS OF THE BRAIN

Hemisphere dominance for language and the particular functions of the language centers are revealed in at least three ways.

2.1. Aphasias

First, and the original evidence for Broca's and Wernicke's areas as language centers, is the correlation between injuries or damage in these areas and apparently resulting loss of linguistic abilities, known as **aphasia**. Broca, for example, found that eight consecutive aphasic patients whom he treated had left-hemisphere brain injuries.

Aphasias of particular types are typically found to be associated with injuries in either Broca's or Wernicke's areas.

a. Persons with injury in Broca's area often are:

1. able to comprehend language well, but
2. have difficulty speaking with fluency, especially showing
3. limited ability to use grammatical morphemes.

b. Persons with injury in Wernicke's area often:

1. have difficulty comprehending language, but
2. talk fluently if incomprehensibly, especially showing
3. poor access to lexical morphemes, especially nouns.

2.2. Clinical procedures

2.2.1. Sodium amytal injection

Various procedures are employed in hospitals and clinics to determine the location and extent of brain injuries. In preparation for possible surgery on epileptic patients, a procedure involving the injection of sodium amytal into the left or right carotid artery has been employed. This induces paralysis in the brain hemisphere opposite that of the injection, and resulting aphasic symptoms would show that the language-dominant hemisphere had been affected. Table 10.1 shows the results of this procedure as reported for 119 patients differing in handedness and, for lefthanders, experience of left-brain injury (Milner et al. 1968, p. 369).

Notice the greater likelihood of right-hemisphere dominance for left-handed or ambidextrous subjects, in 27 (18 + 9) out of 71 (27 + 44) or 38% of these patients. The category 'left or ambidextrous' is appropriate, since so-called left-handers do not usually have such strong hand preference as right-handers. These results emphasize another important factor: whether or not the patient suffered left-brain injury as a young child. Notice that if there was such injury the patient is strongly likely – 21 out of 27 subjects – to have some right (including bilateral)

Table 10.1 Hemisphere dominance for language determined by sodium amytal procedure in 119 patients

Handedness of patient	No.	Hemisphere dominance for language		
		Left	Bilateral	Right
Right	48	43 (90%)	0 (0%)	5 (10%)
Left or ambidextrous:				
with early left-brain damage	27	6 (22%)	3 (11%)	18 (67%)
without early left-brain damage	44	28 (64%)	7 (16%)	9 (20%)
	119			

dominance for language. That is, the bilateral or right dominance may result from the injury, as the right hemisphere takes over for the left. Notice, finally, that 64% of left-handers without early left-brain damage (28 out of 44) have left-hemisphere language dominance.

2.2.2. Computer-assisted tomography

A number of high-technology procedures for analyzing and mapping brain function by electronic sensors have been developed recently and have become the source of important new and detailed information about brain function: positron emission tomography (PET) and magnetic resonance imaging (MRI) have been combined with computer analysis (**computer-assisted tomography** or **CAT** or **CT scanning**) to provide newly detailed looks at brain response in specific tasks, and a great advance over previously available information.

See the diagram of figure 10.2 (Raichle 1994) which presents results of PET + CT analysis of the left-brain during subjects' performance of four different language activities: (a) reading written nouns, (b) hearing spoken nouns, (c) speaking nouns, with the areas active in reading and hearing deleted, and (d) 'generating verbs', for example, saying *decide* upon hearing the noun *decision*. The five top views of the brain show the five layers or cross-sections indicated in the lateral view at the left. Notice that the temporal lobes become evident in the third and fourth cross-sections.

The author described these results as follows:

> When subjects passively view nouns (a), the primary visual cortex lights up. When nouns are heard (b), the temporal lobes take command. Spoken nouns minus viewed or heard nouns (c) reveal motor areas used for speech. Generating verbs (d) requires additional neural zones, including those in the left frontal and temporal lobes corresponding roughly to Broca's and Wernicke's areas. (Raichle 1994, p. 60)

The linguistically most creative task, producing verbs given nouns, involves the most involvement of the brain's language centers.

2.3.   Dichotic listening

Dichotic listening is a test which may be administered in a phonetics laboratory as evidence of a person's hemisphere dominance for language. In dichotic listening, subjects listen to a two-track stereo recording, one track per ear, of a random list of syllables, numbers, or words, hearing different signals on each track, so that different syllables, numbers, or words are heard simultaneously in the two ears, for example, *ba* vs. *ka*, 75 vs. 59, *dog* vs. *cat*. See the diagram of dichotic listening in figure 10.3.

For most subjects, dichotic listening of such pairs reveals a **right ear advantage**: the signal heard in the right ear tends to be recalled. Right-handers have shown about 80% left-dominance for language in dichotic listening, whereas other

a. Subjects view written nouns.
b. Subjects hear spoken nouns.
c. Subjects speak nouns, with effects of a and b subtracted.
d. Subjects generate verbs from nouns.

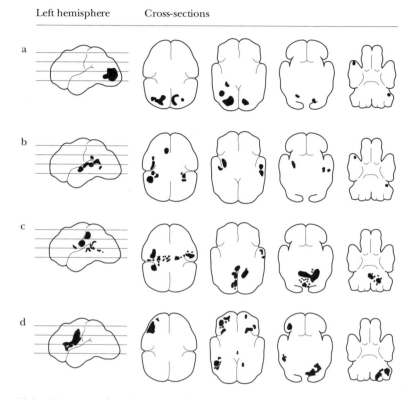

Figure 10.2   Diagram of PET/CAT analysis of four language activities
Source: Raichle 1994

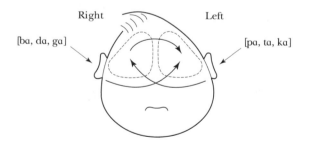

Figure 10.3   Diagram of dichotic listening

evidence, such as that of table 10.1 from the sodium amytal test, suggests this is 90% (Bryden 1988, p. 25).

This right ear advantage is attributable to hemisphere dominance for language. The language-dominant hemisphere (usually the left, that is) presumably pro-

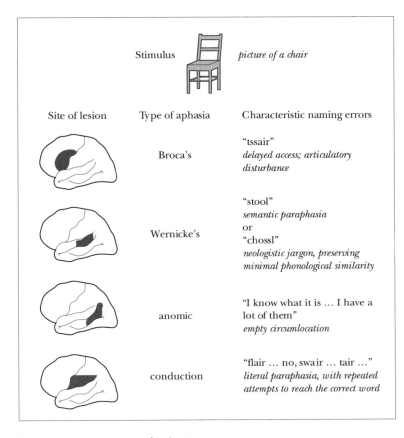

Figure 10.4   Four major types of aphasia
Source: Goodglass 1980

cesses the signal received from the contralateral (right) ear better, whether because of (a) better attention or more efficient processing by the dominant hemisphere, (b) interference by the dominant hemisphere in processing by the non-dominant hemisphere, and/or (c) the slight delay of time while the non-dominant hemisphere passes the signal via the corpus callosum to the dominant hemisphere. Thus dichotic listening shows the language-dominant hemisphere to be that opposite whichever ear tends more accurately to perceive the signal. Dichotic listening in children shows that hemisphere dominance for language is typically well established by about five years of age.

3. APHASIAS

The symptoms of aphasias tend to differ according to location of the injury in different parts of the brain, and may differ in extent or seriousness according to handedness and age. Two major types of aphasia are associated with injury to the two major language centers, Broca's area and Wernicke's area. See in figure 10.4. a diagram of the four major types of aphasia (Goodglass 1980), which shows for each type the location of injury in a patient, a language task for the patient (naming a picture, such as of a chair), and a typical response.

3.1.   Broca's aphasia

Injury in Broca's area results in a type of aphasia known as **Broca's aphasia,** which, as noted above in §2.1, is typically characterized by effortful speech and an absence of grammatical morphemes (so-called agrammatism). An example of Broca's aphasia is as follows. Asked to describe the week's events, the patient with an injury to Broca's area says (from Goodglass 1968):

> Yes . . . ah . . . Monday . . . ah . . . Dad and Peter Hogan, and Dan . . . ah . . . hospital . . . and, ah . . . Wednesday . . . Wednesday, nine o'clock and ah Thursday . . . ten o'clock ah doctors . . . two . . . two . . . and doctors and ah . . . teeth . . .

The short quotation illustrates both effortful speech and the absence of grammatical morphemes, which inserted (underlined) may yield well-formed sentences, such as 'Yes, <u>on</u> Monday Dad and Peter Hogan <u>were at the</u> hospital, and <u>then</u> Wednesday <u>at</u> nine o'clock . . .'.

3.2.   Wernicke's aphasia

Injury to Wernicke's area results in a type of aphasia known as **Wernicke's aphasia,** which is characterized by verbal fluency without coherence, as mentioned above. An example of Wernicke's aphasia is as follows. Asked to describe his difficulties since the brain injury, the patient says (Goodglass 1968):

> Well, I had trouble with . . . oh, almost everything that happened from the eh, eh . . . Golly, the word I can remember you know is ah . . . When I had the . . . ah biggest . . . ah . . . that I had trouble with, you know . . . that I had the trouble with, and I still have a . . . the ah different . . . The things I want to say . . . ah . . .

This short quotation illustrates a major difference from Broca's aphasia, the ready access to grammatical morphemes, but the corresponding difficulty in accessing lexical morphemes and so in creating coherent sentences. Wernicke's aphasia is also often associated with difficulty in comprehending language.

3.3.   Other types of aphasia

Quite specific language difficulties have been reported from specific injuries generally in Wernicke's area. Injury toward the rear of Wernicke's area, where it neighbors the occipital lobe, may result in **anomic aphasia,** inability to name things seen. Injury in the area between Wernicke's area and the motor strip results in **conduction aphasia,** seeming inability to pronounce words (difficulty 'conducting' information from Wernicke's area to the motor areas to implement pronunciation).

Aphasias may have extremely specific effects, such as inability to speak read words, but to speak instead synonyms and other closely associated words. A patient has been reported to say *balloon* for *parachute*, *insect* for *gnat*, and *duke* for *earl*. Other aphasic effects reported concern specifically nouns, verbs, or adjectives. **Alexia** or **acquired dyslexia** is the inability specifically to read (acquired dyslexia is distinct from dyslexia genetically acquired), and results particularly from injury behind Wernicke's area, adjacent to the occipital lobe. Injury to the right brain, in persons with general left-hemisphere dominance for language, has been reported to result in inability to understand intonation and the emotional tone of utterances, and in an inability to understand non-literal language, such as *kick the bucket* or *bury the hatchet*.

3.4. Other aphasic effects

3.4.1. Aphasias in left-handers
The aphasias of left-handers (or non-right-handers) are often not so severe or long-lasting as those of right-handers. This is presumably owed to the fact that hemisphere dominance in left-handers is usually not so complete, language functions often being more evenly distributed in left-handers. As a negative effect of bilateral distribution of language functions in left-handers, however, they are more likely to suffer aphasia from either right- or left-brain injury.

3.4.2. Aphasias in children
Children also may suffer less severe or long-lasting aphasia. Rough generalizations concerning childhood aphasia are that:

a. up to about four years of age, an injury to either the left or right brain is unlikely to result in long-lasting aphasia;
b. from about four to eleven, aphasias resulting from injury to either hemisphere can be overcome with time and practice, but
c. after about 11, some permanent effects may often result from injury to the language-dominant hemisphere.

Such results have been interpreted as showing three stages of development of language-hemisphere dominance:

a. birth to about 4: both hemispheres are equally engaged in language learning;
b. 4 to about 11: the left hemisphere becomes progressively dominant;

c.   after 11: the non-dominant hemisphere loses full capability for language learning.

The apparent loss of some capability for language learning of the left hemisphere after age 11 is evidence for a **critical period** for language, a time after which language learning becomes difficult or, some would argue, even impossible. The likelihood of a critical period for language learning is a topic of the next chapter.

4.   LANGUAGE AS AN ANALYTIC ACTIVITY

4.1.   General characteristics of the hemispheres

The two hemispheres generally appear to differ not just in their capability for language, but in their general 'personalities', as follows:

a.   Left hemisphere, typically better at:

1.   **analytic and temporal activities** such as:
2.   mathematics, jigsaw-type puzzles, music in musicians, alphabetic reading.

b.   Right hemisphere, typically better at:

1.   **intuitive and holistic activities** such as:
2.   recognizing faces, guessing games, music in non-musicians, logographic reading.

Brain injury in one of the two hemispheres thus has typical effects other than on language ability. A person with a right-hemisphere injury, whose language ability may be more or less intact, may have difficulty recognizing faces and, if a non-musician, may lose enjoyment for music. Persons with right-hemisphere injuries may sometimes seem generally emotionless (the left side of the face, by the way, is typically more emotionally expressive than the right). A person with a left-hemisphere injury, by contrast, besides suffering language loss, may have difficulty with mathematics and, if a musician – for whom presumably music has become an analytic activity – may lose some musical ability.

4.2.   Aphasic effects

The general characteristics of the hemispheres, the analyticness of the left and intuitiveness of the right, are somewhat consistent with aspects of the relation between language and the brain. Since language is analytically and temporally organized knowledge or behavior, it is not surprising that the language centers should be found typically in the left hemisphere, which characteristically favors such activities.

A couple of right-hemisphere linguistic abilities, which are revealed in aphasias resulting from right-hemisphere injury, were mentioned above: intonation, and non-literal language. Intonation carries emotional overtones of language such as doubt, certainty and neutrality about what is said, and non-literal language, for example idioms such as *kick the bucket* or *bury the hatchet*, are non-analytic and presumably holistically represented in the mental lexicon. The meaning of idioms is not based on an analysis of their structure; the meaning 'die', for example, does not follow from an analysis of *kick the bucket* into the separate parts *kick* and *the bucket* nor the fact that *the bucket* is the direct object of the verb *kick*. Instead, interpretation is holistic; the whole phrase just means 'die'. (The etymology goes back to death by suicide, in which the victim stands on a bucket, attaches the rope, then kicks away the bucket.)

One approach to therapy for those suffering from adult left-hemisphere aphasias is to provide practice in holistically and emotionally rich aspects of language, for example songs and poems, as a stimulus to enriching and restoring the linguistic abilities of the right hemisphere.

The mentioned difference between alphabetic and logographic reading (the former often impaired in left-hemisphere aphasias and the latter in right-hemisphere aphasias) is similarly explained. Alphabetic reading, as of a word such as *five*, may involve some analysis of its letter/sound relationships (f = [f], $i \ldots e$ = [ay], v = [v]), and assembling these temporally (left-to-right) into the meaning 'five' – an analytic, left-hemisphere-type, activity. A logographic representation of the same meaning is '5', which has no parts to recognize and assemble as [fayv], and may be interpreted nonanalytically and holistically as 'five' – an intuitive, right-hemisphere-type, activity.

4.3.   Analyticness of language learning

A number of findings about hemisphere activity in language learning reinforce this understanding of language as an analytic activity. In fact, perhaps language is the preeminent and most typical analytic activity of our species. Only three such findings are mentioned here.

First, from birth, babies tend to favor their right ear for speech sounds, whereas they favor their left ear for other types of sound (remember: contralateral control). If, for example, speakers in their cribs broadcast a speaking voice versus sounds such as music or street noises, babies will tend to orient themselves so that their right ear is closest to the voice-speaker.

Second, it was mentioned that at the outset of first-language learning, and up to about age four, both hemispheres are approximately equally engaged in the learning task. After about four years the left hemisphere becomes dominant. This is consistent with the initial intuitiveness but increasing analyticness of our knowledge of language. Recall, for example, the child's early learning of irregular past tense forms such as *went* and *saw* (which lack a recognizable past tense morpheme), which later for a time the child replaces by *goed* and *seed* (with their analytic structure).

Third, in contrast to child first-language learning, it has been found that in typical classroom foreign-language learning left-hemisphere dominance may be present in learners from the beginning. This is consistent with the greater analyticness of both the older students found in classrooms, and of the deductive methods often employed in teaching foreign languages in school. Finally, aphasias which often result in thorough or complete loss of second and foreign languages may less thoroughly affect the first language, knowledge of which has been registered and retained in the non-dominant, usually right, hemisphere.

Suggestions for
ADDITIONAL READING

Most introductory textbooks present the topic of brain and language, but among these especially the discussion in *An Introduction to Language* (1993), by Victoria Fromkin and Robert Rodman, should be mentioned. An introduction to the structure and organization of the brain is *Inside the Brain* (1980) by William H. Calvin and George A. Ojemann. Two books focussed on many of the topics of this chapter are *Neurolinguistics and Linguistic Aphasiology: an Introduction* (1987), and *Language: Structure, Processing, and Disorders* (1992), by David Caplan. A collection of articles on these and related topics is the *Handbook of Neurolinguistics* (1998) edited by Brigitte Stemmer and Harry Whitaker.

The evolutionary links between language and the brain are discussed in *The Symbolic Species: the Co-evolution of Language and the Brain* (1997) by Terrence W. Deacon. Presenting the method and some recent findings in computer-assisted positron emission tomography (PET) is 'Visualizing the mind', by Marcus E. Raichle, in *Scientific American* for April, 1994. Findings concerning the interesting but puzzling relationship of lateral preferences including handedness and behavior, including language, are thoroughly surveyed in *Lateral Preferences and Human Behavior* (1977) by Clare Porac and Stanley Coren.

IMPORTANT CONCEPTS AND TERMS IN THIS CHAPTER

- contralateral control
- cortex
- temporal lobe
- frontal lobe

- parietal lobes
- occipital lobes
- corpus callosum
- Sylvian fissure

- longitudinal fissure
- central fissure
- motor strip
- Broca's area
- Wernicke's area
- aphasia
- computer-assisted tomography
- CAT/CT scanning
- dichotic listening
- right ear advantage
- Broca's aphasia

- Wernicke's aphasia
- anomic aphasia
- conduction aphasia
- alexia
- acquired dyslexia
- critical period
- analytic activity
- temporal activity
- intuitive activity
- holistic activity

OUTLINE OF
CHAPTER 10

1. **Structure of the brain**
    1. General structure
    2. Language centers
2. **Types of evidence for language centers of the brain**
    1. Aphasias
    2. Clinical procedures
        1. Sodium amytal injection
        2. Computer-assisted tomography
    3. Dichotic listening
3. **Aphasias**
    1. Broca's aphasia
    2. Wernicke's aphasia
    3. Other types of aphasia
    4. Other aphasic effects
        1. Aphasias in left-handers
        2. Aphasias in children
4. **Language as an analytic activity**
    1. General characteristics of the hemispheres
    2. Aphasic effects
    3. Analyticness of language learning

EXAMPLES AND PRACTICE

1. Broca's and Wernicke's aphasias. Following are quotations from two persons suffering from aphasias (Allport 1983). Each is asked to describe a picture illustrating various 'household dangers'. One has Broca's aphasia and the other Wernicke's.

A. You never do that with a place there, you push it and do that . . . That is the same thing underneath; there's a little one to that as well. That you don't have to do either . . . I don't know what's happened to that, but it's taken that out. That is mm there without doing it, the things that are being done. . . .

B. Fire . . . open . . . matches . . . light matches . . . naughty boy . . . ha, ha, shut the door . . . knife . . . water . . . tablets . . . shut (pointing to high shelf) up . . . children . . .

Which of the above appears to represent Broca's aphasia and which Wernicke's aphasia? What are the linguistic characteristics of the two texts which indicate these major types of aphasia?

2. Five types of lateral preference. In addition to 88% left-brain preference for the language centers, humans show other lateral preferences, also generally for the right side, but in diminishing strength, (a)–(d), as follows:

a. right hand: 88%
b. right foot: 81%
c. right eye: 71%
d. right ear: 59%

These are percentages for a sample of 5,147 Americans and Canadians who completed a questionnaire about their preferences for hand, foot, eye and ear use (Porac and Coren 1977, p. 34).

Unfortunately, there is no simple way to discover in individuals their brain hemisphere preference for language. Using the following questions (adapted from those of Porac and Coren 1977), ask ten people including yourself about their lateral preferences for hand, foot, eye, and ear, and calculate the percentages for each.

The task tells nothing about language, but about other types of dominance. When fifty or more randomly selected subjects are averaged, they are likely to show the general reliability of the test, and the percentages above should generally be supported.

1. Which hand do you prefer:
    a. to write?
    b. to throw a ball?
2. Which foot do you prefer:
    a. to step first onto a chair?
    b. to kick a can?

3. Which eye do you prefer:
    a. to look through a telescope?
    b. to sight a gun?
4. Which ear do you prefer:
    a. to listen through a door?
    b. to place a single earphone?

EXAMPLE

3. Face recognition. The following task has little directly to do with language, but reinforces the important point about the functional asymmetries of the hemispheres, and, in comparison to the typical linguistic/analytic dominance of the left, the emotional/holistic dominance of the right, in tasks such as face recognition. Consider the two pairs of pictures of figure 10.5 (Bradshaw and Rogers 1993, p. 11). Each lower face is identical to that above it, except is left/right reversed. Ask yourself which face of these vertical pairs is happier: the top or bottom face?

Figure 10.5   Which faces, upper or lower, are happier?
Source: Bradshaw and Rogers 1993

Most people choose the bottom face of each pair, an effect which Bradshaw and Rogers explain as a perceptual preference: 'We take more notice of the face seen on the left' – the one most directly judged by our right hemispheres. The effect must be perceptual, because, with use of both positive and negative (reversed) prints of just two photographs, the person's left face appears on both the left and right in the pictures.

PRACTICE

Confirm the described effect by asking ten persons to look at the two pairs of pictures and say whether the upper or lower pair presents happier faces.

ADULT LANGUAGE LEARNING

This chapter concerns the most important issue concerning foreign and second language learning: whether after childhood we retain the natural ability to learn other languages as we did our first. Some reasons are noted for the obvious differences between child and adult language learning, and evidence is surveyed concerning whether we can or cannot learn languages in the natural way of children.

1. FOREIGN AND SECOND LANGUAGE LEARNING

Let's let 'after childhood' mean after the age of 12, and, for simplicity's sake, refer to persons over 12 as 'adults'. When as adults we take up the learning of another language, it is common to call this a 'foreign language'. However, there is a helpful distinction to be made between a foreign language and a 'second language'.

1.1. Foreign language learning

A **foreign language** is learned outside of the community in which it is spoken. In the US, for example, German and French are learned as foreign languages, whereas in Germany and France English is learned as a foreign language.

1.2. Second language learning

A **second language** is learned in a community in which it is a commonly used language. Thus immigrants to the US learn English as a second language, and English speakers study French in France as a second language. In the southwest of the US, it might be reasonable to speak of learning Spanish as a second rather than foreign language, and, in border communities of Mexico, English may be more reasonably thought of as a second than a foreign language.

1.3.   Major differences between foreign and second language learning

Learning languages as either second or foreign languages can be significantly different for at least four reasons. In second language learning:

a.   One can receive input for learning both inside and outside the classroom.
b.   One can readily put to use what is learned, as can the child learning its first language, so lots of naturalistic practice is possible.
c.   Also as for the child, what is learned may be essential for getting along in the community. A second language may even be essential for getting and keeping a job.
d.   Partly for these reasons, adults are ordinarily better motivated toward learning a second than a foreign language.

Therefore, when considering the issue of whether adults can learn languages as successfully as children, the better examples will be found in second rather than foreign language learning.

2.   REASONS FOR THE SUPERIORITY OF CHILD LANGUAGE LEARNING

There is little doubt that adults are, as a group, ordinarily less successful in learning languages, even second languages, than are children. Three sorts of evidence show this:

a.   Rate of success: almost all children fully succeed in learning their first language, whereas many adults fail to learn well the second languages which they study.
b.   Degree of success: children acquire their first language completely fluently and without accent, whereas most adult learners continue to make errors, however minor, and have a persistent accent in using their second language.
c.   Effort and spontaneity: adults typically have to work hard at second language learning, whereas children seem to acquire their first language almost effortlessly.

Three sorts of explanation may be offered for this generally observed superiority of children in language learning: cognitive, affective, and biological differences between children and adults.

2.1. ⌐Cognitive differences⌐

Cognitive differences have to do with knowledge and the processing of know-ledge. Language-learning adults are obviously different from children by already having knowledge of a language. In addition, they have analytic abilities, and metalinguistic knowledge: ability to talk about the language and how it works. Adults use this knowledge to try to figure things out. Finally, adults have expecta-tions about learning, including an expectation, generally, for things to make sense – and language often doesn't, at least superficially.

2.1.1. Transfer

Earlier knowledge influences the acquisition of later knowledge, and this in-fluence is termed **transfer**. Adults already know a language, whereas children acquiring their first language are, by contrast, completely naive in this regard.

Transfer in language learning can be good or bad, positive or negative. **Positive transfer** results when categories of second or foreign language are very similar to those of the first language. Such similarity is rarely perfect, though. Categories of the first and later-learned language are usually different in one of three ways, the third of which, reinterpreted categories, results in problems of transfer.

a.   Categories of the first language may be **absent** in the second language. These won't present a problem for learning the second language.
b.   Categories of the second language may be **new**, being absent in the first language. These present problems for learning, but not of transfer.
c.   Categories of the first language may be **reinterpreted** in the second, being similar in some ways but different in others. These may present persistent problems of transfer.

Here are examples of the three types concerning phonemic categories.

a.   A phoneme /æ/ is an absent category for English-speaking learners of Spanish, and a phoneme (trilled) /r/ is an absent category for Spanish-speaking learners of English.
b.   English /æ/ is a new category for Spanish-speaking learners of English, and Spanish trilled /r/ is a new category for English-speaking learners of Spanish.
c.   Spanish /d/ is a reinterpreted category for English-speaking learners of Spanish, and English /d/ is a reinterpreted category for Spanish-speaking learners of English. Recall that Spanish /d/ has the allophone [ð] and [d], of which the latter is absent after vowels, where [ð] occurs (chapter 3, §2.4), whereas both /d/ (= [d]) and /ð/ (= [ð]) are phonemes of English, both of which occur after vowels.

Reinterpreted categories result in **negative transfer**, also known as 'interference'. Here are two examples of negative transfer concerning phonemes.

    a. Spanish speaking learners of English transfer their /d/ into English and pronounce their allophone [ð] in words such as [liðər] 'leader' and [læðər] 'ladder' (instead of [lidər], [lædər]).

    b. English speaking learners of Spanish transfer their /d/ into Spanish and pronounce their allophone [d] in words such as [kada] 'each' and [lado] 'side' (instead of [kaða], [laðo]).

Here are two examples of negative transfer concerning categories other than phonemes:

    c. Spanish speaking learners of English transfer their possessive constructions with *de* 'of' as in *palacio del rey* 'King's palace' and thus underuse or lack altogether English possessives with -'s, saying *sister of Helen* not *Helen's sister*.

    d. English speaking learners of Spanish transfer their [__ NP] subcategorization feature for transitive verbs (chapter 7, §3.2), and thus say, for example, *llamé mi madre* instead of *llamé a mi madre*, omitting the Spanish direct object preposition *a* used with human direct objects.

Positive transfer, which contributes to success in adult language learning, usually goes unnoticed, but negative transfer results in errors. **Foreign accent,** which typifies adult language learning, is largely owed to negative transfer of phonological categories.

2.1.2. *Metalinguistic knowledge*

Adults have **metalinguistic knowledge**: conscious, analytic, knowledge of their use of language, and often also formal knowledge of the terminology of grammar. This gives them the means to learn in conscious and analytic ways seemingly quite different from those of children. They are also able, to some extent, to monitor their speech – comparing their utterances with their conscious knowledge, and correcting accordingly. The learning style of children is more intuitive and, it is reasonable to say, more 'natural'.

The different learning styles of adults and children have been distinguished as 'learning' and 'acquisition'. The conscious and analytic approach of adults has been termed **language learning,** and the unconscious and spontaneous approach of children **language acquisition.**

Some language teachers doubt whether adults, in speaking, can actually apply such rules as (for English speakers learning Spanish) 'the allophone of /d/ after vowels is [ð]' or even 'use *a* with human direct objects'. But learning such rules and using them in doing classroom practice and homework may be useful as a way to obtain experience with the language, and practice which child learners obtain naturally.

2.2. Affective differences

Besides cognitive differences, **affective differences,** having to do with attitudes, emotions and personality, distinguish children and adults as language learners. Perhaps the most important such affective differences between children and adults concern motivation and acculturation.

2.2.1. Motivation

It is not clear that children learning their first language can reasonably be said, even, to HAVE motivation in the usual sense of this word. Language learning is just something we DO as children – in the nature of a biological drive, like eating and sleeping. Eating and sleeping, like language, are essential for survival in human society, and we have evolved the natural motivaters hunger and sleepiness to ensure that we get them. In chapter 10, it was noted that the spontaneity of language learning is evidence for the innateness of language. For adults, two sorts of motivation can, to some extent, provide a substitute for this spontaneity or drive.

a. Integrative motivation. **Integrative motivation** is the desire to integrate into the society of speakers of the language one attempts to learn. Integrative motivation is often characteristic of successful foreign language learning, as of French by American university students.

b. Instrumental motivation. **Instrumental motivation** is the desire to get something practical or concrete from language learning, typically a job, higher pay, or higher social status. Instrumental motivation is often characteristic of second language learning. It is, for example, difficult to get a good job, or even to know where to find one, in a society in which you don't speak the language of the majority. Immigrants to Great Britain and the US have always had strong instrumental motivation to learn English.

2.2.2. Acculturation

First language learning is an aspect of enculturation: becoming a member of one's cultural group; every normal human being becomes a member of some culture, of which its language is an integral part and perhaps the richest expression. In first language learning, language learning is permeated with learning about family, society, and the world.

Adult language learning, by contrast, may have an aspect of **acculturation:** adding a culture, or at least becoming identified with a new social group. For those who don't welcome it, this can be a trying experience. After taking up residence in a foreign country, for example, many persons are known to suffer from culture shock, a result of which is profound longing for the homeland and for things of the homeland. Later, with success in learning the second language, they may feel anomie, alienation from even their own culture, and, eventually, a resulting feeling of culturelessness and isolation.

Because of the intrinsic relation between a language and its society or culture, advanced adult language learning has been reported to lead, sometimes, to a lesser degree of culture shock for learners. English speakers, for example, remark on the stress they feel with uncertainty about use of the French or Spanish familiar and polite pronouns (French *tu* and *vous*, Spanish *tu* and *usted*). Native French and Spanish speakers have little or no distress about making these distinctions. Adults learning English as a second language never master the use of slang and fast-speech variants in our casual language.

2.3. Biological differences

Biological difference between child and adult language learners may concern a **critical period** for language learning (chapter 10, §3.4.2). In learning, a 'critical period' is a time during which something must be learned, for after that time the neurophysiological basis for that learning will be lost or weakened. There is a critical period, for example, for many birds to learn to sing: they may sing incompletely and abnormally, or not at all, if they live their first months of life without hearing the characteristic singing of mature birds of their species (see chapter 12, §3.2.2). Nest-building in some bird species is similarly sensitive to a critical period. In humans, for example, it is known that certain vision problems of children, unless treated early, will be untreatable later in life.

Evidence of a critical period for first language learning are the facts that:

a. aphasias after age 11 or so often result in permanent loss of some language ability, and
b. persons who do not acquire their first language before this age often appear to be unable to do so with success later (see §3.1.4, below).

There are two main versions of the critical period hypothesis for language learning: the 'maturation' and 'exercise' versions.

a. **(Maturation version)** According to the maturation version of the critical period hypothesis, after the critical period (age 11 is reasonably its approximate end) we lose the biological basis to learn in the spontaneous and effortless way of children.

b. **(Exercise version)** According to the exercise version, there is a critical period for language learning, but this is valid only for learning the first language. The experience of learning a first language stimulates and sufficiently establishes the biological basis for subsequent learning of other languages.

According to the exercise version of the critical period hypothesis, adults should be as able as children, at least biologically, to learn languages. The maturation version, by contrast, provides an explanation of the seeming difficulty of adult language learning.

3. EVIDENCE THAT ADULTS CAN AND CANNOT LEARN LIKE CHILDREN

There is evidence on both sides of the issue of whether adults retain the natural language learning powers of children. Here we consider first the evidence against this, and then the evidence for it.

3.1 Evidence that adults cannot learn like children

3.1.1. *Variable success*

The clearest evidence against the proposition is the variable success of strenuous adult language learning in comparison to the near perfect success of effortless child language learning. Cases are always mentioned of adults who live for years in a foreign country, surrounded by a language which they try to learn with only limited success. But within a few months their children, in the same circumstances, may master the new language so well that they are called upon to help their parents as translators.

Some who believe they know of unusual cases of fully successful adult language learning, if foreign accent is ignored, say that these prove that adults have the necessary ability, and only usually lack sufficient opportunity including a suitably supportive environment with personal circumstances that free them, like child learners, from other responsibilities. Opponents say that such exceptional individuals only 'prove the rule'. Some claim, in fact, that examination would show that these adults have unremediable shortcomings in their command of subtleties of morphology or syntax.

3.1.2. *Significance of motivation*

Children learn their first language so naturally that they don't need any motivation for the task. There is evidence, however, that in areas where a language is learned as a second language, as, for example, English is learned in French Canada or French in English-speaking communities in or near French Canada, integrative motivation is particularly important. Thus English speakers who don't particularly like French Canadians tend not to be so successful at learning French, but those who do succeed at a better rate.

Consider the following research findings from Canada (Gardner 1980). Hundreds of students of grades 7–11 took the Modern Language Aptitude Test (MLAT), and also completed a 98-item questionnaire called the 'Attitude Motivation Index' (AMI). The MLAT is a standard test of word-memory and linguistic-analytic skills which has been shown to predict, with significant confidence, the likelihood of success in language learning in school. The AMI questionnaire elicited students' attitudes toward and motivation for learning French, including attitudes toward Canadian French and European French people. The MLAT and AMI scores were then compared with the students' grades actually obtained in high-school French classes, and with each other. Table 11.1 presents the resulting

Table 11.1 Comparison of three measures of language learning ability

Area	AMI and grades	MLAT and grades	AMI and MLAT	Three-way correlation
1	0.43	0.59	0.23	0.66
2	0.42	0.23	0.16	0.45
3	0.15	0.50	0.05	0.52
4	0.45	0.48	0.20	0.60
5	0.35	0.39	−0.03	0.52
6	0.44	0.21	0.09	0.47
7	0.23	0.27	0.04	0.47
Median	0.37	0.41	0.13	0.52

Source: Gardner 1980

correlations for 11th-grade students in seven regions of Canada, and the median correlations for students of all grades in all seven regions. Higher numbers are better correlations. The higher the number, the better the correlation.

Notice that attitudes and motivation as expressed in the little AMI questionnaire correlate with grades generally about as well as does the much more lengthy MLAT. The AMI and MLAT don't correlate well with each other, but the combination of AMI and MLAT correlates with grades much better than does either of these alone.

3.1.3. Fossilizations

Even adults who <u>acquire fluent command</u> of a second language are typically perceived to make <u>persistent and seemingly uncorrectable errors of usage of sorts unnoticed in child language learning.</u> Such persistent errors have been called fossilizations. Some examples are:

a. Native speakers of Chinese who are very fluent second language speakers of English often persist in mixing up the third-person pronouns *he/she* and *him/her*.

b. Native speakers of English who are very fluent second language speakers of Spanish typically fail, nevertheless, to use Spanish subjunctive verbs, or use them incorrectly.

c. Native speakers of various non-Indoeuropean languages who are very fluent speakers of English often continue to make errors in the use of the English definite article *the*. The grammar of English *the* is indeed complex and often puzzling, but the fact remains that four-year-old native speaking children have almost errorless command of *the*.

In fact, there is little evidence that fossilizations persist when the learner benefits from continued good teaching and relevant practice. But most advanced adult learners don't.

3.1.4. *Feral children*

There have been cases of abandoned and isolated children who grow up without the normal conditions for language learning, and so without language. These are termed **feral** ('wild') **children**. An American child of six and a half was discovered in 1937 to have been isolated from language acquisition. With care and instruction, however, she is said to have passed through the usual stages of language acquisition at a rapid pace, and within two years was 'not easily distinguished from ordinary children of her age' (Brown 1958: 192). Two cases of feral children discovered at a later age, near the end of or after the hypothetical critical period, are particularly well known.

Until recently, the most famous case was a boy of 12 named **Victor**, who came to the attention of authorities in Aveyron, France, in 1798. Victor seems to have been abandoned in the woods some years before, perhaps after an attempt to kill him (he had the scar of a severe wound on his neck). He had no command of language, and subsequently, even after years of patient instruction, was able to acquire little.

A 1970s case in the US concerned a girl known as **Genie**, who from her second year until she was 13 had been isolated by her parents and deprived of normal human contacts by which she might have acquired language. Despite several years of language instruction accompanied by attempts also to assist her social development, and despite initial evidence of good progress, Genie never progressed much beyond child-like command of language.

At age 13, Genie's syntax was at the two-word stage, about like that of an 18-month-old child. Though her command of syntax improved in the next three and a half years, until she was producing complex sentences like (d)–(f), below, she never showed more than sporadic use of the frequent grammatical morphemes of English, and her linguistic development seemed to remain at the telegraphic stage. Following are some of her sentences at age 18, five years after her 'discovery' (Curtis 1977). Notice the absence of grammatical morphemes *doesn't*, *the*, *a*, etc. in these sentences.

EXAMPLES OF GENIE'S SENTENCES AT AGE 18

a. Ellen not work at school.
b. Mama not have baby grow up.
c. I want you open my mouth.
d. Mr. W say put face in big swimming pool.
e. Genie upset teacher said outside.
f. Teacher said Genie have temper tantrum outside.

It is also of interest that Genie was found to be right-dominant for language, when, given her and her family's right-handedness, she normally would have

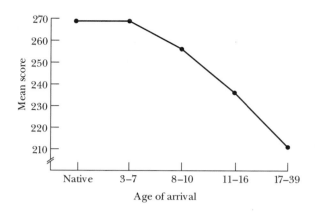

Figure 11.1   Graph of relationship between age of arrival in the US and total score on
the test of English grammatical morphology
Source: Johnson and Newport 1989

been expected to be left-dominant, like 90% of right-handers. An interpretation
of this fact is that, because her natural left-brain language centers were not
exercised in the critical period, these became unavailable for subsequent use, and
Genie had to depend for language learning on her less adept right brain.

While Victor and Genie seem to support the correctness of the critical period
hypothesis – they support the maturation version but offer no evidence for the
exercise version – some doubt remains whether their language learning difficulties are strictly the result of loss of linguistic ability or may be additionally or
entirely attributed to more pervasive and even more devastating damage to general learning ability, personality, and social personhood.

3.1.5.   Research on learning

Recently there has been a lot of research attempting to test the language learning ability of adults. Consider the following findings from one of these studies
(Johnson and Newport 1989). Forty-six native speakers of Chinese and Korean,
living in the US for from 3 to 26 years, were given a test of their mastery of 12
points of English grammatical morphology. The most important results of this
research are seen in the graphs of figures 11.1–3.

Figure 11.1. This graph compares age of arrival in the United States with
scores on the test. Notice in the graph both the general correlation between age
of arrival and test scores, and the sudden decline in scores for subjects who
arrived after age 7. Age of arrival and length of residence in the US are said not
to correlate with one another, so results cannot be explained by the latter. Nor
did attitudes of the subjects, as expressed in a simple questionnaire, correlate
with the language test results.

Figure 11.2. This graph compares scores for each of the 12 points of English
morphology for 6 age-of-arrival groups of Chinese and Korean-speaking subjects
and one group of native speakers of English. The same steady decline in scores is

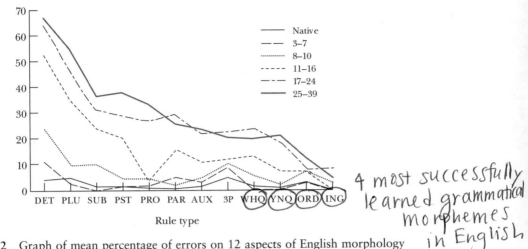

4 most successfully learned grammatical morphemes in English for L2

Figure 11.2   Graph of mean percentage of errors on 12 aspects of English morphology by six age-of-arrival groups

DETerminer, PLUral, SUBcategorization, PaST tense, PROnouns, PARticles, AUXiliaries, 3rd Person singular, WH-Questions, Yes/No Questions, wORDer, ING-progressive suffix

Source: Johnson and Newport 1989

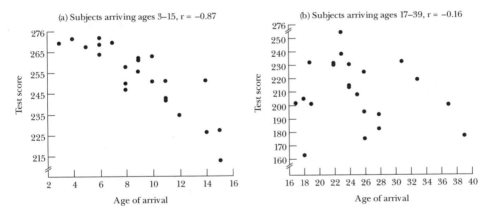

Figure 11.3   Graphs of test scores in relation to age of arrival for subjects before and after puberty

Source: Johnson and Newport 1989

seen, generally, for each of the 12 grammar points in relation to age of arrival. Notice that those who arrived in the US before age 8 generally do as well as native speakers, and those who arrived from ages 8–10 do almost as well.

Figure 11.3. The left-hand graph here shows test scores for subjects who arrived from ages 3 to 15. Notice how these array themselves diagonally in the graph according to age of arrival, with the earlier arrival age correlating with higher scores. The right-hand graph shows test scores for those who arrived after age 15. Here all the scores are relatively low, and there is no apparent correlation with age, suggesting that after 15 something other than age is the determining factor in language learning.

In another recent study (Bongaerts et al. 1997) 5 native speakers of Dutch, who had begun their study of English at age 12, were judged to be native speakers of British English by judges hearing tape recordings of their speech, randomly included among recordings which also included native speakers of British English and clearly non-native speakers who were also native speakers of Dutch.

Experimental results are somewhat mixed, and controversial. It remains unclear both whether convincing cases of adult or post-critical period language learning exist, and what would constitute convincing evidence of such cases.

3.2.   Evidence that adults can learn like children

3.2.1.   Creative construction

Adult learners are usually reluctant to make mistakes (another affective difference from children that should be noted). They typically avoid occasions in which they have to take chances in using their foreign or second language. When they do, however, they give evidence of **creative construction**, the parallel in adult language learning of the child's creative utterances such as *mommy sock* and *I have not rided a horse*. Like children, adult learners are observed to test hypotheses about the language, which results in novel and 'creative' utterances.

EXAMPLES OF ADULT CREATIVE CONSTRUCTION

They won't have no fun.	The bird was shake his head.
He putted the cookie there.	We too big for the pony.
He put it in the his room.	After that we walked, we felt warm.
He not play anymore.	I bought in Japan. (Dulay et al. 1982)

3.2.2.   Natural orders

Natural orders are patterns of development of grammar which occur in learners without or despite instruction. For example, both adults and children learning English as a second language – like first-language learning children, in fact – go through a stage in which their negative sentences have simply a negative word, *no*, *not* or *don't*, before the verb, for example, *I no like this one*; *I don't can explain*; *You no swim*. There is evidence that children and adults are similar in their patterns of mastery of grammatical morphology. See figure 11.4 (Bailey et al. 1974), a graph which compares a group of 73 adults, ages 17–55, and three groups of children (total 152), ages 5–8, all learning English as a second language in the US, according to their relative accuracies in using 8 English grammatical morphemes. Notice that the grammatical morphemes have been

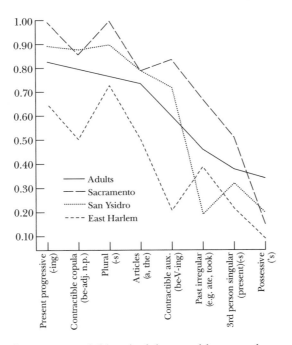

Figure 11.4 Graph comparing child and adult second-language learner relative accuracies for eight English grammatical morphemes
Source: Bailey et al. 1974

listed, left-to-right, according to the adult order of mastery. The rough similarity between adults and children is somewhat apparent in the graph, and said to be statistically significant.

3.2.3. *Successful adult learners*

It was mentioned above that successful adult learners are rare, and fully successful adult learners, who achieve a command of a second language equivalent to that of native speakers, may not even exist. If they do, however, and if there are enough such successful cases that they cannot be considered mere oddities, they may be considered to disprove the proposition that adults lack the language acquisition powers of children.

The example of the Polish–British novelist **Joseph Conrad** (1857–1924) is often mentioned. Conrad is believed to have known only a few words of English when he arrived in London at the age of 20. Although he eventually settled in England and wrote over a dozen English novels including *Lord Jim* and *Heart of Darkness*, he always spoke English with a prominent Polish accent.

We have seen that language is a complex and often abstract system of knowledge, while an accent may reflect nothing more than one's command of the medium of language, speech. Readers may know of persons like Conrad whose late-acquired non-native ability in English is notable only in their 'foreign accent'. Still at issue is whether such persons always have subtle and rarely noticeable deficits in their knowledge of syntax (such as that a sentence like 'Who did you know the book that wrote?' is ungrammatical).

Suggestions for
ADDITIONAL READING

Topics of this chapter are extended in a number of good textbooks in the field of second language acquisition, of which among the best and most recent are *Second Language Acquisition: an Introductory Course* (1994) by Susan Gass and Larry Selinker, *An Introduction to Second Language Acquisition Research* (1991) by Diane Larsen-Freeman and Michael H. Long, and *In Other Words: the Science and Psychology of Second Language Acquisition* (1994) by Ellen Bialystok and Kenji Hakuta.

Evidence for the existence of a critical period for second language learning is reviewed in *Language Acquisition after Puberty* (1994) by Judith R. Strozer. Focussed on the social aspects of second language acquisition is *Sociolinguistics and Second Language Acquisition* (1989) by Dennis Preston, and on the contribution of linguistic theory in this field is *Linguistics and Second Language Acquisition* (1993) by Vivian Cook. Genie's story is told by Russ Rymer (1992) as 'Silent childhood' in *The New Yorker*. Victor's story is told by Harlan Lane (1976) in *The Wild Boy of Aveyron*.

IMPORTANT CONCEPTS AND TERMS IN THIS CHAPTER

- foreign language
- second language
- cognitive differences
- transfer
- positive transfer
- absent category
- new category
- reinterpreted category
- negative transfer
- foreign accent
- metalinguistic knowledge
- monitor
- language learning
- language acquisition
- affective differences

- integrative motivation
- instrumental motivation
- acculturation
- culture shock
- anomie
- critical period
- maturation version
- exercise version
- fossilization
- feral children
- Victor
- Genie
- creative construction
- natural orders
- Joseph Conrad

OUTLINE OF CHAPTER 11

EXAMPLES AND PRACTICE

EXAMPLE

1. Creative construction. Creative construction in language learning is saying things which could not possibly have been heard, or learned by imitation. For example, children learning English as a first language say things like *I didn't goed* and *It's a bad news*. Typically, such creative constructions are based on generalization of patterns of the language being learned. For example, the error *goed* follows the pattern of so-called regular verbs, like *open* and *walk*, which form their past tense by adding /d/ to the basic form: *opened* and *walked*. *Didn't goed* shows mastery of the rule of *do*-insertion, but absence of knowledge that *did* is marked for past tense, which therefore need not be marked in the main verb, *go*.

PRACTICE

For five of the following seven common errors of adult learners of English, explain briefly, as in the example above, why the error might be expected. Hints are given for 1–3.

1. He said me no. (Consider verbs with meaning similar to *say*.)
2. I cannot fine it. (Consider the pronunciation of words like *find* when the following word begins with a consonant.)
3. We did not reach. (Consider the pattern of verbs with meaning similar to *reach*.)
4. Your both hands are dirty.
5. My foot is paining.
6. Write it with ink.
7. He prevented me to go.

EXAMPLE

2. Transfer. Transfer is relying, consciously or not, on forms and rules of one's native language to make guesses about how another language works. This can be good or bad depending on the degree of similarity between the two.

Learners typically expect syntax to be similar in another language, but not bound morphology. They may be misled by 'false cognates': words of the other language that sound or look like words of their own language. English speakers, for example, expect the Spanish word *parentela* to mean 'parent', but it just means 'relative/kin (fem.)'; similarly, Spanish speakers expect English *parent* to mean 'relative/kin'. Consider Spanish sentences 2–7 below. A literal word-by-word translation is given for each; you can guess what the free translation would be.

PRACTICE

(a) Give the free English translation of Spanish sentences 2–7, and then suggest an error that would be expected because of transfer of the Spanish language forms (lexicon, morphology, or syntax). One of 2–7 is very like English, and should result in positive transfer. The first item is completed, as an example.

1. Juan está estudiando para medico.
   John is   studying for   doctor
   Free translation: 'John is studying to be a doctor'.
   Predicted transfer error: 'John is studying for doctor.'

2. Mi hermano no ha vivido en México antes.
   my brother no has lived in Mexico before
3. El está detrás de la mesa.
   he is behind of the table
4. El muchacho y su primo están estudiando la lección para mañana.
   the boy   and his cousin are studying the lesson for tomorrow.

5. Los niños son amados de sus padres.
   the children are loved of their parents
6. Él quiere que yo vaya.
   he wants that I go
7. Asistimos en una conferencia.
   attended(we) in a lecture

(b) Given their similarity of form to English words, an English speaker will guess that meanings of the following words and phrases are also similar. Give the English 'false cognate,' and, using a Spanish dictionary, the actual meanings of 8–15.

8.	simpatico	12.	ropa
9.	en efecto	13.	vaso
10.	contestar	14.	contento
11.	jornalero	15.	limpio

EXAMPLE

3. Absent, new, and reinterpreted categories. Examples of these types of language comparison were illustrated in §2.1.1, above.

PRACTICE

For English and another language you know or have studied, try to list additional examples of each of these three categories, but especially in realms of language other than phonology, for example, morphological categories (of word formation, for example, noun plurals and verb tense), and syntactic categories (of sentence formation, for example, negative sentences and questions). Discuss your examples in terms of their seeming difficulty for learners of either language, in your personal experience and from observing other learners.

ANIMAL LANGUAGES?

This chapter presents some language-like and nonlanguage-like forms of natural communication in three animal species, monkeys, birds, and bees, with emphasis on the evidence for the interpretation of these signs. It considers the results and success of research in which chimpanzees have been taught aspects of human language.

1. ANIMAL LANGUAGES?

1.1. Two important questions

In this chapter as in ordinary usage, let 'animal' mean 'non-human animal'. Regarding communication by animals, in this sense, there are two important questions the answers to which may provide insight into the fundamental nature of human language:

a. Do animals have human-like languages?
b. If not, can they be taught such languages?

Regarding the first question, it seems clear that animals lack human-like languages, which are characteristic of the human species or of human societies. Regarding the second question, if animals cannot be taught human languages, then it appears that languages are truly characteristic of our species, and explained by factors unique to human nature and evolution.

Indeed, in ingenious research of recent decades, animals have learned some aspects of human language. However, there is a lot of controversy about the extent and significance of these achievements. The issue importantly reflects on the basic nature of human language: whether this is a unique ability of the human species or just an elaboration – if complex – of more general cognitive abilities which we share, if differentially, with other species. This question stimulates research on the nature and structure of human language as well as on other aspects of human and animal knowledge.

1.2.   Sign, communication, language

Recall that a **sign** is 'a relation between a form and a meaning'; **communication** is 'the use of signs'; and **language** is 'a sign system'. Animals certainly communicate with signs, and certainly their use of signs is systematic. In this sense animals certainly have languages, though it seems equally certain that these are not languages of the highly structured and unboundedly expressive nature of human languages.

2.   SIGNS SHARED BY HUMANS AND OTHER ANIMALS

Humans share some signs with non-human animals: iconic and indexical signs whose physical and emotional bases we also share with them. For example, see as figure 12.1 the picture of an angry dog (Darwin 1872 [1955, p. 3]). Two things which a human may notice about this dog are (a) the hair standing up on its back, and (b) its stiff tail. These signs (forms with meanings), which mean to us and to other dogs that the dog is angry, are iconic or indexical signs. That is, they are actual characteristics of, or characteristics naturally associated with, the

Figure 12.1   Dog giving 'I'm angry' signs
Source: Darwin 1872

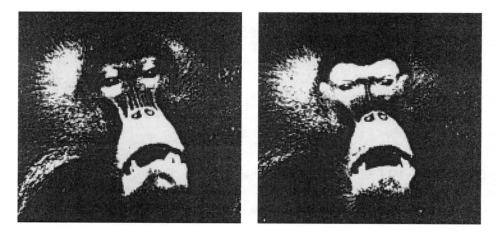

Figure 12.2   Gelada monkey, at right, giving 'I'm angry' sign
Source: Andrew 1965

dog's anger. Probably we readily recognize these signs in dogs because they result from the same sort of bodily arousal and preparation for a fight that also affect us, when we are angry or threatened. For example, it is a universal of human and animal communication that hostility is communicated by lower rather than higher pitched vocalizations, perhaps because of the indexical association of lower pitch with a bigger, more threatening body (Morton and Page 1992, p. 104).

For a second example, see figure 12.2, two pictures of a Gelada monkey (Andrew 1965). Both faces look quite fierce, but only the right-hand picture shows a Gelada monkey more likely to be given space by another Gelada monkey. This face presents a sign, obvious to other Geladas, that the monkey is angry. Notice the light coloring above the eyes, which appear when the monkey stiffens its scalp, and lowers its brow. The natural basis of this sign may not be obvious, but the sign is presumably indexical nevertheless, resulting from the lowering of the brow which comes with narrowing the eyes and focusing vision, both naturally associated with the presence or approach of an enemy.

Most animal communication, it seems, uses signs of this iconic/indexical sort, which are also found in the human species, as when we raise our eyebrows when we see something surprising, look down when embarrassed, and narrow our eyes when physically threatened. Other humans may get the meaning of these signs quite clearly, but surely they are the basis of a small if important (and mainly unconscious) proportion of human communication. Such signs are not ordinarily voluntary in humans, and presumably are rarely if ever so in animals. On the contrary, the signs of our language, morphemes combined as words and sentences, are seemingly voluntary in humans. As emphasized in chapter 1 (§3.4), these are **symbolic signs**, having entirely conventional association with their meanings. Furthermore, we use them with **displacement**, to comment on events past and future which may even be imaginary, and on emotions which we may not even feel.

3. COMMUNICATION IN THREE ANIMAL SPECIES

3.1. Vervet monkeys

Monkeys of course have human-like characteristics which have sometimes been thought to underlie language: imaginative intelligence, lengthy dependence on the family, large and structured social groups, and the ability to vocalize. In addition to posture, facial expression, and other channels of communication which they share with humans, some species of monkeys are thought to use as many as 30 'calls' (barks, squeals, grunts, etc.) with meanings (here perhaps somewhat inappropriately expressed in human terms) such as 'Hello!', 'It's me', 'I'm contented', 'I'm discontented', 'Look out for the eagle!', and 'Look out for the snake!'. Distinct cries for different predators and other threats are the largest number of these calls. The effectiveness of the calls is apparent in the fact that others in the group who hear them behave appropriately. Hearing the 'snake' call, for example, vervet monkeys gather round and search the ground, and hearing the 'eagle' call they look to the sky and run for cover. Hearing the 'leopard' call, they climb trees.

3.1.1. Language-like aspects of vervet calls

The 'snake', 'leopard', and 'eagle' calls of vervets have been described (by Seyfarth et al. 1980, p. 802) as follows:

   a. Snake: 'high-pitched chutter'
   b. Leopard: 'short tonal call'
   c. Eagle: 'low-pitched staccato grunt'

These vocal signs appear to illustrate **arbitrariness**, the human language-like use of **symbolic** signs. A 'high-pitched chutter', for example, seems neither snake-like nor to be naturally associated with snakes.

In the human language characteristic of **cultural transmission**, signs are learned. The calls of young vervets gradually increase in accuracy: young vervets but never adults may, for example, give the 'eagle' call upon seeing a harmless large bird such as a stork. This alone does not prove learning. More evidence for learning, however, is that infant vervets appear to check the response of adults before responding to alarm calls themselves. Also as in human language learning, comprehension precedes production: young vervets learn to respond appropriately to the signs before they give them accurately (Seyfarth and Cheney 1986, p. 1656).

3.1.2. *Non-language-like aspects of vervet calls*

Since the predator calls appear to be used only when the threat that they announce is real or is thought to be (Cheney and Seyfarth 1990, p. 196), the use of these signs doesn't illustrate the human language characteristic of **displacement**. Other signs are rarely used deceptively, or falsely, as when a monkey presents the posture and other sign of submissiveness, then bites a rival misled by these signs. This is not clear evidence of displacement, but might present a secondary, if opposite, use of the undisplaced sign. Nor is there evidence for **openness**: new signs don't appear. Also, the calls appear to be unanalyzed wholes – you can't break them down into pieces of sound which get arranged differently in the different calls, so they appear to lack **duality**. Finally, there is no evidence for **creativity**: no novel and extended use of the calls or of combinations of calls to express new meanings.

3.2. Birds

Birds do a lot of vocalizing, especially just before sunrise, before most of us are up. It is natural to ask 'What are they talking about?' assuming, indeed, that they may be appropriately said to be talking. Birds can produce a variety of vocal sounds, and many species don't just talk, but sing, sometimes in duets. The nightingale is thought to sing as many as 200 different songs (Todt and Hultsch 1996, p. 79).

It appears that bird-song (and the rhythmic pecking or drumming of woodpeckers) often has two purposes: to mark the territory of the singer and to attract a mate. Evidence that singing is for mating is that, upon mating, birds cease a lot of their singing. Evidence that the song is for marking territory is that birds sing more when a strange bird enters their chosen territory.

3.2.1. *Language-like aspects of bird-songs and calls*

Young birds gradually acquire perfection in their songs, depending on experience with adult singing, which could be evidence of **cultural transmission**, or learning. Some chaffinches appear to improvise on songs they learn by imitation, which shows some **creativity** (Bright 1984, p. 95). Another language-like aspect of bird-song which suggests learning is **dialects**. Dialects are regional varieties of a language, and the songs of several bird species have been found to vary from region to region, much like dialects of a language (Mundinger 1982). Presumably the dialectal aspects of song must be learned, even if the basic song is known by genetic transmission. Finally, there is evidence for a **critical period**, a time during which exposure to adult song is necessary for subsequent mastery (Kroodsma 1982, pp. 14–18).

3.2.2. *Non-language-like aspects of bird-songs and calls*

Different species sing different songs, and despite the evidence for cultural transmission mentioned above, the songs appear to be largely innate, with cultural

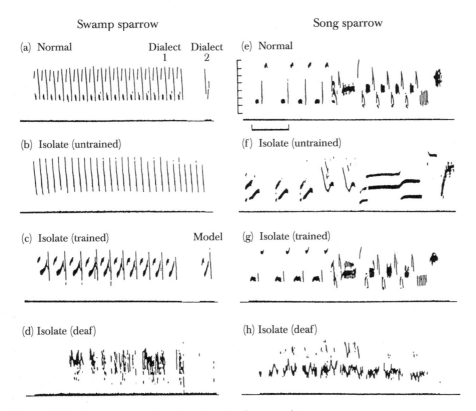

Figure 12.3 Sparrow song produced under four conditions

Source: Reprinted by permission of Lawrence Erlbaum Associates, Inc. from 'The instinct to learn' by Peter Marler, in *The Epigenesis of Mind* (1991)

transmission serving to improve and elaborate the song. See as figure 12.3 the comparison of the acoustic images of the songs of two species of sparrow (Marler 1991, p. 49). The first row of this figure shows normal song, in the wild, and the second that produced by sparrows unexposed to adult singing. The obvious similarities between these two rows can be attributed to innateness of the song. The third row shows the song of sparrows who heard only recorded songs of their species, and the fourth the song of those who have no aural experience of singing. The role of learning is apparent in comparisons of the first row with these other rows.

Birds also have calls (whistles, chirps, screeches, etc.), some of which appear to have specific associations if not meanings: 'alarm', 'food', 'predator', etc. An interesting example concerns the comparison of 'mobbing' and 'aerial predator' calls of species including the wren and robin (Thorpe 1961; Bright 1984). The effect of mobbing calls is that all the birds of the flock gather round, for example when an owl is seen in a tree nearby. Mobbing calls consist of a sharp chirp, a quick rise and fall of pitch and intensity. See at the left in figure 12.4 an acoustic representation of the mobbing call. There is an **indexical** nature to this call: its

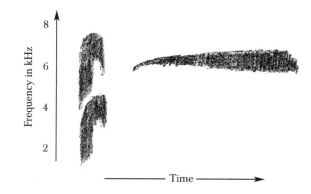

Figure 12.4   Acoustic images of mobbing and aerial predator bird-calls

form has a natural if indirect association with its meaning. Because it becomes loud quickly, and at low pitch, it is perceived immediately by the ear nearest the call and a split-second later, differently, by the other ear, which makes it possible to calculate the direction of origin of the mobbing call. This localizability of the call makes its meaning, 'mobbing', or 'Gather round!' effective.

Calls which warn of aerial predators such as hawks are somewhat opposite in form, but similar in their indexical nature. See at the right in figure 12.4 an acoustic representation of such a warning call. It begins relatively higher in pitch, and increases slowly in loudness. This makes it difficult for predators (other than owls) to locate the source of the call, and birds which respond to the call, by taking cover, don't need to know its source. Because it becomes perceptible slowly and at relatively high pitch, when such a call is perceived by one ear it tends to be perceived nondistinctly by the other. The calling bird warns others without giving away its own location. The nonlocalizability of the call is in natural or indexical association with its 'predator warning' meaning.

3.3.   Bees

Bees are insects, with tiny insect brains, yet their characteristic system of communication has an aspect of complexity missing in other species. Bees put four signs together in a **'tail-wagging dance'** about something very important in bee life as it is in ours: food. This four-part sentence of the European Carniolan bee is known from ingenious research in the 1940s by **Karl von Frisch** (Frisch 1993).

The bee goes out and finds food. If the food is a hundred yards or more away, it returns to the hive and repeatedly 'dances' a figure-8 in the pattern shown in figure 12.5, a complex sign with four meanings:

a.   The direction of the diagonal part of the dance tells the direction to food, calculated in relation to the angle of the hive wall to the sun.

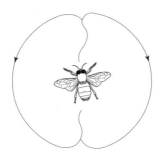

Figure 12.5   Figure-8 dance of the honeybee

b. The duration of the diagonal portion of the dance tells how far the food is: the longer the farther.
c. The bee's tail-wagging and wing-buzzing during the diagonal tells how good the food is: the more wagging/buzzing the better.
d. Finally, the bee carries some of the food, such as flower pollen, on its body, and during the dance other bees come up and have a taste for themselves.

3.3.1.   Language-like aspects of the bee's dance

The dance shows some **displacement**, and some limited **creativity** too, of a sort. The bee has to perform the dance somewhat removed in time and space from the food, though not by more than a few minutes or more than a few hundred meters. The creativity of the dance is limited to different degrees of distance, direction, and quality. Finally, knowledge of the dance may be somewhat **culturally transmitted**, but not much, as evidenced by the fact that young bees tend, more than adults, to misunderstand the direction and distance messages: after witnessing the dance, they don't fly as accurately to the food as they do later in life, upon getting more experience.

3.3.2.   Non-language-like aspects of the bee's dance

Arbitrariness is generally lacking, since the separate signs of the dance are not purely symbolic signs. The message about the nature of the food which inspires the dance is perfectly **iconic**, actual particles of the food carried on the body of the bee. Other signs of the dance appear to be **indexical**:

a. the angle of the diagonal is in regular if indirect relation to direction to the food;
b. the rate of completion of the diagonal is in regular relation to time, hence distance, to the food;
c. the amount of tail-wagging is in regular natural relation to the quality of the food.

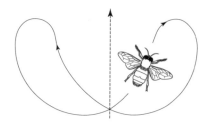

Figure 12.6   Open figure-8 dance of the Italian honeybee

Finally, the dance involves little if any **cultural transmission,** as noted above. Instead, the dance is known mostly by genetic transmission. There are two sorts of quite clear evidence for this:

First, bees raised apart from the hive and without experience of the dance, and so without opportunity to learn it, can perform and interpret the dance when they are restored to the hive.

Second, is a difference between gray Carniolan and striped Italian bees. The Italian bee does the same tail-wagging dance as the Carniolan bee, but for short distances it dances an elongated or open figure-8 pattern shown in figure 12.6, in which the opening points the way to food (dotted arrow). When the two varieties are cross-bred, the latter dance is mostly known only by the offspring that also have the striped marking of the Italian bee, which is evidence that knowledge of the dance is part of the genetic material that also provides the cross-bred bee's stripes.

4.   TEACHING LANGUAGES TO ANIMALS

It appears that animals in the wild don't have much to say to one another, at least compared to humans, who are talking most of their waking hours. And what animals do say is quite simply expressed, largely with iconic and indexical signs. Perhaps, however, they are capable of learning human languages. This hypothesis has been tested with aspects of the manual language of American deaf communities, known as **ASL,** taught to chimpanzees and to a gorilla, and more recently with potentially human-like laboratory languages taught to chimpanzees.

4.1.   ASL

ASL, **American Sign Language,** is the manual-gestural language of American deaf communities. It should be emphasized that ASL is a fully expressive language, with all the lexical and grammatical complexity of other human languages. There is a popular but false idea that ASL signs are iconic or indexical modelings of meanings by the hands. The sign for 'eat', indeed, is **iconic,** formed

Eat   Candy   Jealous

Figure 12.7   Three ASL signs: 'eat', 'candy', and 'jealous'
Source: Reprinted by permission of Harvard University Press from *The Signs of Language* by Edward Klima and Ursula Bellugi, Harvard University Press, copyright © 1979 by the President and Fellows of Harvard College

like taking a bite of food held in the fingers, as shown in the left-hand picture of figure 12.7. The middle picture is a possibly **indexical** sign, for 'candy'. These are the exceptional cases, however, since typical ASL signs are **symbolic**, having forms with no obvious qualities of or natural association with their meanings, as in the right-hand picture of figure 12.7, the sign for 'jealous' (all three from Klima and Bellugi 1979, pp. 29, 42).

Meanings like 'jealous', as compared with such as 'eat' or 'candy', cannot be readily modeled with the hands, whether iconically or indexically. Most signs of spoken human language are like this, yet, as one can see by watching deaf people converse or by seeing the simultaneous translation of a speech into ASL, one can say in ASL anything that can be said in a spoken language, and just about as fast.

Signs of ASL consist of combinations of choices among three **parameters**, termed 'primes':

a.   **Place**, or space in which the sign is made; about 12 place primes can be distinguished,
b.   **Handshape**; about 19 possible handshape primes, and
c.   **Movement**; about 24 possible movement primes.

These primes function somewhat like **phones** of vocal language (or perhaps more like phonological features, which are introduced in chapter 14), in that they are meaningless but make up meaningful wholes, **morphemes**, as do phonemes. In this regard ASL, like spoken language, has the human language characteristic of **duality** (chapter 1, §3.4.4):

a.   they recombine systematically in the creation of signs, as do phonemes in words like /pɑt/, /tɑp/, and /ɑpt/;
b.   they contrast different signs, as phonemes contrast morphemes in minimal pairs like [sɪt] and [zɪt]; as seen in the signs for 'candy' and 'jealous' (figure 12.7), which differ just by handshape; and
c.   they influence one another in adjacent signs, as nasal consonants may influence the occurrence of adjacent nasalized vowels.

Notice that $12 \times 19 \times 24$ primes gives a total of 5,472 signs, a number which, augmented by aspects of ASL communication which cannot be taken up in this introductory account, is a more than adequate vocabulary for human language purposes.

4.2. Teaching ASL to chimpanzees

In the 1940s, two psychologists Katherine and Keith Hayes, brought up a baby chimpanzee, Viki, alongside their own child for 16 months, in order to see what it would learn in comparison to the human baby. Viki was claimed to have learned to recognize about a hundred spoken words, but is said to have voiced, with difficulty, only a few, including *poppa*, *momma*, *cup* and *up*. It seemed clear that this animal species, that closest to humans, with whom indeed we share perhaps 99% of genetic structure, is unable, for lack of the right physiology of speech if not for other reasons, to learn human vocal language.

However, partly inspired by the gestures that Viki seemed naturally to associate with her spoken words, another pair of psychologists, Beatrice and Allen Gardner, decided to try the experiment with a non-vocal human language, ASL. After all, chimps have vision comparable to ours for acuity, form-recognition, and color, and hands more adept than ours. Their chimp was named **Washoe**, and they reported that by the end of the experiment in 1975 Washoe had learned to use 150 ASL signs, far short of a human vocabulary after comparable time, but a notable achievement nevertheless.

But training chimps to recognize, shape, and remember ASL signs is a laborious process, and not many animal researchers are also fluent in ASL. A third pair of researchers, David and Ann Premack, began to train their chimp Sarah to use plastic tokens as words. She is reported to have learned to understand sentences as advanced as 'If Sarah takes the banana, Mary won't give Sarah chocolate'; see figure 12.8 (Premack and Premack 1972, p. 96). Notice that except for that meaning 'Sarah', the tokens of the sentence are entirely symbolic signs.

Eventually this method was improved with the use of a computerized board of light-up signs such as used by the chimp Kanzi, taught by Sue Savage-Rumbaugh; see a portion of these signs as figure 12.9 (Savage-Rumbaugh and Lewin 1994, p. 141). Notice the symbolic nature of these signs.

Washoe, Kanzi, and other chimps trained in the use of ASL and these artificial symbolic signs have used them, to some extent, in language-like ways, though interpretation of some of these claims remains controversial:

a. They use their signs spontaneously, not just in response to their trainers' signs to them.

b. Besides concrete lexical morphemes like *eat* and *banana*, they use grammatical morphemes like *if* and *not*.

c. Like human children, they **overgeneralize** the meaning of signs, using the *flower* sign for 'tobacco', for example, and the *key* sign for 'can opener'.

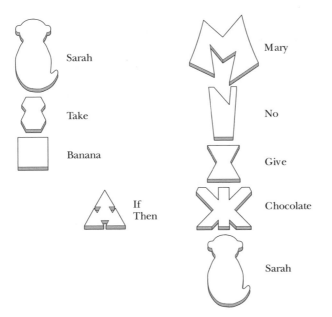

Figure 12.8 Conditional sentence understood by Sarah
Source: Premack and Premack 1972

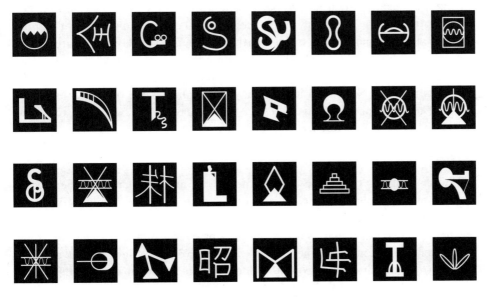

Figure 12.9 Part of Kanzi's computerized sign-board
Source: Savage-Rumbaugh and Lewin 1994

d. They string the signs together in 'sentences' (often rather repetitious sentences, indeed) like *More please fruit more gimme, more you, please more gimme, please fruit, more you gimme fruit, gimme more, gimme fruit gimme, Roger.*

e. They seem even to employ some minimal syntax, observing word order rules and using grammatical morphemes, as in *Sarah give apple Mary,* and even *If Mary take banana, Sarah take apple.*

f. They learn signs – a few, at least, it seems – by watching other chimps (especially claimed for Kanzi by Savage-Rumbaugh 1994, pp. 135ff).

g. Individuals are reported to sign to themselves, when no one else is around.

h. They spontaneously create new sign combinations, such as Washoe's combination of *water-bird* for 'swan', the San Francisco gorilla Koko's combination of *finger-bracelet* for 'ring', and Kanzi's sentence *Liz get cold food.*

i. Perhaps showing displacement, Koko is reported to have lied, signing *Kate there bad* to blame one of his trainers for a broken toilet.

4.3. Is this language learning?

There is disagreement concerning whether the resulting use of signs by chimpanzees is really or significantly language-like.

4.3.1. Pessimistic view

Many, especially linguists, are pessimistic about what this work shows. For example, they note the great difference in language learning rates of human children and chimpanzees, in mean length of utterance (**MLU**). See figure 12.10, a graph (Terrace 1979, p. 211) which compares MLU in five children (two hearing children, spoken language learners, and three deaf children, ASL learners) and a chimpanzee Nim, who in forty months (from the age of four months) of intensive teaching acquired an expressive vocabulary of 125 ASL signs and comprehended 200. The difference of MLU is extreme.

The critics argue that:

Chimps still don't carry on conversations with one another using their signs, as do human children just two years old. Chimps learn very slowly compared to human children, and, also unlike children, only with intensive training. Their reliable vocabularies are probably not over a hundred signs, and their rare sentences don't grow beyond a length of five or six signs – quite a difference from the dramatic growth of language in a human child within three years.

One linguist (Pinker 1994, p. 333), thinking of language as if it were an organ of the body, believes that a chimpanzee is no more likely to perform like a

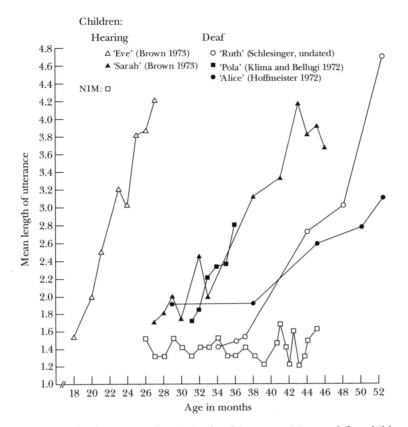

Figure 12.10 Graph of increase of MLU in the chimpanzee Nim, and five children
Source: Reprinted by permission of Alfred A. Knopf, Inc. from *Nim* by Herbert S. Terrace, copyright © 1979 by Herbert S. Terrace

human, using language, than a hyrax, a small, rodent-like animal but the nearest relative to an elephant, is likely to perform like an elephant, using a trunk.

4.3.2. *Optimistic view*

Others, especially most of those who have worked with the signing animals, are more optimistic. They prefer to emphasize what has been accomplished rather than what has not. They argue that:

> Chimpanzees are using more and more symbolic signs of a human language, and beginning to use them in more and more complex ways. There is indication that they are beginning to use their newly acquired knowledge with others of their species, and even to pass it on in families. There is still much to learn about appropriate teaching methods for chimpanzees and other animals, so greater success is likely. More time is needed to really know what is possible, and, after all, the chimpanzees are learning something quite new to them, even if it is potentially within their nature.

Suggestions for
ADDITIONAL READING

Communication in monkeys is surveyed in *How Monkeys See the World: Inside the Mind of Another Species* (1990) by Dorothy Cheney and Robert Seyfarth, communication in birds in *Acoustic Communication in Birds* (1982), 2 vols, edited by Donald E. Kroodsma, Edward M. Miller, and Henri Ouellet, and communication in bees in *The Dance Language and Orientation of Bees* (1993) and *Bees: their Vision, Chemical Senses, and Language* (1971) by Karl von Frisch. Animal communication generally is well and readably surveyed in *Animal Language* (1984) by Michael Bright and *Animal Talk: Science and the Voices of Nature* (1992) by Eugene S. Morton and Jake Page.

ASL is described, illustrated, and explained in *The Signs of Language* (1979) by Edward Klima and Ursula Bellugi. The stories of the chimpanzees Viki, Washoe, Sarah, Kanzi, and Nim are told, respectively, in *The Ape in Our House* (1951) by Cathy Hayes, 'Two-way communication with an infant chimpanzee' (1971) by Beatrice T. and R. Allen Gardner, *The Mind of an Ape* (1993) by David Premack and Ann James Premack, *Kanzi: the Ape at the Brink of the Human Mind* (1994) by Sue Savage-Rumbaugh and Roger Lewin, and *Nim* (1979) by Herbert S. Terrace.

IMPORTANT CONCEPTS AND TERMS IN THIS CHAPTER

- sign
- communication
- language
- symbolic sign
- displacement
- arbitrariness
- cultural transmission
- openness
- duality
- creativity
- dialects
- critical period
- indexical sign
- tail-wagging dance

- Karl von Frisch
- iconic sign
- indexical sign
- ASL
- American Sign Language
- prime
- place
- handshape
- movement
- phoneme
- morpheme
- Washoe
- overgeneralize
- MLU

OUTLINE OF
CHAPTER 12

EXAMPLES AND PRACTICE

EXAMPLE

1. Some ASL signs. Signs in ASL are rarely iconic, like the 'eat' sign seen in figure 12.7, and occasionally indexical, like the 'candy' sign in figure 12.7, the form of which, like candy itself, is associated with the mouth. Surely, however, one would never be able to guess such meanings – the indexicality is too distant or slight.

PRACTICE

Match the nine ASL signs of figure 12.11 (from Klima and Bellugi 1979) with meanings (a)–(i). If you get some right, think about how you were able to do it. Consider whether you could ever have guessed the meanings, even roughly, given the nine forms.

a.	chair	d.	dry	g.	star
b.	apple	e.	home	h.	tape
c.	summer	f.	ugly	i.	train

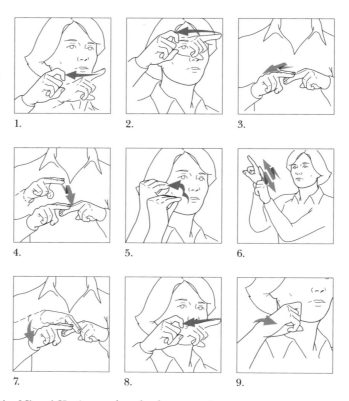

Figure 12.11   Nine ASL signs: what do they mean?
Source: Reprinted by permission of the publisher from *The Signs of Language* by Edward Klima and Ursula Bellugi, Harvard University Press, copyright © 1979 by the President and Fellows of Harvard College

EXAMPLE

2. Primes in ASL signs. It was noted above that the forms of ASL signs have been analyzed as made up of the finite possibilities determined within the three parameters of (a) place, (b) handshape, and (c) movement.

PRACTICE

Describe five of the nine signs of figure 12.11 in terms of these three aspects. The first, for example, might be described as:

Place: off right chin
Handshape: fist with extended index finger
Movement: the hand moves back and the finger curls in

EXAMPLE

3. Repetition in chimpanzee ASL signing. One characteristic of chimpanzee use of ASL signs – and of the use of natural and learned signs by animals generally – is repetitiveness. This contrasts sharply with the practice of human child-

language learners. Both child and chimp three- and four-sign utterances appear to be combinations involving one or more two-sign utterances, but the child learner omits the repetitive element in such combinations. For example, the child's subject–verb and verb–object combinations become subject–verb–object combinations: *Baby eat + Eat pudding → Baby eat pudding*. Following are ten representative three- to four-word utterances of human children from 2 to 3 years old (Menyuk 1969):

Count a buttons.	Daddy uh New York.
No write this name.	Nose hurt you.
How bout this part.	I makin cake too.
Going on floor.	Here she is.
Put in head.	No show you mommy.

PRACTICE

Consider the following representative list of 20 frequent three- and four-sign combinations of the ASL-sign-learning chimpanzee Nim (Terrace 1979, pp. 212–213), from age 18 to 35 months. (a) Calculate the percentage of four-sign combinations which have repetition. (b) Besides their repetitiveness, what are some other generalizations true of these utterances?

Frequent three-sign combinations	Frequent four-sign combinations
1. Play me Nim.	Eat drink eat drink.
2. Eat me Nim.	Eat Nim eat Nim.
3. Eat Nim eat.	Banana Nim banana Nim.
4. Tickle me Nim.	Drink Nim drink Nim.
5. Grape eat Nim.	Banana eat me Nim.
6. Banana Nim eat.	Banana me eat banana.
7. Eat me eat.	Banana me Nim me.
8. Me Nim eat.	Grape eat Nim eat.
9. Hug me Nim.	Nim eat Nim eat.
10. Yogurt Nim eat.	Play me Nim play.
11. Me more eat.	Drink eat drink eat.
12. More eat Nim.	Drink eat me Nim.
13. Finish hug Nim.	Eat grape eat Nim.
14 Banana me eat.	Eat me Nim drink.
15. Tickle me eat.	Grape eat me Nim.
16. Apple me eat.	Me eat drink more.
17. Eat Nim me.	Me eat me eat.
18. Give me eat.	Me gum me gum.
19. Nut Nim nut.	Me Nim eat me.
20. Drink me Nim.	Tickle me Nim play.

EXAMPLE

4. A language experiment with dolphins. An interesting experiment to test the language ability of dolphins was conducted by J. Bastian in 1967 (described in Herman 1980, pp. 178–180).

Bastian trained a male and female bottlenosed dolphin to get food in either of two conditions: when both pushed certain paddles when a flashing light came on, and when both pushed certain other paddles when a steady light came on. The female had to push the correct paddle first. Then Bastian put a separation in the tank, between the two dolphins, so that only the female could see the light. He found that when the light came on, blinking or steady, the female was usually heard to vocalize to the other, and the dolphins performed nearly flawlessly, getting food again and again by pushing the right paddles according to whether the light was blinking or steady.

Later, when he removed the separation so that both dolphins could again see the light, they continued to perform perfectly to get food, but the female continued to vocalize in the same way. Furthermore, when the light was moved and could be seen only by the male, the dolphins were unable, without retraining, to perform successfully.

PRACTICE

In about 250 words, discuss the validity, or not, of this experiment as evidence for the language ability of dolphins.

PHONOLOGICAL RULES

This chapter presents phonological rules of the two basic types, which concern noncontrastive (allophonic) and contrastive (phonemic) aspects of pronunciation. Phonological rules often affect phones in one of a number of common ways, and almost always refer to broad classes of phones defined by shared features, such as [voiced], [labial], etc.

1. TWO TYPES OF PHONOLOGICAL RULE: ALLOPHONIC AND MORPHOPHONEMIC

Recall that a **morpheme** is a **sign** of language, an association of a simple meaning and its form. The word *coat*, for example, consists of the single morpheme *coat*, which has the meaning 'coat' and the form /kot/. The form /kot/ is **phonemic**: it consists only of qualities of pronunciation associated with the meaning 'coat'. In our understanding of the structure of grammars, the phonemic qualities, those associated with the meanings of morphemes, are encoded as the form aspect of entries of the **lexicon**, or **mental dictionary**.

When the words *coats* and *rulls* are pronounced, their lexical forms are elaborated and take on additional and perhaps different qualities, as in the following diagram.

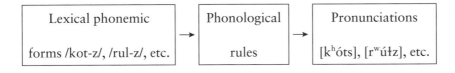

Pronunciations thus consist of the phonemic form of morphemes plus additional and/or alternative aspects of form assigned by **phonological rules**.

There are phonological rules of two types, according to their functional role in yielding pronunciations from lexical forms. (A third type is introduced in the next chapter.)

✳ a.   **Allophonic rules** fill in qualities of pronunciation which are absent in the lexical forms of morphemes but are required by their circumstances in speech, like the aspiration of word-initial /k/ in *coats* and the rounding of word-initial /r/ of *rules*.

✳ b.   **Morphophonemic rules** (also known as morphonemic rules and as morpho-(pho)nological rules) change or choose between meaningful qualities given as part of the lexical entries of morphemes, as where voicing of the /z/ of the plural suffix is replaced by voicelessness, giving /s/, in words like /kots/ *coats* and /saks/ *socks*.

1.1.   Allophonic rules

As an illustration of **allophonic rules,** consider the example of the English word *coat*, with the phonemic or lexical form /kot/. When we say the word *coat*, its pronunciation [kʰót] includes qualities which are absent in its lexical form, and which are added by allophonic rules of English. Two such allophonic qualities are:

a.   aspiration of the /k/, shown as [kʰ], and
b.   stress on its vowel /o/, shown as [ó].

1.1.1.   *English stop* (aspiration)

Coat has an aspirated /k/, a /k/ whose articulation is released with a little puff of air which sounds a lot like [h], and so is appropriately represented as [kʰ] (as discussed in chapter 3, §2.3.1). Aspiration of voiceless stops in English cannot be associated with the meaning of words, or (thus) with their lexical forms, because it results from the requirement of a rule of English phonology:

[k] [p] [t]

Rule 1: Voiceless stops are aspirated when initial in stressed syllables.

1.1.2.   *English* (stress)

Like all monosyllabic English nouns, *coat* [kʰót] has a stressed vowel, another aspect of pronunciation which is not associated with this particular morpheme. Stress in such words is owed to the following phonological rule of English:

*think of examples for rules

Rule 2: Nouns, main verbs, adjectives and adverbs have at least one stressed vowel.

Because of the rule, the single vowel of the lexical forms of English one-syllable nouns, main verbs, adjectives, and adverbs lacks any marking for stress. *Coat* is such a morpheme. Rule 2 provides the necessary stressed vowel of *coat* – and the stressed vowel provides the condition for aspirating /k/ of *coat* by rule 1. The application of the two rules to /kot/ yields [kʰót]:

	/kot/
Rule 2	ó
Rule 1	kʰ
	[kʰót]

1.2. Morphophonemic rules

Instead of filling in qualities which are absent in the lexical entries of morphemes, as do allophonic rules, **morphophonemic rules** seem to have the effect of changing phonetic qualities given in the lexicon. Some morphophonemic rules apply under conditions which, like allophonic rules, can be stated in strictly phonological terms. Others of these rules also include morphological conditions, stated in terms of grammatical or lexical categories. Some morphophonemic rules apply only in particular morphemes, which the rules must specify.

1.2.1. *Phonological conditioning of morphophonemic rules*

Like all allophonic rules, some morphophonemic rules apply under conditions expressed strictly in phonological terms. We say they have **phonological conditioning**. Here are two examples of such rules of English: devoicing of the plural suffix, and voicing of alveolar stops.

1.2.1.1. *English (plural) suffix devoicing.*

The English plural suffix is sometimes pronounced /s/ as in *coats* /kots/ and sometimes /z/ as in *codes* /kodz/. The difference of form of the suffix is owed to phonological rule 3:

[handwritten margin note: obstruent = stop, fricative]

Rule 3: A word-final obstruent (stop or fricative) has the value for voicing (voiced or voiceless) of a preceding obstruent.

According to rule 3, the plural (suffix) morpheme of nouns with final voiceless obstruents is /s/, as in *coats* /kots/, and the plural suffix of nouns with final voiced obstruents is /z/, as in *codes* /kodz/.

In order to know the effect of the rule, we need to know the 'basic' or lexical form of the plural morpheme, on which the rule applies. Consider the following **minimal pairs**:

Word with final /z/		*Word with final /s/*	
peas	/piz/	*peace*	/pis/
lies	/lajz/	*lice*	/lajs/
fears	/fɪrz/	*fierce*	/fɪrs/
dens	/dɛnz/	*dense*	/dɛns/

Such minimal pairs show that word-finally either /s/ or /z/ may follow a vowel, glide, liquid or nasal consonant. Thus when /s/ or /z/ is pronounced in such words, this is meaningful, ~~or~~ contrastive, and must be lexically determined. The lexical or basic form of the suffix is considered to be /z/, because when the suffix follows a vowel, glide, liquid or nasal consonant, it is pronounced [z], and this pronunciation is not required by phonology.

basic form = /s/z/ [handwritten annotation]

Then, when this /z/ follows a voiceless obstruent as in *coats*, *socks*, *caps*, etc., and [z] is impossible because rule 3 requires [s], we understand the rule to change /z/ to [s]. This is **devoicing**. Devoicing does not apply in the derivation of *codes* [kʰódz]:

	/kot-z/ 'coats'	/kod-z/ 'codes'
Vowel stress	ó	ó
Aspiration	kʰ	kʰ
Devoicing	s	–
	[kʰóts]	[kʰódz]

(Devoicing could apply at any time, but the stress rule must apply before the aspiration rule can.)

As in this example, morphophonemic rules concern two (or more) forms of the same morpheme, in this case /z/ (input to the rule) and /s/ (= [s], output by the rule). The two forms are termed **alternants** and their relation within a single morpheme is termed an (**alternation**) *alternates, allophones* [handwritten annotation]

Compare allophonic rules, which concern allophones of a phoneme, such as [kʰ] and [k] of the English phoneme /k/, and [o] and [ó] of the phoneme /o/. Allophonic qualities are considered to be absent in the lexicon, and are provided by allophonic rules, upon pronunciation.

1.2.1.2.   *English alveolar stop voicing.*   As a second example of a phonologically conditioned morphophonemic rule of English, consider the alternation of /t/ and /d/ in words like *coat* /kot/ and *coating* /kodɪŋ/. Notice that the /t/ of *coat* is voiced, and pronounced [d], in *coating*. In fact, the [d] of *coating* is an especially quick and relaxed articulation, sometimes called a 'flapped *t*', but one of its qualities is voicing, and, in fact, it is the same in most American English casual pronunciations as the [d] of *coding*. So a morpheme like *coat* has the two phonemic forms, /kot/ and /kod/, the latter resulting from **voicing** the /t/ to /d/, when a suffix with an unstressed vowel follows, such as *-ing* /ɪŋ/ of verbs.

The English phonological rule concerning this alternation is morphophonemic rule 4:

Rule 4: An alveolar stop is (flapped and) voiced when after a stressed vowel and before an unstressed vowel.

Following are a few more words which show the same alternation of /t/ and /d/:

Word *in isolation, with* /t/		Word *with unstressed suffix, with* /d/	
boat	/bót/	boating	/bódɪŋ/
heat	/hít/	heated	/hídəd/
hot	/hát/	hotter	/hádər/
fit	/fít/	fittest	/fídəst/

Notice that the lexical form of morphemes like *boat* and *heat* must have final /t/, since it is this which contrasts them with others like *bode* and *heed*, respectively, with final /d/.

1.2.2. *Morphological conditioning of morphophonemic rules*

The conditions of application of some morphophonemic rules refer to morphology, or categories of grammar, as well as to phonology. We say these rules have **morphological conditioning**.

1.2.2.1. *English stress-attracting suffixes.*

In English certain derivational suffixes require primary stress to be on the vowel before the suffix. For example, when -*al*, which forms adjectives from nouns, is suffixed to *government* [gávərnmənt], with stress on the first syllable, the pronunciation is [gəvərnméntəl]; stress has shifted one place to the right. Similarly, when -*ity*, which forms nouns from adjectives, is suffixed to *fatal* [fétəl], with stress on the first syllable, the pronunciation is [fètǽləti] (or [fətǽləti]). (The vowel changes are accounted for by other rules.)

Phonology alone – the pronunciation of the adjective and/or the suffix – is a factor insufficient to produce this effect, as evident in words like *edible* [édəbəl] and *beautiful* [bjútəfəl], which end in [əl] without stress shift: stress is on the first syllable. Nor does just any suffix have this effect; thus *govern* [gávərn] and *random* [rǽndəm] are unchanged when -*ment* and -*ize*, respectively, are added: *government* [gávərnmənt], *randomize* [rǽndəmàjz]. The rule must refer to certain suffixes.

certain suffixes only ex. -al, -ity,

1.2.2.2. *Amharic palatalization.*

In Amharic, an Ethiopian Semitic language, first-person singular verbs of a form known as 'conjunctive' have a suffix /e/ and, also, the final consonant of these verbs is long. Furthermore, if the verb ends in a coronal (tongue-tip articulated) consonant, this consonant becomes alveopalatal. Such a change is called 'palatalization'. See the following examples, in which first-person singular conjunctive forms with palatalization are compared with third-person masculine singular forms without it.

Verb stem	1st sg.		3rd m.sg.	
lɨs-	lɨšš-e	'I licking'	lɨs-o	'he licking'
jɨz-	jɨžž-e	'I holding'	jɨz-o	'he holding'
kɨd-	kɨjj-e	'I denying'	kɨd-o	'he denying'
sɨm-	sɨmm-e	'I kissing'	sɨm-o	'he kissing'
lɨk-	lɨkk-e	'I sending'	lɨk-o	'he sending'

Notice that in the last two rows, in which the verbs end in labial /m/ and velar /k/, there is no palatalization. The palatalization of coronals in the first three rows is morphologically conditioned, by the grammatical categories of 'conjunctive' + 'first-person singular subject'. The palatalization is not phonologically conditioned: it doesn't happen with any /e/ or even any suffix /e/. This is evident in words like /zəde/ 'method' and /wɨze/ 'my sweat', the latter of which has the suffix /-e/ 'my'.

1.2.3. Suppletion

Some alternations are found only in particular morphemes or arbitrary sets of morphemes. Morphemes with such alternations must be considered to have both pronunciations in their lexical entries. One pronunciation is the general case, and the other replaces, or 'suppletes' the general case under stated conditions. Here are two examples of such **suppletions** in English.

The verb *go* is /go/ in the present tense but, peculiarly, /wɛnt/ in the past tense. No other verb has such an unlikely and extreme alternation. Therefore we must say that the lexical entry for 'go' has two forms, {/wɛnt/, /go/}, and a special rule for 'go' chooses /wɛnt/ in the past tense, leaving /go/ to occur otherwise.

A number of English nouns have alternations of /f/ and /v/, where /f/ appears in the singular form and /v/ in the plural: for example *loaf* /lof/, *loaves* /lovz/; *knife* /najf/, *knives* /najvz/; and *calf* /kæf/, *calves* /kævz/. This sort of alternation is limited to a fixed set of words; it doesn't appear in other nouns whose singulars end in /f/: not in *fife, oaf, cuff,* etc. We say that the lexical entries for *loaf, knife,* etc. have two forms, with /f/ and /v/, /lo{f, v}/, /naj{f, v}/, etc., and a special rule for these morphemes chooses /v/ in the plural, leaving /f/ to occur otherwise. (Sometimes such morphemes are said to have a special feature which encodes their exceptional alternation, but the special feature is just an abbreviation of the fact of the two pronunciations /f/, /v/ in these words.)

1.2.4. *Difference between suppletions and other alternations*

Notice how suppletions like {/wɛnt/, /go/} 'go' or {/f/, /v/} in nouns like 'knife' are different from alternations such as that between /s/ and /z/ of the English plural suffix. The latter follows a general requirement of English phonology, rule 3, above. There are no exceptions to rule 3, which, indeed, affects the third-person singular suffix of verbs (/wɔks/ *walks* vs. /rənz/ *runs*), the possessive of nouns (/pæts/ *Pat's* vs. /nɛdz/ *Ned's*), the contraction of *is* /ɪz/ (/pæts/ *Pat's* = *Pat is*), and the past tense of verbs (/wɔkt/ *walked* vs. /opənd/ *opened*).

Suppletions, on the other hand, are peculiar to the morphemes in which they occur. Therefore the existence of the suppletion, including the two (or more) forms which appear, has to be a part of the form aspect of the lexical entry of the affected morphemes (whose meanings are 'go', 'knife', 'loaf', etc.).

1.3. Redundancy rules

There are phonological rules of a third type, redundancy rules, which can only be illustrated when we have gone somewhat deeper into phonology, in the following chapter on phonological features.

2. ASSIMILATION, DELETION, AND OTHER RULE TYPES

Allophonic and morphophonemic rules differ in the nature of their environment of application and in the general nature of their effects. The effect of many, and perhaps most, phonological rules is to make phones similar to neighboring phones. This is called assimilation. Another common type of phonological rule deletes whole phones, and some provide a few other effects including inserting phones, moving them, and modifying them in ways that are not assimilatory. Following are a few examples of each type.

2.1. Assimilation

Many phonological rules, both allophonic and morphophonemic rules, are assimilations. The rule of English by which vowels which precede nasal consonants are nasalized, as in [bĩn] *bin* and [sɔ̃ŋ] *song*, is an assimilation, as is the English rule by which consonants are rounded before the rounded glide [w], as in [kʷwæk] *quack* and [tʷwɪnz] *twins*. (The [ʷ] follows [k, t] in the phonetic writing, but rounding actually begins before the consonant is articulated.)

Following are four more assimilation rules of English, and four assimilation rules of other languages:

EIGHT ASSIMILATION RULES

(handwritten annotation: assimilates:)

a. In English, /t/ is voiced between vowels (which are voiced) the second of which is unstressed, so *water* is pronounced [wádər], and *rating* [rédɪŋ]. The rule (rule 4, above) brings about a voiced consonant in a voiced (vowel) environment. *(handwritten: voicing)*

b. In English, the negative prefix *im-* is pronounced [ɪm], with a labial consonant, before other labial consonants, as in *impossible, impractical, imbalance.* *(handwritten: point of articulation)*

c. In English, the past tense /d/ and noun plural /z/ suffixes are voiceless, [t] and [s] respectively, when they follow voiceless consonants, as in *pick*[t], *walk*[t], *goat*[s], *cat*[s], etc. (Rule 3, above.) *(handwritten: voicing)*

d. In English, the nasal consonant of words like *symphony* and *invade* may be pronounced labiodental [ɱ], like the following consonant [f] or [v]: /sɪɱfəni/, /ɪɱved/. *(handwritten: place of articulation)*

e. In Spanish, the consonants spelled *b*, *d*, and *g* are pronounced as fricatives, or continuants, when they are between other continuant phones, including vowels and /r/, as in *saber* 'to know', *padre* 'father', and *lago* 'lake': [saβér], [paðre], [laɣo].

f. In Japanese, unaccented short vowels between voiceless consonants may be voiceless, as in *h*[i̥]*to* 'person', and *s*[u̥]*ki* 'like, love' (the small circle under a vowel represents voicelessness).

g. In German, the fricative spelled *ch* is fronted as palatal [ç] after front vowels including [i], and backed as velar [x] after back vowels including [u], as in *Licht* [liçt] 'light', *Buch* [buːx] 'book'.

h. In Brazilian Portuguese, the phoneme /t/ has the high affricate allophone [č] before the high vowel [i], and is [t] otherwise: [parči] 'party', [natu] 'born'.

Probably every language has one or more assimilation rules. Many more assimilation rules could have been mentioned, in fact, just in English.

2.2. Deletion

Rules which delete phones are, appropriately, called deletions. A deletion rule of English affects word-final /d/ which follows /n/ and precedes /z/, in words like *lends* and *brands*, which are pronounced /lɛnz/ and /brænz/. In ordinary casual speech, indeed, a word-final /d/ after /n/ will be deleted before any consonant beginning the following word, as in /lénmìədálər/ 'lend me a dollar'. The spelling of words like *climb* /klɑjm/ and *lamb* /læm/ is evidence that in the past word-final /b/ was deleted in English when it followed /m/.

Following are six more examples of deletion rules in English and other languages:

SIX DELETION RULES

a. In English casual speech, the unstressed vowel /ə/ or /ɪ/ is ordinarily deleted in the middle of words when the preceding vowel is stressed, so we tend to say /víktri/, instead of /víktəri/ *victory*, and /ízli/ instead of /ízɪli/ *easily*.

b. In English grammatical morphemes, initial /h/ before unstressed vowels is ordinarily deleted in casual speech, so that *him* is pronounced /ɪm/ and *her* is pronounced /ər/ – for example, /gɪvɪm/ *give him* and /siər/ *see her*.

c. In French, many adjectives have two forms, one with a final consonant, the 'feminine form', with feminine nouns, and one without the final consonant, the 'masculine form', with masculine nouns, for example, /vɛrt/ 'green', feminine, and /vɛr/, masculine, and /fɔrt/ 'strong', feminine, and /fɔr/, masculine. Final consonants are usually understood to be deleted in the masculine forms.

d. In Russian, /t/ or /d/ are deleted at the end of verb stems when the past tense suffix -/l/ is added, so for the verb /mot/- 'sweep', 'he swept' is /mol/, and for /vʲod/- 'lead', 'he led' is /vʲol/. (/vʲ/ represents palatalized /v/.)

e. Also in Russian, the past tense suffix -/l/ is deleted when it follows consonants other than /t/ or /d/. Thus for the verb /pʲok/- 'bake', 'he baked' is /pʲok/, and for /nʲos/- 'carry', 'he carried' is /nʲos/.

f. In Hindi, the vowel /ə/ is deleted before a single consonant when a suffix beginning with a vowel is added. When the plural suffix /õ/ is added to words like /kəmər/ 'lesson', the result is /kəmrõ/, and the plural of /suːrət/ 'shape' is /suːrtõ/. (There are words like /fikr/ 'worry' which lack /ə/ in the singular and whose plural is /fikrõ/, which show that /ə/ is not added in the singular but deleted in the plural.)

Probably every language has some deletion rules, particularly evident in fast or casual speech. An extreme case of casual speech deletion is illustrated by English /jítjèt/ *Did you eat yet?*, which comes from /dìdjuítjèt/. The underlined phones are deleted, and /dj/ and /tj/ assimilate.

2.3. Other rule types

Other phonological rules modify phones in other ways, inserting and inverting phones, and modifying phones in ways which are not assimilatory. These rules often apply at the beginnings and ends of words. Following are six examples of rules of these other types, in English and other languages.

SIX PHONOLOGICAL RULES OF OTHER TYPES

a. In English, an insertion rule provides /ɪ/ when the third-person singular suffix /z/ follows a verb ending in a sibilant /s, z, š, ž/, as in *kisses*, *raises*, *pushes*, and *nudges* /kɪsɪz, rezɪz, pušɪz, nədžɪz/.

b. In most varieties of English syllable-final /l/ is velarized – the back of the tongue is raised toward the velum – in words like *call* and *tell*: ca[ɫ], te[ɫ].

c. In English, voiceless stops are aspirated before stressed vowels, as in *call* [kʰáɫ] and *tell* [tʰέɫ].

d. In German, Russian, Turkish, and many languages, stops and fricatives are voiceless at the end of words. Thus in German *und* is [unt] 'and' and *Hund* is [hunt] 'dog'. 'Dogs', with the plural suffix [ə], is *Hunde* [hundə], with [d] because this is not at the end of its word as in singular *Hund* [hunt]. (This phonological rule is also discussed below.)

e. In Puerto Rican Spanish, word-final non-labial nasal consonants are velar, [ŋ], as in *pa*[ŋ] 'bread' (compare *pa*[n]*es* 'breads') and *ve*[ŋ] 'Come!' (compare *ve*[n]*ir* 'to come').

f. In Hebrew, reflexive verbs – those which have 'oneself' as an object – are formed by prefixing /hit-/, as in /hitkonen/ 'prepare onself' and /hitlabeš/

'dress oneself'. But when the prefix occurs with a verb with initial /s/ (or /š, z/), there is inversion, or **metathesis**, of the /t/ and /s/; thus /hit/ + /salek/ 'remove' is /histalek/ 'remove oneself', and /hit/ + /sapek/ 'satisfy' is /histapek/ 'satisfy oneself'.

3. DERIVATIONS

The step-by-step application of rules to a lexical or phonemic form, to yield a pronunciation or phonetic form, is a **derivation** (chapter 3, §5). Figure 13.1 shows derivations of the words *coats* [kʰóts] and *coating* [kʰódɪŋ] by application of rules 1–4.

	/kot-z/	/kot-ɪŋ/
Rule 2:	ó	ó
Rule 1:	kʰ	kʰ
Rule 3:	s	–
Rule 4:	–	d
	[kʰóts]	[kʰódɪŋ]

Figure 13.1   Derivation of *coats* and *coating*

The derivations begin with the phonemic representations /kot-z/ and /kot-ɪŋ/, which result from rules of English word-formation (morphological rules). The input to a derivation is sometimes called an '**underlying form**'. Rule 2 puts stress on /o/, which provides the necessary condition for rule 1, which aspirates /k/ at the beginning of a stressed syllable. Rule 3 devoices the suffix /z/ in *coats*, and rule 4 voices the /t/ in *coating*. Rules 3 and 4 must apply after stress is assigned by rule 2, but they could apply along with or before rule 1.

4. TWO MORE EXAMPLES

Here are additional examples of allophonic and morphophonemic rules: an allophonic rule of Spanish, and a morphophonemic rule of German.

4.1. Spanish voiced obstruents

[β], [ð], and [ɣ] are voiced labial, dental, and velar fricatives, respectively. (English has [ð] ([ðɪs] 'this', [ðæt] 'that', etc.) but not [β] or [ɣ].) In Spanish, [β], [ð], and [ɣ] are allophones of the phonemes /b/, /d/, and /g/ respectively (as discussed in chapter 3, §2.4). These phonemes are pronounced as stops [b], [d], and [g] except when they follow a vowel, /r/ (and sometimes /l/), or another fricative, in which case the fricative allophones [β], [ð] , and [ɣ] appear, as in the following words.

/b/: *beber* /beber/ [beβér] 'to drink', *pobre* /pobre/ [póβre] 'poor', *bebé* /bebé/ [beβé] 'baby'

/d/: *dedo* /dedo/ [déðo] 'finger', *lado* /lado/ [láðo] 'side', *padre* /padre/ [páðre] 'father', *sed* /sed/ [séð] 'thirst'

/g/: *gargara* /gargara/ [gárɣara] 'gargle', *trigo* /trigo/ [tríɣo] 'wheat', *lago* /lago/ [láɣo] 'lake', *rasgo* /rasgo/ [rásɣo] 'characteristic'

All three of these allophones are accounted for by Spanish rule 5:

Rule 5: Voiced obstruents are fricatives when they follow vowels, /r/, or another fricative.

4.2. German word-final obstruents

Another example of a morphophonemic rule concerns German words like:

Tag /taːk/ 'day' vs. *Tage* /taːgə/ 'days', and
Eid /ajt/ 'oath' vs. *Eide* /ajdə/ 'oaths'.

The German spellings of these words, with *g* and *d*, do not show the actual pronunciations with both [k] and [g] and [t] and [d] – just as the spelling *s* of the English plural suffix does not show its two pronunciations /z/ and /s/. The alternations in these and many other German words are owed to the following phonological rule:

Rule 6: Obstruents are voiceless at the ends of words.

Many languages including Turkish and Russian also have this phonological rule. English-learning children tend to follow the same rule, too, before they learn to pronounce word-final voiced obstruents, and have pronunciations like [ɛk] for 'egg', and [təp] for 'tub' (as seen in practice 2 of chapter 8).

Given this rule, consider the following derivations of *Tag* 'day'/ *Tage* 'days', *Fleck* 'spot'/ *Flecke* 'spots', *Eid* 'oath'/ *Eide* 'oaths', and *Scheit* 'log'/ *Scheite* 'logs', in which /-ə/ is the plural suffix.

	/tag/	/tag-ə/	/flek/	/flek-ə/	/ajd/	/ajd-ə/	/šajt/	/šajt-ə/
Rule 6:	k				t			
	[tak]	[tagə]	[flek]	[flekə]	[ajt]	[ajdə]	[šajt]	[šajtə]

Rule 6 changes the /g/ of *Tag* to [k] and the /d/ of *Eid* to [t]. In all the other words, lexical or underlying forms are unaffected by the rule.

Notice how the derivation shows the grammar to be an interaction of lexical form and rules of the grammar. Pronunciations are the product of this inter-action. The lexical form of German 'day' must be /tag/ not /tak/ because, while the combination of lexical /g/ and rule 6 appropriately yields [k] in the singular, the plural is [tagə]. We know the latter can't result from a voicing rule (/tak-ə/ becoming [tagə]), because of words like *Flecke* [flekə] 'spots', in which /k/ does not become [g] between vowels. The pronunciation [tɑk] 'day' can result from /tag/ by devoicing, but [tɑgə] 'days' cannot result from /tak/ by voicing.

5. RULES AND CLASSES OF PHONES

None of the rules discussed above affect a particular single phone, or some arbitrary or miscellaneous set of phones. Instead, they affect general **phonetic classes**, including the following:

a. voiceless stops (English rule 1)
b. vowels (English rule 2)
c. obstruents (English rule 3 and German rule 6)
d. alveolar stops (English rule 4)
e. voiced obstruents (Spanish rule 5)

If we surveyed other phonological rules of English and other languages, we would find that phonological rules almost always affect such phonetically defined classes of phones – such as consonant, vowel, fricative, nasal, voiceless consonant, high vowel, etc. Only very rarely do rules affect particular phones or some odd collection of phones.

The necessity for phonological rules to refer to classes of phones shows that the sound structure of languages, phonology, is not based on phones but on the features by which phones form classes with other phones. Phones are made up of these **phonological features**, which cross-classify the phones with one another in different ways, to determine the classes.

Take the phone [b], for example. This is:

a. a consonant, like [d], [n], [r], etc.
b. an obstruent, like [d], [f], [g], etc.
c. a stop, like [d], [p], [g], etc.
d. labial, like [m], [p], [v], etc.
e. voiced, like [d], [l], [ɑ], etc.

Or take the phone [i], which is:

a. a vowel like [ɑ], [o], etc.
b. a high vowel like [u], [ɪ], etc.
c. a front vowel like [e], [æ], etc., and
d. a 'tense' vowel like [e], [u], etc.

[n] is a consonant, a nasal, an alveolar, etc. The phonological features include some of those features which describe the classes of phones in a place and manner of articulation chart of consonants and a vowel chart of vowels (such as shown for English consonants and vowels in figure 2.3 of chapter 2), plus other features.

The set of phonological features for languages must fulfill two conditions: (a) they must accurately describe phones, and (b) they must differentiate the classes of phones which figure in phonological rules. Also, of course, (c) they should do this in an efficient way; we don't want to have more phonological features than are necessary. The definitions and roles of the phonological features are the topic of the next chapter.

Suggestions for
ADDITIONAL READING

The form and organization of phonological rules is the main concern of phonological theory, which is introduced in textbooks such as *Understanding Phonology* (1998) by Carlos Gussenhoven and Haike Jacobs, *An Introduction to Phonetics and Phonology* (1990) by John Clark and Colin Yallop, *Phonology: Theory and Description* (1996) by Andrew Spencer, and *Phonology* (1993) by Philip Carr. Thorough presentation of most

topics in phonological theory is found in *The Handbook of Phonological Theory* (1995) edited by John A. Goldsmith.

For English phonology, see *The Pronunciation of English: a Coursebook in Phonology* (1989) by Charles W. Kreidler, *English Phonology: an Introduction* (1992) by Heinz J. Giegerich, and *English Sound Structure* (1994) by John Harris.

IMPORTANT CONCEPTS AND TERMS IN THIS CHAPTER

- morpheme
- sign
- phonemic
- lexicon
- phonological rule
- allophonic rule
- morphophonemic rule
- aspiration
- stress

- phonological conditioning
- minimal pair
- devoicing
- alternant
- alternation
- voicing
- morphological conditioning

- suppletion
- assimilation
- deletion
- insertion
- metathesis
- derivation
- underlying form
- phonetic classes
- phonological feature

OUTLINE OF CHAPTER 13

2. Morphophonemic rules
   1. Phonological conditioning of morphophonemic rules
      1. English plural suffix devoicing
      2. English alveolar stop voicing
   2. Morphological conditioning of morphophonemic rules
      1. English stress-attracting suffixes
      2 Amharic palatalization
   3. Suppletion
   4. Difference between suppletions and other alternations
3. Redundancy rules

2. Assimilation, deletion, and other rule types
   1. Assimilation
   2. Deletion
   3. Other rule types
3. Derivations
4. Two more examples
   1. Spanish voiced obstruents
   2. German word-final obstruents
5. Rules and classes of phones

EXAMPLES AND PRACTICE

EXAMPLE

1. English negative prefix. Many English negative adjectives have a negative prefix, as in the following examples:

impossible	illegal	irreplaceable	intolerable	inordinate
impractical	illegible	irrevocable	indecent	inaccurate
imprecise	illegitimate	irresolute	indelible	inexorable
imbalanced	illiterate	irregular	insensitive	inedible

PRACTICE

Answer the following questions about these negative adjectives.

1. Why does the prefix have these different forms? What is this process called?
2. How are the words of the last column different from those of other columns?
3. Which of the forms is most reasonably considered to be lexical, or underlying? Why?

EXAMPLE

2. Yoruba progressive verbs (Cowan and Rakušan 1987, p. 79). In Yoruba, the progressive tense verb has the form of the present tense verb plus a prefix, as in the following phonemically written words:

Pres.	Prog.		Pres.	Prog.	
bá	m̀bá	'meet'	bé	m̀bé	'cut off'
bù	m̀bù	'cut'	bèrù	m̀bèrù	'fear'
dé	ńdé	'arrive'	dà	ńdà	'pour'
dì	ńdì	'tie'	dúró	ńdúró	'stand'
ká	ŋ́ká	'fold'	kàn	ŋ́kàn	'touch'
kɔ̀	ŋ́kɔ̀	'reject'	kù	ŋ́kù	'remain'

PRACTICE

Answer these questions.

1. Why does the prefix have three different forms? What is this process called?
2. Think of some English adjectives with the negative prefix *in-*, where the basic adjective begins with *k* or *g*. Does the English negative prefix *in-* have a pronunciation with [ŋ] before velars, like the progressive prefix in Yoruba?

EXAMPLE

3. Arabic definite article. The definite article, meaning 'the', in Arabic has different forms, as in the following phonemically written words ([ʕ] is a voiced pharyngeal fricative):

al-qamr	'the moon'	ar-rajal	'the man'
al-bint	'the girl'	aš-šams	'the sun'
al-walad	'the boy'	ad-daar	'the home(land)'
al-kitaab	'the book'	as-saʕat	'the hour'
al-fuul	'the beans'	an-nahr	'the river'
al-malik	'the king'	at-tiin	'the figs'

PRACTICE

Answer these questions.

1. What do the words in the second column illustrate?
2. What phonological characteristic distinguishes the nouns in the second column from those of the first column?
3. What is the lexical, or underlying, form of the Arabic definite article?

EXAMPLE

4. French masculine and feminine adjectives. Many French adjectives have two forms, one with a final consonant, the feminine form, and one without a final consonant, the masculine form. Consider the following phonemically written adjectives:

Feminine	Masculine		Feminine	Masculine	
vɛrt	vɛr	'green'	fɔrt	fɔr	'strong'
tut	tu	'all'	pətit	pəti	'small'

kurt	kur	'short'	fos	fo	'false'
ot	o	'high'	movɛz	movɛ	'bad'
bas	ba	'low'	frɛš	frɛ	'fresh'

PRACTICE

If the lexical form is the feminine, the final consonant is deleted in pronouncing the masculine. If the lexical form is the masculine, the final consonant is added. Which makes more sense, and why?

EXAMPLE

5. English allophonic rules. Look at the list of 25 English allophonic rules for consonants and vowels in chapter 3, §3.1. From those lists, the allophonic rules which apply in the derivation of the pronunciation of

[ǽntʰísɪpʰèʔtðətʰɛ́ɲθbìːd] from the phonemic form

/ǽntísɪpètðətén θbìd/ 'anticipate the tenth bid'

are (1), (2), (4), (17), (19), (20), and (23).

PRACTICE

Using the list of 25 allophonic rules of English in chapter 3, list those which apply in deriving each of sentences 1–3. In the third, the phonemic form is given and not the phonetic form. List the allophonic rules which apply and also write the sentence phonetically.

1. [gì:vmĩð̀ò:zpʒ̥tʰéʲDəz] 'Give me those potatoes.'

2. [hʷʷɪ̥čtʰʷʷ̥ɪ̃nz̥łísn̩] 'Which twins'll listen?'

3. /dóntfìlbǽd ɛ́mfəsà̀jzprǽktɪs/ 'Don't feel bad; emphasize practice.'

EXAMPLE

6. Sidamo assimilation rule. Sidamo is a language of Ethiopia. Consider the following Sidamo verbs, written phonemically.

/umí/	'he dug'	/untú/	'she dug'
/umanno/	'he digs'	/untanno/	'she digs'
/faní/	'he opened'	/fantú/	'she opened'
/fananno/	'he opens'	/fantanno/	'she opens'
/rumí/	'he cursed'	/runtú/	'she cursed'
/rumanno/	'he curses'	/runtanno/	'she curses'

The grammar of these verbs has two parts: lexicon and rules. The lexicon has seven morphemes and there are two rules:

Lexicon:	/-anno/	'he, present'	/um-/	'verb, dig'
	/-í/	'he, past'	/rum-/	'verb, curse'
	/-tanno/	'she, present'	/fan-/	'verb, open'
	/-tú/	'she, past'		

Rules: a. The 'present' and 'past' morphemes are suffixed to verbs.
        b. /m/ becomes /n/ when /t/ follows.

PRACTICE

Answer these three questions about Sidamo.

1. What process does rule b illustrate?
2. Suppose the underlying forms of 'dig' and 'curse' were /un-/ (not /um-/) and /run-/ (not /rum-/), respectively. How would the rules have to be changed?
3. What difficulty does /fan-/ 'open' present to the latter analysis?
4. How is the analysis with underlying /um-/ and /rum-/ simpler or more economical?

EXAMPLE

7. Phonological rules and English derivational suffixes. It was noted (§1.2.2.1) that certain English derivational suffixes including -ity and -al require primary stress on the vowel before the suffix. For example, normal is [nármǝl], but normality is [nàrmǽlǝti]; sacrifice is [sǽkrǝfàjs], but sacrificial is [sǽkrǝfíšǝl].

PRACTICE

Consider words with the following eight suffixes of English (given as spelled forms). Think of words which have these suffixes and ask whether they illustrate the stress-attracting characteristic of -ity and -al. For each suffix: (a) Give an example of a two-syllable word, with stress on the first syllable, which may have the suffix. (b) Give the word with the suffix, and mark the stress. (c) Say whether stress is changed in the word.

For example: for the suffix -ly, a two-syllable word with stress on the first syllable is happy /hǽpɪ/; with the suffix this is happily /hǽpɪlɪ/; stress doesn't change.

1.	-ation	5.	-ate
2.	-ment	6.	-ify
3.	-ous	7.	-ly
4.	-ness	8.	-ian

PHONOLOGICAL FEATURES

This chapter presents the fundamental, atomic, units of linguistic form: phonological features. Twelve phonological features are defined and exemplified, particularly in their use to explain and define the structure of syllables, and to give general and maximally economical expression to English phonology.

1.   PHONOLOGICAL FEATURES ARE BINARY AND FEW

Phones are not the smallest units of sound. Phones are made up of **phonological features**, which are the fundamental or atomic elements of linguistic sound, for example [labial], [voiced], and [nasal] (chapter 1, §3.2.1). There are a relatively small number of these, perhaps not more than about twenty, fewer certainly than the typical number of phonemes of a language, and many fewer than the traditional place and manner of articulation terms of articulatory phonetics, like 'consonant', 'vowel', 'stop', and 'fricative'.

The phonological features may generally be considered **binary** – that is, they have one of two values, positive or negative, + or –, for a given phone. Consider the phones [p], [m], and [b], for example:

a.   [p] contrasts with [b] by the feature [voiced]; [b] is [+voiced] and [p] [–voiced];

b.   [m] contrasts with [b] by the feature [nasal]; [m] is [+nasal] and [b] [–nasal];

c.   [m] contrasts with [p] by the two features [voiced] and [nasal]; [m] is [+voiced] and [+nasal], and [p] is [–voiced] and [–nasal].

2. PHONOLOGICAL FEATURES FOR ENGLISH

The 36 American English phonemes may be considered to be composed of only 12 phonological features of three types: (a) airstream features, (b) articulator features, and (c) tongue body features. Below, these are listed, defined and illustrated with the English phonemes. Notice how the features define phones and classify them into sets. There are other features, relevant for English as well as other languages, but these 12 go far toward explaining how we are able to process English speech so rapidly and effectively.

2.1. Six airstream features

The six **airstream features** are [vocoid], [syllabic], [sonorant], [continuant], [voiced], and [strident]. According to its definition, each feature sorts the 36 English phonemes into two groups, as follows:

1. [+vocoid], articulated with an unobstructed airstream: /j, w, i, ɪ, e, ɛ, æ, ə, ɑ, ɔ, o, ʊ, u/. These are the glides and the vowels. The traditionally recognized similarity of glides and vowels, which the feature [vocoid] expresses, is suggested by the name 'semivowels' for glides.

    [–vocoid] are /p, b, f, v, θ, ð, t, d, s, z, č, ǰ, š, ž, k, g, ʔ, h, m, n, ŋ, l, r/. These are what traditionally have been called the 'true consonants' – that is, consonants not including glides. (American English /r/ is sometimes considered to be [+vocoid].)

2. [+syllabic], articulated with the duration of a syllable: /i, ɪ, e, ɛ, æ, ɛ, ə, ɑ, ɔ, o, ʊ, u/.

    [–syllabic] are ordinarily the consonants, /p, b, f, v, θ, ð, t, d, s, z, č, ǰ, š, ž, k, g, ʔ, h, m, n, ŋ, l, r, j, w/, but there are also syllabic consonants, such as in English the [ṇ] of *button* [bətṇ], and the [ḷ] of *little* [lɪdḷ], which are the second syllable of these pronunciations of these words.

3. [+sonorant], articulated with no obstruction or an obstruction less than friction: nasals, approximants, and vowels /m, n, ŋ, l, r, j, w, i, ɪ, e, ɛ, æ, ə, ɑ, ɔ, o, ʊ, u/. These phones have sonorous airstreams, and are termed **sonorants**. They are typically voiced.

    [–sonorant] are stops, fricatives, and affricates /p, b, f, v, θ, ð, t, d, s, z, č, ǰ, š, ž, k, g, ʔ, h/. [–Sonorant] phones have non-sonorous airstreams, and are termed **obstruents**.

```
        p f θ t s š k ʔ h m n ŋ l r j w i ɪ e ɛ æ ə ɑ ɔ o ʊ u
voc     – – – – – – – – – – – – – – – – + + + + + + + + + + +
syl     – – – – – – – – – – – – – – – – + + + + + + + + + + +
son     – – – – – – – – – + + + + + + + + + + + + + + + + + +
cnt     – + + – + + – – + – – – + + + + + + + + + + + + + + +
vcd     – – – – – – – – – + + +
str     – + – – + + – – – – – – – – – – – – – – – – – – – – –
```

Figure 14.1 Feature matrix of airstream features and English phonemes (affricates and voiced obstruents omitted)

4. [+continuant], articulated with an uninterrupted – if perhaps obstructed – oral airstream: /f, v, θ, ð, s, z, š, ž, h, l, r, j, w, i, ɪ, e, ɛ, æ, ə, ɑ, ɔ, o, ʊ, u/. These are the fricatives, approximants, and vowels.

    [–continuant] are /p, b, t, d, k, g, ʔ, m, n, ŋ/. Recall that affricates have stop onsets, which are [–continuant], and fricative offsets, which are [+continuant] (/č, ǰ/ = [tš, dž]).

5. [+voiced], articulated with vibrating vocal folds: /b, v, ð, d, z, ǰ, ž, g/ and, ordinarily, the sonorant phonemes /m, n, ŋ, l, r, j, w, i, ɪ, e, ɛ, æ, ə, ɑ, ɔ, o, ʊ, u/. English sonorant consonants may be [–voiced] when they follow syllable-initial voiceless obstruents as in *plane* [pʰl̥ējːn] and *truck* [tʰr̥ək] (allophonic rule 3 of chapter 3, §3.1), and English unstressed vowels may be voiceless when they are between voiceless consonants as in *petunia* [pə̥tʰúnjə] (allophonic rule 20 of chapter 3, §3.1; IPA shows voicelessness by a small circle under a phonetic symbol, as in [m̥, l̥, e̥]).

    [–voiced] are /p, f, θ, t, s, č, š, k, ʔ, h/.

6. [+strident], having acoustic stridency: /f, v, s, z, š, ž, č, ǰ/. Stridency is the sound of high pitched friction, which, for example, distinguishes alveolar [s] from interdental [θ], and labiodental [f] from bilabial [ɸ]. Pronounce [sssss] and [θθθθθ], and hear the difference of stridency, which is prominent in [sssss]. Stridency is a characteristic of fricatives only, including of those affricates which like /č, ǰ/ have strident fricatives offsets.

    [–strident] fricatives of English are /θ, ð, h/, and all the non-fricative phonemes are [–strident]: /p, b, t, d, k, g, ʔ, m, n, ŋ, l, r, j, w, i, ɪ, e, ɛ, æ, ə, ɑ, ɔ, o, ʊ, u/.

If we list the phonemes of American English horizontally and the phonological features vertically, the result is a **feature matrix,** in which the values of the phonemes for each feature are shown in the cells, as in figure 14.1, the feature matrix of the six airstream features and 36 phonemes. For lack of space, the voiced obstruents and the affricates are omitted. The voiced obstruents /b, v, ð, d, z, ž, g/ are like their voiceless counterparts /p, f, θ, t, s, š, k/ except for being [+voiced] instead of [–voiced], and the affricates /č, ǰ/, recall, are stop + fricative sequences [tš] and [dž], respectively.

Notice in figure 14.1 the empty cells for [voiced] in the column of [+sonorant, +continuant] phones /l, r, j, w, i, ɪ, e, ɛ, æ, ə, ɑ, ɔ, o, ʊ, u/, which are ordinarily [+voiced] but, allophonically, may be [–voiced], as in *clue* [kʰḷú], *quick* [kʷw̥ík], and *potato* [pə̥tʰédə].

Also notice how the nasal consonant phonemes [m, n, ŋ] are defined: as [+sonorant, –continuant]. These phones are also [+nasal], a feature defined as 'articulated with lowered velum'. The feature [**nasal**] was not listed among the airstream features because it is not necessary for defining this set of phonemes; if a phoneme is [+sonorant, –continuant], then it is also, redundantly, [+nasal].

2.2. Three articulator features

Three **articulator features** are [**glottal**], [**labial**], and [**dorsal**], defined as follows:

7. [+**glottal**], articulated with the glottis: /h, ʔ/.

   [–**glottal**] are /p, b, f, v, θ, ð, t, d, s, z, č, ǰ, š, ž, k, g, m, n, ŋ, l, r, j, w, i, ɪ, e, ɛ, æ, ə, ɑ, ɔ, o, ʊ, u/.

8. [+**labial**], articulated with the lips: consonants /p, b, f, v, m, w/, and vowels /o, u/ plus sometimes /ɔ, ʊ/. /p, b, f, v, m/ have labial contact; labial vowels, /w/, and labialized consonants as in *quick* [kʷw̥ík] and *rip* [rʷíp] have lip rounding.

   [–**labial**] are consonants /θ, ð, t, d, s, z, č, ǰ, š, ž, k, g, h, ʔ, n, ŋ, l, j/ and vowels /i, ɪ, e, ɛ, æ, ə, ɑ/ plus sometimes /ɔ, ʊ/. American English /r/ is [+labial] when word initial (chapter 3, §3.1, allophonic rule 11).

9. [+**dorsal**], articulated with the body of the tongue: velar consonants /k, g, ŋ/, the labiovelar glide /w/, velarized /l/, and the central and back vowels /ə, ɑ, ɔ, o, ʊ, u/. Vocoids /w, o, u/ and, if rounded, /ɔ, ʊ/, are [+dorsal] as well as [+labial]. Velarized /l/ (chapter 3, §3.1, allophonic rule 12) is [+dorsal] as well as [+coronal].

   [–**dorsal**] are consonants /p, b, f, v, θ, ð, t, d, s, z, č, ǰ, š, ž, h, ʔ, m, n, r, j/ plus unvelarized /l/, and vowels /i, ɪ, e, ɛ, æ/.

The tongue tip is a fourth and indeed the most frequent articulator. Consonants which are not glottal, labial, or dorsal are articulated with the tongue tip.

	p	f	θ	t	s	š	k	ʔ	h	m	n	ŋ	l	r	j	w	i	ɪ	e	ɛ	æ	ə	ɑ	ɔ	o	ʊ	u
glt	–	–	–	–	–	–	–	+	+	–	–	–	–	–	–	–	–	–	–	–	–	–	–	–	–	–	–
lab	+	+	–	–	–	–	–	–	–	+	–	–	–		–	+	–	–	–	–	–	–	–		+		+
dor	–	–	–	–	–	–	+	–	–	–	–	+		–	+	–	–	–	–	–	–	–	+	+	+	+	+

Figure 14.2   Feature matrix of articulator features and English phonemes (affricates and voiced obstruents omitted)

These phones, termed '**coronal**', may be described as [+**coronal**], but the coronal consonants are here represented as having minus values for other articulator features, thus: [–glottal, –labial, –dorsal]. The English coronal consonants are /θ, ð, t, d, č, ǰ, s, z, š, ž, n, ŋ, l, r/ (velarized /l/ is [+coronal, +dorsal], and word-initial /r/ is [+coronal, +labial]).

See figure 14.2, the feature matrix of the three articulator features and English phonemes, again less the voiced obstruents and the affricates.

Notice the empty cells of figure 14.2: (a) [dorsal] for /l/, which, velarized, is [+dorsal] and otherwise [–dorsal]; (b) [labial] for /r/, which is rounded and [+labial] at the beginning of words and otherwise unrounded and [-labial]; (c) [labial] for /ɔ, ʊ/, which may or may not be [+labial] (rounded) in some environments and in the speech of some.

2.3.   Three tongue body features

The three **tongue body features** are [**high**], [**low**], and [**peripheral**], defined as follows.

10.   [+**high**], articulated with the tongue body raised: /č, ǰ, š, ž, k, g, ŋ, r, j, w, i, ɪ, ʊ, u/. In /č, ǰ, š, ž, r/ the tongue tip is also raised.

[–**high**] are /p, b, f, v, θ, ð, t, d, s, z, h, ʔ, m, n, l, e, ɛ, æ, ə, ɑ, ɔ, o/.

11.   [+**low**], articulated with the tongue body lowered: the three vowels /æ, ɑ, ɔ/.

[–**low**] are all the rest, /p, b, f, v, θ, ð, t, d, s, z, č, ǰ, š, ž, k, g, h, ʔ, m, n, ŋ, l, r, j, w, i, ɪ, e, ɛ, ə, o, ʊ, u/.

12.   [+**peripheral**], articulated with the tongue body fronted or backed, toward the periphery of oral vowel space; /i, e/ are fronted and /ɔ, o, u/ are backed. For English, this feature is only relevant for vowels, characterizing the five vowels which can occur at the end of words and are traditionally termed 'tense' (chapter 2, §5.2).

[–**peripheral**] are all other phonemes /p, b, f, v, θ, ð, t, d, s, z, č, ǰ, š, ž, k, g, h, ʔ, m, n, ŋ, l, r, w, j, ɪ, ɛ, æ, ə, ɑ, ʊ/.

	p	f	θ	t	s	š	k	ʔ	h	m	n	ŋ	l	r	j	w	i	ɪ	e	ɛ	æ	ə	ɑ	ɔ	o	ʊ	u
hi	–	–	–	–	–	+	+	–	–	–	–	+	–	+	+	+	+	–	–	–	–	–	–	–	–	+	+
lo	–	–	–	–	–	–	–	–	–	–	–	–	–	–	–	–	–	–	–	–	+	–	+	+	–	–	–
per	–	–	–	–	–	–	–	–	–	–	–	–	–	–	–	–	+	–	+	–	+	–	–	+	+	–	+

Figure 14.3   Feature matrix of tongue body features and English phonemes (affricates and voiced obstruents omitted)

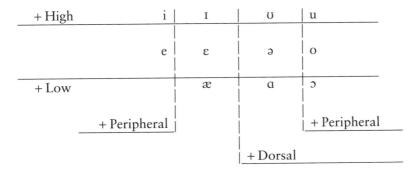

Figure 14.4   English vowels characterized by articulator and tongue body features

See figure 14.3, the feature matrix of the three tongue body features and American English phonemes (less the voiced obstruents and affricates).

The American English vowels are fully sorted with one articulator feature, [dorsal], and the three tongue body features. This is shown in figure 14.4, a chart in which the features define cells in a cross-section of English vowel-space. In fact, there is considerable disagreement about the feature description of English vowels.

3. SYLLABLES

3.1. The typical structure of syllables

The phonological airstream features provide an understanding of what we traditionally call 'syllables'. Syllables always include one [+syllabic] phone, ordinarily a vowel, with zero or more [–syllabic] phones on either side. Typically the phones on either side of the [+syllabic] phone are progressively less open than the vowel – they limit the airstream more. More openness corresponds, generally, to greater acoustic **sonority**. The **sonority scale** of phones may be expressed with phonological features as in figure 14.5.

Typical syllables (there are exceptions) consist of an up and down cycle of sonority, in which only a [+syllabic] phone (usually a vowel), the **syllable nucleus**, is obligatory. Consonant sequences which rise in sonority, before the nucleus, are the **syllable head**, and those which fall in sonority, after the nucleus,

More sonorous ↑ ↓ Less sonorous	1	[+ vocoid, + syllabic]	Vowels
	2	[+ vocoid, – syllabic]	Glides
	3	[+ sonorant, + continuant]	Liquids
	4	[+ sonorant, – continuant]	Nasal stops
	5	[– sonorant, + continuant]	Fricatives
	6	[– sonorant, – continuant]	Oral stops

Figure 14.5   Sonority scale

	6 [– cnt]	5 [– son]	4 [– cnt]	3 [+ son]	2 [+ voc]	1 [+ syl]	2 [+ voc]	3 [+ son]	4 [– cnt]	5 [– son]	6 [– cnt]
print:	p			r		ɪ			n		t
quark:	k				w	ɑ		r			k
clasp:	k		l			æ				s	p
bright:	b			r		ɑ	j				t
swerve:		s			w	ə		r		v	
smile:		s	m			ɑ	j	l			

Head — Nucleus — Coda

Rhyme

Figure 14.6   Sonority structure of some English words

are the **syllable coda**. The nucleus plus the optional coda is the **rhyme**. In figure 14.6, notice this rise and fall of sonority across the five phonemes of six English one-syllable words.

To the possibilities of syllable composition determined strictly by sonority sequencing, as in the words of figure 14.6, English adds two:

a.   syllable-initial /s/ may precede the voiceless stops /p, t, k/, as in *splash* /splæš/, *strict* /strɪkt/, and *squeeze* /skwiz/, and,

b.   syllable-final /s, z, t, d/ may follow stops in word-final syllables; these consonants almost always represent the inflectional suffixes, as in *sprints* /sprɪnts/, *builds* /bɪldz/, *clasped* /klæspt/, and *grabbed* /græbd/.

These additions are sometimes said to be syllable 'affixes', or 'extrasyllabic'.

3.2. Syllabification

Often different syllabifications of a word are possible, each of which fulfills the requirements of the sonority cycle. The word /sɪlæbɪfɪkéšən/ *syllabification*, for example, could be syllabified as /sɪ • læ • bɪ • fɪ • ké • šən/, /sɪl • æb • ɪf • ɪk • éš • ən/, or many other ways, but there is usually evidence that the preferred syllabification is that which favors the maximal number of consonants as heads.

In the pronunciation of this word, for example, /l/ is unvelarized as if it was at the beginning of a word (hence syllable-initial), and /k/ is aspirated [kʰ] as if it was at the beginning of a word (hence syllable-initial). Such facts favor the syllabification / sɪ • læ • bɪ • fɪ • ké • šən /.

Thus a generally successful procedure for syllabifying most words of most languages is as follows:

> Each peak and optional associated rise and fall of sonority, maximizing the rise, is a syllable.

The word *subtraction*, then, is syllabified as /səb • træk • šən/; *algebra* /ælǰəbrə/ is syllabified as /æl • ǰə • brə/; and *calculus* /kælkjələs/ as /kæl • kjə • ləs/.

4. FEATURE PHONOLOGY

4.1. Phonemic and phonetic representations

The basic or lexical form of a morpheme, as this appears in the mental dictionary, is a **phonemic representation**, which includes only the **phonemic features** of the form of a morpheme, those which are contrastively or distinctively associated with its meaning (chapter 13, §1).

The system of phonological features is very efficient, and relatively few phonological features are needed to specify phonemic (lexical) form. In pronunciations, phonological rules apply to the phonemic form, and the result is a **phonetic representation**, which includes features which persist from the lexicon and also many features added by the phonological rules, perhaps including a few phonemic values which are changed by the rules. This is illustrated below, in some detail, by an example from English: the phonology of the sentence *Cats will play*.

4.2. Feature phonology of English

Figure 14.7 is a feature matrix which combines all twelve phonological features and the American English phonemes, less the voiced obstruents and affricates. Cells with feature values supplied by allophonic rules are left empty.

4.2.1. Redundancy rules

Many pluses and minuses included in the feature matrix of figure 14.7 are redundant. That is, they are fully predictable from other feature values of the matrix. **Redundancy rules** for these features, including those true for all languages and those specific to English, are:

a.   Phones of any language which are [+vocoid] are [+sonorant, +continuant].
b.   Phones of any language which are [+sonorant] and not made [−voiced] by a more specific (allophonic) rule are [+voiced].

	p	f	θ	t	s	š	k	ʔ	h	m	n	ŋ	l	r	j	w	i	ɪ	e	ɛ	æ	ə	ɑ	ɔ	o	ʊ	u
voc	−	−	−	−	−	−	−	−	−	−	−	−	−	−	−	−	+	+	+	+	+	+	+	+	+	+	+
syl	−	−	−	−	−	−	−	−	−	−		−			−	−	+	+	+	+	+	+	+	+	+	+	+
son	−	−	−	−	−	−	−	−	−	+	+	+	+	+	+	+	+	+	+	+	+	+	+	+	+	+	+
cnt	−	+	+	−	+	+	−	−	+	−	−	−	+	+	+	+	+	+	+	+	+	+	+	+	+	+	+
vcd	−	−	−	−	−	−	−	−	−	+	+	+															
str	−	+	−	−	+	+	−	−	−	−	−	−	−	−	−	−	−	−	−	−	−	−	−	−	−	−	−
glt	−	−	−	−	−	−	−	+	+	−	−	−	−	−	−	−	−	−	−	−	−	−	−	−	−	−	−
lab	+	+	−	−	−	−	−	−	−	+	−	−	−	−	−	+	−	−	−	−	−	−	−	−	+	−	+
dor	−	−	−	−	−	−	+	−	−	−	−	+	−	−	−	+	−	−	−	−	−	−	+	+	+	+	+
hi	−	−	−	−	+	+	+	−	−	−	−	+	−	+	+	+	+	+	−	−	−	−	−	−	−	+	+
lo	−	−	−	−	−	−	−	−	−	−	−	−	−	−	−	−	−	−	−	−	+	−	+	+	−	−	−
per	−	−	−	−	−	−	−	−	−	−	−	−	−	−	−	−	+	−	+	−	−	−	+	+	−	−	+

Figure 14.7 Feature matrix of 12 features and English phonemes (affricates and voiced obstruents omitted)

c. Phones of any language which are [+sonorant, −continuant] (nasal consonants, English /m, n, ŋ/) are [+nasal]. But the row for [nasal] is not shown in figure 14.7.

d. Phones of English which are [−sonorant, +continuant, +labial] (/f, v/) are labiodental and therefore [+strident].

e. Phones of English which are [+vocoid, +dorsal, −low, +peripheral] (/w, o, u/) are [+labial], as are, sometimes, phones which are [+vocoid, +dorsal] and [+peripheral] or [+high] (/ɔ, ʊ/).

f. Phones of English which are [−continuant, +dorsal] (/k, g, ŋ/) and those which are [+vocoid, −syllabic] (/j, w/) are [+high].

g. In all languages, feature values not filled in by other rules are [−].

The redundancy rules permit the omission in the lexical forms of morphemes of the features which they provide. Thus the lexicon need not include values for [sonorant] or [continuant] for [+vocoid] phonemes, nor values for [voiced] for [+sonorant] phonemes, etc., nor, indeed, any minus values.

4.2.2. Allophonic rules

Allophonic rules permit further omission of feature values from figure 14.7. Among the **allophonic rules** of English (chapter 3, §3.1), four are:

h. [−syllabic, +sonorant, +continuant] (approximant) phones are [−voiced] when they follow [+aspirated] phones (so /l/ of *play* is [l̥]).

i. [−sonorant, −continuant] (voiceless stop) phones are [+aspirated] when initial in their syllables and before a stressed vowel (so /k/ of *cats* and /p/ of *play* are [kʰ] and [pʰ]). The feature [+aspirated] is entirely allophonic in English, and has been omitted in the feature matrices.

	p	f	θ	t	s	š	k	ʔ	h	m	n	ŋ	l	r	j	w	i	ɪ	e	ɛ	æ	ə	ɑ	ɔ	o	ʊ	u
voc																+	+	+	+	+	+	+	+	+	+	+	+
syl																	+	+	+	+	+	+	+	+	+	+	+
son										+	+	+	+	+													
cnt		+	+		+	+			+				+	+													
vcd																											
str					+	+																					
glt								+	+																		
lab	+	+								+																	
dor							+					+				+							+	+	+	+	+
hi							+									+	+	+								+	+
lo																					+		+	+			
per																	+		+				+		+		+

Figure 14.8 Lexical feature matrix of English phonemes (affricates and voiced obstruents omitted)

j. [−vocoid, +sonorant, +continuant, −high] (/l/) is [+dorsal] (velarized) when at the end of syllables (so /l/ of *will* is [ɫ]).

k. [+syllabic, −dorsal, −high, +peripheral] (/e/), when stressed, is followed by a high off-glide (so /e/ of *play* is [eʲ]).

4.2.3. *Lexical representations*

The redundancy rules and allophonic rules permit omission of numerous feature values from phonemic feature matrices, and thus very economical lexical representations. Columns of the matrix remain distinct from one another, while including information sufficient to allow the grammar, by the application of the redundancy and allophonic rules, to convert these into representations of fully detailed phones. Figure 14.8 is a feature matrix of just the **phonemic features** of English phonemes, including only those values necessary in the lexical representations of morphemes to distinguish phonemes from one another and to predict other values. After the omissions of values which the redundancy and allophonic rules permit, only 66 feature values remain for the 324 cells of figure 14.8 (66/324 = 20%).

The syntax and morphology of English assemble the four morphemes of the sentence /kætswɪlple/ *Cats will play* as the four-part phonemic feature matrix shown in figure 14.9. Notice how few feature values are necessary in the representation of these four morphemes of ten phonemes: 20, or 16.7% of 120 cells of the four matrices.

4.2.4. *Morphophonemic rules*

In addition to rules (a)–(k) above, **morphophonemic rules** (chapter 13, §1.2) apply, including:

	'cat'	'Plural'	'will'	'play'
voc	+		++	+
syl	+		+	+
son			+	+
cnt		+	+	+
vcd		+		
str		+		
glt				
lab				+
dor	+		+	
high			+	
lo	+			
per				+

Figure 14.9   Phonemic feature matrix of *Cats will play*

l. A [−sonorant] phone following a [−sonorant] phone within a syllable has the value for [voiced] of the preceding obstruent; /z/ of the plural suffix follows a voiceless obstruent in its syllable, so its lexical feature [+voiced] must be [−voiced]. (It was discussed in the preceding chapter, §1.2.1.1, why we consider this suffix to be lexically [+voiced].) We assume this rule changes [+voiced] of /z/ to [−voiced].

m. Stress is assigned by phonological rules we have not discussed: in English secondary stress on the vowel of /kæts/ and primary stress on that of /ple/. This is shown in figure 14.10 as a '2' and a '1', respectively, in the column of these vowels in the row of the feature [stress] ([sts]). Stress is generally assigned by rules in English, so this feature is generally absent in English lexical/phonemic forms. (There are other ways to represent stress, which it is convenient to include here as a phonological feature.)

After all relevant phonological rules of the three types apply, the result is the phonetic form written in IPA symbols [kʰǽtswɪɫpʰléi], and represented in phonological features as the phonetic feature matrix of figure 14.10. At the bottom of figure 14.10, the IPA phonetic representation is provided just as a guide to reading the unfamiliar columns of features.

From this example of the short English sentence *Cats will play*, it may be apparent that pronunciations are the product of surprisingly simple lexical phonological form and intricately interacting phonological rules. But this is fully apparent only when phonology is understood in terms of features rather than phones.

5.   FUNCTIONS OF PHONOLOGY

The two aspects of phonology, lexical phonological representations and phonological rules, have distinct purposes evident in the example of *Cats will play*.

$$
\begin{bmatrix}
\text{voc} & - & + & - & - & + & + & - & - & - & + & + \\
\text{syl} & - & + & - & - & - & + & - & - & - & + & - \\
\text{son} & - & + & - & - & + & + & + & - & + & + & + \\
\text{cnt} & - & + & - & + & + & + & + & - & + & + & + \\
\text{vcd} & - & + & - & - & + & + & + & - & - & + & + \\
\text{str} & - & - & - & + & - & - & - & - & - & - & - \\
\text{glt} & - & - & - & - & - & - & - & - & - & - & - \\
\text{lab} & - & - & - & - & + & - & - & + & - & - & - \\
\text{dor} & + & - & - & - & + & - & + & - & - & - & - \\
\text{hi} & + & - & - & - & + & + & - & - & - & - & + \\
\text{lo} & - & + & - & - & - & - & - & - & - & - & - \\
\text{per} & - & - & - & - & - & - & - & - & - & + & + \\
\text{asp} & + & - & - & - & - & - & - & + & - & - & - \\
\text{sts} & & 2 & & & & & & & 1 & &
\end{bmatrix}
$$

$$([\text{k}^\text{h} \; \text{æ} \; \text{t} \; \text{s} \; \text{w} \; \text{ɪ} \; \text{ɫ} \; \text{p}^\text{h} \; \text{l̥} \; \text{é} \; {}^\text{j}])$$

Figure 14.10 Phonetic feature matrix of *Cats will play*

Lexical phonological representations need to be no more extensive or complete than is necessary to distinguish one morpheme from another. Fulfillment of this requirement is evident in the simple and economical representation given in figure 14.9 for the four morphemes *cat*, *s* (plural), *will* and *play*, which employs only 12 features and 20 feature values (all '+').

As for phonological rules, these are typically of four types.

5.1. Universal rules

Some rules reflect the simple realities of the physiology of speech common to all languages, according to which one feature value necessarily implicates another. Redundancy rule (a), above, is an example of a phonological rule of this type: [+vocoid] phones have an uninterrupted airstream, so these are necessarily also [+sonorant] and [+continuant]. Redundancy rules (b) and (c) are also of this type. Universals of language are the topic of chapter 20.

Redundancy rule (g) fills empty cells with minus values. This rule simply reflects the fact that the phonological features may be defined in such a way that fewer cells, whether in phonemic or phonetic matrices, have plus values. Thus all phonemic feature values are pluses, and, except for this rule and in exceptional environments, phonological rules need only supply additional plus values. (This rule is only implicit in writings on phonology, but it is very generally true, and very useful in the present introductory discussion because of the considerable simplification which it allows.)

5.2. Language particular feature choices

Some rules reflect the different choices of languages among the phonological features and their possibilities of cooccurrence. Redundancy rule (d) is an example of a phonological rule of this type, for English. According to this rule [–sonorant, +continuant, +labial] phones (the labial fricatives) are [+strident] (labiodental). (English, that is, has [f, v] and not [ɸ, β], a characteristic shared with many other languages (chapter 20, §2.1.1.1).) Redundancy rules (e)–(f) are also of this type.

5.3. Assimilatory rules

Some rules blend one phone into another, as a natural result of efficient speech, in which feature values persist from one phone to another or anticipate feature values of following phones. Allophonic rule (h) is an example of a phonological rule of this type: [–syllabic, +sonorant, +continuant] (approximant) phones are [–voiced] when they follow an aspirated (voiceless) phone in their syllable. Morphophonemic rule (l), which makes adjacent obstruents identical in voicing, is also of this type.

5.4. Marking rules

Other rules cannot be confidently identified as having any of the above three roles, but often these rules have the effect of making phones more acoustically prominent, particularly where such prominence may mark the beginning or end of a morpheme or word. Rule (i) is an example of such a 'marking' rule: [–sonorant, –continuant, –voiced] phones are [+aspirated] before a stressed vowel. Aspiration adds a phenomenon of prominent 'burst' to many stressed syllables of words of English. Allophonic rules (j)–(k) and morphophonemic rule (m), which assigns stress, mainly to lexical not grammatical morphemes, are also of this type.

Suggestions for
ADDITIONAL READING

Phonological features, some different from those employed here, are introduced in most current textbooks on phonology, such as those suggested at the end of the previous chapter. In *The Handbook of Phonological Theory* (1995), edited by John A. Goldsmith, the chapter on 'The internal organization of speech sounds', by G. N. Clements and Elizabeth V. Hume, reviews work on the nature of features and their interdependencies.

Also in *The Handbook of Phonological Theory* is an article on the syllable: 'The syllable in phonological theory', by Juliette Blevins. Regarding the syllable, also see *Preference Laws for Syllable Structure, and the Explanation of Sound Change* (1988) by Theo Vennemann.

IMPORTANT CONCEPTS AND TERMS IN THIS CHAPTER

- phonological features
- binary
- airstream features
- [vocoid]
- [syllabic]
- [sonorant]
- obstruent
- [continuant]
- [voiced]
- [strident]
- feature matrix
- [nasal]
- articulator features
- [glottal]
- [labial]
- [dorsal]
- [coronal]
- tongue body features

- [high]
- [low]
- [peripheral]
- syllable
- sonority
- sonority scale
- syllable nucleus
- syllable head
- syllable coda
- rhyme
- phonemic representation
- phonemic features
- phonetic representation
- redundancy rules
- allophonic rules
- morphophonemic rules
- universal rules
- assimilatory rules

OUTLINE OF CHAPTER 14

5. Functions of phonology
1. Universal rules
2. Language particular feature choices
3. Assimilatory rules
4. Marking rules

EXAMPLES AND PRACTICE

EXAMPLE

1. Feature characterization of sets of phones. The set of phones [s, l, w] share at least the positive feature [+continuant] and many negative features including [−glottal]. The set [m, o, a] share at least the positive feature [+sonorant] and many negative features including [−glottal].

PRACTICE

Mention at least one positive feature and one negative feature shared by each of the three-phone sets 1–12. The set [d, n, r], for example, is [+voiced] and [−labial].

1. [m, w, j]   5. [e, ə, o]   9. [ð, i, e]
2. [s, z, l]   6. [p, f, w̥]   10. [ʊ, ə, ɑ]
3. [v, b, m]   7. [f, s, r]   11. [k, w, u]
4. [g, č, w]   8. [i, u, ɪ]   12. [m, n, õ]

EXAMPLE

2. Phone classes. The phonological features classify phones variously.

PRACTICE

Match phone sets 1–10 with feature sets (a)–(l) with which they are consistent. Two of (a)–(l) are not answers. Use each answer only once.

1. [f, θ, s, š, h]   6. [m, n, ŋ, j̃, w̃, ĩ, ẽ, ɔ̃, ã]
2. [p, b, t, d, k, g, ʔ]   7. [l, r, j, w]
3. [w, ə, ɑ, ɔ, o, ʊ, u]   8. [θ, ð, h, z, š, ž]
4. [č, š, k, ŋ, j, i, ɪ, ʊ, u]   9. [æ, ɑ, ɔ]
5. [p, f, θ, t, č, s, š, k]   10. [e, ɛ, ə, o]

a. [+vocoid, −high, −low]   g. [+high]
b. [−syllabic, +sonorant, −nasal]   h. [−voiced, −glottal]
c. [−sonorant, −continuant]   i. [−sonorant, +continuant, −voiced]
d. [+vocoid, +high]   j. [+vocoid, +dorsal]
e. [+continuant, −labial, −dorsal]   k. [+labial, −voiced]
f. [+nasal]   l. [+vocoid, +low]

3. Features and English phonemes. The feature specification [+vocoid, −syllabic, +dorsal] describes only /w/ of the English phonemes, and the feature specification [−sonorant, +continuant, −voiced, −glottal, −labial, −strident] describes only /θ/ of the English phonemes.

For each feature specification 1–10, say which English phoneme it describes.

1.   [−sonorant, −continuant, +voiced, +labial]
2.   [+sonorant, −continuant, +dorsal]
3.   [+vocoid, +syllabic, −dorsal, +high, +peripheral]
4.   [+vocoid, −syllabic, −dorsal]
5.   [+vocoid, +syllabic, +dorsal, +low, +peripheral]
6.   [−sonorant, +continuant, +glottal]
7.   [−sonorant, +continuant, +voiced, +labial]
8.   [+sonorant, +continuant, +voiced, +labial]
9.   [+vocoid, +syllabic, +dorsal, −high, −low, −peripheral]
10.   `[−sonorant, −continuant, −glottal, −labial, −dorsal]

4. English words expressed as phonological feature matrices.

Match meanings 1–15 with phonetic feature matrices (a)–(o) of figure 14.11. For example, matrix (a) is 'end' (1). These are phonetic feature matrices, so they include some non-lexical information, such as [+dorsal] for the velarized /l/ of 'old' and [+labial] for word-initial rounded /r/ of 'red' and 'read'.

1. 'end'	5. 'sigh'	9. 'road'	13. 'read'
2. 'nick'	6. 'then'	10. 'door'	14. 'tree'
3. 'seem'	7. 'red'	11. 'old'	15. 'soon'
4. 'shoot'	8. 'hang'	12. 'move'	

5. English syllablification. Recall the procedure for syllabifying words, given in §3.2.

Following the procedure, syllabify the following words (given in the author's pronunciations, less stress marking). Then check your syllabifications against those given by a dictionary and mention any differences.

1. Argentina /àrȷ̌əntínə/	4. Colombia /kəlámbiə/
2. Brazil /brəzíl/	5. Costa Rica /kòstəríkə/
3. Canada /kǽnədə/	6. Guatemala /gwàdəmálə/

	a	b	c	d	e
voc	+ − −	− + −	+ − −	− + −	− + −
syl	+ − −	− + −	+ − −	− + −	− + −
son	+ + −	+ + −	+ + −	− + +	+ + −
cnt	+ − −	+ + −	+ + −	+ + −	+ + −
vcd	+ + +	+ + +	+ + +	− + +	+ + +
str	− − −	− − −	− − −	+ − −	− − −
glt	− − −	− − −	− − −	− − −	− − −
lab	− − −	+ − −	+ − −	− + −	+ + −
dor	− − −	− − −	+ + −	− + −	− + −
hi	− − −	+ − −	− − −	− + −	+ − −
low	− − −	− − −	− − −	− − −	− − −
per	− − −	− − −	+ − −	− + −	− + −

	f	g	h	i	j
voc	− + −	− + −	− + −	− + −	− + −
syl	− + −	− + −	− + −	− + −	− + −
son	+ + −	+ + −	− + +	− + +	− + +
cnt	− + −	+ + −	− + +	+ + −	+ + −
vcd	+ + −	+ + +	+ + +	+ + +	− + +
str	− − −	− − −	− − −	− − −	+ − −
glt	− − −	− − −	− − −	− − −	− − −
lab	− − −	+ − −	− + −	− − −	− − +
dor	− − +	− − −	− + −	− − −	− − −
hi	− + +	+ + −	− − +	− − −	− + −
low	− − −	− − −	− − −	− − −	− − −
per	− − −	− + −	− + −	− − −	− + −

	k	l	m	n	o
voc	− + +	− − +	− + −	− + −	− + −
syl	− + −	− − +	− + −	− + −	− + −
son	− + +	− + +	− + −	+ + −	− + +
cnt	+ + +	− + +	+ + −	− + +	+ + −
vcd	− + +	− − +	− + −	+ + +	− + +
str	+ − −	− − −	+ − −	− − +	− − −
glt	− − −	− − −	− − −	− − −	+ − −
lab	− − −	− − −	− + −	+ + +	− − −
dor	− + −	− − −	− + −	− + −	− − +
hi	− − +	− + +	+ + −	− + −	− − +
low	− + −	− − −	− − −	− − −	− + −
per	− − +	− − +	− + −	− + −	− − −

Figure 14.11 Phonetic feature matrices of 15 English words

7. Honduras /hùndúrəs/   9.   Nicaragua /nìkərágwə/
8. Mexico /méksiko/   10. Panama /pǽnəmɑ/

6. Syllables and non-syllables of English. The sonority cycle described in §3.1, above, which is generally consistent with syllable heads and codas of English, allows some syllables which do not occur in English, such as /pmæ/ and /dlo/ – but there is /æmp/ and /old/; English has more different codas than heads. However, with the two exceptions mentioned exceptions mentioned of initial /s/ and final /s, z, t, d/, it does not disallow any which do occur in careful speech.

Consider the possible English syllable heads consisting of a phone of the vertical axis of table 14.1 followed by a phone of the horizontal axis of the table. Number consecutively each cell which describes an actual syllable head of English. Then list English words, one for each number (spelled and written phonemically), which have the word-initial syllable heads. The first row is done as an example; the words 1–3 are:

Table 14.1   Two-consonant sequences of English syllable heads

	p	b	f	v	θ	ð	t	d	s	z	š	ž	k	g	ʔ	h	m	n	ŋ	l	r	j	w
p																				1	2	3	
b																							
f																							
v																							
θ																							
ð																							
t																							
d																							
s																							
z																							
š																							
ž																							
k																							
g																							
ʔ																							
h																							
l																							
r																							
m																							
n																							
ŋ																							
j																							
w																							

1. play /ple/
2. pray /pre/
3. pure /pjʊr/

7. Phonological rules and representations I. Ignoring stress and vowel length, the fully specified phonetic feature matrix for *Ring the bell, please*, according to typical American speech, is figure 14.12.

$$
\begin{array}{lccccccccccccc}
\text{voc} & - & + & - & - & + & - & + & - & - & - & + & - \\
\text{syl} & - & + & - & - & + & - & + & - & - & - & + & - \\
\text{son} & + & + & + & - & + & - & + & + & - & + & + & - \\
\text{cnt} & + & + & - & + & + & - & + & + & - & + & + & + \\
\text{vcd} & + & + & + & + & + & + & + & + & - & - & + & + \\
\text{str} & - & - & - & - & - & - & - & - & - & - & - & + \\
\text{glt} & - & - & - & - & - & - & - & - & - & - & - & - \\
\text{lab} & + & - & - & - & - & + & - & - & + & - & - & - \\
\text{dor} & - & - & + & - & + & - & - & + & - & - & - & - \\
\text{hi} & + & + & + & - & - & - & - & + & - & - & + & - \\
\text{low} & - & - & - & - & - & - & - & - & - & - & - & - \\
\text{per} & - & - & - & - & - & - & - & - & - & - & + & - \\
\text{nas} & - & + & + & - & - & - & - & - & - & - & - & - \\
\text{asp} & - & - & - & - & - & - & - & - & + & - & - & - \\
\end{array}
$$

([rʷ ĩ ŋ ð ə b ɛ ɬ pʰ ḷ i z])

Figure 14.12   Phonetic feature matrix of *Ring the bell, please*

Considering rules (a)–(m), above, and allophonic rules 1–25 of chapter 3, §3.1, provide the lexical or phonemic matrix for this sentence, a matrix like figure 14.12 but with all the minuses and the redundant pluses omitted.

8. Phonological rules and representations II. Consider the short English sentence *Dogs shouldn't fight*. Ignoring stress, its phonemic representation in typical American speech might be /dɔgzšʊdntfɑjt/ (with a syllabic /n/).

Provide a phonetic feature matrix for this sentence. Then, using the 12 features presented in this chapter, and considering redundancy and allophonic rules, provide its lexical form.

SIX WAYS TO GET NEW WORDS

This chapter presents an important principle which tends to limit the possibilities of new word formation, and, using mainly English examples, presents four ways to give new form to old, or established, meanings, and two ways to get new meanings in new forms.

1. OPENNESS

An important aspect of the general characteristics of language known as **creativity** (chapter 1, §3.4.3) is **openness**, which concerns the fact that all languages continually get new morphemes, and have a variety of ways to do this. New ideas, new tools and products, and unique events occur all the time, and all languages cope readily and richly with this novelty by having several ways of creating new morphemes and new words to express them.

2. NEW WORDS NOT USUALLY ALL NEW

Morphemes, recall, are relationships of form and meaning, so there are three senses in which a morpheme may be new, and so be the basis of a new word: the new morpheme may have (a) new meaning in new form, (b) new meaning in old form, or (c) old meaning in new form.

2.1. New meanings in new forms

In relatively rare cases, languages require the expression of new meaning in new form. An example of this is the word *karaoke*, a Japanese word introduced into English along with the technology which it concerns: 'sing along with video display of recorded music'. Both the meaning of the word and its form are new – in English. (In Japanese, by the way, this word is also a case of new meaning in new form: *kara* 'empty' + *oke*, a shortened or clipped form of the Italian word *orchestra*, which perhaps reaches Japanese through English.) This chapter will discuss two ways to express new meanings in new forms.

2.2.   New meanings in old forms

In many cases, new meanings are expressed by use of old forms of the language, if sometimes in new combinations. An example of this is the relatively recent but already well established use of the words *log* and *on*, as *log on*, to mean 'access electronic communication networks via computer'. The meaning is new, but the forms are old. The following chapter presents seven such ways to express new meanings by use of old forms.

2.3.   Old meanings in new forms

2.2.1.   *New forms in syntax*

We have seen that syntax is a rich and ready source of creative expression in languages. New thoughts can be given form, if rather lengthily, through new sentences. In this case, the form of the thought, the sentence, may be quite routine. Consider the first occasions of electronically transmitted mail by computer, which may naturally have been described, in English, by use of a 'relative clause' (explained in chapter 18, practice 5; the relative clause of the following noun phrase is bracketed): *mail [which is sent and received electronically, by computer]*. This suggests a much simpler adjective + noun phrase: *electronic mail*. But when such a new meaning is no longer so new, and has been proven useful with much repetition, it may usefully be condensed further by processes of new word formation of the language. (In English, most new morphemes are new words.)

2.2.2.   *New forms in morphology*

New morphemes also result when old and everyday things and events are expressed in clever new ways, as new words, sometimes by child learners, but more importantly by adults who in this way assert their creativity and individuality. This too is going on all the time in languages: old meanings are given new form. An example of this is *e-mail*, a shortened form of *electronic mail*. The first part of the form of this new word, *e-*, is new but, at least at first, the meaning, basically, is old: 'electronic'. The new, shortened, form has a convenience and flexibility absent in the old, two-word, form. For example, it can readily be used as a verb, as in 'Please e-mail your order right away' (compare 'Please electronically mail your order right away'). In fact, by now this new form has almost completely replaced the old two-word phrase. The present chapter presents four examples of such ways to express old meanings with new forms.

2.4. Principle of limited novelty

The infrequency of new words with both new meaning and new form, versus the frequency of new words with just new meaning or new form, illustrates a **principle of limited novelty** generally effective in the formation of new morphemes:

New meanings are preferred in old forms, and new forms are preferred in old meanings.

As the result of this principle, rarely are new morphemes entirely new, and this partial familiarity of most new words, being familiar in either form or meaning, presumably helps to make them more effective and therefore more acceptable than they would be otherwise.

2.4.1. Limits of new form: phonology

The grammar of languages places strict limits on the possibilities of new phonological form. New morphemes must ordinarily follow the phonological pattern of old morphemes and consist of phonemes of the established inventory of phonemes, ordered according to the established patterns. The Japanese word mentioned above, *karaoke*, provides an example. The part *oke* /oke/ appears to come from the first two syllables of Italian or English *orchestra*. Words of Japanese phonology do not have the syllable-final /r/ of these languages, and this phoneme is therefore lost in the Japanese form *oke*. The English word itself comes from Italian *orchestra* /orkéstra/, and Italian phonological characteristics of the word, such as second-syllable stress and the vowels [e] and [a], are modified as /ɔrkəstrə/ (or /ɔrkɛ̀strə/) in English, which prefers stress on the first syllable and disprefers [e] and [a] in unstressed syllables. The adaptation of borrowed words to fit the phonology of the borrowing language is discussed further below (§3.6.3).

2.4.2. Limits of new meaning

It is not evident that language places any limits on imagination, or therefore on new possibilities of meaning. The opposite is as likely: only the possibilities of coherent meaning place limitations on language. Perhaps here the often quoted words of the philosopher Ludwig Wittgenstein (1921 [1974, p. 74]) are relevant: 'What we cannot speak about, we must pass over in silence.' This rather difficult topic, indeed, has to be passed over here.

3. NEW WORDS IN NEW FORMS: SIX WAYS

Of six ways in English to get new words by use of new forms, four yield new forms for old meanings: (1) clipping, (2) acronyming, (3) blending, and (4) wrong cutting. Two are ways to get new words with new meanings as well as new forms: (5) invention and (6) borrowing.

3.1. Clipping

Clipping is shortening or clipping the spoken form of a word. This definition excludes what are traditionally called **abbreviations**, which concern shortening just the written form of words, as in *Mr./Mr* for 'mister', *Tex.* for 'Texas', and *etc.* for 'et cetera'. These don't ordinarily replace the long forms, but just substitute for them. Notice that abbreviations ordinarily end in periods, and often have spellings which would be unsuitable for English words, like *Eng.*, and *govt.* (British English lacks the period after an abbreviation which keeps the final letter of the word abbreviated, as in *Mrs* (*mistress*) and *Dr* (*doctor*), and common scientific abbreviations lack the period, for example, *cm* 'centimeter', *kg* 'kilograms'.)

Clippings, on the other hand, have spellings which have the appearance and pronounceability of English words. With the passage of time, clippings may fully replace their original longer forms. Three examples are:

a. *pub* 'tavern', in British English the clipped form of 'public house'. Americans may recognize and use the term *pub* without knowledge of its original 'public house' form, illustrating that such clippings are not just abbreviations but may become new words.

b. *fan* 'devoted follower, as of sports' is clipped from *fanatic*. Probably most users of this word are unaware of its origin as a shortened form, and many fans will tell you they are not fanatic, so *fan* has become a new word fully separate from *fanatic*.

c. *pet* 'loved household animal' is thought to have been clipped from French *petite* 'small'.

Some clippings, such as *lab*, *intro*, and *econ*, are in wide use on college campuses nowadays without tending to replace their source-words. Those who use them continue to recognize them as abbreviations. Other clippings, perhaps *condo*, *flu*, and *fax*, have probably established themselves as new words, independent of their origins as *condominium*, *influenza*, and *facsimile*, respectively. The clippings have become more common than the long forms, and are sometimes known to the exclusion of the long forms, which may eventually drop out of the language, though *facsimile* can survive in its original general meaning 'copy'. *Pram* 'baby carriage', for example, has almost completely replaced its long form, *perambulator*.

3.2. Acronyming

Acronyming is a sort of clipping in which a phrase is replaced by a word based upon the first letters of its words. There are two types.

3.2.1. Word acronyms

Word acronyms are pronounced as ordinary words, not as spellings. Examples are:

a. *scuba* 'self-contained underwater breathing apparatus'. Hardly anybody knows the origin of this as an acronym. It is very useful as a new word, obviously, since the original phrase is so long and unnecessarily descriptive, just for a name of the apparatus.

b. *RAM* 'random access memory'. This acronym has become common and in the computer literature even tends nowadays to be written in lower-case letters, *ram*.

c. *Unicef* originally 'United Nations International Children's Emergency Fund'. The *i* is preserved even though the word 'International' has now been dropped from the name of this agency.

Some other cases are *MASH* 'mobile army surgical hospital', a term popularized by the television series of this name, *laser* 'light amplification by stimulated emission of radiation', and *NASA* 'National Aeronautics and Space Administration'. People vary in their knowledge of such words as originally acronyms. As long as the spelling is with upper-case letters, as in *NASA*, people may guess they are acronyms even without knowing their phrasal forms. Sometimes, perhaps with deliberate intent to have them replace their longer forms, word-acronyms are written in lower-case letters, for example *laser*, *Unicef*, and *radar*.

3.2.2. Spelling acronyms

Spelling acronyms, or **initialisms**, are read and pronounced as spellings, as a sequence of letters, so their acronymic origin tends to be obvious. Still, if they are useful as abbreviations, they may become much more common than the phrase they are based on, and some people may forget their phrasal, original, forms. Examples are:

a. *PR* 'public relations'

b. *TLC* 'tender loving care'

c. *ID* 'identification'. In this case, the acronym is based not on a phrase but, it seems, on the single word *identification*, which was perhaps too long and felt to be too formal to be suitable in one of its frequent contexts of occurrence: the entrance to bars and at convenience-store counters where alcholic beverages may not be sold to minors.

Notice the similarity and difference between these and ordinary written abbreviations. Both lack the appearance and pronounceability of words, but spelling acronyms lack the period at the end of most abbreviations, and are read as a sequence of letters; *Mr/Mr.*, for example, is not read 'M-R'.

3.2.3. Two-level word acronyms

Acronyming has become very popular in modern English. An increasingly important sort of acronym concerns the names of public interest groups and organizations, which nowadays are often specifically named so that the name will be suitable as an acronym which spells a word which suggests some aspect of the organization's purpose. The acronym thus expresses meaning on two 'levels': as an acronym and as a simple word. For example *NOW* 'National Organization of Women' suggests that members of the organization are getting impatient. The acronym *SMOOSA*, 'Save Maine's Only Official State Animal', suggests which animal this is. *MADD* is an organization of angry mothers. Perhaps a particular inspiration of this phenomenon was an extreme case in Ian Fleming's James Bond novels: *SPECTRE*, 'Special Executive for Counterintelligence, Terrorism, Revenge, and Extortion'.

3.3. Blending

Blending is replacing two words of a phrase with parts of both, ordinarily the first part of the first and the last part of the other. Like clippings and acronyms, these may start out as merely abbreviations, but, perhaps because they more often look like ordinary words, with the passage of time they can more readily become new words in their own right. Examples are:

  a. *motel* 'motor hotel', *motor + hotel*
  b. *chunnel* 'tunnel under the English Channel', *channel + tunnel*
  c. *glassphalt* 'highway paving material made of glass and asphalt', *glass + asphalt*

These have an effective iconic aspect (chapter 1, §2.1.1): they are blends of form as their meanings are blends of meaning.

Cases like *motel*, *motor + hotel*, and *smog*, *smoke + fog*, whose origins as blends are probably unknown to many people who freely use them, show the potential of blending to create new words and not just clever abbreviations. Undoubtedly many children who play with gobots have no idea of this analysis of this word: *gobot*, 'robot vehicle', *go + robot*.

Gobot and *glassphalt* are cases in which the first word is used in its entirety. They illustrate the usual characteristic of blends to overlap their forms, as *smoke* and *fog* at [ɔ] (in terms of spelling, at the *o*), and *channel* and *tunnel* at [nəl] (*nnel*). *Iff* 'if and only if', used by logicians, looks like a blend but is so only as a spelling; it has to be pronounced in full form, 'if and only if'. In blends like *sitcom* and *edutainment*, there is no such overlap: *situation + comedy*, and *education + entertainment*. *Sitcom* involves the first part of two words instead of the first of one and last of another.

3.4.   Wrong cutting

The phenomenon of **wrong cutting** is a rare source of new word forms, but it is interesting, and should be mentioned for completeness. The English words *apron* and *umpire* come from French *napron* and *nomper*. The French word-initial [n] was misunderstood to be part of the indefinite article with final [n], of either French *un(e)* or English *an*. That is, the word was wrongly identified and wrongly cut from the stream of speech, for example, *a napron > an apron*. Notice that the spelling simply makes obvious the mistaken analysis. Wrong cutting before rather than after the misanalyzed [n] resulted in *nickname* from earlier *ekename*. Related cases are *lute*, from Arabic [al ūd] 'the lute', and *lariat* from Spanish *la reata* 'the lariat'. In these two cases, the misunderstanding must entirely concern morphemes of the source language, Arabic [al] 'the' and Spanish *la* 'the', rather than morphemes of English.

Examples like *nickname* in which there is no influence of a misunderstood foreign language, show that wrong cutting can happen by a process of ordinary language change in which the stream of speech is analyzed in a novel way, known as **metanalysis** (chapter 24, §2.6). Wrong cutting is a subtype of this, in which a word boundary is mislocated.

3.5.   Invention

Because of the above-noted principle of limited novelty, new meanings with new forms are relatively rare. There are, however, two ways to get such new words: by invention and by borrowing.

Invention is just that: inventing a word, more or less from scratch. There is often controversy about possible inventions; some people question whether they are truly invented, or whether another origin for them is simply undiscoverable. Three examples, perhaps, are:

a.   *geek* 'strange looking person'
b.   *snob* 'person over-proud of social status'
c.   *barf* 'vomit' (verb)

Proper names of products and companies may more often be invented, such as *Kodak* and *Exxon*.

3.5.1.   *Logic of inventions*

Inventions are probably not entirely arbitrary or symbolic relations of form and meaning. Their acceptance may sometimes depend on their having an indexical or iconic relation with earlier words. The two zeros of the invented word *googol*, for example, a term in mathematics which means a number with a hundred zeros, has an indexical association through its two *o*'s with the similar two zeros of '100'. *Kleenex* invokes 'clean'. *Zip* sort of sounds like the sound of one of its meanings. *Geek* perhaps has an indexical association through its rhyme [ik] with the rhyme of *freak*. An iconic characteristic of inventions like *geek*, *dork*, *nerd*, and older *goof*, is that their strange (new) form is an actual characteristic of an aspect of their meaning, 'strange looking person'.

3.5.2. *Form constraints on inventions*

Invented words can't be completely new in form. Like all new words they have to conform to the phonological rules of the language, being made up of phonemes of the language ordered in ways consistent with old words. Thus an English invented word that would be pronounced [tlak] or [srilg] would be impossible, but inventions like *dork* [dork] and *zap* [zæp] have unsurprising and completely English-sounding pronunciations. Native words of English rarely end in *o*, so the final *o* of words like *tomato*, *disco*, and *rancho*, suggests that they are not inventions, but are 'borrowings' from other languages: in fact, Nahuatl, Italian, and Spanish, respectively. Borrowing is the likely source of words which look and sound so uniquely new in form.

3.6. Borrowing

Borrowing is just taking a word from another language. The borrowed words are called **loanwords**. It is somewhat misleading to call this 'borrowing', since we can't return the borrowed words. In fact, probably the original intent of the first 'borrower' of a word of another language is to use it just for the occasion, when speaking with persons who, like the speaker, know the source language. But when a word is so borrowed, and when others hear the borrowing and find it useful, they repeat it, and with repetition the foreign word becomes familiar in the borrowing language. Unless the word is phonologically or orthographically odd in the borrowing language, subsequent users often won't know that the word comes from another language.

Borrowing is further discussed in chapter 23, §2.1, as an important cause of language change.

3.6.1. *English examples*
Consider:

a. *disco* 'light rock music especially intended for dancing'. This is probably clipped from the French word *discothèque*, 'dance hall with recorded music played on *discos* (from Italian?) 'records, disks with recorded music'.

b. *gung-ho* 'spirit, enthusiasm'. This is from Chinese, in which language it means 'work together'. How it came to describe the ideal military fighting spirit, in 1940s World War II, seems to be unknown.

c. *passé* 'out of style, old fashioned', borrowed from French, a favorite source
of new English words having to do with style and fashion. In writing, the
accent on the final vowel reveals this as a borrowed word.

3.6.2. Loanwords as evidence of history

Loanwords give evidence of the nature of political, social, or cultural relations
between language groups. Here are three examples.

3.6.2.1. French words in English.

A lot of languages have food vocabulary
borrowed from French, like English's *mutton, pork, beef* (compare *sheep, pig,*
and *cow*, the native English words, whose meanings now exclude the eaten forms
of these animals), *du jour, soufflé*, and even *restaurant*. This suggests, correctly,
that the French have been very influential in the realm of cuisine (another French
word), for many years.

3.6.2.2. English words in Japanese.

The Japanese got baseball from the US,
and along with this game most of their baseball vocabulary, including *hoomuran*
'homerun', *sutoraiku* 'strike', *faasuto* 'fast', and *faaru* 'foul'. Even 'third', when
this means 'third base', is a loanword: *saado*.

3.6.2.3. Italian words in Amharic.

Amharic, of Ethiopia, has lots of words of
Italian origin concerning automobiles, because Ethiopia was occupied by Italy in
the 1930s, when automobiles became common in that part of the world: [fren]
'brake' from Italian *freno*, [gomːa] 'tire' from Italian *gomma*; [benzina] 'gasoline'
from Italian *benzina*; and [makina] 'car' from Italian *macchina* 'machine, engine'.

3.6.3. Nativization

Nativization is changing the pronunciation of borrowed words so they conform to the pronunciation rules of the borrowing language. This is very evident
in the Japanese baseball vocabulary above, such as *hoomuran* 'homerun' and
sutoraiku 'strike', *faasuto* 'first'. Japanese phonology disallows consonant sequences such as *mr* of *homerun* and *st* of *strike*, which must be separated by a
short vowel, *u* in this case, and Japanese also disallows final consonants except *n*,
so 'strike' gets a final *u*. A notable example of nativization is the Hawaiian phrase
melikalikimaki 'Merry Christmas', which results from the facts that Hawaiian
lacks [r] and [s], for which it substitutes its nearest equivalents [l] and [k], respectively; it has no consonant sequences such as [kr] and [sm], for which it substitutes
[kɑl] and [kim], and it has no word-final [s], for which it substitutes [ki].

There is also nativization of spelling, as where the accent on vowels of borrowings from French are dropped, for example *saute* from *sauté*, or the dieresis (two
dots) is omitted in *naive* from *naïve*, also from French.

3.6.4. English history in loanwords

Some languages borrow words more than others, depending on their history,
and on their desire for whatever the words are about. At times in its history

English has borrowed lots of words from Latin, Danish, French, American Indian, and other languages. The result is that it is estimated that over 60% of the words of most English texts were borrowed since 500 AD (following Williams 1975).

3.6.4.1.   From Latin.   Britain was the westernmost fringe of the Roman Empire, and little influenced by it. Latin words including *monk, school, martyr, creed, ounce, purse,* and *mass* date from these times (Williams 1975, p. 57), and the relatively high proportion of religious vocabulary among these words is evidence of the nature of greatest Roman influence.

Inhabited since prehistory by speakers of Celtic languages including Irish, Scots Gaelic, and Welsh, Britain was invaded by West Germanic tribes, including the Angles and Saxons, from about 450 AD, whose Anglo-Saxon dialects evolved into Old English.

3.6.4.2.   From Danish.   As soon as the Anglo-Saxons were settled in their new land, another wave of Germanic tribes, from Denmark, invaded, and before 900 occupied much of eastern Britain. Among the Danish words which survive in English from that time are *sky, sister, thing* (originally, 'council of elders'), *odd, egg,* and *both*. The everyday basicness of the meanings of such loanwords is evidence of the thoroughness of Danish influence in ordinary realms of English life.

3.6.4.3.   From French.   After the Norman French victory at the battle of Hastings in 1066, French influence became pervasive. In the following hundred years, French became the second language of cultured Britons, and French loanwords from this period especially reflect the influence of the Normans in political and economic affairs: *duke, rent, market, cost, labor, calendar, pay,* etc. The thoroughness of Norman influence is also evidenced in many Norman French loanwords in the basic, ordinary, vocabulary, including *poor, uncle, aunt, story, fruit,* and *easy.*

3.6.4.4.   From Latin and Greek.   During the Middle Ages and the Renaissance (10th to 16th centuries), European languages including English freely borrowed Latin and Greek words, since these were the languages of educated people, so were favored for the creation of vocabulary for philosophical discourse and scientific discoveries of the period. From this era we have words like *necessary, legal, popular, solar, gravity, telescope,* and *history.*

3.6.4.5.   From Native American languages.   In America, speakers of English encountered a New World of places, plants, and animals, and most of these kept the names which Native American peoples had given them: *Michigan, Illinois, Chicago,* and *Texas; maize, tobacco,* and *tomato; moose, caribou, cougar,* and *skunk.* Borrowings of this sort unquestionably show the unusual combination of new meaning and new form.

4. ETYMOLOGY

Etymology is the origin, or the study of the origin, of words. The etymology of *etymology* is the Greek word *etymos* 'truth'. Etymologies of many words even in thoroughly studied English remain unknown. Inventions and borrowings are exceptions which 'prove the rule' of the general principle that new meanings are preferred in old forms. The inspiration for inventions in particular is often mysterious, and it is difficult, later, to guess what inspired them. Some words that are thought to have been invented may in fact have other origins, perhaps as borrowings or blends. New-word formations of the other types, however, are sometimes so natural or reasonable that they may have appeared separately and independently at several times and places before catching on in the broad language community.

OK is an interesting case. The etymology of *OK*, or *okay*, has been convincingly argued to be the ca. 1839 acronym of 'oll korrect' (= 'all correct'), a deliberate misspelling of a sort considered amusing at the time, subsequently reinforced in the 1839 presidential campaign by its use to abbreviate '*Old Kinderhook*,' the nickname of US President (1836–40) Martin Van Buren, of Kinderhook, NY (Read 1964).

Nowadays, the editors of the major dictionaries are always on the look-out for new words, and new English words are noted in every issue of the journal of the American Dialect Society, *American Speech*, including, in the first number for 1997, *bugbot* 'small mobile robot', *cyber addiction* 'frequent use of the Internet as a psychological problem', *hotel* (v.) 'use an office on a part-time basis', *infonaut* 'user of the Internet', and *v-mail* 'video-mail'. Until recently, however, the first appearance of new-word formations was rarely recorded and often the inspiration of these was not subsequently discoverable.

Suggestions for
ADDITIONAL READING

Word formation in English is broadly examined in *The Categories and Types of Present-day English New Word Formation* (1969) by Hans Marchand, and *English Word-formation* (1983) by Laurie Bauer. For examples of new words entering English since 1941, see the section 'Among the new words' in every issue of the journal *American Speech*.

The history of word borrowing in English is treated in a number of textbooks on the history of English, including *The Origins and Development of the English Language* (1993) by Thomas Pyles and John Algeo, and *Origins of the English Language: a Social and Linguistic History* (1975) by Joseph M. Williams. These books also survey other means of getting new words in English; in the book by Joseph Williams, see especially chapter 6, 'Creating new words'.

IMPORTANT CONCEPTS AND TERMS IN THIS CHAPTER

- openness
- principle of limited novelty
- clipping
- abbreviation
- acronyming
- word acronym
- spelling acronym
- initialism

- blending
- wrong cutting
- metanalysis
- invention
- borrowing
- loanword
- nativization
- etymology

OUTLINE OF CHAPTER 15

      3. Nativization
      4. English history in loanwords
         1. From Latin
         2. From Danish
         3. From French
         4. From Latin and Greek
         5. From Native American languages

4. Etymology

EXAMPLES AND PRACTICE

EXAMPLE

1. Ways to get new words with new forms.

PRACTICE

Classify the underlined words in 1–10 as one of acronyming, blending, clipping, invention, or borrowing. You might find it necessary to make some educated guesses.

1. The results of the <u>urinalysis</u> were negative.
2. The economy experienced eight years of <u>Reagonomics</u>.
3. This book stimulates a certain sense of <u>deja vu</u>.
4. Police arrested four <u>coke</u> dealers.
5. I always <u>zap</u> soap operas and comedy reruns.
6. Some new <u>DJs</u> prefer to play old rock.
7. Send it to me on a <u>floppy</u>.
8. There'll be a <u>quiz</u> every week.
9. The local <u>FM</u> station may be heard at 90.5.
10. Let's try to <u>meld</u> the two plots into a single story.

EXAMPLE

2. Clipping or abbreviation? Let 'abbreviation' mean a shortened form which is pronounced or read as the full word or phrase it replaces. Let 'clipping', on the other hand, mean a shortened form which is pronounced or read according to its shortened form. Thus *Tex.* is an abbreviation since it is read [téksəz], but *Frisco* is a clipping since it is not read as [sǽnfrənsísko] (or even [frənsísko]).

PRACTICE

Are 1–12 clippings or abbreviations?

1. Ger.
2. etc.
3. limo
4. hifi
5. univ.
6. R.I.P. (on a gravestone)
7. bsmt.
8. intro
9. Dr (British punctuation)
10. econ
11. D (like offense, half of the game)
12. Yank

EXAMPLE

3. Explaining examples of new forms for old meanings. Consider the following three examples, and their explanations.

Affluenza. Negative environmental effects of over-consumption.
Explanation: Blend of *affluence* and *influenza*, overlapped at *-fluen-*.

AC/DC. The two types of electric current.
Explanation: Acronym of *alternating current/direct current*.

The House. The House of Commons in Britain, and the House of Representatives of the US Congress.
Explanation: Clipping of *House of Commons* and/or *House of Representatives*.

PRACTICE

Similarly explain the following six examples of new-word formation in English. You may need the help of a good dictionary.

1. *Fridge*, as in 'The fridge is always full of leftovers.'
2. *Snafu*, as in 'Running out of paper was just another snafu.'
3. *Selectric*, as in 'My last and favorite typewriter was an IBM Selectric.'
4. *Radar*, as in 'radar can detect incoming aircraft hundreds of miles out'.
5. *Infomercials*, as in 'Did you see the infomercial about flu vaccinations?'
6. *Teens*, as in 'This magazine is written for teens.'

EXAMPLE

4. Japanese borrowing + clipping. Japanese has an unusual way of getting new words, which combines borrowing with nativization incorporating a very systematic sort of clipping. Useful phrases are borrowed from languages including English and nativized and clipped so that they consist of two parts, each of which has one of the structures (C)VCV, (C)V:, or (C)V[n], where C is a consonant and V a vowel. (Each word, that is, has four time units, termed *morae*, where (C)V, vowel length, or syllable-final [n] is one *mora*.) Examples are [waːpuro] 'word processor' (CVːCVCV) and [konbeni] 'convenience store' (CV[n] CVCV).

Match 1–10 with (a)–(j).

1.	[masukomi]	a.	'personal computer'
2.	[rimokon]	b.	'patrol car'
3.	[famikon]	c.	'panty stockings'
4.	[sekuhara]	d.	'sexual harassment'
5.	[patokaː]	e.	'air-conditioning'
6.	[hansuto]	f.	'mass communication'
7.	[pansuto]	g.	'remote control'
8.	[raǰikase]	h.	'radio cassette'
9.	[eakon]	i.	'hunger strike'
10.	[pasokon]	j.	'family computer'

5. English Latinate borrowings. The influence of Latin was so strong in its time that English borrowed lots of Latin words (some via French) for which there are also perfectly good native English equivalents, like *assist*, for which there is native *help*, and *excavate*, for which there is native *dig*. Such loanwords are probably owed to the usage of classically educated English speakers who knew Latin so well that they introduced prestigious Latin words freely into their English speech and writing to others who also knew Latin well.

For each native English word 1–5, provide an English word of Latin origin and the same approximate meaning, and for each word of Latin origin 6–10, provide a native English word with the same approximate meaning. You may wish to use a thesaurus.

1.	ask	6.	dismiss (from job)
2.	give up	7.	masticate
3.	talk	8.	abduct
4.	see	9.	purchase
5.	tell	10.	reply

6. Borrowings in English. English has words it has borrowed from many languages. Often the reason for the borrowing is apparent: the borrowed word expresses a meaning which was absent in English until it was encountered in the territory of the lending language. The new meaning came into English along with its form.

Look up the following English words in a good etymological dictionary and identify the source language of each. There are four groups of words, each representing a different stage in the history of English-speaking people. Try to identify and chronologically order the four historical periods.

1.	furnish	9.	chamber
2.	whiskey	10.	penguin
3.	raccoon	11.	hickory
4.	siesta	12.	corral
5.	ranch	13.	cigar
6.	criminal	14.	slogan
7.	poncho	15.	potato
8.	declare	16.	plaid

7. Giving form to new meanings. For some years, each issue of the journal *American Speech* includes an article titled 'Among the new words', in which new English words are noted and discussed, and the American Dialect Society every year chooses, from the new words nominated by its members, its 'Word of the Year' – in 1997 *millennium bug* and in 1996 *soccer-mom*. The new technology section of current events magazines, such as *Newsweek*'s 'Cyberscope', and, of course, science fiction novels are particularly good sources of new meanings being given form. In *Always Coming Home*, by Ursula Le Guin (1985, p. 366), is the sentence 'The Dayao were always particular about people's ages, because they had a numerical system of lucky and unlucky days that started with your birthday.' Notice that the phrase 'a numerical system . . . birthday' is the syntactic expression of a new meaning.

In the new technology section of news magazines or science fiction novels, find five or so new meanings. Discuss how these new meanings are given form, whether syntactically, in phrases, by borrowing or invention, or by other processes of new-word formation, such as *soccer-mom*, above, by combining words (this is called 'compounding', which with other new-word formation processes is discussed in the next chapter).

Chapter 16

SEVEN MORE WAYS TO GET NEW WORDS

Using English examples, this chapter presents seven ways to use established forms of the language to express new meanings, and some of the sub-types of these.

1. NEW MEANINGS IN OLD FORMS

In the previous chapter were presented six sorts of new-word formation which employ new forms of words. In four of these, old meanings are given new forms (clipping, acronyming, blending, and wrong cutting), and, in two, new meanings are given new forms (invention and borrowing). This chapter presents seven means of new-word formation in which new meanings are given old or established forms: (1) derivation, (2) zero-derivation, (3) compounding, (4) extension, (5) narrowing, (6) bifurcation, and (7) backformation.

2. SEVEN WAYS TO EXPRESS NEW MEANINGS WITH OLD FORMS

2.1. Derivation

Derivation is the creation of new words by the use of derivational affixes.

2.1.1. Derivational vs. inflectional affixes

Inflectional and **derivational affixes** are different in a number of ways (a topic introduced in chapter 4, §5). Inflectional affixes have very customary or even obligatory use, and the word-types they form are therefore very frequent and accustomed. There are relatively few such affixes (about eight in English: chapter 4, §6), and their meanings are well predicted from the combination of the meaning of the affix and the word or stem to which this is added. English noun plurals are an example. When a new noun is pluralized in English by affixing the inflectional suffix /z/ (or its allomorphs), the result is a meaning completely predictable from that of the noun and the suffix. For this reason, except for exceptional forms like *children* or *geese*, there is no need to include inflectional forms in dictionaries.

The use of derivational affixes, by contrast, is not obligatory, and occasions of their use much less frequent. They tend to form words the meaning of which is narrower than that of their parts. Result nouns in English are an example. These tend to be formed with *-ment*, for example, *government*, the result of governing; but *settlement* tends to mean the result not just of settling but of settling a new community. *-Able* forms adjectives from verbs, in the meaning 'able to be verbed'; *readable*, however, means not just 'able to be read' but 'able to be read easily'. *Unbalanced* tends to mean not just 'not balanced' but 'mentally unbalanced, insane'. (These are narrowings; §2.5, below.) Thus derivational forms ordinarily must be listed in dictionaries, with their particular meanings.

2.1.2. Heads and modifiers in derivational affixing

One understanding that can be given to the fact that some derivational affixes seem to bring about changes of part of speech is that they are actually, despite being just affixes, the **heads** of their words. Recall that in a noun phrase the head is a noun, and in a verb phrase the head is the verb – the head is the essential element of a phrase, toward which other elements are **modifiers**. In this understanding, *excitement* would have the structure at the left, and *energize* would have the structure at the right, below.

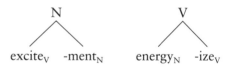

$$\text{excite}_V \quad \text{-ment}_N \qquad \text{energy}_N \quad \text{-ize}_V$$

That is, *-ment* is a sort of N, which obligatorily combines with verbs, and as the head of its phrase naturally yields a noun. If *-ize* is a verb, as head of its construction with a noun the result is a verb.

2.1.3. English examples

Three English examples of recently noticed words newly formed by derivation are:

a.   *geosynchronous* (*geo* + *syn* + *chron* + *ous*) 'in time with the orbit of the earth' (of communications satellites which stay over one point on the earth's surface). *Geo-* 'earth', *-syn-* 'alike', *-chron-* 'time', *-ous* 'suffix forming adjectives from nouns'. Like typical derivations of new words in the technical fields, all the morphemes have Greek or Latin origins.

b. *cabledom* (*cable* + *dom*) 'the cable television business and its sphere of influence'. The suffix *-dom* is pretty rare, probably most encountered in the word *kingdom*, but in a few other words including *stardom* and *serfdom*. This recent formation, perhaps first in a magazine article about the cable television business, suggests that *-dom* still has some life in the language.

c. *energizer* (*energ(y)* + *iz* + *er*) 'which causes to have energy'. The suffix *-ize* is added to nouns to form verbs with the meaning 'cause to have the quality of the noun', as in *synchronize* (*synchron(y)* + *ize*) and *sympathize* (*sympath(y)* + *ize*). *-Er* is added to verbs to make noun instruments or agents, causers of the verb, as in *walker* 'instrument to help walking'.

Derivation is perhaps the most common way to express new meanings in English, especially in technical fields including computer science, medicine, and the physical and natural sciences, in which new discoveries, new technology, and new ways of thinking are regular occurrences which necessitate a ready means of expression.

2.2. Zero-derivation

Zero-derivation is also known as 'functional shift' or 'conversion'. Zero-derivation is using a word as another part of speech, without any affix or change of form at all. For example, a noun may be used as a verb or a verb may be used as a noun. This is quite common in English, especially to get new verbs based on nouns and new nouns based on verbs.

2.2.1. *English examples*
Three English examples are:

a. *trail*, basically a noun (as in 'a trail through the woods'), may be used as a verb in sports-talk, as in 'The Pistons trailed until the second period.'

b. *swim*, basically a verb (as in 'Can you swim?'), may be used as a noun, as in 'have a swim'.

c. *fun*, basically a noun (as in 'Are we having fun yet?'), may be used as an adjective, as in 'That would be a fun thing to do.'

Verb-to-noun and noun-to-verb cases are common; others are rarer.

2.2.2. *Zero-derivation as metaphor*
Novel or creative occasions of zero-derivation may be thought of as metaphoric. A **metaphor** is an implicit comparison based upon the obvious similarities between the meanings of words. A common example of a metaphor is 'The ship plows the sea', where the similarity of plowing and what a ship does when

similarly moving through the sea results in the word for the former being used to describe the latter. In the zero-derivation of 'take a swim', the verb-like process of swimming is very similar to a noun-like occasion or event of swimming, and the use of the verb as a noun is a metaphoric comparison which takes advantage of the obvious similarity. Like other metaphors, and like derivations (use of the derivational affixes), zero-derivations often take on unpredictable aspects of meaning, as when *trail* as a verb takes on the meaning of 'follow (behind)', or *vacuum* means 'clean with a vacuum cleaner'.

2.3. Compounding

Compounding is combining words as a word.

The meaning of the resulting word is not predictable as the simple combination of the meanings of the two combined words.

2.3.1. English examples

Three English examples are:

a. *greenhouse* (*green* + *house*, adjective (or noun) + noun) 'a building for nurturing plants' (noun).
b. *soccer-mom* (*soccer* + *mom*, noun + noun) 'a mother whose time is occupied with children who play soccer' (the American Dialect Society's Word of the Year for 1996).
c. *dry-clean* or *dryclean* (*dry* + *clean*, adjective + verb) 'clean by a dry process' (verb).

Notice how one could probably not predict the meanings of some of these compounds just from their pronunciation or spelling. A *greenhouse* is not green and *soccer-moms* don't play soccer. Compounds really yield new meanings, even though the words they are made of are old and familiar.

Many languages disfavor compounding as a means of deriving new words. German is a language which, more than English, exploits compounding, with examples like:

a. *Erdkarte* 'map of the earth' (*Erd* 'earth' + *Karte* 'map'),
b. *Lastkraftwagen* 'truck' (*Last* 'load', *Kraft* 'power', *Wagen* 'vehicle'),
c. *Akademikerarbeitslosigkeit* 'unemployment of graduates' (*Akademiker* 'college graduate', *Arbeitslosigkeit* 'unemployment'),
d. *Bundesausbildungsförderungsgesetz* 'National Law for the Advancement of Education' (*Bundes* 'national', *Ausbildung* 'education', *Förderung* 'advancement', *Gesetz* 'law').

2.3.2. Stress in English compounds

Some compounds are written as a single word, without a space between the words, like *football* and *dryclean*; others have a hyphen, like *hand-ball* and *drip-dry* and some are written with a space between, like *rugby ball*, or *spot clean*. But unlike phrases, compounds, even those written as two words, usually have main stress on the left-hand word and secondary stress on the right-hand word: [fútbɔ̀l] a noun compound, but [rə̀bərbɔ́l] a noun phrase; *greenhouse* [grínhàws] a noun compound, but [grìnháws] a noun phrase. Notice that the stress pattern [rə́bərbɔ̀l] is possible, but presents a contrastive meaning, which singles out balls of rubber vs. balls of other materials. And the stress pattern [fùtbɔ́l] is unlikely for *football*.

2.4. Extension

Extension is the widening or extending of the meaning of a word. Three English examples are:

a. *red* 'a person with socialist political/economic beliefs', as in 'a red was elected mayor'. The word *red* came to be associated with socialism because of the use of the color red in flags and banners of the International Socialist movement.

b. *silverware* 'table utensils: knives, forks, etc.', whether made of silver or not. Manufacturers must use the word 'tableware', so as not to seem to lie about their product, which are usually stainless steel, but in ordinary usage many of us just say 'silverware', sometimes even for the plastic versions!

c. *holiday* 'customary day of no work', or, in British English, 'vacation' (= 'days of no work'). The first part of *holiday* comes from 'holy'. On many 'holy days' there is or was traditionally no work, and the term was extended to mean both religious and non-religious work-less days.

2.4.1. *Extension as metaphor*

As in zero-derivation, the first occasions of extensions of meaning are **metaphors**, in which a word or phrase sharing qualities of meaning with another replaces the other. When such metaphors are used repeatedly, the extended usage may become ordinary; the metaphor loses its novelty and its metaphoric origin may even be lost and forgotten. Notice the metaphor in *understand*, and *holiday* (< holy-day).

A common sort of extension involves taking the name of a popular first or early version of a new product and extending its name to all subsequent such products, as in *Xerox* ® 'photo-copy', *Kleenex* ® 'tissue paper', *Band-aid* ® 'adhesive medical dressing', etc. These extensions may start out as clippings of phrases: the phrase *Xerox (photo)copier*, for example, is first clipped as *Xerox*, and then the single word is extended to other copiers. Although such extensions certainly reflect honor on the products whose names are extended, the makers of these products try to discourage the practice, because the extended usage, when it becomes common, makes it impossible to distinguish, especially in advertising, between theirs and the products of others.

2.4.2. Idioms

Idioms are whole phrases extended in meaning (though sometimes the word 'idiom' is used for customary extensions of single words). Some examples of English idioms are *get up on the wrong side of the bed* 'be in a bad mood', a verb phrase; *in the dog house* 'accused and disfavored', a prepositional phrase; *green with envy* 'very envious', an adjective phrase; and *birds of a feather* 'very similar people', a noun phrase.

2.5.   Narrowing

This is the opposite of extension: the narrowing of the meaning of a word.

2.5.1.   English examples

Three English examples of narrowing are:

a.   *band* 'a group of persons, especially one which performs music'. The narrowed meaning of *band* is the latter sense. The earlier broader meaning is found in phrases such as 'Robin (Hood) and his merry band' and 'a band of outlaws', both of which now have an archaic ring, whereas the narrower meaning, in phrases like 'a band concert' and 'the Bob Seeger band', seems completely ordinary. The meaning 'group of persons' has diminished (replaced by *group*, *party*, in phrases like 'a party of five', and, in colloquial language, *bunch*, 'a bunch of kids'), except in the narrowed sense of 'group of musicians'. Naturally people have begun to think of *band* as concerning particularly this narrowed meaning.

b.   *building* 'something built to enclose and cover a large space'. The verb *build* clearly suggests the earlier broader meaning of *building*, 'a result or occasion of *building*', as *fishing* very broadly concerns the verb *fish* and *working* the verb *work*, etc. The meaning 'result (or product) of an act of building' was narrowed to concern only a particular sort of product, excluding cases like fences and dams; even the Eiffel Tower seems not to be a 'building' in the current narrowed sense of this word.

c.   *doctor* 'one holding a doctorate degree in medicine or other field'. The tendency of ordinary language is for this word to mean specifically one holding a doctorate in medicine (MD). Thus if a person faints at a college faculty meeting and the cry 'Get a doctor!' is heard, all the doctors of chemistry, education, law, etc. don't rush to offer assistance. The narrowed sense has not become widespread enough, however, to replace the word *physician* in the 'yellow pages' of telephone directories (the *yellow pages* is another case of narrowing).

2.5.2.   Elevation, pejoration, and lateral shifts

Words may be extended or narrowed to yield a more pleasant or positive meaning, or to yield a more unpleasant or negative one. Change in the former direction is termed **elevation**. Three English examples of elevation of meaning are:

a. *brave*, which earlier meant 'bright, gaudy' (as in Shakespeare's phrase 'brave new world').

b. *prize*, which earlier meant 'price'.

c. *great*, which now tends to mean 'wonderful', recently was more likely to mean just 'large, important'.

An opposite shift of meaning toward a more unpleasant or negative meaning is termed **pejoration**. Three English examples of pejoration are:

a. *mean*, which nowadays tends to mean 'malicious, selfish', but earlier was more likely to mean 'stingy' or even 'common, inferior'.

b. *idiot*, which earlier meant simply 'ignorant'.

c. *criticize*, which earlier meant 'give a critique', but now tends to mean 'give a negative critique'.

Strictly speaking, elevations and pejorations are the result of extension plus narrowing: there is extension of meaning to the more positive or negative sense with subsequent narrowing to just this sense.

Extension plus narrowing may also lead to a merely **lateral shift** of meaning, with neither elevation nor pejoration apparent. Three examples of this are:

a. *harvest*, which originally meant 'autumn', but was extended to mean also the autumn activity of 'bringing in crops' and was then narrowed to mean just this.

b. *trade*, originally meaning 'track' (as noun form of the verb *tread*), was extended to mean also 'path,' and then 'path or means of livelihood'; later it was narrowed to mean just this.

c. *bead*, earlier spelled *bede*, meant 'prayer', and took on its present meaning with the close association of prayers and beads, as in rosary beads; the meaning 'prayer' was taken over by *prayer*, at first a noun form of the verb meaning 'beg, implore'.

2.5.3. *Euphemism*

Euphemism is the extension of ordinary words and phrases to express unpleasant or embarrassing ideas. The indirectness of form is felt to diminish the unpleasantness of the meaning. The words so extended are called **euphemisms**, and some examples are *bathroom* (often used in American English even for rooms without bathing facilities), *intercourse*, *undertaker*, and *dentures*. Acronyms, clippings, derivations, and compounds are also sources of euphemism, as in *VD*, *bra*, *pre-owned*, and *pass away*, respectively. Notice, in examples like *intercourse* and *undertaker*, the tendency for euphemistic extensions to become narrowed and lose their broader sense, so that, in an economics lecture, mentioning 'intercourse between nations' tends to distract the audience.

2.6. Bifurcation

In **bifurcation** a word or morpheme develops two forms and its meaning is eventually divided between the two forms. Bifurcations are cases of narrowing in which often the original, broader, meaning survives in one of the forms. The two forms of words which may lead to bifurcation are of three types: morphological, phonological, and orthographic (spelled).

2.6.1. English examples

The following English examples illustrate one each of these three types of form-splitting.

a. *Hanged* and *hung* are variant morphological forms of the past tense of *hang*. By bifurcation, *hanged* tends to be favored (by some dictionaries and style manuals) in the meaning 'executed by hanging' and *hung* is favored for other past tense senses of *hang*. The regular form *hanged* results from **analogical change**, on the model of the majority of regular verbs which form their past tense with -*(e)d*; the form of the analogy yielding *hanged* is '*hang* is to X as *bang* is to *banged*'. Analogical change (which comes up again in chapter 23, §2.2.2.3) solves for X.

b. *Some* has two pronunciations each with a different meaning. Without stress, *some* has become a plural indefinite article, the plural equivalent of *a/an*, as in 'I bought [səm] potatoes' (notice that the meaning of the sentence is not significantly changed if *some* is omitted). With stress, *some* has the meaning 'certain (not all)', as in 'I like [sə́m] potatoes (but not all)' (here the meaning is changed if *some* is omitted).

c. *Metal* 'class of chemical elements' and the differently spelled (identically pronounced) *mettle* 'capability', in the archaic phrase 'test/try one's mettle', both derive from Latin *mettal(um)* 'metal' (as, indeed, does *medal*, via French). With the narrowing of meaning of *mettle*, these have been sorted into the two meanings.

Here are additional examples of bifurcation, one of each of the three types.

d. Morphological form variants: *flied* and *flew*, past tense forms of *fly*. The regularized past tense form *flied* is used in baseball, where it means 'hit a fly ball' ('the first three batters flied to left'). (Even the regular plural of *leaf*, *leafs*, is found in the name of the Toronto professional hockey team, the Maple Leafs.)

e. Pronunciation variants: [hæf] and [hæv] of *have*. *Have* in the phrase *have to*, 'obligated to', is pronounced [hæf], with [−voiced] [f] by assimilation to the [−voiced] [t] which follows. But *have* of 'have two' is [hæv].

f. Spelling variants: *shoppe* and *shop*. The former spelling may be found where quaintness is part of the desired meaning, as in 'olde antique shoppe'.

2.6.2.   *One form/one meaning principle*

Ordinarily, people don't purposefully produce bifurcations, though use of spellings like *shoppe* and *olde* might be rare cases of such purposefulness. Bifurcations ordinarily just happen, over time, as the product of unconscious application of a general principle of language learning and language change known as the **one form/one meaning principle**:

Let one form have one meaning and one meaning one form.

Bifurcations fulfill the principle by yielding two meanings for two forms. (The principle comes up again in chapter 24, §2.4.1.)

2.6.3.   *Homonyms and synonyms*

Homonyms and synonyms appear to be exceptions to the one form/one meaning principle. **Homonyms** are cases of one form having two meanings, such as English [bi], [fláwər], and [rayt]. But English spelling usually distinguishes these as written forms: *be/bee, flower/flour, right/write*. (There are also homographs, words with the same spelling but different pronunciation, like *wind*: [wɪnd], [waynd] (see chapters 19, §2.1, and 22, §2.4.3). **Synonyms** are cases of one meaning having two forms, like *twelve* and *dozen*, and *sick* and *ill*. But the two forms of so-called synonyms rarely have just the same meaning: *twelve* and *dozen*, for example, may seem completely synonymous, but only one of these continues the series *nine, ten, eleven*, and only one can be *a baker's __*.

2.7.   Backformation

It was noted that 'wrong cutting' (chapter 15, §3.4) can result in a slightly new form for an old meaning, as in *apron* from *napron* and *nuncle* for *uncle*. But wrong cutting can also result in a new meaning. This is called **backformation**. Here are three examples.

a.   *Televise* results from falsely analyzing *television* as *televise* plus the suffix *-ion*. In fact, *television* comes from *tele* plus the noun *vision*. The false part *televis-* was taken to be the stem of a verb *televise*, a useful verb, which, as a result of this novel analysis, now actually exists. Notice the logic of the word **backformation** to describe such a case: instead of the word *television* being formed 'forward' from preexistent *tele + vision*, previously nonexistent *televise* is formed 'back', from *television*.

b.   *Burger* results from falsely analyzing *hamburger* as *ham + burger* instead of historical *hamburg + er*. The original word *hamburger* was first applied to a sandwich at the 1891 St Louis World's Fair, where it meant 'of the type of the city of *Hamburg* (Germany)'. People sensibly understood the first part, *Ham*, to be to the meat of the sandwich (even though it was actually beef), which left *-burger* to refer to the type of sandwich. *Burger* being a useful morpheme, it survived and spread, and now we have *fishburgers, cheeseburgers,* etc.

c. *-athon,* as in *eatathon* and *talkathon,* results from falsely analyzing *marathon* 'long distance foot race' as *mar + athon. Marathon* already is an extension of the name of the Greek plain of Marathon, 20 or so miles from Athens, from which a messenger ran to announce the Athenian victory at the Battle of Marathon in 490/491 BC. Some creative person has lately imagined *-athon* of *marathon* to be a suffix having to do with any long-lasting event. So now we have *walkathons, talkathons, kissathons,* etc.

Recently much noted is the backformed new suffix *-gate* 'scandal', whose source is *Watergate,* the name of the building where the burglary that started this political scandal took place. *Water* being obviously a word, someone creatively but surely with intentional cleverness metanalyzed *-gate* to be a suffix, and now we have *Irangate, Koreagate,* etc. That the English language seems to have need for a suffix meaning 'scandal' may be an interesting fact about recent US political life.

Also significant as evidence of our changing needs for morphemes is the newly discoverd suffix *-oholic,* meaning 'addiction to'. This is backformed from *alcoholic,* as if *alc-* and not *alcohol* meant 'alcohol'. The new suffix is attached to words, as in *workaholic,* and to a backformed new stem *choc-,* in *chocoholic.*

Like other 'wrong cuttings', backformation results from **metanalysis**, a process generally at work in language change, since, in each generation, learners (including adults) analyze the data of their language somewhat differently than did the previous generation. Metanalysis, a general cause of language change, is the topic of chapter 24, §2.6.

Suggestions for
ADDITIONAL READING

For English resources in word formation, especially derivational affixes, see *English Vocabulary Elements* (1995) by Keith Denning and William R. Leben. A workbook treating English derivational morphology is *The Structure of English Words* (1985) by Clarence Sloat and Sharon Taylor. For theoretical aspects of inflectional and derivational morphology, see *Word Formation in Generative Grammar* (1976) by Mark Aronoff. Extension and narrowing, as well as other types of lexical change in language, are discussed in historical linguistics textbooks, such as *Understanding Language Change* (1994) by April M. S. McMahon, and *Historical Linguistics* (1996) by Larry Trask.

IMPORTANT CONCEPTS AND TERMS IN THIS CHAPTER

- derivation
- derivational affix
- inflectional affix
- head
- modifier
- zero-derivation
- metaphor
- compounding
- extension
- idiom
- narrowing

- elevation
- pejoration
- lateral shift
- euphemism
- bifurcation
- analogical change
- one form/one meaning principle
- homonym
- synonym
- backformation
- metanalysis

OUTLINE OF CHAPTER 16

    6. Bifurcation
       1. English examples
       2. One form/one meaning principle
       3. Homonyms and synonyms
    7. Backformation

EXAMPLES AND PRACTICE

EXAMPLE

1. Identifying examples of the seven ways to get new words with new meanings.

PRACTICE

For each sentence circle one of DE, ZE, CO, etc., which its underlined word best illustrates. Consider the use of the underlined word in the context of the whole sentence. Some educated guessing may be necessary, and people might reasonably disagree about the interpretation of some items. Each of the seven ways to get new words with new meanings is intended to be illustrated at least twice.

DErivation   ZEro-derivation   COmpounding   EXtension
NArrowing   BIfurcation   BAckformation

1.	I h[æv] two cars, so I <u>h[æf] to</u> sell one.	DE	BI	ZE	CO
2.	<u>Symptomologically</u> speaking, he has a cold.	DE	CO	ZE	NA
3.	If it's not feasible, you can't <u>fease</u> it.	CO	BA	BI	EX
4.	The weather in Texas is <u>murderous</u>.	BI	EX	NA	ZE
5.	They filed a legal <u>brief</u> with the court.	ZE	BI	DE	BA
6.	Be sure to <u>dryclean</u> this sweater.	NA	ZE	BI	CO
7.	He's only <u>bowing</u> to modern taste.	EX	NA	BI	ZE
8.	The team will then <u>bus</u> to Des Moines.	NA	EX	DE	ZE
9.	We want to hire two new <u>professors</u>.	BA	EX	NA	CO
10.	These small nations are engaged in <u>minisummitry</u>.	CO	DE	EX	BI
11.	On weekends I'm a <u>sportsoholic</u>.	BI	BA	CO	ZE
12.	My <u>business</u> is selling furnaces.	BA	DE	BI	ZE
13.	These <u>sneakers</u> don't fit.	DE	CO	NA	BA
14.	Do you see that <u>stoplight</u>?	ZE	CO	EX	BI

EXAMPLE

2. Identifying examples of the 12 ways to get new words with new meanings and/or new forms. (The 13th type, wrong cutting (chapter 15, §3.4), is omitted here.)

ACronyming	BOrrowing	INvention
DErivation	CLipping	BAckformation
BIfurcation	COmpounding	NArrowing
BLending	EXtension	ZEro-derivation

PRACTICE

For each sentence circle one of AC, DE, BI, etc., which its underlined word best illustrates. For example, 'Man U are playing the Hammers' represents CLipping. (For non-fans of British football: Man U is the Manchester United team; for non-fans of baseball: the Bosox are the Red Sox team of Boston.) Consider the use of the underlined word in the context of the whole sentence. Some educated guessing may be necessary, and reasonable disagreement is possible about the interpretation of some items. Each of the twelve types is intended to be illustrated at least once, and most twice.

1. The candidate used a <u>bull-horn</u> to address the crowd. CO NA ZE DE
2. More funds are needed for <u>AIDS</u> research. CL AC BA NA
3. They have many <u>supernaturalist</u> beliefs. BA DE ZE BO
4. Put your dirty dishes on the <u>trayveyor</u>. BA ZE IN EX
5. What a <u>dork</u>! CL BI NA IN
6. White <u>penned</u> two novels. DE NA ZE BO
7. A new cellular phone on a <u>plaine olde</u> table. BI DE EX BL
8. The series is about mythology <u>à la</u> Joseph Campbell. BO NA BA BL
9. <u>Exam</u> week will soon be here again. DE NA BO CL
10. The <u>trial</u> should take place next week. BO NA DE ZE
11. Does your system have the <u>wysiwyg</u> feature? CO BL EX AC
12. This new model is more <u>user-friendly</u>. BL BA CO DE
13. Police seized the funds of the <u>drug</u> dealers. NA CL EX BO
14. Mazola oil is said to have <u>cornthenticity</u>. CO BA EX ZE
15. Maybe they need <u>perestroika</u> at General Motors. CO BO EX NA
16. These new fashions are <u>hot</u>! NA AC CL EX
17. The <u>chunnel</u> connects England and France. AC BL BO ZE
18. Morgan was <u>flanked</u> by McGill and Roberts. BI ZE NA DE
19. The <u>Bosox</u> are playing the Yankees. CL AC BL EX
20. All three batters <u>flied</u> to left. DE NA BO BI

EXAMPLE

3. Explaining examples of new-word formation. Consider these examples of zero-derivation, compounding, and extension.

Zero-derivation: 'One minute to *lift-off*.'
Explanation: *lift-off* is a verb (a compound, in fact), but here it is used as a noun (as object of a preposition), without an affix or other change of form.

Compounding: 'Geraldo's *talk-show* is on at 4 p.m.'
Explanation: *talk* and *show* are combined as one word with the specific meaning 'show based on talk'.

Extension: 'We went to a *Broadway* show in Chicago.'
Explanation: *Broadway* is the name of a street in New York City, where many theatres of stage-shows of this type are located, and this name has been extended to stage-shows of this general type.

PRACTICE

Similarly explain five of the following seven examples of new-word formation in English. You may want or need to use a dictionary.

1. Narrowing: '*Unfaithfulness* is grounds for divorce.'
2. Backformation: 'Don't just sit there *emoting*.'
3. Bifurcation: 'You can use this studio for *dubbing* the words.'
4. Extension: 'Lansing is in Ingham *County* in Michigan.'
5. Zero-derivation: 'These trees are trying to *root* on the hillside.'
6. Derivation: 'We need to *anthemize* our campaign.'
7. Compounding: 'Carelessness in typing addresses results in a lot of *oops-mail*.'

EXAMPLE

4. Narrowings. The word *demonstration* tends to be narrowed to mean 'public display, protest', as in 'I'm going to a demonstration at the state capitol'. But the broader meaning 'a performance' of the verb *demonstrate* is also still effective, as in 'A chem lab demonstration resulted in a small explosion'.

PRACTICE

Give two sentences or phrases which illustrate the tendency in the following words toward narrowing: one sentence which illustrates the narrowed meaning, and one which illustrates the older, broader, meaning.

1. operation   4. conductor
2. prescription   5. criticism
3. readable   6. professor

EXAMPLE

5. New-word formation in current English I. Between June 1968 and August 1977 the appearance of the following new words was noticed (by Norris Yates 1981).

a. biographoid   Derivation: the derivational suffix *-oid* is added to *biograph* clipped from *biography*

b. Californicated   Blend: *California* overlapped with *fornicated* at their common part *-forni-*

c. Koreagate   Backformation: *-gate*, from *Watergate*, is used as a suffix meaning 'scandal'

PRACTICE

Weekly newsmagazines like *Time*, *Newsweek*, and the *Economist*, computer magazines, and *Rolling Stone* are especially fond of such new words. Following are listed some more examples from *Time* during the same period. For five of these, say what type or types of new-word formation they appear to illustrate, and explain your answers as in the examples above.

1.	amorific	'extremely amorous'
2.	Arkahoma	'general area of Arkansas and Oklahoma'
3.	Carterphobia	'dislike of Jimmy Carter'
4.	eco-activists	'activists for natural ecology'
5.	gymnophiliac	'extreme admirer of exercise'
6.	kitchencarnation	'revival of an old recipe'
7.	librarified	'filled with books'
8.	petroglitter	'ostentatious oil wealth'
9.	roadies	'those who follow rock bands on their road-tours'
10.	space-bopper	'young admirer of space exploration'

EXAMPLE

6. New-word formation in current English II. *Newsweek* for 17 July 1995 included the following novel words:

a. *E. coli burger* 'sandwich with E. coli bacteria', a compound of *E. coli* and *burger*, with *burger* metanalyzed from *hamburger*

b. *crazoid* 'somewhat crazy person', an affixation with *-oid* suffixed to a stem from *crazy*

c. *boom car* 'car with extra loud speakers (boomboxes)', a clipping *boom*, from the compound *boombox*, used in another compound with *car*

d. *warnography* 'obscene writing about war', backformed, presumably, by wrongly cutting *pornography* as *por ± nography* and suffixing *-nography* to *war*.

PRACTICE

Look through one or two issues of the above-mentioned magazines and find ten words new to you and exemplifying four different types of new-word formation. List them, with full references (magazine, date, and page number), and explain your interpretation of them, as in the examples above.

EXAMPLE

7. English derivational affixes. Some of the English derivational affixes have limited productivity (chapter 4, §5): they have limited possibility of combination with other morphemes to form new words. Others, like inflectional affixes, are quite productive: they form new words quite regularly, including:

re-:   'again', usually prefixed to verbs, as in *reattach* and *rethaw*

-ate: 'having the quality of', usually suffixed to nouns, as in *affectionate* and *passionate*

PRACTICE

For ten of the English derivational affixes 1–15, say as in the examples above what sort of word it is usually affixed to and give two examples. You may need to use a dictionary. Give examples as above, in which the affix is clearly attached to a word of the class you claim it is usually attached to. Unsatisfactory examples for *re-* would be *repeat*, in which *peat* is not meaningful, and *renew*, in which *new* is not a verb; bad examples for *-ate* would be *insulate* and *cultivate*, in which *insul* and *cultiv* are not words or stems.

1.	dis-	6.	en-	11.	-ist
2.	non-	7.	-ity	12.	-eer
3.	-ive	8.	-ly	13.	-y
4.	-able	9.	-ment	14.	un-
5.	-(i)fy	10.	-ize	15.	-burger

EXAMPLE

8. Three types of change of word meaning: elevation, pejoration, and lateral shift. It was noted in §2.5.2 above, that changes or extensions of word meaning may be classified as *elevations*, when a word gets a more positive or pleasant meaning, *pejorations*, when a word gets a more negative meaning or unpleasant meaning, or simply *lateral shifts*, when a word changes its meaning in a neutral way, neither positively or negatively.

PRACTICE

The following 12 English words are given with their old meanings, from Old or Middle English times, before 1600. Classify 3–12 as one of elevation, pejoration, or lateral shift of meaning. The first two are already classified, as examples. There are intended to be four cases of each type, but there is room for differences of interpretation concerning some.

1. stool 'throne' – Pejoration
2. ambassador 'messenger' – Elevation
3. deer 'animal'
4. stink 'smell'
5. silly 'blessed'
6. queen 'woman'
7. dirt 'excrement'
8. worm 'dragon'

9. thing 'council'
10. spill 'destroy'

11. starve 'die'
12. journey 'one-day trip'

9. Synonyms. It was noted in §2.6.3, above, that synonyms, words which 'mean the same', seem to go against the one form/one meaning principle. But rarely (if ever), in fact, do they have the same meaning exactly. Here are some pairs of words commonly thought of as synonyms.

a. ache, pain
b. aid, help
c. attractive, handsome
d. big, large
e. dinner, supper

f. little, small
g. place, location
h. teach, educate
i. too, also
j. sad, unhappy

Show how the members of each pair slightly differ in meaning or usage by giving a sentence in which each can be used but not the other. Also try to explain any slight difference of meaning you find; use a dictionary if you wish.

For example, consider the pair *find, locate. Locate* means 'find' but also 'find a place to live', as in 'We want to relocate to the west coast.' One can't say 'We want to refind to the west coast.' One can say, 'Hey, I found a dollar!' but not 'Hey, I located a dollar.' *Locate* means 'find upon searching'.

Chapter 17

SENTENCE MEANING

This chapter presents two relationships of form and meaning, compositional and noncompositional, and a problematic form of compositionality, discontinuous constituents. It contrasts grammatical relations with semantic roles, and shows how a number of aspects of meaning may be explained by semantic roles.

1. COMPOSITIONAL MEANING

Probably most of the meaning of most sentences is **compositional meaning**. Compositional meaning results from adding up or relating the meanings of morphemes and words within their phrases, and adding up or relating the phrases, phrase by phrase. For example, consider the English sentence *Beavers in the pond by the river eat tasty fish with gusto*, with the phrase structure or tree diagram of figure 17.1.

The meaning of this sentence can be understood as built up, progressively, out of the meanings of its phrases, which are built up out of the meanings of their words and morphemes: that is, as seen in figure 17.1, from bottom to top:

a. *the river*: a noun phrase with *river* as its head
b. *by the river*: a prepositional phrase with *by* as its head
c. *the pond by the river*: a noun phrase with *pond* as its head
d. *in the pond by the river*: a prepositional phrase with *in* as its head
e. *beavers*: a plural noun consisting of the noun *beaver* plus the plural suffix
f. *beavers in the pond by the river*: a noun phrase with *beavers* as its head, the subject of the sentence
g. *with gusto*: a prepositional phrase with *with* as its head
h. *tasty fish*: a noun phrase with *fish* as its head

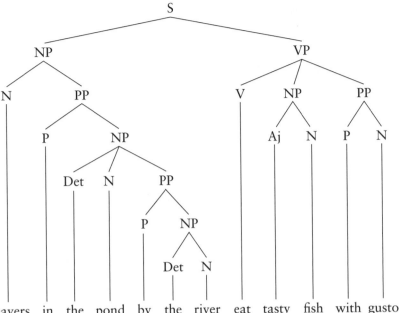

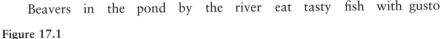

Figure 17.1

i. *eat tasty fish with gusto*: a verb phrase with *eat* as its head, the predicate of the sentence

j. The noun phrase subject (f) and verb phrase predicate (i) make up the sentence.

1.1. Linear compositionality

In such analysis, the meaning of the sentence is reasonably the sum of the parts, including the word and morpheme meanings. In this case, each phrase combines with that before or after it to form the next highest constituent, up to the sentence.

It may be difficult to imagine that by application of so many atomic analytic operations we synthesize for pronunciation our own sentences and analyze in comprehension the sentences of others. Of course, each operation doesn't have to be done separately from others, and many or all might be done simultaneously, with so-called 'parallel processing'. Furthermore, since the brain, in fact, is probably better at such operations than the very best computer, and since we have no conscious knowledge of its workings, maybe we can deal with compositional meaning in approximately this linear bottom-to-top way.

1.2. Nonlinear compositionality: discontinuous constituents

Not all meaning is compositional and not all compositional meaning is linear. Sometimes the compositionality of a phrase is nonlinear: its constituents are

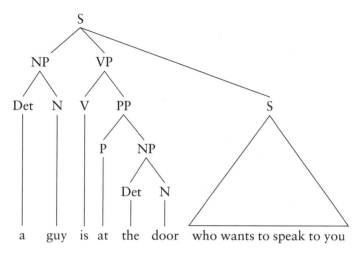

Figure 17.2

discontinuous. **Discontinuous constituents** are phrases the members of which are separated from one another by words of other phrases. Consider two such cases of discontinuous constituents in English, **extraposition** and **wh-fronting**.

1.2.1. Extraposition

For example, in *A guy is at the door who wants to speak to you*, the clause *who wants to speak to you* is plainly not about *door*, which it immediately follows. Instead, *a guy who wants to speak to you* is the subject noun phrase whose head is *guy*, which the clause *who wants to speak to you* is understood to be about – to modify as a relative or adjective clause. But *a guy* and *who wants to speak to you* are separated by the other words of the sentence, the verb phrase *is at the door*. The structure of the sentence is perhaps as seen in figure 17.2, in which the relative clause is suggested to be a dependent of the sentence, with the subject NP, and VP.

This sort of discontinuity, in which a clause is separated from the subject noun phrase which it modifies, and appears at the end of a sentence, is known as **extraposition**. The clause is said to be 'extraposed'.

1.2.2. Wh-fronting

You may think separating constituents in sentences like this is just carelessness, and even 'bad English', even though people do say such things. Instead, we could say *A guy who wants to speak to you is at the door*, if we thought about it.

But what about an ordinary English question like *Who(m) will you ask?* Here *who(m)* is the direct object of the verb *ask*, but it precedes *you*, the subject of the sentence. So-called **wh-words** of English, like *who*, *when*, *what*, and *how*, are typically 'fronted', to the beginning of questions, even when, in terms of compositional meaning, they are part of the verb phrase, and upon fronting are separated from the verb by the subject and an auxiliary verb, as in *When are they going?* and *What do those people want?* This is known as **wh-fronting**.

Since they violate compositional meaning, our ability readily to understand and allow discontinuous constituents in our questions appears to require some sort of processing additional to that required for getting and giving compositional meaning. Some other cases of discontinuous constituents in English will be discussed in the next chapter.

2. NONCOMPOSITIONAL MEANING: IDIOMS

Noncompositional meaning cannot be built up as the sum of its parts. This exists in **idioms**, which are phrases derived by metaphor and other types of semantic **extension** (chapter 16, §2.4). *Get up on the wrong side of the bed*, for example, is a verb phrase with the structure seen in figure 17.3, but its meaning is fully noncompositional, 'be surly/be in a bad mood'. The meaning 'be surly/be in a bad mood' seems unrelated to the compositional meaning of *get up on the wrong side of the bed*, as analyzed in the figure 17.3. Other English examples of this include *in the doghouse*, *kick the bucket*, and *face the music*.

Idioms can be understood to be listed in the lexicon, already formed, where they are associated with their noncompositional meanings, for example:

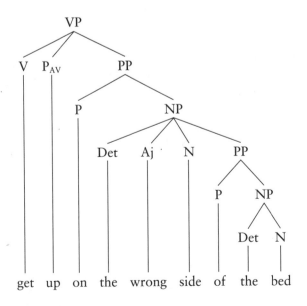

Figure 17.3

a. [in$_P$ [the$_{Det}$ doghouse$_N$]] 'accused and disfavored'
b. [green$_{Aj}$ [with$_P$ envy$_N$]] 'very envious'
c. [get$_V$ up$_{PAv}$ [on$_P$ [the$_{Det}$ wrong$_{Aj}$ [side$_N$ [of$_P$ [the$_{Det}$ bed$_N$]]]]]] 'be surly'
d. [get$_V$ up$_{PAv}$] 'arise, especially from sleep'

Up in *get up* is a prepositional adverb (P$_{Av}$), an adverb which may also be a preposition, for example *over*, *up*, and *out*. English has a lot of idioms which, like *get up*, combine a verb and a prepositional adverb, for example *look over* 'examine', *look up* 'find in a dictionary', *fill out* 'complete (as a form)', etc. The idiomatic prepositional adverb is sometimes called a 'particle'.

3. SEMANTIC ROLES

Some aspects of the meaning of sentences may be understood to result from the **semantic roles** of their nouns or noun phrases. Nouns or noun phrases may have various semantic roles in their relation to a verb. In the sentence *Birds fly*, for example, *birds* is said to be in the role of **agent** of the verb.

At least ten semantic roles may generally be recognized in the sentences of all languages. These ten seemingly universal semantic roles (a)–(j), here provided with approximate definitions suitable for present purposes, are illustrated in sentences 1–6. Theoretically the semantic roles need no definitions, but are themselves basic unreducible meanings.

TEN COMMON SEMANTIC ROLES

a. **Agent:**   Doer, actor
b. **Patient:**   Entity affected by deed of agent or cause
c. **Location:**   Location of deed/event
d. **Instrument:**   Entity employed by an agent in a deed
e. **Time:**   Time of deed/event
f. **Recipient:**   Receiver of result of deed of agent
g. **Experiencer:**   Perceiver of a stimulus
h. **Stimulus:**   Entity perceived/experienced by an experiencer
i. **Cause:**   Cause not an agent
j. **Goal:**   Targeted location

Examples of the Ten Common Semantic Roles

       Ag   Pa   Re
1. Farmers raise crops for cityfolk.

       St   Ex   Ca   Pa
2. Rain pleases the farmers but too much rain harms the crops.

       Ti   Ag   In   Pa   Lo

3.   In the summer, they use trucks to bring crops from the fields.

   Ag   Pa   Go   In

4.   They may send their crops to market through cooperatives.

     Pa   In   Go   Lo

5.   The crops are sent by train to distribution centers in large cities.

     Ca   Pa Ag   Ti

6.   Market value determines which crops farmers will plant the next spring.

Notice the clear difference of semantic role in English sentences with *listen to* and *hear*, or *watch* and *see*, sentences which otherwise express an identical event.

7.   The farmer listened to the tree fall.
8.   The farmer heard the tree fall.

9.   The farmer watched the tree fall.
10. The farmer saw the tree fall.

In the the former of each of these pairs the subject actively or voluntarily participates, as an agent. In the latter of each pair the subject is only passively involved, as an experiencer.

A recipient who benefits from the receiving may be termed a 'beneficiary'. Two other semantic roles that have been suggested are 'possessor', such as *I* in *I have a new watch*, and 'source', such as *acorns* in *Acorns grow into oak trees*. Sometimes a noun or noun phrase appears to have another semantic role different from any of these, like *weather* in *The weather changes often*, *the economy* in *The economy is expected to rebound in the third quarter*, or *he wouldn't play* in *He said he wouldn't play*.

4.   VERB CLASSES ACCORDING TO SEMANTIC ROLES

Part of the meaning of verbs lies in their relationship to the semantic roles of the nouns which are their complements – which cooccur with them in sentences. In (a)–(e) are listed, with examples, five types of English verbs according to the semantic roles with which they associate.

a.   Verbs with an agent and a patient: *open*, *eat*, *fill*, etc.

1.   Mom opened a box of cornflakes.
2.   Beavers eat fish.

    b. Verbs with an agent and no patient: *resign, smile, wake up*, etc.

      3. Nixon resigned.
      4. This little kid is always smiling.

    c. Verbs with an agent, patient, and recipient: *give, award, send*, etc.

      5. Every year we give something to the United Fund.
      6. The committee awarded the prize to the boss's cousin.

    d. Verbs with an agent and goal: *walk, go, travel*, etc.

      7. I can walk home in about an hour.
      8. Don't go into that bar alone.

    e. Verbs with a recipient (no agent) and a patient: *win, get, receive*, etc.

      9. Five people won a magazine subscription.
      10. Did you get a strange telephone call last night?

One can recognize numerous such classes of verbs, perhaps more than fifty in English, based upon the semantic roles of nouns with which they characteristically form sentences.

5. GRAMMATICAL RELATION VS. SEMANTIC ROLE

Grammatical relations include subject, object, and object of preposition. Unlike semantic roles, these are formal – or grammatical – relations, based on sentence structure rather than on the meanings of noun and verb. In English, agents are most often subjects and patients are typically objects. Other semantic roles are ordinarily expressed in English as objects of particular prepositions: recipients as the object of *for* or *to*, instruments as the object of *with*, locations as the object of *on, at, near, beside*, etc.

But grammatical relations and semantic roles are different, in at least three ways: (1) their formal or structural nature, (2) their constancy in paraphrase, and (3) their means of expression in languages.

5.1. Formal nature of grammatical relations

Grammatical relations may be considered strictly to reflect constituent relations in phrase structure, whereas semantic roles reflect meaning. Thus in the

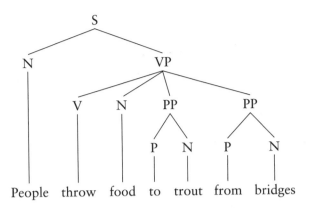

Figure 17.4

phrase structure of *People throw food to trout from bridges*, figure 17.4, *people* is the subject, as the N immediately under S, and *food* is the direct object or object of the verb, as the N immediately under VP. *Trout* and *bridges* are objects of prepositions, since they are immediately under PP.

5.2.   Constancy of semantic roles in paraphrases

Paraphrases are synonymous sentences, and synonymous sentences 'say the same thing'. When either one is true so, necessarily, is the other. In paraphrases, the semantic roles of the nouns are the same even though the grammatical relations of these nouns may be different. Consider the following paraphrases, in which its semantic role and grammatical relation is noted above each noun phrase:

      Ag/Subj   Pa/Obj   Pa/Subj   Ag/ObjPrep
11.   Beavers eat fish. → Fish are eaten by beavers.

      Ag/Subj   Lo/ObjPrep   Lo/Subj   Ag/ObjPrep
12.   Ants swarmed in the garden. → The garden swarmed with ants.

The role of such paraphrases in understanding meaning is a topic of the next chapter.

5.3.   Formal expression of grammatical relations

5.3.1.   *Subjects and objects in English*
Unlike semantic roles, grammatical relations often have regular concrete, formal, properties of word order or morphology, according to requirements of the grammar of a language. That is, grammatical relations are expressed by the grammar, in some way. Subjects in English, for example, have at least five such characteristics, as follows:

FIVE CHARACTERISTICS OF SUBJECTS IN ENGLISH

a. Subjects ordinarily precede the verb in statements: *Beavers eat fish*, not *Eat beavers fish*.

b. A present tense verb has a special suffix if the subject is third-person singular. We say *A beaver eats fish*, but *Beavers eat fish*.

c. Subjects are replaced from the set of pronouns *I, you, he, she, they*, and *we* (and objects from the set *me, you, him, her, them*, and *us*): *Beavers build dams / They build them*.

d. The auxiliary verb precedes the subject in yes/no questions: *Beavers can swim under water / Can beavers swim under water?*

e. The tag of a 'tag question' includes a pronoun with the person and number of the subject: *A beaver eats trees, doesn't it? Pigs eat slop, don't they?*

Unlike subjects, English objects are not so variously marked by the grammar. Their most obvious characteristics are typically to follow verbs in declarative sentences, and to be replaced by the object pronouns *me, us, him, her*, and *them* (versus subject pronouns *I, we, he, she*, and *they*, respectively). (*You* and *it* are both subject and object pronouns.)

5.3.2. Subjects and objects in five other languages

Languages differ in how they express subjects and objects. The data of practice 5 of chapter 5, for example, showed how in Samoan animate subjects of transitive verbs are introduced by *e*. Let's take note of some ways that subjects and objects are marked in five other languages.

5.3.2.1. Amharic.

In Amharic, subjects are marked as affixes on verbs, and definite direct objects (those presumed to be known to the hearer) are marked as suffixes on verbs and also by the suffix /-n/.

13. innat-e ingida-w-n rədda-čč-iw
     mother-my visitor-the-DO helped-she-him
     'My mother helped the visitor.'

14. innat-e səw rədd-ačč
     mother-my person helped-she
     'My mother helped someone.'

In sentence 13, the verb has a subject suffix /-čč/ for the singular feminine subject, [innat-e] 'my mother', and another suffix /-iw/ for the definite direct object /ingida-w-n/ 'the visitor'. The direct object /ingida-w-n/ is definite (it has the suffix /-w/ 'the'), and therefore also requires the definite direct object suffix /-n/. Compare the second sentence, in which the direct object of the verb /sɔw/ 'someone' is indefinite, and lacks the suffix /-n/, and also is not represented as a suffix on the verb.

Unlike English, Amharic does not consistently employ word order to distinguish subject and object: the first sentence above can be paraphrased /ingida-w-n innat-e rədd-ačč-iw/. Despite the different word orders, it is clear who is subject and who direct object, because the /-n/ suffix is usually present to show what is an object, and the /-iw/ direct object suffix of the verb is in the masculine form.

5.3.2.2. Japanese. In Japanese the subject is marked by following /ga/ and the direct object by following /o/.

15. ǰon ga jooko ni eego o ošieta
     John Subj Yoko to English DO taught
     'John taught English to Yoko.'

In addition to subject and object, Japanese also has the grammatical relation **topic** (chapter 5, §1.4.4), which is marked by the particle /wa/. Topics in English are not marked morphologically but syntactically, as in the translation of sentence 16, with *as for*:

16. jooko wa kinoo ǰon ni hana o ageta
     Yooko Top yesterday John to flowers DO gave
     'As for Yoko, yesterday she gave flowers to John.'

5.3.2.3. Spanish. Direct objects in Spanish, if they are definite and human, tend to be marked by preceding *a*. Another way to think of this is that such definite human nouns are not, in fact, direct objects but objects of this preposition *a*, so *a* is not the grammatical marker of direct objects but a preposition, as it is historically.

17. Visit-é a mis amigos.
     visited-I 'to' my friends
     'I visited my friends.'

19. Visit-é las ciudades grandes.
     visited-I the cities big
     'I visited the big cities.'

18. Juan vió a Maria anoche.
     Juan saw 'to' Maria last night
     'Juan saw Maria last night.'

20. Juan vió los ciudades grandes.
     Juan saw the cities big
     'Juan saw the big cities.'

When they are pronouns, however, direct objects in Spanish are marked by word order or as affixes: they typically follow the subject and precede the verb, except when the verb is an infinitive or imperative, in which case they are suffixes of the verb.

21. Juan le preguntó.
    Juan her/him asked
    'Juan asked her/him.'

23. Me visit-ó dos veces el año pasado.
    me visited-he two times the year past
    'He visited me two times last year.'

22. Da-me-lo.
    Give-me-it
    'Give it to me.'

24. El quiere comprar-lo.
    He wants tobuy-it.
    'He wants to buy it.'

5.3.2.4. Latin. In some languages there are different suffixes for a number of different grammatical relations, traditionally called **cases**. There are suffixes for subject, so-called **nominative**, for direct object, **accusative**, for possessive, **genitive**, and for various other cases which are usually expressed in English by prepositions. Latin is such a language. Consider the following Latin sentences (Langacker 1972, pp. 204–205):

25. puella bona amīcum bonum audit
    girl good friend good hears
    'The good girl hears the good friend.'

26. amīcus beātus puellam beātam audit
    friend happy girl happy hears
    'The happy friend hears the happy girl.'

Notice that 'girl' has the suffix *-a* when subject, in the first sentence, and the suffix *-am* when object of the verb in the second sentence. 'Friend' has the suffix *-us* when subject and the suffix *-um* when direct object. Latin adjectives have the case suffixes, too – of their head noun, as in 'good friend': *amīcus bonus* subject/nominative, and *amīcum bonum* direct object/accusative.

Word order varies a lot in Latin and in other case languages. A sentence can begin with the verb, the direct object, or the subject, or some other word. This does not result in misunderstanding, because the verb suffixes show who is the subject and who is the direct object.

5.3.2.5. Nepali. In Nepali (spoken in Nepal), the subjects of transitive and intransitive verbs have different suffixes (that is, they are grammatically different), whereas the subject of an intransitive verb and object of a transitive verb have the same suffixes (that is, they are grammatically identical), as in the following pair of Nepali sentences (Givón 1995, p. 253).

27. kitaab tebul-ma thi-j-o
     book table-on be-past-3msg.
     'The book is on the table.'

28. Raĵ-le kukhura poka-j-o
     Raj-Erg chicken cook-past-3msg.
     'Raj cooked the chicken.'

Notice that the subject *Raj* of the transitive verb 'cooked' has the suffix *-le*, but the subject *kitaab* of the intransitive verb 'is' and the direct object *kukhura* of 'cooked' are the same, without suffixes. Languages with this pattern of grammatical morphology are called **ergative** languages, and the subject of a transitive verb, here marked by *-le*, is said to have **ergative case**.

6. PARAPHRASES AND SEMANTIC ROLES

Paraphrases may be regularly possible for sentences with verbs of certain types according to the semantic roles of their associated nouns. Here are five English examples.

6.1. Verbs with cause/agent and patient

These are so-called **transitive verbs**, which usually have the cause/agent as subject, and the patient as object:

29. Beavers eat trees.
30. Noise may frighten the fish.

Sentences 29–30 are **active sentences**, with **active verbs**. In English these can ordinarily be paraphrased as **passive sentences**, in which the patient is the subject and the agent may appear as object of the preposition *by*. A passive sentence has a **passive verb**, which consists of a form of *be* plus a past tense or past participle form of the verb. Sentences 31–32 are passive versions of 29–30, respectively.

31. Trees are eaten by beavers.
32. Fish may be frightened by noise.

Notice that there is no passive paraphrase of *Beavers swim home*, even though this seems to have the same structure as *Beavers eat trees*: we can't say *Home was swum by the beavers*. Also, we can say *This book costs five dollars*, but not *Five dollars is cost by this book*. The verb of a passive sentence must have a cause or agent as active subject, and a patient as direct object.

6.2.   Change of state verbs

Verbs whose patient undergoes a change of state may have the patient as active verb subject, with no agent expressed. This requires presence of a 'manner' adverb – here, *quickly* and *easily*:

33.   These logs light easily. (= Someone lights these logs easily.)
34.   The gas tank in my car empties quickly on long trips. (= Long trips empty the gas tank in my car quickly.)

There are some exceptional extensions of this usage, with verbs that don't obviously involve a patient (entity affected by an agent or cause), as in *This book reads easily*.

6.3.   Verbs with agent, patient, and recipient

These may have the patient as direct object and the recipient as object of *to*, or both patient and recipient as co-objects, without *to*:

35.   The buyer still hasn't sent the check to me. (= The buyer still hasn't sent me the check.)
36.   The committee awarded the prize to the boss's cousin. (= The committee awarded the boss's cousin the prize.)

In the parenthesized paraphrase of 35 and 36, *me* and *the boss's cousin* are sometimes called **indirect objects**. (Sometimes, *me* and *the boss's cousin* are termed indirect objects in the unparenthesized versions too, although grammatically they are objects of the preposition *to*.)

A goal may look like a recipient, but doesn't permit such a paraphrase: *I sent my little brother to the store*; **I sent the store my little brother*. The paraphrase is dependent on meaning, not form.

6.4.   Verbs with source and goal

Source is a semantic role additional to the ten listed in §3, above. In sentences 37–38, *acorns* and *egg* are in the source role. If the source is subject, the goal is object of *into*. If the goal is subject, the source is object of *from*, as in the parenthesized paraphrases.

37.   Little acorns grow into mighty oaks. (= Mighty oaks from little acorns grow.)
38.   A softball-sized egg develops into a 200 lb. ostrich. (= A 200 lb. ostrich develops from a softball-sized egg.)

6.5.   Verbs with agent = patient

These have the agent as a subject, and the same noun phrase agent may be optionally expressed as an object **reflexive pronoun.**

39.   Fred shaved. (= Fred shaved himself.)
40.   The cat is washing. (= The cat is washing itself.)

There may be very many such classes of verbs, defined according to the dozen or so semantic roles of the noun phrases with which they form sentences. These numerous possibilities challenge our abilities to provide formal understandings of language structure, meaning, and use. Our fluent and effortless ability to understand and form new sentences with such variable structure and complex semantic relations must, however, be underlain by our unconscious knowledge of strict linguistic generalizations which relate meaning and form.

Suggestions for
ADDITIONAL READING

Most topics of this chapter are discussed and extended in textbooks of semantics, such as *Linguistics Semantics* (1995) by John Lyons, *Semantics* (1997) by John Saeed, *Semantics: a Coursebook* (1983) by James R. Hurford and Brendan Heasley, and on English *Introducing English Semantics* (1998) by Charles W. Kreidler. Topics in semantics are treated more deeply in *The Handbook of Contemporary Semantic Theory* (1996) edited by Shalom Lappin. Semantic roles are the topic of *Syntax and Semantics* Vol. 21: *Thematic Relations* (1988) edited by Wendy Wilkins. Also see the works on syntactic theory suggested at the end of chapter 18.

For the types of grammatical relations and how these are differently employed and marked in different languages, see *Functionalism and Grammar* (1995) by Talmy Givón, and *Fundamentals of Linguistic Analysis* (1972) by Ronald W. Langacker. The many types of English verb are surveyed and exemplified in *English Verb Classes and Alternations* (1993) by Beth Levin.

IMPORTANT CONCEPTS AND
TERMS IN THIS CHAPTER

- compositional meaning
- discontinuous constituent
- extraposition
- wh-word

- goal
- grammatical relation
- paraphrase
- topic

- wh-fronting
- noncompositional meaning
- idiom
- extension
- semantic role
- agent
- patient
- location
- instrument
- time
- recipient
- experiencer
- stimulus
- cause

- ergative
- case
- nominative case
- accusative case
- genitive case
- transitive verb
- active sentence
- active verb
- passive sentence
- passive verb
- indirect object
- source
- reflexive pronoun

OUTLINE OF CHAPTER 17

1. **Compositional meaning**
    1. Linear compositionality
    2. Nonlinear compositionality: discontinuous constituents
        1. Extraposition
        2. Wh-fronting
2. **Noncompositional meaning: idioms**
3. **Semantic roles**
4. **Verb classes according to semantic roles**
5. **Grammatical relation vs. semantic role**
    1. Formal nature of grammatical relations
    2. Constancy of semantic roles in paraphrases
    3. Formal expression of grammatical relations
        1. Subjects and objects in English
        2. Subjects and objects in five other languages
            1. Amharic
            2. Japanese
            3. Spanish
            4. Latin
            5. Nepali
6. **Paraphrases and semantic roles**
    1. Verbs with cause/agent and patient
    2. Change of state verbs
    3. Verbs with agent, patient, and recipient
    4. Verbs with source and goal
    5. Verbs with agent = patient

EXAMPLES AND PRACTICE

1. Semantic roles associated with verbs. Verbs are associated by meaning with certain semantic roles of nouns. These verb + semantic role associations may be formally represented as below for *jump* and *hear*, where the blank represents where the verb stands in a constituent with the noun of the stated semantic role. Each verb is illustrated by two example sentences:

		Examples:
1.	*jump*, V, [agent __]	Fleas jump.
		The kids jumped into the puddle.
2.	*hear*, V, [experiencer [__ stimulus]]	I smell a rat.
		We heard the bell.

The interpretation of the notation is as follows:

'*jump* is a Verb which takes a noun in the semantic role of agent as its subject' (preceding it in a sentence of the form [NP V]);

'*hear* is a Verb which takes a noun in the semantic role of experiencer as its subject (preceding it) and a noun in the semantic role of stimulus as its direct object' (following it in a sentence of the form [NP [V NP]]).

Give two examples each for ten of the twelve verb + semantic role relationships 3–14.

3. *walk*, V, [agent __]
4. *hit*, V, [agent [__ patient]]
5. *feel*, V, [experiencer [__ Aj]]
6. *feel*, V, [agent [__ patient]]
7. *give*, V, [agent [__ patient [P recipient]]]
8. *write*, V, [agent [__ patient [P recipient]]]
9. *live*, V, [experiencer [__ [P location]]]
10. *use*, V, [agent [__ instrument]]
11. *load*, V, [agent [__ location [P patient]]]
12. *fall*, V, [experiencer __]
13. *break*, V, [instrument [__ patient]]
14. *put*, V, [agent [__ patient [P location]]]

EXAMPLE

2. Semantic roles associated with prepositions. Like verbs, prepositions may be considered to be associated by meaning with certain semantic roles of nouns. These preposition + semantic role associations may be formally represented as in the left column, below, where the blank represents where the preposition stands as a constituent with the noun/semantic role. Each is illustrated by two example sentences:

		Examples:
1.	*to*, P, [__ goal]	I went to the store.
		He ran to first base
2.	*at*, P, [__ time]	We left at 2 o'clock.
		I will arrive at noon

In the interpretation of these, '*to* is a Preposition which takes as its object a noun in the semantic role of goal' (= follows it in a prep phrase), and '*at* is a Preposition which takes as its object a noun in the semantic role of time'.

PRACTICE

Give two example sentences which illustrate ten of the preposition + semantic role relationships 3–14.

3.	*to*, P, [__ recipient]	9.	*by*, P, [__ instrument]
4.	*for*, P, [__ recipient]	10.	*with*, P, [__ instrument]
5.	*for*, P, [__ time]	11.	*with*, P, [__ (co-)agent]
6.	*at*, P, [__ location]	12.	*from*, P, [__ agent]
7.	*in*, P, [__ location]	13.	*from*, P, [__ location]
8.	*toward*, P, [__ goal]	14.	*by*, P, [__ location]

EXAMPLE

3. Ten common semantic roles are agent, recipient, cause, experiencer, goal, instrument, location, patient, stimulus, and time.

PRACTICE

In sentences 3–18, label each underlined noun according to its semantic role, as in the examples. Each of the ten semantic roles appears at least three times. Sentences 1 and 2 are done as examples. There may be room for disagreement about some of these.

  C   P   T
1. The bell awakened me at 6 a.m.

    A   L   S
2. My sister was sitting under a tree listening to music.

3. The truck was loaded with hay by the farmers.

4. This <u>morning</u>, the <u>men</u> used <u>shovels</u> to fill the <u>truck</u> with <u>sand</u>.

5. <u>Mary</u> got a <u>letter</u> from her <u>father</u>.

6. The <u>children</u> put away their <u>books</u>.

7. My <u>mom</u> sent a <u>check</u> to a professional <u>association</u> in <u>Chicago</u>.

8. <u>I</u> felt hot all <u>day</u>.

9. The <u>door</u> slammed.

10. <u>Winter</u> brings <u>snow</u> which refills the <u>mountain</u> <u>lakes</u>.

11. A <u>sorcerer</u> can change a <u>lizard</u> into a <u>princess</u>.

12. <u>Inflation</u> drives up <u>prices</u>, and gives <u>consumers</u> <u>headaches</u>.

13. <u>We</u> heard the <u>bell</u> of the <u>church</u>.

14. The <u>midday</u> <u>sun</u> feels hot to <u>me</u>.

15. <u>She</u> sent her <u>father</u> a quick <u>reply</u>.

16. <u>Dad</u> took a <u>train</u> to <u>Los Angeles</u>.

17. The <u>sun</u> melted the <u>ice</u>.

18. The <u>wind</u> closed the <u>door</u>.

Chapter 18

SENTENCE FORM

This chapter presents two types of relation between paraphrases, and parts of the grammar of paraphrases, through English examples. It shows how paraphrases are related by syntactic rules, and provides explanations of the apparent function of some of these rules.

1. PARAPHRASES

Paraphrases exist for some of the sentences of all languages. In English, for example, we have paraphrases like:

Version 1	*Version 2*
This modem can send faxes.	Faxes can be sent by this modem.
Ants are swarming on the porch.	The porch is swarming with ants.
It is time to go?	Is it time to go?
You saw what?	What did you see?
What I saw was penguins.	It was penguins that I saw.

As in other aspects of language we have seen, the grammar of paraphrases involves aspects of both form and meaning. Some sorts of paraphrases are possible for sentences with particular meanings, while others are possible for sentences with particular forms. In this chapter we will examine the grammar of three English examples of paraphrases of the type based on meaning, and two of the type based on form.

1.1. Paraphrases dependent on meaning

In the previous chapter it was noted that verbs may be understood to differ according to the semantic roles of their associated nouns. Here are three examples of paraphrases dependent on such verb types.

1.1.1. Open-type verbs

Verbs of the *open*-type include *open, eat, frighten,* and *see,* which form sentences with nouns in the semantic roles of agent and patient, as in 1 and 2.

1.   Mom opened a box of Wheaties.
2.   Beavers eat fish.

Verbs of this type are traditionally known as **transitive verbs** (chapter 7, §3.2).

Transitive verbs may be either **active** or **passive.** Sentences 1 and 2 have **active verbs,** of which the agent is the subject (*Mom, beavers*) and the patient is the direct object (*a box of Wheaties, fish*). **Passive verbs** of the *open* type are seen in sentences 3 and 4. In these sentences, paraphrases of 1 and 2 respectively, the patient is the subject and the agent is the object of the preposition *by.*

3.   A box of Wheaties was opened by Mom.
4.   Fish are eaten by beavers.

1.1.2. Spray-type verbs

A second example of paraphrase dependent on meaning concerns verbs of the type of *spray, stuff, spread, smear,* and *paint,* which involve filling a space or covering an area. *Spray*-type verbs form sentences with an agent, a patient, and maybe a location. In the sentences of *spray*-type verbs, either the patient (*paint, cotton*) or location (*the wall, the pillow*) may be the direct object. If the patient is direct object, as in 5 and 6, the location is object of some preposition. If the location is direct object, as in sentences 7 and 8, the patient is object of the preposition *with.*

5.   They sprayed paint on the wall.
6.   We stuffed cotton into the pillow.

7.   They children sprayed the wall with paint.
8.   We stuffed the pillow with cotton.

1.1.3. Give-type verbs

English verbs of this type, including *give, tell,* and *send,* have agents, patients and recipients. In sentences 9 and 10 *a little* and *a story* are patients and *the Salvation Army* and *the kids* are recipients. The recipient may be object of the preposition *to,* as in 9 and 10, or co-object with the patient and preceding the patient, as in 11 and 12.

9.   They give a little to the Salvation Army.
10.   The teacher told a story to the kids.

11.   They give the Salvation Army a little.
12.   The teacher told the kids a story.

Recipient nouns of some languages are termed **dative** (*dat-* is a stem of the Latin verb 'give'), and the difference between sentences like 9–10 and 11–12 is said to result from **dative movement,** as if the recipients of 9–10 lose their preposition and 'move' before the patient in 11–12.

1.2. Paraphrases dependent on form

Other cases of paraphrases exist for sentences with nouns in all sorts of semantic roles, and depend only on the form of the sentences. Two examples of English paraphrases dependent on the form of sentences are yes/no questions and information questions.

1.2.1. Yes/no questions

All languages have **yes/no questions.** Yes/no questions ask for a *yes* or *no* answer, such as English sentences 13, 14, 15, and 16, of which 15 and 16 are paraphrases of 13 and 14, respectively:

13. Beavers can swim?
14. Beavers are likely to chew all the trees around a pond?

15. Can beavers swim?
16. Are beavers likely to chew all the trees around a pond?

English yes/no questions have a rise of pitch at the end (on *swim* or *pond* in 13–16), and, typically, as in 15 and 16, also an **auxiliary verb** first in the sentence and separated from the rest of the verb phrase by the subject NP. The auxiliary verbs in 13–16 are *can* and *are*.

Auxiliary verbs include the forms of *be* (*am, is, are, was,* etc.), forms of *have* and *do* when these are not the main verb (as in *has gone, have eaten, doesn't like,* etc.), and so-called **modal verbs** such as *can, may, should,* and *must*. Modal verbs express notions like ability (*can*), permission (*may*), likelihood (*should*), and obligation (*must*). (The word *modal* includes the stem *mod-* of *mood,* the traditional name of such aspects of verb meaning.)

1.2.2. Information questions

All languages also have **information questions.** In English, information questions involve **wh-words** such as *who(m), which, when,* and *how* (which, however, lacks a *wh*), and are also termed **wh-questions.** The wh-word of an information question ordinarily precedes the subject, as in 19 and 20, which are paraphrases of the less likely questions 17 and 18.

17. We shall eat what?
18. You will get the book from who(m)?

19.   What shall we eat?
20.   Who will you get the book from?

There is rising pitch on the wh-word in 17 and 18, but not in 19 and 20.

If the wh-word is the subject of the sentence, as in 21, there is no paraphrase, because as subject the wh-word already precedes the subject:

21.   Who broke this window?

Notice that, according to the compositional meaning of sentences 17–20, the wh-word is part of the verb phrase, as direct object of *eat* in 17 and 19 and as object of the preposition *from* in 18 and 20. In sentences 19 and 20, however, the wh-word is sentence-initial and separated from the other members of the verb phrase, which is thus a **discontinuous constituent**.

2.   THE GRAMMAR OF PARAPHRASE RELATIONS

It was noted in chapter 7 that rules of syntax concern grouping, function, and word order. More generally, syntax is concerned with the systematic relations of meaning and form of sentences, so syntactic rules must also concern paraphrases, in which noun phrases in the same semantic roles are in different grammatical relations, as expressed by differences of word order and grammatical morphemes. Let's consider the syntactic rules which can account for the five cases of paraphrase discussed above.

2.1.   Paraphrases dependent on meaning

Paraphrases dependent on meaning are dependent on the meaning of verbs as expressed by their relations of cooccurrence with noun phrases of particular semantic roles. We have seen paraphrases involving *open*-type, *spray*-type, and *give*-type verbs.

2.1.1.   Open-type verbs

Open-type or transitive verbs have as part of their lexical entry the specification [__, Agent, Patient], a formula which expresses their cooccurrence with an agent and a patient.

Now it is perhaps true of all languages (there are said to be exceptions) that if a sentence has an agent, this is typically the subject, a generalization which we can express as rule 22:

22.   [V, Agent, X]   →   [Agent, [V, X]$_{VP}$]

According to 22, of a construction consisting of a verb, agent, and other material represented by X (which may be zero), V is grouped with X as the VP.

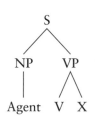

Figure 18.1

With the phrase structure rule that S → NP VP (chapter 7, §1.1), the agent is thus subject NP of the sentence, and with the phrase structure rule that VP → V . . . (chapter 7, §1.4), V is first in the VP. The rule is a generalization; there are exceptions to it, which need their special rules, one of which we shall see below.

As a result of rule 22 and the phrase structure rules, the construction [Agent [V, X]] takes the form of figure 18.1, in which with *open*-type verbs X is a patient noun phrase, as in sentences 1 and 2.

Open-type verbs may, however, be passive instead of active, and if they are, as in sentences 3 and 4, above, English has rule 23 for their structure:

23. $[V_{pass}$, Agent, Patient] → [Patient [be$_{Aux}$ [V$_{ppart}$ ([*by* Agent])]$_{VP}$]$_{VP}$]

Notice the rather complicated requirements of rule 23:

a.   the verb is passive in meaning (shown as V_{pass})
b.   the patient is subject,
c.   a (suitable) form of *be* is introduced as an auxiliary verb head of its verb phrase,
d.   the main verb, V, is a past participle (shown as V_{ppart} – *opened* and *eaten* in sentences 3 and 4) and head of its verb phrase,
e.   the agent, if present, is object of the preposition *by* (but may be absent, as shown by the parentheses).

This rule, if the agent is present, yields the sentence structure of figure 18.2, which is that of passive sentences 3 and 4, above.

The paraphrase relation between sentences 1 and 3, and 2 and 4, is the product, then, of the lexical specification of *open*-type verbs as [__, Ag, Pa], and the possibility of realization of such a construction according to either rule 22 or rule 23. What decides between the two possibilities is discussed in §5, below.

2.1.2.   *Spray-type verbs*

Spray-type verbs also have agents and patients: [V, Ag, Pa]. Like all verbs with agents, *spray*-type verbs may have locations; this is the rule [V, Ag, X] → [V, Ag, X, (Lo)]. Typically the agent of a spray-type verb is subject by rule 22, and the location is the object of a preposition. This leaves the patient as direct object; that is: [Ag [V Pa [P Lo]]]. Sentence 5, for example, fulfills this structure as in 24.

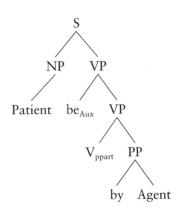

Figure 18.2

24.   [They [sprayed paint [on [the wall]]]$_{VP}$]

Spray-type verbs also fulfill conditions for rule 23, allowing (with slight modification of the above analysis) passive-verb sentences like *Insecticide was sprayed on the grass by those guys.*

English *spray*-type verbs, however, have the special characteristic that they are specified for the paraphrase [__ Lo [*with* Pa]], which allows them to form sentences like 7, which has the structure 25.

25.   [They [sprayed [the wall] [with paint]$_{VP}$]

2.1.3.   Give-type verbs

Give-type verbs have agents, patients, and recipients, so are specified [__, Ag, Pa, Re]. Typically, again (by rule 22), the agent is the subject and the patient is the direct object. Recipients in English are typically objects of the preposition *to*, as expressed by rule 26:

26.   [V, Pa, Re] → [V Pa [*to* Re]]

Rule 26 results in sentences like 9, which has the structure 27.

27.   [They [give [a little] [to [the Salvation Army]]]$_{VP}$]

Another peculiarity of English *give*-type verbs is their possibility of alternatively fulfilling, by rule 28, a structure with two objects, in which the recipient follows the verb as the so-called **indirect object**.

28.   [V, Pa, Re] → [V Re Pa]

Rule 28 results in sentences like 11, which has the structure 29.

29.   [They [give [the Salvation Army] [a little]$_{VP}$]

Paraphrases of the type of 9 (= 27) and 11 (= 29) are those traditionally described as resulting from **dative movement** (§1.1.3). Notice, however, that in our present understanding there is no movement, just alternative possibilities of structure and word order for *give*-type verbs. Similarly, paraphrases of *open*-, and *spray*-type verbs may be understood to result from syntactic rules which specify alternative structures for verbs of the types.

2.2. Paraphrases dependent on form

2.2.1. *Preliminaries: specifiers of verbs and sentences*

2.2.1.1. Specifiers of verbs. In order to understand paraphrases dependent on form, or phrase structure, let's review the basic rules of phrase structure presented in chapter 7, and extend these somewhat. Recall that two hypothetically universal rules provide for the expansion of major categories, noun, verb, etc., as phrases, and interpret the phrases to consist of maybe a single specifier, the head, and zero or more modifiers. These rules are repeated here as 30 and 31. Rule 31 gives the branching structure 32.

30. X → XP   32.   XP

31. XP → (Spec) X M^n Spec   X M^n

For nouns, rules 30 and 31 are fulfilled in English as 33 and 34, where the specifier (Spec) of 31 is the determiner of 34, and modifiers (M^n) include adjective phrases (AjP) and prepositional phrases (PP):

33. N → NP

34. NP → (Det) (AjP) NP (PP)

English word order is a bit different from that of the hypothetically universal rule 31: adjective modifiers in English don't follow but precede their head nouns. (Some Spanish NPs, for example, exemplify 31 more exactly, as in *la comida famosa de Madrid* 'the famous food of Madrid'.)

In chapter 7 we deferred consideration of how 30 and 31 are exemplified in the grammar of English for the categories V and S. There is controversy about this, but, here, let's consider a verb to fulfill the rules as in 35, with an auxiliary verb in the role of specifier of V:

35.   VP

Aux   V

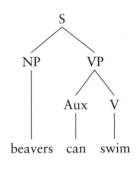

Figure 18.3

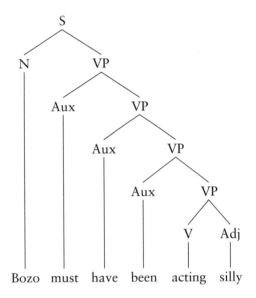

Figure 18.4

Thus sentence 13, *Beavers can swim*, will have the structure of figure 18.3.

Verb phrases, like other structures governed by rules 30 and 31, may be recursive, and have verb phrases within themselves. This is appropriate, since, in English for example, there may be multiple auxiliary verbs, with each one the head of its phrase. The sentence *Bozo must have been acting silly*, for example, with three auxiliary verbs, has the structure of figure 18.4.

2.2.1.2. Specifiers of sentences. We shall consider sentences to fulfill rule 31 as in 36, in which the specifier of S is termed a **complementizer** (Comp):

36.

In all languages, **conjunctions** are typical such complementizers (there is, however, great disagreement about the grammatical categories of language at this level of abstractness and hypothetical universality). In English, for example, *that*, *if*, *because*, and *so* show the role of a dependent clause as, respectively, a noun clause, a condition, a cause, and a result, as in 37(a)–(d).

37. a. I hope [that_{Comp} [it won't rain]].
     b. We will come [if_{Comp} [it doesn't rain]].
     c. We stayed at home [because_{Comp} [it rained]].
     d. It rained, [so_{Comp} [we stayed at home]].

Some languages, though not English, have words or morphemes which mark sentences as questions. In the classical variety of Arabic, for example, yes/no questions (in the written language, ordinarily) may begin with /hal/ (or/ʔa/). In Japanese yes/no questions end with *ka*, and in Sidamo verbs of yes/no questions are suffixed by /ni/.

38. a. Arabic: hal al-qaahira madiinatun kabiiratun
                    Ques Cairo city big
                    'Is Cairo a big city?'

     b. Japanese: tookjoo wa ookii machi desu ka
                    Tokyo Topic big city is Ques
                    'Is Tokyo a big city?'

     c. Sidamo: kiʔne roduwaa-nsaa-ti-ni
                    you(pl.) brother-their-are-Ques
                    Are you their brothers?

With this background, we are ready to analyze paraphrases dependent on form.

2.2.2. *Grammar of paraphrases dependent on form*

2.2.2.1. *Yes/no questions.*   Somewhat as Arabic yes/no questions begin with a question word, English yes/no questions begin with an auxiliary verb. The auxiliary verb is first in the verb phrase in questions like 13 and 14, but first in the sentence, preceding the subject, in more typical questions like 15 and 16, where it introduces the sentence as a question. This is a role of complementizers, in structures like 36.

Yes/no question 15, then, has the structure of figure 18.5. Notice that this includes within it the simpler structure which underlies 13 (that is, figure 18.3).

Can beavers swim? results from movement of the auxiliary verb to the Comp position, as shown by the arrow in figure 18.5. This movement is traditionally termed **auxiliary inversion**, because as a result the auxiliary verb and subject are

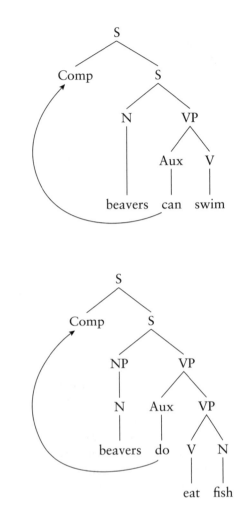

Figure 18.5

Figure 18.6

inverted. The movement accounts for the discontinuity of the verb phrase. The unraised, lower, position provides the interpretation of the auxiliary verb as specifier of V, and its raised, higher, position provides its role in question marking as complementizer/specifier of S.

Another peculiarity of English grammar is **do-insertion:** if there is no auxiliary verb to mark a question, one must be provided as a form of *do.* Thus the yes/no question of *Beavers eat fish* is *Do beavers eat fish?* The structure of this is as in figure 18.6, in which Aux is filled by *do,* which rises to Comp of S, as the arrow shows. (There are morphological peculiarities of *do,* which takes the form *does* /dəz/ with present tense 3rd person singular subjects, and *did* /dɪd/ in the past tense.)

2.2.2.2.   Information questions. English information questions have a wh-word at the beginning of the sentence (*what* and *who* in 19 and 20), which like

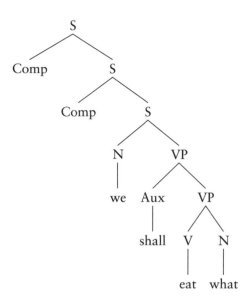

Figure 18.7

auxiliary verbs introduce these as questions. Like the auxiliary verb, the wh-word is part of a discontinuous constituent, and fulfills a semantic role and grammatical relation in the basic or lower sentence. Consistent with our analysis of yes/no questions, we consider the structure of 19 to be as in figure 18.7.

Rules of English require the structure of figure 18.7 to undergo two raisings: *what* to Comp of the highest S, and the auxiliary verb *shall* to Comp of the lower S. The rise of *what* or other *wh*-word as complementizer of the higher S is traditionally known as **wh-fronting**, and the similar rise of the auxiliary verb was seen above as **auxiliary inversion**. Notice how wh-fronting gives form to our understanding of wh-words in compositional meaning: *what* is the patient and direct object of *eat* in figure 18.7 despite its position, after wh-fronting, at the beginning of the sentence and outside the VP.

3.   DEEP AND SURFACE STRUCTURES OF SENTENCES

Sentence structures as in figures 18.5–18.7 are often termed **deep structures**: the analytically justified form of sentences in which meaning is fully compositional, phrase groups are all whole, without discontinuities, and verbs and their complements fulfill the grammatical relations fixed by the phrase structure rules. A deep structure is thus the **underlying form** of a sentence, before rules like auxiliary inversion and wh-fronting apply. After all raisings apply, plus relevant morphological and phonological rules (as for forms of *do*), the result, along the bottom of the tree, is the linear, concrete, **surface structure** of sentences, ready to be given **phonetic form**.

4. THE TRANSFORMATIONAL METAPHOR

We have talked about paraphrases as involving transformation of one structure into another. For example, dative movement is said to delete *to* and move a recipient NP before a patient NP, and auxiliary inversion is said to raise an auxiliary verb to Comp of S. In such cases the deep structure of a sentence is related to its surface structure by so-called **transformational rules**.

In fact, in the case of dative movement the paraphrases with and without the recipient preposition *to* were described above as alternative grammatical forms provided for a verb and its cooccuring noun phrases in the agent, patient, and recipient semantic roles, as either [Ag [V Re Pa]] or [Ag [V Pa [to Re]]]. Neither is changed or transformed into the other. If we consider the latter structure to be more basic, or more precise in having *to* as a marker of the recipient role, then dative movement is a metaphor in which the basic or deep structure is transformed into an alternative non-basic and surface structure.

In the case of paraphrases based on form, again we may think of the transformational understanding as helpfully concrete, but still metaphoric. Our thinking could be more abstract. Our understanding in each case of paraphrase based on form may be considered to involve two structures: an analytic one (the deep structure) in which morphemes are organized in non-discontinuous but non-linear constituents, and an actual one (the surface structure), which is linear and phonetically interpretable.

5. WHY PARAPHRASES?

Why do languages have paraphrases, two or more ways, it seems, of saying the same thing? Isn't this inefficient? Doesn't the existence of paraphrases make language unnecessarily redundant and complex?

In fact, paraphrases may often if not always be considered useful. Paraphrases arise in languages for reasons including some discussed in chapter 24, below. Once they arise, however, they may persist because they play useful roles in communication, (1) in organizing the information of sentences as background and foreground, and (2) in distinguishing sentence types.

5.1. Paraphrases based on semantic roles

Paraphrases sensitive to semantic roles of nouns, such as *Fish are eaten by beavers* vs. *Beavers eat fish*, and *The porch is swarming with bees* vs. *Bees are swarming on the porch* play the role of **backgrounding** and **foregrounding** information. By choosing among the paraphrases we can fit our sentences, with appropriate word order, into a discourse so that background is early in the sentence, and foreground is late. Notice how the passive sentence *Fish are eaten by beavers* is suitable to a context in which *fish* is **background**, as old or given information, and *beavers* is **foreground**, as new or asserted information. The question 'Tell me something about fish,' rather than 'Tell me something about beavers,' favors *Fish are eaten by beavers*. Similarly, *The porch is swarming with bees* is suitable to the context in which, say, someone comes rushing in from the porch, which thus is present as background, and *bees!* is the new focus of interest, or foreground.

5.2. Paraphrases based on phrase structure

Paraphrases based on phrase structure may play the same role of backgrounding/ foregrounding, and also the role of distinguishing sentence types. Notice that yes/ no questions are suitable in contexts in which nothing of the question is present as background known to a hearer; for example, out of the blue, we might hear 'Hey! Have you seen the new James Bond movie?' In this context, auxiliary inversion reasonably has the effect of announcing a yes/no question, and making this clearly distinct from a statement.

Raising wh-words in information questions, wh-fronting, may play a similar role, since the result is a sentence-initial question word. However, wh-fronting also has the effect of dividing a sentence into a focus, the wh-word, and the presupposed information which a hearer shares with a questioner, and out of which the question arises. Thus when *What shall we eat?* (= 19, above) is asked, the questioner presumes the hearer knows that 'we shall eat'; at issue is what, which is highlighted by initial position.

5.3. Prepositional adverb inversion

Let's consider one more paraphrase peculiarity of English. Prepositional adverbs are preposition-like adverbs which, however, don't have objects, like *up* in *She looked up*, and *down* in *He sat down*. English has frequent verb idioms which consist of a verb and a **prepositional adverb**, for example *tune in*, *turn on* and *throw up*. The prepositional adverbs are sometimes called 'particles'. As idioms, the meaning of verb + prepositional adverb compounds is not the sum of the two parts: *throw up*, for example, doesn't involve either throwing or a direction up.

Prepositional adverbs can precede or follow the direct object of the verb phrase of which they are a part, as in the sentence pairs 39–40, 41–42, and 43–44:

39. My cat threw a hairball up.
40. My cat threw up a hairball.

41. Turn the light out.
42. Turn out the light.

43. I have to take the garbage out on Tuesday.
44. I have to take out the garbage on Tuesday.

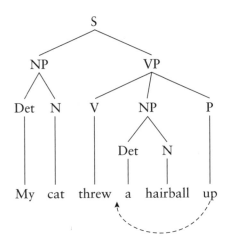

Figure 18.8

Since adverbs ordinarily follow the object of the verb (*I bought the car yester-day*, not *I bought yesterday the car*), and our rule for introducing prepositions (as PP) has these after a direct object (chapter 7, §1.4: rule 5), we will say that the basic or underlying word order of these pairs is as in 39, 41, and 43, respectively. See as figure 18.8, the deep structure of 39–40. A word order rule of English allows prepositional adverbs to switch positions with the object NP, as the dotted arrow shows in figure 18.8, and yields the phrase *threw up a hairball*. This is termed **prepositional adverb inversion**.

Prepositional adverb inversion foregrounds an object NP and/or backgrounds the verb by backgrounding its associated prepositional adverb, moving it to the left. This is apparent when we consider cases where the direct object is a pronoun. Use of a pronoun shows that the speaker assumes that the hearer knows what noun is being mentioned, so pronouns must, ordinarily, be backgrounded information. In the case of pronoun direct objects, prepositional adverb inversion is impossible, as in sentence 45:

45.   The cat threw it up. *The cat threw up it.

This shows that, at least relative to the ordinarily backgrounded pronoun, the prepositional adverb is foregrounded. (In a related phenomenon, in Spanish a pronoun object must ordinarily, as background, precede its verb: *Juan le preguntó* 'Juan asked him', not *Juan preguntó le*.)

Suggestions for
ADDITIONAL READING

See books suggested for chapters 6 and 7. Recommended introductory syntax textbooks include *Syntax: a Linguistic Introduction to Sentence Structure* (1991) by E. K. Brown and J. E. Miller, *From Word to Sentence* (1998) by David Pesetsky, *Transformational Grammar: a First Course* (1988) by Andrew Radford, and *Syntax: Structure, Meaning, and Function* (1997) by Robert D. Van Valin Jr. and Randy J. LaPolla. On English syntax are *Syntactic Theory and the Structure of English: a Minimalist Approach* (1997) by Andrew Radford, and *English Grammar* (1998) by Liliane Haegeman and Jacqueline Gueron.

IMPORTANT CONCEPTS AND TERMS IN THIS CHAPTER

- paraphrase
- transitive verb
- active
- passive
- active verb
- passive verb
- dative
- dative movement
- yes/no question
- auxiliary verb
- modal verb
- information question
- wh-word
- wh-question
- discontinuous constituent
- indirect object
- complementizer
- conjunction
- auxiliary inversion
- do-insertion
- wh-fronting
- deep structure
- underlying form
- surface structure
- phonetic form
- transformational rule
- backgrounding
- foregrounding
- background
- foreground
- prepositional adverb
- prepositional adverb inversion

OUTLINE OF CHAPTER 18

1. **Paraphrases**
   1. Paraphrases dependent on meaning
      1. *Open*-type verbs
      2. *Spray*-type verbs
      3. *Give*-type verbs

EXAMPLES AND PRACTICE

EXAMPLE

1. Five paraphrase rules I. Five paraphrases discussed above concern syntactic rules known as auxiliary inversion, do-insertion, dative movement, prepositional adverb inversion, and wh-fronting. Any or even all of these might apply in some sentences.

PRACTICE

Indicate which if any of these five rules (AI, DI, DM, PI, and WF, respectively) have applied in sentences 3–10. 1–2 are marked as examples.

   1. Can beavers give their young protection?   <u>AI</u> DI <u>DM</u> PI WF
   2. Do beavers cut down trees?   <u>AI</u> <u>DI</u> DM <u>PI</u> WF
   3. What do beavers eat for breakfast?   AI DI DM PI WF
   4. Some beavers live out their lives in obscurity.   AI DI DM PI WF
   5. Why did the beaver cross the pond?   AI DI DM PI WF
   6. Beavers in ponds near forests eat fish for fun.   AI DI DM PI WF
   7. Who cut down the trees near the pond?   AI DI DM PI WF
   8. Farmers fed the beavers tranquilizers.   AI DI DM PI WF
   9. Did the farmers hand out pills to the beavers?   AI DI DM PI WF
  10. What do beavers cut down trees with?   AI DI DM PI WF

EXAMPLE

2. Five paraphrase rules II.

PRACTICE

Indicate which, if any, of the five syntactic rules have applied in sentences 3–20.
1–2 are marked as examples.

1.	The farmers gave the beavers fish.	AI DI *DM* PI WF
2.	Did the farmers give fish to the beavers?	*AI* *DI* DM PI WF
3.	Will the farmers give fish to the beavers?	AI DI DM PI WF
4.	The beavers scarfed the food down.	AI DI DM PI WF
5.	What will the beavers scarf down?	AI DI DM PI WF
6.	Did the beavers scarf down the fish?	AI DI DM PI WF
7.	Who gave fish to the beavers?	AI DI DM PI WF
8.	What did the beavers scarf down?	AI DI DM PI WF
9.	Can the beavers scarf the fish down?	AI DI DM PI WF
10.	Will the farmers give the beavers grief?	AI DI DM PI WF
11.	What did the farmers give the beavers?	AI DI DM PI WF
12.	What will the beavers eat?	AI DI DM PI WF
13.	Who gave the beavers fish?	AI DI DM PI WF
14.	What did the farmers give to the beavers?	AI DI DM PI WF
15.	The beavers scooped the fish up.	AI DI DM PI WF
16.	The beavers scooped up what?	AI DI DM PI WF
17.	The farmers gave the beavers what?	AI DI DM PI WF
18.	The beavers can scarf down the fish.	AI DI DM PI WF
19.	Who did the farmers give the fish to?	AI DI DM PI WF
20.	Who will give the beavers fish?	AI DI DM PI WF

EXAMPLE

3. Deep structure tree diagrams I. Sentences with discontinuous constituents have
deep structures in which the discontinuities are only potential, and in which all
constituents are continuous and grammatical relations are fixed by the phrase
structure rules (as in chapter 7, §1).

Notice how this is so in the deep structure tree diagrams of figure 18.9 for the
following two sentences:

a.   Should the kids sweep out the barn?
b.   What has the cat thrown up?

PRACTICE

Match deep structure tree diagrams (a)–(d) of figure 18.10 with four of sentences
1–5, and provide the deep structure tree diagram of the remaining sentence.

1.   Who will sweep out the barn?
2.   What should the pigs eat their slop from?

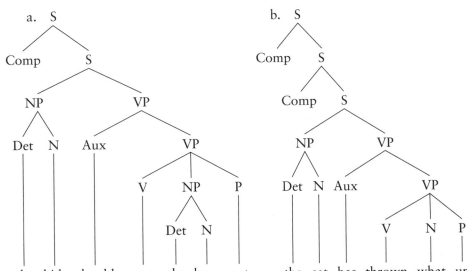

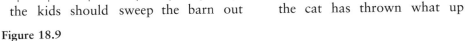

Figure 18.9

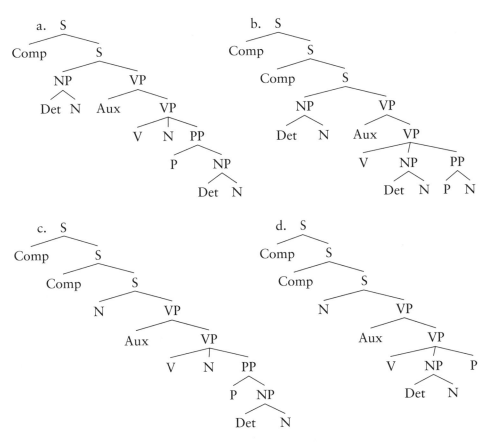

Figure 18.10

3. What do the kids eat like?
4. What do farmers feed to their pigs?
5. May the kids play games in the barn?

EXAMPLE

4. Deep structure tree diagrams II. Consider the tree diagram of figure 18.11, the deep structure of the sentence *Who(m) do the anglers give their fish to?*

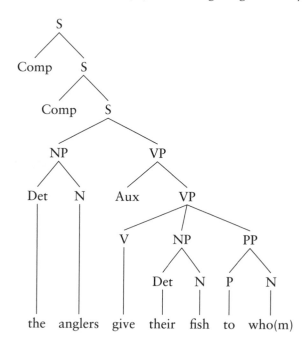

Figure 18.11

PRACTICE

Give deep structure tree diagrams for question sentences 1–3:

1. What will the beavers eat?
2. Did the beavers scarf down the fish?
3. What did the beavers scarf down?

EXAMPLE

5. Relative clauses. All languages have **relative clauses,** also known as adjective clauses, embedded sentences which are modifiers of nouns. In the following English sentences, for example:

1. The beaver that the farmer chased jumped into the pond.
2. The beaver that jumped into the pond got away.

that the farmer chased and *that jumped into the pond* are relative clauses.

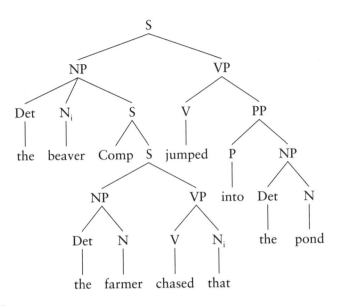

Figure 18.12

Recall the phrase structure rule for noun phrases from chapter 7 (§1.3), which allows adjective phrases and prepositional phrases as modifiers of nouns within noun phrases. A third possibility for such a modifier is a relative clause, a sentence within the noun phrase:

a.   NP → (Det) N (S)

There are certain requirements of S in such a structure, in any language:

b.   the relative clause S of course has to be about the head noun, N, of the NP;
c.   this is assured by the requirement that the relative clause includes a noun with the same reference as N; the two nouns are said to be **coreferential**; furthermore,
d.   the S has to be composed of Comp S, as in 36, above.

Also, in an English relative clause:

e.   the coreferential N of S fills the Comp position and is completed as an appropriate *wh*-word, or *that*, or, if not a subject, may be deleted.

The structure of the sentence *The beaver that the farmer chased jumped into the pond* is shown in figure 18.12. In figure 18.12, the subscripts on the N's show that these nouns are coreferential. According to condition (d), above, *that* (or *which*), as a non-subject of the clause, can be deleted, giving *The beaver the farmer chased jumped into the pond*.

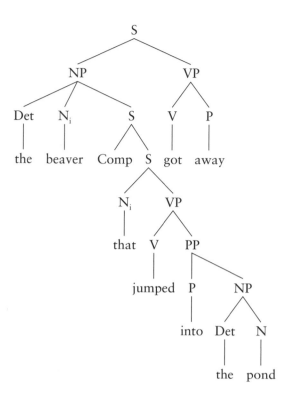

Figure 18.13

The structure of *The beaver that jumped into the pond got away* is shown in figure 18.13. According to condition (e), above, *that* of figure 18.13, as subject of its S, cannot be deleted.

PRACTICE

(a) Identify the relative clauses in the following sentences, and (b) provide tree diagrams like those above for three of the sentences. In many languages, relative clauses share characteristics with wh-questions. (c) Mention some characteristics which English relative clauses share with wh-questions.

1. Sentences that have relative clauses are fun.
2. I love sentences which have relative clauses.
3. The wh-word which the third sentence has is in a relative clause.
4. The sentence I drew a diagram of is a toughy.

EXAMPLE

6. An unbounded sentence using one word. The word /báfəlo/ *buffalo/Buffalo* can be a noun or a verb:

    a. Noun: 'wild ox(en), bison'; 'US city in New York state'
    b. Verb: 'bamboozle, trick'

Thus the three-word sentence *Buffalo buffalo buffalo* means 'Bison bamboozle bison'. We could expand the sentence with noun compounds as *Buffalo buffalo buffalo Buffalo buffalo* 'Buffalo bison bamboozle Buffalo bison', which has the (slightly simplified) structure

[Buffalo buffalo]$_{NP}$ [buffalo$_V$ [Buffalo buffalo]$_{NP}$]$_{VP}$

Furthermore, because in English a wh-word which represents a non-subject of a relative clause may be absent or omitted, as where *books which I like* may be shortened as *books I like*, a sentence consisting of only /bə́fəlo/ can be expanded unboundedly, for example: *Buffalo buffalo Buffalo buffalo buffalo buffalo buffalo* (= *buffalo from Buffalo which buffalo buffalo from Buffalo buffalo other buffalo*) has the structure

[Buffalo buffalo [[Buffalo buffalo] $_{NP}$ buffalo$_V$]$_S$]$_{NP}$ [buffalo$_V$ [buffalo]$_{NP}$]$_{VP}$

PRACTICE

As above, bracket and label the NP's, S (relative clause) and VP's in the sentence *Buffalo Buffalo buffalo buffalo buffalo buffalo buffalo buffalo.*

PRAGMATICS: INFERRING MEANING IN CONTEXT

This chapter concerns five important ways that we infer meanings beyond those of the forms of language, and how a few principles of language structure and language use make this possible.

1. PRAGMATICS

In a movie, Dean Martin takes an interest in a woman on an elevator. Noticing that she doesn't have a watch, he says, 'Excuse me, do you know what time it is?' When she says no, he looks at his watch and says, 'It's three twenty-five.' This was amusing because his question violates our usually reliable expectations about the **pragmatics** of language. (Pragmatics) is the relation between language and its context of use (and the study of this relation).

Pragmatics is important in the understanding of how language works, because linguistic form alone fails to explain all the meanings that we readily get from language – for example, that when people ask if we know what time it is, they wish to know the time. What happens is that meanings which are absent in the forms of language may be inferred from the context, given certain principles about how we use language.

2. FIVE SORTS OF LANGUAGE REQUIRING PRAGMATIC INFERENCE

Here we will consider five sorts of meanings which can be inferred by comparing language with its context of use: (1) ambiguous words, phrases, and sentences, (2) deictics, (3) figures of speech, (4) indirect illocution, and (5) presupposition.

2.1. Ambiguity

Ambiguity exists when a form has two or more meanings. Ambiguity is different from **vagueness**. With vagueness, the number of possible meanings is quite open. For example, there is vagueness when I say 'I bought a dog.' The dog could be male or female, brown or white, big or small, St Bernard or Chihuahua, etc. But in 'Can you see the [bič]?' two meanings contrast quite crisply: 'Can you see the beech?', and 'Can you see the beach?' Pragmatics, ordinarily, would make clear which meaning is appropriate – in the forest the former and at the seashore the latter.

There are two kinds of ambiguous language: lexical ambiguity and structural ambiguity.

2.1.1. Lexical ambiguity

[handwritten: general term]

Lexical ambiguity is ambiguity in the form of a morpheme or word. Lexical ambiguity results from the existence of **homonyms**, cases in which a single form has two or more meanings, as in English [tu] (*to*, *too*, and *two*), and *tear* ([tɪr] and [tɛr]). These two examples represent the two sorts of homonyms: **homophones**, like [tu], and **homographs**, like *tear*.

[handwritten: one form, 2+ meanings]

2.1.1.1. Homophones.

A **homophone** is a single pronunciation with two or more meanings. English examples in addition to [tu] are [fláwər], which could be either *flower* or *flour*, [sajt], [fli], and [sɛnt]. *[handwritten: [ðɛr] = there, the ir, they're]*

[handwritten: one sound, 2+ meanings]

2.1.1.2. Homographs.

A **homograph** is a single spelling with two or more meanings. English examples in addition to *tear* are *read*, which could be either [rid], the present tense form of *read*, or [rɛd] the past tense form of *read*, and *wind*, *does*, and *use*. Some homographs are also homophones, like *bat* [bæt] 'club for hitting in baseball' and 'type of flying rodent', and *hide* [hajd] 'skin (noun)' and 'conceal (verb)'.

[handwritten: one spelling, 2+ meanings]

2.1.1.3. Homonymy vs. polysemy.

Homonymy may often be distinguished from polysemy. **Polysemy** occurs when the form of a word suggests different meanings but the meanings are all related by semantic extension. English examples of polysemy are *drive*, as in 'drive animals' and 'drive a car', and *wave*, which can be a verb or a noun.

[handwritten: more examples?]

Homonymy and polysemy are not always clearly distinct, because it isn't always apparent whether or not different meanings are related by semantic extension. *Cool* [kul], 'low in temperature' and 'calm in mind/demeanor', is historically an example of polysemy, but nowadays some might feel that these meanings are so different that it better represents homonymy, like *bat*. *Ear* 'listening organ of the body' and *ear* as in 'ear of corn' are historically different words which came to be pronounced and spelled the same with the passage of time, but some may reasonably now consider this a case of polysemy, supposing 'ear of corn' to be a metaphoric extension of 'ear for listening'.

2.1.2. (*Structural ambiguity*)

Structural ambiguity exists when a phrase or sentence has two or more meanings because of structure, either of grouping or function (grammatical relations).

2.1.2.1.   Grouping ambiguity.   A case of (**grouping ambiguity**) is *The police searched for the car with broken headlights.* This sentence has two structures, one in which the prepositional phrase *with broken headlights* is about the car, and is grouped with *car* in a noun phrase, and another in which it is about the searching, and is grouped apart from the noun phrase but still with *searched* in the verb phrase. See the two tree diagrams, one for each of these meanings, in figure 19.1. Other examples of grouping ambiguity are *nutritious food and drink* and *We feed the pigs in clean clothes*, the two tree diagrams of each of which were compared in chapter 6, §4.1.3.

2.1.2.2.   Function ambiguity. (**Function ambiguity**) is less common than grouping ambiguity. This exists when a word or phrase potentially fulfills two or more grammatical relations, and morphemes and groupings are the same for both meanings (chapter 6, §4.2). Examples are *the shooting of the hunters* and *Visiting professors can be boring*. See the tree diagrams for these in figure 19.2.

The shooting of the hunters is a noun phrase which concerns either hunters who are shot by someone – so *hunters* is object of the verb *shoot*, or hunters who shoot – in which case *hunters* is subject of the verb. There are no homonyms, and grouping is the same on both interpretations.

Visiting professors can be boring, in which *visiting* is the present participle of *visit*, is a sentence concerning either professors who visit (that is, *professors* is the subject of *visit*), or professors who get visited (in which case *professors* is direct object of *visit*). Again there is no lexical ambiguity and there is only one grouping. Another understanding of the difference of function concerns head/modifier relations: if *professors* is head, the professors visit; if *visiting* is head (a so-called gerund), the professors get visited.

2.2.   Deictics

All languages have deictics. (**Deictics**) are morphemes with variable referential meaning, whose specific reference varies with each context of their use. Deictics include pronouns, adverbs that refer to space and time, and definiteness morphemes including the 'definite article' *the* in English. If it weren't for pragmatics, which ordinarily makes their reference clear, deictic usage could result in a lot of vagueness. In fact we are seldom puzzled by deictic usage, even though deictics are among the most frequent words and morphemes of a language.

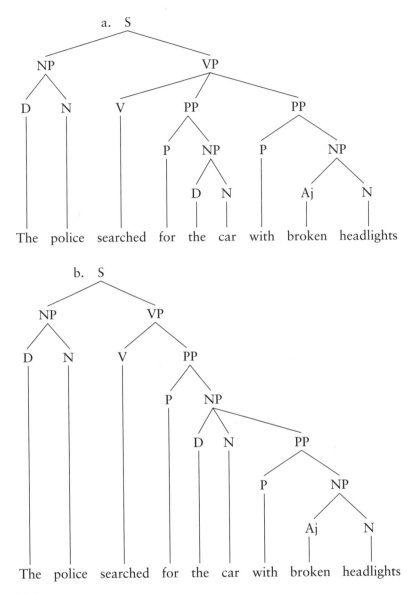

Figure 19.1

2.2.1. (Personal deictics)

These are the personal pronouns, English *I*, *me*, *she*, *your*, *they*, etc. The set of personal pronouns may distinguish person, number, gender, and grammatical relation, so *I* may be said to mean 'the person speaking (or writing) who is subject of the verb', *you* 'the person or persons addressed (subject or object)', and *her* 'the female person spoken of who is a possessor or object'. But just who this person is varies with the particular occasion of use of the pronoun. Of course, there can be vagueness and ambiguity in the use of these or any of the

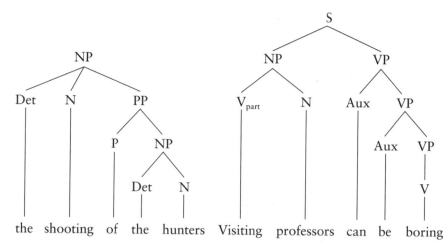

Figure 19.2

deictics. Notice how *we* in English can mean 'I and the person(s) spoken to', or 'I and some other person(s) not spoken to'. These are termed the 'inclusive' and 'exclusive' senses, respectively, of this pronoun.

2.2.2. (Spatial deictics)

These are the demonstrative pronouns, including English *this, that, these,* and *those,* and some frequent adverbs including English *here* and *there. This,* for example, in *I'll take this* can mean a rose, an ice cream cone, a rainy day, or whatever, depending on the context of its use. *Here* may mean a place in Chicago when spoken in Chicago, a place on Michigan Avenue when spoken on Michigan Avenue, or a place in this book when used in this book.

2.2.3. (Temporal deictics)

These are adverbs which refer to time, like English *then, now, today,* and *yesterday. Today* means 'this day' when spoken today, 'yesterday' when spoken yesterday, 'tomorrow' when spoken tomorrow, and June 1, 1647 when spoken on June 1, 1647. Tomorrow, *tomorrow* will mean the day after tomorrow.

2.2.4. (Definiteness)

This is communicated in various ways in languages. English communicates definiteness particularly with the definite article *the,* with demonstratives including *this,* and *that,* and with the personal pronouns *my, your, her, his,* etc.

A speaker says 'I went to a wedding' and, later, 'The wedding was last Saturday'. The second sentence, with *the,* assumes or presupposes the hearer's knowledge of the wedding. When someone says, 'Have you heard that song?' *that* shows that the hearer is assumed to know what song is being referred to. As in interpreting personal, temporal, and spatial deictics, interpreting definiteness requires us to consider the context, particularly the speaker, and the knowledge which we share with the speaker, part of which has been created by conversation that has gone immediately before. Recall that *the* is the most frequent word of English, so it must play a very important role in marking a speaker's understanding of what they consider to be knowledge shared with hearers. (Definiteness is a type of presupposition, discussed in §2.5, below.)

2.3. Figures of speech

It is common, if not always easy, to distinguish literal and non-literal or figurative language. We usually take certain meanings to be basic, expected, or **literal language**. Figurative, or **non-literal, language** is novel and creative, and suggests other meanings, like English *Drop me a line*, *Give me a break*, and *Get a life!* Non-literal language is frequent and part of everyone's ordinary speech, but by pragmatic inference hearers/readers ordinarily recognize non-literal language, and readily make reasonable inferences about its meaning.

The different types of such creative language use are termed '**figures of speech**'. Six commonly encountered figures of speech are metaphor, metonymy, synecdoche, personification, hyperbole, and irony.

2.3.1. *Metaphor*

[handwritten: icon – actual charact. shared]

This is substituting words for others with which they share characteristics of meaning.

1. The ship plows the sea. (The ship moves through water like a plow through soil.)
2. The red car won by a nose. (The leading part of the red car crossed the finish-line first, like the nose of the winning horse in a horse-race.)

2.3.2. *Metonymy*

[handwritten: index – association found in nature]

This is substituting words for others with which they share associations of meaning in time and/or space.

3. Hollywood won't buy this story. (*Hollywood* substitutes for the *movie industry*, which is importantly located in Hollywood.)
4. Can you lend me some bread? (*Bread* substitutes for *money*, which, importantly, money buys.)

*[handwritten: * come up with examples]*

Metonymy is to metaphor as index is to icon (chapter 1, §2.1.2). A metaphor is an iconic sign, effective because of actual characteristics it shares with what it substitutes for. Metonymy is an indexical sign, effective because of a natural association, in time or space, with what it substitutes for. As icons and indexes are not always clearly distinct, neither are metaphor and metonymy. *Bread*, for example, can substitute for *money* because of the natural association of bread and money (money buys bread), or, perhaps, because of the characteristic of meaning of practical necessity for life which it shares with *money*. The difference is particularly unclear in the case of complex meanings which may be considered to consist of a set of associations, such as 'Paris' and 'Christmas'.

2.3.3. *Synecdoche* /sɪnékdoki/

This is using a part to mean the whole, a type of metaphor or metonymy:

5. Can I borrow your *wheels*? (wheels = car)
6. There is still great respect for the *crown*. (crown = monarchy)

The latter example is a type of metonymy if crown is not part of the meaning of *monarchy*, but just an association with it.

2.3.4. *Personification*

This is a type of metaphor in which human characteristics are attributed to something non-human, which shows similar characteristics:

7. This drawer *refuses* to open. (refuses to open = is stuck)
8. My goldfish is *begging* to be fed. (is begging to be fed = looks very hungry)

2.3.5. *Hyperbole*

This is a type of metaphor in which comparison is implied to a similar but extravagant case:

9. *Drop dead*!
10. I'd rather *kill myself* than watch music videos.

2.3.6. *Irony*

This is a type of metaphor in which comparison is implied to an opposite or unreasonably extreme case:

11. That's cute! (Said of something not cute at all)
12. Let's keep the noise down to an uproar, please. (When the noise is not at 'uproar' level.)

Some figures of speech are **idioms**. Idioms are figures of speech, especially phrases, which have become common and even routine. A couple of examples are *stand up for*, meaning 'assert or insist on', as in *Stand up for your rights!* (a case of metonymy, standing up usually associated with but not otherwise similar to insistence or assertion), and *Necessity is the mother of invention* (a case of metaphor, in which necessity 'gives birth' to invention).

Many idioms become the customary way of expressing some meanings, and as a result have fully lost their sense of non-literalness. For example:

[handwritten marginal notes:] idiom: can't infer the meaning by putting pieces together "kick the bucket"

[handwritten annotation next to 2.3.6:] (sarcasm)

13. *understand*, literally 'stand under'; metaphorically speaking, to become knowledgeable/aware of something is to 'stand under' it.
14. *run for* 'actively seek' political office; metaphorically speaking, actively to seek political office is to 'run for office' like a runner for a prize.

Neither of these usages, as idioms, any longer has any novelty or demands interpretation as a figure of speech.

2.4. Indirect illocution

2.4.1. *Locution and illocution*

In the terminology of the philosopher J. L. Austin (1955), simply to speak is to perform a **locution,** but to speak with an intent, such as to ask, promise, request, plead, assert, demand, order, apologize, warn, or threaten, is to perform an **illocution.** This purpose, or illocutionary intent, is meaningful and will ordinarily be recognized by hearers (or readers), whether it is directly (overtly) expressed or indirectly (inovertly) expressed.

2.4.2. *Direct and indirect illocution*

2.4.2.1. (*Direct illocution.*) Direct illocution is making the intent of speech evident in the overt form of sentences. There are two ways to make overt or *being direct w/ intent* direct illocutions:

a. By use of special grammatical forms which directly express the intent, as in English yes/no questions in which an auxiliary verb precedes the subject as in *Can I go now?* (vs. *I can go now?*), or in imperative sentences in which the subject pronoun *you* is absent as in *Have it on my desk by Monday morning* (vs. *You have it on my desk by Monday morning*).
b. By use of a **performative verb,** the main verb of a sentence of which the rest of the sentence is the direct object, as in:

15. I warn you not to do that again.
16. I promise that I'll be there.
17. We request a booth in the back.

Warn, promise, and *request* are the performative verbs in 15–17.
confess, inquire, name, declare

2.4.2.2. (*Indirect illocution.*) **Indirect illocution** is leaving the intent of speech unexpressed or unovert in the form of sentences. Consider the example of the common English question *Do you know what time it is?* This has the form of a yes/no question, but everybody understands it to be an information question. An appropriate answer to this question is not 'Yes' or 'No', but a time, like 'Two twenty-five', or 'A quarter to eight'. The sentence is directly or overtly a yes/no

question, but indirectly it is an information question, and, by pragmatic inference, almost everyone understands it so.

There is usually no special grammatical form for an illocution, though in some
languages there is more grammatical marking of illocutions than in English. Nor
is a performative verb usually used. Instead the illocution is **indirect,** as in:

18.	Don't do that again.	– an indirect warning
19.	I'll be there.	– an indirect promise
20.	A booth at the window would be nice.	– an indirect request
21.	OK, team, let's get started.	– an indirect command

Like ambiguities, deictics, and figures of speech, indirect illocutions are very
common, and ordinarily they are readily recognized by hearers/readers, who interpret them by pragmatic inference.

2.4.3.   Declarative speech acts

There are cases in which to say something is not just to say it (a locution) or
to say it with an intent (an illocution), but actually to bring about some new
situation. These unusual cases are called **declarative speech acts.** The wonder of
declarative speech acts is suggested by the children's story in which any wish can
be made a fact just by uttering *Abracadabra.* But declaratives are performed in
real life by a few persons with special rights and authority, such as policemen,
judges, and umpires. A judge, for example, says *I sentence you to 90 days in jail,*
and the sentence is fixed. In baseball, an umpire says *You're out!* and the base-
runner is out.

2.4.4.   Felicity conditions

Appropriate grammatical form or use of performative verbs, however, do not
guarantee an illocution. There are, for example, rhetorical questions, which do
not ask for or expect an answer, and imperative verbs in advertisements (*Get one
today! Call now!*), which everyone ignores. The request by a lawyer for a mis-
trial, while it has the form of a request, may be knowingly futile and merely
a formality to justify a subsequent appeal. Valid or sincere illocution, as for a
promise to be accepted as a promise or for a request to be taken as a request,
depends on the fulfillment of certain conditions within the context of speech.

The conditions which validate an illocution are termed **felicity conditions.**
Following are some felicity conditions for questions, requests, promises, and
warnings.

a. Questions about X
  1. The speaker wants to know something about X
  2. The speaker believes the hearer may know something about X
b. Requests for X
  1. The speaker desires X
  2. The speaker believes the hearer is able and willing to provide X

c. Promises that X
   1. The speaker believes the hearer desires X
   2. The speaker is able and willing to bring about X
d. Warnings that X
   1. The speaker is knowledgeable about X
   2. The speaker believes the hearer does not desire X

Felicity conditions may be thought of as part of the meaning of the performative verbs which express an illocution, but whether they are fulfilled or not must be judged by pragmatic inference. For example, do we consider something to be a promise if the speaker is certainly unable and/or unwilling to fulfill it? And if the speaker is unable or unwilling to fulfill a promise, is it then a 'false promise' or not a promise at all? In either case, our ability to recognize an indirect illocution, as well as a direct one, depends on our understanding of its felicity conditions.

2.5. Presupposition

2.5.1. Presupposed and asserted information

A presupposition is something assumed (presupposed) to be true in a sentence which asserts other information. For example, sentence 22a presupposes 22b, 23a presupposes 23b, and 24a presupposes 24b.

22. a. Christopher realized that Winnie was gone.   *usually linked to verbs
    b. Winnie was gone.
23. a. Christopher stopped looking.
    b. Christopher had been looking.
24. a. The owl sneezed again.
    b. The owl had sneezed before.

That the information of the second sentences is presupposed, rather than entailed or included some way in the first, is apparent in the fact that if the first sentence is negated the truth of the second sentence is unchanged: 25, 26, and 27 also presuppose 22b, 23b, and 24b, respectively.

25. Christopher didn't realize that Winnie was gone.
26. Christopher didn't stop looking.
27. The owl didn't sneeze again.

In presupposition, furthermore, if the second sentence is false the first is false or unreasonable. Thus the respective truth of 28, 29, and 30 makes 22a, 22b, and 23b false or unreasonable.

28. Winnie wasn't gone. (So Christopher could not have realized that he was.)
29. Christopher had not been looking. (So he could not have stopped looking.)
30. The owl hadn't sneezed before. (So it could not have sneezed again.)

2.5.2.   *Presupposition vs. synonymy and entailment*

It is helpful to distinguish presupposition from **synonymy** and **entailment**.

Synonymy is the relationship between paraphrases (chapter 18, §1), such as 31a and 31b, and 32a and 32b.

31.   a.   Kanga gave Piglet a bath.
       b.   Kanga bathed Piglet.
32.   a.   Pooh was too short to reach the honey.
       b.   Pooh wasn't tall enough to reach the honey.

If either of two synonymous sentences is true so is the other, and if either is false so is the other.

Entailment is the relationship of logical inclusion between the circumstances described by pairs of sentences, as where 33a entails 33b, and 34a entails 34b.

33.   a.   Christopher has a bear and a pig.
       b.   Christopher has a bear.
34.   a.   Christopher dropped Winnie.
       b.   Winnie fell.

In these relationships, if the first sentence is false the second could be either true or false, and if the second sentence is false so is the first. Thus if Christopher doesn't have a bear and a pig he might or might not have a bear (or a pig, though not both), but if he doesn't have a bear, then he certainly doesn't have a bear *and* a pig. Likewise, if Christopher didn't drop Winnie, then Winnie may still have fallen, some way, but if in fact Winnie didn't fall, then it cannot be the case that Christopher or anyone else dropped him.

These understandings result because an entailed sentence describes a broader or more inclusive circumstance than an entailing sentence. In these examples: having a bear is a circumstance which includes having a bear and a pig, and falling may result from a number of circumstances besides being dropped.

2.5.3.   *The pragmatic nature of presupposition*

Presuppositions unlike synonyms and entailments concern knowledge which a speaker/writer does not assert but presumes as part of the **background** of a sentence, knowledge (presumed to be) already known to the hearer/reader (chapter 18, §5.1). This explains why negating a presupposing sentence (or making a negative presupposing sentence affirmative) does not affect the truth of a presupposition, which remains as mere background, and why the falsity of a presupposition makes a presupposing sentence unreasonable, or false. When a presupposing sentence wrongly assumes knowledge of the hearer, it is based on a mistaken assumption, if not a false one.

Presuppositions have to be recognized by hearers, so their validity has continually to be confirmed or rejected by hearers. The validity of assertions is important too, of course, but knowledge of the validity of assertions is not imputed to hearers by a speaker, and doesn't have to be accepted in order for conversation to proceed normally. Checking the validity of presuppositions is an important application of pragmatic inference.

3. PRINCIPLES OF CONVERSATION

3.1. Cooperative principle

Given an utterance, or locution, and its lexical meanings related to one another through grammatical structure, the possibility of pragmatic inference necessary to interpret ambiguity, deictics, figures of speech, indirect illocutions, and presuppositions depends, importantly, on the assumption that speakers honor what the philosopher of language Paul Grice (1975) termed the (cooperative principle,) simply and in short:

> Cooperative principle: contribute meaningfully to the accepted purpose and direction of conversation.

Hearers are also speakers, ordinarily, so both speakers and hearers recognize the principle, and, accepting it, can use it as a basis for inferring what is meant even when this isn't overt in a message. Thus when someone says 'The heat is killing me', and they seem otherwise quite healthy, we readily infer that the speaker is not about to die, but wishes to emphasize his or her discomfort from the heat (a case of the hyperbole figure of speech).

connected

3.2. Four conversational maxims

There are four sub-principles of the cooperative principle, termed **conversational maxims**:

1. **Maxim of relevance:** be relevant. Thus:
   a. When we hear that someone 'kicked the bucket', we ordinarily presume that the person died, which is likely to be relevant, and not that they kicked a bucket, which is unlikely and probably irrelevant.
   b. When someone asks, with a yes/no question, 'Do you know what time it is?', we suppose they want to know what time it is, not just whether we know, and instead of answering just 'Yes', we provide a time.

*think of examples

Does it fit?

on point w/conversation

2. **Maxim of quality:** be truthful; don't lie (unless you have to!). Thus:
   a. When a friend says 'If I hear that song again I'm gonna kill myself', we accept this as hyperbole, and don't turn the radio off.

true/ honest

answer: what is being violated? why is this being violated? → intention

b.   Hearing 'The boss has lost his marbles', we imagine a mental problem, not actual marbles.

3.   **Maxim of <u>quantity</u>**: be informative, say neither too much nor too little. Thus:

normal length

a.   Asked how many children so-and-so has, we may reply 'Three' but never 'Two' if three is correct, even though if three is true so is two (by entailment).

b.   On June 23 when asked the date, we may say 'The twenty-third', or maybe 'June twenty-third', but we normally don't include the year in such an answer.

4. **Maxim of <u>manner</u>**: be clear and orderly. Thus:

normal way

a.   Although it would be possible to arrange things in other than chronological order, a recipe will say 'Bake about 50 min. at 400°, check after 40 min.; when brown, remove from oven and put on a cookie sheet'.

b.   Instructions to assemble a bicycle begin with a statement about how to orient oneself to the pieces, for example: 'Front, back, right and left are determined as if you were sitting on the bike.'

The maxims may seem like applications of ordinary common sense and not worth mentioning, and maybe they are. But just think how chaotic and unhelpful conversation would be if the maxims were often flouted or disobeyed (and they are flouted, often enough). Their general validity and our consequent ability to rely on them as strategies of interpretation explains much of the effectiveness of most talk, and our ability, by pragmatic inference, to get a lot of overtly unexpressed but important meanings.

Suggestions for
ADDITIONAL READING

Important topics in pragmatics are developed further in *Pragmatics and Natural Language Understanding* (1996) by Georgia Green, *Understanding Utterances: an Introduction to Pragmatics* (1992) by Diane Blakemore, and *Pragmatics: an Introduction* (1993) by Jacob L. Mey. Presenting principles of conversation, a topic not raised above, is *Approaches to Discourse: Language as Social Interaction* (1993) by Deborah Schiffrin.

Some of the most important readings in pragmatics are collected in *Pragmatics: a Reader* (1991) edited by Steven Davis.

Concerning indirect illocutions, an important article is 'Indirect speech acts' by John R. Searle (1975), and concerning principles of conversation 'Logic and Conversation' by H. Paul Grice (1975); both of these are included in the volume *Pragmatics: a Reader*.

IMPORTANT CONCEPTS AND TERMS IN THIS CHAPTER

- pragmatics
- ambiguity
- vagueness
- lexical ambiguity
- homonym
- homophone
- homograph
- polysemy
- structural ambiguity
- grouping ambiguity
- function ambiguity
- deictic
- personal deictic
- spatial deictic
- temporal deictic
- definiteness
- literal
- non-literal
- figure of speech
- metaphor
- metonymy
- synecdoche

- personification
- hyperbole
- irony
- idiom
- locution
- illocution
- indirect illocution
- direct illocution
- performative verb
- declarative speech act
- felicity condition
- presupposition
- synonymy
- entailment
- background
- cooperative principle
- conversational maxim
- maxim of relevance
- maxim of quality
- maxim of quantity
- maxim of manner

OUTLINE OF CHAPTER 19

1. **Pragmatics**
2. **Five sorts of language requiring pragmatic inference**
   1. Ambiguity
      1. Lexical ambiguity
         1. Homophones
         2. Homographs
         3. Homonymy vs. polysemy
      2. Structural ambiguity
         1. Grouping ambiguity
         2. Function ambiguity

EXAMPLES AND PRACTICE

EXAMPLE

1. Ambiguity. The sentence *May I try on that dress in the window?* is structurally ambiguous, having two understandings, (a) or (b).

   a.   May I try on that dress which is in the window.
   b.   May I get into the window and try on that dress.

I found a bat in the attic contains a lexical ambiguity, *bat*, so it could mean either (c) or (d):

   c.   I found a baseball bat in the attic.
   d.   I found a flying rodent in the attic.

PRACTICE

Rewrite each of the following five ambiguous sentences in two ways, each of which makes clear one of the two (or more) meanings.

1. She gave her dog meat.
2. The chickens are ready to eat.
3. Scientists put their glasses on their noses.
4. What gets wetter the more it dries?
5. Leave the chairs on the veranda.

EXAMPLE

2. Grouping ambiguity.

PRACTICE

Sentences 1–7 are ambiguous, each having (at least) two meanings depending on how words and phrases are grouped. Provide one pair of parentheses to show one of the two meanings. The result does not need to be the more likely meaning! The first two are done as examples. Provide a pair of parentheses for 3–7.

1. There's a café in the theatre district which I like.

   There's a café in (the theatre district which I like).

2. Oh, that's just a crazy lawyer's idea.

   Oh, that's just a (crazy lawyer)'s idea.

3. The FCC intends to eliminate sex and race bias in TV advertising.
4. You should eat more nutritious food.
5. Realizing that it was late, he rushed out and forgot the papers.
6. We discovered that they lost the election by chance.
7. He said he didn't tell you because he wants to make you mad.

EXAMPLE

3. Directness and literalness. Consider sentences 1–2 and sentence descriptions (a)–(b). Sentence 1 is an indirect request for aspirin. Sentence 2 is an indirect promise (not to 'miss it') and non-literal, being a case of hyperbole, since, presumably, one really wouldn't turn down the whole world to be there!

1. I wonder if you have some aspirin.   – a literal indirect request
2. I wouldn't miss it for the world.   – a non-literal (hyperbolic) indirect promise

PRACTICE

Match 3–7 with (a)–(e), 8–12 with (f)–(j), and 13–17 with (k)–(o). Use one answer one time. Make the best match, considering the five choices.

3. Will you be quiet? (said by the boss)
4. Don't you think it's too dark in here?
5. Yeer out! (said by a baseball umpire)
6. I wouldn't do that if I were you.
7. Do you know what time it is?

    a. Literal indirect request
    b. Literal indirect command
    c. Literal indirect warning
    d. Literal indirect information question
    e. Declarative speech act

8. The Pistons murdered the Knicks.
9. Can you hold it down a little, kids? (said by the kids' father)
10. I wonder what time it is.
11. Go ahead and try, buddy.
12. You can bet I'll be there.

    f. Literal indirect promise
    g. Literal indirect warning
    h. Literal indirect information question
    i. Non-literal (metaphoric) indirect command
    j. Non-literal (metaphoric/hyperbolic) direct statement

13. A table by the window would be nice.
14. Drop dead.
15. Hold your horses!
16. I do appreciate all this peace and quiet, kids.
17. If you wanna make an omelette you hafta break eggs.

    k. Non-literal (hyperbolic) direct command
    l. Non-literal (metaphoric) direct statement
    m. Non-literal (ironic) indirect request
    n. Non-literal (metaphoric) direct command
    o. Literal indirect request

EXAMPLE

4. Figures of speech. Six types of figure of speech defined and exemplified above are:

Hyperbole:	Exaggeration
Metaphor:	Substitution based on similar characteristics
Metonymy:	Substitution based on other associations
Personification:	Extension of human characteristics to non-human

Irony: Substitution of opposite
Synecdoche: Substitution in which part = whole

PRACTICE

Identify the figure of speech represented by sentences 1–18. You should be able to find three sentences for each figure of speech, though some of 1–18 may represent more than one type, and the difference between metonymy and metaphor is often unclear.

1. A black and white is parked outside.
2. Get a life!
3. Can I borrow your wheels?
4. I just love having cat hair all over my lap.
5. The Lions smashed the Packers' hopes.
6. The used car I bought is a lemon.
7. I paid a fortune for this book.
8. The engine coughed and died.
9. Out of gas? Oh, great!
10. The Green and White will now play Penn State.
11. I'm so hungry I could eat anything.
12. The house had a very inviting floorplan.
13. The pen is mightier than the sword.
14. My hopes rose.
15. Get your tail outa here.
16. This pen refuses to write.
17. Two heads are better than one.
18. Your neck brace is very stylish.

EXAMPLE

5. Synonymy, entailment, and presupposition. We saw (§2.5) that a sentence is true if a synonymous sentence is true, and false if a synonymous sentence is false; that an entailed sentence may be either true or false if an entailing sentence is false; and that a presupposed sentence may be true even when the presupposing sentence is false.

PRACTICE

Identify each of the sentence pairs 1–24 as showing one of synonymy, entailment, or presupposition. There are eight examples of each type.

1. Jill turned off the alarm. It was Jill that turned off the alarm.
2. Jill neglected to let the cat out. The cat was in.
3. Jill's sister is staying at her place. A member of Jill's family is staying at her place.
4. Jill did twenty pushups. Twenty pushups were done by Jill.
5. Jill did twenty pushups. Jill did ten pushups.

6. Jill bought the one that has batteries. Jill bought the one with batteries.
7. Jill accused Jack of xantheism. Xantheism is bad.
8. Something startled Jill. Something got Jill's attention.
9. Are we going to invite Jill? We are going to invite Jill?
10. Jill broke an arm in the game. Jill was injured in the game.
11. Jill began to exercise. Jill was not exercising before.
12. Jill sent Jack a letter. Jill sent a letter to Jack.
13. It rained every day of the week. It rained on Wednesday.
14. Jill regrets cancelling her Sunday paper. Jill cancelled her Sunday paper.
15. It was surprising how Jill ducked the question. Jill ducked the question.
16. Jill let the cat out. Jill let out the cat.
17. Jill read up to page 275. Jill read page 200.
18. Jill was happy that it was Friday. It was Friday.
19. Jill sprayed the chair with varnish. Jill sprayed varnish on the chair.
20. The drawer is stuck. The drawer won't open.
21. A blow on the head knocked Jill out. Jill was unconscious.
22. Jill managed to disconnect the burglar alarm. Disconnecting the burglar alarm was hard.
23. Jill finished mowing the grass before dark. Jill mowed the grass.
24. It's time to go now. Now it's time to go.

EXAMPLE

6. Presuppositions. Recall that if a presupposing sentence is negated its presupposition remains, and that if a presupposition is false, its presupposing sentence is unreasonable or false.

PRACTICE

Provide a presupposition of each of sentences 1–10.

1. When Jack arrived, we began to eat.
2. Jack repeated the story for latecomers.
3. Jack returned to Mayberry.
4. Jack was finally able to open the door.
5. It wasn't Jack that wrecked the car.
6. Jack can't find those gadgets anymore.
7. Jack likes those gadgets too.
8. It surprised Jack that the game was so lopsided.
9. What did you say that Jack likes?
10. Jack agreed to go.

THE UNITY OF
LANGUAGES

This chapter concerns some of the ways and the extent to which languages are all the same, and explanations for this similarity or unity of languages.

1. PREREQUISITES TO THE DISCOVERY OF LANGUAGE UNIVERSALS

Language universals, principles of language valid for all languages, reasonably concern features which are essential for the function and/or structure of language and thus for human communication. For two reasons, the discovery of language universals has not been easy. First, linguists have only in recent decades agreed, informally, on the terminology and practical descriptive framework of grammar within which all languages can be described and compared. Second, considerable time has been required to provide dictionaries and grammars of a representative number of the thousands of languages of the world. Just a few decades ago, indeed, many linguists believed that there might be no language universals, and that languages might vary from one another unpredictably.

Today, however, the languages of the world, even if many remain unstudied and others are only partially known, are at least largely identified and cataloged (as in Grimes 1996). Linguists have largely agreed upon the descriptive categories and framework of universal grammar (by formal consensus, indeed, in the important case of the International Phonetic Alphabet), though this remains tentative in many details, and probably a reliably representative sample of the world's languages are described in significant depth.

Following is a survey of language universals of various kinds, discovered by broad comparison of languages and language types. This is followed by discussion of some hypothetically innate universal principles of language discovered by a quite different method: comparison of principles of language with the seemingly insufficient data available to children during acquisition. The universal regularities of acquisition suggest that child learners share important principles of acquisition or of language itself, or both. Finally, some explanations of language universals are presented.

2. SOME LANGUAGE UNIVERSALS

Below, let the comment that some feature is or appears to be universal 'in languages' be understood to mean 'in languages that we know sufficiently'. With this condition some language universals are absolute, seemingly true without exception, while many others are only tendencies, generally true but with a few exceptions. Some language universals must be stated as implications: they concern features which are present only if some other feature is present.

The two characteristics of absoluteness and implicationalness determine universals of four types:

1.   Absolute non-implicational universals,
2.   Non-implicational universal tendencies,
3.   Absolute implicational universals, and
4.   Implicational universal tendencies.

The absolute universals are often controversial; they would be demoted to the status of tendencies by confirmation of the existence of a single language in which they are violated. The universal tendencies may more reasonably be considered true, given the broadly representative sample of the world's languages for which they now seem valid.

Following, for each of the four types, are examples of universals concerning phonology, morphology, and syntax.

2.1. Absolute non-implicational universals

Absolute non-implicational universals concern features which appear to be found without exception in languages. Some of these concern **markedness**, the relationship of relative expectedness, likelihood, and, often, evident simplicity between contrastive phonological or morphological features of language.

2.1.1. *Phonology*

2.1.1.1. Markedness universals.   An important type of absolute non-implicational universal of phonology and morphology concerns markedness between contrastive phones or features of phones. The phone or phonetic feature which is more common and has other characteristics expected of the more common and presumably more basic category is said to be **unmarked**. The phone or feature which contrasts with the unmarked phone or feature is said to be **marked**. Some unmarked and marked phonological categories are:

	Unmarked	Marked
a.	[−aspirated] stops	[+aspirated] stops
b.	[−voiced] obstruents	[+voiced] obstruents
c.	[+voiced] sonorants	[−voiced] sonorants
d.	labiodental fricatives	bilabial fricatives
e.	[−nasal] vowels	[+nasal] vowels
f.	[+round] back vowels	[−round] back vowels

Unmarked categories have some or all of the following characteristics, which explain their relative commonality.

a. greater frequency (likelihood of occurrence) across languages
b. greater frequency within a language
c. less restricted context of occurrence
d. presence in contexts where marked categories are absent (for example, voiceless obstruents appear word-finally where voiced stops and fricatives are absent in many languages, including Russian, German, Turkish, etc.)
e. greater number of variants; thus there are more coronal consonant phonemes than consonant phonemes at other places of articulation. (English, for example, has coronal (alveolar) stops and fricatives, a nasal /n/, and alveolar /l/; the labials, dorsals (velars), and glottals are considerably fewer.)
f. simpler or lesser form

The term 'unmarked' is most appropriate for a category with lesser form, which may be said to be lesser in form by lacking the mark of a marked category. The correlation of greater frequency and lesser form is itself a universal tendency, known as **Zipf's Law** (Zipf 1935, p. 38). Often unmarked categories are found to fulfill the additional characteristic of being earlier learned by children. English-learning children, for example, often have voiceless obstruents for adult word-final voiced obstruents (as in data from the child Paul in practice 2 of chapter 8).

The characteristic of lesser form is expressed in phonology by lexical absence of the phonological feature for the unmarked category. Thus in chapter 14 (§2.2), it was suggested that the feature [coronal] is absent in lexical representations of consonants, with consonants lacking any of the features [+labial], [+dorsal], or [+glottal] understood to be coronal. Likewise the features [−voiced] in obstruents, [+voiced] in sonorants, and [−nasal] in vowels are lexically absent and provided by general rules. The presence of the rule supplying the unmarked category explains its lexical absence.

2.1.1.2. Other absolute non-implicational phonological universals.   Among other absolute non-implicational phonological universals are:

a. All languages have consonants and vowels.
b. All languages have at least one voiceless stop, such as [p, t, k].
c. All languages have syllables consisting of a consonant followed by one vowel (CV syllables).

2.1.2. Morphology

2.1.2.1. Markedness universals. Among the contrastive morphological categories are singular versus plural, masculine versus feminine, and animate versus inanimate. For each of these, the former is unmarked and the latter marked. Concerning singular versus plural, for example:

a. Singulars are much more frequent than plurals, across languages.
b. Singulars often occur where plurals are absent; thus in many languages when a plural number is present the plural form of nouns is avoided, as in Amharic where one says /assïr bïrr/ not /assïr bïrr-očč/ for 'ten dollars', where /-očč/ is the plural suffix. In English, plurality must ordinarily be marked on plural count nouns; however, when speaking of measurements we say, for example, *a seven foot door* and not *a seven feet door*.
c. Singulars typically have more variants, as in English third-person pronouns, which distinguish masculine, feminine, and neuter singular *he*, *she*, *it* versus only *they* for the plural.
d. Singular nouns are typically unaffixed while plurals are affixed. Exceptional languages are quite rare, such as Ethiopian Cushitic Sidamo which has a singular suffix /-ččo/ as well as plural suffixes. In all such languages, noun number may go unexpressed, so the singular suffix is still less frequent than the plural suffix of other languages.

Regarding the unmarkedness of masculine versus feminine, notice in English the presence of *he* among the ten most frequent words (see chapter 1, practice 3), and the use of *he* to refer to people and animals when the gender of these is irrelevant and/or unknown: 'That's a nice puppy. What's his name?'

Regarding the unmarkedness of animate versus inanimate, notice, in addition to the greater frequency of animate over inanimate references of all sorts in languages, the greater number of form distinctions among animates, as in English masculine and feminine *he* and *she* versus neuter and inanimate *it*, and a special possessive question word *whose* just for animates – thus we can say *Whose book is this?* but not *Whats box is this?*

2.1.2.2. Other absolute non-implicational morphological universals. All languages have nouns and verbs. That is, all languages have two morpheme classes with characteristics ordinarily recognized as those of nouns and verbs – nouns, for example functioning as subjects and objects of verbs, forming plurals, taking determiners, etc., and verbs expressing tense, aspect and modality, often showing agreement with a subject, etc. Also, all languages have a negative morpheme, whether for verbs or nouns, or both.

2.1.3. *Syntax*

All languages have **relative clauses** (**adjective clauses**), clauses within noun phrases which modify the head noun of the clause (see practice 5 of chapter 18). Examples of relative clauses in three languages are, in square brackets:

1. English: the girl [who played the violin]
2. Spanish: la muchacha [que ve-o] 'the girl that I see' the girl that see-I
3. Amharic: [məs'ɨhaf jə-sətt'ə-hw-at] lɨj 'the girl I gave a book'
              book that-gave-I-her child

2.2.   Non-implicational universal tendencies

Universal tendencies concern features which strongly tend to be found in languages. For example:

2.2.1. *Phonology*

Languages tend to have fricatives. That is, not all but certainly almost all languages have at least one fricative, a [−sonorant, +continuant] phoneme, whose major allophone is such as [f, v, θ, ð, s, z, x, ɣ] (the latter pair are voiceless and voiced velar fricatives).

2.2.2. *Morphology*

Languages tend to have adjectives. That is, not all but certainly most languages have in addition to nouns and verbs a class of morphemes which describes or modifies nouns within the noun phrase and which can be compared in constructions like 'this one is bigger (than that one)'. In a number of languages, in fact, the adjectives are relatively few and appear to be a closed class.

2.2.3. *Syntax*

An important universal syntactic tendency concerns the basic or typical word order of sentences. Among subject (S), verb (V), and object (O) there are six possibilities of word order of which three are common and three are uncommon, as follows (Tomlin 1986):

a. SOV, about 44% of languages
b. SVO, about 33% of languages
c. VSO, about 18% of languages
d. VOS ⎫
e. OSV ⎬ , about 5% of languages
f. OVS ⎭

Thus in 95% of languages, those of the SOV, SVO, and VSO types, subjects precede objects.

English and Spanish are **SVO languages**, in which the most common word order of sentences is subject before verb before object (or other verb complement); Japanese and Amharic are **SOV languages**, in which the usual word order is subject before object (or other verb complement) before verb; and Irish and Standard Arabic are **VSO languages**, in which the usual word order is verb before subject before object (or other verb complement).

4. English: The man opened the door.
5. Amharic: səwïjjə-w bər-u-n kəffətə 'The man opened the door.'
                      man-the door-the-Obj opened
6. Classical Arabic: fataħa l-rajul-u l-baba. 'The man opened the door.'
                      opened the-man-Subj the-door

2.3. Absolute implicational universals

Absolute implicational universals concern features which are found without exception in languages, if some other feature is found.

2.3.1. *Phonology*
If a language has mid vowels, then it has high vowels. Thus not all languages have one of /i, u/, but if a language has a mid vowel /e, o, ɛ, ɔ/, then it has at least one of /i, u/.

2.3.2. *Morphology*
If a language distinguishes the categories 'dual' (= 'exactly 2 in number') and 'singular' in its pronouns, it distinguishes the category 'plural' as well. Many languages distinguish singular and plural pronouns, as in English *he/she* versus *they*, and *I* versus *we* (a distinction absent in the 2nd person: *you* singular and plural). But relatively few languages distinguish singular and dual, as does Arabic, which also has plurals. See the Arabic independent pronouns in table 20.1.

Table 20.1 Arabic independent pronouns

	Singular	*Dual*	*Plural*
1	ʔanā		nahnu
2 masc.	ʔanta	ʔantumā	ʔantum
2 fem.	ʔanti		ʔantunna
3 masc.	huwa	humā	hum
3 fem.	hija		hunna

2.3.3. *Syntax*

If a language has relative clauses, it has relative clauses whose heads are coreferential with the subject of the clause, as in the first example of 7–10, below. In the three other examples, the head of the clause is coreferential with a direct object, indirect object, and object of a preposition, respectively.

7.   people [who lend their cars to friends for dates]
8.   cars [which people lend to friends for dates]
9.   friends [who people lend their cars (to) for dates]
10. dates [which people lend their cars to friends for]

Even though all languages have relative clauses, an absolute non-implicational universal mentioned above, not all of the types of relative clauses are found in all languages. Only the first, subject type, is always found. If one of the other types is found, the types above it in the hierarchy are also found, as in the following ranking:

    1   2   3   4
subject < object < indirect object < other prepositional object

If there are relative clauses of type 4, then there are such clauses of type 3, etc. This hierarchy of possibilities is known as **noun phrase accessibility**. (This universal, like other similarly complex ones, is subject to a lot of controversy concerning the understanding and analysis of the data of little-known languages.)

2.4. Implicational universal tendencies

Implicational universal tendencies concern features which strongly tend to be found in languages, if some other feature is found.

2.4.1. *Phonology*

If a language has a nasal consonant, this is probably /n/. That is, the major allophone of the one nasal consonant phoneme is [n].

2.4.2. *Morphology*

If a language distinguishes the singular and plural of nouns by an affix, this is probably the plural rather than singular morpheme, an implication which follows from the unmarkedness of singulars. English is a typical case, with a plural suffix. Sidamo is one of the exceptional languages with a **singular** affix (as mentioned above, §2.1.2.1).

2.4.3. *Syntax*

If a language has VO order (the direct object or other verb complement follows the verb), then **modifiers** tend to follow their **heads** generally in the language. We may understand a direct object to be modifier of its verb, which is the head

Table 20.2 Correlations between VO order and other word orders in 534 languages

V-O/O-V	Other word order	% Correlation
V-O	Auxiliary verb – Main verb	88
O-V	Main verb – Auxiliary verb	92
V-O	Subordinator – Clause	98
O-V	Clause – Subordinator	69
V-O	Adposition – NP	94
O-V	NP – Adposition	85
V-O	Article – Noun	71
O-V	Noun – Article	60
V-O	Noun – Possessor	70
O-V	Possessor – Noun	90
V-O	Adjective – Comparison	97
O-V	Comparison – Adjective	81

Source: Dryer 1992

of VP. OV order, then, is a case – perhaps the leading case – of the generalization that modifiers tend to precede their heads. Thus VO and OV languages tend to have the opposite word order for heads and modifiers. Notice in 11–13, sentences of English, an SVO language, and Amharic, an SOV language, the opposite orders of auxiliary verb and main verb, relative clause and head noun, and comparison phrase and adjective:

11. a. English: The train had left the station.
     b. Amharic: babur-u kə-t'abija-w hedo nəbbər
                   train-the from-station-the left had

12. a. English: the city which I like is Paris.
     b. Amharic: jəmmɨ-wədda-hu-t kətəma Paris nəw
                   which-like-I-it city Paris is

13. a. English: Addis Ababa is higher than Denver.
     b. Amharic: addis abəba kə-denvər kəffɨtəɲɲa nəw
                   Addis Ababa than-Denver high is

Table 20.2 (from Dryer 1992) shows just six of a number of these significant correlations between verb and direct object and other word orders (from a survey of 534 languages of about 247 language groups around the world). The correlations of table 20.2 range from 60 to 98%. For example – looking at the first rows of the table – of languages with VO order (that is, those of SVO, VSO, or VOS types) 88% have auxiliary verbs before main verbs, whereas of languages with OV order (those of the SOV, OSV, or OVS types) 92% have auxiliary verbs after main verbs.

3. HYPOTHETICALLY INNATE LANGUAGE UNIVERSALS

In chapter 9 were noted four general characteristics of child language learning which are consistent with the hypothesis of some innateness of linguistic know-ledge in the human species: (1) absence of a history of development of language, (2) absence of variation of acquisition, (3) evidence of predisposition for language acquisition, and (4) physiological correlates of language, especially left-brain centers. Accepting this hypothesis of the innateness of some aspects of language, one method of seeking language universals attempts to identify features of lan-guage which seemingly cannot have been acquired by learning in the absence of innateness. These features, altogether, may be said to make up **universal grammar**.

Specific evidence of features of such a universal grammar are cases of errorless acquisition of complex and often quite abstract rules in spite of seeming **poverty of the stimulus** – inadequate data on the basis of which, reasonably, a child might discover and hypothesize the rules.

We know, for example, that English-learning children readily hypothesize the existence of words like *rided* and *mans*. This seems understandable given the plentiful analogical evidence for such words, such as *lighted*, and *cans*. Further-more, learners may be helped to overcome these 'wrong' hypotheses by **negative evidence** – adult displeasure with *rided* and *mans* and corrections in favor of *rode* and *men*.

Other such analogies seem equally reasonable or more so, yet even in the absence of negative evidence for these, children don't seem to consider them. For example, on the basis of pairs like 14(a)–(b), 14(d) represents such a reasonable but seemingly untested analogy.

14. a. Mom baked a cake for Jill.
     b. Mom baked Jill a cake.

     c. Mom opened the door for Jill.
     d. *Mom opened Jill the door.

Maybe children know, somehow, perhaps innately, that *opened* is not ana-logous to *baked*, since Jill is a **recipient** (of the cake) in 14(a), but not a recipient (of the door) in 14(c), and that **dative movement** is only possible with *give*-type verbs like *bake*, which have recipient complements (noted in chapter 18, §2.1.3).

Following are discussed two other rules or principles which seem to involve even more abstractness, but which English-learning children learn without apparent difficulty and despite apparent poverty of the stimulus.

3.1. Structure dependency: auxiliary inversion

English-learning children, whose powers of pattern recognition and generalization inevitably lead to creative utterances like *mans* and *rided*, acquire the rule for yes/no questions, **auxiliary inversion** (chapter 18, §2.2.2.1), apparently without supposing that the rule for these is to front the *first* auxiliary verb of the sentence. This is a simple and reasonable hypothesis, consistent with all the evidence of questions with one auxiliary verb, such as:

15. a. Are we home yet?
     b. Can I have an ice cream cone?

Yet when children first ask questions with two clauses and two auxiliary verbs, they don't construct these on the pattern of 16(a), whose uninverted equivalent is 16(b) and whose correct form is 16(c):

16. a. *Are what we going to eat is vanilla pudding?
     b. What we are going to eat is vanilla pudding.
     c. Is what we are going to eat vanilla pudding?

That is, their hypothesis is revealed to refer, correctly, not to the first auxiliary verb but to the highest auxiliary verb, or that of VP of S. This is something structurally not linearly recognized: Aux in the hierarchically organized structure 17(a) rather than in the fully linear 17(b).

17. a. $[_{NP} [_{Aux} [\ldots]_{VP}]_{VP}]_S$

     b. $[X^n_{-Aux} \text{ Aux} \ldots]_S$ (where X^n_{-Aux} means 'does not include Aux')

But because simple sentences such as *Can I have an ice cream cone?* have only one verb, the question-forms of such sentences provide no evidence to the child that what one fronts is Aux in 17(a) rather than in 17(b). Furthermore, if a child should say 16(a), it is doubtful that an adult would understand the error and be able to correct it, providing negative evidence. (In fact, children may be heard to say 'Is what we are going to eat is vanilla pudding?', suggesting a hypothesis to COPY rather than move the auxiliary verb of 17(a).)

The child's experience with simple questions provides inadequate evidence on the basis of which to make the correct hypothesis, and all the evidence of simple sentences is consistent with an alternative (some would say simpler) hypothesis. In this sense there is **poverty of the stimulus**. Nevertheless, when they begin to form questions of two-clause sentences, children seem to ignore the wrong hypothesis and go directly to the right one.

One reason could be that children innately know that 16(a) is not a possible question because it violates the language-universal principle of **structure dependency**:

Syntactic rules recognize hierarchical not linear structures.

We saw in chapter 6 that phrase structures as evidenced in the recognition of ambiguities like *more nutritious food and drink* are abstract (unevidenced in the stream of speech), and in chapter 18 that syntactic rules refer to phrase structure. Thus child learners must employ abstractions and acquire abstract knowledge. Innateness is an explanation of this, and what is hypothetically innate are language universals such as structure dependency.

3.2.   C-command: the interpretation of pronouns

Another example of this approach to the discovery of language universals concerns the interpretation of pronouns. Consider the sentences of 18:

18.   a.   It embarrassed Tarzan that he forgot his credit card.
     b.   Tarzan left because he wanted to.
     c.   That he forgot his credit card embarrassed Tarzan.
     d.   Because he wanted to, Tarzan left.

In the four sentences 18(a)–(d), *he* and *Tarzan* can be the same person, whether *he* precedes (in 18(c)–(d)) or follows *Tarzan* (in 18(a)–(b)). *Tarzan*, if considered to be the same person, is said to be the **antecedent** of *he*, whether *Tarzan* precedes *he* or not. (The antecedent of a pronoun is the non-pronoun noun phrase with which a pronoun co-refers.)

But in 19(a)–(b) *Tarzan* cannot be the antecedent of he, and *he* and *Tarzan* must be different persons.

19.   a.   He knew that Tarzan had forgotten his credit card.
     b.   He left because Tarzan wanted to.

The explanation of such facts of pronoun interpretation is not simple, but it seems that English-learning children have no difficulty reaching the right analysis.

A principle thought to be involved and hypothetically valid in all languages (though of course these facts have not been checked for the majority of languages of the world, and are somewhat controversial), is that:

A pronoun cannot **c-command** and precede its antecedent.

C-command is the relationship in a phrase structure between two nodes X and Y such that the first node over X, which c-commands Y, is also over Y. Thus in the following structure, A and C c-command each other, A c-commands D and E, and D and E c-command each other, but D and E don't c-command A.

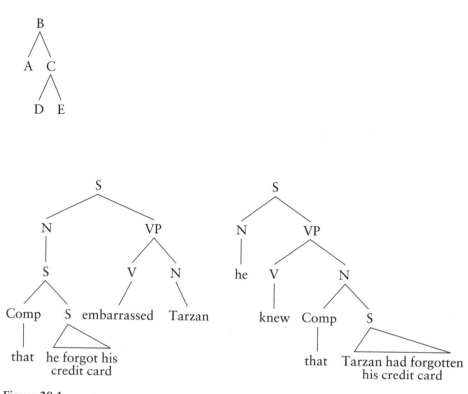

Figure 20.1

As seen in figure 20.1 in the tree diagrams for sentences 18(c) and 19(a), respectively, the c-command relationship explains why *Tarzan* can be antecedent of *he* in the first but not the second. Notice that 19(a) is a perfectly good, grammatical, sentence, but can't mean that Tarzan himself knew about the forgotten credit card.

Children seem to have plentiful evidence of sentences with ambiguous pronoun antecedents. Also, adults can't reasonably recognize and correct children's sentences in which there are pronoun/antecedent errors – if, indeed, children produce such errors. So how children figure out c-commands is quite a mystery. Innateness of the c-command relationship for pronoun interpretation could explain the mystery.

4.   EXPLANATION OF LANGUAGE UNIVERSALS

There are four sorts of explanation of language universals: (a) phylogenetic unity of language, (b) functional unity of language, (c) physiological unity of the species, and (d) innateness of language. For some universals one or the other explanation seems reasonable; for others no explanation seems now possible.

4.1. Phylogenetic unity

If all languages descend from the same original human language, forms and principles of the grammar of that language could, even after the passage of many thousands of years, persist in all or most of its descendants. For example, if verbs preceded objects in that hypothetical first language, then verbs might reasonably tend to precede objects in languages today. However, since we have no knowledge of the first language, or even of how long ago it might have been spoken (and 50,000 years is perhaps minimal), the phylogenetic explanation of language universals remains utterly speculative.

4.2. Functional unity

Maybe the universal *functions* of language, to carry out very similar requirements of communication across human communities, determine similarities of linguistic *structure*. Some functionally reasonable language universals which can be explained this way are:

a. the tendency for subjects to precede verbs and objects in over 75% of languages (SOV + SVO languages). This is functional because it tends to establish within a sentence what one is talking about before one talks about it.

b. the tendency within a language for heads of various sorts (such as nouns, verbs, adjectives) consistantly to precede or follow their modifiers (such as determiners, objects, and intensifiers, respectively). This is consistent with a functional principle of economy to employ similar means for similar purposes, an application of the principle of one form/one meaning noted in chapter 16, §2.6.2.

c. the tendency for frequent (unmarked), categories to be lesser in form than marked categories (known as **Zipf's Law** (Zipf 1935)). A language like other mechanisms is reasonably more efficient (functional) if its more frequently used parts are easier to use.

Such functional explanations of language universals could be very effective, over time, because of their regular effect in language change. That is, when language change produces variants, unless both are preserved (by bifurcation (chapter 16, §2.6) or for reasons to be discussed in chapters 26 and 27), in the absence of some force regularly favoring the non-functional variant, the choice between these forced by the one form/one meaning principle will tend to favor that which is functionally superior.

4.3. Physiological unity

Maybe universally human speech physiology determines phonetic (speech) similarities. Shared brain neurophysiological structures might explain more abstract language universals, though this remains speculative. Some physiologically reasonable phonetic universals of language are:

a. The universality of consonants and vowels. Vowels are just shapings of the pulmonic airstream necessary as the basis of an audible speech signal, and consonants are the reasonable result of interruptions which modulate the airstream more audibly.

b. The unmarkedness of coronal consonants. Coronals are reasonably unmarked since the tongue tip is the most flexible and adept articulator, which, unlike others, reaches a number of places of articulation.

c. The unmarkedness of voiceless word-final obstruents. Final obstruents involve significant sustained blockage of the airstream, and upon such interruption air pressure increases rapidly within the vocal cavity. This equalizes pressure from below, which tends to stop the airstream upon which voicing (vocal fold vibration) depends.

Like functional explanations, such physiological explanations of language universals could be very effective, over time, because of their regular effect in language change. That is, when language change produces variants, in the absence of some force regularly favoring physiologically unmotivated variants, the choice between these forced by the one form/one meaning principle will tend to favor that which is physiologically motivated.

4.4.   Innateness of language

Other universals are not obviously explained by functional or physiological naturalness, such as the noun/verb dichotomy, and c-command. Complex functional and other explanations have been proposed for these, but their abstractness or complexity and the noted universalities of the general nature of first language learning (chapter 9, §4.1.2) are evidence that, whatever their original motivation, some universals of language may have become encoded in the genetic makeup of the human species as part of a **universal grammar** of more or less abstractness and detail.

Suggestions for
ADDITIONAL READING

Two books which concern the types and universals of language are *Language Universals and Linguistic Typology* (1981) by Bernard Comrie, and *Introduction to Typology: the Unity and Diversity of Language* (1997) by Lindsay J. Whaley. Somewhat more advanced is *Typology and Universals* (1990) by William Croft. The languages of the world are surveyed for phonetic and phonological universals in *The Sounds of the World's Languages* (1996) by Peter Ladefoged and Ian Maddieson.

Explanations of many language universals in terms of the functions of language are provided in *Functionalism and Grammar* (1995) by Talmy Givón, and, concerning word order in particular, *Basic Constituent Orders: Functional Principles* (1986) by Russell Tomlin. The theory of innate universal grammar is introduced for students in *Chomsky's Universal Grammar: an Introduction* (1995) by Vivian Cook and Mark Newson. A variety of universals and their possible explanations are discussed in *Explaining Language Universals* (1988) edited by John A. Hawkins. Many findings and theories concerning universals of language are found in the four volumes of *Universals of Language* (1978) edited by Joseph Greenberg.

IMPORTANT CONCEPTS AND TERMS IN THIS CHAPTER

- language universals
- absolute non-implicational universals
- markedness
- unmarked
- marked
- Zipf's Law
- relative/adjective clause
- non-implicational universal tendencies
- SVO language
- SOV language

- VSO language
- absolute implicational universals

- noun phrase accessibility
- implicational universal tendencies
- singular
- modifier
- head
- universal grammar
- poverty of the stimulus
- negative evidence
- auxiliary inversion
- structure dependency

- antecedent
- c-command

OUTLINE OF CHAPTER 20

    2. Non-implicational universal tendencies
       1. Phonology
       2. Morphology
       3. Syntax
    3. Absolute implicational universals
       1. Phonology
       2. Morphology
       3. Syntax
    4. Implicational universal tendencies
       1. Phonology
       2. Morphology
       3. Syntax

3. Hypothetically innate language universals
   1. Structure dependency: auxiliary inversion
   2. C-command: the interpretation of pronouns

4. Explanation of language universals
   1. Phylogenetic unity
   2. Functional unity
   3. Physiological unity
   4. Innateness of language

EXAMPLES AND PRACTICE

EXAMPLE

1. Possible and impossible languages. Languages could imaginably differ in three very general ways from languages we know: (a) they could use known features of language in novel ways; (b) they could have new features so far unknown in languages; and (c) they could lack features known in all languages. For example:

   a. as novel use of a known feature, there might be general use of manual signs, in the languages of hearing as well as non-hearing people.

   b. as a new feature, there might be word inversion without structure dependency, for example, a language in which yes/no questions are formed by reversing the first two words of statements, so that, if the language was English, the yes/no question of *You are going* would be *Are you going* and the yes/no question of *This book is good* would be *Book this is good*.

   c. as absence of a universal linguistic feature, there might be a language without a single voiceless stop. (But we would reasonably wonder why such an obviously useful sort of consonant should be absent!)

PRACTICE

Imagine and describe one or two additional examples of each of these three ways that languages could differ from known languages as you now understand them.

EXAMPLE

2. The unmarkedness of coronals. Coronal (tongue-tip articulated) consonants are generally considered to be unmarked in relation to labials (lip articulated), dorsals (tongue-body articulated) and glottals. In terms of the criterion of frequency, this is quite clear for English, since the coronals include the interdentals, alveolars, and alveopalatals.

PRACTICE

Provide frequency evidence for or against the unmarkedness of the English alveolars /t, d, s, n/ by counting the number of occurrences of the phonemes /t, d, s, n, p, b, f, m, k, g, h, ŋ/ (that is, four alveolars, four labials, and four others, three of which are velars): (1) in pronunciations of the ten most frequent words of English given in practice 3 of chapter 1, (2) in the phonemically written text of practice 4 of chapter 2, and, (3) going just by spelling where the phonemes above are equated with respective spellings t, d, s, n, p, b, f/ph, m, k, g, h, and ng, in a 250-word newspaper text which you provide.

EXAMPLE

3. Word orders. Consider the following sentences of Sidamo, a language of Ethiopia. Notice how Sidamo word order differs from that of English. Thus English has *on foot* where Sidamo has /lekkate nni/ 'foot on' (item (f)). A word-by-word translation is given, followed by a free translation. (Some Sidamo morphemes shown as words are probably better considered to be suffixes.)

a. samaago kaajjite laʔi
    Samaago Kaajite saw
    'Samaago saw Kaajite.'

b. dangiso nna ledamo danca
        jaalaa ti
    Dangiso and Ledamo good
        friend are
    'Dangiso and Ledamo are
        good friends.'

c. tini saada lowillaadda te
    these cows big are
    'These cows are big.'

d. ooso se barru tuk'a hajšitanno
    children her days all washes
    'She washes her children every
        day.'

e. waare baaramo ra diina ho
    Waare Baaramo to enemy is
    'Waare is an enemy to
        Baaramo.'

f. baaramo lekkate nni dajnó
    Baaramo foot on came
    'Baaramo came on foot.'

g. kabiico heeʔranno manni
        fiit'aʔ jaa ti
    here live people relatives mine
        are
    'The people who live here are
        my relatives.'

h. bisso insera se waj nni wanšitino
    Bisso pot her water with filled
    Bisso filled her pot with water.'

i. samaago doda no
    Samaago running is
    'Samaago is running.'

j. annu mini ra eʔi wate waare
        ita nnino
    father home to came when
        waare eating was
    'When his father came home,
        Waare was eating.'

Table 20.3 Vowel inventories of 24 languages

	Front vowels	Central vowels	Back vowels
1. Greek:	i, ɛ,	a,	ɔ, u
2. Pashto:	i,	ə, a,	u
	eː,		oː
3. Finnish:	i, y, ɛ, ø, æ,	a,	o, u
	iː, yː, eː, øː, æː,	aː,	oː, uː
	([y] is high, front, rounded; [ø] is mid, front, rounded.)		
4. Japanese:	i, e,	a,	o, ɯ
	([ɯ] is high, back, unrounded.)		
5. Bambara:	i, e, ɛ,	a,	ɔ, o, u
	iː, eː, ɛː,	aː	ɔː, oː, uː
6. Swahili:	i, e,	a,	o, u
7. Fur:	i, e, ɛ,	a, ə,	ɔ, o, u,
	iː,	aː,	uː
8. Luo:	i, ɪ, e, æ,	a,	ɒ, o, ʊ, u
	([ɒ] is low, back, rounded.)		
9. Amharic:	i, e,	ɨ, ə,	ɑ, o, u
	([ɨ] is high, central, unrounded.)		
10. Hausa:	i, e,	a,	o, u,
	iː, eː,	aː,	oː, uː
11. Mundari:	i, e,	a,	o, u
12. Vietnamese:	ɪ, e, ɛ, æ,	ə,	ɔ, o, ɣ, ʊ, ɑː, ɯ
	([ɣ] is mid, back, unrounded.)		
13. Bardi:	i,	a,	ɔ, u,
	iː,	aː,	uː
14. Aranda:	i,	a,	u
15. Thai:	i, e, æ,	ɨ, ə, a,	ɔ, o, u
16. Malay:	i, e,	a, ə,	o, u
17. Mandarin:	i, y,	ə, a,	ɣ, u
18. Lahu:	i, e, ɛ,	ɨ, ə, a,	ɔ, o, u
19. Nimboran:	i, e,	ɨ, ɑ,	ɣ, ɯ
20. Dani:	i, ɪ, e,	a,	o, ʊ, u
21. Navaho:	ɪ, ɛ,	a,	ɔ,
	ĩ, ɛ̃,	ã,	ɔ̃,
	ɪː, ɛː,	aː,	ɔː
	ĩː, ɛ̃ː,	ãː,	ɔ̃ː
22. Ojibwa:	ɪ,	a,	ʊ,
	iː, ɛː,	aː,	oː,
	ĩː, ɛ̃ː,	ãː,	õː
23. Aleut:	i,	a,	u
24. Basque:	i, e,	a,	o, u

PRACTICE

In addition to English *on foot* and Sidamo /lekkate nni/ 'on foot', list five word-order differences of English and Sidamo. Discuss these differences in light of the language universal described in §2.4.3, above.

EXAMPLE

4. Manifestation of some universals in English. Here are some more morphological markedness universals:

    a. Subjects are less marked than objects.
    b. Affirmative is less marked than negative.
    c. Masculine is less marked than feminine.
    d. Third person is less marked than first person.
    e. First person is less marked than second person.
    f. Present tense is less marked than past tense.

One of the characteristics of less marked categories is lesser form, a characteristic typically apparent for each of the universals (a)–(f), above, in English as in other languages. For example, English subject pronouns are somewhat shorter in terms of number of phonemes than are object pronouns:

Subject pronouns	/aj, ju, hi, ši, ɪt, wi, ðe/:	14 phonemes
Object pronouns	/mi, ju, hɪm, hər, ɪt, əs, ðɛm/:	17 phonemes

Furthermore, subject pronouns can often be omitted, as in *Don't know*, in answer to *What happened?* But object pronouns can't: *Where's the money? *I lost* (for *I lost it*).

PRACTICE

Discuss how other markedness universals (b)–(f) above are or are not exemplified by lesser-form characteristics of English.

EXAMPLE

5. Phonemic systems. Table 20.3 presents the vowel inventories of 24 languages, two each of 12 language families (most taken from Maddiesen 1984).

PRACTICE

Of the many generalizations true about the 24 vowel inventories of table 20.3, two are given below as 1–2. Study the 24 vowel inventories and discover at least six more generalizations about them which are universal, for these inventories. Also classify each of your universals and the two examples 1–2 according to the four types (1) absolute non-implicational, (2) absolute implicational, (3) non-implicational tendency, and (4) implicational tendency. Try to find at least one example of each type.

1. There is at least one high front unrounded vowel (/i/ or /ɪ/).
2. If there are long vowels, there are short vowels.

THE BASIC HISTORY OF WRITING

This chapter describes the history of writing, including theories of its origin and important principles of its development and diversification. It surveys and contrasts some of the major types of writing and writing systems from Sumerian to English.

1. PREWRITING: PICTURES

Throughout the world in prehistoric times people made pictures on stone, by carving and painting. Some of these pictures, especially on the walls of caves, have survived until today, and some of these are dated from 35,000 years ago. Reproduced as figure 21.1 is an example of cave painting from Altamira, Spain, estimated to date from about 15,000 BC.

But pictures are not writing. In **writing**, visual signs are in a regular relation to language, and persons who know a writing system will interpret its signs very similarly. Pictures may be in a more or less regular relation to reality but in no regular relation to language: one person will interpret a picture in certain words and another in others. Those who made prehistoric paintings probably hoped their work would be seen and understood, but in the absence of such a regular relationship with language, their thoughts in painting the pictures are unlikely to be reproduced in the minds of persons seeing the pictures later.

To regularly and reliably reproduce one's ideas in the minds of others, later, writing would be needed, and writing evolved a little over 5,000 years ago, perhaps from pictures.

Figure 21.1   Cave painting, Altamira, Spain, ca. 15,000 BC
Source: Brevil and Obermaier 1935

2. LOGOGRAPHIC WRITING

2.1. The earliest writing

Human societies have almost certainly been using languages for at least 40,000 years (and much, much, longer, according to most opinions), but the earliest known writing dates from perhaps 3200 BC, or 5,200 years ago. This first writing is **Sumerian**, which was used in the kingdom of Sumer in the region of modern-day Iraq.

Sumerian writing was basically **logographic**. In logographic writing a sign or character of the writing system, a **logogram**, stands for a morpheme or simple word. Many of the earliest logograms of the earliest writing systems were picture-like, which is evidence that these writing systems evolved from pictures. Notice the picture-like qualities of the seven logograms of the four early logographic writing systems Sumerian, Egyptian, Hittite, and Chinese, shown in figure 21.2 (Carter and Schoville 1984, p. 3).

Picture-like characters at the early stage of logographic writing are sometimes termed **pictograms**. At this early stage, it is likely that pictographic characters were often somewhat broad in interpretation. The Sumerian character based on the picture of a mouth, for example, could mean 'mouth', 'tooth', 'speak', or 'word' (Green 1989, p. 46). Pictographic characters with this quality are sometimes termed **ideograms**.

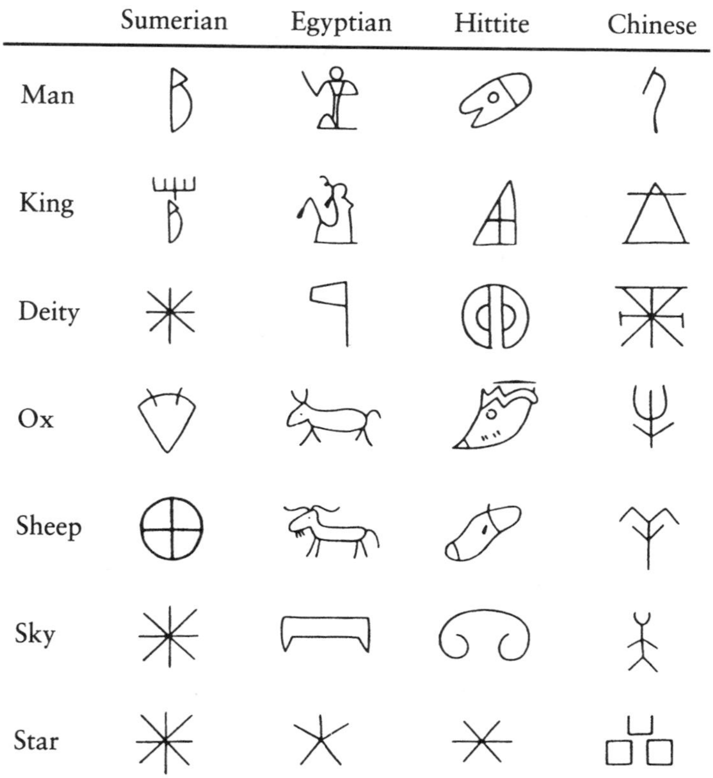

	Sumerian	Egyptian	Hittite	Chinese
Man				
King				
Deity				
Ox				
Sheep				
Sky				
Star				

Figure 21.2   Seven logograms of four early logographic writing systems
Source: Carter and Schoville 1984

The earliest Egyptian writing is not quite as old as Sumerian, from perhaps 3000 BC. It is possible that Egyptian writing was originally inspired by Sumerian, but underwent quite independent development. Probably a fully independent development was Chinese writing, from about 1200 BC, as probably also was Mayan writing, which arose in Mexico and Central America from about AD 250.

2.2.   Token inventory representation

There is a theory (Schmandt-Besserat 1989) that writing does not originate directly from pictures, but from 'tokens' – small, variously shaped, clay objects. From about 8,000 years ago, the Sumerians and subsequent ancient peoples of Mesopotamia employed a method of inventory keeping which used small clay tokens to represent commodities, for example vases, and sheep. The tokens were distinct by shape and sometimes were carved, and were symbolic signs – not recognizably likenesses of the commodity they represented.

Figure 21.3 Sumerian clay tablet (ca. 4000 BC) with sheep sign and impressions
Source: Schmandt-Besserat 1989

Sometimes, probably for the purpose of recording transactions or to show specific ownership, the tokens were sealed in spherical clay envelopes. At a later period these clay envelopes were impressed with the shapes of the tokens they enclosed, presumably as a helpful redundancy or accuracy-check on their contents.

Then, over 5,000 years ago, before the appearance of Sumerian writing, the tokens were omitted altogether. Their shapes in the surface of the clay ex-envelope, now just a tablet, had apparently been found simpler and even superior for the record-keeping purpose. As figure 21.3 is a picture of such a clay tablet, of six thousand years ago; the tablet has the Sumerian logogram for sheep ⊕, with five impressions next to it (Schmandt-Besserat 1989, p. 38). These shapes or impressions in clay may have evolved into characters of the Sumerian writing system.

This theory explains the steps from iconic representation – in this case not pictures but little sculptures – to logographic writing, an explanation in which each step was a reasonably small and perhaps inevitable one.

2.3. Sumerian cuneiform writing

Sumerian writing is known as **cuneiform**, for the wedge-shaped tool (Latin *cuneus* 'wedge') used to inscribe characters in wet clay. Curves and angles of the early pictographic signs were straightened and details were omitted in the evolution of these into cuneiform symbolic signs, as seen in the chart of figure 21.4, which shows such evolution in six cuneiform characters (Green 1989, p. 45).

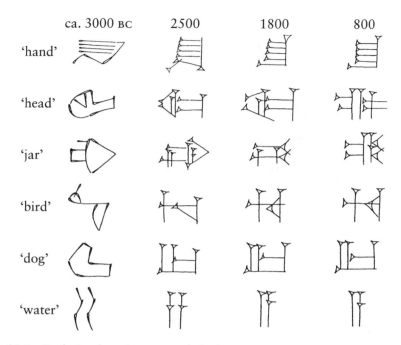

Figure 21.4   Evolution from icon to symbol of six Sumerian cuneiform characters, ca. 3200 to 800 BC

Source: Reprinted from *The Origins of Writing* edited by Wayne M. Senner by permission of the University of Nebraska Press, copyright © by the University of Nebraska Press

2.4.   Monogenesis of writing?

By gradual selective narrowing of meaning and stylizing and simplifying of form, the most useful and repetitious pictures, or token imprints, must have evolved interpretation as words, and eventually came to have full and fixed meanings as words. The result is writing – logographic writing.

Persons who consider this development an extraordinary human achievement, unlikely to have been duplicated at different times and places, tend to favor a Sumerian inspiration for all subsequent writing. Others, inclined to think that writing must have been a necessary and/or natural outcome of the human experience of language-use, picture-making, and socio-economic development, favor the likelihood of independent origins for Sumerian, Chinese, Egyptian, and other ancient writing systems.

Mayan writing, which dates from about AD 250 in southern Mexico and Central America, presumably arose beyond the influence of the ancient Asian and Middle Eastern ancient writing systems – at least there is so far no convincing evidence of such influence. As Mayan and other ancient writing systems have become deciphered and better known, showing unique original forms but considerable similarities of development with those of the ancient Middle East, the likelihood of the **monogenesis** of writing, a unique origin of writing subsequently copied elsewhere if in greatly transformed ways, seems less likely.

Modern pronunciation/ meaning	Oracle-bone form (Shang dynasty)	Greater seal (W. Chou)	Lesser seal (E. Chou-Han)	Modern form (3rd cent. AD on)
Objects				
1. *jen* / man				
2. *nü* / woman				
3. *erh* / ear				
4. *yü* / fish				
5. *jih* / sun				
6. *yueh* / moon				
7. *yü* / rain				
8. *ting* / cauldron				
9. *ching* / well				

Figure 21.5 Evolution from icon to symbol of nine Chinese characters, ca. 1200 BC to AD 300

Source: Reprinted from *The Origins of Writing* edited by Wayne M. Senner by permission of the University of Nebraska Press, copyright © by the University of Nebraska Press

2.5. Chinese logographic writing

A largely logographic writing system in use today is Chinese, a direct descendant of the ancient Chinese logographic system the earliest traces of which date from about 3,200 years ago. In Chinese as in Sumerian, there was evolution from the iconic to the symbolic, as shown in figure 21.5, which shows this sort of change, over time, in nine Chinese characters. The first column of figure 21.5 presents pictures of which the characters of the third to fifth columns are thought to be simplifications (Keightley 1989, p. 173).

2.6. Logograms used in English writing

Numerals like *1* 'one', *2* 'two', *3* 'three', and symbolic word substitutes like $ 'dollar(s)', and *&* 'and' are logograms, and are good illustrations of the usefulness of logograms, at least for very frequent meanings. Other mathematical logograms used around the world and found on a standard keyboard are # 'number', % 'percent', + 'plus', – 'minus', and = 'equal(s)'.

3. PHONETIC EXTENSIONS OF LOGOGRAMS

3.1. Rebus writing

The meanings of many words are not easily represented by pictures, notably emotions and abstract ideas. Thus in all the ancient writing systems ways were discovered to derive characters for use for words which were not so easily pictured. Characters were combined to represent some related meanings, so that, for example, Sumerian cuneiform 'eat' was the combination of the logograms for 'head' and 'food', and Egyptian 'leave' was the combination of its logograms for 'house' and 'walk'.

Another method employed the **rebus**, a sign which stands not for the meaning but for the sound, or the approximate sound, of a word. For example, a picture of the sun could, as a rebus, mean 'son' in English, and the numeral '4' is a rebus in a 'for sale' sign written *4 sale*. Interpreted as a rebus, the letters *F U M N X* can mean 'Have you ham and eggs?' Sumerian 'arrow' and 'life' were pronounced approximately [ti], so the character for concrete picturable 'arrow' was extended to mean abstract hard-to-picture 'life'; Egyptian 'ear', the consonants of which were [msdr], is represented as a combination of the logograms for 'fan' [ms] and 'basket' [dr].

3.2. The acrophonic principle

Another way to extend logograms according to the sounds of their words employed the **acrophonic principle** (Greek *akros* 'highest'), according to which a character was extended to mean not the sound of a whole word but just one of its important phones, typically the first consonant. By the acrophonic principle, for example, the logographic character ∀ for the word 'ox(en)', the ancient Semitic pronunciation of which was approximately [ʔalef], took on the phonetic value [ʔ] (glottal stop), and the logographic character ⊓ for the word 'house', with approximate pronunciation [bajt], took on the phonetic value [b].

3.3. Chinese extended logograms

Chinese makes extensive use of compounded logograms and of logograms extended to mean a pronunciation only sort of like that of the word which they at first represented. See figure 21.6 (Pederson 1967, p. 144), which shows the Chinese character for 'work' in its combination with eight other characters. The character for 'work' provides the meaning 'sounds sort of like [kung¹]' (the raised number represents the word's tone (chapter 2, §6.3.1)) and the other character contributes the meaning 'having to do with', so that, for example, the combination of 'sounds sort of like [kung¹]' and 'having to do with a human being' means 'big belly', the pronunciation of which is [hung²].

1. *kung*[1] 'work'

   hung[2] 'big belly'

2. *k'ung*[1] 'impatience'

3. *k'ang*[2] 'carry on the shoulders'

4. *kang*[4] 'sedan chair'

5. *kiang*[1] 'river'

6. *hung*[2] 'red'

7. *hung*[4] 'quarrel'

8. *hung*[2] 'quicksilver'

'human being'

'heart'

'hand'

'wood'

'water'

'silk'

'word'

'water'

Figure 21.6   Rebuses in Chinese character compounds

Source: Reprinted by permission of the publisher from The Discovery of Language by Holger Pederson, translated by J.W. Spargo, Cambridge, Mass.: Harvard University Press, copyright © 1931 by the President and Fellows of Harvard College; copyright © 1957 by John Webster Spargo

3.4.   Egyptian writing

Egyptian classical writing, **hieroglyphic** (Greek *hiero* 'sacred' + *glyphic* 'writing'), was ordinarily cut in stone or painted on wood or plaster, although a cursive, simplified, style was later inked on papyrus paper. Hieroglyphic writing made extensive use of logograms, phonograms following the acrophonic principle, and rebuses. A picture of a swallow meant both 'swallow' [wr], and 'big', also [wr], and a picture of a beetle [hprr] could also mean 'to become' [hpr] (Coulmas 1989, p. 63). Only consonants were represented. For the phrase 'Great woman, mother of God', see the hieroglyphic characters of figure 21.7 (Coulmas 1991, p. 66), which include the logogram for 'God', two rebuses, and pure 'phonograms' following the acrophonic principle.

4.   SYLLABIC WRITING

By the rebus principle, a logogram which meant the sound of a single-syllable word often came to have the value of that syllable, as where Sumerian 'arrow'

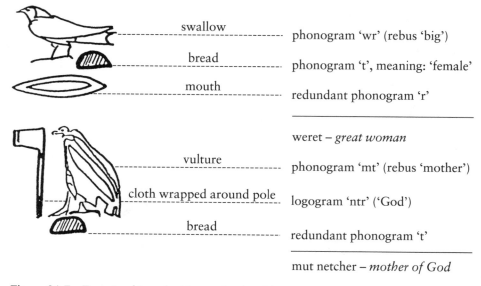

swallow	phonogram 'wr' (rebus 'big')
bread	phonogram 't', meaning: 'female'
mouth	redundant phonogram 'r'
	weret – *great woman*
vulture	phonogram 'mt' (rebus 'mother')
cloth wrapped around pole	logogram 'ntr' ('God')
bread	redundant phonogram 't'
	mut netcher – *mother of God*

Figure 21.7   Egyptian hieroglyphic: a mixed writing system
Source: Coulmas 1991

[ti] could also serve for the single-syllable word meaning 'life'. Many words in Sumerian and in Chinese are words of one syllable. Other logograms extended by the rebus principle were just abbreviated or rounded off to single syllable value. The extension of these developments results in **syllabic writing**, in which a character stands for a **syllable** (chapter 14, §3), a vowel plus its associated consonants.

4.1.   Greek Linear B

By about 1400 BC, a Greek-speaking people of Crete and the Agean Sea adapted cuneiform writing into a syllabic writing system known as **Linear B**, which was perhaps derived from an even earlier still undeciphered syllabic writing system, Linear A, of non-Greek peoples who had established the Minoan civilization on Crete and neighboring islands. The only examples of Linear B which survive are inventories, lists of goods and valuables. This writing system had about ninety signs with quite consistent syllabic, CV values. The early Greek language it recorded, however, had syllables both with and without final consonants – of form CVC as well as CV, and the syllable-final consonants were simply ignored in Linear B representations. See the Linear B sentence of figure 21.8 (Sampson 1985, p. 73), an inventory-list of footstools. Notice that only CV syllables are written, so word-final and syllable-final *s* is ignored in the first, second, and third words, and syllable-final *n* is ignored in the third and fourth words.

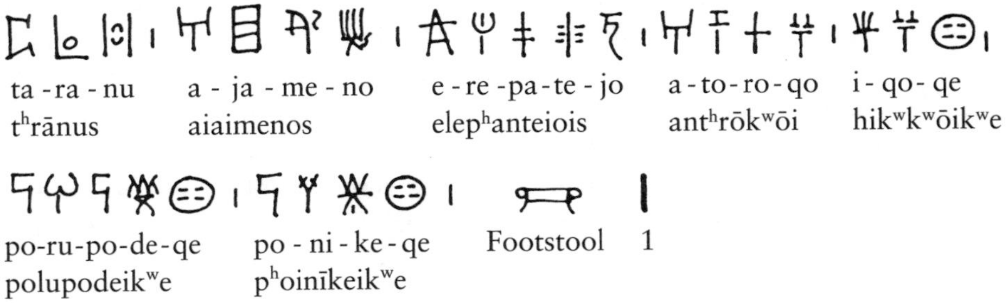
ta - ra - nu
t^{h}rānus
a - ja - me - no
aiaimenos
e - re - pa - te - jo
elep^{h}anteiois
a - to - ro - qo
ant^{h}rōk^{w}ōi
i - qo - qe
hik^{w}k^{w}ōik^{w}e
po-ru-po-de-qe
polupodeik^{w}e
po - ni - ke - qe
p^{h}oinīkeik^{w}e
Footstool
1

Figure 21.8 Linear B sentence with unrepresented syllable-final consonants
Source: Reprinted from *Writing Systems* by Geoffrey Sampson with the permission of the publishers, Stanford University Press, © 1985 by Geoffrey Sampson

Chinese	宇	加	仁	女	呂
Katakana	ウ	カ	ニ	メ	ロ
Hiragana	う	か	に	め	ろ
Phonetic	u	ka	ni	me	ro

Figure 21.9 Japanese syllabic characters and their Chinese logographic character basis

4.2. Japanese *kana*

A modern syllabic writing system in Japanese, which employs Chinese characters termed *kanji*, plus two additional sets of characters *katakana* and *hiragana*, each character of which represents a syllable – usually a consonant and a vowel. These syllabic *kana* characters were derived, beginning about a thousand years ago, as simplifications of Chinese characters with the same or similar phonetic values. Typical Chinese words – like typical Sumerian words – are monosyllabic, so the rebuses of these have the phonetic value of syllables. As figure 21.9 are shown five examples each of Japanese *katakana* and *hiragana* characters, with the Chinese characters from which they were derived.

5. CONSONANTAL WRITING

The Semitic-speaking peoples in several places of the ancient Middle East appear to have copied, adapted, and thoroughly transformed Egyptian writing.

The most striking characteristic of Semitic languages (and of Egyptian, which is distantly related to Semitic) is their systematically different use of consonants and vowels: consonants to express lexical meanings, and vowels to express grammatical meanings. Arabic is perhaps the most famous example of this Semitic language type. In Arabic, for example, the consonants *ktb* and *drs* mean basically 'write' and 'study', respectively, and these three-consonant 'skeletons' are fleshed out with prefixes, suffixes, and various vowels between the consonants to express derivations of basic or root meanings, as in these examples:

kataba	'he wrote'	*darasa*	'he studied'
yaktubu	'he writes'	*yadris*	'he studies'
uktub	'Write! (masc. sing.)'	*darrasa*	'he taught'
kitaab	'book'	*dars*	'lesson'
maktab	'office'	*madras*	'school'
kaatib	'writer'	*mudarras*	'teacher'

The Arabic writing system, dating from about AD 300, is one of several ancient writing systems developed in the ancient Middle East to represent Semitic languages. It is unusual in having early evolved a basic cursive style, the characters of which are usually connected within words. Because of the restricted role of vowels in Semitic grammars, and perhaps also because vowels were relatively few (Arabic /i, a, u/, plus long counterparts /iː, aː, uː/), application of the rebus and acrophonic principles for writing Arabic resulted in basically **consonantal writing**, in which regularly the twenty-eight consonants are written and only the long vowels but not the more frequent short vowels. Arabic is written from right to left, as shown below for several words of the morpheme *ktb* 'write', for which phonemic writing and translations are given in the first two columns. The short vowels /i, a, u/ may be written with small symbols above and below the line, as in the fourth column, but these dots are usually provided only in texts for teaching.

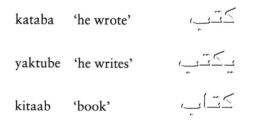

kataba	'he wrote'	كَـتَـبَ
yaktube	'he writes'	يَـكْـتُـبَ
kitaab	'book'	كِـتَـابْ

Writing with consonants alone is perhaps not something which is possible only for Semitic languages. In modern English also, with eleven vowel phonemes represented by just five vowel letters *a, e, i, o, u*, prhps wth prctc w cld lrn t wrt wtht th vwls nd stll b rsnbl wll undrstd.

6. ALPHABETIC WRITING

A little less than three thousand years ago (about 850 BC), the Greeks began to adapt the consonantal writing system of Semitic eastern Mediterranean peoples, especially that of the Phoenicians (of approximately modern-day Lebanon), for use in writing Greek. See as figure 21.10 a comparison of Egyptian characters with their adaptations in Protosinaitic (early writing systems of the Sinai Peninsula), Phoenician, early Greek, Greek, and Latin.

The important contribution of the Greeks was to adapt some of the consonantal characters, for Semitic phonemes absent in Greek, to represent their five vowels /ɑ, e, i, o, u/.

a. Characters for Phoenician [ʔ, ʕ, j], which Greek lacked, were used to represent vowels [ɑ, o, i] which, respectively, were commonly associated with these consonants.

b. The character for [w] also served for [u], and later the two forms of this character, with one and two loops ('double-u'), were bifurcated to distinguish these completely.

c. Phoenician like other Semitic languages had two voiceless fricatives of 'h' quality: glottal [h] and pharyngeal [ħ]. The character for [ħ] was used for Greek [h] and that for Semitic [h], which was apparently often associated with a vowel of [ɛ] quality, became E.

The result was the first **alphabetic writing**, with separate representation of both the consonant and vowel phonemes. The word *alphabet* combines the Greek names of the first two letters in the fixed recitation order of letters, (*alpha, beta, gamma, delta,* etc.) but the source of the letter-names is Semitic: *alpha* from Semitic **alep* 'ox' and *beta* from Semitic **bayit* 'house', the pictograms of which evolved into the Greek letters A and B.

The early Semitic consonantal writing systems, often termed Canaanite or Sinaitic, were written left-to-right, right-to-left, and top-to-bottom, variability which was typical of logographic writing and often persisted in early post-logographic writing systems. Phoenician was usually written right-to-left, and Greek was so written at first. After a period of **boustrophedon** writing ('ox turning' as in plowing a field), the **Greek alphabet** eventually came to be written only left-to-right, probably because when writing on paper the right-to-left direction was found problematic for the usually dominant right hand. The symbols of early Greek writing were oriented to the left or right depending on the direction of the line, and this change of direction explains the reversed orientation of some of the Greek successors to Semitic symbols, for example, B, E, K, P (see figure 21.10).

Egyptian	Protosinaitic	Phoenician	Early Greek	Greek	Latin
					A
					B
					G
				E	E
				K	K
				M	M
				N	N
				O	O
				P	R
				T	T
					S

Figure 21.10   Comparison of Egyptian, Sinaitic, Phoenician, early Greek, Greek, and Latin characters
Source: Davies 1987, © the British Museum, British Museum Press

7. ENGLISH WRITING

7.1. Spread of Latin

Greek writing of the variety of western Greece was adopted by the Romans, before 600 BC, via the Etruscans, the people who preceded the Indoeuropeans in the Italian peninsula. The language of the Etruscans lacked voiced stops, so they used Greek C (from Γ, for phonetic [g] in Greek) for their [k], which necessitated a modification as 'G' when, later, a letter for [g] was needed for Latin.

During the Roman Empire, at its peak from about AD 0–300, the Romans spread knowledge of Latin writing throughout Europe, North Africa and the Middle East. Latin writing, or **orthography** (Greek *orthos* 'right', *graphein* 'write'), was eventually adapted for use for most European languages, including, before AD 900, English.

7.2. Modifications of the Greek–Latin alphabet

Latin had consonants and vowels somewhat different from those of Greek, so there was not a perfect match of letter–phoneme relationships between the two languages, and some adaptation was necessary. The Old English language from which modern English descends and for which Latin orthography was adopted is an Indoeuropean language very distantly related to Greek and Latin, but Old English had consonants and vowels even more different, so again some adaptation was necessary. The eventual development of the consonant and vowel letters of English orthography from Greek via Latin is summarized in figure 21.11.

7.3. English divergence from alphabetic writing

English spelling has never perfectly fulfilled the logic of an alphabetic writing system – one letter for each phoneme, consonant or vowel – and probably no basically alphabetic writing system can do so for long. But modern English spelling in particular seems unsystematic, for basically three reasons: lack of standardization, changes in pronunciation, and word borrowing.

7.3.1. *Lack of standardization*

At its outset English spelling showed Latin influence, such as *c* usually for [k]. At first some characters from the ancient Germanic writing system Runic were used for Old English /θ/ and /w/, absent in Latin, but these were later replaced by *th* and *w*, the latter at first a pair of *u*'s. When printing came along around 1475, many of the first printers, even of English books, were Dutch, who wrote English irregularly. They introduced the Dutch spelling of word-initial /g/ as *gh*, in *ghost* and other words now spelled with just *g*.

Greek	Latin	English
A	A	A
B	B	B
Γ	C, G	C, G
Δ	D	D
E	E	E
⅂*	F	F
Z	Z	Z
H	H	H
Θ	–	–
I	I	I, J
K	(K)	K
Λ	L	L
M	M	M
N	N	N
Ξ	–	–
O	O	O
Π	P	P
ϙ*	Q	Q
P	R	R
Σ	S	S
T	T	T
Y	V	U, V, W, Y
Φ	–	–
X	–	X
Ψ	–	–
Ω	–	–

Figure 21.11   Greek via Latin sources of English letters
* These did not survive in classical Greek, but survive in Latin owing to their adoption by the Etruscans, the pre-Indoeuropean people of the Italian peninsula, some of whose adaptations of Greek were continued by the Romans, for Latin.

English-speakers did not recognize a spelling authority, such as the government, or church, which might have imposed a **standard**, which would tend to be copied. Old English spelling was quite consistent and phonemic, but by Middle English times, with the start of the extensive change of English vowels known as the Great Vowel Shift (chapter 23, §2.2.1.1) and the appearance of French spellings for English words, different spellings competed for the same phoneme, including k and c for /k/, and ea and ee for /i/. Many of these variants persist today. Neither the introduction in 1476 of printed books in English (by William Caxton, 1422?–91), nor in 1755 the first authoritative dictionary (by Samuel Johnson, 1709–84), were able to standardize English spelling. Caxton himself took note of the variability of English spelling, and joked that this reflected the influence of the cycles of the moon (see practice 3, below).

In the US, partly with the political purpose to separate British and American spelling, Noah Webster (1758–1843) proposed through his dictionaries many simplifications of English spelling, but only some of these were eventually successful, including *-or* for *-our* as in *color/colour*, and *-er* for *-re*, as in *center/centre*. In 1935 the *Chicago Tribune* newspaper introduced a number of simplified spellings including *thru* for *through* and *catalog* for *catalogue*. The suggestions were controversial and only a few were successful, such as *catalog*; others, including *thru*, *nite*, and *tho*, survive in regular usage only in informal writing.

7.3.2. Sound changes

Languages are always systematically changing their pronunciations, but these changes have rarely been reflected in English spelling as they have in other languages. Thus /b/ at the end of a word after /m/ was lost, but we still write it, as in *climb* /klɑjm/ and *thumb* /θəm/. Old English had a velar fricative, /x/, in words like *right*, which was spelled *gh*; this /x/ was lost altogether, but we kept the *gh* spellings. The vowel of this word was /iː/ (long /i/), and over hundreds of years this vowel lowered and became a diphthong, so that *right* /rixt/ became /rɑjt/, but we persist in writing the *i*.

7.3.3. Borrowed words

Thousands of words borrowed from other European languages have kept the spellings of the lending languages, including for example, *debut* /dɛbju/ from French, which keeps its French *u* (pronounced [u] though with an English [j] onset) and (unpronounced) final *t*, and *tomato* /təmeto, təmɑto/ from a Mexican language (probably Nahuatl) via Spanish, which keeps its Spanish spelling. Latin influence is seen in *island* /ɑjlənd/, whose 'silent' *s* was inserted into Old English *iland* on analogy with Latin *insula*, and *phoenix* for *fenix*. Words from Greek via Latin mostly have their Latin spellings, for example with *ph* for Greek φ, as in *philosophy*, and *c* for Greek κ as in *cardiac*.

English spelling as a result is now a hybrid in which influences of its alphabetic Greek–Latin origins plus a few partially adopted reforms are mixed with a logographic tendency according to which the spelling of a word, once fixed, is retained in all forms of the word, regardless of their changed pronunciation. This is discussed further in the next chapter.

7.3.4. Smileys

Very recently has arisen something quite innovative in writing, in computerized or e-mail communication, the **smiley**, a means of expressing some of the emotional quality which spoken language expresses with intonation, or which is communicated by the speaker's face. Smileys (also termed *emoticons*), for example : -) and its variants : -(and :→, originated in e-mail messages whose authors don't have or won't take time to qualify or elaborate their messages with the traditional resources of written language for expressing emotions. Instead of writing 'I'm only kidding, really', or 'Don't take this seriously', one types ':-)'.

In fact, it is not clear that smileys are a part of writing, since they are not in any regular relationship to language. Time will tell whether smileys will make their way into standard written language, where they would probably develop some narrowed symbolic preciseness of meaning, or whether they will remain little icons of emotion inserted into an e-text like doodles in the margin of a letter.

Suggestions for
ADDITIONAL READING

There are a number of good books which present the writing systems of the world and their history, including the *The Blackwell Encyclopedia of Writing Systems* (1996) by Florian Coulmas, the *Handbook of Scripts and Alphabets* (1997) by George L. Campbell, and *Writing Systems: a Linguistic Introduction* (1985) by Geoffrey Sampson. Detailed discussion on each writing system is provided in *The World's Writing Systems* (1989) edited by Peter Daniels and William Bright. Papers focussed on origins of a number of systems are in *The Origins of Writing* (1989) edited by Wayne M. Senner. The stylistic development of the Greek alphabet up to English is surveyed in *Ancient Writing and Its Influence* (1969) by Louis B. Ullman.

Two very enjoyable accounts of the discovery and decipherment of ancient writing systems are *The Decipherment of Linear B* (1976) by John Chadwick, and *Breaking the Maya Code* (1993) by Michael D. Coe.

Particular writing systems of interest are treated in *Visible Speech: the Diverse Oneness of Writing Systems* (1989) by John DeFrancis (especially concerning Chinese), *Egyptian Hieroglyphics* (1987) by W. V. Davies, *Cuneiform* (1987) by C. B. F. Walker, and *The Early Alphabet* (1990) by John Healey. The history of American spelling reforms is described in chapter 8 of *The American Language* (1937) by H. L. Mencken.

Regarding the practice and implications of computer-mediated writing, see *Computer-mediated Communication: Social and Cross-cultural Perspectives* (1996) edited by Susan C. Herring.

IMPORTANT CONCEPTS AND TERMS IN THIS CHAPTER

- writing
- Sumerian
- logographic writing
- logogram
- pictogram
- ideogram
- cuneiform

- hieroglyphic
- syllabic writing
- syllable
- linear B
- consonantal writing
- alphabetic writing
- boustrophedon

- monogenesis
- Chinese logographic writing
- rebus
- acrophonic principle

- Greek alphabet
- orthography
- standard
- smiley

OUTLINE OF CHAPTER 21

1. **Prewriting: pictures**
2. **Logographic writing**
   1. The earliest writing
   2. Token inventory representation
   3. Sumerian cuneiform writing
   4. Monogenesis of writing?
   5. Chinese logographic writing
   6. Logograms used in English writing
3. **Phonetic extensions of logograms**
   1. Rebus writing
   2. The acrophonic principle
   3. Chinese extended logograms
   4. Egyptian writing
4. **Syllabic writing**
   1. Greek linear B
   2. Japanese *kana*
5. **Consonantal writing**
6. **Alphabetic writing**
7. **English writing**
   1. Spread of Latin
   2. Modifications of the Greek–Latin alphabet
   3. English divergence from alphabetic writing
      1. Lack of standardization
      2. Sound changes
      3. Borrowed words
      4. Smileys

EXAMPLES AND PRACTICE

> **EXAMPLE**

1. Amharic root and pattern morphology. This example and practice illustrates **root and pattern morphology** in a Semitic language, Amharic, to show the appropriateness of consonantal writing for such a language.

Below are 45 Amharic words in 9 sets A–I of five words each. Each set of five words illustrates a particular grammatical form. For example, set A shows present tense first-person singular forms of the verb, and set B shows verb infinitives. Looking at the first row of three words, you may see that the consistent phonetic material which means 'take' is just the three consonants *wsd*. This is the 'root' of the verb. Looking at the sixth row, you can see that the consistent phonetic material which means 'break' is just the root *sbr*.

Looking at set A, you can see that the pattern of first-person singular verb forms is *ɨCəCC*, where C represents any consonant ([ɨ] is a high central vowel). Thus 'I break' would be *ɨsəbr*. Looking at set B, you can see that the pattern of the infinitive, 'to-form', is *məCCəC*, so 'to break' would be *məsbər*.

	A			B			C	
ɨwəsd	'I take'		məwsəd	'to take'		wəsda	'she, taking'	
ɨdəgm	'I repeat'		mədgəm	'to repeat'		dəgma	'she, repeating'	
ɨkəft	'I open'		məkfət	'to open'		kəfta	'she, opening'	
ɨməls	'I return'		məmləs	'to return'		məlsa	'she, returning'	
ɨrəfd	'I am late'		mərfəd	'to be late'		rəfda	'she, being late'	

	D			E			F	
tɨsəbr	'she breaks'		səbari	'breaker'		səbro	'he, breaking'	
tɨnədf	'she stings'		nədafi	'stinger'		nədfo	'he, stinging'	
tɨsəbk	'she preaches'		səbaki	'preacher'		səbko	'he, preaching'	
tɨqərb	'she approaches'		qərabi	'approacher'		qərbo	'he, approaching'	
tɨrəgm	'she curses'		rəgami	'curser'		rəgmo	'he, cursing'	

	G			H			I	
jɨfərdu	'they judge'		fɨrəd	'Judge!'		jɨfrəd	'let him judge'	
jɨwəsdu	'they take'		wɨsəd	'Take!'		jɨndəf	'let it sting'	
jɨzəllu	'they jump'		zɨləl	'Jump!'		jɨsbək	'let him preach'	
jɨkərmu	'they graze'		kɨrəm	'Graze!'		jɨqrəb	'let him approach'	
jɨdərsu	'they arrive'		dɨrəs	'Arrive!'		jɨrgəm	'let him curse'	

PRACTICE

Analyze the Amharic data further and provide the correct Amharic roots or words for 3–12, below. Answers of 1–2 are provided as examples.

1. root of 'take':   wsd
2. root of 'break':   sbr
3. 'I break':
4. 'to break':
5. root of 'repeat':
6. 'repeater':

7. 'he, repeating':
8. root of 'preach':
9. 'to preach':
10. 'she, preaching':
11. root of 'curse':
12. 'Curse!':

2. Chinese characters. Characters of the Chinese writing system started out as pictographic logograms. Over the three thousand years of their use, their pictographic origin has been obscured and forgotten – or forgotten and obscured, depending on which comes first; the two developments were probably often simultaneous.

Listed in figure 21.12 are twenty Chinese logograms, at the left the original forms of about 1200 BC, as 1–20, and at the right, in a different order, the simplified and stylized modern forms, as (a)–(t). The meaning given is the approximate original meaning, not of the modern character. By making reasonable comparisons, knowing that the left-hand characters are pictograms (plus, finally, some thoughtful guessing on the hard ones), match 1–20 with (a)–(t).

3. English spelling in 1490. Here is a text written about English spelling by William Caxton in 1490; it has Caxton's spellings; þt in the fifth line is an abbreviation of 'that' (Lounsbury 1907, p. 159).

And when I had aduysed me in this sayd boke, I delyvered and concluded to translate it in to Englysshe, and forthwyth toke a penne and ynke and wrote a leef or tweyne, whyche I oversawe agayn to corecte it. And whan I sawe the fayr and straunge termes therin, I doubted that it sholde not please some gentylmen whiche late blamed me, sayeng þt in my trsnslacyons I had ouer curyous termes whiche coulde not be understande of comyn peple, and desired me to vse olde and homely termes in my translacyons; and fayn wolde I satysfye euery man and so to doo toke an olde booke and redde therin, and certaynly the Englysshe was so rude and brood that I ooude not wele vnderstande it. And also my lorde Abot of Westmynster ded do shewe to me late certayn euydences wryton in olde Englysshe for to reduce it in to our Englyssehe now vsid. And certaynly it was wreton in suche wyse that it was more lyke to Dutche than Englysshe. I coulde not reduce ne brynge it to be vnderstonden. And certaynly our langage now vsed varyeth ferre from that whiche was vsed and spoken when I was borne. For we Englysshe men ben borne vnder the domynacion of the mone, whiche is neuer stedfaste but ever wauerynge, wexynge one season and waneth and dycreaseth another season.

Translate the above text into modern English, as completely as you can. You will have to guess some of Caxton's meaning, and perhaps leave a few words untranslated, in brackets ([ ]).

1	⊠
2	☺
3	𝄞
4	𝄢
5	人
6	玄
7	⊔
8	𝄡
9	𝄢
10	从
11	𝄞
12	𝄢
13	𝄢
14	𝄢
15	𝄢
16	囚
17	𝄢
18	𝄢
19	𝄢
20	𝄢

a. 若 ʐuò 'yield, conform'

b. 言 jén 'flute'

c. 奻 nuàn 'quarrel' (two women)

d. 好 xàu 'love' (woman and child)

e. 兼 ciēn 'to have two at once' (hand holding two arrows)

f. 其 cī 'winnowing-basket'

g. 眉 méi 'eyebrow'

h. 水 ʂuěi 'river/water'

i. 辟 pì 'prince'

j. 女 nʏ̄ 'woman'

k. 魚 ý 'fish'

l. 木 mù 'tree'

m. 雨 ʏ̌ 'rain'

n. 日 ʐùɪ 'sun/day'

o. 囚 ciōu 'prisoner' (man in cell)

p. 目 mù 'eye'

q. 口 kʰǒu 'mouth'

r. 人 ʐə́n 'man' (i.e. human being)

s. 子 çǔ 'child'

t. 東 tūŋ 'east' (sun behind tree)

Figure 21.12 Twenty Chinese pictograms and their modern character descendants
Source: Reprinted from *Writing Systems* by Geoffrey Sampson with the permission of the publishers, Stanford University Press, © 1985 by Geoffrey Sampson

4. Dates in the history of writing. Some of the dates given in this chapter are worth taking note of, to get a good sense of the antiquity of writing and of the relation in time of important steps in the history of writing.

Listed in chronological order, as 1–6, are six important steps in the basic history of writing. Listed as (a)–(f) are approximate dates (as years BP, 'Before the Present) of these six steps. Match 1–6 with (a)–(f).

1.	English adapted from Latin	a.	5,200
2.	Sumerian writing	b.	5,000
3.	Cave pictures	c.	2,850
4.	Chinese writing	d.	3,200
5.	Egyptian hieroglyphic	e.	35,000
6.	Greek alphabet	f.	1,100

Chapter 22

THE ECOLOGY OF WRITING

This chapter concerns differences between speech and writing, and how writing systems reasonably differ according to the languages and communities they serve. Even English spelling, though much criticized, is generally quite systematic and may be considered well fitted to its purposes.

1. THE LANGUAGE OF WRITING IS DIFFERENT

1.1. Writing is secondary

Writing is secondary to speech, in history and in the fact that speech and not writing is fundamental to the human species. It is sometimes said that writing is just a visual representation of speech. Thus, for example, it employs punctuation to do some of what speech does with pitch, stress, and pauses. The sentence

John where Bill had had had had had had had had had had had a better effect on the teacher.

needs punctuation in order to be sensibly read, but when this is provided, it can be read as it would be said, which helps to make the meaning clear.

John, where Bill had had 'had', had had 'had had'; 'had had' had had a better effect on the teacher.

But in addition to punctuation, which substitutes for some of the prosodic qualities of speech, writing and speech are different in a number of ways. In the past, at least until the invention of audio recording, writing was more permanent than speech, and the usual language of writing has characteristics based on this fact.

1.2. Six ways that the language of writing differs from that of speech

a. Writing is better planned. Writing is better planned than speech, and as a result the language of writing is more 'bookish', ordinarily using longer sentences, bigger and lower-frequency words, and a wider range of tenses and other forms of grammar than speech. Speech can do the same, but usually only after it has been planned and prepared in writing.

b. Writing employs special forms of language for its unique purposes. There are special forms of presentation of some of the things that must be expressed in writing, like letters ('Dear...', 'Sincerely yours,...'), laws and decrees, inventories, diaries, statistics, letters, and dictionaries and grammars.

c. Writing lacks some of the personal qualities of speech. In writing, the phonological features are absent which in speech reveal the age, gender, dialect and sometimes features of the social status of speakers.

d. Writing cannot express the non-discrete emotional qualities expressed non-discretely in speech. Some of these qualities can be captured by use of different print-size (*I said NO!*) and innovative spellings (*He sez 'Pleeeze!'*). Speech expresses the continuum of emotions with a continuum of voice qualities, including pitch, loudness, and rate, a flexibility which writing lacks.

e. Writing, however, expresses some distinctions absent in speech. For example,

   1. Direct and indirect speech are distinguished in writing, as in English *He said, 'He went'* (direct), vs. *He said he went* (indirect). Speech can distinguish these with pauses, stress, and pitch, but in doing so perhaps speech is a secondary representation of writing.
   2. English distinguishes singular and plural possession with punctuation, as in *my friend's idea* vs. *my friends' idea* (both pronounced [majfrènzajdíə], and proper nouns and other words with capitalization: *Bill Wood hit it* vs. *Bill would hit it*.
   3. Spanish distinguishes certain homophones with accent marks, for example *el* 'the' and *él* 'he', and *si* 'if' and *sí* 'yes', meaning differences which often but not always correspond to stress differences.
   4. French orthography similarly contrasts homophones such as *la* 'the, her' and *là* 'there', and *sur* 'on' and *sûr* 'secure', but in other cases these do reflect pronunciation differences, for example in *achète* [ašté] 'bought' vs. *achete* [ašɛt] 'buy', and *moule* [mul] 'mussel' vs. *moulé* [mulé] 'moulded'.

    f.   Writing readily shows the organization of discourse including the raising, grouping, and change of topics, by such devices as indentation, spacing, numbering, and font differences.

2. FOUR ADAPTATIONS OF WRITING TO SOCIETY

The variation in writing systems around the world is not just the result of accidental differences in the way writing was invented or developed here and there through history. Instead, differences of writing systems correlate, to some extent, with differences in the languages and societies they serve.

2.1. Chinese

2.1.1. *Chinese logographic writing*

Chinese writing is at least generally speaking logographic: the original and persistent basic meaning of a character is basically a word (with, however, the adaptation of these by rebuses, noted in chapter 21, §3.3). There are many thousand such basically logographic characters.

A basically logographic writing system, however, even one as thoroughly extended and adapted as is Chinese, has two important disadvantages:

    a.   First, it's a lot to learn, particularly when rebus syllabic-readings of characters are added to logographic readings, and, in fact, it appears that fluent reading is not mastered by Chinese-speaking children as quickly as in societies with alphabetic systems.

    b.   Second, with logographic writing one cannot predict with confidence the written representation of a new word which is heard, or the pronunciation of a new word which is written. There is a system for phonetically writing, as rebuses, the syllables of Chinese, which then may combine as the syllables of new words and substitute for the syllables of foreign words, but this cannot be predictably applied to all new and foreign words.

2.1.2. *Suitability of Chinese writing*

A logographic writing system like Chinese is in fact quite learnable, as its widespread and completely fluent use clearly shows. We are easily able to learn arbitrary form–meaning correlations, well beyond the thousands needed to read Chinese fluently. For example, long before we begin to write, we learn tens of thousands of arbitrary relationships of pronunciation and meaning for spoken words.

Furthermore, the most common Chinese language, **Mandarin Chinese**, and related varieties of Chinese (all of which go by the name 'Chinese' in the rest of the world), have little grammatical morphology; they are so-called **isolating languages**, in which a word usually consists of only one lexical morpheme, as in the Chinese sentence:

我不會說英文。

wo bu   hui   shuo ying   wen.
I   NEG know speak English language
'I don't know how to speak English.'

Associating a largely arbitrary written representation to these words of the Chinese writing system is not different from learning other symbolic aspects of form and meaning, as in learning the morphemes of any other language, such as English, many of which have two or more syllables.

More importantly, the Chinese writing system is particularly suited to China, where it serves a vast geographic area bigger than Europe, and a vast population (more than two billion) which speaks scores of languages, many of which, such as the most common Chinese languages, Mandarin (north and central China), Wu (centered on Shanghai), and Yue/Cantonese (centered on Canton), are substantially different from one another. They are largely unintelligible to one another in speech. But by use of the Chinese logographic writing system, meanings are written in these different languages much the same. Besides, China has an ancient and important literature, and, being written in logographic rather than alphabetic characters, Chinese writing hundreds of years old can be read today, despite the thoroughly changed pronunciations.

An alphabetic or even syllabic writing system, dependent on pronunciations, could not unite this area or make the literature of the past accessible, except by the requirement that one of the languages, including its most widespread or standard pronunciations, be learned by all the people, and that the old literature be translated into modern Chinese spellings.

2.2. Arabic

2.2.1. *Arabic consonantal writing*

We saw in the previous chapter that in the Arabic writing system, most of the characters represent just consonants, and the short vowels typically go unexpressed – though these may be written, for children and foreigners, with the use of superscripts and subscripts added to the consonantal characters.

2.2.2. *Suitability of Arabic writing*

A largely consonantal writing system is suitable for the Arabic-speaking world, because Arabic is a language in which, certainly in verb formation, the consonants play the important primary role of expressing the lexical morphemes, and the vowels the secondary role, generally, of expressing the grammatical morphemes. Thus it is natural that in Arabic the vowels should go generally unwritten, as in the following Arabic words, in which only the phonemes in the left column in capitals, the consonants and the long vowels, are represented:

KaTaBa   'he wrote':   كتب

KiTAAb   'book':   كتاب

KAATiB   'writer':   كاتب

KuTiBa   'it was written':   كتب

Furthermore, the consonants are many, 29, and the vowels are few (3 short and 3 long) – and, besides, the long vowels cannot ordinarily appear in syllables which end in consonants. The vowels are thus said to 'carry a low functional load'.

The classical Arabic language, preserved in the Koran during the generations after Mohammed (570–632), had a vast geographic expansion during the Muslim conquests of much of the Middle East and North Africa from about 650 to 1400, with the result that many varieties of Arabic subsequently developed in geographically and politically separated areas. These modern Arabic languages are only marginally intelligible or even unintelligible to one another today. Vowels in particular are much changed from classical Arabic times.

However, the standard variety of Arabic serves universally in the Arab world as the **lingua franca**, language of choice in the absence of a shared first language, throughout the Arab world. Typically only Standard Arabic is written, or taught in schools, or serves the full range of writing purposes. Thus though people speak Arabic quite differently in Casablanca, Cairo, Beirut and Baghdad, newspapers and books published in these cities all employ Standard Arabic, which most literate Arabic-speakers read and can also speak.

2.3. Japanese

2.3.1. Japanese syllabic writing

Japanese has a rather complex writing system, which employs three different sets of characters:

a. *Kanji* logographic characters, borrowed from Chinese from 1,200 years ago; one needs to recognize at least about two thousand of these. Some of the Chinese words (pronunciations) for these were also borrowed. Some are read (pronounced) as native Japanese words. Most may be read both ways: as Chinese words and as native Japanese words.

b. *Katakana* syllabic characters, 46 in all; these were created from parts of *kanji* characters.

c. *Hiragana* syllabic characters, 46 in all; these were created by cursively writing *kanji* characters.

See the illustration of five each of these in chapter 21, §4.2.
The three character sets are generally used in different functions.

a. *Kanji* logographic characters are used to write lexical morphemes, including nouns, verbs, and adjectives.

b. *Hiragana* syllabic characters are used to write Japanese grammatical morphemes including verb tense and postpositions, which have no Chinese equivalents.

c. *Katakana* syllabic characters are used to write unfamiliar names, and borrowed and foreign words.

The two latter sets are together termed *kana* (*hiragana* < *hira-kana*). Members of all three character sets may often appear in a single sentence, as follows, in which, in the phonemically written second row, the words in *kanji* are in capitals and the borrowed word 'coffee', in *katakana*, is underlined:

私 は 喫茶店 で コ ー ヒ ー を 飲ん だ 。
WATASHI wa   KISSATEN de koohii o   NOn-da.
I   TOP café   at coffee OBJ drink-PAST
'I drank coffee at a café.'

In fact, Japanese readers nowadays are also familiar with the basic Latin alphabet, termed *romaji*, words written in which (mainly foreign words, but also names of Japanese products) commonly appear in many modern texts, especially advertisements in newspapers and magazines.

2.3.2. *Suitability of Japanese writing*

Syllabic writing is quite suitable for a language with the phonological structure of Japanese. Most words consist of syllables of the structure CV, one consonant followed by one vowel, and possibilities for syllables other than this are very limited. There are few consonant sequences. Thus the number of *kana* characters needed to write syllables of the language is not so great.

Despite the availability of the two syllabaries, lexical morphemes are ordinarily written in *kanji* logographic characters. The Ministry of Education requires that a Japanese high school student know at least 1,945 *kanji* characters. However, until they learn the *kanji* forms of words, students substitute their *hiragana* syllabic spellings.

The resulting combination of writing systems and mix of character sets is complex but quite functional and richly expressive. A glance at a Japanese text, as in the sentence above, quickly reveals the three morpheme types and provides a lot of information about grammatical structure: the core of lexical morphemes in *kanji*, the grammatical morphemes in *hiragana*, and foreign words in unfamiliar and/or technical usage in *katakana*.

2.4. English

2.4.1. *Suitability of English writing*

English, like the other long evolved writing systems introduced above, is something of a hybrid. Still, its basically alphabetic nature, with symbols for each consonant and vowel phoneme, is sensible for the language, because a syllabic or logographic system would be less suitable.

a.   Syllabic writing would be problematic if not completely impossible because the language has so many different syllable types: V, CV, CVC, CCV, CCCV, VC, CVC, CCVC, etc. With 24 consonants and 11 vowels to work with, there are over 50,000 possible English syllables. An English syllabary would have as many characters as Chinese has logograms.

b.   Logographic writing would be problematic because of the difficulty noted for Chinese of representing new or borrowed words, which are frequent in English, and, with the growing role of English as a world language, surely as expected in the future as in the past.

2.4.2. *Graphs, allographs, and graphemes*

We could term the characters of an alphabetic writing system 'letters', but in English *letter* usually doesn't include things like $, @, & etc., so it will be helpful to have the concept of **graph**, with its associated terms **grapheme** and **allograph**, parallel in meaning to the previously introduced concepts of phone/phoneme/allophone, and morph/morpheme/allomorph.

A **graph** is a separate symbol or character of a writing system, whether logographic, syllabic, consonantal, alphabetic, or mixed – for example in our alphabet, g, i, h, r, G, N. Always some of the graphs are (somewhat) similar to others with which they are in complementary distribution, for example, English G and g, of which G is found at the beginning of names (proper nouns) and at the beginning of sentences, or in assertive texts written entirely in capital letters. A set of such graphs is a **grapheme**, and the members of such a set are **allographs** of the grapheme. Thus {g, G, *g*, *G*, . . . } is the set of allographs of the grapheme we might represent as simply G, and {*i*, I, *i*, *l*, . . . } is the set of allographs of the grapheme we might represent as simply I. Let **letter** be a member of the set of graphemes of an alphabetic system.

2.4.3. Nonphonemicness of English writing

The letters of English writing are not employed in a strict one-to-one relation to phonemes, as in a perfect phonemic transcription. There are four sorts of violation of such strict phonemicness:

a. One grapheme may correspond to two or more phonemes; for example, *c* = /k/ in *coat*, /s/ in *certain*, and /š/ in *ocean*; and *e* = /ɛ/ in *bet*, /i/ in *be*, and /a/ in *sergeant*. Thus we have **homographs**, words spelled the same but pronounced differently, like *wind* (/wɪnd/ and /waynd/), and *sow* (/so/ and /saw/).

b. One phoneme may correspond to two or more graphemes; for example, /k/ = *k* in *kin*, *c* in *can*, and *q* in *quick*; and /i/ = *e* in *we*, *ee* in *seen*, and *ea* in *dream*. Thus we have **homophones**, words pronounced the same but spelled differently, like *we* and *wee*, and *so* and *sow*, and *sew*.

c. A grapheme may correspond to nothing in speech, a so-called 'silent letter'; for example *h* in *hour* /awr/, *c* in *scene* /sin/, and *b* in *doubt* /dawt/.

d. A phoneme may correspond to nothing in writing, an 'invisible phoneme'; for example /w/ in *one* [wən] and *Qantas* [kwantəs], and /j/ in *use* /juz/ and *music* /mjuzɪk/.

English has only 26 letters but there are 69 'grapheme units', many of two letters and one of three, including *ee* /i/, *qu* /kw/, *que* [k], *ch/tch* /č/, and *wh* /hw/, and there are 166 different correspondences between these 69 units and pronunciations (Venezky 1970). Because of such inconsistency, George Bernard Shaw (1856–1950) claimed that in English the word *fish* could be spelled *ghoti* (*gh* as in *enough* /ənəf/, *o* as in *women* /wɪmən/, and *ti* as in *nation* /nešən/), and Anthony Burgess (1964, p. 79) accused our spelling practice of 'a total lack of logic'.

2.4.4. English spelling rules

But of course English is not totally illogical, and we could not reasonably write /fɪš/ *ghoti*. *Gh* may be read [f] only in the few words where it is preceded by *ou*, like *enough*, and *tough*; at the beginning of words, *gh* is always read /g/. *Women* is an utterly exceptional spelling of [ɪ], and *ti* can spell [š] only when followed by another vowel grapheme as in *nation* and *Dalmatian*.

And while most of the regularities of English spelling have exceptions, and the most common words are the most irregular, for example *does* (compare *do*), *says* (compare *say*), and *of* /əv/, there ARE regularities – typical ways to spell, and limits to how innovatively one can spell. Among the generally followed rules here are five.

a. A single consonant after a stressed 'lax' vowel should be doubled before an unstressed suffix: *big/bigger*, *stop/stopped*, but *write/writer*, and *pencil/ penciled*. (*Write* has a tense vowel, and the second vowel of *pencil* is unstressed.)

b. Word-final silent *e* follows a tense (peripheral) vowel and a single consonant, as in *cede, rode, gate, lute*.

c. Of the vowels, only *e* and *o* are written double, with the values [i] and [u] or [ʊ], respectively (*seed, keep; root, loom*).

d. A Latinate foreign spelling is usually retained, especially if the word would otherwise be spelled the same as another word, as in *aide* (vs. *aid*), *belle* (vs. *bell*).

e. The most typical or otherwise basic spelling of a morpheme tends to be retained in all its allomorphs, as where the past tense suffix is spelled *ed* in all of *opened* (in which it is pronounced /d/), *walked* (pronounced /t/), and *waited* (/əd/). This logographic tendency of English writing, perhaps its main source of irregularity, may nevertheless be considered a strength of the system.

2.4.5. *Logographic tendency of English writing*

In its thousand-year history, English writing has moved away from rather than toward the alphabetic principle of a one-to-one relationship between graphemes and phonemes, which was well approximated in Greek and Latin writing. As a result, the spelling of an English morpheme or basic word tends to be the same in all words which include the morpheme or basic word, despite the different pronunciations of these. For example:

a. The word *photograph* is pronounced /fótəgrǽf/, and this spelling is unchanged when the word is suffixed by *-y* or *-ic* even though with the suffixations the vowels are pronounced quite differently: *photography* /fətágrəfi/, *photographic* /fòtəgrǽfɪk/.

b. The word /sɑjn/ 'symbol, marker' is spelled *sign* (not *sine*), an archaic spelling also found in the related word *signal*, even though in *signal* the pronunciation of this morpheme is /sɪgn/, with the spelled /g/ pronounced, and a different vowel.

c. The verb *fine* /fayn/ is spelled *fined* in the past tense, a spelling which makes this distinct from the homophonous present tense verb *find* /fɑjnd/.

There are many exceptions to the tendency of the above examples, because of the different histories in the language of words which seem to have the same basic morpheme: for example instead of *truely, pronounciation,* and *equalitarianism,* we have *truly, pronunciation,* and *egalitarianism.* But the logographic tendency is prevalent, so English orthography is an unusually thorough mix of alphabetic and logographic practice. It might be termed **logo-alphabetic** or **morphophonemic writing**: it is alphabetic (or phonemic) in that it generally if only roughly establishes letter-to-phoneme relationships, but it is logographic (or morphemic) in that it favors letter-to-basic word relationships in contradiction of the letter–phoneme relationships.

2.4.6. *Spelling pronunciations*

The desire for alphabetic readings of words has, in some cases, encouraged new pronunciations of words to make these more alphabetically accurate. Instead of changing the spelling to suit the pronunciation, the pronunciation is changed to suit the spelling! These are called **spelling pronunciations**, and some examples are *often*, now often pronounced with a [t], [ɔftən], instead of earlier [ɔfən], *Theo* and *Catherine* pronounced with [θ] instead of earlier [t], and *hospital*, formerly with a 'silent' h as in *hour* and *honest*, now [háspɪtl]. The opposite is a **pronunciation spelling**, like *nite* instead of *night*, and *civilize* with a z (vs. British *civilise* with s), and still slangy looking *sez* for *says*.

3. SHOULD ENGLISH SPELLING BE REFORMED?

3.1. For spelling reform

Calls for a reform of English spelling, to make it consistently alphabetic, have been heard for over two hundred years. George Bernard Shaw, who sarcastically suggested the *ghoti* spelling of *fish*, was nevertheless serious enough about the issue to leave funds in his will to promote the use of a 40-letter phonetic alphabet for English.

There are two clear arguments for English alphabetic writing, the opposites, in fact, of the above-mentioned disadvantages of the basically logographic system of Chinese writing:

3.1.1. *Learnability*

Presumably children would learn to read a consistent, phonemic, system faster, since, theoretically, there would be only as many letter–sound correspondences to learn as there are phonemes, 36, instead of the 166 now found, many of which compete with one another, like *ea* and *ee* for /i/, and *ph* and *f* for /f/. The 'see and say' method of reading would be unnecessary, since a strict 'phonics' system would be perfectly applicable to all words. Perhaps also this would result in less stress for children in the early grades, who then would suffer less hyperactivity, and behave better.

3.1.2. *Applicability to new words*

Everyone would know how to spell new words, given their pronunciation, and everyone would know how to pronounce new words, given their spelling.

3.2. Against spelling reform

More and perhaps more persuasive arguments can be arrayed against a consistent alphabetic system:

3.2.1. Which dialect?

Since alphabetic writing is supposed to reflect pronunciation, a difficult question would arise of whose pronunciations would be found in standard English writings. There is general consensus nowadays on 'standard' English pronunciations (upper midwestern in the US and 'RP' in Britain), but our logo-alphabetic writing reflects lots of pronunciations inconsistent with these varieties, which perhaps would have to be changed. And certainly British and American writers would not be happy writing each other's pronunciations, even if they knew what these were. Perhaps everyone would write their own dialect. As was noted concerning the suitability of logographic writing in China, in a linguistically diverse area served by a standard language, non-phonetic writing can be a unifying factor; phonetic writing could be a divisive factor.

3.2.2. Readability of older literature

Since pronunciations are always changing (the constancy of language change is emphasized in the next chapter), to make spellings reflect current pronunciations would mean that writings from an earlier time of different pronunciations would be stranger looking than they are, and these would become unreadable sooner. Certainly, if we began to write alphabetically, writing would not look like it does today; it might look like this:

Thu kwik brown foks jumpt ovur thu layzy dawgz.

3.2.3. Homophones

By such reform, non-homophonic homographs would disappear, so that the noun *lead* would no longer look like the present tense verb *lead* – and would look like the past tense verb *led*! *Be* would look like *bee*, *rose* and *rows* would look the same, and both *do* and *due* would be *doo*! All the relationships of morphological identity now made clear in our logo-alphabetic writing would vanish. *Sign* and *signal* would be quite different in appearance, fodugrafs would be taken by futagruferz, and (in some dialects) meri meri would meri, instead of merry Mary marrying. In short, phonetic transparency would create morphological opacity.

3.2.4. Loss of stylistic and individual differences

A means of expressing individuality, novelty, and style would disappear. The *olde antique shop* would just be *old*. *Amerika* would be the standard spelling, and no longer available as a political statement, and 'Who sez?' could not suggest an assertive version of 'Who says?'; both would be *hu sez*.

3.2.5. Cost

Finally, such a reform of English spelling would be expensive. Voters who won't approve a tax increase for school music programs probably won't approve one for spelling reform. Publishers, who would have to lead the way, probably wouldn't expect to make enough money to pay for their great costs in such a change.

3.3. Reform or not?

In short, it is hard to say that our logo-alphabetic writing is so bad. It represents a complex and long evolved solution to the need for compromise between the conflicting needs, basically, for (1) predictable spellings that don't have to be learned word by word, and (2) spellings that can be read by people who speak the same language but differently, whether from generation to generation or from region to region.

Suggestions for
ADDITIONAL READING

The ecology of languages and societies and their writing systems is discussed by Florian Coulmas in *The Writing Systems of the World* (1991), and Geoffrey Sampson in *Writing Systems: a Linguistics Introduction* (1985). The difference between speech and writing, particularly English, is shown by M. A. K. Halliday (1989) in *Spoken and Written Language*. Concerning the creation and development of writing systems, see *Advances in the Creation and Revision of Writing Systems* (1977), edited by Joshua Fishman.

For the system of English spelling see *A Survey of English Spelling* (1997) by Edward Carney, and *American English Spelling: an Informal Description* (1988) by D. W. Cummings. Important statistical background to these works is *The Structure of English Orthography* (1970) by Richard L. Venezky. Concerning just punctuation is *The Linguistics of Punctuation* (1990) by Geoffrey Nunberg.

Concerning the learning of English reading and spelling is *Why Our Children Can't Read, and What We Can Do About it* (1997) by Diane McGuinness, *Beginning to Spell* (1993) by Rebecca Treiman, and *Learning to Spell* (1997) edited by Charles A. Perfetti, Laurence Rieben, and Michel Fayol. A comparative perspective is found in *Scripts and Learning: Reading and Learning to Read Alphabets, Syllabaries, and Characters* (1994) edited by Insup Taylor and David R. Olsen.

IMPORTANT CONCEPTS AND
TERMS IN THIS CHAPTER

- Mandarin Chinese
- isolating language
- lingua franca
- graph
- allograph
- grapheme
- letter

- homograph
- homophone
- logo-alphabetic writing
- morphophonemic writing
- spelling pronunciation
- pronunciation spelling

OUTLINE OF
CHAPTER 22

1. **The language of writing is different**
   1. Writing is secondary
   2. Six ways that the language of writing differs from that of speech
2. **Four adaptations of writing to society**
   1. Chinese
      1. Chinese logographic writing
      2. Suitability of Chinese writing
   2. Arabic
      1. Arabic consonantal writing
      2. Suitability of Arabic writing
   3. Japanese
      1. Japanese syllabic writing
      2. Suitability of Japanese writing
   4. English
      1. Suitability of English writing
      2. Graphs, allographs, and graphemes
      3. Nonphonemicness of English writing
      4. English spelling rules
      5. Logographic tendency of English writing
      6. Spelling pronunciations
3. **Should English spelling be reformed?**
   1. For spelling reform
      1. Learnability
      2. Applicability to new words
   2. Against spelling reform
      1. Which dialect?
      2. Readability of older literature
      3. Homophones
      4. Loss of stylistic and individual differences
      5. Cost
   3. Reform or not?

EXAMPLES AND PRACTICE

EXAMPLE

1. Arabic writing. Arabic is written from right to left. Characters have somewhat different form when they are at the beginning, middle, or end of a word. As

beam بیـم	bim بِـمِ	bum بَـم	boom بـوم
Mease مـیس	miss مِـس	muss مَـس	moose مـوس
meet مـیت	mit مِـت	mutt مَـت	moot مـوت
mean مـین	sin سِـن	munn مَـن	moon مـون
neat نـیت	knit نِـت	nut نَـت	knute نـوت
bean بـین	bin بِـن	bun بَـن	boon بـون
teen تـین	tin تِـن	ton تَـن	tune تـون
beat بـیت	bit بِـت	but بَـت	boot بـوت
Steen سـتین	bits بِـتـس	stun سـتَـن	suits سـوتـس

Figure 22.1 English words written in the Arabic writing system

figure 22.1 are 36 English words written in the Arabic writing system. The words employ only the five consonants /b, m, s, t, n/ and the four vowels /i/, /ɪ/, /ə/, and /u/. These English vowels are equated with the somewhat similar Arabic vowels /iː/, /i/, /a/, and /uː/, respectively. Notice that a superscript mark shows the short vowel /ə/, and a subscript mark shows the short vowel /ɪ/.

PRACTICE

Analyze the 36 examples and then provide (a) the English words written in Arabic as 1–12, and (b) the Arabic writing of the English words 13–16.

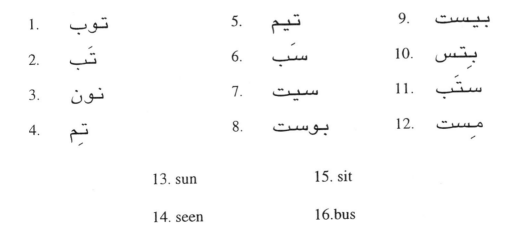

1. تـوب
2. تَـب
3. نـون
4. تِـم

5. تیـم
6. سَـب
7. سـیت
8. بـوسـت

9. بیـسـت
10. بِـتـس
11. سـتَـب
12. مِـسـت

13. sun
14. seen

15. sit
16. bus

EXAMPLE

2. Amharic writing. Amharic, the major Semitic language of Ethiopia, is written from left to right. Like Phoenician writing, which Greek borrowed and adapted, Amharic writing descends from a Semitic Sinaitic script, and therefore has similarities with Greek, such as ተ [tə] and ለ [lə]. Amharic is a somewhat consonantal system in that basic characters represent consonants, but it is somewhat alphabetic in that vowels are regularly represented as certain modifications of the basic consonantal characters. As figure 22.2 are 36 English words written in the Amharic writing system.

ባፕ	bop	ኦት	Ott	ሳፕ	sop	ዳን	Don
ቤት	bait	ኤት	ate/8	ሴት	sate	ይት	date
ቢት	beat	ኢዝ	ease	ሲት	seat	ዲን	dean
ቦት	boat	ኦዝ	owes	ሶፕ	soap	ጶፕ	dope
ቡት	boot	ኡዝ	ooze	ሱፕ	soup	ዱን	dune
ካፕ	cop	ሻት	shot	ላት	lot	ጾዝ	doze
ኬፕ	cape	ሼፕ	shape	ሌት	late	ጄን	Jane
ኮን	cone	ሺን	sheen	ሊፕ	leap	ዲፕ	deep
ዞን	zone	ሺፕ	sheep	ሉት	loot	ጄክ	Jake

Figure 22.2   English words written in the Amharic writing system

PRACTICE

Analyze the 36 examples, and then (a) provide the English words written in Amharic as 1–12, and (b) the Amharic writing for the English words 13–16.

1. ሌን   4. ሹት   7. ዳት   10. ጾን

2. ኮት   5. ቦዝ   8. ኢት   11. ሼክ

3. ኩፕ   6. ኦን   9. ዲን   12. ቢን

13. soon   15. Duke

14. sheet   16. cane

3. Devanagari writing. Devanagari is a writing system in use in India for over two thousand years. It was used to write the ancient language Sanskrit, and is now used for writing a number of modern languages of India including Hindi.

As figure 22.3 are 40 English words written in the Devanagari writing system. Analyze the 40 examples and then provide the Devanagari writing for the English words 1–8.

1. cod
2. pad
3. dope
4. seed
5. sewn
6. leap
7. case
8. gnawed

1. पट putt	11. सप sup	21. कप cup	31. डुन dun
2. पाट pot	12. साप sop	22. काप cop	32. डान Don
3. पिट pit	13. सिट sit	23. किप kip	33. दिन din
4. पीट peat	14. सीट seat	24. कीप keep	34. डीन dean
5. पुट put	15. पुस puss	25. कुक cook	35. कुड could
6. पूप poop	16. सूप soup	26. कूप coop	36. डून dune
7. पेट pate	17. सेट sate	27. केप cape	37. डेन Dane
8. पैट pat	18. सैट sat	28. कैप cap	38. डैन Dan
9. पोप pope	19. सोप soap	29. कोप cope	39. डोल dole
10. पौन pawn	20. सौट sought	30. कौल call	40. डौन dawn

Figure 22.3   English words written in the Devanagari writing system

4. Korean writing. The Korean **hangul** writing system was invented in about AD 1444 by King Sejong (reigned 1418–1450) to replace Chinese writing, which yet continues to be learned in Korea. The system presents consonants and vowels in regular form–sound relationships and is very efficient and learnable.

As figure 22.4 are 46 English words written in the Korean writing system. By figuring out the character–sound correspondences of those 46 words, supply the Korean writing for the 14 English words at the bottom of the chart.

	m	p	b	k	t	h	n
-en	men	pen	Ben	ken	ten	hen	—
-an	man	pan	ban	can	tan	—	net
-et	met	pet	bet	—	tat	hat	gnat
-at	mat	pat	bat	cat	—	hatch	natch
-atch	match	patch	batch	catch	tap	—	nap
-ap	map	—	—	cap	tin	—	—
-in	—	pin	bin	kin	ton	—	none
-un	—	pun	bun	—	—	—	nut
-ut	mutt	putt	but	cut	—	hut	—
-it	mitt 1	pit 4	bit 7	kit 9	tub 11	hit 13	nub 3
-ub	—	pub 5	—	cub 10	tuck 12	hub 14	—
-uck	muck 2	puck 6	buck 8	—	—	—	—

Figure 22.4 English words written in the Korean writing system

5. English logo-alphabetic writing. A morpheme in English may typically keep its spelling even when, in another word, usually in combination with an affix or other morpheme, it is pronounced differently – for example, *bomb* and *bombard*. *Bomb* is pronounced /bɑm/ but when *bomb* appears in *bombard*, the final /b/ is pronounced.

For the following words 3–12, write another word in which the word appears, with the same spelling but a different pronunciation. Also write the phonemic transcription of the second word. Two examples are shown as 1–2. If you can't think of a second word for any of those given, you may substitute a different word with its differently pronounced homograph.

1.	use (verb)	/juz/	use (noun)	/jus/
2.	malign	/məlɑjn/	malignant	/məlɪgnənt/
3.	reciprocate	/rəsɪprəkət/		
4.	conduct	/kɑndəkt/		
5.	medicate	/mɛdɪket/		
6.	rebel	/rɛbəl/		
7.	act	/ækt/		
8.	do	/du/		
9.	electric	/əlɛktrɪk/		
10.	resign	/razajn/		
11.	Paris	/pærɪs/		
12.	edit	/ɛdɪt/		

6. English major and minor spelling patterns. Every English phoneme except /θ/ and /ð/, both always spelled *th*, has more than one spelling. For example, /f/ is spelled *f* in *fish*, *ph* in *phone*, and *ff* in *daffy*; /ɪ/ is spelled *i* in *hit*, *ee* in *been* (usual American pronunciation), *u* in *busy*, *y* in *myth*, *o* in *women*, and *ie* in *sieve* ([sɪv]). Furthermore, almost every English letter has more than one pronunciation. For example, *e* is pronounced /ɛ/ in *bet* and /i/ in *be*, and *t* is pronounced /t/ in *ton* and, with help from following *i*, /š/ in *action*.

For each of the English phonemes 1–12 give two words in which different spellings represent the phoneme. For each of the English letters or letter pairs 13–24, give two words in which the spelling represents different pronunciations. Numbers 1 and 13 are done as examples.

1. /k/: *k* in *kick* and *c* in *can*
2. /l/:
3. /ŋ/:

4. /š/:
5. /h/:
6. /č/:

7. /f/:   10. /o/:
8. /æ/:   11. /ə/:
9. /e/:   12. /j̃/:

13. x: /ks/ in *next*, /z/ in *xylophone*   19. *i*
14. *b*   20. *o*
15. *s*   21. *ee*
16. *h*   22. *ou*
17. *th*   23. *ei*
18. *ch*   24. *y*

EXAMPLE

7. Child spellings. Children learning to spell English words naturally sometimes pick up the idea that spellings are, in fact alphabetic. This is a good guess, which represents a reasonably good generalization. But the guess often leads to wrong results, as in the following child spellings (Read 1975).

a. nooigland   'New England'   f. bedr   'better'
b. prede   'pretty'   g. mitl   'middle'
c. riden   'riding'   h. chruk   'truck'
d. adsavin   'eighty-seven'   i. myn   'mine'
e. convenshun   'convention'   j. bkos   'because'

PRACTICE

For five of these, suggest how or why the child might have come up with such a spelling.

EXAMPLE

8. Holo-phonemic sentence. A **holo-alphabetic** sentence is one which includes all the letters of the alphabet. A famous holo-alphabetic sentence, notoriously useful for practicing typewriting, is 'The quick brown fox jumps over the lazy dog.' Following is confirmation that the sentence includes all 26 letters.

a lazy   j jumps   s jumps
b brown   k quick   t the
c quick   l lazy   u quick, jumps
d dog   m jumps   v over
e over, the   n brown   w brown
f fox   o brown, fox, over, dog   x fox
g dog   p jumps   y lazy
h the   q quick   z lazy
i quick   r brown, over

PRACTICE

Write an English **holo-phonemic** sentence, one which includes 35/36 (American/British) phonemes of English. These are listed below; the glottal stop phoneme is problematic and may be omitted. For review of English phonemes, see chapter 3, §3.

Try to make your sentence as efficient as the holo-alphabetic sentence above, which uses a total of just 35 letter-graphs to illustrate the 26 different letter-graphemes of the alphabet. (a) Write the sentence both as spelled, and phonemically, and (b) mention the total number of phonemic symbols that you use. (c) Then, to confirm that your result is complete, for each phoneme provide a word of your sentence, written phonemically, which includes the phoneme.

PHONEMES OF ENGLISH

/p/	/ǰ/ (= /dʒ/)	/š/(= /ʃ/)	/r/	/i/	/ɒ/ (British)
/b/	/f/	/ž/(= /ʒ/)	/j/	/ɪ/	/ɔ/
/t/	/v/	/h/	/w/	/e/	/o/
/d/	/θ/	/m/		/ɛ/	/ʊ/
/k/	/ð/	/n/		/æ/	/u/
/g/	/s/	/ŋ/		/ə/	
/č/ (= /tʃ/)	/z/	/l/		/ɑ/	

Chapter 23

THREE CHARACTERISTICS OF LANGUAGE CHANGE

This chapter introduces language change and illustrates its three important characteristics of constancy, pervasiveness, and systematicness.

1. CONSTANCY OF LANGUAGE CHANGE

Language change is constant but it is often imperceptible. It is slow enough that the replacement of forms and rules is rarely noticeable within one generation, but fast enough that we are often aware that generations before and after ours speak differently, preferring forms and rules different from those we prefer and even having some different ones. Whenever a language at some point in time is compared with its descendant language even a few hundred years later, the change is obvious. This is apparent in the three texts of figure 23.1 (Matthew 8, 1–5; Old and Middle English versions from Marckwardt 1951), which illustrate three commonly recognized periods of the history of English:

a. Old English, up to about 1100, 455 – 1066 (Norman french conquest)
b. Middle English 1100 to about 1500, and 1476 (printing)
c. Modern English 1500 to the present.

(Some of the differences in the three texts of figure 23.1 reflect revisions in the translation from Greek, not changes in the English language.)

The date 1100 is not an entirely arbitrary dividing line between Old and Middle English. It is 34 years after 1066, the year of the battle of Hastings and the Norman French conquest of Britain. Even something as politically cataclysmic as this can't suddenly and drastically change a language, but the Norman conquest did result, eventually, in a lot of French word-borrowings and other

Old English, Gospels (ca. 1000)

(þ and ð usually distinguish [θ] and [ð], respectively; c is usually [k]; y is [y], a high, front, rounded vowel; and vowels with [¯] are long vowels.)

1. Sōþlīce þā sē Hǣlend of þǣm munte nyþer āstāh, þā fyligdon him micele menigu.
2. þā genēalǣhte ān hrēofla to him, and hine tō him geēaðmēdde, and þus cwaeð: Dryhten, gif þū wilt, þū miht mē geclǣnsian.
3. ðā āstrehte sē Hǣlend his hand, and hrepode hine, and þus cwaeð: Ic wille; bēo geclǣnsod. And his hrēofla waes hradlīce geclǣnsod.
4. ðā cwaeð see Hǣlend to him: Warna þē þaet þū hit nǣnegum men ne secge; ac gang, aetīewe þē þǣm sacerde, and bring heom, þā lāc þe Moyses bebēad on heora gecȳðnesse.
5. Sōþlīce þā sē Hǣlend in ēode on Capharnaum, þā genēalǣhte him ān hundredes ealdor, hine biddende.

Middle English, Wycliffe Bible (ca. 1389)

1. Forsothe when Jhesus hadde comen doun from the hil, many cumpanyes folewiden hym.
2. And loo! a leprouse man cummynge worshipide hym, sayinge, Lord, ȝif thou wolt, thou maist make me clene.
3. And Jhesus, holdynge forthe the hond touchide hym, sayinge, I wole, be thou maad clene. And anoon the lepre of hym was clensid.
4. And Jhesus saith to hym, See, say thou to no man; but go, shewe thee to prestis, and offer that ȝifte that Moyses comaundide, into witnessing to hem.
5. Sothely when he hadde entride in to Capharnaum, centurio neiȝide to hym, preyinge hym.

Modern English, King James Version Bible (1611)

1. When he was come down from the mountain, great multitudes followed him.
2. And, behold, there came a leper and worshipped him, saying, Lord, if thou wilt, thou canst make me clean.
3. And Jesus put forth his hand, and touched him, saying, I will; be thou clean. And immediately his leprosy was cleansed.
4. And Jesus saith unto him, See thou tell no man; but go your way, shew thyself to the priest. And offer the gift that Moses commanded, for a testimony unto them.
5. And when Jesus was entered into Capernaum there came unto Him a centurion, beseeching Him.

Figure 23.1 Old, Middle, and Modern English texts

French influence on English, and 1100 is the approximate time of the height of this influence.

The date 1500 is 24 years after 1476, the year of the introduction of printing in England and 64 years before the birth of Shakespeare. An advance in technology, even one as influential as the printing press, or an author, even one as influential as Shakespeare, can't change a language much either, but the beginning of printing and the rise of popular literature did promote literacy and recognition of a standard English language, and 1500 is the approximate time of the onset of these important influences.

From 1100 to 1500 is 400 years, and another 500 years has now passed since 1500, so the third, Modern English, era is now relatively advanced. Perhaps the growth and influence of electronic communication in the present generation could represent the onset of the next, post-modern, stage in the history of English.

2. PERVASIVENESS OF LANGUAGE CHANGE

As in the history of English, in all languages change is pervasive as well as constant, affecting the lexicon (the inventory of morphemes) and all aspects of the grammar: phonology, morphology, and syntax. Old English is completely unintelligible to modern-day speakers and readers of the language, and such pervasive change is not peculiar to the history of English. Similar change over similar periods of time is known for other languages for which we have a significant record of history, such as Latin to Italian, Sanskrit to Hindi, Old Chinese to Modern Chinese, and ancient Egyptian to Coptic.

Following are some illustrations of how change has affected the lexicon and grammar of English, including grammatical change in each of phonology, morphology, and syntax. In fact, change in one part of the grammar is usually not isolated from change in others.

2.1. Lexical change

New morphemes, in the form of new words, are being continually added to a language (chapters 15 and 16), and old morphemes are disappearing. Recent years have seen the appearance of *byte*, *CAT-scan*, *geek*, *e-mail*, and *cybertalk*, for example, and, scanning a book published in 1864, in New York, I soon see the word *knacker*, the meaning of which is unknown to me, at least.

Borrowing is a prominent source of new words in times of drastic externally driven societal change. English has borrowed much of its vocabulary, over 60% of the words of typical written texts, from Greek and Latin, from French, and from Latin and Greek via French, much of this in the era of Norman political superiority in Britain. Only the most frequent and basic words were unaffected by this borrowing, which was especially prominent in sectors of society in which the French dominated, for example, government and cuisine. The preference for

French cuisine and so for French words for foods (chapter 15, §3.6.2.1) balanced against the frequency of native English words on the farm and in the fields resulted in bifurcations (chapter 16, §2.6) of words for edible animals, in which the French word was narrowed to mean the meat (on the table) and the English word preserved to mean the living animal (on the hoof):

French	English
mutton	sheep
pork	pig
beef	cow
veal	calf
venison	deer

At least *poultry* (French) and *chicken* (English) each persist in both senses of the words.

Relic forms of a word generally lost from a language may survive in specialized uses in which their meaning has become well extended, for example, Middle English:

a. *let* 'hinder', survives in the tennis term *let (ball)* (hindered by the net);
b. *plumb* 'lead (metal)' survives in the carpenter's *plumb line*, a weight on a string for judging verticality, and in chemistry's *Pb*.
 c. *wer* 'man' survives in *werewolf*, literally 'manwolf'.

The word *knack* of *knacker*, mentioned above, survives in the idiom to *have the knack* (skill) of doing something (but not in the original meaning).

2.2. Grammar change

2.2.1. *Phonological change*

2.2.1.1. Phonetic change. Phonetic change is imperceptible at first. In fact, pronunciations are always changing, and after hundreds of years it often can be seen that the changes were, with exceptions, of a very general or regular nature, according to which all phones of a type in a given environment changed identically. This **regularity of phonetic change** is clearly evidenced in two well studied cases: Grimm's Law and the English Great Vowel Shift.

a. Grimm's Law. The stop consonants of the language known as **Indoeuropean** – the predecessor language of English and most of the European languages, spoken over 6,000 years ago – changed in a regular pattern with the result that one finds regular correspondences between phonemes of English and Latin in cognate words. **Cognates** are words of different languages descended from a word of a mutual ancestor language. In the case of English and Latin, the ancestor is the Indoeuropean language. As seen in table 23.1, in English–Latin cognates English /t/ corresponds to Latin /d/, English /k/ to Latin /g/, etc.

Table 23.1 Regular consonant correspondences in English and Latin cognates

English		Latin	
/t/:	two, tooth, teach	/d/:	duo, dens, dīco
/k/:	corn, kin, acre	/g/:	grānus, genus, ager
/b/:	bear, brother, beech	/f/:	ferō, frāter, fāgus
/d/:	door, do, deer	/f/:	forus, fēcī, fera
/g/:	guest, greedy, garden	/h/:	hospes, hortārī, hortus
/f/:	foot, father, few	/p/:	pes, pater, paucus
/θ/:	three, thin, thrill	/t/:	trēs, tenuis, terebra
/h/:	hundred, head, horn	/k/:	centum, caput, cornū

examples.

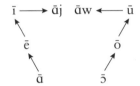

Figure 23.2 The English Great Vowel Shift

There is controversy about the nature of the Indoeuropean stops which became those of English and Latin, in the example words in table 23.1. The important point is that, whatever these were, they changed regularly, or systematically, in the different languages that separated and diverged over hundreds of years to become the Germanic language (which again separated and evolved into English, German, Swedish, etc.) and Latin (which then separated and evolved into French, Italian, Spanish, etc.).

The regular consonant phoneme correspondences that result reflect the sound change known as **Grimm's Law**, named for the early Indoeuropeanist linguist **Jacob Grimm** (1785–1863) who discovered them, and in doing so helped establish linguistics as a field of scientific study, based upon the discovery of systematic or lawful natural phenomena.

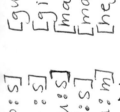

b. **Great Vowel Shift**. In a systematic phonetic change lasting hundreds of years up to about 1700, the Old English non-high long vowels /ē, ā, ɔ̄, ō/ moved up in articulation, and the highest long vowels /ī, ū/ became **centralized** and **diphthongized**, as in the somewhat simplified chart of figure 23.2.

Later, vowel length contrasts were also lost, and the eventual result is that there are very regular correspondences between modern pronunciations and those of Old English, as in the examples of table 23.2 (in which Old English word-final vowels are ignored). Notice how, in several rows of table 23.2, the modern English spellings still reflect the old English phonetic vowels: a, e, i in the first three rows, and oo in the fifth.

Table 23.2   Examples of the English Great Vowel Shift

	Old English	*Modern English*
ā > e	/blām, nām, māk/	/blem/ blame, /nem/ name, /mek/ make
ē > i	/wēp, spēk, hē/	/wip/ weep, /spik/ speak, /hi/ he
ī > aj	/blīnd, fīr, līf/	/blajnd/ blind, /fajr/ fire, /lajf/ life
ɔ̄ > o	/stɔ̄n, hɔ̄m, gɔ̄t/	/ston/ stone, /hom/ home, /got/ goat
ō > u	/mōn, tōθ, fōd/	/mun/ moon, /tuθ/ tooth, /fud/ food
ū > aw	/fūnd, sūθ, hūs/	/fawnd/ found, /sawθ/ south, /haws/ house

2.2.1.2. Phonemic change.   Sound change can lead to complete loss and change of phonemes. Most of the consonant phonemes of Old English survive in Modern English, but the set of vowel phonemes is thoroughly changed because of the effects of the Great Vowel Shift, loss of vowel length, and vowel reduction. Voiced and voiceless fricatives [f, v], [θ, ð] and [s, z] were allophones of /f/, /θ/, and /s/ in Old English times, as described below, but in Modern English the voiceless fricative phonemes /f, θ, s/ contrast with the voiced fricative phonemes /v, ð, z/ in minimal pairs like *fine/vine*, *ether/either*, and *bus/buzz*.

2.2.1.3. Alternations.   Sound changes may result in different pronunciations of a single morpheme, known as **alternations** (chapter 13, §1.2.1.1). Probably every language has some of these phonological relationships. Here is a brief history of two alternations in English.

   a. Vowel reduction. Many English morphemes have alternations resulting from vowel reduction, a phonetic change according to which, since Middle English times, vowels in fully unstressed syllables became centralized as [ə]. The result is alternations such as seen in the following pairs of words:

photograph	/fótəgræf/	photography	/fətágrəfi/
Canada	/kǽnədə/	Canadian	/kənédiən/
neutral	/nútrəl/	neutrality	/nùtrǽləti/
metal	/métəl/	metalic	/mətǽlɪk/

Notice in these word-pairs that /o/, /æ/, /e/, /a/, /u/, and /ɛ/ appear when their syllable is stressed, but these are centralized (said to be 'reduced'), and /ə/ appears whenever this syllable fully lacks stress, when suffixes are present. (In English, words may be stressed differently depending on the presence of certain suffixes, as in words of the right column above.)

   b. Fricative voicing. There are some alternations in English concerning voiced and voiceless fricatives at the end of morphemes which survive from Middle

English (mentioned in chapter 13, §1.2.3). The voiceless fricative is heard in singular nouns, and, in the speech of some (this is quite variable – readers should consider their own pronunciations, and check that of others), the voiced fricative is heard in plural nouns, verbs, and adjectives; for example:

* examples:

Singular noun		*Plural noun*	
/nɑjf/	knife	/nɑjvz/	knives
/buθ/	booth	/buðz/	booths
/hɑws/	houses	/háwzɪz/	houses

Noun		*Verb*	
/strɑjf/	strife	/strɑjv/	strive
/bæθ/	bath	/beð/	bathe
/jus/	use	/juz/	use

Noun		*Adjective*	
/lɑjf/	life	/lájv/	live
/sawθ/	south	/sə́ðərn/	southern
/laws/	louse	/láwzi/	lousy

These alternations of voiced and voiceless fricatives go back (with some simplification) to a stage of English after a sound change of **fricative voicing** according to which the <u>fricatives were voiced between voiced phones</u>, especially vowels. The phonemes which were voiceless fricatives at the ends of words were voiced when the vowel of a suffix followed, as it did in plurals of nouns and in many verbs and adjectives. At that time in the history of English there was thus no contrast between voiced and voiceless fricatives, which were in complementary distribution and were **allophones**.

The modern pronunciations and spellings still to some extent suggest this distribution of fricatives: words in the right column, except for the plural nouns, are always spelled and sometimes pronounced with a vowel after the fricative (*houses, bathe, southern*), while words in the left column are sometimes spelled but never pronounced with a final vowel.

Borrowings from French during the Middle English period included words in which voiced fricatives occurred other than between vowels, for example French *verai* 'true', which was borrowed and broadened in meaning as *very*. Also, certain unstressed vowels began to be omitted, with the result that complementarity between voiced and voiceless fricatives was lost, and these came to be **contrastive** – corresponding to meaning differences seen today in minimal pairs like *ferry* (Old English) and *very* (French), and *ice* /ajs/ (singular) and *eyes* /ajz/ (plural). At this stage voiced and voiceless fricatives are different **phonemes**.

The old pronunciations, in which voiced and voiceless fricatives appeared in different allomorphs of a morpheme, survived as the alternations exemplified in the words above. Words which have entered the language since the time of the rule of fricative voicing, such as *chief* (plural *chiefs*), *toss* (*tosses*), and *nice* (adverb *nicely*), don't have the voiced/voiceless alternation.

2.2.2. Morphological change

2.2.2.1. *Derivational morphology.* The flood of French words into English brought with it lots of words with their derivational affixes attached, including *-able*, *-ment*, *dis-*, and *re-*, which, because the words they were part of became accepted within the English lexicon, eventually themselves became recognized within English grammar, and were extended for use with English words, as in *drinkable, settlement, dislike*, and *rebuild*.

We get new derivational affixes also by compounding, as in *street-wise* 'wise in the ways of the street' and *vacation-wise* 'as for vacation'. Such is the source of *-ly* coming from Middle English *lic* 'like' (from Old English *gelic*), a process which repeats itself today in compounds like *child-like* and *quick-like* (whose novelty is evident in their being written with the hyphen). Even if the suffixes *-oholic* 'addiction' and *-gate* 'scandal concerning' (chapter 16, §2.7) are short-lived in English, they clearly illustrate the possibility also of getting derivational affixes by backformation.

In an opposite change, some Old English derivational affixes dropped out of use, such as *a-* 'in, on' (roughly), which survives, now unrecognized as a prefix, in words including *awake, arise*, and *asleep*. Another Old English prefix, *for-* 'very (intensification of meaning)', survives unrecognized in words including *forgive, forbid*, and *forlorn*. Still fading from the language is the French-origin suffix *-age* as in *bondage, freightage* and *equipage*; the latter two have now been replaced by *freight* and *equipment*.

2.2.2.2. *Inflectional morphology.* As was noted in chapter 4, §5.2.1, it is a characteristic of grammatical morphemes that new ones appear rarely. Loss of inflections (bound grammatical morphemes) is often the result of competing patterns, in which the competition is resolved by **regularization,** according to which **irregular forms** of less frequent and, sometimes, later-learned morphemes are replaced by **regular forms** of more frequent and earlier learned morphemes. For example, the regular plural *fishes* tends to replace irregular *fish*, and the regular plural /pæθs/ tends to replace irregular plural /pæðz/, in which /ð/ is a survival of fricative voicing. Such regularizing changes are especially promoted by child learners, but adults too may regularize low-frequency irregular words with which they are unfamiliar.

fishes instead of fish

Rules which are extended to new words are said to be **productive**. The rule which adds the basic /z/ suffix to singulars, as for *dog*/z/ and *cat*/s/ (with assimilated /z/), for example, is productive: it applies to new words like *clone* and *ET* (plurals /klonz/ and /itiz/). Rules which tend to be curtailed by extension of productive rules are **nonproductive.** The rule by which the plural of a noun is the same as the singular, as for *fish* and *deer*, is, generally, nonproductive.

2.2.2.3. *Rule extension.* **Rule extension** is the application of productive rules to cases formerly subject to nonproductive rules. In this understanding, on the basis of frequent earlier encountered words like *cat/cats* and *dish/dishes*, the child acquires productive rules for forming plural nouns, including:

a.   The plural of nouns is formed by suffixing /z/ to the singular form.
b.   /z/ at the end of words after a voiceless consonant is replaced by /s/.
c.   /ɪ/ is inserted between a strident coronal fricative and word-final /z/.

These rules apply to words new to the learner and new in the language, as well as to those the irregularities of which a learner may not have mastered, such as *path* /pæθ/ and *fish* /fɪš/, which may be pluralized as /pæθs/ and *fishes* /fɪšɪz/.

Such regularizations are also known as **analogical change**, or analogical extension. This may be thought of as an aspect of **hypothesis testing** by the learner (chapter 9, §3), who sets up hypothetical analogies such as:

a.   /pæθ/ 'path' is to plural X as /kæt/ 'cat' is to plural /kæts/.
b.   /fɪš/ 'fish' is to plural X as /dɪš/ 'dish' is to plural /dɪšɪz/.

Solving for X gets /pæθs/ and /fɪšɪz/.

2.2.2.4.   Leveling.   The loss of irregular cases as the result of extending productive rules to cover these cases is termed (leveling) distinctions or contrast between different forms for the same meaning are 'leveled' – for example the contrast of /pæθ/ and /pæð/ both meaning 'path' (the latter in plurals, the former otherwise) is being leveled as /pæθ/.

Fully irregular forms, outside any pattern (termed **suppletive**: chapter 13, §1.2.3), are especially targets of leveling. For example *kine*, the Middle English irregular plural of *cow*, has almost vanished, replaced by regular *cows*. Past tense *went* resists replacement and survives because it is part of early-learned very frequent vocabulary, but it is under attack by children who say *goed* (noted in practice 4 of chapter 8).

A leveling now underway in English concerns an irregularity in the past participles of verbs. According to the productive rule for past participles, these are equivalent to the past tense form, for example: *opened, has opened*. In Old English, past participles were suffixed with /ɛn/, and these forms survive in many frequent and early-learned verbs, for example *eaten, taken*, and *seen*. But the past participles in /n/ have long been replaced in many verbs, including *comen* by *come*, and *shotten* by *shot*, and some have recently or are now being regularized, as in the following five verbs which have undergone this change in the past fifty or so years.

Present	Old present perfect	New present perfect
wake	has woken	has waked
strive	has striven	has strived
thrive	has thriven	has thrived
chide	has chidden	has chided
sow	has sown	has sowed

Others are now changing, including *swell, forget, saw* ('use a saw'), and *mow*. (The old past participles may survive as adjectives; for example, we say *the apple has rotted* not *the apple has rotten*, but the result of rotting is *rotten apples*; we say *a ball was struck*, not *a ball was stricken*, but very frightened people are *terror stricken*.)

Notice that leveling of some rules implies extension of others: the productive rule gets new cases (for example *waked*), as the number of cases of the nonproductive rule (such as *woken*) is reduced.

2.2.3. *Syntactic change*

2.2.3.1. *Word order change.*
Since Old English, somewhat variable word order among subject, object and verb has changed to quite rigid **SVO** (subject-verb-object) order. Consider the following Old English sentences (recall that þ = [θ] and [ð]):

a. Castelas hē lēt wyrcean.   'He caused castles to be built.'
    castles he made built
b. þā sende se cyning þone disc.   'Then the king sent the dish.'
    then sent the king the dish
c. Hēo hine lǣrde.   'She advised him.'
    she him advised

The first Old English sentence has OSV order, the second VSO order, and the fourth SOV, but the three modern translations all have SVO order.

2.2.3.2. *Loss of case suffixes.*
Such variation enabled Old English to express backgrounding and foregrounding (chapter 18, §5.1) by word order alone. The variable position of subject and direct object did not cause misunderstanding because Old English nouns in these functions had suffixes to indicate their grammatical function, as seen in table 23.3. Such inflectional morphemes express the grammatical category known as **case** (case suffixes of Latin were exemplified in chapter 17, §5.3.2.4). In Old English, the form of the case suffix varied depending on whether the noun was of the so-called masculine, feminine or neuter class. Table 23.3 presents examples of two nouns of each class, in the six case forms; notice the different case suffixes of the three classes. 'Masculine', 'feminine', and 'neuter' are not natural classes but grammatical classes, since a stone, for example, is not masculine in nature, nor is a care feminine.

The typical case suffix of masculine plural nouns had an *s*, and presumably because this class was the most frequent, these case endings were extended and survive as the Modern English plural suffix spelled *s*. Similarly, the most frequent case suffix of possessive singulars had an *s*, which was extended and survives as the Modern English possessive suffix spelled *'s*.

Table 23.3   Old English noun classes

	Masculine		Feminine		Neuter	
Singular	'stone'	'end'	'care'	'wound'	'horse'	'ship'
Subject	stan	ende	caru	wund	hors	scip
Object	stan	ende	care	wunde	hors	scip
Possessive	stanes	endes	care	wunde	horses	scipes
Plural						
Subject	stanas	endas	cara	wunda	hors	scipu
Object	stanas	endas	cara	wunda	hors	scipu
Possessive	stana	enda	cara	wunda	horsa	scipa

In Old English times, however, short word-final vowels, which were unstressed, as many of the case suffixes were, were gradually lost. At about the same time, perhaps in order to keep the subject, object and possessive roles distinct despite loss of the case suffixes, word order became fixed in the SVO pattern, which persists in Modern English.

There are syntactic relics of the old word orders, in traditional and poetic wordings, for example:

> With this ring I thee wed.
> Here endeth the reading.
> Whose woods these are I think I know.
> ('Stopping by Woods on a Snowy
> Evening', Robert Frost)

2.2.3.3.   Syntactic rules.   Syntactic rules may be added and lost. An example concerns English do-insertion in Modern English one adds a form of the verb *do* when there is no auxiliary verb but one is needed for the formation of yes/no questions, negatives, and emphatic sentences. For example, for the simple statement *They speak English*, we have:

Yes/no question:	Do they speak English?
Negative statement:	They do not speak English.
Emphatic statement:	They do speak English.

In early Middle English, *do* was used as a causative verb, about as *make* is used today in sentences like 'You made me do it': *Sche dede hym etyn & drynkyn & comfortyd hym* 'She made him eat and drink and comforted him' (*dede* 'did'). This usage was not very common though, and in about 1400 *do* began to be used in questions and negative sentences with increasing frequency. See the graph of

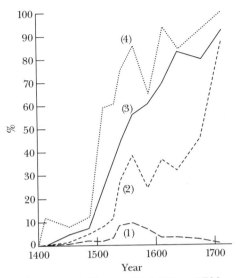

Figure 23.3   The rise of *do* as an auxiliary verb, 1400 to 1700

In: (1) affirmative statements; (2) negative statements; (3) affirmative questions; and (4) negative questions

Source: Ellegård 1953

figure 23.3 (Ellegård 1953, p. 162). *Do* gradually increased in frequency until, about 300 years ago, it achieved today's frequencies in these sentence types, in which *do* is usually obligatory unless another auxiliary verb is present.

One understanding of this thorough syntactic change is as follows:

1. Perhaps when *make* began to take over its function as a causative verb, *do* came to be interpreted as a marker of emphatic sentences, as in today's *I did try*, meaning 'Certainly I tried!'

2. Questions and especially negative questions were, and are, often emphatic, so that there were two ways of forming negatives and yes/no questions: with and without emphatic *do*:

Yes/no question	Like they tobacco?
	Do they like tobacco? (Emphatic)
Negative yes/no question	Like they not tobacco?
	Do they not like tobacco? (Emphatic)

3. *Do* in such cases soon became greatly overused, as intensifiers are often overused (for example *awful* in *I'm awful glad* and *really* in *It's really hot today*), with the result that it lost its emphatic force (as *awful* and *really* have become only slightly stronger than 'very').

4. Its frequency in questions and negatives, however, caused new generations of learners, hearing *do* often in these sentence types, to begin to

interpret it as the simple unemphatic way of forming negative questions, affirmative questions, and then simple negatives.

5. Generation after generation has extended this usage until *do* is now almost obligatory for questions and negatives without auxiliary verbs.

The old way of forming yes/no questions, by fronting the main verb, is still used if this is a form of *be*: *Was it a hot summer? Is the election next week?*; and in British English *have* continues to be fronted as a main verb: *Have you a pen I could borrow?*

3. SYSTEMATICNESS OF LANGUAGE CHANGE

Language change is systematic as well as constant and pervasive. It seeks out and follows patterns, with the result that after a change has been effective for sufficient time, all utterances within its pattern are affected.

Even lexical change, which by definition affects one morpheme at a time, shows general tendencies at any point of history. We noted that Middle English borrowed French vocabulary of the cultural realms in which the French were dominant. Vocabulary is especially affected in realms in which technological and cultural change take place. Thus new words are especially being created for English nowadays in the fields of computer science and robotics.

Phonetic change, like Grimm's Law and the English Great Vowel Shift, is regular: it tends, with time, to be completely exceptionless. Morphological change is regular in its own way: typically analogical and simplifying, with the spread of productive rules at the expense of unproductive rules.

With sufficient passage of time, analogical change will completely transform a morphological system. Today, for example, only the third-person-singular subject-suffix of the present tense spelled *-s* – descended from Old English *-eþ* – survives from the extensive Old English **inflectional suffixes** of **subject–verb agreement**, seen in figure 23.4. Old English had four forms of the present tense verb, exemplified in figure 23.4 by the verb 'sing' (recall that *þ* spells Old English [θ]). Relics of the

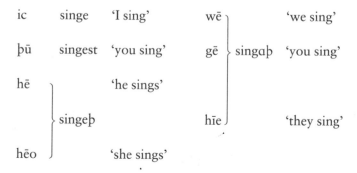

Figure 23.4 Old English verb inflections

2nd and 3rd person singulars -st and þ survive in Biblical language, as in *thou goest* and *thus saith the Lord*.

Since language change is systematic, the result of language change is always a modified and, eventually, new system. Even when its parts are thoroughly changed, the systematic relationships of language are preserved, and no language has ever been known to break down or to become at all dysfunctional as the result of change. Languages disappear, of course, but because their speakers begin to speak other languages. There is no evidence that English, though it changed extensively in the early Middle English period, ever became a hindrance to communication in England. If it did, indeed, it is surprising that England became a major European nation during that time, and that Middle English literature flourished and is still greatly valued and read.

Suggestions for
ADDITIONAL READING

Most of these topics are extended in textbooks of general historical linguistics such as *Historical Linguistics* (1996) by R. L. Trask, *Understanding Language Change* (1994) by April M. S. McMahon, *An Introduction to Historical Linguistics* (1992) by Terry Crowley, *Historical Linguistics and Language Change* (1997) by Roger Lass, and *Historical and Comparative Linguistics* (1989) by Raimo Anttila.

For the history of English, see *A History of the English Language* (1996) by Geoffrey Hughes, *The Origins and Development of the English Language* (1993, 4th edn) by Thomas Pyles and John Algeo, and *Origins of the English Language: a Social and Linguistic History* (1975) by Joseph M. Williams. With focus on the recent period, and British English, is *A History of the English Language* (1996) by Norman Blake. For the history of American English, see *A History of American English* (1992) by J. L. Dillard.

IMPORTANT CONCEPTS AND
TERMS IN THIS CHAPTER

- Old English
- Middle English
- Modern English
- relic form
- regularity of phonetic change
- Indoeuropean
- cognate
- Grimm's Law

- phoneme
- regularization
- irregular form
- regular form
- productive
- nonproductive
- rule extension
- analogical change

- Jacob Grimm
- Great Vowel Shift
- centralized
- diphthongized
- alternation
- vowel reduction
- fricative voicing
- allophone
- contrastive

- hypothesis testing
- leveling
- suppletive
- SVO
- case
- do-insertion
- inflectional suffix
- subject–verb agreement

OUTLINE OF CHAPTER 23

1. **Constancy of language change**
2. **Pervasiveness of language change**
   1. Lexical change
   2. Grammar change
      1. Phonological change
         1. Phonetic change
         2. Phonemic change
         3. Alternations
      2. Morphological change
         1. Derivational morphology
         2. Inflectional morphology
         3. Rule extension
         4. Leveling
      3. Syntactic change
         1. Word order change
         2. Loss of case suffixes
         3. Syntactic rules
3. **Systematicness of language change**

EXAMPLES AND PRACTICE

EXAMPLE

1. Indoeuropean languages. It was noted that borrowing is unlikely to affect words in the most frequent or basic vocabulary. Thus, if we compare only basic words in different languages, the presence of many phonetic similarities between cognates shows that the languages are likely to be related as co-descendants

of an earlier language. (This exercise anticipates a point to be raised in chapter 25, §4.)

Of the eighteen languages labeled A–R in figure 23.5, whose numerals for 1–10 and 100 are shown in simplified phonetic writing (from Algeo 1972, p. 95), ten are Indoeuropean. Try to find the ten Indoeuropean languages, by noticing phonetic similarities to English words of the same meanings, and/or to such words of any other Indoeuropean language you may be familiar with, such as Spanish, French, and German.

2. Recent change in English. English has of course changed since the King James version of the Bible was published in 1611. Look again at the lines from the King James Version Bible in figure 23.1, at the beginning of this chapter. The first verse is 'When he was come down from the mountain, great multitudes followed him', which in present-day English would be 'When he had come down from the mountain, great multitudes followed him'.

Rewrite the other four verses according to your understanding of appropriate Modern English usage.

3. Change since Old English. Consider the following Old English sentences (from Williams 1975 and Blakeley 1976), many words of which have recognizable similarity to modern words.

a.	Eart þū se cyning?	'Are you the king?'
b.	þā begann hē tō mōdgenne.	'Then he began to be proud.'
c.	Hīe ealle wurdon āwende.	'They were all changed.'
d.	Hwæt sægst þū?	'What do you say?'
e.	Hwilce fixas gefehst þū?	'Which fish do you catch?'
f.	Hū gefehst þū fixas?	'How do you catch fish?'
g.	Hwæt canst þū scieppan?	'What can you create?'
h.	Hæst þū hafoc?	'Do you have a hawk?'
i.	þā āscodon hīe hine hwæt se mann wære.	'Then they asked him what the man was.'

Answer these questions concerning differences, evident in these sentences, between Old and Modern English.

1. How has 'King' changed, in pronunciation and spelling?
2. What other word in (a)–(i) illustrates a spelling change concerning *c* and *k*?
3. The modern descendant word of *þū* is not exactly *you*, but what?

	A	B	C	D	E	F
1	en	un	bir	jedyn	egy	ūn
2	twene	doui	iki	dwaj	két	duos
3	thria	trei	ūç	tři	három	trais
4	fiuwar	patru	dört	štyri	négy	quatter
5	fif	cinci	beş	pjeć	ŏt	tschinch
6	sehx	şase	altı	šěsć	hat	ses
7	sibun	şapte	yedi	sedm	hét	set
8	ahto	opt	sekiz	wosm	nyolcz	och
9	nigun	nouă	dokuz	dźewjeć	kilencz	nouv
10	tehan	zice	on	dźesać	tíz	dêsch
100	hunderod	sută	yūz	sto	száz	tschient

	G	H	I	J	K	L
1	nigen	mot	unan	mek	i	aeva
2	khoyar	hai	daou	yerku	liang	dva
3	ghorban	ba	tri	yerek	san	þrayo
4	durben	bon	pevar	čors	ssu	caþwaro
5	tabon	nam	pemp	hing	wu	panca
6	jirghoghan	sau	c'houec'h	vec	liu	xšvaš
7	dologhan	bay	seiz	yot	ch'i	hapta
8	naiman	tam	eiz	ut	pa	ašta
9	yisun	chin	nao	innə	chiu	nava
10	arban	muoi	dek	tas	shih	dasa
100	jaghon	tram	kant	haryur	pai	satem

	M	N	O	P	Q	R
1	ichi	hana	eka	yaw	eden	echad
2	ni	tul	dvau	daw	dva	shnayim
3	san	set	trayas	dree	tri	shlosha
4	shi	net	catur	tsaloor	četiri	arba'a
5	go	tasŏt	pañca	pindze	pet	chamishsha
6	roku	yŏsŏt	şaş	shpazz	šest	shishsha
7	shichi	ilgop	sapta	uwe	sedum	shiv'a
8	hachi	yŏdŏl	aşta	ate	osum	shmona
9	ku	ahop	nava	ne	devet	tish'a
10	ju	yŏl	daça	las	deset	'asara
100	hyaku	paek	çata	sulu	sto	mea

Figure 23.5 Numerals for 1 to 10 and 100 in 18 languages

Source: Excerpt from *Problems in the Origin and Development of the English Language*, 2nd edn, by John Algeo and Thomas Pyles, copyright © 1972 by Harcourt Brace & Company

4. How has 'fish' changed?
5. How is inversion in the yes/no questions different from that of Modern English yes/no questions?
6. How is inversion in wh-word questions different from that of Modern English?
7. Are there differences of word order in the statements as well?
8. Which words illustrate the English Great Vowel Shift (§2.2.1, above)?
9. What suffix regularly marks second-person ('you') forms of verbs in these Old English sentences?
10. What about the indefinite article, Modern English a/an?

EXAMPLE

4. An Old English text. You may be able to recognize many words of this Old English version of 'The Lord's Prayer'.

PRACTICE

Make a list of the fifty words of the text in order of their appearance in the text, and, for as many as you can, give modern English translations. The first two words are shown as examples. For many of the words the translations are their descendant Modern English words. Mark these with an arrow, as in the examples.

Ūre Faeder, ðū ðe eart on heofonum, sī ðīn nama gehālgod. Tōcume ðīn rice. Geweorthe ðīn willa on eorðan swā-swā on heofonum. Sele ūs tō-daeg ūrne daeghwāmlican hlāf. And forgif ūs ūre gyltas, swā-swā wē forgifað ūrum gyltendum. And ne lǣd ðū ūs on costnunge. Ac ālȳs ūs fram yele.

1. Ūre > our
2. Faeder > father

EXAMPLE

5. English Great Vowel Shift. Because of the regularity of phonetic change, given an Old English word which survives into Modern English, if we know the Old English vowels, we can generally predict the Modern English vowel.

PRACTICE

Determine the Modern English pronunciations of Old English words 1–16, and then match them with meaning clues (a)–(n).

1. bōn	9. hwī	a. broad	i. create
2. māk	10. hōm	b. *dent* in French	j. part of a skeleton
3. nū	11. dīk	c. where the heart is	k. fire
4. fēd	12. blāse	d. for what reason	l. sacred
5. hōlig	13. mōd	e. toward	m. not in
6. ūt	14. hē	f. give food	n. state of mind
7. wīd	15. cū	g. river wall	o. *him* as subject
8. tō	16. tōθ	h. milk source	n. at this time

EXAMPLE

6. Schwa deletion in current English. English appears to be in the process of losing the unstressed vowel [ə] in the medial syllable of many words. The word *every*, for example, is always pronounced [évri] and never [évəri], while the word *victory* has the two pronunciations [víktri] and [víkətri], but [víktri] is common in fast or casual speech. The [ə] is likely to be omitted (i) in more frequent words, (ii) in faster speech, and (iii) only if the consonants which precede and follow it in the word can be adjacent.

PRACTICE

(a) Underline letters which represent unstressed medial [ə] in the following words. (b) Put a line through those which are deletable in fast or casual speech. (c) Circle letters which represent schwas which seem to you undeletable. (d) Notice the consonants which precede and follow unstressed [ə] in these words, and try to find generalizations about the relation between these and deletability of [ə].

prisoner	balloting	happening	remarkable
leveling	hickory	easily	scenery
candidate	opener	gossiping	marginal
factory	chocolate	boundary	finally
personal	capacity	definite	rocketing
awfully	celery	family	separate

EIGHT CAUSES OF LANGUAGE CHANGE

This chapter concerns why languages change, and presents eight reasons for this, with examples.

1. WHY DO LANGUAGES CHANGE?

Languages have always changed in the past and they certainly continue to change today. The result of language change may occasionally be miscommunication, when users of new forms of language mistakenly expect others to recognize them, so it is reasonable that language change has long and often been deplored, especially by the older generation. The characteristic of language change that it is systematic suggests that it is unlikely to be harmful. Its characteristics of constancy and pervasiveness suggest that language change is necessary, and perhaps even useful.

Except for the obvious necessity to get new morphemes to express new meanings and to get rid of the obsolete ones, we might expect language change to be resisted more successfully. In fact, we are unable to predict the occasions and forms of language change, though the spread of language changes, once underway, can often be expected. Often, also, after a language change has been noticed, we can reasonably identify a probable cause or causes for it.

A number of causes of language change have been recognized, including some which are controversial, but eight of the least controversial are these:

a. Ease of articulation
b. Expression of new meanings
c. Desire for novelty
d. Regularization or rule extension
e. Redundancy reduction
f. Metanalysis
g. Obsolescence of meanings
h. Language contact

2. EIGHT CAUSES OF LANGUAGE CHANGE

In discussion below, each of the eight causes listed above is explained and exemplified, from the history of English and other languages. More than one cause may often be effective in a particular language change.

2.1. Ease of articulation

Ease of articulation seems to be the reason for the two most common phonological changes: (1) **deletion**, by which whole phonemes are lost, in some or all environments, and (2) **assimilation**, by which neighboring phonemes become like or more like one another. Loss of phonemes makes pronunciations shorter, and assimilations make them simpler.

Even when a phonological change is initiated by ease of articulation, it may spread partly by a desire for new ways of speaking, in order to attract attention to one's speech and to one's ideas. Ease of articulation suggests the new way of speaking, which spreads because of its social function of making ourselves more noticed.

2.1.1. Deletion

Deletion or loss of phonemes is probably found in the history of all languages. Some examples were mentioned in chapter 13, §2.2. Here are three more, two in English and one in Amharic.

a. English voiced stops after nasals. Word-final /b/, which was pronounced in Shakespeare's time, has been deleted at the end of words after nasal consonants. The old spellings survive, so we have words such as *thumb* /θəm/, *limb* /lɪm/, and *climb* /klɑjm/. Word-final /g/ has similarly been lost in most English dialects, as in *long* /lɔŋ/, *strong* /strɔŋ/, and *hang* /hæŋ/.

The earlier presence of the stop is shown not only by the spellings but by related words such as *thimble* /θɪmbəl/, *limber* /lɪmbər/, *longer* /lɔŋgər/, and *stronger* /strɔŋgər/, in which the stop survives. In these, with the presence of suffixes, the word-final environment of the deletion was not fulfilled.

Unlike labial /b/ and dorsal /g/, coronal /d/ was not invariably lost at the end of words after nasal consonants. But pronunciations without final /d/ are likely when a consonant follows, as in (a)–(d), but if a vowel follows the /d/ remains, as in (e)–(h):

Without [d]		*With [d]*	
a.	/hǽnkɑ̀rt/ handcart	e.	/hǽndi/ handy
b.	/sǽnglæ̀s/ sandglass	f.	/sǽndi/ sandy
c.	/hǽnðæ̀ttəmi/ Hand that to me.	g.	/hǽndɪtəmi/ Hand it to me.
d.	/ðəwìnstɑ́pt/ The wind stopped.	h.	/ðəwìndɪzstrɔ́ŋ/ The wind is strong.

The result of the historical (or **diachronic**) phonological change which deleted /d/ is an **alternation** (chapter 13, §1.2.1.1) in current English of /d/ and zero, an alternation which requires expression by a rule of the present-day (or **synchronic**) grammar of English. The rule is, approximately:

/d/ is deleted after /n/ before a consonant within the word or in the next word.

Recall that terms like '/d/', '/n/' and 'consonant' should be understood as feature sets; /d/ = [−sonorant, −continuant, +voiced], /n/ = [−continuant, +nasal], and consonant = [−vocoid] (as in chapter 14, §4.2).

b. English unstressed medial vowels. The loss of unstressed medial (neither initial or final) vowels has happened repeatedly in the history of English. It is apparent in the presence of contractions such as *can't, don't, I've, he'd,* and *it's*. These examples (out of many) show a deletion of unstressed vowels (and, in two cases, loss of word-initial /h/): /kænt/ < *cannot,* /dont/ < *do not,* /ɑjv/ < *I have,* /hid/ < *he had* (also /híəd/), and /ɪts/ < *it is*.

The earlier loss of unstressed vowels is apparent in the past tense suffix of words like *opened* /opənd/ and *washed* /wašt/, where the spelling shows the old vowel, which is preserved in words like *needed* /nídəd/ and *waited* /wétəd/, where loss would have resulted in a disallowed sequence of word-final coronal stops (and in a few relic adjectives including *naked* /nékəd/ and *wretched* /réčəd/).

Nowadays as well, unstressed medial vowels are lost in casual speech, if the result is an allowable sequence of consonants (see practice 6 of chapter 23). Words with such vowels have two pronunciations, in fast speech without the /ə/, and in careful speech where it is retained, as in *victory* /víkt(ə)ri/, *finally* /fájn(ə)li/, *happening* /hǽp(ə)nɪŋ/, and *probably* /práb(əb)li/ (in the latter, loss of /ə/ yields /bb/, which becomes /b/). The medial /ə/ has been lost in almost all pronunciations of the very frequent word *every* /évri/.

c. Amharic vowel deletion. In Amharic, an Ethiopian Semitic language, the high central vowel /ɨ/ is always lost when, historically, it was adjacent to other vowels, and synchronically when a morpheme with initial /ɨ/ follows another vowel. Two nouns that end in vowels are /bəqlo/ 'mule' and /wiša/ 'dog', and the 2nd person singular suffixes begin with /ɨ/: /-ɨh/ 'your, masculine' and /-ɨš/ 'your, feminine'. When these combine, ordinarily only the preceding vowel survives: /bəqloš/ 'your (f.) mule', /wišah/ 'your (m.) dog'. Two nouns that begin with /ɨ/ are /ɨwnət/ 'truth' and /ɨnč'ət/ 'wood', and two prefixes that end in vowels are /bə-/ 'in' and /jə-/ 'of'. When these combine, ordinarily only the prefix vowel survives: /bəwnət/ 'in truth' and /jənč'ət/ 'of wood'.

2.1.2. *Assimilation*

In **assimilation**, phones become like neighboring phones. Like deletions, assimilations are very common in the history of languages, and the history of probably every language involves some examples. Some examples were mentioned in chapter 13, §2.1, and here are three more, two in English and one in Amharic.

a. English obstruent voicing assimilation. Assimilation in the English plural (and past tense) suffix has been noted several times in preceding chapters (including chapter 13, §1.2.1.1). The suffix is [–voiced] after a voiceless consonant (a)–(c) and [+voiced] everywhere else (d)–(f):

a.	/bʊks/	books	d.	/bəgz/	bugs	
b.	/læmps/	lamps	e.	/pɪlz/	pills	
c.	/ræts/	rats	f.	/biz/	bees	

It was argued (chapter 13, §1.2.1.1) that /z/ must now be considered the basic form of the suffix, because /z/ appears where /s/ could also appear – in words ending in sonorants, like /kawz/ *cows* and /bʊlz/ *bulls*. This means the [–voiced] value of the final consonant in words like *book*, *lamp*, and *rat* spreads into the suffix. Such forward spread of a feature in assimilation is termed **progressive assimilation**.

b. English **nasal place assimilation**. In many languages, nasal consonants typically have the place of articulation of a following obstruent (stop or fricative). The English negative prefix *in-*, for example, is:

a. labial /ɪm/ before labial /p, b, m/, as in *impossible*, *imbalanced*, and *immovable*; and
b. velar /ɪŋ/ before velar /k/ and /g/, in fast speech, as in *incompetent* and *ingracious*. (In slow speech, /n/ and not /ŋ/ is pronounced.)
c. coronal /ɪn/ before coronal /t, d, s, z, n/ as in *intolerant*, *indecisive*, and *insincere*, and /ɪn/ before vowels, as in *ineligible* and *inactive*.

Such backward spread of a feature in assimilation is termed **regressive assimilation**. (That /n/ is pronounced before vowels, as in *ineligible*, where /m/ or /ŋ/ could also appear, shows that /ɪn/ is basic for the suffix.)

c. Amharic coronal palatalization. Another common phonological change is **palatalization**, by which consonants get an (alveo-)palatal articulation by assimilation to following high front vowels. In Amharic (as mentioned in chapter 13, §1.2.2.2), this assimilation affects coronal consonants including /t, d, s, z, n/, which become /č, ǰ, š, ž, ɲ/, respectively, when a suffix with initial /i/ or /e/ follows, as in the following 2nd person singular feminine imperatives with suffix /i/:

	'You-sg.m. __ !'	'You-sg.f. __ !'	
a.	/kɨfət/	/kɨfəč-i/	'open!'
b.	/wɨsəd/	/wɨsəǰ-i/	'take!'
c.	/lɨbəs/	/lɨbəš-i/	'put on!'
d.	/jɑz/	/jɑž-i/	'grab!'
e.	/zɨfən/	/zɨfəɲ-i/	'sing!'

A similar palatalization happens in English, when word-final /t, d, s, z/ precede /j/ in casual speech (recall that /j/ is like /i/ but [–syllabic]):

	Careful speech		Casual speech
a.	/hɪtju/	hit you	/hɪču/
b.	/sɛndju/	send you	/sɛnǰu/
c.	/kɪsju/	kiss you	/kɪšu/
d.	/rezju/	raise you	/režu/

2.1.3. Other phonological changes

Some phonological changes do not appear to fulfill a tendency toward easier articulations. Phones (a) get inserted (termed 'insertion'), (b) become different from neighboring phones ('dissimilation'), (c) are inverted ('metathesis'), and (d) change as part of a set of parallel changes in so-called 'chain shifts'. Here are a couple of examples of each of these.

2.1.3.1. Insertion.

An English example of **insertion** of a phone concerns the [b] of *number* and the [d] of *thunder*, which were inserted in these words in Middle English times: [numrə] became [nəmbər], and [θunrə] became [θəndər]. The change is somewhat mechanical, phonetically: notice that [m] and [n] have the characteristics of [b] and [d], except for the position of the velum, which is open in [m] and [n] allowing air to exit nasally during their articulation. If in the passage of [m] and [n] to following non-nasal [r] the velum is closed while the stop articulations remain, the result is [b] and [d]. While it is not obvious, it is possible that the result with inserted [b] and [d] is easier to articulate.

As the rarity of these examples suggest, in language change, insertions are much less common than deletions.

About the only common sort of insertion is of glides between vowels, as in Amharic, in which /j/ or /w/ is inserted between some vowel sequences. If the first vowel is /u/ or /o/, /w/ is inserted; if the first vowel is /i/ or /e/, /j/ is inserted: thus /fəlləgu-at/ 'they searched for her' becomes /fələguwat/, and /fəlligi-at/ 'Search (you, fem.) for her!' (imperative) becomes /fəlligijat/. Such insertions don't obviously contribute to easier articulation, but at least the glide seems to be a natural transition between the adjacent vowels.

2.1.3.2. Dissimilation.

Dissimilation is when neighboring phones become less like one another. Dissimilation is uncommon, but an example from child speech is the pronunciation /čɪmli/ for *chimney* /čɪmni/; here a nasal consonant after a nasal consonant is replaced by a lateral. An example of dissimilation between nonadjacent phones is *colonel* /kərnəl/, in which an /r/ replaced the first /l/ of original Italian *colonello*, a change which happened in French, from which English borrowed the word.

2.1.3.3. Metathesis.

In **metathesis** adjacent phones are inverted. The English word *ask* provides an example; it has two pronunciations: /æks/ and /æsk/, which appear to have been around for hundreds of years. The latter is typical, but /æks/ is regularly heard in some English dialects, including that of many

African Americans. The two pronunciations may seem equally 'easy', but one is easier when the past tense suffix is added: compare /ækst/ and /æskt/.

In Hebrew, /t/ of the reflexive ('self') prefix /hit-/ ordinarily precedes the verb stem, as in (a)–(c) below, but metathesizes with the initial /s, z, š, ts/ of the verb stem, as in (d)–(g) (Bolozky 1997):

a.	/-nages/	'collide'	/hitnages/	'collide (mutually)'
b.	/-pina/	'remove'	/hitpana/	'remove oneself'
c.	/-konen/	'establish'	/hitkonen/	'get ready'
d.	/-saken/	'endanger'	/histaken/	'take a risk'
e.	/-zaken/	'get old'	/hizdaken/	'grow old'
f.	/-šameš/	'be used as'	/hištameš/	'use'
g.	/-tsamek/	'shrivel' (vt.)	/hitstamek/	'shrivel up'

By providing potential syllable heads of /st, zd, št/ versus /ts, dz, tš/, this metathesis rule perhaps yields preferable syllable structures (chapter 14, §3.2), but this is not obvious.

2.1.3.4. Chain-shifts. Systematic far-reaching sound changes like the English Great Vowel Shift (chapter 23, §2.2.1.1) may transform a whole set of phonological distinctions. Another **chain-shift** of English vowel qualities has been found underway today in northern American cities, according to which /æ/ becomes /eᵊ/ or even /iᵊ/, so that *that* is pronounced /ðeᵊt/, and /ɑ/ becomes fronted as /æ/, so that *lock* is pronounced /læk/. Such changes do not seem to result in easier articulations, just different ones. It is not known what causes such changes.

2.2. Expression of new meanings

Because societies change, there is always a need to express new meanings in languages. The characteristic of **openness** (chapters 15 and 16) enables languages readily to create new words to express the new things, events, and ideas that come along.

2.2.1. New things

Open for business in 1993 was the *Channel Tunnel*, a name immediately shortened to *Chunnel*. Of course there are words for new technology, including for the central processing units of personal computers, *CPUs* of *PCs*, which are acronyms, *fax*, clipped from *facsimile*, and for a new medical procedure, *electroencephalography*, a derivation. Unfortunately, also among the new things are new diseases, for example *bird flu*, a compound (with *flu* clipped from *influenza*), and another compound *acquired immune deficiency syndrome*, immediately shortened as *AIDS*, an acronym.

2.2.2. New events

Meetings between heads of state become common, called *summits*, clipped from *summit meeting*, a compound with metaphoric extension of *summit*, and spectacular sports events are held, such as the *Super Bowl*, whose name is a compound which combines hyperbole (*super*) and metaphor (*bowl*). An important cyclic weather event has been recognized and named *El niño*, a borrowing from Spanish 'the child', short for 'the Christ child', a metonymic extension (association in time), since the warm ocean current which is this weather event's basis gets underway around Christmas time.

2.2.3. New ideas

Words for new ideas include *stagflation*, a blend of *stagnation* and *inflation*, and *e-mail*, a partial acronym-compound. Among the new words for types of entertainment are *soaps*, clipped from *soap operas*, a compound with extension ('opera for selling soap'), *sexploitation*, blended from *sex* and *exploitation*, and *edutainment*, another blend.

The ideas of other societies may be adopted along with the words that name them. The words are said to be **borrowed** from the other language, and the other language is said to 'lend' the words (though, unlike other borrowings, the words don't have to be returned to the lender). Borrowed words, if they become common, soon cease to be recognized as borrowings. A hundred years ago, French words in use in English including *amateur*, *envelope*, and *unique* were perhaps as recognizably foreign as *double entendre* and *discotheque* are today.

2.3. Desire for novelty

New words especially arise in two social contexts which suggest that their purpose, at least partly, is not a need to express new meanings, but a simple desire for novelty of expression: in **jargon** and **slang**.

2.3.1. Jargon

All the devices of getting new words (13 of which were discussed chapters 15 and 16) are employed in creating **jargon**, the specialized vocabulary of professional and occupational groups. The words of specialists often seem unnecessarily novel, and even obfuscatory, to those outside a specialization, but they are probably considered useful by the specialists.

2.3.1.1. Linguistic role of jargon.
Computer programmers, for example, regularly need to refer to unidentified problems in computer programs, and reasonably extended, by metaphor, the word *bug* for this. Linguists need often to refer to the specialized meaning aspect of grammars, distinct from the ordinary, broad, sense of 'meaning', and have derived the term *semantics* for this. The police need

saddle 'seat'

roller skate 'small car'

four '10–4' (= 'end of message')

XYL 'wife' (< ex-young lady)

coax 'coaxial cable for antenna'

rodadio 'CB radio' (< road radio)

Popeye 'vehicle with one headlight'

shake the trees 'look out for police'

greenstamps 'money'

slick top 'police car without roof lights'

Figure 24.1   Some words of truckers' jargon
Source: *Jason's Authentic Dictionary of CB Slang* 1976

often to refer to the characteristic means and practice of criminals, and for this purpose have shortened the Latin phrase *modus operandi* as the acronym *MO*. In the 1970s, long-distance truck drivers in the US using their CB (citizen's-band) radios developed an extensive jargon including the words of figure 24.1.

Some English-speaking professions have traditionally had knowledge of foreign languages, such as the medical profession (German), musicians (Italian), and linguists (French), and their members have used words from these languages when writing and speaking to others of their profession who are expected to recognize them. When this happens often and repeatedly, the foreign words may become customary. (This starts out as 'code-switching', discussed below in chapters 26, §3.3.2, and 27, §2.3.1.5.) The terminology of English linguistics, for example, includes French *portmanteau*, *calque*, and, recently, *tableau* (the meanings of which are unimportant here). Of course, if the foreign word doesn't add any meaning not fully available in the borrowing language, its use is just 'showing off'.

2.3.1.2.   Social roles of jargon.   Besides its linguistic purpose to express new meanings, jargon is motivated by at least three probably unconsciously fulfilled social purposes of its creators.

a.   Argot. Jargon may play the roll of an **argot** to obfuscate – to keep others from understanding. (The French word *argot* is sometimes used as synonymous with jargon.)

b.   Euphemism. In some cases, jargon may be intended to make objectionable meanings less objectionable. This is called **euphemism**. Examples of euphemism are *preowned car* for *used car*, *pass away* for *die*, *Department of Defence* for *Department of War*, and *protection* for *condom* (cases of derivation, compound, extension/metonymy, and extension/metaphor, respectively).

c.   In-group markers. Jargon which fulfills any of the above purposes also serves the additional purpose, if again an unconscious one, of **in-group marking**, enabling members of the occupational group to announce themselves as such, and to recognize each other by how they talk. In-group markers, whether pins, uniforms, or special forms of language, promote solidarity or cohesiveness, as well as exclusivity and snobbery, within the group.

2.3.2. Slang

Slang is the specialized vocabulary of social groups, especially young social groups. Like jargon, slang also illustrates all the means of new word formation: extension, derivation, clipping, borrowing, etc. Unlike jargon, slang perhaps rarely has the linguistic purpose of expressing new meanings, but ordinarily starts out as just clever alternative ways of saying things which the language has other ways of saying. Examples include *wheels* for *car*, *rad* for *radical*, and *ID* for *identification* (cases of extension/synecdoche, clipping, and acronyming, respectively). In figure 24.2 are presented some reported examples of 'Los Angeles gang talk'. Perhaps this could be considered a 'thieves' argot', except that many of the words don't necessarily concern this line of work.

The need for marking one's speech, to attract attention to what one is saying, is particularly present in close social groups. We especially want our friends to pay attention to us. Also, within close social groups very familiar things are discussed, such as fun, food, friends, and enemies. This gets old, of course, so there is good reason to try to create some novelty. Also, the main purpose of a lot of casual talk among friends is social play and building social relationships ('grooming', in the animal world), in which cleverness or cuteness are valued. The new words, if cute and clever or useful enough, may spread within the social group, and come to serve as markers of the group.

Since its purpose is the creation of novelty and the display of cleverness, slang, unless it spreads into the common language and displaces old words, usually fades quickly with repetition (like *groovy* and *rad*). Cleverness depends on novelty, and the novelty wears off.

Slang will be perceived as excessively informal and even crude by those outside the social group in which it originates. But if it is found helpful or clever enough by the general population, it may spread and eventually cease to be slang. Some examples of English words which started out as slang and made their way into the ordinary language are *bus*, *throw up*, *gay*, *ID*, *jazz*, and *marijuana* (clipping, compound, extension, acronym, invention (?), and borrowing, respectively).

bud 'marijuana'	g-ride 'stolen car'
bullet 'one year in jail'	hooptie 'car'
drag 'flirt with'	jacked 'hassled by police'
dope 'good' ('play that dope tape')	pisto 'drunk'
drop a dime 'inform (to the police)'	rata 'informer, snitch'
double deuce '22 caliber'	smack 'African American gang talk'

Figure 24.2 Some words of Los Angeles gang slang
Source: Los Angeles Times Magazine, May 5, 1991

2.4. Regularization

2.4.1. Regularization in morphology: rule extension

A principle which was mentioned as generally at work in the creation of new words is the **one form/one meaning principle**: one form should have one meaning, and one meaning one form (chapter 16, §2.6.2). Especially child learners don't expect there to be two ways of saying the same thing, and when there seem to be (potentially) two forms for some meaning, for example, *rided* or *rode* and *feeded* or *fed*, they favor the more regular, or that formed by the more general or frequently applying rule, a tendency overcome only when the irregular form is very frequent. Illustrating the human language characteristic of **creativity** (chapter 1, §3.4.3), child learners come up with words which they haven't heard, by applying the rule for similar frequent words the formation of which they know; thus the English past tense verb *dreamt* is being replaced by *dreamed* and *lit* by *lighted*, and plural noun *fish* is being replaced by *fishes* and *thieves* by *thiefs*. (*Fish/fishes* also illustrates an alternative to replacement, bifurcation (chapter 16, §2.6), *fish* now established as the regular plural with *fishes* preserved in the narrower meaning 'varieties or species of fish'.)

Adults, though more experienced than children and somewhat more tolerant of variation, can't be expected to know their language perfectly, either, especially concerning the use of rare and even low frequency words and constructions, for example, *striven* as the past participle of *strive*, and *lit* as the past tense of *light*. Like child learners, they tend to extend the general rule in such cases, favoring *strived* and *lighted*.

The result of **rule extension** by children and adults is **regularization** of the grammar, as productive rules encompass more cases and nonproductive rules fewer (chapter 23, §2.2.2.2–3).

2.4.2. Regularization in the lexicon: leveling

We saw that with rule extension the contrast of different forms, resulting from the coexistence of productive and nonproductive rules for the same meaning, is lost or 'leveled' (chapter 23, §2.2.2.4).

The result of **leveling**, again whether by children or adults, is regularization or **simplification** of the lexical entries of morphemes with suppletive allomorphs. For example, English verbs with *-(e)n* past participles, such as *strive/striven*, *wake/woken*, and *mow(n)*, have to be lexically complex, including both the frequent basic form and the infrequent past participle: 'strive' /strɑjv, strɪvən/, 'wake' /wek, wokən/, and 'mow' /mo(n)/. In leveling, such a complex lexical entry is simplified by loss of the infrequent or secondary form: /strɑjv/, /wek/, and /mo/. (Common parts should be shared between allomorphs in the representation, for example /str{ɑj, <ɪ>}v<ən>/; that is, /str...v/ is shared, /ɑj/ contrasts with /ɪ/, and /ɪ/ goes with /ən/.)

2.4.3. Regularization in syntax

The analogical extension of *do*-insertion for negative sentences and questions was mentioned in the previous chapter. A more recent case of regularization in syntax concerns the rise of *hopefully* in sentences like 1, below, in which *hopefully* describes the attitude of the speaker (hopeful) towards the timely arrival of the train.

1. Hopefully, the train will be on time.
2. They waited hopefully for the train.
3. Hopefully, they waited for the train.

Sentence 2 shows the older use of *hopefully*, in which it describes the attitude of those who waited. Sentence 3 is ambiguous between these two uses (they were hopeful about the arrival of the train, or the speaker hopes that they waited). Perhaps because of such ambiguities, usage as in 1 has arisen, with resulting objection by critics of language change.

But *hopefully* as in 1 follows perfectly the pattern of adverbs like *sadly* and *certainly*, as in 4 and 5:

4. Sadly the train is always late;
5. Certainly the train is always late;

and the parallelism of 4 and 5 suggests a regularity which English speakers will readily extend to new cases, as follows, where 'S' is for 'sentence', for example, *the train will be late/on time*:

I am certain that S.:   Certainly S.
I am sad that S.:   Sadly S.
I am hopeful that S.:   ____ S.

2.5. Redundancy reduction

Redundancy is excess. Languages have redundancy when there are two forms, usually two pronunciations, for the same meaning: violations of the one form/one meaning principle. **Redundancy reduction** eliminates the violations by eliminating one of the forms, and in this sense all regularizations and levelings are redundancy reductions.

2.5.1. *Bifurcation as redundancy reduction*

One solution to the existence of two forms for one meaning is **bifurcation** (chapter 16, §2.6), by which the single meaning of two forms is split into two meanings each with its form. *Fish* and *fishes*, for example, tends to be split as 'plural fish' and 'varieties of fish' respectively. Such a development shows that redundancy is not necessarily bad, since, by one interpretation of the one form/one meaning principle, there should be two meanings for two forms, so the two forms may motivate the discovery of new meanings (though it is never clear how and when this happens in language change). Similarly, *e-mail*, originally an acronym for *electronic mail*, is now understood as a very specific sort of electronic mail (not a fax message, for example, which also arrives electronically).

2.5.2. *Simplification as redundancy reduction*

Redundancy also exists in language when part of the form of a word or morpheme is predictable from or duplicates the function of another part. **Redundancy reduction** is losing the predictable or duplicating part. For many English speakers, there are fast-speech pronunciations of past tense verbs like *kept* [kɛpt] and *slept* [slɛpt] in which the past tense suffix is omitted: [kɛp], and [slɛp]. But this deletion of [t] does not happen in similar verbs like *reaped* and *heaped*. The important difference between the two sets of verbs is that the former have a vowel alternation in addition to suffixation to mark the past tense: *keep/kept, sleep/slept* versus *reap/reaped, heap/heaped*. The presence of the lower vowel [ɛ] in past tense forms apparently makes the suffix [t] redundant and dispensable.

Following are three more examples of probable redundancy reduction in language change.

a.   English voiceless stop deletion after nasals. We saw that English word-final voiced stops were lost after nasals, as in [lɪm], [lɔŋ], and, before consonants, [lɛn], pronunciations respectively of *limb*, *long*, and *lend* (§2.1.1, above). Voiceless stops are not completely lost in the same environment, but, in some dialects, when these are word-final except before initial vowels of following words, they are 'reduced' to a glottal stop, as in [læmʔ] *lamp*, [lɪŋʔ] *link*, and [lɛnʔ] *lent*. This may be understood as redundancy reduction because the missing place of articulation of each stop is reflected in the nasal consonant of each word: [m] before [p], [ŋ] before [k], and [n] before [t].

b.   Amharic palatalization. We saw that Amharic coronal consonants /t, d, s, z, n/ are palatalized before the suffix /i/ (§2.1.2c, above). Furthermore, the suffix may be absent when the palatalizations are present, so that besides /kɨfəči/ 'open! (fem. sg.)' and /wɨsə̌ji/ 'take! (fem. sg.)', also heard are /kɨfəč/ and /wɨsəǰ/. The palatalizations appear to have become understood as forms of the meaning originally expressed by the suffix /i/. This makes the suffix itself redundant and omissible.

c.   French *ne...pas*. Standard French negative verbs have *ne* before the verb and *pas* after: *il parle*, 'he speaks', *il ne parle pas*, 'he doesn't speak', *tu vends*, 'you sell', *tu ne vends pas*, 'you don't sell'. Like perhaps *do* in English questions and negatives, the use of *pas* arose as a marker of emphaticness. In current colloquial spoken French, however, *ne* may be omitted: *il parle pas, tu vends pas*. It appears that *pas*, which tends to receive stress versus *ne* which doesn't, has become recognized as the primary marker of negation, and *ne* as secondary, redundant, and unnecessary.

2.6. Metanalysis

Metanalysis was noted (in chapters 15, §3.4 and 16, §2.7) as the process involved in **backformation**. Learners and even mature users of a language analyze a word, phrase, or sentence in a new way, and then start using the parts of that analysis. They may do this as a way of being clever, or because of imperfect learning.

2.6.1. Clever metanalysis

A case of presumably clever metanalysis has recently resulted in the new suffix -*oholic*: the word *alcoholic* was analyzed, perhaps jokingly, as *alc-oholic*, and the resulting suffix now appears in *chocoholic*, *workaholic*, etc. Another is -*festation*, seen in *fleafestation* and *tickfestation* and probably originating in metanalysis of *infestation* as *in* + *festation*.

Some bifurcations (chapter 16, §2.6) may be cases of clever metanalysis, as, for example, *shoppe* used in names of shops which sell antique or traditional goods (versus a *shop*, which sells ordinary goods). This may show recognition of archaicness of spelling with a doubled consonant plus *e*, in words like *programme*, which spelling is then employed as a visual suffix meaning 'authentic, traditional'.

2.6.2. Naive metanalysis

Naive metanalysis, resulting not from cleverness but from misunderstanding, has given us a number of English nouns with initial vowels, when their original initial /n/ was metanalyzed as part of the indefinite article: *a nadder* > *an adder*, and *a napron* > *an apron* (chapter 15, §3.4). A case of naive metanalysis now underway is apparent when contractions like *would've* and *should've* are written *would of* and *should of*, because, quite reasonably, the [əv] of such words ([wʊdəv], [šʊdəv]) is identified with *of*. Indeed, *have* is a purely grammatical morpheme here, with only historical connection to lexical *have* 'possess', and no more sensible than *of*.

2.7. Obsolescence of meanings

Obsolete meanings disappear from language as obsolete things and ideas disappear from use. Almost gone from English in recent years, for example, are the words *icebox*, *choke* (of an automobile), and *telegram*, following the things they express into history and old movies.

2.8. Language contact

The causes of language change noted above are all **internal causes**, forces from within the language. But perhaps the most important force in language change is an **external cause: language contact**. Prolonged and intimate contact between languages – actually, of course, between speakers of the languages – often results in extensive language change, especially when one of the languages is numerically or politically dominant, and especially also when much of the population speaks both languages. There are many cases of thorough language change under the influence of language contact. Following are examples illustrating contact-induced change in each of lexicon, phonology, morphology, and syntax.

2.8.1. Lexicon

It was mentioned (chapter 23, §2.1) that English has a surprising number of French loanwords dating from the time of intense English–French contact after the Norman conquest of Britain. The earlier present language is termed the **substratum** language, in this case English. The later arriving language is the **superstratum** language, in this case French.

Even earlier, language contact resulting from the Danish occupation of eastern Britain from about 850 AD resulted in borrowings in Old English of a number of common words of basic vocabulary, including those which come down to us as *get, give, take, they, both, dirt, egg, seat, sister, skin,* and *sky*.

2.8.2. Phonology

The Indoeuropean languages of southern India (Hindi the most populous) have coronal retroflex consonants (IPA [ʈ, ɖ, ɳ]) in which the tongue tip 'retroflects', and contacts the roof of the mouth behind the alveolar ridge. Outside India, Indoeuropean languages lack these consonants, which, however, are common also in the non-Indoeuropean Dravidian languages spoken in southern India (of which Tamil and Telugu are the most populous). The Indoeuropean languages must have acquired the retroflex consonants as a result of contact with Dravidian substratum languages.

2.8.3. Morphology

The Cushitic language Ma'a is somewhat separated from other Cushitic languages of East Africa, and has long been neighbor to a number of Bantu languages in southern Tanzania. Probably as a result of this contact, a variety of Ma'a employs characteristically Bantu noun class prefixes (illustrated from Swahili in chapter 5, §1.4.2), such as [mu-/βa-] and [iʔ-/maʔ-], which distinguish singular and plural in words like:

a. [mu-he] 'a man', [βa-he] 'men'
b. [iʔ-ila] 'eye', [maʔ-ila] 'eyes'

Extensive borrowing of grammatical morphology is rare, except in contexts of long and close language contact.

2.8.4. Syntax

The Ethiopian Semitic languages including Amharic, exemplified often above, are intimate neighbors of Cushitic languages in Northeast Africa. Ethiopians are often bilingual, and many speak Semitic and Cushitic languages. Semitic languages outside Ethiopia typically have prepositions, as does the usually representative Semitic language Arabic. By contrast, the Ethiopian Semitic languages have a number of postpositions, as seen in Amharic. Postpositions are common in the Cushitic languages of Ethiopia, such as Sidamo, and it is likely that Ethiopian Semitic languages have acquired postpositions under the influence of Cushitic contact languages.

a. Arabic prepositions
   1. [min bajtī]   'from my house' ([bajt] 'house')
   2. [ʔila l-baħri]   'to the sea' ([baħr] 'sea')
b. Amharic postpositions
   3. [bet wɨst']   'in the house' ([bet] 'house')
   4. [ɨne ga]   'with me' ([ɨne] 'me')
c. Sidamo postpositions
   5. [mini-ra]   'to the house' ([mini] 'house')
   6. [faraššo-nni]   'on a horse' ([faraššo] 'horse')

3. CONFLICTING DIRECTIONS OF LANGUAGE CHANGE

Some language changes tend to simplify forms, as when deletion shortens words, such as [prábli] from *probably*, and when regularization eliminates minority patterns of grammar, as where *striven* is replaced by *strived*. Other changes, however, produce opposite effects, as when derivation yields new, long, words such as *symptomologically*, and metanalysis produces new patterns of grammar, for example *would of* as an alternative to *would have*.

Language change regularly presents new possibilities, which users of language evaluate and choose among, if ordinarily unconsciously. It is reasonable to suppose that, overall, the result of language change is language continually renewed and maximally well fitted to its purpose.

Suggestions for
ADDITIONAL READING

Textbooks of historical linguistics mentioned at the end of the previous chapter ordinarily offer explanations of language change as well as examples of change. The book *Language Change: Progress or Decay?* (1991), by Jean Aitchison, argues against the common, popular, belief that language changes for the worse. Much of Aitchison's book is concerned, also, with presenting the causes of language change. The book *Language: the Loaded Weapon* (1980) by Dwight Bolinger is an entertaining exposition of how we twist and change language, often purposefully, to trick and persuade others.

IMPORTANT CONCEPTS AND TERMS IN THIS CHAPTER

- ease of articulation
- deletion
- assimilation
- progressive assimilation
- regressive assimilation
- palatalization
- insertion
- dissimilation
- metathesis
- chain-shift
- openness
- borrowed words
- jargon
- argot
- euphemism
- in-group marker

- slang
- one form/one meaning principle
- creativity
- rule extension
- regularization
- leveling
- simplification
- redundancy reduction
- bifurcation
- metanalysis
- backformation
- internal causes
- external causes
- language contact
- substratum
- superstratum

OUTLINE OF CHAPTER 24

4. Regularization
   1. Regularization in morphology: rule extension
   2. Regularization in the lexicon: leveling
   3. Regularization in syntax
5. Redundancy reduction
   1. Bifurcation as redundancy reduction
   2. Simplification as redundancy reduction
6. Metanalysis
   1. Clever metanalysis
   2. Naive metanalysis
7. Obsolescence of meanings
8. Language contact
   1. Lexicon
   2. Phonology
   3. Morphology
   4. Syntax
3. **Conflicting directions of language change**

EXAMPLES AND PRACTICE

EXAMPLE

1. Sidamo past tense verbs. Sidamo is a language of Ethiopia. Some of the following Sidamo data were seen in practice 6 of chapter 13.

A. Sidamo past tense verbs are formed by suffixing, as in (a)–(d).

a.	murí	'he cut'	murtú	'she cut'
b.	ganí	'he hit'	gantú	'she hit'
c.	malí	'he advised'	maltú	'she advised'
d.	ití	'he ate'	ittú	'she ate'

PRACTICE

Answer these questions about Sidamo verb formation.

1. What are the four verb stems of (a)–(d)?
2. What are the suffixes for 'he' and 'she'?

B. Sometimes there is assimilation, as in (e)–(h).

e.	agí	'he drank'	aggú	'she drank'
f.	k'aafí	'he walked'	k'aaffú	'she walked'
g.	hasí	'he sought'	hassú	'she sought'
h.	ledí	'he added'	leddú	'she added'

3. What are the four verb stems of (e)–(h)?
4. What kind of rule applies in the second column?

C. Sometimes there is an insertion, as in (i)–(l).

i.	dandí	'he was able'	danditú	'she was able
j.	sirbí	'he sang'	sirbitú	'she sang'
k.	wiʔlí	'he cried out'	wiʔlitú	'she cried out'
l.	ofollí	'he sat'	ofollitú	'she sat'

5. What are the four verb stems of (i)–(l)?
6. What kind of rule applies in the second column, and what characteristic generally distinguishes these verb stems from those of (a)–(h)?

D. Consider these 'we' forms.

m.	dandinummo	'we were able'
n.	sirbinummo	'we sang'
o.	wiʔlinummo	'we cried out'
p.	ofollinummo	'we sat'

7. Assuming the same insertion rule of (i)–(l), what is the 'we' suffix?

E. Now consider the verbs of (q)–(t).

q.	agummo	'I drank'	aŋgummo	'we drank'
r.	k'aafummo	'I walked'	k'aamfummo	'we walked'
s.	hasummo	'I sought'	hansummo	'we sought'
t.	ledummo	'I added'	lendummo	'we added'

8. What is the first person singular, 'I', suffix?
9. What happens when the 'we' suffix is added to these verb stems?
10. Why does the 'we' suffix appear with [ŋ] in 'we drank' and with [m] in 'we walked'?

EXAMPLE

2. Trucker's jargon/CB jargon. Here are five more examples of truckers' jargon, in addition to those in §2.3.1.1, above.

Charlie	'FCC' (Federal Communication Commission)
ptomaine palace	'bad place to eat'
thin	'weak' (of radio signal)
post	'mile post' (post marking one-mile distance)
negatory	'no, negative'

Of the 12 ways to create new words noted in chapters 15 and 16, CB or truckers' jargon uses several. For example, perhaps *negatory* illustrates derivation (*negate* + *ory*).

PRACTICE

Mention five more different types of new-word formation, with examples, exemplified in the words of truckers' jargon above and in §2.3.1.1.

EXAMPLE

3. Deletions and assimilations in casual English speech. Consider the following phonetically written English sentence, as spoken in ordinary casual speech:

[d ì ǰ ʊ r g r ǽ m p ɑ ī n ó r g ə̄ n p è ɪ z f è̱ ɖ r ə l ɪ́ ŋ k ə̄ m t ǽ k s l ǽ s č ɪ r]

'Did your grandpa in Oregon pay his federal income tax last year?'

PRACTICE

List examples of 10 deletions and/or assimilations by which the sentence above differs from a pronunciation of the same sentence in slow and careful speech. For example:

[d] of 'grand' is deleted.

EXAMPLE

4. Borrowings in English. English has borrowed words from many other languages, and the borrowings are evidence of significant events and periods in the history of the English-speaking people. For example, *bungalow* and *bandana*, from Hindi, reflect the need to express the tropical life encountered by the British in their Indian colony, and *karaoke*, from Japanese, reflects the prevalence of Japanese electronics goods in current life.

PRACTICE

Look up the following words in a dictionary that gives etymologies, and for each give its source language and suggest what historical contact between English speakers and others might have led to its having been borrowed by English: *curry*, *satan*, *coffee*, *almanac*, *okra*, *safari*, *typhoon*, *sarong*.

EXAMPLE

5. Obsolete meanings. Some nouns fading from English in recent decades are *telex*, *phonograph*, and *telegram*. *Fountain pen* may be fading as well.

PRACTICE

Think of at least five more such words which you think are obsolete or likely to become so. Explain why you think the words are or might soon become obsolete (even though you may consider the reasons to be obvious).

LANGUAGE FAMILIES

This chapter concerns the classification of languages into descent groups, or families, how these are known and established, and how the forms of ancient unwritten languages may be known. Pidgin languages are shown to have exceptional origins.

1. HOW MANY LANGUAGES ARE THERE?

Estimates of how many languages there are in the world range from four to six thousand, but there is yet no complete census of the world's languages, and accurate descriptions, grammars and dictionaries are still lacking for most of these. Even distinguishing one language from another is a problem, because one language may have several names, including the names of its dialects, and different languages may be known by the same name.

Especially three sorts of cases make an accurate count of the world's languages difficult:

1.1. Chinese-type cases

Different languages may be thought of as one language. Properly, mutually intelligible varieties of one language are best thought of as dialects of the language, for example, British and American English. But mutually unintelligible varieties are different languages, for example Mandarin Chinese and Cantonese, also often known as 'Chinese'. Because of the long political unity of their speakers and the fact that they both use the same Chinese writing system (chapter 22, §2.1), Mandarin, Cantonese, and a number of quite different languages including some quite populous, such as Shanghai and Taiwanese, are all commonly called 'Chinese'.

1.2. Swedish/Norwegian-type cases

Mutually intelligible varieties are sometimes counted as different languages, especially if their speakers are politically separated. Swedish and Norwegian, for example, are dialects of one language. Another example is Hindi, of India, and Urdu, of Pakistan, one language with two names, spoken in different countries and using different writing systems. Hindi is written with the Devanagari writing system, while Urdu, whose speakers are mostly Muslim, is written with the Arabic writing system.

1.3. Arabic-type cases: diglossia

Sometimes there is mutual unintelligibility between the casual or vernacular variety and the formal or standard variety of a single language. This circumstance is called **diglossia**, and it exists to some degree in many widespread speech communities: imagine a lawyer who cannot be fully understood by her teenage children when she talks in legalese to other lawyers, and who cannot fully understand her teenagers when they talk familiarly to others. Diglossia is extreme in the Arab world, where the casual language of everyday affairs and the formal language of newscasts and newspapers are quite different, as if these were different languages. However, a speaker of Arabic is ordinarily a speaker of both varieties, so there is little mutual unintelligibility between speakers of the two.

2. Language families

The explanation of the multiplicity of languages in the world today is the combination of social separations between people and constant language change, over many thousands of years. Languages are always changing, and populations speaking one language have, at least in the past, repeatedly split up, with the result that the separated peoples eventually speak different languages. The result of social separation plus language change is at first **dialects**, mutually intelligible varieties of a language. With the passage of time, however, wider social separation between dialect groups and continued language change results in new **languages**, mutually non-intelligible varieties, as suggested in the the diagram of figure 25.1.

The result of this simple process of separation and differentiation, taking place time after time over thousands of years, is the thousands of languages of the world, many of which have been classified into **language families**, each of which consists of the languages descended from an earlier language. The map of figure 25.2 (from Ruhlen 1987) shows one rather controversial classification of the languages of the world into 19 families plus a number of **isolates**, languages not yet shown to be part of the larger groups; for another such map, which presents 29 families, see Crystal (1987, p. 294).

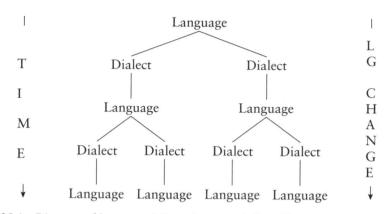

Figure 25.1   Diagram of language differentiation and diversification

See as figure 25.3 a list of ten widespread language families with representative languages, and as figure 25.4 the list of the world's 12 most populous languages (from various recent estimates).

English is an **Indoeuropean** language, descended from the Indoeuropean **protolanguage** spoken at least six thousand years ago perhaps in southeastern Europe, perhaps northeastern Turkey. The speakers of this ancient language spread and separated from one another, resulting, at some intermediate time, in several Indoeuropean languages, which themselves fragmented resulting in more languages and, eventually, the hundred or so Indoeuropean languages whose hypothetical historical relationships of progressive divergence are suggested in the **family-tree** diagram of figure 25.5.

The **Afroasiatic** family of languages, which includes Arabic, Hebrew, and Egyptian, began to diverge perhaps over seven thousand years ago, probably in northeastern Africa. The Afroasiatic protolanguage was probably spoken in northeastern Africa, and spread and differentiated as suggested by the Afroasiatic family tree, shown as figure 25.6.

A language family, then, is the set of co-descendant languages of an earlier language. Every modern language is a member of a language family, even if the family has only one known member, and every language family consists of descendants of a language spoken in prehistoric times. A language family is somewhat like a human family, except that there is just one parent, not two. The member languages of a language family are sometimes called **sibling languages** (in older terminology, 'sister' languages), and the language from which sibling languages descend is the **parent language**, or **protolanguage**.

3. ORIGIN OF LANGUAGE

At one or more times and places in the prehistory of humankind, people began to associate meanings with vocalizations, and elaborated their use of these verbal

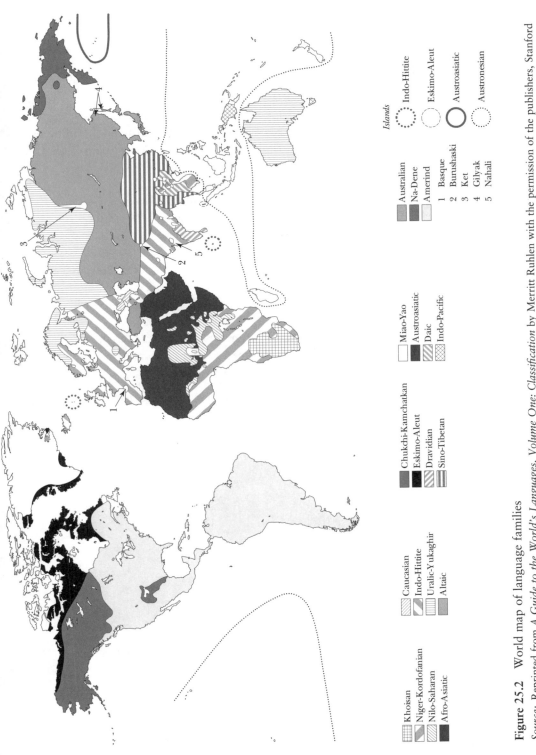

Figure 25.2 World map of language families

Source: Reprinted from *A Guide to the World's Languages, Volume One: Classification* by Merritt Ruhlen with the permission of the publishers, Stanford University Press, © 1987, 1991 by the Board of Trustees of the Leland Stanford Junior University

Family	Three languages of the family
1. Afroasiatic	Arabic, Hebrew, Hausa (Nigeria)
2. Amerind	Navajo (Arizona), Mayan (Mexico), Quechua (Bolivia, Peru)
3. Altaic	Japanese, Turkish, Mongolian
4. Austroasiatic	Vietnamese, Thai, Khmer (Cambodian)
5. Austronesian	Indonesian/Malay, Hawaiian, Tagalog (Philippines)
6. Dravidian	Tamil (India and Sri Lanka), Malayalam (India), Telegu (India)
7. Indoeuropean	
a. Germanic	English, German, Swedish/Norwegian
b. Celtic	Irish, Welsh, Breton (France)
c. Italic	Spanish, French, Portuguese
d. Slavic	Russian, Polish, Czech
e. Indo-Iranian	Hindi, Bengali (India, Bangladesh), Persian/Farsi (Iran)
8. Niger-Khordofanian	Swahili, Yoruba (Nigeria), Wolof (Sierra Leone)
9. Sino-Tibetan	
a. Sinitic	Mandarin Chinese, Cantonese, Hunanese
b. Tibeto-Burman	Tibetan, Burmese, Lahu (Thailand)
10. Uralic	Finnish, Hungarian, Estonian

Figure 25.3   Ten widespread language families and example languages

1.	Mandarin Chinese (UN)	775 million speakers
2.	English (UN, IE)	345
3.	Spanish (UN, IE)	300
4.	Hindi (IE)	160
5.	Arabic (UN)	160
6.	Portuguese (IE)	150
7.	Indonesian/Malay	150
8.	Russian (UN, IE)	150
9.	Bengali (IE)	150
10.	Japanese	125
11.	French (UN, IE)	115
12.	German (IE)	100

Total: 2,690 million (2.69 billion)*

Figure 25.4   The world's 12 most populous languages

* About 55% of world population

UN: One of six official languages of the United Nations

IE: Indoeuropean language

Population figures are 1990 estimates of numbers of native speakers of the languages, based on various sources

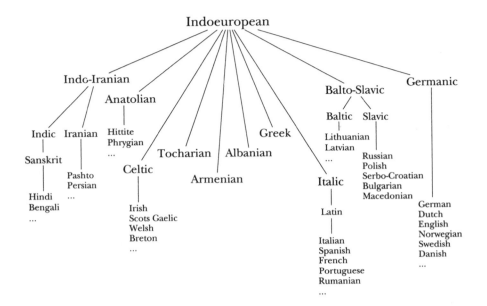

Figure 25.5 Indoeuropean

signs into languages as we know them. This development of language almost certainly evolved over thousands of years. How and how long ago it happened remains quite speculative, since there is little agreement concerning underlying issues: (1) the definition of *language* or of 'language as we know it', (2) the biological and social conditions necessary for its development, and (3) the nature of archaeological evidence that would support the presence of language in pre-historic societies, such as use of tools and the employment of decoration and art. Guesses about the approximate time of origin of language range from 50,000 to a million years ago.

We saw in chapter 12 that there is no evidence of language as we know it in the nearest relatives of humans, chimpanzees, from whom we separated about six million years ago, a fact which is evidence that language must have arisen since the time of that separation. Anatomically modern humans, *homo sapiens sapiens*, appear to date from about 200,000–150,000 years ago, an event followed shortly by an increase of brain size, and the use of fire, finely shaped tools, ornamentation, and art, all from about 75,000–50,000 years ago.

According to the hypothesis of **monogenesis** of language, language was invented or developed only once in human history, so all languages descend from that one original language. The hypothesis of monogenesis is favored by those who believe that language is an extraordinarily unique achievement and unlikely to have arisen more than once. Those who believe that language must be the inevitable result of the natural drive for communication in human societies everywhere tend to favor the contrary hypothesis of **polygenesis**, that languages derive from multiple origins. It is possible that all modern languages are descendants of

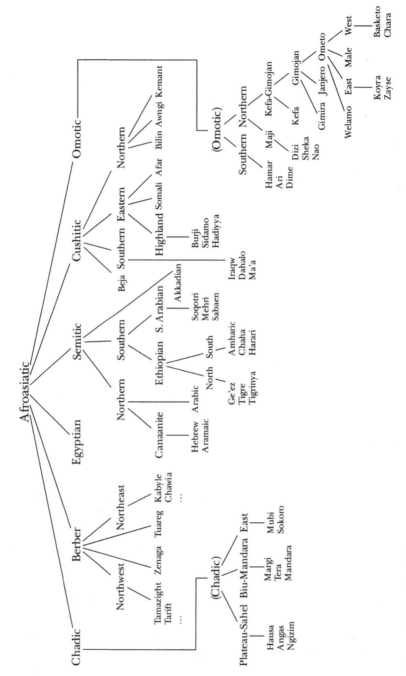

Figure 25.6 Afroasiatic

one language even if language was invented/developed on multiple occasions – if descendant languages of only one of the occasions happened to survive.

4.   METHODS OF HISTORICAL LINGUISTICS

4.1.   The limits of history

Language classification, sometimes called genetic language classification, is the process of determining the grouping of languages on the basis of their shared descent from a parent language. Remember that writing is only about 5,000 years old, so only relatively recent language splits and separations are recorded in history. History records, for example, the spread of Latin and its separation into the so-called Italic languages, including Italian, Spanish, and French, as the result of the spread of the Roman Empire, from about 0–400 AD, and the diversification of Arabic into its modern varieties now spoken from Morocco in the west to Iran in the east, as the result of the Muslim conquests from 700 to 1200 AD. We know what classical Latin and classical Arabic were like, because there are documents written in these ancient languages, and over time the written record shows the gradual change of these into the geographically separated modern Italic languages and varieties of Arabic.

Large language families, however, are the result of movements of people which happened long before writing was invented, such as that of the Indoeuropean and Afroasiatic peoples hypothesized in figure 25.7. The membership of such families can only be known by inference from linguistic evidence (with help from archaeology, and, controversially, biogenetic evidence). The linguistic evidence is largely the product of two methods of analysis: **mass comparison** and **language reconstruction**.

4.2.   Mass comparison

The first step toward discovery of a language family is a simple comparison of vocabulary between languages suspected to be related by common descent. Such comparison seeks evidence of similarities of a sort which would support a more confident hypothesis of common descent. Because several languages are compared, the method is called **mass comparison**. In this method, words of the **basic vocabulary** of the languages in question are compared to find words of different languages which have **semantic and phonetic similarity**. Basic vocabulary includes only words thought to be essential to human societies, such as for lower numerals, body parts, kinship relations, etc., excluding **mimetic words** (chapter 1, §2.2.3.4).

A lot of semantic and phonetic similarity in their basic vocabulary is evidence that two or more languages are members of a family. This is so because there are

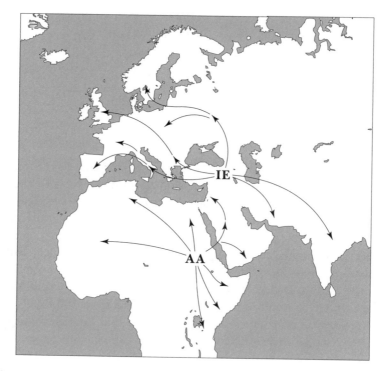

Figure 25.7   Hypothetical spread of Indoeuropean 6000 + years ago and of Afroasiatic 7000 + years ago

only four reasons for such similarity, and the limitation of comparison to basic vocabulary tends to exclude all but the last of these:

1. **Borrowing**. A recently borrowed word is of course very similar in meaning and sound to the equivalent word of the lending language, and the similarities may persist after thousands of years of language change. But words of basic vocabulary, like 'one' and 'sky', compared with non-basic words which express specifics of culture or technology, such as *television* and *Christmas*, are unlikely to be borrowed.

2. **Onomatopoeia**. Onomatopoeic or mimetic words like *crash*, *bow-wow*, and *sneeze*, are iconic signs (chapter 1, §2.2.3.4), which naturally tend to share meaning and sound from language to language. But such words are excluded from the list of basic vocabulary.

3. **Chance**. Because of the characteristic of language known as **arbitrariness** (chapter 1, §3.4.1), chance similarities of form and meaning of words from language to language are very unlikely. There are so many possibilities of sound and meaning that words which sound and mean about the same in different languages must occur only rarely by chance. Some linguists believe, nevertheless, that after a separation of 10,000 years between

languages such chance similarities are as likely as similarities resulting from common descent.

4. **Common descent.** Shared membership in a language family results in **cognates**, words whose similarities of meaning and form are explained by common origin.

Here is an example of the method of mass comparison. Below, written phonetically, are the numerals 'one' to 'five' in five geographically widely separated languages: English, Italian, Hindi (India), Amharic (Ethiopia), and Japanese.

	'one'	*'two'*	*'three'*	*'four'*	*'five'*
English	wən	tu	θri	for	fajv
Italian	uno	due	tre	kwɑtro	činkwe
Hindi	eːk	doː	tiːn	čaːr	pãːč
Amharic	ɑnd	hulət	sost	ɑrat	amːist
Japanese	iči	ni	san	ši	go

Notice the phonetic similarities and regular correspondences between some words of a column. Some of these are obvious, and some which are not so obvious would be noticed by a linguist who has knowledge of a variety of languages (not all linguists do). The similarities especially appear in the English, Italian, and Hindi words for 'one', 'two', and 'three' – for example English and Italian [wən] and [uno] 'one', and English, Italian and Hindi [tu], [due] and [doː] 'two'.

Phonetic similarity in the columns of 'four' and 'five' is not so obvious, but, significantly, concerning English, Italian, and Hindi there is an interesting similarity of form in the first consonant of 'four' and the last consonant of 'five': [f] or [v] corresponding to [kw] and [č]:

	'four'	'five'
English	[f] ...	... [v]
Italian	[kw] ...	... [kw]
Hindi	[č] ...	... [č]

On the basis of these and other similarities we should guess, if we didn't know otherwise, that English, Italian, and Hindi are sibling languages. In fact, more comparisons would soon show similarities to other languages of the Indoeuropean family, suggesting that the three are Indoeuropean languages, and many similarities of form would occur repeatedly, as **regular phonetic correspondences**, which are the natural product of common origin plus the **regularity of phonetic change**, the strong tendency for all phones of a type in a given environment to change identically (chapter 23, §2.2.1.1).

4.3.   Language reconstruction

Mass comparison provides the first evidence of a language family and its members, and additional evidence is provided by methods of **language reconstruction**, by which the forms of a protolanguage are hypothesized by undoing the sound changes by which cognates are related. Two important methods of language reconstruction are the comparative method, and internal reconstruction.

4.3.1.   Comparative method

By the **comparative method** one identifies regular phonetic similarities between the phones of cognates and hypothesizes the original phone (of the protolanguage) from which these evolve. Here is an example: English, Italian, and Hindi are members of the Indoeuropean language family, and the words provided above of these three languages are descendants of Indoeuropean words. From the evidence of these cognate words plus many others, linguists have proposed that these five words in the Indoeuropean language were as follows:

	'one'	'two'	'three'	'four'	'five'
Indoeuropean	*oino	*duwo	*trei	*k^wetwer	*penk^we

Words of the **reconstructed protolanguage** (*proto* 'first' in Greek) are written with an asterisk, as above, to show that they are hypothetical and known only by reconstruction. Making good guesses depends on having very reliable data and knowing very well the sorts of language change that are possible and likely.

Here is another example, concerning just five words of four Ethiopian languages of the Cushitic subfamily of Afroasiatic, written phonetically.

	'one'	'two'	'three'	'four'	'five'
Gedeo	mitːe	lame	sase	šoːle	onde
Hadiyya	mato	lamo	saso	soːro	onto
Kambaata	matu	lamu	sasu	šoːlo	onto
Sidamo	mite	lame	sase	šoːle	onte

There is a lot of similarity among these words, supporting the tentative grouping of the languages in a family, and we may even hypothesize, if more tentatively, the following protolanguage words:

Protolanguage	*mite	*lama	*sasu	*šoːlo	*onto

In comparative reconstruction, protolanguage words such as these are guessed to have existed (historical linguists like to say 'posited' rather than 'guessed to have existed') because they can reasonably be the basis, before language change, of the cognate words. For these five words (though we would want many more such comparisons) our initial reasoning might be as follows:

*mite   because all four cognates have *m*; four have *t*; three have *i*; and two have final *e*.

*lama   because *lam* is found in all four and final vowels other than *a* can be understood to result from a tendency in some of the languages to regularize the final vowel within this set of numerals – notice the regularity of final *e* in Gedeo and Sidamo and *o* in Hadiyya, and the tendency for final *u* in Kambaata.

*sasu   because *sas* is found in all four words and final *e* in two, and, if we reconstruct final *u*, the vowels of languages other than Kambaata may again be explained as regularizations within the numerals.

*šo:lo   because four have *šo:* and *š* can become *s* by typical phonetic change; *l* of three of the languages can become *r* in Hadiyya (in fact, the sound correspondence *l* vs. Hadiyya *r* is pervasive in these languages); final *o* because it occurs in two of the languages and the *e*'s may again be understood as regularizations.

*onto   because all four have initial *on*; Gedeo *d* can result from *t* by assimilation to voicing of the preceding *n*; and the final vowels other than *o* can again be understood as regularizations.

Because of the **regularity of phonetic change**, if we identify cognate words accurately and accumulate enough comparisons, it is often possible to reconstruct the form of protolanguage words with good confidence.

Some linguists consider the partial reconstruction of the protolanguage to be the only reliable evidence that languages which appear to have cognates are members of a language family. Others, pointing out that reconstruction can only proceed on the basis of reasonable hypotheses of language relationships, have more confidence in the method of mass comparison.

4.3.2. Internal reconstruction

Internal reconstruction is similar to the comparative method, but it reconstructs only earlier forms of a single language, by making comparisons within that language. This is possible because within a single language, as well as between languages of a family, one finds cognate words related by common origin and systematic language change. Let's look at two examples of internal reconstruction.

In English there are regular and **irregular verbs**. The past tense form of regular verbs is the present tense form plus /t/, /d/, or /əd/, whereas the past tense form of irregular verbs shows a vowel alternation, as in the following examples:

Regular verbs		Irregular verbs	
Present tense	*Past tense*	*Present tense*	*Past tense*
/waš/ 'wash'	/wašt/	/kæč/ 'catch'	/kɔt/
/opən/ 'open'	/opənd/	/rən/ 'run'	/ræn/
/nid/ 'need'	/nidəd/	/rajd/ 'ride'	/rod/

Some verbs have both regular and irregular past tense forms:

/stɪŋk/ 'stink'   /stɪŋkt/ or /stæŋk/
/šajn/ 'shine'   /šajnd/ or /šon/
/lɛnd/ 'lend'   /lɛndəd/ or /lɛnt/

Because of the tendency for **analogical change** or **rule extension** to replace irregular forms by regular forms (chapter 23, §2.2.2.3), the regular past tense forms of verbs like 'stink', 'shine', and 'lend' are probably the result of change, and we can guess that in the past only /stæŋk/, /šon/, and /lɛnt/ were used. In fact, written records of less than a hundred years ago show this to be so.

As a second example of internal reconstruction, consider these verbs of the Ethiopian language Sidamo (seen in chapter 24, practice 1):

agí   'he drank'   aggú   'she drank'   aŋgí   'we drank'
tumí   'he pounded'   tuntú   'she pounded'   tummí   'we pounded'
sirbí   'he sang'   sirbitú   'she sang'   sirbiní   'we sang'

Analysis of these verbs plus knowledge of how languages typically change makes it possible to internally reconstruct earlier Sidamo forms of these words as follows:

*agí   'he drank'   *agitú   'she drank'   *aginí   'we drank'
*tumí   'he pounded'   *tumitú   'she pounded'   *tuminí   'we pounded'
*sirbí   'he sang'   *sirbitú   'she sang'   *sirbiní   'we sang'

Reconstructions in the first column are identical with modern words. Others are the result of undoing six hypothetical but likely phonological changes:

(1) Word-medial vowel loss, which was blocked in *sirbitú and *sirbiní, where this would have created a sequence of three consonants, resulted in:

*agtú   'she drank'   *agní   'we drank'
*tumtú   'she pounded'   *tumní   'we pounded'

Then, (2) Inversion of the g and n of *agní (**metathesis**, chapter 24, §2.1.3.3) resulted in *angí, and, finally, (3) four **assimilations** (chapter 24, §2.1.2):

aŋgí from *angí by assimilation of [n] to the following velar [g],
aggú from *agtú by assimilation of [t] to preceding [g],
tuntú from *tumtú by assimilation of [m] to following [t], and
tummí from *tumní by assimilation of [n] to preceding [m].

5.   PIDGIN AND CREOLE LANGUAGES

5.1.   Pidgin languages

There are exceptions to the ordinary process of language diversification of figure 25.1. In the ordinary process, new languages result from the splitting of one language (similar to asexual reproduction, by cell division). In the exceptional cases, two languages come together and combine to create a third (similar to sexual reproduction).

The exceptional cases occur when speakers of a foreign language, who are few in number, have business with speakers of a number of other local languages, who are many. The need for communication between the two groups may result in the creation of a rudimentary language typically consisting of:

a.   words of the foreign language
b.   pronounced according to the phonology of the local languages, and
c.   combined in simple sentences according to the syntax of the local languages.

Such a rudimentary language is called a **pidgin language** (*pidgin* is perhaps a changed older form of the word for *business*). Following are four sentences of 'Tok Pisin', spoken in New Guinea, which originated as a pidgin language.

a.   Mi wokim haws.   'I am building ('working') a house.'

b.   Husat i wokim haws?   'Who is building a house?'
c.   Yu wokim bret? (with rising intonation)   'Are you making bread?'
d.   Em i gat planti moni.   'He has lots of money.'

At first a pidgin language has no native speakers, and is used just for doing business with others with whom one shares the pidgin language and no other. In time, most pidgin languages disappear, as the pidgin-speaking community develops, and one of its established languages becomes widely known and takes over the role of the pidgin as the **lingua franca**, or language of choice of those who do not share a native language.

5.2.   Creole languages

However, because it is the only language, rudimentary though it is, which people share, a pidgin language may become a native language. Marriage between those who share only the pidgin language can result in the pidgin becoming the language of many homes, in which children will grow up with the pidgin as their native language. In such cases the children expand and elaborate the pidgin language, adding vocabulary and a grammar with grammatical functions expressed by grammatical morphemes. The result is a **creole language**, with the range of expression of other languages evolved in the ordinary way, including verb tenses, conjunctions, articles, and word derivation, as exemplified in Tok Pisin sentences 1–9 (from Murphy 1989).

a. Verb tense
   1. I go. [i go] 'He goes.'
   2. I bin go. [i bin go] 'He went.'
   3. bai em i go. [bɑy ɛm i go] 'He will go.'
b. Conjunctions
   4. Yu ken go sapos you wok gut. 'You can go if you work well.'
   5. I krai bilong dok i dai. 'He is crying because a dog died.'
c. Articles
   6. Mi lukim sampela man. 'I am looking for some men.'
   7. Yu save dispela man? 'Do you know this man?'
d. Word derivation
   8. Kiap mekim dai dok. 'Kiap killed a dog.' ('make die' = 'kill')
   9. I wokim haus. 'He is making a house.' (Compare *I wok.* 'He is working'; -*im* suffix of transitive verbs)

The future tense morpheme *bai* of sentence 3 comes from English *by and by*. That this has become the Tok Pisin grammatical morpheme of future tense is evident in the facts that it is (a) very frequent, (b) unstressed, and (c) obligatory. Its obligatoriness is apparent in its seemingly redundant use, when time adverbs like *naw* 'now' and *klostu* 'soon' are present. Such appearance of grammatical morphemes is typical in the evolution of a creole language from a pidgin.

5.3. Mixed languages?

The usual sort of borrowing by one language from another does not produce a pidgin language, and the result does not change the language family membership of the borrowing language. English, for example, has borrowed as much as 60% of its words of typical texts from Latin and French, but its basic vocabulary, including all of its grammatical morphology, is inherited from the Proto-Germanic language.

Creole languages are more thorough cases of **mixed languages**, although they are apparently exceptional cases. Nevertheless they challenge the usual understanding of language diversification as resulting from separations between speakers of one language plus ordinary language change. The written record of human history goes back less than five thousand years, and the likelihood in prehistoric times of conditions which might have encouraged the creation of pidgin languages and their evolution into creole languages is difficult to judge.

6. DEEP LANGUAGE RELATIONS

Some believe that the Indoeuropean family is part of a much older family, named **Nostratic** (Latin *nostra* 'our'), which includes Uralic, Altaic, Eskimo-Aleut, and perhaps Afroasiatic, and stretches across the entire northern hemisphere from Finland across Europe, Asia, and North America to Greenland. Other combinations of language families into bigger and older families have been proposed, which would reduce the number of the world's language families to as few as ten or so. It has also been claimed that membership in these greater language families significantly corresponds to shared blood types of peoples around the world. There is great controversy about these claims, and some argue that the linguistic evidence which would support them – confidently recognizable cognates – could not survive in languages with more than 10,000 years of separation, and that apparent cognates which suggest proto-words older than this could as well be accidental similarities. These skeptics are willing to believe in such ancient proto-languages when they are partly reconstructed, but not before. The next few years will probably see increasing agreement either for or against the claims of deep language relationships.

Suggestions for
ADDITIONAL READING

The languages of the world are cataloged, including basic information about them, in *Ethnologue: Languages of the World* (1996) edited by Barbara F. Grimes and others. A worldwide survey of languages with information on the grammar of many is provided in *An Introduction to the Languages of the World* (1997) by Anatole V. Lyovin. An ambitious attempt to group the world's languages into families is *A Guide to the World's Languages*, vol. 1 (1987) by Merritt Ruhlen. Brief descriptions are provided for some of the most important languages in *The World's Major Languages* (1990) edited by Bernard Comrie. The *Concise Compendium of the World's Languages* (1998) by George L. Campbell, provides brief grammatical description and other information on the hundred or so most populous languages. Indoeuropean languages are well surveyed and their major characteristics described in *Comparative Indo-European Linguistics* (1995) by Robert S. P. Beekes. Very complete information about the languages of the world is available on the internet at a site of the Summer Institute of Linguistics, publishers of *Ethnologue*, mentioned above: http://www.sil.org/ethnologue/ethnologue.html.

The methods of language classification and reconstruction are described in most textbooks of historical linguistics, such as those listed at the end of the chapter 23. Focussed on reconstruction in particular is *Linguistic Reconstruction* (1995) by Anthony Fox. For a controversial attempt to reconstruct aspects of the earliest human languages see *The Origin of Language* (1994) by Merritt Ruhlen. *The Rise and Fall of Languages* (1997) by R. M. W. Dixon presents a theory of language diversification and an overview of the problem of language classification.

The origin of human language is the topic of a number of recent books, including *The Symbolic Species: the Co-evolution of Language and the Brain* (1997) by Terrence W. Deacon, *The Seeds of Speech: Language Origin and Evolution* (1996) by Jean Aitchison, *Human Evolution, Language and Mind* (1996) by Iain Davidson and William Noble, *Grooming, Gossip, and Evolution of Language* (1996) by Robin Dunbar, and *Language and Species* (1990) by Derek Bickerton.

An introduction to pidgin and creole languages is *Pidgins and Creoles* (1990) by Loreto Todd, and an anthology of readings on the topic is *Pidgins and Creoles: an Introduction* (1995) edited by Jacques Arends and others.

IMPORTANT CONCEPTS AND TERMS IN THIS CHAPTER

- diglossia
- dialects
- languages
- language family
- isolate
- Indoeuropean
- protolanguage
- family tree
- Afroasiatic
- sibling language
- parent language
- protolanguage
- monogenesis
- polygenesis
- language classification
- mass comparison
- basic vocabulary
- semantic similarity
- phonetic similarity
- mimetic words
- borrowing

- onomatopoeia
- chance
- arbitrariness
- common descent
- cognates
- regular phonetic correspondences
- regularity of phonetic change
- language reconstruction
- comparative method
- reconstructed protolanguage
- internal reconstruction
- irregular verbs
- analogical change
- rule extension
- metathesis
- assimilation
- pidgin language
- lingua franca
- creole language
- mixed language
- Nostratic

OUTLINE OF
CHAPTER 25

EXAMPLES AND PRACTICE

EXAMPLE

1. Mass comparison I. The method of mass comparison compares basic vocabulary of languages as evidence of the membership of the languages in a family or families. See in table 25.1 the sample of seven words of basic vocabulary from

Table 25.1 Seven words in eight languages

	'one'	'two'	'three'	'head'	'eye'	'ear'	'mouth'
a.	sang	su	soti	jung	sing	–	a
b.	wate	iba	tati	ju(le)	no(do)	to(go)	jabodo
c.	toro	ču	agozo	daho	samo	sumo	či
d.	ili	iwa	ita	ilɔ	ewu	ɔtɔ	ɛnu
e.	mwe	bali	tato	(li)to	(le)iso	(ku)toi	(mu)njwa
f.	tilo	ndi	jasko	kela	sim	sumo	či
g.	kiet	iba	ita	ɛte	enjin	utong	inua
h.	lakoi	swe	we	taha	i	kebbe	a

eight African languages (a)–(h) of two families (Greenberg 1966, p. 4), written phonetically. Words of the first three columns, indeed, might provide sufficient evidence for the two groups.

PRACTICE

By identifying numbers of probable cognates, try to group the languages into two language families, each of which consists of four languages.

EXAMPLE

2. Mass comparison II. Consider the word comparisons of table 25.2, of 20 words of basic vocabulary in six Ethiopian languages, written phonetically. The six languages are historically related to one another approximately as in the family tree of figure 25.8, as even these few vocabulary comparisons may suggest.

Table 25.2   Fifteen words in six Ethiopian languages

		Amharic	Oromo	Gedeo	Hadiyya	Kambaata	Sidamo
a.	'chicken'	doro	indaaŋk'o	lukko	antaba?a	antabe?u	lukko
b.	'dry'	dərək'	gogaa	bago	goballa	moola	moola
c.	'dust'	abwara	awaara	buko	dira	dira	buko
d.	'eye'	ajn	ija	ille	ille	illi	ille
e.	'hand'	iǰǰ	harka	aŋga	aŋga	aŋga	aŋga
f.	'honey'	mar	damma	malebo	marabo	malabu	malawo
g.	'hot'	muk'	buluk'aa	eebba	iibba	iibba	iibbado
h.	'house'	bet	mana	mine	mine	mine	mine
i.	'knee'	gulbət	ǰilba	gulubo	gurubbo	gulube	gulube
j.	'male'	wənd	d'iira	labba	goona	goonu	labba
k.	'six'	siddist	ǰi?a	ǰaane	loho	leho	leje
l.	'soil'	afər	bijoo	buttina	bučča	bučča	bušša
m.	'soul'	nəfs	lubbuu	lubbo	foore	fooli	lubbo
n.	'tree'	zaf	muka	hakk'a	hakk'a	hakk'o	hakk'e
o.	'wet'	irtib	ǰiida	šamo	aašalla	mut'a	šama

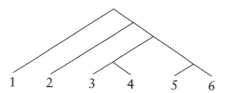

Figure 25.8   Family tree of the six Ethiopian languages

PRACTICE

(a) Count the number of likely cognates for each pair of languages of table 25.2, and fill in these numbers in table 25.3. For Amharic and Oromo, one should be able to recognize two probable cognates (that is, /abwara/ and /awaara/, and,

Table 25.3 Probable cognates among the six Ethiopian languages

	Sidamo	Kambaata	Hadiyya	Gedeo	Oromo	Amharic
Amharic	____	____	____	____	_2_	X
Oromo	____	____	____	_3_	X	
Gedeo	____	____	____	X		
Hadiyya	____	____	X			
Kambaata	____	X				
Sidamo	X					

not so obviously, /gulbət/ and /jilbɑ/), and for Oromo and Gedeo three. These numbers are supplied in the table. Other language pairs have a greater number of probable cognates. (In fact, this work is quite speculative for those who are unfamiliar with the languages and with principles of language change. Try it, though, as an exercise in the general practice of the method of mass comparison.)

(b) On the basis of the numbers you supply in table 25.3, try to say which languages correspond to which numbers 1–6 in the family tree of figure 25.8.

EXAMPLE

3. Comparative method. The comparative method compares cognate words of a family to enable guesses about the pronunciation of the source-word of the parent language. The reconstructed language is called a protolanguage. In the case of the so-called Italic or 'Romance' languages, we have actual knowledge of the parent language, Latin.

PRACTICE

Compare the phonemically written Spanish, Rumanian, and Italian words of table 25.4 and, on the basis of these comparisons and the principles discussed in

Table 25.4 Eleven words in five Romance languages

		Spanish	Rumanian	Italian	Latin
a.	'air'	ajre	aer	arja	—————
b.	'bone'	weso	os	osːo	—————
c.	'ear'	oreha	orekjo	orekːjo	—————
d.	'grey'	gris	gri	grijo	—————
e.	'honey'	mjel	mjere	mjele	—————
f.	'man'	ombre	om	womo	—————
g.	'month'	mes	luna	mese	—————
h.	'sad'	triste	trist	triste	—————
i.	'saddle'	sijːa	se	selːa	—————
j.	'three'	tres	tre	tre	—————
k.	'water'	agwa	akwa	akːwa	—————

§4.3.1, above, try to guess the form of the word of the protolanguage, Latin. Keep in mind a point of chapter 24, §2.1.3.1, that in language change deletions are more likely than insertions. After making your guesses, you can look the actual words up in a Latin dictionary.

EXAMPLE

4. Internal reconstruction. English has a prefix for deriving the negative of adjectives. This prefix has a number of pronunciations: [ɪn]*decisive*, [ɪm]*possible*, [ɪn]*eligible*, and in fast speech [ɪɱ]*fallible* and [ɪŋ]*credible*. All but one of these pronunciations can be understood as resulting from assimilation of place of articulation: we find alveolar [n] before [d] of *decisive*, labial [m] before [p] of *possible*, labiodental [ɱ] before [f] of *fallible*, and velar [ŋ] before [k] of *credible* (in slow speech one can also say [ɪn]*credible*). The remaining pronunciation, [n] before *eligible*, is unexplained, and this is evidence for a reasonable guess that the [n] pronunciation is original – as the modern spelling suggests, and old documents show. (This prefix is pronounced just [ɪ] in *illegal* and *irrational*, which have just one [l] and one [r], despite the spellings. In these words the [n] assimilated to the following [l] yielding [ll] and to the following [r] yielding [rr], respectively, as the spellings show, and later the long consonants were shortened.)

PRACTICE

a. Noun stems with *-ion*. Consider the different pronunciations which some verbs have when they are suffixed by *-ion*, to form nouns:

Verb with final [d]	*Verb with final [t]*	*Verb with final [z] or [s]*
decide, deci[ž]ion	sedate, seda[š]ion	revise, revi[ž]ion
elide, eli[ž]ion	inflate, infla[š]ion	precise, preci[ž]ion
persuade, persuasion	negate, negation	confuse, confusion

Think of some other verbs which accept the *-ion* suffix: *rebel*, with final [l], *prevent*, with final [nt], and *abstract*, with final [kt], etc. Consider whether the pronunciation with *-ion* is earlier, or that without the suffix. What type of phonological change is at work here?

EXAMPLE

5. Word borrowing. Cognate words – words of sibling languages which descend from the same word of their common parent language – are semantically and phonetically similar. Borrowed words of different languages which were borrowed from a common language are also semantically and phonetically similar. However, borrowed words are not usually found in the basic vocabulary. Thus semantically and phonetically similar words in languages of different families are likely to be borrowed words, especially if they concern areas of likely cultural and/or technological influence.

Swahili, Persian, and Indonesian are members of very different language families, and all three have borrowed a lot of words from Arabic. Consider the words of Swahili, Persian, and Indonesian in table 25.5 (written phonetically; [x] is a voiceless velar fricative). Try to identify the borrowings from Arabic (Gleason 1964, p. 86).

By the way, is it apparent why languages don't borrow words of basic vocabulary?

Table 25.5 Ten words of Swahili, Persian, and Indonesian

		Swahili	*Persian*	*Indonesian*
a.	'child'	mwana	bačeh	anak
b.	'fire'	moto	ateš	api
c.	'leg'	mguu	saq	kaki
d.	'news'	habari	xæbær	xabar
e.	'prophet'	nabij	næbij	nabi
f.	'rain'	mvua	baran	huǰan
g.	'soldier'	askari	æskær	askar
h.	'speech'	hutoba	xutbæh	xutbah
i.	'temple'	hekalu	hæjkil	rumah
j.	'two'	bili	do	dua

Source: Gleason 1964

Chapter 26

DIALECTS AND OTHER SOCIOLECTS

This chapter takes note of societal factors which influence language change, and the role of variant forms of language, which arise in language change, as identifying markers of social groups. Social groups distinguished by language are based upon factors including geography, socioeconomic status, and gender.

1. THREE DIMENSIONS OF LANGUAGE VARIATION

There is a principle of language which values one form for one meaning and one meaning for one form (chapter 16, §2.6.2 and chapter 24, §2.4.1). This is a good principle from the perspective of the language learner. From the perspective of society, however, there is usefulness to having multiple ways of saying more or less 'the same thing'. This multiplicity, or **linguistic variation**, is also perhaps an important and even necessary aspect of the nature of language.

There are three dimensions along which linguistic variation comes about and within which it persists: the dimensions of *time*, *society*, and the *individual*. The three dimensions intersect as suggested in figure 26.1.

language variety – broad term

2. VARIATION IN TIME

The horizontal dimension of the figure 26.1 shows one-directional time. Along this dimension languages are constantly, pervasively, and systematically changing (chapter 23). In the lexicon, new words are always appearing; in the grammar, restructuring is always underway (as where *lighted* arises as an alternative to *lit*). The result is **linguistic variation**, different ways of saying about the same thing. While this variation may be undesirable from the point of view of an efficient grammar, it proves useful to social groups, for differentiating and marking

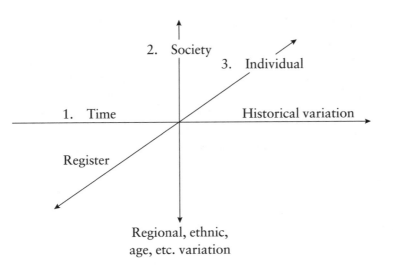

Figure 26.1 Three dimensions of language variation

themselves, and to individuals, to express their awareness of varying social circumstances. The individual response to language variation is the topic of the following chapter.

2.1. Speech communities

Language change starts and spreads in a **speech community,** a group or network of people whose language is more or less the same because, to the relative exclusion of others, they learn from and influence one another in all sorts of behavior including language. Language change is accelerated in certain speech communities, at certain times, for example under the influence of language contact, as in 11th century Britain, with the influence of French after the Norman conquest, and in 16th century America, in the English-speaking community somewhat isolated from the influence of the British homeland.

Modern diverse societies consist of embedded and overlapping speech communities. Just about everybody is a member of more than one of these, and people often join new speech communities and leave their old ones. Speech communities are based on factors including geography, religion, age, and gender, and may be more or less cohesive, and recognizable by their characteristics of language.

2.2. Centers of change

The evidence is disputed, but a few generalizations are possible about the relation between language change and speech communities of different types. Factors which influence the rise and spread of change in speech communities are: (1) population size, (2) tightness of social networks, (3) removal from linguistic standards of the broader community, and (4) bilingualism.

2.2.1.   More populous speech communities

In more populous speech communities more people are contributing change, including linguistic change. Thus language change is generally greater in cities than in the countryside, and probably greater in the US than in the UK (to the extent the two nations represent different speech communities; also, other factors than population size are relevant, such as the history of greater regional variation in the UK). Similarly, change is slower among the less numerous wealthier elites (who furthermore naturally value conservative speech, are sufficiently educated to recognize it, and seek to preserve it against changes 'from below' which could affect its usefulness as a social symbol).

2.2.2.   Tight social networks

In tighter or more cohesive social networks, whose members all know and interact with each other for most societal purposes, language changes, when these arise, tend to spread. Members of the speech community have more exposure to the innovations, they value in ~~~~~~~~~~~~~~~~~ d forms of language are more likely to be put to ~~~~~~~~~~~~~~~~se members of such networks interact with each o *ex: individual college campuses* nteract with others less, which lessens their aware ~~~~ ~~~ ~~~~~~~ or the broader community and its value to them. For this reason also, language change tends to be greater in urban than rural areas, and, for example, greater among college students than among college professors, who form a less cohesive social network.

2.2.3.   Groups removed from linguistic standards

In groups isolated from the broader community (whether these are tight networks or not) there is less pressure to maintain the standards of that community. In more populous groups there is more room, socially speaking, to be removed from standards of the center. A tight interpersonal network in particular, within which one may talk uninhibitedly, receives greater loyalty than a looser traditional one within which one must 'say the right thing'. Thus a college student is less likely than a college professor to be ridiculed for saying, for example, *Did you and them go out last night?* Mere geographic separation from the traditional community (England) and its linguistic standards, in a time before modern communication could tend to neutralize this, explains to a considerable extent the divergence of American and Australian from British English, though other factors mentioned here are also relevant.

2.2.4.   Subordinate bilingualism

In communities which use two or ~~~~ ~~~~~~~~~, ~~~ ~~ ~~~~~ is typically dominant in more important contexts of use. One language may be preferred in public schools, in the church, or at work, and children growing up bilingual often use one language at home and another at school. Among the different linguistic domains which can often be distinguished are (a) home, (b) school, (c) church, (d) neighborhood, (e) region, and (f) nation, and one or the other

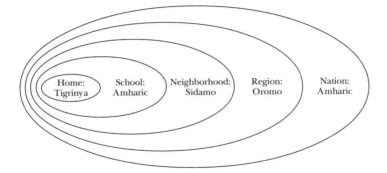

Figure 26.2   Five domains of language in a multilingual Ethiopian community

language will be often be favored in each of these. For example, the typical language of some of these domains for a Tigrinya-speaking family living in a Sidamo-speaking neighborhood of a town in Bale province in southern Ethiopia is as in figure 26.2.

Such inequalities of use can result in **subordinate bilingualism**, as in the example of figure 26.2 in which the language of the school and nation are the same, which tends to render the other languages subordinate, especially if these have fewer speakers. The result of subordinate bilingualism is lots of word-borrowing by the subordinate language in the realms of dominance of the other. Thus English vocabulary and, eventually, derivational morphology was strongly influenced by French in the period of English–French bilingualism after the Norman conquest of Britain, when French was the language of high culture and government. Similarly, Japan was strongly influenced by China for several centuries after AD 800, resulting in a lot Chinese words in Japanese, and adoption of the Chinese writing system.

In **coordinate bilingualism**, by contrast, both languages are generally used for all purposes. Perfectly coordinate bilingual societies and individuals are rare or even nonexistent, however, since the two (or more) languages must ordinarily play at least somewhat different roles within a society or even within a home. Compare the relatively coordinate roles of French and German in Switzerland, versus the subordinate role of Spanish in the US, or the relatively coordinate roles of English and French in Montreal, versus the subordinate role of French in Toronto.

Language maintenance in bilingual groups is undermined by the three factors of (a) subordinate bilingualism, especially in which one language is subordinate within the peer group of its child speakers, (b) a population insufficient to provide a rich social network for one of the languages, and (c) removal of one of the languages from the influence of the linguistic standards of its traditional community. All three of these factors can explain the loss within one or two generations of homeland languages by immigrant groups, as traditionally in the American 'melting pot'.

2.3.   Societal interpretation of linguistic variation in time

Language change continually produces variants of linguistic form. Those which spread beyond the speech community in which they arise, into the language of the larger society, are often employed in the larger society to distinguish different degrees of familiarity or formality of language, as when slang (chapter 24, §2.3.2) spreads out of the speech community of young people into the society at large, and is characteristic, early in its spread, of a very casual and informal register – for example, *bro* clipped from *brother*, as a familiar form of address. These different levels of formality, or styles, are termed **registers** and are the topic of the next chapter.

Other variants which arise through language change may be restricted to the social groups in which they arise or in which they become typical, as where syllable-final *r*-lessness characterizes regional speech, or jargon (chapter 24, §2.3.1) characterizes a professional or occupational group. Such characteristic forms of the language of social groups are termed **sociolects**. The rest of this chapter is concerned with the characteristics of seven sociolects.

3.   SEVEN SOCIOLECTS

Sociolects arise within social groups based upon factors including seven which will be discussed here: (1) geography, (2) socioeconomic status, (3) ethnicity/race, (4) age, (5) occupation, (6) religion, and (7) gender.

3.1.   Geography

When linguistic innovations arise and spread in a particular geographic region, their unity and relative isolation may focus and limit their spread, and, as a result, the innovations may become typical of the region. The regional varieties of a language which result, if these become recognizably distinct, are termed **dialects**. Geography doesn't directly cause dialect differences, but the social separation which geography can cause, plus ordinary constant language change, does. Geographic features which severely limit travel, like wide bodies of water and mountain ranges, can result in particularly distinct dialects, in the US, for example, those of the Ozark mountains and the Carolina and Georgia coastal islands.

3.1.1.   Two senses of 'dialect' and 'language'

With the passage of time, and if they are sufficiently isolated from each other, people who start out speaking one language begin to lose **mutual intelligibility**. Their different dialects become separate languages. This is how languages like English and German, which started out as dialects of Germanic, and Spanish and French, which started out as dialects of Latin, in time became languages (chapter 25, §2).

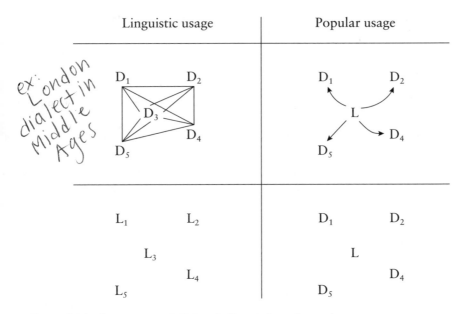

ex London dialect in Middle Ages

Figure 26.3   Language and dialect in linguistic and popular usage

Often in English popular usage, speakers of a politically or socially advantaged or empowered region are said to speak a language, while others speak dialects of the language. In this usage, both Danish and Norwegian, and Serbian and Croatian, even though they are mutually intelligible with one another, are considered languages, while the different minority languages within linguistically diverse nations such as China or Nigeria may be termed dialects. As a caricature of this popular usage, it has been said that a language is a dialect with an army and a navy.

Every language of any geographic extent has regional varieties, or dialects, and every dialect is a variety of a language. In the terminology of linguistics, a language is a set of dialects, and every speaker of the language speaks one of its dialects. Consider a region with five dialects of one language, as in the upper left diagram of figure 26.3, one of which, D_3, is the most prestigious, and recognized as preferred. In popular usage of the words, D_3 is a 'language', and all but speakers of D_3 are said to speak 'dialects', as in the upper right diagram. Or consider a hypothetical nation where five languages are spoken, as in the lower left diagram of figure 26.3. If only one of these, L_3, is commonly written, used in government, and taught in the schools, in popular usage only this may be considered a 'language' while everybody else would be said to speak a 'dialect', as in the lower right diagram.

3.1.2. Mutual intelligibility

Mutual intelligibility is not an either/or matter, but a continuum, so linguists may reasonably differ about whether two regional varieties of speech ought to be considered dialects or languages. Being spoken in separate nations has tended in the past to lead, eventually, to mutual nonintelligibility between varieties – though not yet completely in the case of Danish and Norwegian, or Hindi (of India) and Urdu (of Pakistan).

Two varieties of speech may be mutually intelligible in some contexts and not in others. When the topic is one familiar to speakers of one dialect of a language but not to listeners who are speakers of another dialect of the language, intelligibility may nevertheless break down. Thus Americans can usually understand the British prime minister speaking on world affairs, but may not understand familiar conversation between young people in a British movie. Ordinarily, when speakers of different dialects of a single language speak to one another, being unfamiliar with one another socially, they assure mutual intelligibility by speaking about shared topics, and by using standard forms of vocabulary and grammar which both tend to know. Speakers of different varieties will usually also make themselves more mutually intelligible in writing, which uses forms which they are likely to share.

Since languages are always changing, and longer settled areas tend to be more populous and to have evolved more and tighter social networks, dialect differences are usually more prominent in longer-settled areas. Thus there is more dialect differentiation in British than in American English, and more dialect differentiation on the American East Coast than in the western states. Thus also dialects of Maine, Boston, and New York are clear and recognizable to many Americans, but differences between Los Angeles, San Francisco, and Seattle are minor and unrecognizable.

3.1.3. Standard dialect

Often one of the dialects of a language will be recognized as the **standard dialect**. This is usually the dialect which has most prestige and thus more acceptance by speakers of the others. Typically such prestige and acceptance derives from the greater cultural and/or economic influence of the region of the standard. Since the traditional US economic and cultural center is the northeast, a region typified by a number of recognizable but not widespread dialects, the American English standard dialect is something of an abstraction, a collection of features generally common in the northeast and more typical, in fact, of the speech of the upper Midwest.

3.1.4. American dialects

Individuals ordinarily recognize a few characteristics of other dialects of their language. American English speakers are likely to be aware of a few prominent regional characteristics of American English, for example these six:

a.   In the Massachusetts area and in states of the 'deep' south including Virginia and Georgia, [r] before consonants and at the end of words is ordinarily absent, so that I parked the car in the yard is typically pronounced in Boston, Massachusetts as [ay pakt ðə kar ɪn ðə yad], and in Richmond, Virginia as [ɑy pɑkt ðə kɑ ɪn ðə yɑd] ([a] is not as front as [æ], and [ɑ] is a back vowel).

b. In northeastern r-less dialects, word-final [r] is absent before words beginning with consonants but may be present before following words beginning with vowels, so *car* is [kar] in *car in the yard*, but [ka] in *car-port*.

c. In the northeast, people pronounce *greasy* [grísi], but in the south [grízi].
    ↳ *and everywhere outside the South*

d. In New York City, typically in the speech of those native to the borough of the Bronx, consonants are rounded before [ɔ], so that *bought*, and *taught* and *caught* are pronounced [bʷɔt], [tʷɔt], and [kʷɔt], respectively.

e. In the southwest including Texas and Oklahoma, [ɛ] and [ɪ] are merged before nasal consonants, so that both *pen* and *pin* are pronounced [pɪn]. Texans also use *you all*, and its contraction *y'all*, for *you*-plural: *Y'all come back now.*

f. West of the Great Lakes, /ɔ/ and /ɑ/ are typically merged as /ɑ/, so *caught* and *cot* are both pronounced /kɑt/.

3.2. Socioeconomic status

The populations of most large societies are to some extent stratified according to socioeconomic status, **SES**. But SES is ordinarily a quite gradual continuum, and well-defined speech communities are not based upon SES. Most persons have numerous and frequent linguistic interactions up and down on this SES continuum, and vary their speech accordingly.

An influential study by the sociolinguist William Labov (Labov 1966), nevertheless clearly showed the reality and regularity of SES-based differences of language. Labov asked clerks in three New York City department stores a question such as 'Excuse, me, where are women's shoes?', to which the answer was 'Fourth floor', both words of which have a potential **post-vocalic r**, [r] preceded but not followed by a vowel. In New York City, post-vocalic r is **variable**: New Yorkers may or may not pronounce it, saying [fɔθ flóə] sometimes, and [fɔrθ flor] at others. In New York City, post-vocalic r is prestigious, unlike, for example, in Boston, Richmond, Virginia, and England. In this research the question eliciting post-vocalic r was asked at the three department stores Saks', Macy's, and Klein's, respectively stores with higher, moderate, and lower prices. After the first answer, Labov pretended not to hear, and sought a repetition, saying 'Excuse me?'. Table 26.1 presents the results concerning variable post-vocalic r in the two words of the two answers at the three department stores.

One can see variation of three sorts in these numbers: that corresponding to the word, *fourth* or *floor*; that corresponding to the answer, first or second; and that corresponding to the store, Saks', Macy's, or Klein's. The word *floor*, in which r, if it occurs, is word-final, always gets more r's than in *fourth*, in which

Table 26.1   Variable post-vocalic *r* in New York City

| | First answer | | Second answer | |
	Fourth	Floor	Fourth	Floor
Saks'	30	63	40	64
Macy's	27	44	22	61
Klein's	5	8	13	18

[handwritten margin notes: "Ross" and "r-lessness is lowclass"]

it is before a consonant ([θ]), and the second answer, which Labov termed 'emphatic', always gets more *r*'s than the first answer, which Labov termed 'casual'.

The greater number of *r*'s in *floor* than *fourth* presumably concerns a phonological factor related to ease of articulation or perception which favors word-final over preconsonantal consonants (a factor probably also evidenced in the absence of [l] in words like *talk* and *calm* versus its presence in *tall* and *call*).

The greater number of *r*'s in second answers presumably concerns individual variation of a sort which will be discussed in the next chapter, concerning so-called **register**.

Our emphasis here is on the difference between department stores, the explanation of which is reasonably associated with the SES of clerks and customers of the stores. Clerks have their own SES, and are influenced by the presumed and perceived SES of their customers. The more prestigious the store, the more occasions of the prestigious pronunciations with *r*. Notice another fact about the numbers of *r*'s, which also concerns variation probably related to SES: the minimal increase in second-answer *r*'s at Saks', versus the marked increase at Klein's and Macy's, the middle-class stores. Much research has shown that a characteristic of SES middle-class speech is not just presence or absence of a variable like post-vocalic *r*, but a wider range of variation between presence and absence of the feature, which may be explained by the wider-ranging class identities of members of the middle class.

3.3.   Ethnicity/race

Three populous and often separate racial groups in the US are African Americans, Hispanic Americans, and European Americans. Each group forms a speech community only to some extent correlating locally with geographic isolation from one another. The speech of each group tends plainly to differ from that of the others. The speech of African Americans, particularly, has been a focus of controversy concerning the historical reason for its marked difference from other varieties of American English.

3.3.1.   *African American English*

Lately known popularly as **Ebonics**, the characteristic speech of African Americans, especially of big cities including New York, Philadelphia, and Detroit, is sometimes called by linguists **BEV**, Black English Vernacular, to emphasize the point that African Americans who know this variety may use it only as vernacular or casual speech with other African Americans, switching to more standard forms in other circumstances. BEV is spoken in discontinuous African American communities, in northern cities as well as the south, so it is not a regionally but an ethnically based variety.

3.3.1.1. Characteristics of BEV.   Three characteristics of BEV are:

a.   *Be*-**deletion**. One variety of African American English gets along without the *be*-verb except in two contexts. First, where in other varieties of English the *be*-verb is stressed, it will be present in BEV. Thus in BEV one can say *He goin* as a statement and *He goin?* as a question (with rising intonation), but in answering one will say *Yes, he is* (or *Yes, he be*), and never *Yes, he*. In other words, where in the casual speech of other varieties the *be* verb is unstressed and contracted, as in *she's, we're, I'm*, etc., it may be absent in BEV, but where it is stressed and uncontracted in other varieties, it is present in BEV. That is, BEV carries the weakening or reduction of the *be* verb one step further than contraction.

b.   **Habitual *be*.** The second environment for presence of *be* in BEV is where its meaning is 'habitually be'. Thus a BEV speaker says *He late (this morning)*, but not *He late (all the time)*, which is *He be late (all the time)*.

c.   Consonant deletion. Another way that BEV extends a feature of casual English speech is word-final consonant deletion. Where in casual speech most English speakers will say *I foun' something*, not *I foun*[d] *something*, dropping the word-final stop between consonants (especially, indeed, in an irregular verb like *found*, where the vowel also shows past tense), BEV usually lacks this consonant even before vowels: *I foun' it*. (In fact, consonant deletion in BEV is sensitive to the morphemic significance of final consonants: 'find' will probably be [fɑjn], but 'fined' ('assessed a fine') in which [d] represents past tense, is more likely to be [fɑjnd].)

3.3.1.2. Origins of BEV.   Three explanations have been offered for the uniqueness of vernacular African American speech. Perhaps all three are partly true.

a.   It might represent an extension of features of regional American Southern dialect. Final consonant deletion (including post-vocalic *r*-lessness), for example, is common in Southern speech, generally, as well as in BEV.

b.   It might have features which arose in the pidgin English likely to have been fashioned in the first, 17th century, African speech communities in America, the members of which came from different regions of Africa and typically shared no language but English, which they must at first have known very incompletely. This would have been a typical setting for the invention of a **pidgin language** (chapter 25, §5), which in time would have been replaced by a variety of English preserving characteristics of the pidgin.

c. It might include characteristics of African languages. An example could be habitual *be*. English and other Indoeuropean languages don't have a special grammatical form for this meaning, but some West African languages do. (Notice that Standard English has no habitual morpheme, but the so-called 'simple present tense' is ordinarily habitual in meaning, as in *Who plays poker?*, versus *Who's playing poker?*)

3.3.2. *Chicano English*

Most speakers of Chicano English are also speakers of Spanish, and Chicano English is especially characterized by the influence of Spanish (this is **transfer**: chapter 11, §2.1.1).

a. For example, there are double negatives, like *I don't want nothing*, for which the Spanish equivalent also employs two negatives: *No quiero nada* 'I don't want anything'.

b. The English vowel phonemes tend to be reinterpreted in terms of the five Spanish vowel phonemes /a, i, e, o, u/, so that *I will have to*, standard English [ày wɪl hǽftə], will be [ay wil hɑftu], also without the large stress differences of standard English.

c. Spanish doesn't distinguish /č/ and /š/, and this is true of Chicano English, so that both *cheap* and *sheep* are pronounced [čip].

Chicano English is also characterized by **code-switching**, switching from language to language within an utterance. Chicano English code-switchers employ Spanish words within their English speech, when addressing other Spanish speakers, and English words in their Spanish speech, when addressing other Chicano English speakers. Following is a short sample of this code-switching (Espinosa 1975 [1917]).

Well boys, vamanos ('let's go').
Esta team tiene ('has') un fine pitcher.
Well, compadre, how is your vieja ('old one' (f.) = mother?)?
Que hombre tan sporty. ('What a sporty guy!')

3.4. Age

Age-stratification is not very obvious in most societies, including the English-speaking world. Still, the generations are members of different speech communities, to a small extent, and to the same extent speak somewhat differently. In particular the speech of teenagers is often noted by older people as different (usually objectionable, in fact), since it is typically characterized by what they consider to be an excessive use of **slang** (chapter 24, §2.3.2).

Users of slang usually don't write slang, and when non-users try to write down the slang that they hear, often the result is not very authentic, as probably the case in the following said-to-be teenager sentence reported by *USA Weekend* (May 18–20, 1990): 'I was lampin' at the alley yesterday and a home boy started scamming with me; "Hey, wanna hook up and scoop?" he asked', which was translated, 'I was hanging out at the bowling alley yesterday and a guy from the neighborhood started flirting with me; "Hey, do you want to go steady and kiss?" he asked.'

A clear example of the age difference in speech concerns what male teenagers used to say (or so the author recalls) when getting into a car, to mean 'I'll sit in front next to the driver!': *I got shotgun!* (In the American old west, a stagecoach guard sat next to the driver, armed with a shotgun.) After about age 17, we probably wouldn't say this except as a deliberate attempt at youthful or cute speech.

3.5. Occupation

Occupational groups have their characteristic **jargon** (chapter 24, §2.3.1), but the sociolect of occupational groups is more than just vocabulary. A couple of examples are the sociolects of those in the legal and medical professions:

Legal discourse, or legalese, is partly characterized by the <u>avoidance of pronouns</u>, at least partly as a way to avoid the costly occasional ambiguities that imperfect pronoun reference may cause. Instead of pronouns, jargon vocabulary may appear, such as *party of the first part*.

Medical discourse, medicalese, has a lot more passive verbs than ordinary language, at least partly because of the relative importance in the medical field of events in which indefinite agents, who would be represented by indefinite pronouns including *one*, *someone*, or *anyone*, are unimportant, and avoided as subjects, for example in sentences like:

a.   Mometasone furoate should not be used near the eyes.
b.   It is not known whether calcipotriene is excreted in human milk.

As sociolects, however, jargons like legalese and medicalese are not always motivated just by the objective professional needs of their users. Instead, the language becomes an end in itself, as a marker of membership in the profession, and displayed like a white laboratory coat or pale green surgical clothing ('scrubs') unnecessarily worn to lunch. Legal discourse could reasonably have occasional pronouns, and medical discourse could have fewer passives:

c.   Don't use mometasone furoate near the eyes.

d.   We don't know whether calcipotriene is excreted in human milk.

3.6. Religion

Religion is obviously a frequent basis of social networks and so of speech communities. However, religious differences seem not to result in language differences as marked as for other factors we have seen, except when this results in different political alignments, which result in strict social separation along political as well as religious lines. Religious differences may result in language differences, however, as in these three cases:

a.   Urdu and Hindi are dialects of a language of India and Pakistan, two nations the significant basis of the political separation between which was religion: the Urdu speakers being mainly Muslim and Hindi speakers mainly Hindu.

b.   Serbian and Croatian are dialects of a language the differences between which probably arose largely owing to religious differences which now generally characterize the ex-Yugoslavian states of Serbia, typically Russian Orthodox, and Croatia, typically Catholic.

c.   Amharic and Argobba, Ethiopian Semitic languages, have only recently diverged from one another to the extent of mutual nonintelligibility. Argobba speakers are almost all Muslim, and Amharic speakers, traditionally, are largely Ethiopian Orthodox Christian. This difference of religion is probably the original basis for divergence between the two languages, one of the differences between which is the larger number of Argobba words borrowed from Arabic.

Specialists in the study of these regions may point out the economic and other old historical differences which underlie the religious divisions among historical neighbors, but religion is a sufficient immediate cause of a split within a speech community which, with time, may naturally result in language differences.

3.7. Gender

Like age and religion, gender is rarely a basis for marked linguistic differences. The two genders, more than two age or religious groups, have good cause to continue to interact linguistically as well as otherwise, and this interaction tends to counteract the rise of marked linguistic differences between men and women.

But there are observable linguistic differences between men and women. In English and usually, these differences concern **gender preferential** features of language, which may be used by either but are preferred by one gender or the other. In some societies, however, the differences concern **gender exclusive** features, used only by men or women.

3.7.1. *Gender preferential differences*
Here are just a few of the **gender preferential differences** in English.

a.   Lexical differences. Men and women make different lexical distinctions in different areas of interest. Women, for example, usually recognize more colors and patterns such as *mauve, rose, paisley,* and *herringbone.* Men usually recognize more types of cars and trucks, such as *Cherokee, Bronco, 5-door,* and *diesel.* In fact, women's vocabulary size is generally greater, as evidenced by higher scores on standard vocabulary tests.

b.   Pitch. The average pitch of women's voices (rate of vocal fold vibration) is considerably higher than that of men: typically in the range 100–400 vs. 80–200 cycles-per-second. It is believed that physiological differences such as size of the larynx and vocal space can't entirely explain the pitch difference, which has become at least partly a linguistic gender marker. Typical men's and women's speech in Japan can differ in pitch even more markedly.

c.   Non-standard usage. Much research in the English-speaking world reveals considerably more adherence to standard language by women. Usage of three sorts of non-standard language were counted in an Australian study (Coates 1993, p. 76): past tense verbs such as *seen* in 'He woke up and seen something'; **double negation** as in 'They don't say nothing'; and **invariable don't** for *doesn't* as in 'Mum don't have to'. Sixteen-year-olds differently used these non-standard forms as follows:

Non-standard past tense:	Males	33.3%
	Females	28%
Double negation:	Males	44.1%
	Females	21.7%
Invariable *don't*:	Males	51.7%
	Females	6.5%

One American study looked at so-called **repetitive pronouns**, such as *he* in *My brother he's pretty good*; the repetitive pronoun repeats the subject. The following figures (from Shuy et al. 1967) report percentage of use of such pronouns observed in interviews of American men and women of four SES levels.

SES	*1 (high)*	*2*	*3*	*4 (low)*
Women	4.8%	9.2	27.2	23.7
Men	5.0	19.3	23.1	25.0

Notice that women generally use repetitive pronouns less, especially in the upper middle SES group (9.2 vs. 19.3), and that the SES level at which this usage markedly increases is lower for women than for men: level 3 vs. 2.

Such differences in non-standard usage have been interpreted to show the greater sensitivity of women to linguistic norms, their preference for standard forms, and corresponding rejection of the 'covert prestige' which may be sought by use of non-standard forms (chapter 27, §2.3.2.1).

d. Conversation. In conversation, there is evidence (if somewhat controversial, at least with men) that women (a) ask more questions, (b) use more **back-channeling** (inserting short comments like *unhuh*, *mmm*, and *yes*, to confirm their attention to a speaker), and (c) interrupt men less than men interrupt women. Such differences have been interpreted as reflecting a greater acceptance by women than men of a facilitative role in conversation, and generally.

3.7.2.   Gender exclusive differences   /*found in Thai*

Two languages with **gender exclusive differences** are Sidamo and Japanese. In Sidamo, an Ethiopian language, there are gender exclusive lexical differences, completely different men's and women's words for the same thing. A few examples are:

Women's word	*Men's word*	
gurda	ado	'milk'
basara	maala	'meat'
rore	šoole	'four'
t'uma	danča	'good'
taalo	darawo	'age-mate'

In Japanese, gender exclusive differences, perhaps not as strictly observed as those in Sidamo, are found in grammatical as well as lexical morphology, so that there are differences like the following: + *Arabic*

Women:	Atashi anata ga suki yo.
Men:	Boku kimi ga suki da yo.
	'I like/love you.'

Women:	Chotto kite.
Men:	Chotto koi.
	'Come here for a minute.'

Here pronouns and verb forms favored by women and men differ: *atashi* 'I' vs. *boku*, *anata* 'you' vs. *kimi*, *suki yo* 'like + emphasis' vs. *suki da yo*, *kite* 'come' vs. *koi*.

Suggestions for
ADDITIONAL READING

Topics of this chapter may be pursued in a number of books which introduce sociolinguistics: *Language in Society: an Introduction to Sociolinguistics* (1994b) by Suzanne Romaine, *Sociolinguistics* (1996) by R. A. Hudson, *The Sociolinguistics of Society* (1984) and *The Sociolinguistics of Language* (1990) by Ralph Fasold, *An Introduction to Sociolinguistics* (1986) by Ronald Wardaugh, and *Sociolinguistics: an Introduction* (1983) by Peter Trudgill. Collections of articles covering important aspects of the field are *The Handbook of Sociolinguistics* (1997) edited by Florian Coulmas, and *Sociolinguistics: an International Handbook of Language and Society* (1988) edited by Ulrich Ammon, Norbert Dittmar, and Klaus J. Mattheier.

Concerning the types and effects of bilingualism and multilingualism, see *Bilingualism* (1994a) by Suzanne Romaine, and *Multilingualism* (1994) by John Edwards.

An unusual approach to the cultural aspects of language is *Understanding Cultures through Their Key Words* (1997) by Anna Wierzbicka. For gender differences and issues see *Women, Men, and Language* (1993) by Jennifer Coates, *Language, Gender, and Society* (1983) by Barrie Thorne, Cheris Kramarae, and Nance Henle, *Words and Women* (1977) by Casey Miller and Kate Swift, and *Language and Gender: a Reader* (1998) edited by Jennifer Coates. For African American English see *African American English: Structure, History, and Use* (1998) edited by Salikoko Mufwene and others.

IMPORTANT CONCEPTS AND TERMS IN THIS CHAPTER

- linguistic variation
- speech community
- subordinate bilingualism
- coordinate bilingualism
- register
- sociolect
- dialect
- mutual intelligibility
- standard dialect

- SES
- post-vocalic *r*
- variable
- Ebonics
- BEV
- *be*-deletion
- habitual *be*
- pidgin language
- transfer

- code-switching
- slang
- jargon
- gender preferential
- gender exclusive
- double negation
- invariable *don't*
- repetitive pronoun
- back-channeling

OUTLINE OF CHAPTER 26

1. Three dimensions of language variation
2. Variation in time

1. Speech communities
2. Centers of change
   1. More populous speech communities
   2. Tight social networks
   3. Groups removed from linguistic standards
   4. Subordinate bilingualism
3. Societal interpretation of linguistic variation in time

3. Seven sociolects
1. Geography
   1. Two senses of 'dialect' and 'language'
   2. Mutual intelligibility
   3. Standard dialect
   4. American dialects
2. Socioeconomic status
3. Ethnicity/race
   1. African American English
      1. Characteristics of BEV
      2. Origin of BEV
   2. Chicano English
4. Age
5. Occupation
6. Religion
7. Gender
   1. Gender preferential differences
   2. Gender exclusive differences

EXAMPLES AND PRACTICE

EXAMPLE

1. English dialect differences: pronunciation. Following is a text phonemically transcribed in a variety of British English (Abercrombie 1964, P. 66) (ˈ marks stressed syllables).

[ðə ˈnɔθ ˈwɪnd ən ðə ˈsən wə dɪsˈpjutɪŋ ˈwɪtʃ wəz ðə ˈstrɒŋgə wen ə ˈtravlə kejm əˈlɒŋ ˈrapt ɪn ə ˈwɔm ˈklowk ðe əˈgrid ðət ðə ˈwən hu ˈfəst səkˈsidəd ɪn ˈmejkɪŋ ðə ˈtravlə ˈtejk ɪz ˈklowk ɔf ʃʊd bɪ kənˈsɪdəd ˈstrɒŋgə ðən ði ˈəðə ˈðen ðə ˈnɔθ wɪnd ˈblu əz ˈhad əz i ˈkʊd bət ðə ˈmɔr i ˈblu ðə mɔ ˈkloslɪ dɪd ðə ˈtravlə ˈfowld ɪz ˈklowk əˈrawnd ɪm ənd ət ˈlast ðə ˈnɔθ ˈwɪnd ˈgejv əp ði əˈtɛmpt ˈðen ðə ˈsən ʃɒn awt ˈwɔmlɪ ənd ɪˈmiˌjətlɪ ðə ˈtravlə ˈtʊk ɔf ɪz ˈklowk ən ˈsow ðə ˈnɔθ wɪnd wəz əˈblajˌjd tə ˈkənfɛs ðət ðə ˈsən wəz ðə ˈstrɒŋgə əv ðə ˈtu]

PRACTICE

Compare the text with your speech and mention seven phonological differences, with examples. Low vowels are back [ɑ] and back rounded [ɒ]; [tʃ] is [č]. Try to find some differences of a general sort evident in more than one word, and list the words. For example, one difference with the author's speech is:

[w] for my [hw] in [wɪtʃ] 'which' and [wɛn] 'when'.

EXAMPLE

2. British and American differences: lexicon and spelling. Among British and American lexical differences are *bonnet/hood*, *torch/flashlight*, and *petrol/ gas(oline)*. Among the spelling differences are *honour/honor*, *travelled/traveled*, and *judgement/judgment*. Everyone has a favorite (favourite) such difference. Mine is a sign which in about 1976 I noticed repeatedly on major English highways before the exits to reststops: 'No football coaches'; 'football coach' is 'an (auto)bus carrying football fans' in British English and 'director of a football team' in American.

PRACTICE

Give six more British/American lexical differences and five more spelling differences. Try to think of spelling differences not on the pattern of examples above, like X*our*/X*or*.

EXAMPLE

3. Australian English. Australia is geographically more separated from the UK and the US than the UK and the US are from each other. Naturally an Australian dialect has evolved there.

PRACTICE

Here are fifteen words of Australian dialect, and fifteen word meanings, according to *Aussie English*, by John O'Grady (1965). Match the words with their meanings. Unless you have some familiarity with the dialect, you will just be guessing at many of these form–meaning correspondences, which, of course, are symbolic signs. Check your answers with an Australian.

1.	arvo	a.	intoxicated, drunk
2.	billy	b.	unruly person
3.	dinkum	c.	be unlucky
4.	dyke	d.	learner, apprentice
5.	full	e.	bed, sleep
6.	galah	f.	scheme, short cut
7.	come a gutzer	g.	my
8.	jackeroo	h.	English
9.	kip	i.	boast
10.	lurk	j.	food
11.	me	k.	complain
12.	pommy	l.	afternoon
13.	skite	m.	tea-pot
14.	tucker	n.	authentic, true
15.	winge	o.	toilet

EXAMPLE

4. *Get*-passives. English has two sorts of passive sentences. For the active sentence *A truck ran over him*, for example, there are:

a.   He was run over by a truck.
b.   He got run over by a truck.

The latter is called a '*get*-passive', and tends to be somewhat different in meaning, if in subtle ways, from the former.

PRACTICE

In the Ozark dialect of English, spoken in the Ozark Mountains of the American South (and perhaps in other dialects), *get*-passives and ordinary passives are distinctly different in meaning. In this dialect sentences (a)–(b) are not paraphrases, sentences (c)–(d), below, are paraphrases, (e)–(f) are unlikely to be heard, and (g)–(h) are respectively a complaint and a confession (Elgin 1979, pp. 122, 126). Given these facts, (a) try to figure out the difference of meaning between the two passives in Ozark dialect. (b) Also discuss whether this difference or some other tends to distinguish the two passives in your dialect or, if you prefer, in the dialect of someone you question.

c.   I got arrested.
d.   I got myself arrested.
e.   The cheese got eaten in the night.
f.   The tree got blown down.
g.   I was kept in after school.
h.   I got kept in after school.

EXAMPLE

5. Language use in bilingual and multilingual communities. The different languages of bilingual and multilingual communities typically have their characteristic contexts of use, as discussed in §2.2.4.

PRACTICE

Consider one of the following multilingual settings, and provide a diagram somewhat like that of §2.2.4, with an essay of particulars appended, concerning the different languages likely to be used. You will probably have to research, in your library, the different national and local language circumstances, and/or interview persons knowledgeable about the setting you choose.

1.   A Japanese-speaking family living in a Quechua-speaking neighborhood of Lima, Peru.
2.   A Korean-speaking family living in a Spanish-speaking neighborhood of Los Angeles.
3.   Another such multilingual circumstance in which you are interested.

REGISTER

This chapter concerns how we use language to express our social identity and social competence, some of the forms of this usage, and the non-linguistic factors which determine it.

1. COMMUNICATIVE COMPETENCE

Complete or mature language use requires at least three sorts of competence:

a. **grammatical competence**, knowledge of the grammar: the lexicon and the phonological, morphological, and syntactic rules of the language,

b. **conversational competence**, knowledge and acceptance of the cooperative principle (chapter 19, §3.1), which obligates one to make a meaningful contribution to the accepted purpose and direction of discourse, and

c. **sociolinguistic competence**, knowledge of the social significance of the choices between some forms of language.

Grammatical, conversational, and sociolinguistic competence are three aspects of **communicative competence**. Grammatical competence concerns grammar including phonological, morphological, and syntactic rules of the language; conversational competence concerns meaningful contribution to the discourse of the moment, and sociolinguistic competence concerns acknowledgement and expression of social relationships and circumstances.

Sociolinguistic competence enables speakers to distinguish among possibilities such as the following. To get someone's attention in English, each of the utterances

1. 'Hey!',
2. 'Excuse me!', and
3. 'Sir!' or 'Ma'am!'

is grammatical and a fully meaningful contribution to the discourse of the moment, but only one of them may satisfy societal expectations and the speaker's preferred presentation of self. 'Hey!' addressed to one's mother or father, for example, often expresses either a bad attitude or surprising misunderstanding of the usually recognized social proprieties, and saying 'Sir!' to a 12-year-old probably expresses inappropriate deference.

Every language accommodates such differences as a non-discrete scale or continuum of recognizably different linguistic 'levels' or styles, termed **registers**, and every socially mature speaker, as part of learning the language, has learned to distinguish and choose among places on the scale of register.

2. REGISTER

2.1. Speech situations

Each occasion of speech, or **speech situation**, determines a different register, and each register favors certain choices among different utterances, each of which may fulfill the requirements of grammaticality and the cooperative principle. Notice in the following three speech situations how each of the three English sentences differently characterizes the speaker's understanding of the social situation and his or her place in it.

a.   Interrupting a passerby to ask the time, one might say any of 1–3:
1.   Hey. What time is it?
2.   Hi. Do you have the time?
3.   Excuse me. Could you tell me what time it is?

b.   Wishing to have the heat turned up, one of 4–6:
4.   Turn the heat up!
5.   Would you turn the heat up, please?
6.   It's sorta cold in here, isn't it?

c.   As the greeting of a letter to a member of the city council:
7.   Dear Betty,
8.   Dear Ms. Jones,
9.   Your excellency,

Registers may range even more broadly, while the basic purpose and raw information of speech remain constant. In figure 27.1 are suggested eleven ways in English to express the desire/demand that someone leave, approximately ordered from very polite to very impolite. Readers will surely disagree with some

Very polite   ↑   a.   Perhaps I should be alone now.

b.   May I be alone now?

c.   I don't suppose you would leave, would you?

d.   Would you be willing to leave?

e.   I'd appreciate it if you would leave.

f.   Please leave.

g.   Don't you wanna leave?

h.   Would you leave?

i.   Get goin', how 'bout it?

j.   Get outa here.

Very impolite   ↓   k.   Get the fuck outa here.

Figure 27.1   An eleven-point scale of politeness

of the rankings, and might even broaden the scale of politeness with additional sentences.

2.2.   Linguistic features of register

As in these examples, mature speakers distinguish registers by an array of linguistic features, across the grammar, from phonology to lexicon and morphology to syntax. Some English examples are:

a.   phonology: rate of speech, and contractions, as in *I do not know* vs. *I dunno*; *Whatcha doin?* vs. *What are you doing?*

b.   lexical morphemes such as *wish* vs. *demand*; *yes* vs. *yeah*;

c.   grammatical morphemes: *I ain't* vs. *I'm not*. Late Middle English had also the pronoun distinction of familiar *thou/thee* (second person singular, subject and object case) vs. polite *ye/you*, which were also and orginally second person plural.

d.   syntax: *I don't suppose you'd leave, huh? Will you leave? Leave!*

2.3.   Three non-linguistic factors influencing register

Differences of register may be thought of as based upon three important non-linguistic factors (S-factors, or F-factors):

a.   *speakers*, especially their relationship of *familiarity* with one another,

b.   *setting*, or the relative *formality* of the occasion, and the

c.   *subject* of discourse, or the *functions*, or purposes, of speaking.

These three factors are ordinarily interdependent. We tend to talk to certain persons in certain settings about certain subjects, and we tend to be more familiar with people in less formal circumstances in which language fulfills certain functions rather than others. Altogether, our linguistic response to the three factors has been termed 'speech accommodation' (Giles 1984), and 'audience design' (Bell 1984).

2.3.1.   Speakers and familiarity

Certainly, speakers address one another differently, particularly according to how familiar they are with one another, and how much information and experience they share. Five characteristics of language which particularly depend on relationships, and perceived relationships, between a speaker and an audience are <u>forms of address</u>, <u>politeness morphology</u>, <u>ellipsis</u>, <u>contractions</u>, and <u>code-switching</u>.

2.3.1.1.   Forms of address.

In probably all languages, speakers acknowledge politeness and familiarity by choice of **forms of address**: in English, for example: 'President Clinton'/'Mr Clinton'/'William'/'Bill'/'Billy'. Choice of one or the other form of address communicates the speaker's acknowledgement of a social circumstance, including the speaker's place in it. This is not always a matter of use or non-use of titles and nicknames. In English, for example, a parent's use of a child's middle name tends to mean trouble for the child: 'John William, come here!' 'Mary Catherine, I saw that!'

2.3.1.2.   Politeness morphology.

Perhaps most languages – though not modern English except in archaic uses of *thou* and *thee*, and potential use of the 'royal *we*' by a monarch – distinguish politeness by choice between grammatical morphemes, especially **familiar** and **polite pronouns**. This distinction is often made in second-person pronouns, for those addressed (English *you*, *your*, *yours*), but may also be in third-person pronouns, for persons spoken about (English *he*, *she*, *it*, *they*, etc.). Spanish has:

		Familiar	Polite
a.	2nd-person singular	tú	usted
b.	2nd-person plural	vosotros	ustedes

Tú and *vosotros* are usually considered to be used for persons of similar age and social status as the speaker, though young people tend to use familiar pronouns for persons of the same age, regardless of social status.

Amharic is a language which has the familiar/polite distinction in singular third-person pronouns: familiar *issu* 'he' and *isswa* 'she' vs. polite *issaččəw*. The polite form is particularly for older persons, but is favored even for persons unfamiliar to the speaker. In languages with such grammatical morphemes, there is **grammaticization** of politeness, since the choice between a familiar or polite pronoun concerns grammatical competence, in the choice of grammatical morphemes, as well as simultaneous sociolinguistic competence, in the expression of social expectations and presentation of self which this choice signifies.

Japanese has other forms of grammaticized politeness, including 'plain' versus polite forms of verbs. Plain forms, for example *miru* 'see,' vs. polite form *mimasu*, and *iku* 'go' vs. polite form *ikimasu*, are used when speaking to close friends, and polite forms when speaking to others, especially older persons and persons one doesn't know.

2.3.1.3. Ellipsis. **Ellipsis** is the omission of major constituents of sentences, as in *I did* (the object of the verb is unstated, vs. *I did what you said*;), and *Can't go* (the subject is unstated, vs. *I can't go*). Persons familiar with one another share a lot of information, so in conversations between them much of this can go unsaid, and ellipsis contributes to fluency in their talk. The fluency and greater rate of speech are also evidence as well of register choice, signaling speakers' judgements of the degree of familiarity in their relationship to one another.

Knowledge of the possibilities of ellipsis is a matter of grammatical competence. English for example does not allow object ellipsis with some verbs: *I understand* is okay but not *I opened*. But the choice to employ ellipsis or not reflects sociolinguistic competence.

2.3.1.4. Contractions. Rate of speech increases with familiarity between speakers. As the result of **grammaticization** of fast-speech deletions of phones, many languages, including English, have customary short pronunciations and spellings of some frequent grammatical morphemes. In English these are the **contractions** of auxiliary verbs including *I'm* and *they're*, and of *not* as in *don't* and *isn't*. One study (Crystal and David 1969) showed the following average occurrence of possible contractions per thousand words in five British English settings:

Telephone conversation between friends	59.9%
Interviews	25.4
Prepared speeches	13.3
Science fiction	6.5
Academic writing	0.1

Knowledge of contractions is an aspect of grammatical competence, but the choice to employ them or not reflects sociolinguistic competence.

2.3.1.5. Code-switching. Switching from language to language within a single speech situation is called **code-switching**, a phenomenon which characterizes the sociolect of bilingual speech communities (chapter 26, §3.3.2), the members of which have the grammatical competence to code-switch when speaking to one another. Some occasions of code-switching may be necessitated by speakers' lesser degree of grammatical competence in one of the languages. For example, one who has received a specialized education in a second language often finds it necessary to switch out of the native language when talking about that specialization.

Although bilingual competence is perhaps never balanced for all subjects and settings, many occasions of code-switching are motivated as aspects of register, since they occur in contexts in which differential grammatical competence cannot be an explanation. These reveal this added dimension of bilinguals for expressing sociolinguistic competence. The following (from the *New York Times*, March 26, 1997) exemplifies, if somewhat exaggeratedly, code-switching by a Spanish/English bilingual:

¿Quieres que te cocine some rice en la hitachi, or should I just get you some confley con leche? By the way, you embarkated me el otro dia. What did you do, pick up some fafu en vez de ir al restaurante where I was waiting? Eres tan chipero.

(¿*Quieres que te cocine* 'Do you want me to cook for you?' *la hitachi* 'the (Hitachi) steam cooker', *confley con leche* 'cornflakes with milk', *el otro dia* 'the other day', *fafu en vez de ir al restaurante* 'fastfood instead of going to the restaurant', *Eres tan chipero* 'You're so cheap').

Here, within an English sentence, Spanish *embarcar* is treated as an English verb, *embarkated*, and within a Spanish sentence, English *cheap* is treated as a Spanish noun *chipero*. *Confley* 'cornflakes' and *fafu* 'fastfood' are English words adapted to requirements of Spanish phonology. The alternating stretches of fluent Spanish and English illustrate well the probable sociolinguistic-affective purpose of code-switching. One such bilingual said she 'often switches into Spanish to convey anger, joy, love or embarrassment' and 'because Spanish is a more descriptive, emotional language', but a phrase like *en vez de ir al restaurante* 'instead of going to the restaurant' is not obviously more descriptive or objectively emotional than the equivalent English. The switches themselves, not their linguistic content, express self-identity and assert shared identity with another Spanish speaker.

Code-switching can be even more affectively expressive when more languages are available to switch among. In multilingual Kenya educated persons typically speak at least three languages: their regional or home language, Swahili, and English. Swahili is the lingua franca of East Africa and the official national language of Kenya, and English is the language of secondary and higher education. Kenyans who share a regional language may switch to English to establish their status as educated persons, and government officials, even when speaking to fellow speakers of a regional language, may switch to Swahili to assert authority and their official status (Myers-Scotton 1993b).

2.3.2. *Setting and formality*

We know special forms of language for use in particular settings often distinguished by their degree of formality. 'Formality' in these cases largely means degree

	Register	*Description*
1.	Intimate:	Conversation of intimates
2.	Casual:	Talk at parties and in games
3.	Consultative:	Ordinary commercial transactions
4.	Formal:	Contributions of participants at meetings, hearings, conferences, etc.
5.	Frozen:	One-directional communication by authorities at meetings, hearings, conferences, etc.

Figure 27.2   A five-point scale of register

of fixedness of social relations between speakers, and this tends to correspond to the socially licensed amount of reciprocity of speech – whether talk tends to be one-way or whether all those present talk more or less equivalently. In the courtroom, for example, the judge has to be addressed in the proper way, even by an old friend, and only the judge speaks at will.

The most established and routinized settings tend also to determine regular or even ritualized, 'one-way', forms of language. For example, the classroom, sports events, and formal meetings have their preferred linguistic forms. 'The meeting will come to order' is the usual and ritualized way of saying, in meetings, 'Hey, let's get quiet and get to work now', and 'Bottom of the sixth, two out, and three-one on Bonds' is the normal way of saying, in the game of baseball, 'It is the bottom of the ninth inning of play; there are two outs, and the count on Bonds is three balls and one strike.'

This scale of register, like the others, is a continuum, but at least five degrees of register based basically upon differences of setting/formality may often be recognized, as in figure 27.2 (adapted from Joos 1961).

Two features of language which particularly depend on the setting within a speech situation are vernacular vs. non-vernacular usage, including use of taboo words, and hypercorrection and malapropism.

2.3.2.1.   Vernacular and non-vernacular language.   **Vernacular** language is that of ordinary, carefree, colloquial speech. Use of vernacular forms in non-vernacular contexts could be evidence of a speaker's ignorance of the socially prescribed 'standard' language, and certain forms in particular are recognized as giving such evidence. These are linguistic **social markers**. An often noted American English example is *ain't*, the originally perfectly well-formed contraction of *am + not*, which fell into disrepute in standard English after it was extended out of first-person singular as in third-person *He ain't*. Other English social markers are third person singular *don't* as in *he don't*, and demonstrative *them* as in *them are mine. Ain't*, for example, is common in the vernacular of many English-speaking communities, and its use in non-vernacular settings tends to guarantee the notice of listeners of other communities.

But such usage may also signal frankness and honesty, and solidarity with others whom speakers recognize as fellow members of their vernacular dialect. When used by obviously well-educated persons, such interpretation is guaranteed. A standard dialect speaker of English who intentionally switches to use of social markers such as *ain't* and *he don't* is said to seek **covert prestige**. Such prestige is 'covert' because its elicitation will often not, if successful, be consciously noted.

Deliberate (as opposed to instinctive) use of **taboo words** such as *fuck* and *shit*, usage which tends to characterize male more than female speech, may also seek covert prestige, but the strength of these as social markers makes this more difficult to achieve.

In a contrasting register, one uses unusually formal non-vernacular forms in vernacular contexts. For example, one will ordinarily say *It's me* to the question *Who is it?* asked by a familiar interlocutor, but, when asked the same question by one from whom one seeks prestige, the same speaker may say *It is I*. Similarly, except after prepositions Americans ordinarily say *who* in preference to *whom*: *Who did you ask?*, not *Whom did you ask?*, but in some circumstances the latter may be substituted. Such usage is said to seek **overt prestige**, because the often dubious prestige one gets from such usage is ordinarily consciously noted, hence 'overt'. One may use jargon similarly seeking overt prestige, saying, for example, *semantics* when nothing more than ordinary *meaning* is intended.

2.3.2.2. Hypercorrection and malapropism.   Language use is such a valuable marker of social competence that one seeking the overt prestige of unfamiliar standard language usage may sometimes produce **hypercorrections**. A common English hypercorrection, for example, concerns the subject pronouns as in *They asked he and I* for traditional standard *They asked him and me*, and after prepositions *just between she and I* for *just between her and me*.

The object pronouns *me*, *him*, *her*, and *them* are more frequent and earlier learned than subject pronouns *I*, *he*, *she*, and *they*, and there is a natural tendency, especially of child learners but persisting in adults, to substitute object pronouns for subject pronouns, especially after *and*, as in *Jack and me were there*, and in some dialects even before *and* as in *Him and me were there*. (Notice that the same speakers would never say *Me was there*, but the presence of *and* in the subject somehow licenses the use of object pronouns.) Though common, such usage is stigmatized as a linguistic **social marker**, and fear of the stigma of this social marker results in the opposite tendency to substitute subject pronouns for object pronouns. That is, as *he and I* may be a correction of *him and me*, *between you and I* is a hypercorrection of *between you and me*.

The lexical-morpheme equivalent of such hypercorrection of grammatical morphemes is known as **malapropism**: substituting similar sounding words for words which one doesn't know well, such as *sympathy* for *symphony* ('I prefer listening to sympathies') or *ravished* for *ravaged* ('Fire ravished much of the business district').

2.3.3. *Subject and function*

Depending on the purpose of speaking, the subject or topic, and functions (as to assert, question, and persuade), we have more or less fluency or facility of grammatical competence, especially concerning vocabulary, and we can put this knowledge to use to express sociolinguistic competence as well.

2.3.3.1. *Jargon and slang.*

Professional and technical topics – including some talk about sports – may encourage the use of **jargon**, whereas familiar and strictly social topics are occasions for **slang** (chapter 24, §2.3). Auto mechanics and physicians, for example, won't often describe the same engine repair or medical condition to one another the way they would to their customers or patients, respectively, nor do gang members or friends talk about their activities among themselves the way they talk about these activities with others.

Jargon and slang provide lexical alternatives to more typical or ordinary usage (for example linguistic jargon *semantics* for *meaning*, and slang *cop* for *policeman*), and the choice of a jargon or slang alternative in preference to the ordinary language choice expresses an acknowledgement or claim of shared group membership in and solidarity with the group which the jargon/slang choice typifies. In the case of the intentionally obfuscatory use of jargon (that is, intending not to be understood), the claim is an assertion of separateness, expertise, and perhaps more general superiority.

2.3.3.2. *Speaking vs. writing.*

Speech and writing have different strengths and weaknesses (chapter 22, §1–2). Certain subjects and/or functions of language tend to favor the use of speech or writing, and certain forms of language are encouraged or discouraged according to whether language is spoken or written. Contractions, vernacular usage, and slang, for example, are often avoided in written styles, which also favor more complex syntax and lower frequency vocabulary. A marked distinction between the language of speaking and writing may have been more apparent in the past, and is perhaps becoming less so today, particularly with the appearance of e-mail, and on-line electronic communication, for which traditional standards and expectations of written form often seem not to apply.

2.3.3.3. *Attention to speech.*

Different functions or purposes of language use tend to determine different degrees of **attention to speech**. In the intimate register friends and family members talking about familiar topics pay almost no attention to how they speak, whereas in the 'frozen' register, as in writing instructions to assemble something complicated, how things are said is almost as critical as what is said. A lot of research has revealed a regular continuum of greater to lesser use of certain linguistic features generally reflecting degree of attention to speech. For example, the frequency of [n] for [ŋ] as in *runnin'* [ɹə́nɪn] for *running* [ɹə́nɪŋ] varies according to whether one is speaking casually, speaking carefully, or reading,

Table 27.1 Representative linguistic features and genres of English

Representative genres (out of 23)	Representative features (out of 67)
1. press reportage	1. contractions
2. biography	2. first-person pronouns (*I, me, . . .*)
3. mystery fiction	3. main-verb *be*
4. humorous writing	4. passive verbs
5. personal letters	5. nominalizations in *-ment, -tion, . . .*
6. planned speeches	6. necessity modals (*must, ought, . . .*)

Source: Biber 1988

as seen in the following percentages of such [n] pronunciations in the speech of three socioeconomic status groups (Wald and Shopen 1981). The less presumed attention to speech, the more [n] pronunciations.

Percentage of [n] in	Casual speech	Careful speech	Reading
Lower SES	80	53	22
Working	49	31	11
Middle	32	21	1

Generally speaking, the more attention to speech the more standard and the less vernacular the language. (But the correlation is not perfect: one concerned with covert prestige may pay more attention in order to maximize vernacular forms, and those for whom the standard is not native have to pay more attention than do those for whom standard forms are habitual.)

2.3.3.4. Linguistic characteristics of genres.   Research supports our intuitions that certain linguistic features tend positively or negatively to characterize discourse of certain types. For example,

a.   contractions tend to occur in conversation and to be absent in formal writing;
b.   passive verbs tend to occur in scientific and technical writing and to be absent in speech and informal writing; and
c.   third-person pronouns and past tense verbs tend to occur in narratives.

Certain sets of linguistic features have been found to characterize certain functionally-defined types of spoken and written language, or **genres**. Biber (1988) analyzed texts totaling 960,000 words representing 23 spoken and written genres, including the six listed at the left in table 27.1, for the occurrence or non-occurrence of 67 linguistic features, including the six listed at the right in table 27.1.

1. (Personally) Involved ↔ Informational *(would not expect to find those)*
    a. first-person pronouns
    b. wh-questions
    c. final prepositions
2. Narrative ↔ Nonnarrative
    a. past tense verbs
    b. third-person pronouns
    c. negative feature: present tense verbs
3. Situation independent ↔ Situation dependent
    a. relative clauses (*a book that I liked, someone whom you know, . . .*)
    b. nominalizations with *-ment, -ness, -tion, -ity*
    c. negative feature: time and place adverbs
4. Persuasive ↔ Nonpersuasive
    a. suasive verbs (*agree, ask, demand,* etc.)
    b. conditional subordination
    c. necessity modals (*must, ought,* etc.)
5. Abstract ↔ Concrete
    a. passive verbs (*is known, was seen, . . .*)
    b. past participial clauses (for example: *Known for such behavior, he . . .*)
    c. high type/token ratio (many different words)
6. More ↔ Less on-line informational elaboration
    a. that-clauses as object of verbs (*know that . . . , believe that . . .*)
    b. demonstratives (*this, that, . . .*)
    c. negative feature: phrase coordination (NP *and* NP, VP *and* VP)

Figure 27.3 Six functional dimensions of language and three features characteristic of each
Source: Biber 1988

By **factor analysis**, a statistical procedure which recognizes those factors/features which significantly tend to cooccur, Biber discovered six sets of linguistic features, which could be understood to characterize six 'functional dimensions' of language. See figure 27.3, in which for each dimension three of its characteristic features are listed, including 'negative features', which characterize the dimension by their significant absence. Notice how the linguistic features of each dimension seem reasonably to characterize the positive aspect as described – for example, in genres high on the more personally involved, less 'informational' dimension, the number of first-person pronouns, wh-questions, and final prepositions increases.

These six dimensions of language purpose or function are found in spoken and written genres, and the set of linguistic features which characterizes each is the same in both sorts of texts.

Suggestions for
ADDITIONAL READING

Introductions to the topic of register are *Dimensions of Register Variation* (1995) by Douglas Biber and *Investigating English Style* (1969) by David Crystal and Derek David. A current collection of readings on the topic is *Sociolinguistic Perspectives on Register* (1994) edited by Douglas Biber and Edward Finegan. Informal essays on register are included in *The Social Art: Language and its Uses* (1994) by Ronald Macauley.

On the dimension of politeness in particular is *Politeness: Some Universals in Language Usage* (1987) by Penelope Brown and S. C. Levinson, and on code-switching is *Duelling Languages: Grammatical Structures in Code Switching* (1993a) by Carol Myers-Scotton. For topics concerning multilingual society see *Multilingualism* (1994) by John Edwards. For a comparision of the register differences of speech and writing see *Spoken and Written Language* (1989) by M. A. K. Halliday.

IMPORTANT CONCEPTS AND TERMS IN THIS CHAPTER

- grammatical competence
- conversational competence
- sociolinguistic competence
- communicative competence
- register
- speech situation
- forms of address
- familiar pronoun
- polite pronoun
- grammaticization
- ellipsis
- contractions
- code-switching
- vernacular
- social marker
- covert prestige
- taboo word
- overt prestige
- hypercorrection
- malapropism
- jargon
- slang
- attention to speech
- genre
- factor analysis

OUTLINE OF CHAPTER 27

1. Communicative competence
2. Register

1. Speech situations
2. Linguistic features of register
3. Three non-linguistic factors influencing register
   1. Speakers and familiarity
      1. Forms of address
      2. Politeness morphology
      3. Ellipsis
      4. Contractions
      5. Code-switching
   2. Setting and formality
      1. Vernacular and non-vernacular language
      2. Hypercorrection and malapropism
   3. Subject and function
      1. Jargon and slang
      2. Speaking vs. writing
      3. Attention to speech
      4. Linguistic characteristics of genres

EXAMPLES AND PRACTICE

EXAMPLE

1. Pronunciations in casual speech. Study the 22-line phonemically transcribed American English casual-speech conversation below (slightly adapted from Carterette and Jones 1974, pp. 398–399). A translation is given in complete-word spellings. Notice the many differences between pronunciations in casual and careful speech.

1. dɪdnjəlajkhɑjskul.
2. oajlajkthajskul bədajθɔtajlajktðijajdiəəvkaləjbedər. ænajlajkðijajdiəəv
3. gowiŋtəjusijɛletu. wɛrdəjuwənətrænsfər.
4. ajmgɔnəprabəblitrænsfərtəohajɔstet. wɛrdjuwonətrænsfər.
5. jusijɛle.
6. gʊd. ajlhævkəmpəni.
7. əladə owəladpipəl ðæʔplesɪzjuj
8. wɛl ðɪskulɪzmorərlɛsgirdfərtrænsfərzovərtəjusijɛle.
9. ɔlðɛrkərɪkjuləmənɛvriθɪŋɪzsɛtəpfərɪt.
10. sætərdinajt wiwɛntuðæʔfolkmjuwzɪkfɛstəvəljunoðehædovərðer.
11. ajhərdəbawʔðæt.
12. ænɪtukəsəbawt o so əbawdənawr drajvɪnərawntrajɪntəfajndəparkɪnspes.
13. ənwifajnəlifajndəparkɪnspes wikəməpənðəsajnsɛz dəpazɪʔtukwərdərz.
14. ənwidɪdənhævɪt wiwɛl judɪdən. wihædbɪlzənčenǰ bədnokwərdərz.
15. soðɛnwihætəgodrajvɪnərawntrajɪntəgetukwərdərz. junočenj kembæk.

16. ajhɚdðæʔðehætɚskɔrtwənəvðijentɚtenɚzɔfðəʔəsteǰ sætɚdenɑjt.
17. wɛl ɑjwʊdənnowəbawʔðætsi bɪkɔzðedəvɑjdədəp ðɚwɚsomɛnipipəl
18. ðæʔkemtəðæʔθɪŋ ðæʔðedɪvɑjdədəpðəpɚformɚz æniʔtɚndawt
19. ðehædənəðɚmidiŋ. ɪnədɪfrənhɔl. sowijonlihæd hæfəvðəpɚfɔrmɚz
20. ðəʔwɚsəpozdəbiðɛrrili.
21. wɛlhawlɔŋdɪdɪʔlæst.
22. tɛnθɚdifɑjv.

1. Didn't you like high school?
2. Oh, I liked high school, but I thought I liked the idea of college better. And I like the idea of
3. going to UCLA, too. Where do you want to transfer?
4. I'm going to probably transfer to Ohio State. Where do you want to transfer?
5. UCLA.
6. Good. I'll have company.
7. A lot of, oh, a lot of people; that place is huge.
8. Well, this school is more or less geared for transfers over to UCLA. All their
9. curriculum and everything is set up for that.
10. Saturday night we went to that folk music festival you know they had over there.
11. I heard about that.
12. And it took us, oh, about an hour driving around trying to find a parking space.
13. And we finally find a parking space; we come up; the sign says deposit two quarters.
14. And we didn't have it. We, well, you didn't, we had bills and change but no quarters.
15. So then we had to go driving around trying to get two quarters. You know change. Came back.
16. I heard that they had to escort one of the entertainers off the, uh, stage Saturday night.
17. Well, I wouldn't know about that, see, because they divided up, there were so many people
18. that came to that thing that they divided up the performers and it turned out
19. they had another meeting, in a different hall. So we only had half of the performers
20. that were supposed to be there really.
21. Well how long did it last?
22. Ten thirty-five.

PRACTICE

Listed below are 15 casual-speech pronunciations found in the text. Find examples of at least 12 of these and, for each, write the line number, and the word (as spelled) in which the pronunciation occurs, with the preceding or following word. 'Ø' in the casual speech column means the careful speech phoneme is omitted in casual speech. Here are two examples:

Careful speech	Casual speech	Line no.	Word and adjacent word
/u/	/ə/	15	to get
/t/	/ʔ/	21	it last

Careful speech	Casual speech	Careful speech	Casual speech
1. /o/	/ə/	9. /v/	Ø
2. /h/	Ø	10. /t/	/d/
3. /d/	Ø	11. /tj/	/ʃ/
4. /e/	/ə/	12. /d/	Ø
5. /ŋ/	/n/	13. /ə/	Ø
6. /t/	Ø	14. /s/	Ø
7. /æ/	/ə/	15. /ɑ/	/ə/
8. Ø (nothing)	/j/		

EXAMPLE

2. Scale of casualness: contractions. In a study of English-language texts of different types, spoken and written, such as telephone conversations, newspaper writing, prepared speeches, and official documents, contractions (such as *I've* for *I have* and *she'll* for *she will*) were found to occur, reasonably, at different percentages (Crystal and David 1969).

PRACTICE

Try to match text-types 1–12 with percentages of contractions (a)–(1) (contractions/possible contractions). For 5 answers of the 12, see §2.3.1.4, above.

1.	Science fiction writing	a.	59.9%
2.	Telephone conversation among friends	b.	49.6
3.	Interviews	c.	48.8
4.	Spontaneous speeches	d.	25.4
5.	Romantic fiction	e.	21.5
6.	Academic journals	f.	19
7.	Telephone conversation among business associates	g.	17.8
8.	Prepared speeches	h.	13.3
9.	Newspaper articles	i.	6.5
10.	Radio broadcasts	j.	1.5
11.	Telephone conversation among strangers	k.	0.1
12.	Official documents	l.	0%

EXAMPLE

3. Scale of politeness: requests I. Probably all speakers in all languages vary their choice of certain words and grammatical forms according to degree of politeness. For example, we express requests differently, directly or indirectly, depending on who we are speaking to.

PRACTICE

Consider the following six ways of expressing a request to borrow ten dollars. Arrange them on a scale of politeness from most polite, 1, to least polite, 6. Comparing answers in class, we can find out whether there tends to be agreement or not, and thus how much shared knowledge we appear to have in such judgements.

1. How 'bout lettin' me borrow ten bucks?
2. Could you lend me ten dollars?
3. Would you please lend me ten dollars?
4. I'd appreciate it if you could lend me ten dollars.
5. Lemme borrow ten bucks!
6. Do you suppose you could let me borrow ten dollars?

EXAMPLE

4. Scale of politeness: requests II. See the eleven-point scale of politeness for asking someone to leave in §2.1, above. Consider whether the given order of requests, from very polite to very impolite, matches your sense of the language.

PRACTICE

Suppose you need to pass through a crowd of people. Suggest a number of ways to ask (or demand) that the people step aside and let you through, arranged on a scale of politeness. After you have written out your different requests or demands, write each one on a separate piece of paper and ask a friend to arrange them on the same scale. Of course, the more different ways to express the request, the more difficult it is to order them confidently and for two people to agree fully on this order.

EXAMPLE

5. Sports announcer talk. Probably all sports have jargon, and sports announcers have special ways of describing them. A study of the language used by announcers at sports events (Ferguson 1983) identified a number of linguistic features of baseball 'sports announcer talk' in English including:

a. *be*-verb deletion, as in *Milburn now at first*, a syntactic feature,
b. use of simple present tense for past events of short duration treated as if ongoing, as in *Jeffries takes a pitch high for ball three*, a morphological feature, and

c. routines or patterns for recurring events of the game such as 'the count' in baseball, the pattern for which is [number *and* number *on* name], as in *two and two on Miller*, an idiom derived by clipping from *The count is X balls and Y strikes on Z.*

Listen to a broadcast of any sports event, and (a) list at least five specialized ways of talking about and describing the sport. You probably have to be a sports fan in order to confidently recognize the features as characteristic of such broadcasts. Listen especially for routines and idioms, like giving the count in baseball or the defensive set-up in football. Also (b) list ten items of specialized vocabulary of the sport.

6. Five levels of language. Recall the five registers roughly described in §2.3.2 above: (a) intimate, (b) casual, (c) consultative, (d) formal, and (e) frozen. The five might be illustrated as follows in the words usable by the Speaker of the US House of Representatives asking members, at the beginning of a session, to cooperate in beginning the session.

1. Sit down and shut up, people!
2. Come on, everybody, sit down and get quiet.
3. Ladies and gentlemen, take your seats and be quiet.
4. Members are respectfully asked to be seated and be silent.
5. The House will come to order.

'The House will come to order' are the traditional and accustomed words used by the Speaker to begin sessions of the House.

Write utterances in the five registers for two speech settings. In order to employ the frozen register, you must think of settings for which the level of very routine, 'frozen' language is established.

7. Six functional dimensions of language. Six feature-sets of language which significantly characterize six functional 'dimensions' of language were noted and exemplified in figure 27.3, above, and are repeated here:

1. (Personally) Involved ↔ Informational
2. Narrative ↔ Nonnarrative
3. Situation independent ↔ Situation dependent
4. Persuasive ↔ Nonpersuasive
5. Abstract ↔ Concrete
6. More ↔ Less on-line informational elaboration

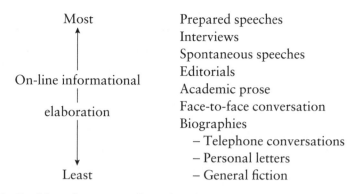

Most

On-line informational

elaboration

Least

Prepared speeches
Interviews
Spontaneous speeches
Editorials
Academic prose
Face-to-face conversation
Biographies
  – Telephone conversations
  – Personal letters
  – General fiction

Figure 27.4   Ranking of genres on dimension 6

A. Academic prose
    Official documents
    Press reviews
    Professional letters
    Biographies
        – Broadcasts
        – Adventure fiction
        – Personal letters
        – Face-to-face conversation
        – Telephone conversations

B. Romantic fiction
    Adventure fiction
    Biographies
    Prepared speeches
    Personal letters
    Face-to-face conversations
        – Interviews
        – Telephone conversations
        – Official documents
        – Broadcasts

C. Official documents
    Professional letters
    Academic writing
    Biographies
    Spontaneous speeches
    Interviews
        – Personal letters
        – Face-to-face conversations
        – Telephone conversations
        – Broadcasts

D. Telephone conversations
    Face-to-face conversations
    Personal letters
    Interviews
    Romantic fiction
        – Broadcasts
        – Humor
        – Biographies
        – Academic writing
        – Official documents

E. Professional letters
    Editorials
    Personal letters
    Telephone conversations
    Official documents
    Face-to-face conversation
    Biographies
        – Adventure fiction
        – Press reviews
        – Broadcasts

Figure 27.5   Five genre scales illustrating five functional dimensions of language
Source: Biber 1988

Biber (1988, pp. 113, 156) described dimension 6 as 'discourse that is informational but produced under real-time conditions . . . [with] an informational focus, but . . . the speaker must contend with real-time production constraints'. 'Real-time production constraints' means that time is limited (or, in writing, space). In figure 27.4, ten genres from prepared speeches to general fiction are ranked in terms of their manifestation of this sixth dimension, the genre at the top of the list most likely to have features of the dimension, and that at the bottom least likely to have them. Genres preceded by minuses are negatively evaluated on the dimension – that is, the linguistic feature-set which characterizes the dimension has below-average occurrence in these genres. The ranking of figure 27.4 may seem reasonable, on consideration: prepared speeches, at the top of the scale, must be very informational to be effective, and must usually be delivered within strict constraints of time. General fiction, on the other hand, at the bottom of scale defined by this dimension, can sacrifice informationalness to entertainment, and take its time in doing so.

PRACTICE

With the above example of dimension 6 and its associated scale of genres, perhaps you can recognize each of the other five dimensions in one of the genre scales A–E of figure 27.5. Try to match dimensions 1–5 with genre-scales A–E.

THE HISTORY OF LINGUISTICS

This chapter surveys the history of linguistics, presenting some of the most important discoveries and events, beginning with the Greeks. It concludes with a brief statement about what the field of linguistics is today and what linguists do.

1. THE HISTORY OF LINGUISTICS

The details of names and dates of this chapter are less important than its attempted showing, very selectively, of the long and gradual development of modern ideas about language, which, as the modern field of **linguistics**, this book has tried to introduce. Also, such a survey must emphasize successful ideas and actual findings, and thus can give little attention to the many false but reasonable ideas, popular in their time, which were eventually left behind. Along with the truthful ideas, false ideas must be present today as they have always been in the past.

1.1. Classical foundations

1.1.1. Greece

The history of linguistics, the study of language, is sometimes and reasonably dated from the first surviving descriptive grammar of a European language, of Greek, written by Dionysius Thrax in about 100 BC. Before this influential little grammar, there had been at least three centuries of Greek philosophizing about language, and some earlier descriptive work, of the so-called Stoic philosophers of Athens, only fragments of which survive.

One of the stories told in about 450 BC by the first historian, Herodotus, concerns an Egyptian king, Psammaticus, who in order to confirm that the original inhabitants of the world were Egyptians isolated two children to see what language they would speak if uninfluenced by the language of their upbringing.

Unfortunately for the Egyptian theory, according to the story their first word, after two years, turned out to be *bekos*, 'bread' in Phrygian, a now extinct Indoeuropean language of Asia Minor.

Perhaps the earliest Greek writing about language concerns speculation about the nature and origin of language. Plato (428–348 BC) in *Cratylus*, the first of the *Dialogues of Plato*, is concerned with the question of whether the forms and meanings of words are naturally related or not – that is, whether words are **iconic** and **indexical signs** (chapter 1, §2.1), or **symbolic signs**. In the dialogue, Plato has Socrates concluding that originally the form–meaning relations of words must have been natural, but convention has subsequently obscured these: 'that objects should be imitated in letters and syllables, and so find expression, may appear ridiculous . . . but cannot be avoided', since no other explanation short of attributing these to God would be reasonable (Salus 1969, p. 58). (The distinction between letter and phone would not become clear in language study for another two thousand years, and is still not clear to those ignorant of phonetics. In fact, the word *grammar* is based on the Greek word for letter, *gramma*.)

Before this period, when Greek interest in language was entirely speculative, in 5th century BC India language description was well underway, and an Indian scholar, Pāṇini, was writing the grammar of Sanskrit, including morphology, phonetics, and morphophemics. But this work would not become known to European scholars for many centuries.

The Greeks begin to analyze their language, with the first rudimentary Greek grammars written by the so-called Stoic philosophers of Athens, around 300 BC, who perhaps became interested in resolving questions about 'correct Greek' when they noticed that their language had changed from that of their earlier writers, such as Herodotus, and had begun markedly to differ from place to place in the Mediterranean world. One of their first realizations concerned the existence of word classes or 'parts of speech'. Plato's student Aristotle (384–322 BC), in his *Poetics*, says that 'to all diction belong the following parts: the letter, the syllable, the conjunction, the noun, the verb, the article, the case, and the discourse or speech' (Salus 1969, p. 60). The verb, for example, Aristotle defined as 'expressing time'. The Greeks, like other ancient peoples, seem to have taken no significant interest in other languages.

The first grammar of Greek which survives was written in the Greek colony of Alexandria, in Egypt, by Dionysius Thrax, in about 100 BC. This included phonetics, though considered strictly in relation to letters of the Greek alphabet, and morphology, dividing words of the language into eight classes or **parts of speech**. Much subsequent work of grammatical description of both Greek and Latin was influenced by this short work, of only about fifteen pages. The first study of Greek syntax, by Apollonius Dyscolus, comes only a hundred years later.

1.1.2. Rome

Based on these Greek foundations the Romans, also concerned with preserving their language in the face of the changes that came with time and geographical spread of the language, wrote grammars of Latin. The significant distinction between **inflectional** and **derivational affixes** (chapter 4, §5) was noted by Varro (AD 116–127) in a multi-volume grammar of Latin only a few parts of which survive. Based on Varro's grammar but more influential were those of Donatus (ca. AD 350), and, in Constantinople as the Roman empire contracted, of Priscian (512–560), a 20-volume work which was adopted as the standard grammar of Latin through much of the Middle Ages (ca. 500–1300). Knowledgeable and complete for its time, the level of sophistication of Priscian's analysis is perhaps suggested by the fact that he equated the two Latin prefixes *in-* 'in' and *in-* 'negative' (Robins 1967, p. 57).

Following Thrax's analysis of Greek, Latin grammars recognized eight parts of speech: nouns, verbs, participles, pronouns, adverbs, prepositions, interjections, and conjunctions. Adjectives, which were then included with nouns because they both carried case suffixes, would not be sorted from nouns in European grammars for another thousand years.

1.2.   European background

1.2.1.   *Study of vernacular languages*

During the Middle Ages, awareness gradually arose of the value and interest of other European languages. These 'vernacular' languages didn't need to be written, since people who could write usually knew Latin. When they were analyzed, this was in the mould of Latin grammar.

Three developments exemplify the gradual increase of the interest of scholars in their native languages. Before 860, the Greek alphabet was adapted for Slavic languages, at first Macedonian, resulting in the **Cyrillic alphabet** (so named for St Cyril (d. 869), who formalized the adaptation). In Britain around AD 1000, an abbot of the church, Aelfric (955?–1020), wrote a grammar of Latin for Anglo-Saxon-speaking children and accompanied it with an Anglo-Saxon and Latin comparative word-list. Then, sometime in the 12th century appeared a short study known as the 'First Grammatical Treatise', whose unknown author has become known as 'the First Grammarian'. The goal of this precocious work was to correct the inadequacy of the Latin alphabet for writing Icelandic (the Germanic language of Iceland), but, along with presenting a brief but original descriptive phonology of Icelandic, it also reveals the first awareness of the difference between **phones** and **phonemes** (chapter 3), and uses **minimal pairs** (chapter 3, §2.5) to show this. Owing to the politically as well as geographically marginal status of Iceland in Europe, the First Grammatical Treatise remained unknown and unable to influence the European study of language for six hundred years.

In this same period, Arabic, like Greek and Latin, had spread widely and changed from that which Mohammed had used in writing the Koran, and concern for 'correct' Arabic stimulated the writing of Arabic grammars, and, eventually, the establishment of a tradition of Arabic descriptive grammar, which included accurate articulatory phonetic observations then unknown in Europe. This Arabic linguistic work was also to remain unknown and unable to influence European language study.

1.2.2. *The relationship of languages*

An issue which continued to be discussed in the Middle Ages was the question of the first language. According to Christian conventional wisdom of the time, this was Hebrew. Gradually, knowledge of the diversity of the world including its languages arose in Europe, and, eventually, this was sufficient to influence an issue that arose in early Renaissance philosophy and continues today (in this book, chapter 9, §4, and chapter 20, §3) – whether we have knowledge innately, or derive all our knowledge by experience (obviously with the exception of that ability, or knowledge, which enables us to encode and analyze experience). The former position was early taken by René Descartes (1596–1650), and goes by the name **rationalism**. Descartes' philosophy emphasized the necessity of doubt in acquiring knowledge by introspection, hence his formula 'I think, therefore I am.' Rationalism inspired a linguistic work known as the *Port Royal Grammar* (1660) by Antoine Arnauld (1612–1694) and Claude Lancelot (1615?–1695). Languages seem to represent basic human knowledge but vary widely from people to people, and this presents an obvious challenge to rationalist philosophy. The Port Royal grammarians tried to show that the grammars of all languages are, in fact, unified at their core by logical structural principles. The alternative to rationalism, **empiricism**, is often represented in the ideas of John Locke (1632–1704), who believed that the mind starts out as a 'blank slate', which we fill with experience and generalizations based on experience.

Gottfried Wilhelm Leibniz (1646–1716) was perhaps the first notable scholar to demand the study of living languages. Leibniz suggested the existence of a European language family, and that European languages might be related to all other languages by **monogenesis** (chapter 25, §3). Broad awareness of the relatedness of European languages spread, and in 1686 Andreas Jäger (d. 1730) hypothesized, quite accurately, that 'an ancient language, once spoken in the distant past in the area of the Caucasus mountains' was the 'mother' of languages including Persian, Greek, Italic, Slavic, Celtic, and Germanic, which were its dialects and, 'in the course of time', mutually unintelligible and its 'daughters'.

But such ideas did not begin to be widely accepted for another hundred years, when the evidence for it finally became widely known with the work of William Jones (1746–94), who as a judge in India had acquired, with the help of Indian teachers and 2,000-year-old Sanskrit grammars, thorough knowledge of this ancient Indian language. Jones noted that Greek, Latin, and Sanskrit showed 'a stronger affinity, both in the roots of verbs and in the forms of grammar, than could have been produced by accident; so strong that no philologer could examine the Sanskrit, Greek, and Latin without believing them to have sprung from some common source, which, perhaps, no longer exists'. Here are a few Latin and Sanskrit words, showing similarities of the sort which Jones believed can only be explained by their being **cognates**, words with a common source in a shared ancestor language (chapter 25, §4.2).

	Latin	Sanskrit			Latin	Sanskrit	
1.	pater	pitar	'father'	6.	domus	dama	'house'
2.	māter	mātar	'mother'	7.	sēmi-	sāmi-	'half'
3.	frāter	bhrātar	'brother'	8.	trēs	trayas	'three'
4.	stēlla	star	'star'	9.	vīra	vir	'man'
5.	ignis	agni	'fire'	10.	vidua	vidhavā	'widow'

Jones' idea had significance beyond its hypothesis of the Indoeuropean language family. He showed that a non-European and non-Biblical language might be an interesting object of study, and he initiated a practical scientific research project, to determine the family relationships among languages. The first findings of this project, mainly concerning Indoeuropean languages, evolved in the hundred years after Jones' 1786 statement and became the basis for the scientific study of languages.

1.2.3.   Indoeuropean diachronic linguistics

With comparison among languages and language families came awareness of the categories and structures for comparison. In evaluating relationships among Scandinavian languages, Rasmus Rask (1787–1832) emphasized the particular importance of grammatical morphology versus lexical morphology, and he noted the importance of **regular phonetic correspondences** (chapter 25, §4.2) in proving such relationships: 'If there is found between two languages agreement in the forms of indispensable words to such an extent that rules of letter changes can be discovered for passing from one to the other, then there is a basic relationship between these languages' (Robins 1967, p. 171). (Letters and phones are still not clearly distinguised in this period.) The validity and interest of non-European languages began to be recognized with Wilhelm von Humboldt (1762–1835), who argued that spoken languages of the world are all intellectually valuable as evidence of the creative powers of humankind. Humboldt was perhaps the first to recognize the **one form/one meaning principle** (chapter 16, §2.6.2), at work in analogical change of languages.

Probably of special importance as a stimulus to the rise of linguistic science from the more general 'study of language', was the discovery by Jacob Grimm (1785–1863) of **Grimm's Law**, which stated regular phonetic correspondences among consonants of European language families as the result of systematic sound changes from the parent Proto-Indoeuropean language (chapter 25, §2). The discovery of many other such regular sound changes led to the formalization of the **comparative method** and principles of **language reconstruction** (chapter 25, §4.3.1), notably by August Schleicher (1821–1868), who used the **family tree diagram** to summarize knowledge about historical relationships among Indoeuropean languages.

Discoveries in this period, which began to include non-European languages, helped to establish the validity of the principle of **regularity of sound change**, which became known as the 'neogrammarian principle', for the group of young grammarians who were using it to establish language families. The principle revealed languages to be natural phenomena, like others subject to natural laws, an idea undoubtely reinforced at this time by the theory of evolution of Charles Darwin (1809–1882), concerning the diversification and natural selection of biological species.

1.3.   Synchronic linguistics

1.3.1.   New data of ancient languages

Three decipherments of ancient writing systems popularized and inspired the study of language in the 19th century. In 1799, the **Rosetta Stone** was discovered in Egypt, inscribed with a Greek and two Egyptian texts including one in **hieroglyphic**. After many had failed, in 1824 François Champollion (1790–1832), by discovering systematic comparisons between the Greek and Egyptian hieroglyphic versions, succeeded in deciphering the hieroglyphic text, and made the Egyptian language with its many ancient writings finally accessible to modern scholarship. The **cuneiform** writing system (chapter 21, §2.3) of **Akkadian** (Assyrian–Babylonian), a Semitic language of Mesopotamia, was deciphered late in the 19th century, and the 'hieroglyphic' writing system of **Hittite**, an extinct Indoeuropean language spoken in the region of central Turkey, began to be deciphered around 1900. These decipherments were largely pursued because of their interest to the field of **philology**, the study of important texts and the cultural insight they provide. But they also generally stimulated popular and scholarly interest in language study, and, because Egyptian, Akkadian, and Hittite texts were from an era as old or older than Greek civilization, the decipherments provided significant new data for a science of language description finally independent of the Greek and Latin model.

1.3.2.   Descriptive linguistics

The continuing search for language family relationships made clear the need for accurate grammars and dictionaries, and naturally encouraged the development of a principled or scientific **descriptive linguistics** or **synchronic linguistics**, distinct from **historical** or **diachronic linguistics**. This initially required an improved and generally accepted system of phonetic description and terminology, which need in 1886 resulted in the founding of the International Phonetic Association. Also, principled and practical phonetics requires an objective appreciation of the difference between **phones and phonemes** (as noted in chapter 3, §2).

Scholars who wanted to understand language change began to think about how languages work, and one of the first of these was Jan Baudouin de Courtenay (1845–1929). After 'the First Grammarian', whose work was mentioned above, he was perhaps the first clearly to understand the phonemic principle, and to conceive of the phoneme, as 'a unitary concept which exists in the mind . . . [and] is connected with a certain sum of individual anthropophonic representations which are . . . articulatory . . . and . . . acoustic' (1895; Stankiewicz 1972, p. 152).

Another who began to work significantly in synchronic as well as diachronic linguistics was Ferdinand de Saussure (1857–1913). Saussure used the comparative method to hypothesize the existence in the Proto-Indoeuropean language of a class of consonants which had merged with others in the descendant languages, and whose presence could be known only by their regular correspondences in the descendant languages. Saussure's controversial hypothesis was eventually accepted when the decipherment of Hittite writing revealed the existence of the class, of laryngeal phonemes, in this extinct Indoeuropean language. This dramatically affirmed the method and thus the validity of the principle of the regularity of sound change.

Saussure is also the author of the *Course in General Linguistics* (Saussure 1916 [English translation 1959]), which was assembled from the notes of his students after his death. Despite his important discovery in diachronic linguistics, because of this influential book Saussure is often considered the most important founder of synchronic linguistics. Among many enduring ideas of the *course* here, are (1) the morpheme as a **sign** (in this book, chapter 1, §1.1), with separate form and meaning aspects; (2) the essential **arbitrariness** (symbolicness) of morphemes (here, chapter 1, §3.4.1), (3) language as having a psychological and abstract structure in addition to its physical and concrete manifestation (which he termed *langue* and *parole*, respectively), and (4) the distinct means of expression of 'paradigms' of morphology, in which meanings derive from oppositions among forms potential at the same place in an utterance, as in *I* vs. *you* vs. *she*, and 'syntagms' of syntax, in which meanings derive from concatenations, as in *airplanes fly* vs. *fly airplanes*.

The distinction of **broad and narrow transcription** was formalized by Henry Sweet (1845–1912). Articulatory phonetics, particularly the description of vowel contrasts, was further refined by Daniel Jones (1881–1967), who also clarified the importance of **contrast** in distinguishing phones and phonemes. The idea that phones contrast by **phonological features**, which are the basic elements of phonology, was emphasized by Nikolai Trubetzkoy (1890–1938). Interest in **universals of language** (chapter 20 of this book) was furthered by an associate of Trubetzkoy, Roman Jakobson (1896–1982), who, among many contributions of a long career, detailed the role of phonological features in child language acquisition and in **aphasias**.

1.3.3. *Structural linguistics*

In Europe the colonial experience encouraged study of non-European languages, while in North America the presence of hundreds of Native American languages, whose grammars typically include morphological categories markedly different from those of European languages, also stimulated the idea that languages might differ in unexpected ways, and therefore have to be understood and described in their own terms. In Great Britain, this emphasis was prominent in the work of J. R. Firth (1890–1960), who had lived in India and studied Indian languages. His method of **prosodic analysis** emphasized units of phonological structure above the phoneme. In the US, studies of languages and cultures combined in the new discipline of anthropology. An anthropologist, Franz Boas (1858–1942) took up linguistics, and trained numerous American linguist-anthropologists in linguistic field work, to whom he passed on his opposition to unsupported but prevalent beliefs such as that languages are influenced by climate, and that there are 'primitive' languages, in which, for example, **alternations** (the different phonemic aspects of allomorphs: chapter 13, §1.2.1.1) are more frequent than in European languages, and unsystematic owing to careless speech.

Linguists were becoming fully aware of the diversity of the world's languages, and of the extent that this diversity was incompatible with Eurocentric and certainly Greek and Latin notions of language structure. A student of Boas, Edward Sapir (1884–1939), wrote a small but influential book, *Language* (1921), and presented a theory of language types which contrasted lexical and derivational means of expression with syntactic and inflectional means.

But mentalistic ideas and perspectives on language grew somewhat into disrepute with the growing success of experimental methods in all the sciences, and the rise of behaviorist and experimental psychology. This new trend was prominent in the influential, long-used, and still rewarding textbook *Language* (1933) by Leonard Bloomfield (1887–1949). In Bloomfield's behaviorist terms, the stimulus and response to speech was not 'meaning' but the 'practical events which [precede and follow] the act of speech' (1933, p. 23). Bloomfield demanded a separation between linguistics and **philology**, with its concern for culturally important texts and their appreciation. He said (1933, p. 22) that 'The linguist studies the language of all persons alike,' and not even especially that of great writers, which 'interest the linguist no more than do the individual features of any other person's speech, and much less than do the features that are common to all speakers'.

This perspective of **structural linguistics** was reflected in the work of linguists like Charles Fries (1887–1967), whose grammar of English (*The Structure of English*, 1952) was not based on the writings of English-speaking authors, but on recorded telephone conversations of ordinary people. He argued that 'all the signals of structure are formal matters describable in physical terms' (1952, p. 8), and he noted that a sentence like 'The vapy koobs dasaked the citar molently' has a 'structural meaning', based upon our ability to recognize the parts of speech of the words (1952, p. 111).

During this period, linguistics became well established in Europe and the US as a field of university study, independent of departments of literature, philology, phonetics, and anthropology in which it had its start, and developed shared interests and cooperative research with other disciplines including foreign and native language study, sociology, philosophy, and psychology. The field of linguistics was much invigorated, even, with the rise of generative grammar in the 1960s.

1.4.   Theoretical linguistics: generative grammar

As in Bloomfield's *Language* (1933), linguistics up to the 1960s paid little attention to two important aspects of language, syntax and meaning, and the theory of **transformational rules** of Noam Chomsky (1928–) contributed to closing both gaps. According to the understanding of Chomsky's small book *Syntactic Structures* (1957), every sentence has a 'level' of representation based on a finite number of phrase structures, on which meaning was, generally, best encoded and interpreted, and, connected to this by transformational rules, a second level of representation on which pronunciation was based. These later became known as **deep** and **surface structure**, respectively. Also later, Chomsky associated his theory with the universal grammar of 17th century rationalist philosophy, according to which language is an innate characteristic of the human species. The theory of generative grammar has the goal of discovering this universal basis and so explaining the unique characteristics of child language learning (typicality, uniformity, spontaneity, and creativity: chapter 9, §4.1.2).

Grammar in this conception was appropriately termed '**generative grammar**', because in it sentences are understood as the products of **derivations** in which phrase structure rules 'generate' an underlying or deep structure, from which a phonetic or surface structure is further derived by the operation of rules. In Chomsky's early theory, for example (1957, pp. 90–91), each of the three sentences:

1. John ate an apple
2. Did John eat an apple?
3. What did John eat?

originates with the string of morphemes 4:

4. John C – eat + an + apple

The latter string of five morphemes, 4, is derived by the phrase structure rules. Sentence 1 is then derived from this by applying a transformational rule according to which C, the past tense morpheme in this case, combines with *eat* to yield *ate*; 2 is derived by applying one transformational rule which interprets C as the auxiliary verb *did* and another which inverts *did* with the subject *John*; 3 is derived by the rule for *did*, again that which inverts *did* with *John*, another which inverts *an apple* with the material that precedes it in the sentence, and a third which replaces *an apple* with *what*.

Chomsky, furthermore, argued (1957, pp. 15–17) that the grammaticality of sentences – that is, their consistency with a derivation according to the rules of the language – is independent of meaning, as seen in the two sentences:

5. Colorless green ideas sleep furiously.
6. Furiously sleep ideas green colorless.

He says that sentences 5 and 6 'are equally nonsensical, but any speaker of English will recognize that only the former is grammatical'. In other words, 'grammar is autonomous and independent of meaning'.

Since 1957, the theory of generative grammar, practiced by a generation of linguists who have largely accepted Chomsky's research program, has undergone much revision, particularly to elaborate and make the theory of deep structure more abstract, incorporating data of more languages, to greatly simplify the theory of transformational operations, and so to make both of these more reasonably universal to all languages.

In this recent period, linguistics has developed additional associations with neurophysiology, computer science, and with the new field of cognitive science, concerned with the structure and acquisition of knowledge.

2. LINGUISTICS TODAY

Much work in linguistics today is inspired by the goals of generative grammar. Much work also is being undertaken by empiricist linguists who, contrarily, expect to discover that the important human universals which explain child language acquisition are universals of general cognition and learning, and, if there are universals of language, these are not autonomous of meaning but concern its universal functional purposes, and are much less analytic or abstract than those being hypothesized within generative grammar.

Linguists are primarily concerned with understanding the basic questions of linguistic theory: how languages are structured and work, and how they are learned. This is proving to be a daunting task. But linguists have broad interests, and many are also trying to answer numerous associated theoretical and practical questions, in subfields of linguistics only some of which have been introduced in this book, including historical linguistics, sociolinguistics, psycholinguistics, and neurolinguistics.

Linguists are also engaged in applying linguistics in practical concerns from traditional ones of language teaching and dictionary writing to, recently, computer science and the law. In the field of language teaching, teachers and authors of teaching materials need complete and accurate information on languages, and, though this is controversial, also understanding of theories of grammar that contribute in determining teaching philosophies and methods. In computer science, linguists are engaged in the effort to program computers to translate, and to give, receive, and process information in ordinary language. Linguists have increasingly been called upon to provide expert consultation in legal questions concerning language use and meaning.

Of course, given the number of languages of the world, most of which still lack adequate documentation and analysis, linguists necessarily continue to be engaged in the traditional basic tasks of language description: writing grammars and dictionaries. This work is especially inspired by the realization that languages, like many plant and animal species, are disappearing almost daily, and that the disappearance of each one means the loss of unique forms of knowledge which have expressed something of significance in human society and perhaps of significance for the full understanding of our species and its development. Some linguists consider it an obligation to encourage the preservation of all human languages, but this is controvesial. (For positions and perspective on this interesting controversy, see Hale et al. 1992; Ladefoged 1992; and Dorian 1993.)

Suggestions for
ADDITIONAL READING

The classical and European basis of the history of linguistics is recently surveyed in *Western Linguistics: an Historical Introduction* (1997) by Peter A. M. Seuren. A more compact survey, up to 1965, is *A Short History of Linguistics* (1967) by R. H. Robins. The major issues and the contributions of important linguists are described in *General Linguistics* (1995) by Francis P. Dinneen. A collection of readings from some of the most important classical and early European works is *On Language: Plato to von Humboldt* (1969) edited by Peter H. Salus.

The story of the development of Indoeuropean historical linguistics was told over sixty years ago in a still very readable account as *The Discovery of Language: Linguistic Science in the Nineteenth Century* (1967) by Holger Pederson. Concerning just phonology, see *Phonology in the twentieth Century: Theories of Rules and Theories of Representations* (1985) by Stephen Anderson, and concerning generative grammar, *Generative Linguistics* (1996) by Frederick J. Newmeyer. The history of non-European grammatical traditions is included in *Universal History of Linguistics: India, China, Arabia, Europe* (1991) by Esa Itkonen.

Among important primary works in the history of linguistics, some which are still very readable and rewarding are the *Course in General Linguistics* (1916, English translation 1959) of Ferdinand de Saussure, *Introduction to the Handbook of American Indian Languages* (1911, reprinted 1966) by Franz Boas, *Language: an Introduction to the Study of Speech* (1921, reprinted 1949) by Edward Sapir, *Language* (1933) by Leonard Bloomfield, and *Syntactic Structures* (1957) by Noam Chomsky.

Compact presentations of what linguistic is are provided in *Invitation to Linguistics* (1984) by Richard Hudson, and *What is Linguistics?* (1985) by David Crystal. For broader and deeper views of its subfields, see *Linguistics: the Cambridge Survey* (1988, 4 vols) edited by Frederick J. Newmeyer. Perhaps the easiest way to get one's own perspective on the field is to survey the contents of two important journals which include a broad range of current research in linguistics, and book reviews: *Language*, the journal of the Linguistic Society of America, and the *Journal of Linguistics*, the journal of the Linguistics Society of Great Britain.

Historical background to the field of cognitive science is entertainingly provided in *The Mind's New Science* (1985) by Howard Gardner. A current survey of the field is *Cognitive Science: an Introduction* (1995) by Neil A. Stillings and others.

On the internet, see the home-pages of the Linguistic Society of America http://www.lsadc.org, which link to a volume of essays on 'The field of linguistics', and of the Linguistics Society of Great Britain http://clwww.essex.ac.uk/LAGB/, linked to a number of essays concerning 'What is linguistics?'. For convenient access to other internet sites dealing with linguistics, including other professional associations, university degree programs in linguistics, home-pages of practicing linguists, and the electronic 'bulletin board' 'LINGUIST', where issues are discussed, new books are announced, and job announcements in linguistics are posted, see the 'WWW Virtual Library' at http://www.emich.edu/~linguist/www-vl.html.

IMPORTANT CONCEPTS AND TERMS IN THIS CHAPTER

- linguistics
- iconic sign
- indexical sign
- symbolic sign
- parts of speech
- inflectional affix
- derivational affix
- Cyrillic alphabet
- phone
- phoneme
- minimal pair
- rationalism
- empiricism
- monogenesis of language
- cognates
- regular phonetic correspondences
- one form/one meaning principle
- Grimm's Law
- comparative method
- language reconstruction
- family tree diagram
- regularity of sound change
- Rosetta Stone
- Egyptian hieroglyphic

- cuneiform
- Akkadian
- Hittite
- philology
- synchronic linguistics
- descriptive linguistics
- diachronic linguistics
- historical linguistics
- sign
- arbitrariness
- broad and narrow transcription
- contrast
- phonological features
- universals of language
- aphasias
- prosodic analysis
- alternations
- structural linguistics
- transformational rule
- deep structure
- surface structure
- generative grammar
- derivation

OUTLINE OF CHAPTER 28

1. **The history of linguistics**
    1. Classical foundations
        1. Greece
        2. Rome
    2. European background
        1. Study of vernacular languages
        2. The relationship of languages
        3. Indoeuropean diachronic linguistics
    3. Synchronic linguistics
        1. New data of ancient languages
        2. Descriptive linguistics
        3. Structural linguistics
    4. Theoretical linguistics: generative grammar
2. **Linguistics today**

EXAMPLES AND PRACTICE

EXAMPLE

1. Early linguistics: parts of speech. It was noted that one of the first discoveries of Greek language study was of the 'parts of speech', or word classes. Over 2,000 years ago in Alexandria, Dionysius Thrax gave the following definitions of the eight parts of speech of Greek (Robins 1967, pp. 33–34):

1. inflected for case, signifying a person or thing
2. without case inflection, but inflected for tense, person, and number, signifying an activity or process performed or undergone
3. sharing the features of the verb and the noun
4. inflected for case and preposed or postposed to nouns
5. substitutable for a noun and marked for person
6. placed before other words in composition and in syntax
7. without inflection, in modification of or in addition to a verb
8. binding together the discourse and filling gaps in its interpretation

These definitions can be roughly matched with the word classes typical of other languages, including English, which may lack the exact grammatical features of Greek. English, for example, lacks the case inflection of Greek (and

Latin; see chapter 17, §5.3.2.4 – though case is distinguished in the pronouns: *I* vs. *me*; *she* vs. *her*).

Try to match definitions 1–8 with parts of speech (a)–(i); one of (a)–(i) is not an answer, being a word-class merged with another by Dionysius: (a) verb, (b) adjective, (c) preposition, (d) adverb, (e) conjunction, (f) noun, (g) pronoun, (h) article, (i) participle.

2. Structural linguistics: form contrasts of English nouns and verbs. Fries (1952, pp. 113–115) presented fourteen ways that English nouns and verbs may contrast in form. For example,

1. verbs of the type of *paint* contrast with nouns of the type of *reader*, as in *paint/painter* and *read/reader*.
2. verbs of the type of *expose* contrast with nouns of the type of *departure*, as in *expose/exposure* and *depart/departure*.

The other 12 contrasts are exemplified in the lists below. Match 12 verbs with 12 nouns as in the examples above. Some verbs and nouns may fulfill more than one type.

Verbs:	accept	decide	adjourn
	deform	break	offend
	catch	assist	use /juz/
	subjéct	deliver	refuse

Nouns:	appearance	division	leakage
	dismissal	servant	defense
	flattery	device	óbject
	perplexity	payment	teaching

3. Transformational analysis of the English verb. In his 1957 book *Syntactic Structures*, Chomsky (p. 39) provided the following analysis of the structure of English verbs (slightly simplified here).

Phrase structure rules: Verb → Aux V
                          Aux → C (have en)(be ing)(be en)

Transformational rule: Af V → V-Af

V is a verb such as *see*, *eat*, *show*, *have* and *be*; C is (1) the present tense suffix usually spelled *s* (when the subject NP is 3rd person singular), (2) the past tense suffix usually spelled *ed*, or (3) Ø (zero); and Af = C, *en*, and *ing*. The result of phrase structure rules and lexical insertions for V and C is such strings as those of the left column, below. After the transformational rule applies to these strings, the result is the verbs of the middle column. (Remember that items in parentheses may or may not be chosen.)

s see	→ see-s	
ed eat	→ eat-ed	→ ate
ed be ing show	→ be-ed show-ing	→ was showing
s have en show	→ have-s show-en	→ has shown

The third column shows morphophonemic rules, which include be-s → is, be-ed → was, have-ed → had, have-s → has, see-ed → saw, and eat-ed → ate, etc.

PRACTICE

According to this analysis:

1. What is the result of the string 's be ing see'?
2. What is the result of the string 'ed have en be ing show'?
3. What is the string underlying 'was eaten'?
4. What is the string underlying 'has been being seen'?

EXAMPLE

4. Vanishing languages. Like endangered species, minority languages are vanishing all around the world. The controversy was noted, above, of whether all languages should be preserved, and whether linguists have responsibility in this. At issue, partly, is whether the collective and unconscious decisions of speakers of minority languages to give up their languages in favor of others ought to be respected.

PRACTICE

Read the short essays of Hale et al. 1992, Ladefoged 1992, and Dorian 1993 (in the journal *Language* for 1992 and 1993; full information is provided in the 'References', below) and write a critique of these arguments, and your own conclusion, in about 500–1,000 words.

REFERENCES

Abercrombie, David. 1964. *English phonetic texts*. London: Faber and Faber.

Aitchison, Jean. 1991. *Language change: progress or decay?* 2nd edn. Cambridge: Cambridge University Press.

Aitchison, Jean. 1992. *Teach yourself linguistics*. Chicago: NTC Publishing.

Aitchison, Jean. 1994. *Words in the mind*. Oxford: Blackwell.

Aitchison, Jean. 1996. *The seeds of speech: language origin and evolution*. Cambridge: Cambridge University Press.

Algeo, John. 1972. *Problems in the origin and development of the English language*, 2nd edn. New York: Harcourt Brace Jovanovich.

Algeo, John and Adele Algeo. 1997. Among the new words. *American speech* 72.1. 84–96.

Allport, D. Alan. 1983. Language and cognition, in *Approaches to language* (chapter 4), Roy Harris, ed., 61–94. Oxford: Pergamon Press.

Ammon, Ulrich, Norbert Dittmar, and Klaus J. Mattheier, eds. 1988. *Sociolinguistics: an international handbook of language and society*. Berlin: Mouton de Gruyter.

Anderson, Stephen. 1985. *Phonology in the twentieth century: theories of rules and theories of representations*. Chicago: University of Chicago Press.

Andrew, Richard J. 1965. The origin of facial expressions. *Scientific American* 213.4. 88–94.

Anttila, Raimo. 1989. *Historical and comparative linguistics*. Amsterdam: John Benjamins.

Arends, Jacques, Pieter Muysken, and Norval Smith, eds. 1995. *Pidgins and creoles: an introduction*. Amsterdam: John Benjamins.

Arlotto, Anthony. 1972. *Introduction to historical linguistics*. Lanham, Maryland: University Press of America.

Aronoff, Mark. 1976. *Word formation in generative grammar*. Cambridge, MA: MIT Press.

Ashby, W. 1981. The loss of the negative particle *ne* in French. *Language* 57. 674–687.

Bailey, N., Carol Madden, and Stephen Krashen. 1974. Is there a 'natural sequence' in adult second language learning? *Language learning* 24. 235–243.

Bauer, Laurie. 1983. *English word-formation*. Cambridge: Cambridge University Press.

Bauer, Laurie. 1988. *Introducing linguistic morphology*. Edinburgh: Edinburgh University Press.

Beekes, Robert S. P. 1995. *Comparative Indo-European linguistics*. Amsterdam: John Benjamins.

Bell, Alan. 1984. Language style as audience design. *Language in society* 13. 145–204.

Bialystok, Ellen and Kenji Hakuta. 1994. *In other words: the science and psychology of second language acquisition*. New York: Basic Books.

Biber, Douglas. 1988. *Variation across speech and writing*. Cambridge: Cambridge University Press.

Biber, Douglas. 1995. *Dimensions of register variation*. New York: Cambridge.

Biber, Douglas and Edward Finegan, eds. 1994. *Sociolinguistic perspectives on register*. New York: Oxford University Press.

Bickerton, Derek. 1990. *Language and species*. Chicago: University of Chicago Press.

Blake, Norman. 1996. *A history of the English language*. London: Macmillan.

Blakeley, Leslie. 1976. *Old English*. London: Teach Yourself Books.

Blakemore, Diane. 1992. *Understanding utterances: an introduction to pragmatics*. Oxford: Blackwell.

Bleile, Ken M. 1991. *Child phonology: a book of exercises for students*. San Diego: Singular Publishing Group.

Bloom, Lois. 1991. *Language development from two to three*. Cambridge: Cambridge University Press.

Bloom, Paul, ed. 1996. *Language acquisition: core readings*. Cambridge, MA: MIT Press.

Bloomfield, Leonard. 1933. *Language*. New York: Henry Holt and Company.

Boas, Franz. 1911. Introduction, *Handbook of American Indian languages* (Bulletin 40, part 1, of the Bureau of American Ethnology), Franz Boas, ed., 1–83. Washington, DC. [Reprinted 1966. Lincoln, NB: University of Nebraska Press.]

Bolinger, Dwight. 1980. *Language: the loaded weapon*. London: Longman.

Bolozky, Shmuel. 1997. Israeli Hebrew phonology, in *Phonologies of Asia and Africa*, vol. 1, Alan S. Kaye, ed., 287–311. Winona Lake, IN: Eisenbrauns.

Bongaerts, Theo, Chantal van Summeren, Brigitte Planken, and Erik Schils. 1997. Age and ultimate attainment in the pronunciation of a foreign language. *Studies in second language acquisition* 19. 447–465.

Bradshaw, John and Lesley Rogers. 1993. *The evolution of lateral assymetries, language, tool use, and intellect*. San Diego: Academic Press.

Brevil, Henri and Hugo Obermaier. 1935. *The cave of Altamira*. Madrid: Tipografía de Archivos.

Bright, Michael. 1984. *Animal language*. Ithaca: Cornell University Press.

Bright, William, ed. 1992. *International encyclopedia of linguistics*. New York: Oxford.

Brown, E. K. and J. E. Miller. 1991. *Syntax: a linguistic introduction to sentence structure*. London: Routledge.

Brown, Penelope and S. C. Levinson. 1987. *Politeness: some universals in language usage*. New York: Cambridge University Press.

Brown, Roger. 1958. *Words and things*. Toronto: Collier-Macmillan.

Brown, Roger. 1973. *A first language: the early stages*. Cambridge, MA: Harvard University Press.

Bryden, M. P. 1988. An overview of the dichotic listening procedure and its relation to cerebral organization, in *Handbook of dichotic listening: theory, methods, and research*, Kenneth Hugdahl, ed., 1–43. New York: John Wiley and Sons.

Burgess, Anthony. 1964. *Language made plain*. New York: Thomas Crowell.

Burquest, Donald A. and David L. Payne. 1993. *Phonological analysis: a functional approach*. Dallas: Summer Institute of Linguistics.

Burton-Roberts, Noel. 1997. *Analysing sentences: an introduction to English syntax*. New York: Longman.

Calvin, William H. and George A. Ojemann. 1980. *Inside the brain*. New York: New American Library.

Campbell, George L. 1997. *Handbook of scripts and alphabets*. London: Routledge.

Campbell, George L. 1998. *Concise compendium of the world's languages*. London: Routledge.

Caplan, David. 1987. *Neurolinguistics and linguistic aphasiology: an introduction*. Cambridge: Cambridge University Press.

Caplan, David. 1992. *Language: structure, processing, and disorders*. Cambridge, MA: MIT Press.

Carney, Edward. 1997. *A survey of English spelling*. London: Routledge.

Carr, Philip. 1993. *Phonology*. New York: St Martin's Press.

Carstairs-McCarthy, Andrew. 1992. *Current morphology*. New York: Routledge.

Carter, Martha L. and Keith N. Schoville, eds. 1984. *Sign, symbol, script: an exhibition on the origins of writing and the alphabet*. Madison, WI: Department of Hebrew and Semitic Studies, University of Wisconsin-Madison.

Carterette, Edward C. and Margaret Hubbard Jones, 1974. *Informal speech: alphabetic and phonemic texts with statistical analyses and tables*. Berkeley: University of California Press.

Chadwick, John. 1976. *The decipherment of linear B*. Cambridge: Cambridge University Press.

Cheney, Dorothy and Robert Seyfarth. 1990. *How monkeys see the world: inside the mind of another species*. Chicago: University of Chicago Press.

Chomsky, Noam. 1957. *Syntactic structures*. The Hague: Mouton.

Clark, Herbert and Eve V. Clark. 1977. *Psychology and language: an introduction to psycholinguistics*. New York: Harcourt Brace Jovanovich.

Clark, John and Colin Yallop. 1990. *An introduction to phonetics and phonology*. Cambridge, MA: Basil Blackwell.

Coates, Jennifer. 1993. *Women, men, and language*, 2nd edn. London: Longman.

Coates, Jennifer, ed. 1998. *Language and gender: a reader*. Malden, MA: Blackwell.

Coe, Michael D. 1993. *Breaking the Maya code*. New York: Thames and Hudson.

Comrie, Bernard. 1981. *Language universals and linguistic typology*. Chicago: University of Chicago Press.

Comrie, Bernard, ed. 1990. *The world's major languages*. New York: Oxford University Press.

Cook, Vivian. 1993. *Linguistics and second language acquisition*. New York: St Martin's Press.

Cook, Vivian and Mark Newson. 1995. *Chomsky's universal grammar: an introduction*. New York: Blackwell.

Coulmas, Florian. 1991. *The writing systems of the world*. Oxford: Blackwell.

Coulmas, Florian. 1996. *The Blackwell encyclopedia of writing systems*. Cambridge, MA: Blackwell.

Coulmas, Florian, ed. 1997. *The handbook of sociolinguistics*. Malden, MA: Blackwell.

Cowan, William and Jaromira Rakušan. 1987. *Source book for linguistics*, 2nd edn. Philadelphia: John Benjamins.

Crain, Stephen and Diane Lillo-Martin. 1998. *Language and mind*. Oxford: Blackwell.

Croft, William. 1990. *Typology and universals*. Cambridge: Cambridge University Press.

Crowley, Terry. 1992. *An introduction to historical linguistics*. Auckland: Oxford University Press.

Crystal, David. 1985. *What is linguistics?* London: Edward Arnold.

Crystal, David, ed. 1987. *The Cambridge encyclopedia of language*. New York: Cambridge University Press.

Crystal, David. 1991. *A dictionary of linguistics and phonetics*. Cambridge, MA: Blackwell.

Crystal, David and Derek David. 1969. *Investigating English style*. London: Longman.

Cummings, D. W. 1988. *American English spelling: an informal description*. Baltimore: Johns Hopkins University Press.

Curtis, Susan. 1977. *Genie: a linguistic study of a modern-day 'wild child'*. New York: Academic Press.

Daniels, Peter and William Bright, eds. 1996. *The world's writing systems*. New York: Oxford University Press.

Darwin Charles. 1955 [1872]. The expression of emotion in man and animals. New York: Philosophical Library.

Darwin, Charles. 1979 [1859]. *The origin of species*. New York: Hill and Wang.

Davidson, Iain and William Noble. 1996. *Human evolution, language and mind*. Cambridge: Cambridge University Press.

Davies, W. V. 1987. *Egyptian hieroglyphics*. Berkeley: University of California Press.

Davis, Steven, ed. 1991. *Pragmatics: a reader*. Oxford: Oxford University Press.

Deacon, Terrence W. 1997. *The symbolic species: the co-evolution of language and the brain*. New York: W. W. Norton.

DeFrancis, John. 1989. *Visible speech: the diverse oneness of writing systems*. Honolulu: University of Hawaii Press.

Denning, Keith, and William R. Leben. 1995. *English vocabulary elements*. New York: Oxford.

Dillard, J. L. 1992. *A history of American English*. Essex: Longman.

Dinneen, Francis P. 1995. *General linguistics*. Washington, DC: Georgetown University Press.

Dixon, R. M. W. 1997. *The rise and fall of languages*. London: Cambridge University Press.

Dorian, Nancy C. 1993. A response to Ladefoged's other view of endangered languages. *Language 69.* 575–579.

Dryer, William. 1992. The Greenbergian word order correlations. *Language 68.* 81–138.

Dulay, Heidi, Marina Burt, and Stephen Krashen. 1982. *Language two*. New York: Oxford University Press.

Dunbar, Robin. 1996. *Grooming, gossip, and evolution of language*. Cambridge, MA: Harvard University Press.

Edwards, John. 1994. *Multilingualism*. London: Penguin Books.

Elgin, Suzette Hayden. 1973. *What is linguistics?* Englewood Cliffs, NJ: Prentice-Hall.

Ellegård, A. 1953. *The auxiliary 'do': the establishment and regulation of its use in English*. Stockholm: Almqvist and Wiksell.

Elman, Jeffrey, Elizabeth A. Bates, Mark H. Johnson, et al., eds. 1997. *Rethinking innateness: a connectionist perspective on development*. Cambridge, MA: MIT Press.

Endo Hudson, Mutsuko. 1994. *English grammar for students of Japanese*. Ann Arbor, Michigan: Olivia and Hill Press.

Ervin, Susan M. 1964. Imitation and structural change in children's language, in *New directions in the study of language*, Eric Lenneberg, ed., 163–189. Cambridge, MA: MIT Press.

Espinosa, Aurelio. 1975 [1917]. Speech mixture in New Mexico: the influence of the English language on New Mexican Spanish, in *El lenguaje de los Chicanos*, Eduardo Hernandez-Chavez,

Andrew D. Cohen, and Authony F. Beltramo, eds., 99–114. Arlington, VA: Center for Applied Linguistics.

Fasold, Ralph. 1984. *The sociolinguistics of society*. Malden, MA: Basil Blackwell.

Fasold, Ralph. 1990. *The sociolinguistics of language*. Malden, MA: Basil Blackwell.

Ferguson, Charles. 1983. Sports announcer talk: syntactic aspects of register variation. *Language and society* 12. 153–172.

Finegan, Edward. 1994. *Language: its structure and use*, 2nd edn. Fort Worth: Harcourt Brace Jovanovich.

Fishman, Joshua, ed. 1977. *Advances in the creation and revision of writing systems*. The Hague: Mouton.

Fletcher, Paul and Brian MacWhinney, eds. 1996. *The handbook of child language*. Oxford: Blackwell.

Foss, Donald J. and David T. Hakes. 1978. *Psycholinguistics: an introduction to the psychology of language*. Englewood Cliffs, NJ: Prentice-Hall.

Fox, Anthony. 1995. *Linguistic reconstruction*. Oxford: Oxford University Press.

Francis, Henry N. and Henry Kučera. 1982. *Frequency analysis of English usage: lexicon and grammar*. Boston: Houghton Mifflin.

Fries, Charles Carpenter. 1952. *The structure of English*. New York: Harcourt, Brace, and World.

Frisch, Karl von. 1971. *Bees: their vision, chemical senses, and language*. Ithaca, NY: Cornell University Press.

Frisch, Karl von. 1993. *The dance language and orientation of bees*. Cambridge, MA: Harvard University Press.

Fromkin, Victoria and Robert Rodman. 1993. *An introduction to language*. Fort Worth, TX: Harcourt Brace Jovanovich.

Fudge, Eric. 1984. *English word-stress*. London: George Allen and Unwin.

Gardner, Beatrice T. and R. Allen Gardner. 1971. Two-way communication with an infant chimpanzee, in *Behavior of non-human primates*, Allan Schrier and Fred Stollnitz, eds, vol. 4, 117–184. New York: Academic Press.

Gardner, Howard. 1985. *The mind's new science*. New York: Basic Books.

Gardner, R. C. 1980. On the validity of affective variables in second language acquisition: conceptual, contextual, and statistical considerations. *Language learning* 30. 255–270.

Gass, Susan and Larry Selinker. 1994. *Second language acquisition: an introductory course*. Hillsdale, NJ: Lawrence Erlbaum.

Giegerich, Heinz J. 1992. *English phonology: an introduction*. Cambridge: Cambridge University Press.

Giles, Howard, ed. 1984. The dynamics of speech accommodation. *International journal of the sociology of language* 46.

Givón, Talmy. 1984. *Syntax: a functional-typological introduction*, 2 vols. Amsterdam: John Benjamins.

Givón, Talmy. 1995. *Functionalism and grammar*. Amsterdam: John Benjamins.

Gleason, Henry A., Jr. 1964. *Workbook in descriptive linguistics*. New York: Holt, Rinehart and Winston.

Goldsmith, John A., ed. 1995. *The handbook of phonological theory*. Cambridge, MA: Blackwell.

Goodglass, Harold. 1968. Studies on the grammar of aphasias, in *Psycholinguistics and aphasia*, H. Goodglass and S. Blumstein, eds, Baltimore: Johns Hopkins University Press.

Goodglass, Harold. 1980. Disorders of naming following brain injury. *American scientist* 68. 647–655.

Goodluck, Helen. 1991. *Language acquisition: a linguistic introduction*. Oxford: Blackwell.

Green, Georgia. 1996. *Pragmatics and natural language understanding*, 2nd edn. Mahwah, NJ: Lawrence Erlbaum.

Green, Georgia and Jerry L. Morgan. 1996. *Practical guide to syntactic analysis*. Stanford, CA: Center for the Study of Language and Information.

Green, M. W. 1989. Early cuneiform, in *The origins of writing*, Wayne M. Senner, ed., 43–57. Lincoln: University of Nebraska Press.

Greenberg, Joseph H. 1966. *Languages of Africa*. The Hague: Mouton.

Greenberg, Joseph, ed. 1978. *Universals of language*, 4 vols. Stanford, CA: Stanford University Press.

Grice, H. Paul. 1975. Logic and conversation, in *Syntax and semantics*, Peter Cole and Jerry L. Morgan, eds, vol. 3, 41–58. New York: Academic Press. [Also in Davis 1991, 305–315.]

Grimes, Barbara F., ed. 1996. *Ethnologue: languages of the world*, 13th edn. Dallas: Summer Institute of Linguistics.

Gussenhoven, Carlos and Haike Jacobs. 1998. *Understanding phonology*. London: Arnold.

Haegeman, Liliane and Jacqueline Gueron. 1998. *English grammar*. Oxford: Blackwell.

Hale, Kenneth, Michael Krauss, Lucille J. Watahomigie et al. 1992. Endangered languages. *Language* 68. 1–43.

Halliday, M. A. K. 1989. *Spoken and written language*, 2nd edn. Oxford: Oxford University Press.

Harris, John. 1994. *English sound structure*. Cambridge, MA: Blackwell.

Hawkins, John A., ed. 1988. *Explaining language universals*. Cambridge, MA: Blackwell.

Hayes, Cathy. 1951. *The ape in our house*. New York: Harper and Row.

Healey, John. 1990. *The early alphabet*. Berkeley: University of California Press.

Herman, Louis M., ed. 1980. *Cetacean behavior: mechanism and functions*. New York: John Wiley and Sons.

Herring, Susan C., ed. 1996. *Computer-mediated communication: social and cross-cultural perspectives*. Philadelphia: John Benjamins.

Hock, Hans H. and Brian D. Joseph. 1996. *Language history, language change, and language relationship*. Berlin: Mouton de Gruyter.

Horrocks, Geoffrey. 1987. *Generative grammar*. New York: Longman.

Huddleston, Rodney. 1995. *English grammar: an outline*. Cambridge: Cambridge University Press.

Hudson, R. A. 1996. *Sociolinguistics*, 2nd edn. Cambridge: Cambridge University Press.

Hudson, Richard. 1984. *Invitation to linguistics*. Oxford: Blackwell.

Hughes, Geoffrey. 1996. *A history of the English language*. Oxford: Blackwell.

Humboldt, Wilhelm von. 1971. *Linguistic variability and intellectual development*, translated by George C. Buck and Frithjof A. Raven. Philadelphia: University of Pennsylvania Press.

Hurford, James R. and Brendan Heasley. 1983. *Semantics: a coursebook*. Cambridge: Cambridge University Press.

Ingram, David. 1989. *First language acquisition: method, description, and explanation*. Baltimore: University Park Press.

Itkonen, Esa. 1991. *Universal history of linguistics: India, China, Arabia, Europe*. Amsterdam: John Benjamins.

Jackendoff, Ray. 1994. *Patterns in the mind: language and human nature*. New York: Basic Books.

Jakobson, Roman. 1959. *On translation*. Cambridge, MA: Harvard University Press. [Also 1971, *On linguistics aspects of translation, Selected writings II*, 260–266. The Hague: Mouton.]

Jason's authentic dictionary of CB slang. 1976. Fort Worth, TX: Jason Press.

Jensen, John T. 1990. *Morphology*. Amsterdam: John Benjamins.

Jensen, John T. 1993. *English phonology*. Amsterdam: John Benjamins.

Johansson, Stig and Knut Hofland. 1989. *Frequency analysis of English vocabulary and grammar*, vol. 1. Oxford: Clarendon Press.

Johnson, Jacqueline and Elissa L. Newport. 1989. Critical period effects in second language learning: the influence of maturational state on the acquisition of English as a second language. *Cognitive psychology* 21. 60–99.

Joos, Martin. 1961. *The five clocks*. New York: Harcourt, Brace and World.

Kaplan, Jeffrey. 1995. *English grammar: principles and facts*, 2nd edn. Englewood Cliffs, NJ: Prentice Hall.

Keightley, David N. 1989. The origins of writing in China: scripts and cultural contexts, in *The origins of writing*, Wayne M. Senner, ed., 171–202. Lincoln: University of Nebraska Press.

Klima, Edward and Ursula Bellugi. 1979. *The signs of language*. Cambridge, MA: Harvard University Press.

Krashen, Stephen. 1982. *Principles and practice in second language acquisition*. Oxford: Pergamon Press.

Kreidler, Charles W. 1989. *The pronunciation of English: a coursebook in phonology*. New York: Basil Blackwell.

Kreidler, Charles W. 1997. *Describing spoken English: an introduction*. London: Routledge.

Kreidler, Charles W. 1998. *Introducing English semantics*. New York: Routledge.

Kroodsma, Donald E. 1982. Learning and the ontogeny of sound signals in birds, in *Acoustic communication in birds*, Donald E. Kroodsma, Edward H. Miller, and Henri Ouellet, eds, vol. 2, 1–23. New York: Academic Press.

Kroodsma, Donald E., Edward H. Miller and Henri Ouellet, eds. 1982. *Acoustic communication in birds*, vols 1–2. New York: Academic Press.

Kučera, Henry and W. Nelson Francis. 1967. *Computational analysis of present-day American English*. Providence: Brown University Press.

Labov, William. 1966. *The social stratification of English in New York City*. Washington, DC: Center for Applied Linguistics.

Ladefoged, Peter. 1992. Another view of endangered languages. *Language 68*. 809–811.

Ladefoged, Peter. 1993. *A course in phonetics*. Fort Worth: Harcourt Brace Jovanovich.

Ladefoged, Peter and Ian Maddieson. 1996. *The sounds of the world's languages*. Cambridge, MA: Blackwell.

Lane, Harlan. 1976. *The wild boy of Aveyron*. Cambridge: Harvard University Press.

Langacker, Ronald W. 1972. *Fundamentals of linguistic analysis*. New York: Harcourt Brace Jovanovich.

Lappin, Shalom. 1996. *The handbook of contemporary semantic theory*. Oxford: Blackwell.

Larsen-Freeman, Diane and Michael H. Long. 1991. *An introduction to second language acquisition research*. London: Longman.

Lass, Roger. 1997. *Historical linguistics and language change*. Cambridge: Cambridge University Press.

Laver, John. 1994. *Principles of phonetics*. New York: Cambridge University Press.

Le Guin, Ursula. 1985. *Always coming home*. New York: Bantam Books.

Lenneberg, Eric. 1964. The capacity for language acquisition. The structure of language: readings, in *The philosophy of language*, Jerry A. Fodor and Jerrold J. Katz, eds, 579–603. Englewood Cliffs, NJ: Prentice-Hall.

Lesser, Ruth. 1978. *Linguistic investigations of aphasia*. London: Edward Arnold.

Levin, Beth. 1993. *English verb classes and alternations*. Chicago: University of Chicago Press.

Lieberman, Philip. 1975. *On the origins of language: an introduction to the evolution of human speech*. New York: Macmillan.

Linden, Eugene. 1976. *Apes, men, and language*. New York: Penguin Books.

Liszka, James Jakob. 1996. *A general introduction to the semeiotic of Charles Sanders Peirce*. Bloomington: Indiana University Press.

Lounsbury, T. R. 1907. *History of the English language*. New York: Henry Holt and Company.

Lyons, John. 1995. *Linguistic semantics*. New York: Cambridge University Press.

Lyovin, Anatole V. 1997. *An introduction to the languages of the world*. New York: Oxford University Press.

Macauley, Ronald. 1994. *The social art: language and its uses*. New York: Oxford University Press.

Maddiesen, Ian. 1984. *Patterns of sounds*. Cambridge: Cambridge University Press.

Malmkjaer, Kirsten, ed. 1992. *The linguistics encyclopedia*. London: Routledge.

Marchand, Hans. 1969. *The categories and types of present-day English word formation*, 2nd edn. Munich: C. H. Beck.

Marckwardt, Albert H. 1951. *Introduction to the English language*. New York: Oxford University Press.

Marcus, Gary F., Stephen Pinker, Michael Ullman, et al. 1992. *Overregularization in language acquisition* (Monograph 57.4 of the Society for Research in Child Development). Chicago: University of Chicago Press.

Marler, Peter. 1991. The instinct to learn, in *The Epigenesis of mind: essays on biology and cognition*, S. Carey and R. Gelman, eds, 37–66. Hillsdale, NJ: Lawrence Erlbaum Associates. [Also 1994. *Language acquisition: core readings*, Paul Bloom, ed., 591–617. Cambridge, MA: MIT Press.]

McCawley, James. 1988. *The syntactic phenomena of English*, 2 vols. Chicago: University of Chicago Press.

McGuinness, Diane. 1997. *Why our children can't read, and what we can do about it*. New York: Free Press.

McLaughlin, Scott. 1998. *Introduction to language development*. San Diego: Singular Press.

McMahon, April M. S. 1994. *Understanding language change*. Cambridge: Cambridge University Press.

McNeil, David. 1966. Developmental psycholinguistics, in *The genesis of language, a psycholinguistic approach*, Frank Smith and George A. Miller, eds, 15–84. Cambridge, MA: MIT Press.

Mencken, H. L. 1937. *The American language*, 4th edn. New York: Alfred A. Knopf.

Menyuk, Paula. 1969. *Sentences children use*. Cambridge, MA: MIT Press.

Mey, Jacob L. 1993. *Pragmatics: an introduction*. Oxford: Blackwell.

Miller, Casey and Kate Swift. 1977. *Words and women*. Garden City, NY: Anchor Books.

Milner, B., C. Branch, and T. Rasmussen. 1968. Observations on cerebral dominance, in *Language*, R. C. Oldfield and J. C. Marshall, eds, 366–378. Harmondsworth: Penguin Books.

Morton, Eugene S. and Jake Page. 1992. *Animal talk: science and the voices of nature*. New York: Random House.

Moskowitz, Breyne Arlene. 1978. The acquisition of language. *Scientific American* 239. 92–108.

Mufwene, Salikoko, John R. Rickford, Guy Bailey, and John Baugh, eds. 1998. *African American English: structure, history, and use*. New York: Routledge.

Mundinger, Paul C. 1982. Microgeographic and macrogeographic variation in acquired vocalizations of birds, in *Acoustic communication in birds*, vol. 2, Donald A. Kroodsma, Edward H. Miller, and Henri Ouellet, eds, 147–208. New York: Academic Press.

Murphy, John J. 1989. *The book of pidgin English: buk bilong Tok Pisin.* Carina, Australia: Robert Brown and Associates.

Myers-Scotton, Carol. 1993a. *Duelling languages: grammatical structures in code switching.* Oxford: Clarendon Press.

Myers-Scotton, Carol. 1993b. *Social motivations for code-switching: evidence from Africa.* Oxford: Oxford University Press.

Napoli, Donna Jo. 1996. *Linguistics: an introduction.* New York: Oxford University Press.

Newmeyer, Frederick J., ed. 1988. *Linguistics: the Cambridge survey,* 4 vols. Cambridge: Cambridge University Press.

Newmeyer, Frederick J. 1996. *Generative linguistics.* London: Routledge.

Nottebohm, F. 1970. Ontogeny of bird song. *Science* 167. 950–956.

Nunberg, Geoffrey. 1990. *The linguistics of punctuation.* Stanford, California: CSLI.

O'Grady, John. 1965. *Aussie English.* Sydney: Ure Smith.

O'Grady, William, Michael Dobrovolsky, and Mark Aronoff. 1993. *Contemporary linguistics: an introduction.* New York: St Martin's Press.

Ohio State University Department of Linguistics. 1994. *Language files,* Stefanie Jannedy, Robert Poletto, and Tracey L. Weldon, eds. Columbus, OH: Ohio State University Press.

Patterson, Francine. 1978. Conversations with a gorilla. *National geographic* 154.4. 438–465.

Patterson, Francine and Eugene Linden. 1981. *The education of Koko.* New York: Holt, Rinehart and Winston.

Pederson, Holger. 1967. *The discovery of language: linguistic science in the nineteenth century.* Bloomington: Indiana University Press.

Peirce, Charles Sanders. 1955. Logic as semiotic: the theory of signs, in *Philosophical writings of Peirce,* Justus Buchler, ed., 98–120. New York: Dover Publications.

Perfetti, Charles A., Laurence Rieben, and Michel Fayol, eds. 1997. *Learning to spell.* Mahwah, NJ: Lawrence Erlbaum.

Pesetsky, David. 1998. *From word to sentence.* Oxford: Blackwell.

Piattelli-Palmarini, Massimo. 1980. *Language and learning: the debate between Jean Piaget and Noam Chomsky.* Cambridge, MA: Harvard University Press.

Pinker, Steven. 1994. *The language instinct.* New York: William Morrow.

Porac, Clare and Stanley Coren. 1977. *Lateral preferences and human behavior.* New York: Springer-Verlag.

Premack, Ann J. 1976. *Why chimps can read.* New York: Harper and Row.

Premack, Ann James and David Premack. 1972. Teaching language to an ape, *Scientific American* 227.4. 92–98.

Premack, David and Ann James Premack. 1993. *The mind of an ape.* New York: W. W. Norton.

Preston, Dennis. 1989. *Sociolinguistics and second language acquisition.* Cambridge, MA: Blackwell.

Pullum, Geoffrey K. 1997. Language that dare not speak its name. *Nature* 386. 321–322.

Pyles, Thomas and John Algeo. 1993. *The origins and development of the English language,* 4th edn. Fort Worth, TX: Harcourt Brace Jovanovich.

Radford, Andrew. 1988. *Transformational grammar: a first course.* New York: Cambridge University Press.

Radford, Andrew. 1997. *Syntactic theory and the structure of English: a minimalist approach.* New York: Cambridge University Press.

Raichle, Marcus E. 1994. Visualizing the mind. *Scientific American* 270.4. 58–64.

Read, Charles Allen. 1964. The folklore of O.K. *American speech* 39. 5–25.

Read, Charles. 1975. *Children's categorization of speech sounds in English*. Urbana, IL: National Council of Teachers of English.

Reich, Peter A. 1986. *Language development*. Englewood Cliffs, NJ: Prentice-Hall.

Robins, R. H. 1967. *A short history of linguistics*. Bloomington: Indiana University Press.

Roitblat, Herbert L., Louis M. Herman, and Paul E. Nachtigall, eds. 1993. *Language and communication: comparative perspectives*. Hillsdale, NJ: Lawrence Erlbaum Associates.

Romaine, Suzanne. 1994a. *Bilingualism*, 2nd edn. Oxford: Blackwell.

Romaine, Suzanne. 1994b. *Language in society: an introduction to sociolinguistics*. Oxford: Oxford University Press.

Ruhlen, Merritt. 1987. *A guide to the world's languages*, vol. 1. Stanford, CA: Stanford University Press.

Ruhlen, Merritt. 1994. *The origin of language*. New York: John Wiley and Sons.

Rymer, Russ. 1992. Silent childhood. *The New Yorker*, April 13 and April 20.

Saeed, John. 1997. *Semantics*. Cambridge, MA: Blackwell.

Salus, Peter H., ed. 1969. *On language: Plato to von Humboldt*. New York: Holt, Rinehart and Winston.

Sampson, Geoffrey. 1985. *Writing systems: a linguistic introduction*. Stanford: Stanford University Press.

Sampson, Geoffrey. 1997. *Educating Eve: the 'language instinct' debate*. London: Cassell.

Sapir, Edward. 1921 [reprinted 1949]. *Language: an introduction to the study of speech*. New York: Harcourt, Brace and World.

Saussure, Ferdinand de. 1959. *Course in general linguistics*, translated by Wade Baskin. New York: McGraw-Hill.

Savage-Rumbaugh, Sue and Roger Lewin. 1994. *Kanzi: the ape at the brink of the human mind*. New York: John Wiley.

Schiffrin, Deborah. 1993. *Approaches to discourse: language as social interaction*. Oxford: Blackwell.

Schmandt-Besserat, Denise. 1989. Two precursors of writing: plain and complex tokens, in *The origins of writing*, Wayne M. Senner, ed., 27–41. Lincoln: University of Nebraska Press.

Searle, John, R. 1975. Indirect speech acts, in *Syntax and semantics*, Peter Cole and Jerry L. Morgan, eds, vol. 3, 59–82. New York: Academic Press. [Also in Davis 1991, 265–277.]

Senner, Wayne M. 1989. Theories and myths on the origin of writing: a historical overview, in *The origins of writing*, Wayne M. Senner, ed., 1–26. Lincoln: University of Nebraska Press.

Senner, Wayne M., ed. 1989. *The origins of writing*. Lincoln: University of Nebraska Press.

Seuren, Peter A. M. 1997. *Western linguistics: an historical introduction*. Malden, MA: Blackwell.

Seyfarth, Robert M. and Dorothy L. Cheney. 1986. Vocal development in vervet monkeys. *Animal behavior* 34. 1640–1658.

Seyfarth, Robert, Dorothy Cheney, and Peter Marler. 1980. Monkey responses to three different alarm calls: evidence of predator classification and semantic communication. *Science* 210. 801–803.

Shopen, Timothy, ed. 1985. *Language typology and syntactic description: grammatical categories and the lexicon*. Cambridge: Cambridge University Press.

Shuy, Roger, Walter Wolfram, and William K. Riley. 1967. *Linguistic correlates of social stratification in*

Detroit speech. East Lansing, MI: Michigan State University.

Sloat, Clarence and Sharon Taylor. 1985. *The structure of English words*. Dubuque, IA: Kendall-Hunt.

Spencer, Andrew. 1991. *Morphological theory*. Cambridge, MA: Blackwell.

Spencer, Andrew. 1996. *Phonology: theory and description*. Cambridge, MA: Blackwell.

Stankiewicz, Edward, ed. 1972. *A Baudouin de Courtenay anthology: the beginnings of structural linguistics*. Bloomington: Indiana University Press.

Stemmer, Brigitte and Harry Whitaker, eds. 1998. *Handbook of neurolinguistics*. New York: Academic Press.

Stillings, Neil A., Steven E. Weisler, Christopher H. Chase et al. 1995. *Cognitive science: an introduction*, 2nd edn. Cambridge, MA: MIT Press.

Strozer, Judith R. 1994. *Language acquisition after puberty*. Washington, DC: Georgetown University Press.

Tallerman, Maggie. 1998. *Understanding syntax*. London: Arnold.

Taylor, Insup and David R. Olsen, eds. 1994. *Scripts and learning: reading and learning to read alphabets, syllabaries, and characters*. London: Kluwer Academic Press.

Terrace, Herbert S. 1979. *Nim*. New York: Knopf.

Terrace, H. S., L. A. Petitto, R. J. Sanders, and T. G. Bever. 1981. Can an ape create a sentence? *Science* 206.4421. 891–902.

Thomas, Linda. 1993. *Beginning syntax*. Oxford: Blackwell.

Thorne, Barrie, Cheris Kramarae, and Nancy Henle. 1983. *Language, gender, and society*. Rowley, MA: Newbury House.

Thorpe, W. H. 1961. *Bird-song: the biology of vocal communication and expression in birds*. London: Cambridge University Press.

Todd, Loreto. 1990. *Pidgins and creoles*, 2nd edn. London: Routledge.

Todt, Dietmar and Henrike Hultsch. 1996. Acquisition and performance of song repertoires: ways of coping with diversity and versatility, in *Ecology and evolution of acoustic communication in birds*, Donald E. Kroodsma and Edward H. Miller, eds, 79–96. Ithaca: Cornell University Press.

Tomlin, Russell. 1986. *Basic constituent orders: functional principles*. London: Croom Helm.

Trask, R. L. 1995. *Language: the basics*. New York: Routledge.

Trask, R. L. 1996. *Historical linguistics*. London: Arnold.

Treiman, Rebecca. 1993. *Beginning to spell*. New York: Oxford University Press.

Trudgill, Peter. 1983. *Sociolinguistics: an introduction*, 2nd edn. Baltimore: Penguin Books.

Ullman, Berthold Louis. 1969. *Ancient writing and its influence*. Cambridge, MA: MIT Press.

Van Valin, Robert D., Jr. and Randy J. LaPolla. 1997. *Syntax: structure, meaning, and function*. Cambridge: Cambridge University Press.

Velten, H. V. 1943. The growth of phonemic and lexical patterns in infant language. *Language* 43. 281–292.

Venezky, Richard L. 1970. *The structure of English orthography*. The Hague: Mouton.

Vennemann, Theo. 1988. *Preference laws for syllable structure, and the explanation of sound change*. Berlin: Mouton de Gruyter.

Vihman, Marilyn May. 1996. *Phonological development: the origins of language in the child*. Cambridge, MA: Blackwell.

Wald, Benji and Timothy Shopen. 1981. A researcher's guide to sociolinguistic variable (ING), in *Style and variables in English*, Joseph Williams and Timothy Shopen, eds, 219–249. Cambridge, MA: Winthrop.

Walker, C. B. F. 1987. *Cuneiform*. Berkeley: University of California Press.

Wardhaugh, Ronald. 1986. *An introduction to sociolinguistics*. Oxford: Blackwell.

Wardhaugh, Ronald. 1995. *Understanding English grammar*. Oxford: Blackwell.

Whaley, Lindsay J. 1997. *Introduction to typology: the unity and diversity of language*. Thousand Oaks, CA: Sage.

White, Lydia. 1989. *Universal grammar and L2 acquisition*. Amsterdam: Jonathan Benjamins.

Wierzbicka, Anna. 1997. *Understanding cultures through their key words*. Oxford: Oxford University Press.

Wilkins, Wendy, ed. 1988. *Syntax and semantics* Vol. 21: *Thematic Relations*. New York: Academic Press.

Williams, Joseph M. 1975. *Origins of the English language: a social and linguistic history*. New York: Free Press.

Winitz, Harris. 1969. *Articulatory acquisition and behavior*. New York: Appleton-Century-Crofts.

Wittgenstein, Ludwig. 1974. *Tractatus logico-philosophicus*, translated by D. F. Pears and B. F. McGuinness. London: Routledge and Kegan Paul.

Yates, Norris. 1981. The vocabulary of *Time* magazine revisited. *American speech* 56. 53–63.

Zipf, Paul. 1935. *The psycho-biology of language: an introduction to dynamic philology*. Boston: Honghton Mifflin.

INDEX

Bradey Powel.
Walter Powel.
Tara Clark.